TO RULE ALL UNDER HEAVEN

TO RULE ALL UNDER HEAVEN

A HISTORY OF CLASSICAL CHINA, FROM CONFUCIUS TO THE FIRST EMPEROR

ANDREW SETH MEYER

OXFORD
UNIVERSITY PRESS

Oxford University Press is a department of the University of Oxford.
It furthers the University's objective of excellence in research, scholarship,
and education by publishing worldwide. Oxford is a registered trade mark of
Oxford University Press in the UK and in certain other countries.

Published in the United States of America by Oxford University Press
198 Madison Avenue, New York, NY 10016, United States of America.

© Oxford University Press 2025

All rights reserved. No part of this publication may be reproduced, stored in a retrieval system,
transmitted, used for text and data mining, or used for training artificial intelligence, in any form or
by any means, without the prior permission in writing of Oxford University Press, or as expressly
permitted by law, by license or under terms agreed with the appropriate reprographics rights
organization. Inquiries concerning reproduction outside the scope of the above should be sent
to the Rights Department, Oxford University Press, at the address above.

You must not circulate this work in any other form
and you must impose this same condition on any acquirer.

CIP data is on file at the Library of Congress.

ISBN 9780197667484

Printed by Marquis Book Printing, Canada

The manufacturer's authorized representative in the EU for product safety is
Oxford University Press España S.A. of Parque Empresarial San Fernando de Henares,
Avenida de Castilla, 2 – 28830 Madrid (www.oup.es/en or product.safety@oup.com).
OUP España S.A. also acts as importer into Spain of products made by the manufacturer.

*Dedicated to Gregory John Taylor (1975–2015) and
to all my students at Brooklyn College*

頌其詩, 讀其書, 不知其人, 可乎? 是以論其世也。是尚友也.
Recite their poems. Read their prose. Will you not understand them as people? In this way you can fathom their age. This is making friends with those of the past.

Mencius 孟子 (ca. 390–305 BCE)

Contents

Acknowledgments ix
Note to the Reader xiii
Maps xvii

Introduction 1

1. Lords and Master: The States of Qi and Lu, 481–479 BCE 7
2. Song of the South: The States of Wu, Chu, and Yue, 527–473 BCE 41
3. The Partition: The State of Jin, 472–453 BCE 73
4. Heaven's Whim versus Heaven's Will: The Extended Zhou Realm, 475–ca. 439 BCE 93
5. The Prince: The State of Wei, 446–396 BCE 109
6. Wanderers: The Extended Zhou Realm, 402–381 BCE 130
7. The Altars of the Soil and Grain are Closer than Kin: The State of Qi, 389–345 BCE 149
8. The West's Awake: The State of Qin, 385–338 BCE 187
9. The Marquis Who Would Be King: The State of Wei, 369–334 BCE 212
10. We Kings: The Extended Zhou Realm, 334–310 BCE 243
11. Better to Give: The State of Qi and the Greater Zhou Realm, 320–294 BCE 290
12. The Harder They Fall: The State of Qi, 294–278 BCE 323
13. The Duel: The States of Zhao and Qin, 307–260 BCE 335
14. Gilded Age: The Various Zhou States, 260–238 BCE 370

15. Unification: The Kingdom of Qin and the Former Zhou States, 256–221 BCE … 400

Epilogue and Conclusions … 434

Appendix A: Historical Timeline … 453
Appendix B: Glossary of Historical Figures … 460
Notes … 471
Bibliography … 509
Index … 527

Acknowledgments

I wrote this book over a period of 16 years. Any project that large must of course be collaborative, and I have many people to thank.

The first debt I must acknowledge is to the Chinese and Japanese scholars who, over many centuries, have preserved, transmitted, discovered, studied, organized, and commented upon the sources upon which this study is built. The list of scholars on whom I have depended would be very long, but I must acknowledge a particular debt to two historians. The work of Qian Mu 錢穆 (1895–1990 CE) in reconstructing the chronology of the Masters was indispensable to my efforts. The scholarship of Yang Kuan 楊寬 (1914–2005 CE) was foundational to everything I have accomplished, as anyone who glances at my endnotes will quickly see.

Closer to home and closer in time, I am very indebted to the many colleagues here in the United States and overseas with whom it has been my privilege to study and learn from for almost four decades. I have profited from exchanges with so many colleagues that any attempt to list them would necessarily fail. Any reader who would like to get a sense of the scope of my debt need only look at the bibliography of this volume. If someone is cited there, there is a good chance that I have met them and benefited enormously from the interaction.

I must give specific thanks to colleagues who assisted directly in the production of this manuscript. My work with John Major, Harold Roth, Sarah Queen, Michael Puett, and Judson Murray on the translation of the *Huainanzi* led me to many sources that were critical to my work on this volume. I collaborated with my friend and classmate Andrew "Dex" Wilson on studies of the *Sunzi bingfa* that informed the discussion of many issues in this text. Paul Goldin was always available to ask questions on issues that arose in my research. Martin Kern lent helpful comments and advice. Li Feng, Carine DeFoort, Moss Roberts, and my 師父 Peter Bol all gave feedback and encouragement to my research on knights (*shi* 士). Sarah Allan and Robin Yates helped shape my work on the intellectual culture of Qi.

My colleagues at Brooklyn College have all been a constant source of personal and intellectual support. Karen Stern assisted me with general questions about ancient history and critical theory. The LAMEM (Late Antiquity Medieval Early Modern) seminar organized by Lauren Mancia has been a persistently stimulating venue in which to work through projects and ideas. Steven Remy, Philip Napoli, David Troyansky, and Margaret King all provided feedback on early drafts of parts of this manuscript or on prior research that made its way into this volume.

I am deeply indebted to those in the publishing field who brought this project to completion. Gerry Krieg drafted the maps that are so crucial to this work's value. Stefan Vranka's editing has made this book a much better piece of writing. Chelsea Hogue and the entire team at Oxford University Press has worked magic by way of making this volume functional and attractive. A special thanks goes to my literary agent, Martha Kaplan, without whose patience and advocacy this project would never have been completed.

Nothing is done over a span of sixteen years without the support of friends and family. My neighbors, high school friends, college friends, camp friends, Broadway friends, graduate school classmates, and extended family have all given encouragement and assistance. A group of camp friends with whom I gather for monthly guitar jamborees baked me a cake. My cousin David Solomon purchased books for me and shlepped them home from Taiwan.

I must give particular gratitude to my "brother from another mother" and fellow history teacher Ron "Hap" Horan. In extended gym sessions and long walks over multiple years, he has heard every chapter of this volume worked and reworked verbally—at least twice. Without his questions and feedback, this would be a poorer offering. His whole family pitched in to this effort, including his wife, Theresa, and their grandson, Kendrick Logan.

My immediate family have been endless wells of love and patience. My father, Melvin, was very excited about this project and asked for updates every time I saw him. I wish he could have lived to see the final product. My brother, Lee, his wife, Marta, and my nephew, Shay, have cheered me on at every step. My mother, Susan Glynn, was, for many years, the only person who had read every word I wrote (in multiple drafts). Her excitement and pride have kept me going through many rough times.

To my wife, Emilie, and my daughter, Ada, I owe deep thanks. They routinely light up my world with joy. Beyond that, they have very graciously allowed me to withdraw into ancient China periodically, and have always welcomed me back with warmth and love.

Finally, I must thank my MA student Gregory John Taylor (1975–2015). This project was in many ways his concept. A history teacher himself, he developed a passion for the study of early China in classes I taught at Brooklyn College and was the first to ask me what type of book I might write for general readers. He then, through a friend, introduced me to my literary agent. I had no idea then how long this project would take me or how little time Greg had. He tragically died of cancer in 2015. This book is dedicated to Greg's memory. I know that he would have liked sharing the dedication with his fellow students.

May 20, 2025

Note to the Reader

If one enters almost any bookstore in the English-speaking world in search of a book about classical Athens, the conquests of Alexander, or the early Roman Republic written for a general reader, one will have many options. But if one looks for such a book about the corresponding period in early Chinese history, there are none. I wrote this book to fill that gap. It presumes no prior or special knowledge of East Asian history or culture.

Any account of early Chinese history, however, poses natural challenges to educated non-specialists in Europe and America, and thus I have tried to make this book as accessible as possible. I have included only the names of persons and places that are central to the narrative, and have used English titles and English translations of place-names wherever possible. A timeline of events and a glossary of historical figures has been provided to help readers navigate through the story as they read along.

Since this is a general work, I have tried to include as much information in my notes and bibliography about sources that readers can consult to learn about the history covered in this book in more depth. I have followed the naming conventions prevalent in East Asia: for all figures in the narrative, the surname (or clan name) is written first, the "given" or personal name is written last. All names and any transcriptions of Chinese terms are romanized using the pinyin system current in the People's Republic of China.

It is conventional in the writing of Chinese history to refer to rulers by their ranks and posthumous titles (for example, King Xuan of Qi) rather than their given names (Tian Pijiang). In this text I will generally use the conventional titles of rulers when it is possible. The Warring States period was a dynamic era, however, and many of the key people I will be discussing started life with one rank and ended it with another. In those cases I generally refer to the figure by his or her personal name, at least until it is no longer anachronistic to do so. The glossary at the back of the volume will list all sobriquets by which any given figure is identified in the course of the narrative.

The romanizations of names in this book reflect current Mandarin pronunciation. Cantonese, Shanghainese, and Fujianese speakers would pronounce these names differently, and they would certainly have been pronounced differently by the people who bore them in ancient times. This is to say that any pronunciation you give to the names you read in this book is only "wrong" as a matter of perspective, and readers should feel free to pronounce the names they encounter in whatever way feels natural and aids in comprehension. For those who would like to be able to discuss the contents of the book using generally conventional Mandarin pronunciations, I provide a pronunciation guide below. Note that Mandarin Chinese has many homophones, so that many names and words that are romanized and pronounced the same in English will not be the same word or name in Chinese.

Vowel Sounds

a	"a" as pronounced in "tra la la"
an	"en" as pronounced in "Zen"
e	"u" as pronounced in "bun"
i	"i" as pronounced in "ski"
o	"aw" as pronounced in "paw"
u	"oo" as pronounced in "food"
ü	purse your lips as if to make the sound "o" as in "low," then vocalize an "e" as in "bee"
ai	"i" as in "pie"
ao	"ow" as in "cow"
ei	"ay" as pronounced in "hay"
ia	"ya" as in "Nadya"
ou	"o" as in "low"
ui	diphthong of "oo" as in food and "ay" as in "hay": oo-ay
uo	"aw" as pronounced in "lawn"

Consonant Sounds

b	"b" as in "bee"
c	"ts" as in "Tsar"
d	"d" as in "dance"
f	"f" as in "fall"
g	"g" as in "go"
h	"h" as in "hello"
j	"j" as in "jiffy"
k	"k" as in "kite"
l	"l" as in "lake"
m	"m" as in "moon"
n	"n" as in "nine"
p	"p" as in "pie"
q	"ch" as in "chick"
r	"r" as in "row"

s	"s" as in "sift"
t	"t" as in "top"
w	"w" as in "way"
x	"sh" as in "ship"
y*	"y" as in "yet"
z	"dz" as in "adze"
~ng	"ng" as in "ring"

*The combination "yi" can be sounded differently in different contexts. The syllable "ying," for example, opens with a "y" consonant sound and rhymes with "sing." The syllable "yi" opens with a slight "y" consonant sound, but rhymes with "see."

Special Sounds

Mandarin has three "hard retroflex" sounds that do not exist in English. These are written:

ch	hard "ch" as in "choke"
sh	hard "sh" as in "shock"
zh	hard "j" as in "joker"

These retroflex sounds are formed by curling one's tongue far back into one's mouth. They are opposed by equivalent "palatal" sounds that are formed by pressing one's tongue against one's upper teeth. The pairs as they are written in pinyin are:

ch	"retroflex ch"	versus	q	"palatal ch"
sh	"retroflex sh"	versus	x	"palatal sh"
zh	"retroflex j"	versus	j	"palatal j"

English speakers might not notice a significant difference in some of the syllables that are formed by these different sounds, and certainly when pronouncing them in English conversation it would be surprising if they did not resemble each other. For example, the syllables written "shu" and "xu" in pinyin might both be pronounced by an English speaker who did not speak Chinese as homophonous with "shoe."

An exception to this pattern is the case when certain consonants are followed by the letter "i" in pinyin transcription. When the hard retroflex sounds are followed by "i," the vowel sound gets "swallowed." For example, one would expect the surname of Zhi Yao to rhyme with "gee," but in Mandarin his surname is simply a voiced "j" sound that rhymes with "brr" (as in "brr, its cold"). The same is true of "Chi" and "Shi," respectively.

A similar pattern occurs when "i" follows the palatal consonants "c," "z," and "s." The "Zi" of "Zixia," for example, is a voiced "dz" sound resembling a shortened version of the onomatopoeia "zzz" (as in "Zzz . . ." she must be sleeping).

Maps

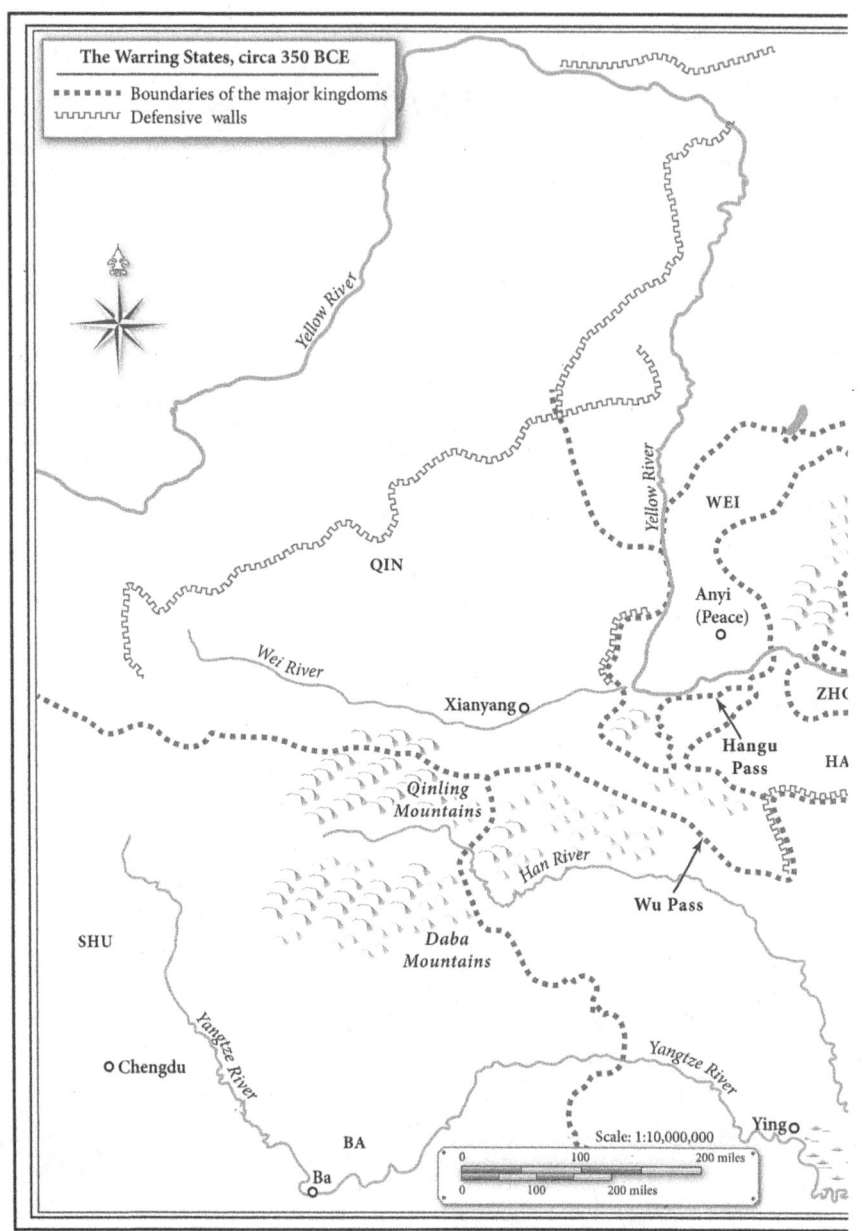

Map 1. Warring States Map

Credit: Map illustrations by Gerry Krieg. The maps were drawn from Tan Qixiang 譚其驤, ed. *Zhongguo lishi ditu ji* 中國歷史地圖集, vol. 1. Beijing: Zhonguo ditu chubanshe, 1982.

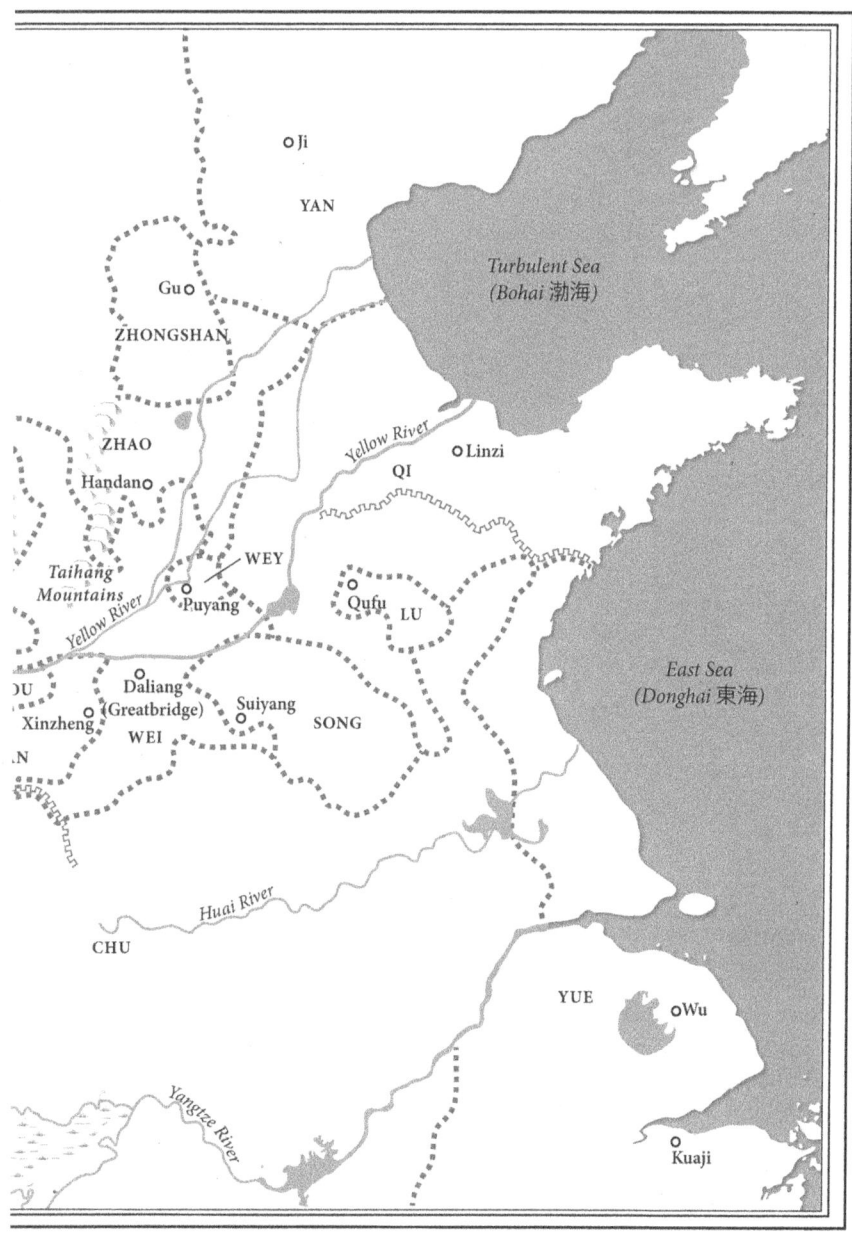

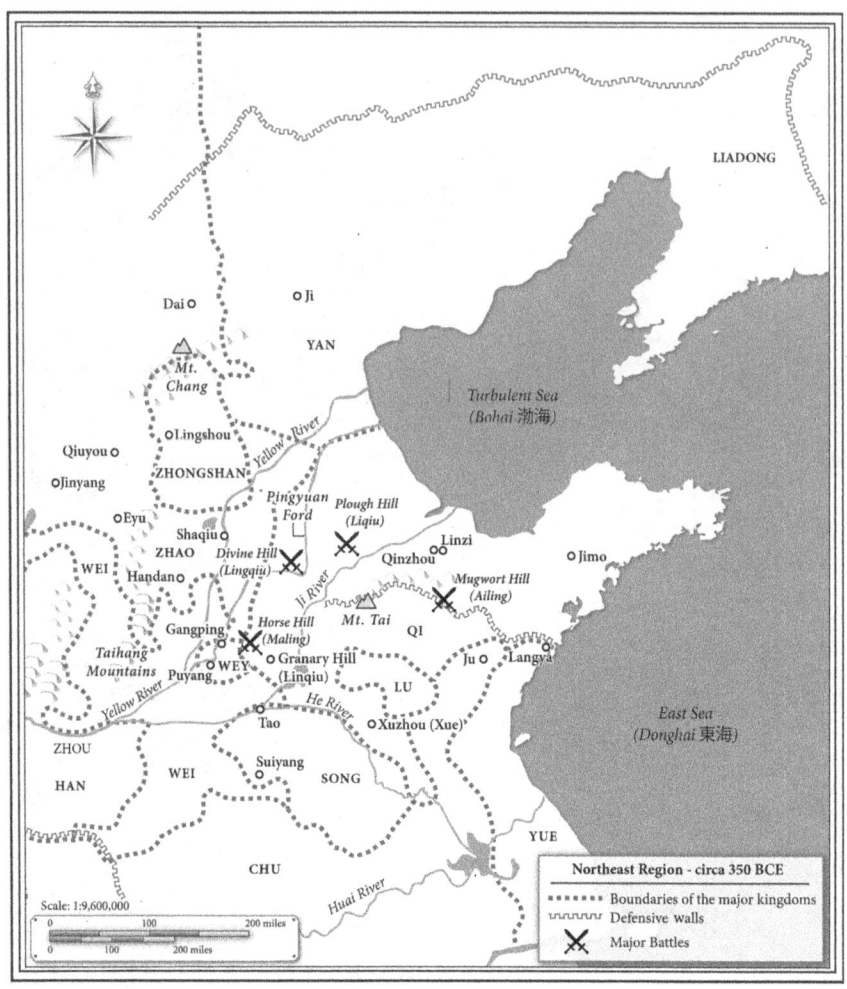

Map 2. Northeast Map

Credit: Map illustrations by Gerry Krieg. The maps were drawn from Tan Qixiang 譚其驤, ed. *Zhongguo lishi ditu ji* 中國歷史地圖集, vol. 1. Beijing: Zhonguo ditu chubanshe, 1982.

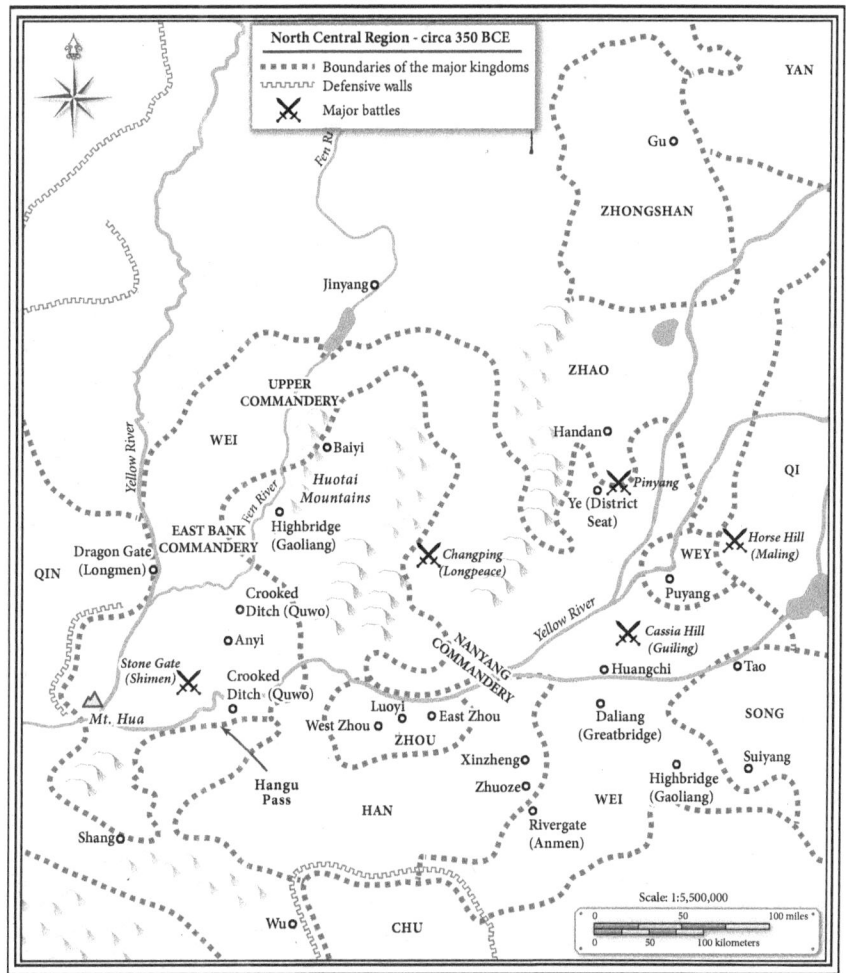

Map 3. North Central Map
Credit: Map illustrations by Gerry Krieg. The maps were drawn from Tan Qixiang 譚其驤, ed. *Zhongguo lishi ditu ji* 中國歷史地圖集, vol. 1. Beijing: Zhonguo ditu chubanshe, 1982.

Map 4. Northwest Map

Credit: Map illustrations by Gerry Krieg. The maps were drawn from Tan Qixiang 譚其驤, ed. *Zhongguo lishi ditu ji* 中國歷史地圖集, vol. 1. Beijing: Zhonguo ditu chubanshe, 1982.

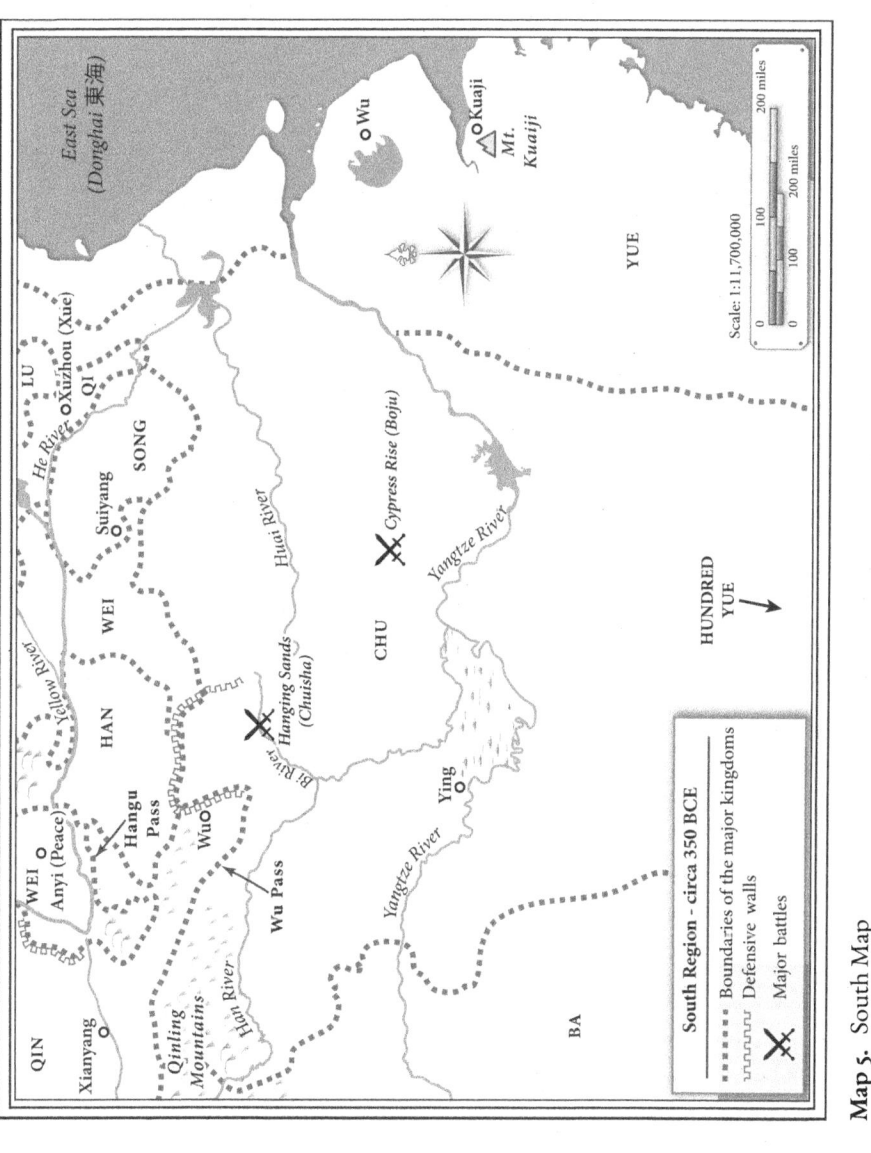

Map 5. South Map

Credit: Map illustrations by Gerry Krieg. The maps were drawn from Tan Qixiang 譚其驤, ed. *Zhongguo lishi ditu ji* 中國歷史地圖集, vol. 1. Beijing: Zhongguo ditu chubanshe, 1982.

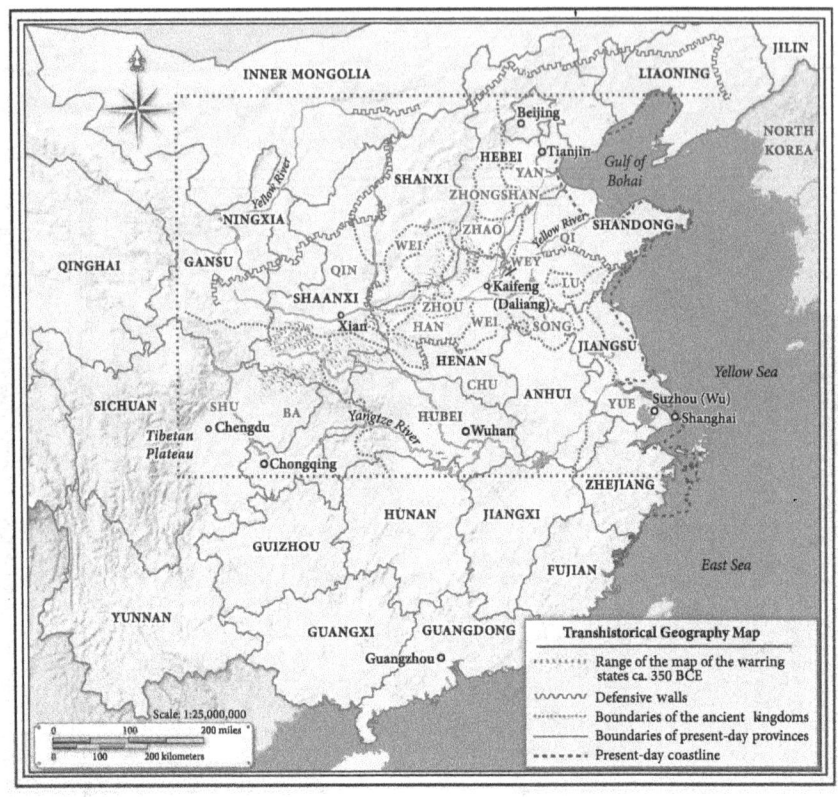

Map 6. Transhistorical Geography
Credit: Map illustrations by Gerry Krieg. The maps were drawn from Tan Qixiang 譚其驤, ed. *Zhongguo lishi ditu ji* 中國歷史地圖集, vol. 1. Beijing: Zhongguo ditu chubanshe, 1982.

The noble man has three joys, and to rule All under Heaven is not among them.
君子有三樂, 而王天下不與焉.

Mencius

One who rules All under Heaven with love eliminates punishments; one who conquers the Lords of the Land with strength sets aside virtue.
以愛王天下者, 并刑; 力征諸侯者, 退德.

The Book of Lord Shang 商君書 (third century BCE)

Introduction

The young men exchanged heartbroken looks, each losing the battle to fend off despair. Having traveled so long, fatigue and frustration had already taken a toll. How could they be blamed for finding this new calamity difficult to bear? Their teacher lay within his carriage, severely ill and approaching death. After years of learning at his mat, this moment felt like the end of the world. He had instructed them in reading, music, and ritual, as was expected of an educator of young knights,[1] but he had also given them much more. With him they had explored the complex questions of human morality and the deeper meanings of ancient tradition. He had exhorted them to the difficult work of forging their own characters, and imparted to them the Dao or Way that gave structure and direction to their lives. Their common sense of purpose, their fervor for grappling with the challenges of the age—all were his inspiration.

His name was Kong Qiu (551–479 BCE). His disciples honored him as *fuzi*, or "Master," thus his name comes down to us in English today as Confucius (a Latinization of Kong *fuzi*, or "Master Kong"). Confucius (Fig. 1) had taught his students that participating in public affairs was the sacred duty of every true *junzi*, or gentleman. But the politics of the regional state of Lu, where Confucius and most of his disciples had been born and where their fellowship had formed, were hopelessly corrupt. The ruling duke was weak and ineffectual, the court dominated by powerful aristocrats who flouted legitimate authority. The upright Confucius had been perpetually frustrated in his attempts to serve in his native state; thus he had set forth in search of a regional ruler who might appoint him to a position of power and responsibility.

His disciples had not hesitated in accompanying him; they would gladly follow him to the wilds of the barbarian steppe if he had asked. Their confidence in their Master's ability was only exceeded by their faith in the Way he had received from the ancient Zhou (ca. 1045–256 BCE) kings, that he would use to heal the strife and violence into which the civilized world had descended.

Fig. 1. Tang dynasty portrait of Confucius (551–479 BCE). Confucius (Kong Qiu, 551–479 BCE) was the first teacher to take the title of "Master" and to profess about "the Way (Dao)." He came to be virtually universally revered in imperial times. This is a famous portrait by the Tang (618–907 CE) painter Wu Daozi (680–740 CE). (Source: worldhistory.org; Creative Commons License.)

The beginning of their journey had been filled with hope and promise, the eager anticipation of seeing so many ideals fulfilled in reality.

Now that promise had become a cruel joke. One after another the rulers they visited had turned Confucius away, often with insults and open scorn. The bitterness of such rejections was made worse by the fact that so many had laughed at Confucius and his disciples from the outset, when they had first set foot upon the path back home in Lu. At this moment it seemed that all the mockers would be proven right. Confucius would not end as a sage leader, remembered as the man who brought order to the chaos of the age. Instead he would die like a stray dog, a poor vagabond cast adrift upon the roads.

The shame was too much to endure. Zilu (ca. 540–480 BCE), one of the oldest of the disciples and the most restlessly impetuous, broke the aching silence. He ordered the others to array themselves around Confucius' carriage as if he was a powerful lord and they were his sworn retainers. In this way they could continue to their next destination, and anyone they encountered on the road would not perceive the despondency of their enterprise. Demoralized and rudderless, the disciples did as Zilu commanded.[2]

After several days of this pantomime, a miracle occurred. The Master regained consciousness, his color and vitality returned. His disciples joyfully welcomed Confucius back from death's brink, but not before he had perceived the way they had been play-acting. Chagrined, amused, and perhaps a bit moved by their well-meaning but misguided charade, he gently rebuked them, saying, "It has been a while that Zilu has been shamming, has it not? In acting as if I have retainers when I have none, whom have we fooled? Have we fooled Heaven? Moreover, would I not rather die in your hands, my friends, than in the hands of retainers?"[3]

Roughly 280 years later, in 210 BCE, another group halted due to mortal illness.[4] Two members of this later group, one a eunuch,[5] stood apart and away from prying eyes, their faces etched with worry as the disciples' had been three centuries prior, though with different cause. The eunuch held a letter he had received from a traveler, with instructions to seal it and send it to the traveler's son. The letter had been sealed, but never sent. Instead the eunuch broke the seal, unrolled the missive, and read it aloud to his companion.

Both men were officials in the service of Ying Zheng (259–210 BCE), known to history as the First Emperor of Qin (r. 221–210 BCE), then in the thirty-seventh year of his reign.[6] Late in the previous year the First Emperor had set out on a grand tour, accompanied by an enormous military escort, hundreds of civilian officials, and a huge staff of personal servants. His route traversed more than 600 miles, taking him from his capital of Xianyang, in present-day Shaanxi Province, as far south and east as Mount Kuaiji in present-day Zhejiang Province.

At that moment the First Emperor was indisputably the most powerful man in the world. When he first assumed the throne of Qin, the former Zhou domain had still been divided between seven mighty regional states, as it had been for more than two hundred years. The First Emperor oversaw the conquest of Qin's six rivals and unified the civilized world under a single throne, the greatest act of conquest and consolidation the world had ever witnessed. If the army of Alexander the Great (356–323 BCE), for example, had encountered that of the weakest of the seven states conquered by the First Emperor, it would have been roundly crushed. To distinguish his unprecedented position of power, Ying Zheng created a new title for himself, *huangdi* or emperor (hence his posthumous designation of "First Emperor"). This grand tour was, in part, a celebration of his imperial enterprise. Along its route, he had pointedly traversed territories where it would have been fatal for him to trespass scant years before, the secure homelands of princes now moldering in unmarked graves. At Mount Kuaiji he had erected a large poetic stele enumerating his achievements and proclaiming the enduring and incomparable significance of his rule.[7]

At Pingyuan Ford, not far from Confucius's birthplace in present-day Shandong Province, the First Emperor had taken seriously ill. Sensing the end was near, he wrote an urgent letter, the one that the eunuch Zhao Gao (d. 207 BCE) now held in his hands. The emperor knew that he was dying. He commanded the Crown Prince, then on campaign on the frontier with the empire's greatest general, Meng Tian (d. 210 BCE), to hasten to the capital and make preparations for a royal funeral. Presiding over his father's funeral was the surest way for the Crown Prince to secure his succession to the imperial throne. The First Emperor knew that the legacy of the institution he had founded depended in large part on the success of this first transmission from father to son.

The emperor had followed protocol in handing the correspondence to the eunuch; as Prefect of Palace Vehicles the tallies and seals of state were in his temporary charge during the course of the tour. Sensing both a danger and an opportunity, however, Zhao had not rushed to carry out the emperor's orders. As the imperial cortege made its way west, the emperor finally died at Shaqiu in present-day Hebei Province. It was here that the eunuch had summoned Chancellor Li Si (ca. 280–208 BCE), head civil official of the First Emperor's government, to a secret meeting.

The Chancellor was a skilled politician; he knew how perilous the moment was for the dynasty he and the eunuch both served. If word got out that the emperor had died on the road, chaos could seize the empire. He also knew that a smooth succession was key to the maintenance of order, and was at first eager to dispatch the Emperor's final letter to the Crown Prince. The eunuch pressed him to reconsider, however. The Crown Prince had little relationship with the Chancellor and was on very intimate terms with General Meng Tian. When the Crown Prince rose to the throne, the Chancellor would certainly be forced to step down. The eunuch reminded the Chancellor that few of his predecessors had met a good end when they had been forced to resign. Moreover, a more malleable younger son of the Emperor was traveling with them. He had been a student of the eunuch in his youth and was already enlisted in the plot.

The Chancellor was finally persuaded, and the two men destroyed the Emperor's last message. Using the official seals in the eunuch's charge, they forged a new edict, ordering the Crown Prince to commit suicide for treasonous negligence and stripping General Meng of his command. They placed the emperor's body in a sealed coffin within an insulated carriage; only the eunuchs under the personal supervision of Zhao Gao were aware that the emperor had died. Meals and official documents continued to be passed in and out of the carriage as if the First Emperor were still attending to the daily business of rule. By now it was late summer, and after a few days the smell of decay began to emanate from the First Emperor's corpse despite the efforts made to contain it. The conspirators cleverly declared that the emperor had developed a craving for fish and ordered a cart of salted fish pulled behind the imperial carriage to cover the smell of the emperor's corruption. The Chancellor and the eunuch may not have fooled Heaven, but their theatrics were otherwise a spectacular success. Placing Huhai (230–207 BCE), the First Emperor's weak-willed younger son, on the throne, they seized control of the imperial court and began a reign of terror that would leave most of the First Emperor's children dead.

On each of these two journeys we thus find two groups of "pretend retainers": Confucius's disciples arrayed around their ill Master as if they were his official subordinates and the First Emperor's actual retainers arrayed around his corpse as if he were still alive. The parallels between these scenes are at once remarkable and deeply ironic, as one could not choose two historical figures more dissimilar than Confucius and the First Emperor. Confucius, for all his labors, could not in his lifetime build a community of more than a few dozen disciples.[8] The First Emperor, by contrast, had managed to forge a unity of the civilized world.

The sheer power and success of the emperor would seem, at first glance, to dwarf that of the old teacher, but a comparison made at these two moments of mortal distress complicates the picture. Small as it was, Confucius's fellowship, held together by ties of affection and respect, guaranteed humane and dignified treatment for all its members, even at their most vulnerable. The First Emperor's huge empire, built on blood and treasure, made everyone within it, even, ultimately, him and his family, subject to the impersonal logic of power upon which it operated. The First Emperor's fate lends eerie prescience to Confucius's judgment, that dying in the hands of friends was preferable to dying in the hands of retainers.

People in China and across East Asia have been left to contemplate, puzzle over, and comment upon the disparity between these two men for more than two millennia. The era they straddled saw one of the most profound revolutions in human history. During this period (481–221 BCE), which historians call the Warring States, through war, diplomacy, debate, commerce, writing, science, and artistic expression, an entire society (indeed, as will be discussed in the next chapters a complex of many diverse, interconnected societies) reinvented and recreated itself. The world through which Confucius traveled was a vastly different one than the one into which he had been born, and the world the First Emperor departed on his death was many times more altered still. In that interval, new traditions of thought and practice were born that continue to this day to draw millions of adherents across the globe. Great monuments of art, literature, and philosophy were created that still inform social life in our own lifetime. The imperial throne that the First Emperor founded persisted, through successive dynasties, for 2,132 years, making it one of the longest-lasting institutions on earth.[9] Though Confucius and the First Emperor were diametrically opposed actors in this seminal drama, the question of which played the greater role is an irresoluble paradox. Millions contributed to the creative maelstrom of the Warring States, but its extraordinary complexity is perhaps best manifest in its encompassing both the world-conquering emperor and the humble teacher among its central agents.

The following pages will tell the story of this revolution, beginning from the time just prior to the death of Confucius in 481 BCE to just after the unification and founding of the empire by the First Emperor and his Qin dynasty (221–206 BCE). It is a centuries-long drama with myriad actors that unfolded across a vast and varied terrain: from the Pacific coast to the foothills of the Himalayas, from the arid Inner Asian steppe to the steamy rainforests of the southern subtropics. Despite the length, breadth, and intricacy of this epoch, it constitutes a sharply pivotal moment in history. Not only the nation we know of today as China, but the entire world was forever transformed by the Warring States.

I

Lords and Master
The States of Qi and Lu, 481–479 BCE

When does a revolution begin? Short, violent revolutions often leave us with an initial moment that can be commemorated by later generations. The "shot heard round the world." The storming of the Bastille.

The Warring States (481–221 BCE) was as violent as and had even greater social and cultural impact than the American and French revolutions. It likewise led to the creation of a radically new, enduring political system that was a model for large parts of the world. But unlike the American and French revolutions, the Warring States unspooled over two and a half centuries, bringing complex changes that transpired at an uneven pace across an enormous and varied geography. Where to start telling the tale?

There is no single moment that can properly be called the "beginning of the Warring States." By the early fifth century BCE the Sinitic (i.e. "ancient Chinese-speaking") world, centered along, between, and extending to the peripheries of the Yellow and Yangzi River valleys (and those great rivers' tributaries) in what is today China, had been ruled by the kings of the Zhou dynasty (1045–254 BCE) for more than half a millennium. This already ancient society was in the throes of a slow-moving crisis that had been going on for several centuries, a time of gradual decline that historians would later label the "Spring and Autumn" (771–481 BCE) period. These two labels, "Spring and Autumn" and "Warring States," served as shorthand for comparing and contrasting states of relative disorder and decay during the long sweep of the Zhou dynasty, the longest-ruling house in the history of China.[1] The question of precisely when one period ended and the other began was not an urgent concern for literati before the twentieth century.

From our current vantage, however, we can choose an event that in retrospect marked a fundamental shift, a "point of no return." Like Caesar's crossing of the Rubicon, it foreclosed old avenues and opened new ones, setting society on a radical new path. It occurred on April 26, 481 BCE, a day that changed the Zhou world, though its impact would only become clear with the passage of time.

That afternoon, Lü Ren, the twenty-sixth Duke of Qi, was relaxing on the Sandalwood Terrace of his palace. It was a fine spring day, and the duke had paused from affairs of state to enjoy some grain wine and fresh air in the company of his wives and concubines. Suddenly, from within, came the sound of a commotion. A scream rang out, the last cry of a palace eunuch, killed trying to prevent intruders from entering the duke's inner quarters.[2]

One of the duke's own guards strolled insolently onto the terrace, his sword stained with blood. The duke was no doubt surprised, but unless he was very daft he could not have lost much time in figuring out what was happening. The guard was a member of the aristocratic Tian clan, and close behind him followed his kinsman and clan head, Tian Chang (fl. ca. 485 BCE), one of two co-prime ministers appointed by the duke to lead the court of Qi. A palace coup had begun.

If we could project ourselves as observers back to that moment, frozen in time, it would have neatly encapsulated the existential situation of the Zhou world on the eve of the Warring States. The comfortable luxury of the Sandalwood Terrace on that spring day would reveal to us the wealth and sophistication of Zhou society. Looking about, we would have seen the duke and his wives dressed in colorful silk garments perfectly suited to the warm weather, eating and drinking from brightly patterned ceramics and lacquer (see Fig. 2) of elegant design.[3] The terrace itself no doubt would have been airy, well-sunned, and cleverly planned, sited to afford a fine view of the palace gardens.[4]

The duke and his wives enjoyed the bounty and refinements of a civilization that was already more than a millennium old in 481 BCE, with roots going back even further into the prehistoric past.[5] The agricultural revolution had taken place in the Yellow River valley by about 6000 BCE, and from that time forward the farmers of the North China plain had cultivated a remarkably diverse and abundant array of grains, vegetables, and fibers.[6] Bronze technology had been developed in the region by about 2500 BCE, and by about 1250 BCE had been perfected to a level of technological and artistic sophistication that has never been surpassed.[7] By the duke's own time iron technology was

Fig. 2. Lacquer box produced in the state of Chu, ca. 316 BCE. Such fine craftsmanship was characteristic of the elite culture of all the most powerful Warring States. (Source: govt.chinadaily.com.)

rapidly developing.[8] Advanced animal husbandry[9] and sericulture[10] had further increased material prosperity, as had organization on a mass scale for the maintenance of dikes and irrigation works to tame the Yellow River and maximize its productive potential.[11] The resulting rich surplus had supported a burgeoning population of skilled and ever more technologically advanced artisans that produced the fine crafts worn and utilized by the elite party on the Sandalwood Terrace.

Politically Zhou civilization was likewise very advanced. The Zhou kings had built and improved upon political foundations laid down by a prior dynasty, the Shang (ca. 1570–1045 BCE).[12] Though (as will be discussed below) their institutions and beliefs would be very alien to our modern-day perspective, in the early centuries of Zhou rule their traditions had fostered stability and prosperity, contributing to the technological sophistication, material abundance, and aesthetic refinement enjoyed by the duke and his entourage.

But as Dickens would later say of eighteenth-century France, and as the blood staining the sword of the duke's guard would have attested, the early fifth century BCE was both the best of times and the worst of times.¹³ Even as—in some respects, because—the material prosperity of Zhou society continued to rapidly increase, the social and cultural traditions that gave structure and predictability to political life were breaking down. It was a sign of the times that the Duke of Qi, a man who was ostensibly one of the loftiest and most powerful rulers in the Zhou world, could not find ease or security in the comfort of his palace and the leisured company of his wives.

It might seem strange to begin the story of a world-altering revolution in the palace of a duke rather than that of a king. There was, of course, a Zhou king in 481 BCE, who bore the title Son of Heaven. His palace was in Luoyi (today known as Luoyang), about 680 kilometers due southwest of the Sandalwood Terrace where the duke was accosted. The king would eventually be apprised of the events of April 26, but few of the people in and around the duke's palace that day would have spared much thought for the king.

By then, the political position of the king had long been a casualty of the changes sweeping the Zhou world. The royal house had at one time been very powerful, and even in the early fifth century BCE the Zhou court enjoyed great symbolic prestige. When the Zhou founders first established their throne in 1045 BCE (at about the same time that King David founded his dynasty at Jerusalem), they had deputized dozens of their kin and close allies to take up posts across the Yellow River plain as regional lords (*hou*). These regional lords, among whom was Lü Ren's ancestor, the first Duke of Qi, were given the task of pacifying the lands of the former Shang kings, whom the Zhou had conquered, and making the Yellow River plain serve as a source of revenue and military support for the defense of the new Zhou domain. For the first centuries of Zhou rule the eastern regional lords were held under the sway of a "king's peace" imposed by the Zhou monarchs from their base area in the Wei River valley to the west, where the kings maintained powerful and well-supplied armies.¹⁴

But in 771 BCE the Zhou suffered a catastrophic defeat. An Inner Asian people known as the Xianyun overran the Zhou capital and drove the dynasty out of its ancestral homeland, destroying the central temples and graves of the founding Zhou monarchs. The royal throne was re-established at Luoyi (which previously had been a subordinate administrative center from which royal deputies had monitored the eastern vassals), but the dynasty was vastly weakened. Without the rich lands and populace of their Wei River base area to draw upon for men and material, the Zhou kings could no longer field armies like the ones that had once enforced their will in the east.¹⁵

By 481 BCE the position of the Zhou king in the larger political web of the regional aristocracy had become largely (though not completely) symbolic. His imprimatur was indispensable to lend legitimacy to affairs, but he had little initiative in the actual conduct of policy. The king claimed to rule under the auspices of the Mandate of Heaven: the gods had sanctioned the Zhou founders' conquest and entrusted them with stewardship over the human realm.[16] Though the military and economic power of the Zhou throne had degenerated, their spiritual mystique remained. The winners of the struggle in the ducal palace at the Qi capital of Linzi in 481 BCE would eventually apply to the Zhou king for his blessing, but until the dust settled the king was effectively a distant, passive bystander. Real power was largely concentrated in the courts of the regional lords, the "states" that give the "Warring States" period its name.[17]

Although the weakened position of the Zhou king explains why we would begin the story of the Warring States revolution in the regional states rather than at the royal court, a modern reader might still wonder why we would first focus upon a palace coup within a single regional state like Qi, rather than a conflict between two or more states. It would seem natural, after all, that a revolution within the "unified" Zhou domain would be driven by the internecine conflicts breaking that domain apart. Indeed, the history of the Warring States did involve radical changes in the relations *between* states that will be discussed here and in subsequent chapters. But just as (or more) central to the revolution of the Warring States were the transformations of political and social relationships *within* states. What made the standoff on the Sandalwood Terrace on April 26, 481 BCE, so significant was that its outcome set off changes that over time impacted thousands of families and individuals throughout the state of Qi, whose relationships with one another would be forever transformed by what had transpired.

The "Warring States," in fact, is the name of both a period and a form of political system. On the one hand, it describes the division of much of what we now know of as "China" into competing regional powers, locked in constant struggle with one another. On the other hand, it describes a new type of polity organized for maximum military power.

This is the significance of the coup of April 26, 481 BCE, as an inception point. Before the coup, most relations in Qi operated along traditional lines dating back to before the Zhou founding, in which those above related to those below simultaneously as lord to vassal and priest to congregant (as implied by the concept of the "Mandate of Heaven"). After April 26, 481 BCE, and over time in the state of Qi, these relationships became more commonly and more intensely like ones familiar to us in the twenty-first century: official to subordinate, patron to client, or employer to employee. In other words, the culmination of this conflict laid the foundations of a radical reorganization of politics and society within Qi, effectively making Qi the first of the "Warring States."

At first blush the events on the Sandalwood Terrace might seem unexceptional when viewed against the recent history of the ducal house of Qi. Just four years before (in 485 BCE) Lü Ren's father, posthumously known as Duke Dao (r. 488–485 BCE), had been murdered by one of his own courtiers in an attempt to appease the invading ruler of another state.[18] That same Duke Dao, on taking the throne in a palace coup of 489 BCE, had murdered his own brother, a child placed upon the throne by an opposing faction.[19] Lü Ren's grandfather had reigned for a remarkable span of 57 years and died of old age, but much of that time was punctuated by brutal infighting among his courtiers,[20] and he himself had come to the throne after the murder of his brother (Lü Ren's great uncle), who had been trapped and killed in the house of his own prime minister, with whose wife he was conducting an affair.[21]

Thus, by 481 BCE instability and violence had become a fixture of life at the Qi ducal court, and in this Qi was far from alone. A survey of the regional lords throughout the Zhou domain in the decades leading up to the confrontation on the Sandalwood Terrace would produce a litany of dukes that had been imprisoned, exiled, or (most often) killed in various ghastly ways.[22] The palace coup of April 26 was thus not exceptionally rebellious or destructive when compared with the politics of the courts of previous Qi dukes or those of other regional lords across the Zhou world. What made the confrontation on the Sandalwood Terrace unique and novel was the nature of its participants and the innovative strategies they pursued.

Among these, the duke himself occupied the most traditional role and pursued the most conservative strategy. The duke was a paragon of the hereditary aristocracy that had ruled the Zhou world since before the establishment of the dynasty, and it was the nature and social dynamics of this aristocracy that would be most drastically changed by the extended revolution of the Warring States.

The conditions of the Zhou aristocracy are often surprising when described to American and European readers. For those whose image of premodern Chinese elites were formed by pop-culture depictions like the detective-novel hero Judge Dee or the pulp fiction villain Fu Manchu,[23] the nature of a typical Zhou aristocrat may seem incongruous. Americans and Europeans who have some knowledge of eras such as the Ming dynasty (1368–1644 CE) are accustomed to imagining Chinese society led by a ruling class who were bookish and quietist in outlook; steeped in poetry, painting, and calligraphy; affecting long lacquer-sheathed fingernails to show their disdain for physical labor. These impressions are (to a degree, as generalizations) accurate for the scholar-officials and scholar-gentry of later imperial times. But the aristocracy of the Zhou dynasty bore little resemblance to this stereotype. The ascent of the scholar-official elite upon which this image is based to become the ruling class of the unified empire was a long-term product of the Warring States revolution. Though Zhou era nobles were expected to display a certain refinement of speech and dress and exhibit an appreciation for music and poetry, these pursuits were ornaments rather than foundations of their status. Prior to the Warring States it is not likely that most of the aristocracy were literate.[24]

The Zhou aristocracy saw themselves first and foremost as warriors. Their world view and ethos was similar to that of the samurai of medieval Japan or the knights of fourteenth-century CE Europe. The duke himself was trained in arms, as the events of April 26 would demonstrate. Courage was viewed as the defining characteristic of noble status. The outcomes of violence might be acknowledged as regrettable, but violence itself was considered a virtue and a necessity, without which an aristocrat was left bereft of purpose. During times of peace the necessary occasions for violence were provided by formal hunts and blood sacrifices. But peace was rare even before the Warring States.[25]

Ideally all armed aggression was to be directed "outward," to the alien people living beyond the frontiers of the Zhou realm, who spoke different languages and did not share the beliefs or customs of the "civilized" world. Such campaigns were frequent, and provided the early Zhou elite with new territories and captives for blood sacrifice and forced labor. But internecine conflict between Zhou vassal states was just as frequent, as were blood feuds between lower-level aristocratic clans and individuals. It was not unusual for two warriors who were ostensibly part of the same army to attack one another during a battle against a "common" enemy, to settle an old offense or point of honor. Duels and bloodshed were so common when aristocrats met that it was conventional to record if a formal encounter between two or more nobles transpired "without incident."[26]

This sounds like a milieu prone to chaos, and in many respects it was. One could be forgiven for wondering how such a society could produce the material luxury and cultural sophistication enjoyed by the duke and his wives on the Sandalwood Terrace. But the relentless belligerence of the aristocracy as warriors was balanced against their other defining social role: that of "priests" to the ancestors and gods.[27]

This priestly vocation of the aristocracy was as or more significant to the authority and prestige of a leader like the duke as his warrior pedigree. The entire Zhou nobility, from the king on down, claimed descent from the nature gods that ruled the cosmos, and from whom the royal house received the "Mandate of Heaven." Each of the ruling clans traced its origins back to a distant female ancestor who had been impregnated by one of the gods. The royal lineage of the prior Shang dynasty (whose descendants still ruled as "dukes" in the regional state of Song) claimed descent from a woman of high antiquity who had become pregnant by swallowing an egg dropped by a black bird, which happened to be the High God Di in corporeal form. The royal clan of the Zhou kings claimed descent from a woman who, on an excursion into the wilds, had become pregnant by stepping into a giant footprint (also that of the High God Di).[28]

This semi-divine parentage, in fact, was what ostensibly gave aristocrats the preternatural courage, strength, and other qualities that made them "noble." It is also what gave them unique spiritual authority to lead: because they were kin to the gods, the ancestral spirits of the nobility were in a unique position to intercede with higher spiritual forces on humanity's behalf, not merely in the interests of the aristocracy, but for all people noble and common. The ancestral spirits of dead aristocrats were believed to occasionally feast and converse with deities like the High God Di, and on those occasions could relay messages and requests sent by their mortal descendants. On this pretext, large portions of the revenue that aristocrats received from their lands and tenants were expended in the maintenance of an elaborate complex of temples, sacrifices, and festivals in support of the spirit realm. The nobility offered grand feasts to their own ancestors, who in turn were expected to gift and flatter the gods in order to secure rain, protection from floods, victory over "barbarians," and other blessings.[29]

This religious dimension of aristocratic life provided the Zhou nobles with a crucial balance against the chaotic violence of their warrior traditions. The rituals of the ancestral cult not only imbued leaders like the duke with great mystique, but also afforded them the opportunity to forge ties and mend breaches with kin, allies, and wayward vassals. If the duke wanted to cultivate the good will of another noble, he could invite him to participate in the sacrifices at Qi's ancestral temple, projecting to the world that the duke now viewed the noble in question as kin (or, if he was already kin, as was often the case, that the bond was even more intimate), and granting him new or enhanced prestige. Conversely, a noble who wanted to cultivate greater intimacy with the duke could offer him gifts of food, gems, bronze instruments, or other treasures to be used in the temples of Qi.[30]

These kinds of ceremonial exchange might seem empty or even hypocritical to our twenty-first-century sensibilities, but they served a significant purpose in the ancient Zhou world. If two aristocrats had a dispute, say, over a piece of territory, they were always faced with a variety of choices. The most obvious one was bloodshed, and there were very few circumstances under which a noble would be condemned for choosing violence. But in almost any instance there were also a number of ritual remedies that could be sought to restore harmony.

In the case of a dispute over territory, for example, the ruler could invite his alienated vassal to a ritual hunt, which would give him the pretext to "reward" the vassal with gifts that might partially compensate him for the surrendered territory. Because permanent records of such ceremonies were invariably kept (very often in the form of inscribed bronze vessels commemorating the occasion, which could literally be counted on to last forever), vassals who peacefully complied with the will of their lords could expect that their loyalty might secure the lord's favor, not only in their own lifetime but in that of their descendants. In this way ritual gave aristocrats the choice of deferring the short-term material benefits to be gained from conflict in favor of a long-term "investment" in the cultivation of a relationship, one that could potentially span generations.[31]

The Zhou aristocracy were acutely aware of the dual nature of their defining traditions. An old adage declared that "the great affairs of the state are sacrifice and warfare,"[32] and ancient writings persistently referred to the opposing dimensions of *"wen* and *wu"* (the civil and the martial).[33] To twenty-first-century eyes this appears like cultural schizophrenia: Zhou aristocrats were constantly being pulled in two directions (war and peace) simultaneously.

But for Zhou society to thrive, it was only necessary that religious and ritual traditions provided aristocrats sufficient incentive to choose peace over war *frequently enough*. Indeed, the scope of Zhou rule steadily expanded, sometimes through conquest, but equally through the influence of Zhou "civil" religious traditions. Non-Zhou elites (leaders of people like the Xianyun who did not speak the same language as the Zhou or share their religious beliefs) often voluntarily elected to become vassals of and participate in the ceremonial practices of the Zhou, seeking enhanced prestige among their own people.[34] Through these tandem processes of "civil" and "martial" expansion, the territory within which Zhou traditions were followed grew to more than twice what it had been at the founding of the Zhou.[35]

In 481 BCE the Duke of Qi ruled his state in the same role of "warrior-priest" that had been fulfilled by 25 of his ancestors. His throne by then was thus more than twice as old as the present-day United States of America. Unfortunately for the duke, by the time of his installation as ruler of Qi, both the martial and civil foundations of his position had been eroding for some time. Some of the forces behind this decay were quite straightforward. On the martial side, the denuding of the power of the Zhou kings had removed a vital prop to the position of the regional lords. Prior to 771 BCE (when the Western Zhou capital was overrun), anyone who defied or violated the authority of a regional ruler like the Duke of Qi had to fear prospective reprisals from the royal armies of the west. That had not been the case for almost three centuries by the time of the confrontation at the Sandalwood Terrace.

But the debasement of civil, religious traditions had been even more corrosive of ducal authority. This was in large part because the internal structure of a state like Qi was quite rudimentary. "Sacrifice and warfare" was more than a statement of values; it described the basic functional organs of government at every level, from that of the Zhou king, through the regional lords, down to the local regimes of the lords' vassals. Each of these courts had the same basic parts: a temple (or complex of temples) and a fortress. The duke's court ostensibly had offices like "Marshal of Horse" and "Master of Punishments," but these were hereditary positions held by courtiers whose duties were very flexible, bound only by their voluntary adherence to custom and tradition. In reality each state like Qi was presided over by a loosely organized oligarchy of warrior-priests.[36]

The duke and his immediate family had control over some lands and soldiers, but in the administration of the state as a whole the duke had to rely on the assistance of the vassal families (known in Chinese as *dafu* or "grandees") with which he shared his domain as *primus inter pares*. These grandee families were a mixed bunch. Some of them were the descendants of very old families that had followed the duke's ancestor from the west when they had first been sent to rule Qi by the founding Zhou kings. Others were the descendants of refugee noblemen that had fled to take shelter with one of the duke's ancestors, or families that had once been "dukes" in their own right but had been conquered and subjugated as vassals of Qi. About half of them were descended from the younger brother of a former Duke of Qi, who had been granted lands to supervise and a special charter to take a new clan name and set up their own noble lineage, to provide a new source of support for the ruling clan.[37]

Each of these grandee families had their own courts with their own temples and fortresses.[38] Thus the structure of the state of Qi (and the other regional states of the Zhou world) resembled nothing so much as a present-day organized crime family, with the duke as "Don" and the grandees as the head of "capo regimes." Just as in today's mafia, each grandee nobleman had sovereign authority over the affairs of his own clan, and could only be restrained to the degree that he deferred to the duke's dignity and authority within the larger Zhou hierarchy. A duke who was displeased with the performance or behavior of a grandee could strip him of a title or an office, but he could never really "fire" a grandee the way one would fire a modern-day employee. A grandee who had been removed from the office of "Master of Punishments," for example, still commanded his own fortress, presided over his own temple, and kept the loyalty of his own kin. If the duke remained displeased with his vassal and the traditional remedies for defusing such conflicts failed (as they did with increasing frequency as decades and centuries passed, for reasons discussed below), the only recourse was a zero-sum war in which either the duke or the grandee in question had to die.

Outside of brute force, the duke thus had no regular and predictable mechanisms to structure his relationship with his courtiers but the complex of sacrifices and other rituals over which he presided as "chief priest" of the state cult, in which he was given clear precedence as lord and superior. These traditions were effectively the currency on which the authority of the duke depended, and by 481 BCE that currency had been radically debased, not only in Qi but throughout the Zhou world. We can see this concretely in the scene on the Sandalwood Terrace.

This moment was not merely a matter of rebellion against a political superior. The blood on the guard's sword as he intruded upon the duke's leisure was that of a eunuch. The eunuch had barred entry to the Sandalwood Terrace because, according to the ritual precepts of Zhou society, the only fertile man allowed to be in the presence of the duke's wives was the duke himself. This was the only way to ensure that the next duke would genuinely be a descendant of the ancestral spirits served in Qi's temples (and therefore authorized to act as their chief priest). Thus, when the rebel male aristocrats trespassed upon the Sandalwood Terrace, they were not only defying the duke's political authority, but profaning the taboos on which his spiritual power within the shared religion of the Zhou world rested—rebelling against both human political authority and the gods. Understood in terms of the old adage about "sacrifice and warfare," the rebel aristocrats were acting solely as warriors and displaying total contempt for the duke's sacrosanct position as chief priest of Qi's temples, under whose aegis they themselves lived as warrior-priests in their own right.

The willingness of the rebels to profane the duke's harem did not make their act particularly "revolutionary" in 481 BCE. Such scenes had become almost routine occurrences across the North China plain and beyond; the martial traditions of the aristocracy were overwhelming and eradicating the strictures of "civil" ritual. The dukes at the head of states like Qi were just as guilty as their vassal grandees in this regard: aristocrats at all levels of the Zhou hierarchy had been systematically violating the taboos of the ancestral religion for decades.

The most common example of such sacrilege was in the ever-rising destructiveness of war.[39] In a common irony that can be seen often in human history, the Zhou elites were victims of their own success. Relative stability and material prosperity produced rapid population growth, especially among the aristocracy. Even with many noble scions "disinherited" (i.e. turned into commoners) in every generation, competition between aristocrats over material resources rapidly intensified. Over time, conflicts between states and clans increasingly ended with the total annihilation of one or more combatants.[40]

None of this is to imply that Zhou society was becoming poorer over time. Quite the contrary was true. As the opulence on the Sandalwood Terrace would have demonstrated, in per capita terms prosperity was growing. But even this development had destabilizing effects. As markets offered increasingly more opportunities for consumption and profit, and as merchants offered greater supplies, quality, and diversity of merchandise, the prestige to be had from elevated titles or intimacy with those of superior rank became progressively less attractive than the immediate, raw purchasing power of convertible wealth.[41]

By April 26, 481 BCE, these trends had been ongoing for decades, if not centuries. Violence had reached into the inner quarters of so many royal and ducal palaces that no member of the pleasure party on the Sandalwood Terrace, even the duke's wives and concubines, could have failed to hear such stories. The duke himself, who had spent much of his life in exile, was well acquainted with the turmoil that had become the norm of court politics. When the rebels broke in upon that day's leisure the revelers were undoubtedly shocked and upset, but they could not have been entirely unprepared.

So what made this incident, so seemingly tawdry and routine, revolutionary? The answer to this question lies in the unique conflict between the figures embroiled in the coup that began on the Sandalwood Terrace on that sunny spring day. The first of these was Tian Chang, co-prime minister of Qi, a "grandee" and head of a noble clan that had served the dukes of Qi for almost two centuries. The events of April 26, 481 BCE, would make him notorious for all time.

The founder of the Tian clan, Tian Chang's seventh-generation ancestor, had arrived as a refugee in Qi in 672 BCE. He had been a prince in the southern state of Chen, in line to inherit the title and throne, but factional battles had forced him into exile.[42] The rulers of Chen claimed descent from the legendary sage-king Shun of high antiquity, a monarch who had supposedly held the title "Son of Heaven" more than a millennium before the Zhou founders.[43] This elevated pedigree, along with all of the breeding he had received as heir apparent of Chen, made him very attractive to the ruler of Qi at the time, one of the most famous and powerful figures to hold the ducal throne of Qi. That duke was so impressed with the refugee prince that he broke precedent by offering the young noble a high office among Qi's most elite courtiers. The prince demurred, but accepted the invitation to stay as a minor vassal.

Over seven generations successive patriarchs of the Tian clan had thrived, achieving the rank of Viscount (*zi*) and a place among the most powerful grandees in the aristocratic oligarchy that ruled Qi.[44] The Tian's lofty pedigree had given them an advantage in the competition between aristocratic houses for wealth and status, but they had not rested complacently in the shelter of their venerable ancestry. As the Zhou world changed, the Tian clan had adapted. Long before Tian Chang ascended to the position of clan head, Tian leaders had realized the direction in which Zhou world was evolving. Particularly, they understood that the growing influence and versatility of material wealth gave new importance to commercial markets and transactions.

Tian Chang's grandfather had been a pioneer in this regard. Grain was one of the commodities that served as currency in the Zhou domain (as in much of the ancient world). The main source of income that the Tian received came in the form of grain from the harvest collected by farmers living on the land under Tian supervision. Most of this grain was used for the Tian's own expenditures, but some of it was given to the ducal court in the form of "tribute," and some of it was held in granaries at the duke's orders, against times of shortage. Disbursements from these public granaries were periodically ordered by the duke, not merely in times of emergency but as a "gift" from the duke to his people. Tian Chang's grandfather ordered that special extra-large measuring ladles be fashioned for use in dispensing "relief grain" from public granaries, so that a "liter" given out from the public store was larger than a "liter" of grain that had been collected at harvest time. This disparity between the "collecting" ladle and the "dispensing" ladle effectively amounted to a cash payment to the farmers, and since the differing measures were only in use on Tian lands, the farmers knew that the Tian clan were their benefactors.

Tian Chang's grandfather adopted similar measures in the markets on Tian lands. He imposed market controls within the areas under Tian control, restricting the markup that locals had to pay on commodities such as lumber, fish, and salt.[45] In these ways the Tian recognized that their elevated status and traditional religious mystique were no longer sufficient to guarantee them the power they would need in the increasingly bitter competition between aristocratic clans. The Tian understood that the changing political economy of the Zhou world had made loyalty a commodity like any other, and that they would have to use their material assets to buy it from the people under their control.

This new outlook did not only shape the manner in which the Tian related to commoners, but to other aristocrats as well. As inter-clan violence became more frequent and more destructive, the sheer numbers and combat effectiveness of a clan's armed forces became more and more important to political survival. Aristocratic clans discovered that the fastest way to increase the number of trained warriors in their ranks was to offer knights from other clans material rewards for transferring their loyalty. There had always been a degree of movement "between clans" in the annals of the Zhou aristocracy. But in the late fifth and early fourth centuries BCE the pace and volume of such movement accelerated dramatically.

This new strategy was largely a spontaneous product of the times. The conditions of the age created a ready "liquid market" for knightly talent. With competition intensifying and quarrels proliferating, there was always a significant pool of young men who had been driven from the ranks of their clan by errant duels or family conflicts, or whose clan had lost its lands and temples to war. In the increasingly violent world of the late sixth and early fifth centuries BCE, offering material support to uprooted knights in exchange for "joining the clan" became a key strategy separating clans that survived from those that perished.[46]

This strategy might seem shockingly obvious to our twenty-first-century sensibilities, but it was a disruptive change. Though there had always been a degree of movement between clans, the traditions that structured aristocratic life made such movement problematic. One source records a conversation of the head of a powerful clan who desired to recruit former vassals of two clans he had defeated in war. On expressing this wish, he is told that good men would not answer such a summons, and that any men who did were not good.⁴⁷ Questions of honor or old blood feuds almost always meant that the recruitment by a lord of a noble from outside his clan entailed a stain upon the good name of one or both. Thus the very tactics that were most imperative for the material survival of the clan posed a threat to its internal logic and cohesion.

Just how jarring this trend was to elite Zhou society can be seen in a story about Tian Chang, the leader of the coup of 481 BCE. He was supposedly so eager to attract client warriors to join the ranks of the Tian clan that he used his own wives and concubines to that end. He searched far and wide to find women of ideal physical proportions to populate his inner household. He then allowed any and all of the warriors that accepted the Tian clan's patronage to enjoy the delights of this harem. As a result, so the story goes, Tian Chang had more than 70 sons, all of dubious paternity.⁴⁸

This story is almost certainly not true, as later commentators have noted.⁴⁹ Times were changing during Tian Chang's lifetime, but not so much that he would have risked casting doubt upon the legitimacy of his own children. But the inner logic of the story (which probably began circulating as slander about the Tian clan during or shortly after Tian Chang's life) communicates the implications of the patronage strategy for Zhou society, and its potential to scandalize even as it was widely adopted throughout the aristocratic world. The idea that clan leaders would give noble-born warriors wealth in exchange for their loyalty offended many of the aristocrats of Tian Chang's time. A bond based on material wealth was equivalent to one based on sexual favors—either kind of relationship was rooted in the selfish needs of patron and client, rather than respect for a higher duty mandated by kinship, tradition, or obligation to the gods and ancestors.

Moreover, filling out the ranks of the clans with retainers was contributing to a world in which kinship no longer counted as much. If strangers who gave an oath in exchange for land or wealth became equivalent to cousins and nephews, what did blood relations matter at all? If that was the case, why would you care if your sons were really your sons? The broadest and most ironically satirical implication of the story about Tian Chang's harem is of course quite straightforward. It translates strictly and simply into colloquial English: "the Tian clan are all a bunch of bastards."

It must be stressed that the Tian was not the only grandee clan experimenting with these new forms of social and political organization in the world of 481 BCE. Virtually all the great clans were adopting similar tactics as the conditions of competition drove aristocrats all over the Zhou domain toward common expediencies. What then made the coup of April 26 such a revolutionary watershed?

One reason is exemplified by the satirical story about Tian Chang's harem: the Tian were enjoying exceptional success in pursuing these developing strategies, and thus were "trendsetters" in the most literal sense of that word. By 481 BCE, through guile, diplomacy, and brute force, the Tian had managed to consolidate enormous wealth and power into their own hands, annihilating and absorbing the assets of several competing grandee clans (some of which were close kin to the Qi ducal house). This had eventually given them effective "veto power" over the succession to the ducal throne itself. They had conspired with other clans to bring the duke and his father home from exile in 489 BCE, so that the duke's father could assume the throne. After the duke's father had been assassinated (by a grandee clan hostile to the Tian), the Tian maneuvered to ensure that the line they favored retained the throne, and so it was with the aid of the Tian clan that the duke had succeeded his father in 485 BCE.[50]

This brings us to the other players in the drama of April 26, and the ultimate reason why that date represented such a turning point for Zhou society. If the duke, on assuming the throne, had "gone with the flow," been ready to acknowledge the ascendant power of the Tian clan, and structured his court accordingly, the tale of his reign would most likely have been unexceptional, and none of the figures or events at his court would have stood out so clearly in later memory. To be sure, his reign would have been marked by the usual infighting and skullduggery that had become a hallmark of Qi politics. Perhaps he would have persisted as a benign puppet for many decades, like his grandfather who grew old on the throne while his grandee vassals warred with one another incessantly. Perhaps he would have met a grisly end like his great uncle, his uncle, or his father. Either way, his reign would not have given us any moments to mark as signifying the beginning of a revolution with global consequences.

But the duke had not proven to be someone content to "go with the flow." In hindsight he might not have been a man of great wisdom, but he was certainly a figure of energy and imagination. He came to the throne determined to make his mark on the state of Qi, and to restore power and dignity to the ducal house. In attempting to do so he induced a crisis that indeed changed Qi (and the entire Zhou world) forever, but not in the ways he had intended.

The explosive element that the duke contributed to the political cauldron of his court in 481 BCE was the product of a twist of fate. The duke and his father spent many years of exile in Lu. Like Qi, Lu was an old state. Its first duke had been the eldest son of one of the most prominent founders of the Zhou throne, thus the state had a very prestigious pedigree. Despite their shared roots in the venerable past, Qi and Lu had been one another's nemeses for many generations. They were often at war, which would explain why the ruler of Lu was quite willing to give shelter to a refugee prince of Qi.

The sojourn would prove fateful for the duke, because during his exile he befriended a man known to history as Zai Wo. Zai Wo was a native of Lu, and by the time he met the future Duke of Qi, he had been swept up in a movement that had begun among the young, lower-ranking aristocrats (again the *shi* or "knights") in his home state. This movement was in its most nascent stages during the duke's exile, but it would expand and spread over time to influence most of what is now China and much of East and Southeast Asia. That development could not have been predicted in 481 BCE. Indeed, few during the whole of the Warring States could have foreseen it.

There are many details we do not know about how Zai Wo and the duke became friends. We are in the dark about how exactly these men met or what about Zai Wo so impressed the duke. Of one thing we can be fairly certain, however: events would have played out very differently if Zai Wo had not been a disciple of Confucius (551–479 BCE).[51]

On assuming the throne, the duke recognized that Tian Chang, as head of the Tian clan, was the most powerful man among his courtiers. In deference to that reality the duke appointed Tian one of two co-prime ministers to lead the other grandees at court. As a counterbalance to Tian Chang's power, however, the duke appointed his friend Zai Wo to serve as co-prime minister.[52]

The enormous audacity of this move on the part of the duke is difficult to exaggerate. Remember that when Tian Chang's ancestor, the refugee prince who founded the Tian clan, had first arrived in Qi in 672 BCE, he had refused an offered position among the high courtiers, only accepting appointment to the court with a minor rank and title. This had been very wise. Though the celebrated duke at that time had been very powerful, and though the young prince had a fine pedigree, leapfrogging over established and longstanding grandee houses would even back then have caused resentment and attracted hostility, perhaps even violence.

By contrast, the duke of 481 BCE, having only a fraction of the power of his famous ancestor, made bold to give a complete newcomer equal status at the very top of the state hierarchy with what was by then an old family of Qi (i.e. the Tian), a clan that had accrued such vast human and material resources that it rivaled any family that had ever served the state. To put Zai Wo on a par with

Tian Chang, the duke granted him land and titles so that he could support his own ancestral temple, which needed to be supplied from the harvest of villages within the state of Qi. This is perhaps the most extraordinary aspect of the duke's plan, because while there is some evidence that Zai Wo's father was a high-ranking grandee back in Lu, he would not have been in line to inherit his father's title. The best he could normally have expected was to enjoy patronage as a *shi* (knight) in the retinue of his family or that of another lord.

In presuming to raise this relative nobody to the pinnacles of Qi society, the duke was assuming a posture that was so conservative it might be called "reactionary." He was, in effect, throwing down the gauntlet and reasserting the ducal house's prerogative to decide who was high and who was low in the state of Qi. The way in which he went about it, however, was shockingly extreme. Even his most exalted and powerful ancestors had shown more deference to the organic hierarchy of aristocratic society. None of them would have attempted to move a person from a position quite so low to one quite so high.

Some of the duke's motivation for this move might have been the simple impulse to avoid his father's fate—and the desire for an ally at court to protect him from rebellious courtiers. Moreover, since the duke almost certainly seized land from the clans that had been implicated in his father's death to support his new prime minister's temple, in one stroke he had managed to strengthen his own hand while weakening that of his likely enemies.

But even if this did form part of the duke's thinking, his move was so unprecedented and fraught with risk (he was doing at least as much to attract enemies among the courtiers as to fend them off, if not more) that he must have had some other source of inspiration. The most logical place to look for this is in the person of the new co-prime minister himself, and in the ideas of his teacher.

Confucius is a figure so diffracted by millennia of myth-making and adulation that it is difficult to recover his historical role in the events of the early fifth century BCE. It is for precisely this reason that he is one of two figures referred to by a Romanized Latin name in this book (the other being his latter-day disciple Mencius, whom we will encounter later). When Jesuit missionaries, who after Marco Polo provided some of the earliest detailed information about China to reach Europe, first traveled to the territory of the Ming dynasty during the sixteenth century, they immediately recognized the reverence in which Kong *fuzi* ("Master Kong") was held by the ruling elite of the imperial court. By then the texts that ostensibly conveyed Master Kong's teachings had been the standard curriculum for exams required of all imperial officials for almost five centuries, and the Master himself had been a figure of almost universal veneration for more than a millennium before that, known by sobriquets such as "the supreme sage" and "the teacher of ten thousand generations." Since the Jesuits' mission required that they communicate the state of imperial religious and ideological belief to the Pope back in Rome, they coined the name "Confucius" for the man held in such awe by Ming rulers and literati. It has been in use in much of the non-Chinese-speaking world ever since.[53]

In 481 BCE Confucius was generally known to his peers by his full name Kong Qiu, or his "style name" Zhongni. There was little sign then of his eventual grandeur. He had evidently become a figure of some fame (or notoriety, depending on one's perspective) in the state of Lu. How far his reputation traveled beyond his home state is difficult to know with any certainty, given the propensity for exaggeration and artifice in even the earliest sources that report on his life. The fact that his name became an eponymous "ism," "Confucianism," might give modern readers the impression that he was a figure akin to Jesus or the Buddha. There are some merits to these analogies, but a key difference. Confucius did attract followers, but he did not attempt to organize them into any kind of strictly regular and hierarchical "church." In this respect his historical role was much closer to that of his near-contemporary Socrates (ca. 470–399 BCE) in ancient Athens, to whom Confucius is often compared.

In the terms of his own time and place, Confucius was an aristocrat, but one of very low status. The Kong clan to which he belonged was a grandee clan descended from the dukes of the state of Song, who were in turn descended from the kings of the Shang, the dynasty that had preceded the Zhou (as mentioned above, in the discussion of these clans' divine ancestry). Confucius's great-grandfather had fled political turmoil in Song and taken refuge in Lu, where the family had been ever since.

Confucius's ancestors had not flourished in Lu in the way that the Tian clan had in Qi. Confucius's father was not a grandee, he served as a knight under the patronage of the Jisun clan, a powerful grandee family descended from a former Duke of Lu. According to one tradition, Confucius's father was an extraordinarily strong warrior. At one battle he held open the portcullis gate of a city from which he and his comrades were retreating so that the forces of Lu could make their escape. Other sources suggest that Confucius's mother was much younger than his father, and that their union may have been illicit. Confucius is said not to have known his father, and had to work to have his knightly heritage recognized by the aristocratic society of Lu.

Though Confucius harbored political ambitions all his life, they remained unfulfilled. He never held a position of high status or substantial responsibility in any regional court. Like his father, he accepted the patronage of the Jisun clan and worked at a number of minor posts as a young man. Despite his career frustrations, he developed a reputation for extraordinary learning, and over time other aristocrats began to send their sons to Confucius for instruction.[54]

This was a common practice, especially for younger sons who were not in line to inherit their father's title and temple altars (such as Zai Wo). All aristocratic scions were expected to have certain refinements that were the hallmark of their status: an appreciation for music, a knowledge of poetry, a familiarity with ritual etiquette, a cultivated manner of speech, dress, and comportment. In addition, those who would not inherit a title found it increasingly useful to learn how to read and write, as these were skills that made them more competitive in attracting the patronage of more powerful nobles. These were the kinds of training that aristocrats hoped their sons would receive at the gate of a teacher like Confucius.[55]

Confucius gave his students all of the ordinary forms of instruction, but he was unlike any of the conventional teachers that had preceded him. He developed a grand doctrine, a set of ideas that tied together all of the component parts of the ordinary aristocratic curriculum.[56] He called this doctrine "the Dao" or (as the word is usually translated into English) "the Way," and he claimed that the Way held the key for saving the entire Zhou world from the cataclysm that was engulfing it.[57]

"I am a transmitter, not an innovator," Confucius declared.[58] He was the first person, to our knowledge, who talked of "the Way" as a grand doctrine, but he insisted that he had not invented it. He had discovered it in the writings, rituals, and music of the ancient kings. It had been lost because over time people had forgotten the deeper meanings of the poems, songs, documents, and rituals that had been passed down from the sage kings of antiquity (especially the founders of the Zhou dynasty, whom Confucius particularly revered),[59] but Confucius could lead people to it if they would follow him. This is what animated his instruction of his students: he exhorted them not to approach their studies as a means to simply become well groomed, sophisticated, and employable, but as a journey to find the Way. The stakes, as he laid them out for his pupils, were supremely high: "It is permissible if one hears of the Way in the morning and dies that night."[60] In other words, if the young men he was teaching achieved some understanding and mastery of the Way they could do great things—potentially save the world. If they did not, their lives would be meaningless.

For Confucius, the power of the Way lay in its potential to provide moral guidance to a society that had lost its bearings. He proposed that the cultural traditions of the Zhou, such as its rituals, music, and poetry, embodied abstract moral values like loyalty, filial piety (the duty owed to parents and ancestors), and humaneness (*ren*).[61] "Humaneness" was especially important to Confucius, signifying for him a kind of total human excellence: the capacity of a person to treat others with sensitivity, compassion, courtesy, and respect.[62]

The relationship Confucius envisioned between Zhou cultural forms and the values of the Way was very profound and subtle. It was not merely the case, for example, that a sacrifice to the ancestors could "teach you about" humaneness. On the one hand, you could never be truly and fully humane unless you not only understood but actually participated in rituals. At the same time, the rituals themselves would not really work unless the people performing the rituals were themselves humane, or were at least making a good-faith effort to become so.[63]

These aspects of the Way explained two things for Confucius. First, it made clear why a society that had become so expansive and prosperous under the auspices of Zhou tradition was, in Confucius's own time, falling apart. The traditions of the Zhou founders no longer provided order and harmony, so Confucius taught, because the people participating in them were only "going through the motions." They expected that the fastidious performance of a ritual could attract blessings from the spirits or foster peace between the living; but they had forgotten the values like harmony and humaneness that made such blessings deserved or peace itself worthwhile. To undertake rituals with selfish, superficial, *materialistic* intentions and then anticipate profound effects was folly. This was why the traditions of the Zhou had become so impotent and why elites had turned increasingly to violence to achieve political goals.[64]

Secondly, an understanding of the Way showed Confucius the path out of the current crisis. The elites of the Zhou world did not need better institutions or better traditions; they needed to become better people. The means to that end was learning, not just of tradition, but of the Way that encompassed and animated the tradition. It was this kind of learning that Confucius offered his students.[65]

A story told about Confucius and his students illustrates what those who believed in Confucius's doctrine imagined it would look like in practice. The *Analects* (*Lun yu*) tells us that two of Confucius's students were given patronage by the head of the Jisun clan. Like the Tian clan in Qi, the Jisun had amassed wealth and manpower enough to make the clan head more powerful that the Duke of Lu himself.

The students came to report to Confucius about a plan that their lord had devised. He envied the rich and strategically important territory of another clan, one that centuries before had been given the charge to oversee sacrifices to the god of a sacred mountain by the Zhou king himself. The Jisun clan head coveted the income to be had in the near term and worried about the strategic threat the terrain might pose in the future, thus he planned to preemptively assault the weaker clan, destroy their temples, and annex their land.

Confucius was apoplectic with outrage and disappointment. He reminded his students of what the Way demanded. To violate the sacred prerogative of both the king and the gods for the sake of military and economic advantage was an abomination. If the Jisun clan head feared a potential threat from the neighboring clan, he should work on developing his own qualities of wisdom and humaneness, so that when he approached the other clan with ceremonial overtures of friendship and good will they would comply gladly, rather than needing to be overcome by force.

As disgusted as Confucius was with the Jisun lord, he blamed his students most of all. They pleaded to their teacher that they opposed the plan, but Confucius did not accept their excuses. "What use to a blind man is the assistant who does not steady him when he totters or support him when he falls?...Whose fault is it when the tiger and the rhinoceros escape from their cages?"[66] Confucius asked. In other words, the fault lay with the students because they were superior to their lord in learning. They understood the Way while the head of the Jisun clan did not, thus they should have been in control of the situation even though he was their superior in status and political authority. If they failed to make their lord see the light, it could only be a sign that they had not been diligent enough in their own studies. Had their learning been more advanced, they would have possessed the moral force of character necessary to sway their lord to the path of the Way.

So how does this story help us to understand the revolution of the Warring States, particularly the part in that revolution played by the coup of 481 BCE? Debates have raged for millennia over whether Confucius was a conservative or whether any part of his doctrine could be considered revolutionary or "progressive." Some of the harshest condemnation of him as a hopeless conservative was voiced in twentieth-century China.[67] But any objective reading of the evidence like the story above must concede that the picture is much too complicated to admit for easy judgments.

On the one hand, we can see that some of the practical ramifications of Confucius's doctrine would undeniably have been conservative in the context of the late Zhou dynasty. First and foremost, Confucius declared that the accelerating trend of territorial consolidation that had been building for several centuries, in which states and clans devoured one another, must stop. The Way demanded that aristocratic families currently in possession of their own temples must be left unmolested and their hereditary privileges respected. If this doctrine had ever been successfully realized, it would have put an end to one of the most common forms of downward social mobility in the Zhou world and helped preserve the status quo.

Beyond ending interstate and inter-clan wars, Confucius and his followers wanted to reinvigorate the traditional Zhou hierarchy. We can see this in the story above, from Confucius's anger at the Jisun clan's disregard for the mandate of the Zhou king. Confucius recognized that one of the worst root causes of disorder was the fact that an individual noble's actual power could no longer be confidently predicted by his hereditary title. Grandees were more powerful than dukes, and dukes more powerful than kings. This had to change, the world needed to go back to being a place where the word of a king or a duke had force: "Let the ruler be a ruler, the vassal a vassal, the father a father, and the son a son."[68] In other words, when each man wielded the powers and fulfilled the responsibilities of his station, harmony would prevail. The gendering of these terms is deliberate: one very conservative aspect of Confucius's teachings was his affirmation of the patriarchal nature of Zhou social norms.[69]

Though these tenets of the Way as Confucius preached it all imply halting the tide of change or turning the clock back, not all of the ramifications of his teachings were so conservative. This can sometimes be difficult to see, because the rhetoric within which Confucius's ideas were broadcast camouflaged some of the most radical aspects of his thought. The story above again gives us clear examples of this principle at work. The story might well seem like an odd example for Confucius's followers to offer of his doctrine in practice, since it was a moment of failure. The *Analects*, in fact, is generally quite candid about Confucius's inability to change the course of politics in Lu (or elsewhere). But if we put the story in the context of Zhou society while Confucius was alive, we see that its candor helps to hide some very shocking assertions it makes about the way social and political relationships *should* operate.

It might seem strange to twenty-first-century readers that two students would come to divulge the secret military plans of their lord and patron to their teacher, and that is no accident. It would have seemed strange to almost all Zhou aristocrats of the fifth century BCE as well. In fact, more than strange, it would have seemed a rank betrayal of the students' oath of loyalty to their lord. The *Analects* is deliberately "normalizing" what the followers of Confucius would have realized was, in fact, deeply aberrant behavior by the conventions of its day.

Confucius's followers understood that the kind of authority they attributed to their teacher was radically new. They believed that their duty to him was profound, and that it might (perhaps often would) trump their allegiance to their rulers and even their families. No one like this had ever (to the best of our knowledge from the historical record) existed in Zhou society before. Confucius occupied a position and filled a role that was newly created and required a new name, just as "philosopher" would later be coined to describe the new vocation of Socrates in ancient Athens. In similar fashion, the followers of Confucius adopted new terms to describe his position and their relationship to him. He was their Master (*fuzi*), they were his disciples (*dizi*).

This new role of "Master" as the followers of Confucius understood it was, as the previous story demonstrates, very powerful. He had the authority, at least within the circle of his disciples, to countermand the orders of their social superiors and even their rulers. Where did such authority come from? From the Way. This was the most radical aspect of Confucius's doctrine. He insisted that the Way was the moral foundation on which the entire social and political order was built. Kings were kings because of the Way. Aristocrats were aristocrats because of the Way. If one aristocrat was born higher in status than another, it was because the Way dictated that it must be so.

But the very existence of the Way created another trait that must, according to Confucius and his followers, be respected: learning. The Way required that people learn, thus in the same manner that the Way made a king a king and a grandee a grandee, it made a Master a Master. Confucius was the inferior of the head of the Jisun clan in both birth and position, and that fact was not within Confucius's power to change. But Confucius had become, through his own effort, vastly superior to the head of the Jisun clan in learning, and that gave Confucius superior moral authority.

The implications of this moral authority were significant. Because the proper powers of a grandee like the Jisun clan flowed to him from the Way, if he used those powers in violation of the Way, then he should be taken to task. Who was equipped to make such a judgment? The man of learning was. This is why it was right for Confucius's students to report the wicked plan of their lord to Confucius and for Confucius to pronounce it anathema.

The socially subversive implications of the Way did not stop with the newfangled authority of the Master. Anyone who was advanced in learning could, according to Confucius, claim authority exceeding that due to them by birth.

We see this in the story of Confucius's two disciples and their Jisun lord. As disappointed as Confucius was in his disciples' failure to curb their highborn patron, Confucius never questioned their legitimate authority to do so: he compared their lord to a blind man or a rhinoceros and his disciples to their lord's "keepers." Like Confucius, the disciples were their lord's superior in learning (they had proven that by at least coming to report his transgression to Confucius), thus whatever their difference in birth they could claim to be their lord's peers as "gentlemen" (*junzi*).

On this score the *Analects* is explicit: in an ideal world the Jisun clan head would have given the disciples his proxy and allowed them to manage affairs on his behalf, in acknowledgment of their superior understanding of the Way. So even though Confucius's doctrine was quite conservative in demanding a halt to common forms of *downward* mobility, it was quite radical in envisioning and advocating new and robust forms of *upward* mobility. Even though the Way demanded that nominal status and authority should remain in the hands of those born to high station, it likewise dictated that actual power and responsibility should be given to those who had improved themselves through learning, no matter what status they had from birth.

This was, in that historical moment, deliberately or not, a message sure to set the hearts of young men like Zai Wo on fire. Though the growing power and changing political strategy of grandee clans like the Jisun and Tian had given young knights new opportunities for patronage and employment, those had come at a social cost. Accepting payment for labor was the hallmark of a commoner, thus even as knights prospered they were forced to suffer the contempt and condescension of highborn aristocrats. Confucius's vision of the Way gave knights like himself and his disciples new dignity and elevated purpose. Confucius denied that the support offered to his disciples by leaders like the Jisun clan head put them under any special onus of gratitude or subservience. He rejected the emerging commercial rationale pursued by leaders like Tian Chang and his forebears in Qi. On this question as others, Confucius's position was a complex mixture of the old and the new. In common with the nobles of Zhou antiquity, Confucius insisted that the relationship between lord and vassal, ruler and minister, could never be transactional, but transcended the petty material interests of those involved. Unlike conventional aristocrats, Confucius did not ground that duty in mere tradition or even the authority of the gods, but in his grand moral vision of the Way.[70]

During the future Duke of Qi's days in exile, did Zai Wo win him over to this vision? The histories do not tell us for sure, but the picture strongly presents itself to us. We know that the duke spent many years of idle exile in Lu. The frustrations of a man of action under those circumstances must have been considerable. The duke and his father most likely lived comfortably—the duke's father married a daughter of the Jisun clan,[71] which suggests that father and son enjoyed the hospitality of wealthy and powerful hosts. But in a society given to petty competition over status and precedence, the duke no doubt suffered frequent slights. He was living among enemies and was down on his luck; there must have been many opportunities for the venal and jealous to snipe at him with impunity.

In that milieu Zai Wo would have been a kindred spirit. Both men's situations were existentially similar. Each was shunted to the sidelines of social life and politics—the duke by exile, Zai Wo by the misfortune of being a younger son. The *Analects* names Zai Wo as one of two of Confucius's disciples famous for being a talented speaker.[72] It is easy to imagine Zai Wo and the duke lounging over wine in the duke's apartments; engaged in late night gab sessions familiar to modern-day college students; commiserating with one another about how they could set the world ablaze if only they were given free scope for their talents. In such discussions Zai Wo might well have described his Master's teachings to the duke, explaining how so much of what was wrong with the world, and of trouble to both young men, would be fixed if only the Master's Way prevailed.

Whether that was in fact what occurred when the two men met we can never know for sure. Whatever the case may be, what happened next proved that Confucius's ideas were combustible. Zai Wo's rise to the position of co-prime minister of Qi was an example of exactly the kind of upward mobility that Confucius had advocated: the ascent of a man of learning to illustrious status and grand responsibility. Moreover, the fact that it was done on the duke's initiative embodied the restored vigor of the traditional Zhou hierarchy that, according to Confucius, the Way demanded. Indeed, the establishment of this regime in Qi was undoubtedly the most robust fulfillment of the Way, as he envisioned it, that Confucius witnessed in his own lifetime.

As the scene on the Sandalwood Terrace with which this chapter opened attests, things did not go well. Zai Wo did his best to serve both his ruler and the teachings of his Master, but he was a babe cast among wolves. Tian Chang predictably despised his co-prime minister from the outset and would glower balefully at Zai Wo during sessions at court. The duke was warned of the hatred between his courtiers, but brushed such alarms aside.[73] It did not take long for actual conflict to arise. On his way to attend an evening convening of the ducal court, Zai Wo witnessed a murder committed by a member of the Tian clan.[74] He arrested the offender and brought him to the palace to be held prisoner. The Tian clan men plied the jail guards with liquor, killed them once they were intoxicated, and sprang their kinsman out of detention.

To head off further violence, Zai Wo came personally to the Tian clan household and entered into a blood covenant with Tian Chang. A covenant involved the participants sacrificing an animal, smearing some of its blood on their lips, and taking an oath of friendship and peace. The spoken words traveled up to the spirits of Heaven, a written copy for each participant was buried along with the carcass of the victim in a pit, as a record for the gods of the earth.[75] Here we see Zai Wo being the good disciple. Confucius would have approved his moral courage: he took his life into his own hands by entering the Tian clan's domain. Beyond this, it was very much in the spirit of the Way to seek reconciliation in ritual and avoid bloodshed.

Tensions between the two prime ministers continued to mount, however, leading inexorably toward a showdown. Zai Wo's final stratagem seems at first glance rather incredible. He had within his own retinue a low-ranking member of the Tian clan.[76] Zai Wo approached him, proposing to drive the current Tian clan leadership into exile and install his man as patriarch of the Tian clan. Given the danger they posed, we might wonder why Zai Wo would seek to preserve the Tian clan to any degree, much less risk leaking them advance knowledge of his intentions. Here again his commitment to the teachings of his Master was instrumental. The Tian were an ancient family of Qi, descended from a sage king. To cut off their ancestral sacrifices entirely would be a terrible violation of Confucius's cherished vision of the Way.

Even if we accept Zai Wo's determination to preserve the Tian clan intact, we might still wonder why he would be so foolish as to entrust his Tian client with such a sensitive secret. Perhaps he had great confidence in his own powers of persuasive speech. But he would also have been applying the teachings of Confucius, who urged his disciples to understand (in the way that his disciples who took up service with the Jisun clan head had not) that learning and moral character have a power of their own. If you possess the Way, others will follow— right can truly make you mighty. It was not only his Tian follower that Zai Wo trusted, but the power of his Master's Way and the force of his own moral character.

That trust, we know in hindsight, was misplaced. However much this low-ranking Tian clan scion may have personally admired Zai Wo, he could have had little doubt as to which prime minister enjoyed the better chances in any struggle to retain purchase in Qi. The scheme itself might well have appeared as naïve to him as it does to our twenty-first-century sensibilities. Given the enormous power accrued by Tian Chang, driving him into exile would never have worked in the long run. As long as he was left alive, Tian Chang would have the ability to strike back at anyone who had crossed him so badly. Zai Wo's Tian clan follower did not want to throw in with what looked surely to be the losing side. He reported Zai Wo's scheme to Tian Chang, setting in motion the preemptive coup of April 26, 481 BCE.[77]

The events of that day demonstrate the degree to which Zai Wo was strategically outmatched. Tian Chang had been preparing for an eventual conflict with his co-prime minister before hearing of Zai Wo's plan. He had placed one of his kinsman in the palace as a member of the duke's guard—the same man who had committed the murder witnessed by Zai Wo some months before, and who wielded the sword that killed the eunuch protecting the Sandalwood Terrace. That man almost certainly provided key intelligence to Tian Chang on the day of the coup.

Because the day was warm, Zai Wo had set up a cloth pavilion outside the palace gates to conduct court business, so that the courtiers could be cool in the airy shade rather than in the musty humidity of the palace halls. Tian Chang arrived while Zai Wo was still hearing business in the tent but the duke had withdrawn to the Sandalwood Terrace within the palace gates. Tian Chang's kinsman inside the palace must have tipped him off to when conditions were just right.

Tian Chang arrived in the company of several of his brothers, riding in four chariots. They would have been accompanied by a sizeable armed retinue. Zai Wo greeted them outside of the cloth pavilion and let them pass through the palace gates, unsuspecting. Once inside the palace compound, Tian Chang ordered the gate barred, trapping the duke inside and putting Zai Wo at a tactical disadvantage. The war between the two co-prime ministers had begun on Tian Chang's terms: Zai Wo would have to assault a fortified position to reestablish contact with the duke.

Tian Chang and his brothers took over the palace and moved immediately to secure the person of the duke. This brings us to the scene on the Sandalwood Terrace. Although he had insolently trespassed on the duke's harem, Tian Chang still hoped to be reconciled with the duke. He almost certainly reported Zai Wo's scheme to the duke, declaring that once Zai Wo was defeated there would be no more need for violence.

This made sense. Tian Chang had not come onto the Sandalwood Terrace intent on making revolution. He was ready to fall back on what had worked in the past. Other dukes, in both Qi and other states, had capitulated to accepting life as a figurehead in a court controlled by a powerful grandee. If the duke had cooperated, the incident might have ended with less noteworthy consequences.

Accordingly, Tian Chang ordered the duke and his wives off of the Sandalwood Terrace and indoors to the palace bedchambers. This was in part to prevent the duke from escaping, but was equally for the protection of both the duke and his wives. The terrace was exposed, and Tian Chang anticipated fighting. If a stray arrow had hit someone on the terrace, the chances for reconciliation might be lost accidently.

But the duke was not willing to cooperate. As Tian Chang and his ruler entered the duke's bedchamber, the duke grabbed a pole-axe and attacked Tian Chang in a fury, intending to kill him. Another courtier intervened and tried to calm the duke by reassuring him of Tian Chang's good intentions.

After this outburst, Tian Chang and some of his men withdrew to the palace armory and set up their headquarters. Tian Chang was shaken. He sent back to know whether the duke was now calm and was told that his ruler was still angry.

This news understandably upset Tian Chang. It meant that the situation was much more volatile and dangerous than he had anticipated. The bloodshed would not be able to end with Zai Wo. The duke himself would have to die, and once that was done it was very difficult to know where the killing would end. More than this, by moving so aggressively to assert his power the duke had forced a very high-stakes showdown. If the duke himself had been willing to back off of the radical implications of his actions, if he had admitted that it had been a mistake to raise a nobody like Zai Wo over the heads of his grandees, then Tian Chang and his ruler might have been able to find a modus vivendi. But if the duke fought Tian Chang now, as it seemed he was determined to do, it would not be enough even to kill the duke and enthrone another member of the Lü clan. Tian Chang would have to take drastic measures to demonstrate that he, his clan, and the other grandees would never tolerate this kind of challenge to their power ever again.

Tian Chang momentarily lost his nerve. He was not ready for the escalating level of destructiveness and risk that the situation was thrusting upon him. "How can I behave as if I have no ruler?" he moaned, and declared his intention to call off the coup and withdraw from the palace. At this, Tian Chang's kinsman drew the same sword with which he had slain the duke's eunuch and brandished it against Tian Chang. "Doubt is the thief of action," he declared. "Which of us is not a member of the Tian clan? Anyone who would not kill you now is no true member of the Tian clan."[78]

It was a pivotal moment and confronted Tian Chang with the brave new world that he and his forebears had been helping to create. Contrary to his words, the man threatening Tian Chang at that moment was showing no respect for traditional Zhou religious values: shedding the blood of a kinsman, particularly someone more senior in the family hierarchy, was a serious transgression under any circumstances. But "the Tian clan" operated under new rules that had been established through several generations of innovation and reform. According to these, Tian Chang could not expect that his position as master of the clan's altars made his person sacrosanct. What made Tian Chang valuable to the clan at this point was the fact that he kept the wealth flowing to all of its clients and dependents, which included the kinsman who was now threatening Chang's life. "Which of us is not a member of the Tian clan?" In other words: all of us are drawing from the same source of revenue, and if you stand in the way of that flow, you will have to be replaced.

The palace guardsman was right, as Tian Chang must have surely realized. In the same way that Tian Chang could not expect deference from his kinsman at this juncture, he could not afford to show any to the duke. The choice was very stark: stand up and do what had to be done, or allow the Tian clan to be destroyed and replaced by another clan with less compunction about being ruthless. Tian Chang withdrew his orders to abandon the coup.

While the altercation had been going on in the palace armory, Zai Wo, realizing too late what was happening, had gone to his own manor and rallied soldiers. He led these men in an assault on the main and side gates of the palace. The assault failed, and Zai Wo's forces broke and fled. Tian Chang and his brothers sallied forth from the palace walls to pursue them.

Zai Wo fled the capital with the remnants of his retinue, Tian Chang hot on his heels. He seems to have hoped to go back to his native state of Lu. Southwest of the capital, in the general direction of home, he lost his way, straying into the village of Fengqiu. The people of Fengqiu were followers of the Tian. This was an occasion in which the investments made by Tian Chang's grandfather in the loyalty of the common people paid dividends. They seized Zai Wo and handed him over to Tian Chang's men. Tian Chang wasted no time in bringing Zai Wo back to the capital and publicly executing him at one of the city gates.

At some point in the melee, perhaps after Tian Chang and his brothers set out in pursuit of Zai Wo, the duke escaped the palace. Tian Chang's forces caught up with him at the town of Xuzhou on May 4. On May 18, after being held prisoner for two weeks, the duke was killed without fanfare at Xuzhou.[79]

The duke's infant brother was enthroned as the twenty-seventh Duke of Qi, known posthumously as Duke Ping (r. 480–456 BCE). Tian Chang was installed as the new duke's sole prime minister, and all of the territory east of Anping (a town just east of the capital of Linzi) was ceded to him as his personal fief.[80] This not only put Tian Chang in control of the ducal court, but in possession of more than half the arable land of the state of Qi. No single aristocrat in the regional states of the Zhou realm, whether duke or grandee, had ever been so wealthy or so powerful.

The aftermath of the April 26 coup gave the first evidence that it represented an important watershed in the history of Zhou society and politics. Though the Zhou king no longer possessed armies to punish usurpers, for form's sake the royal court always condemned the removal of one of the regional lords by a usurper. This was generally enough to initiate a punitive expedition by a coalition of neighboring states, if for no other reason than to use the pretext of a royal mandate to profit from the internal disorder of a rival. In this way almost all usurpers had been made to suffer reprisals in the wake of killing their duke.

That did not happen this time. Tian Chang rode out the shock waves set off by his slaying of the duke and held sway over the state of Qi until his death some years later, when he was succeeded as head of the Tian clan (and de facto ruler of Qi) by his son. Some of this was because Tian Chang displayed political skill. He sent emissaries to neighboring states offering concessions and made pacts with powerful grandee clans.[81] But this diplomacy, however skillful, was underwritten by the radical power-realignment Tian Chang had engineered in the state of Qi. Since he now controlled more than half of the land of Qi he was able to use the massive wealth at his disposal to effectively "buy off" the regional lords and their grandee vassals, making himself into a kind of power broker the Zhou world had never seen before.

This was evident in the scene that transpired in neighboring Lu. On hearing of the death of his disciple and the duke he served, Confucius was distraught.

He fasted for three days to purify himself and presented himself in audience to the Duke of Lu, requesting that an expedition be raised against Tian Chang, to punish him for murdering his ruler. In a moment of deep irony, the Duke of Lu told Confucius to take his request to the head of the Jisun clan. Confucius must have been loath to do so, because it was a concession to the same kind of degeneration of ducal powers in Lu that Zai Wo had been fighting against in Qi. But given the enormity of Tian Chang's transgression, Confucius swallowed his pride and took his plea to the Jisun clan. Here he was again, unsurprisingly, rebuffed. The Jisun clan were the one force in Lu possessed of the material resources needed to move effectively against Tian Chang, but Tian Chang's newly substantial position of power, and the opportunity cost of refusing to accept his material inducements, made the price of enforcing tradition higher than the Jisun clan was willing to pay.[82]

The court of historical memory has not been kind to most of the actors in the coup of April 26, 481 BCE. The duke fared the best. His posthumous title, "Duke Jian," denotes a ruler of "unwavering virtue."[83] This might, however, have been a backhanded compliment, evoking his stubbornness.

Zai Wo's fate was considerably less benign. Though his ascent to the co-premiership of the court of Qi was the greatest political achievement of any of Confucius's disciples, he was not remembered fondly by the fellowship. This alienation may have begun even while Zai Wo was alive. Qi and Lu were at war as the duke assumed the throne, and some of Confucius's leading disciples served in the defense of Lu against Qi's invading armies.

But more than this, Confucius had persistently preached that true "gentlemen" of learning, if allowed to hold the reins of power, could reverse the tide of chaos in the Zhou world. Instead, given high station, Zai Wo had precipitated the murder of his ruler and the collapse of an ancient ducal house. This monumental failure was a blow to the credibility of the Master and his Way.

Whether out of their passionate faith in the Master or a hypocritical urge to defend the "brand" of the fellowship itself, Confucius's followers could not tolerate the contradiction between the Master's message and the facts of Zai Wo's career. The *Analects* thus commemorates Zai Wo as unquestionably the worst of Confucius's disciples. He has the distinction in that text of being depicted in almost purely negative terms. He is lazy, boorish, and callous. He is so insensitive as to feel comfortable shortening the mourning period for his own father,[84] and so lacks discipline that he sleeps during the day, prompting Confucius to compare him to a piece of rotten wood that cannot be carved.[85] Even Zai Wo's name as it comes down to us through the fellowship of

Confucius's disciples is most likely a veiled barb. The logographs "Zai Wo" literally translate out as "Make Me Prime Minister," so it is probable that the disciples and their heirs effaced the man's actual name and replaced it with a phrase deriding his ambition.[86]

Tian Chang came away from the coup of April 26, 481 BCE, with the most infamous reputation of any of its actors. His biography became a cautionary tale for rulers ever after, and his name became synonymous with usurpation and insatiable ambition, serving a function similar to those of "Judas" or "Benedict Arnold" in English literature.[87] If we could go back in time and warn him of this before the coup had been launched he might not have acted any differently, however, given what was at stake, and his relief combined with the material spoils of victory in the aftermath might have afforded him ample consolation.

Confucius himself died less than two years after Zai Wo and one year after the violent death of another of the politically successful among his protégés.[88] By all reports Confucius's mood at death's door was deeply pessimistic. The *Analects* records the Master as lamenting that, "The phoenix does not appear, the River does not give forth its chart (both omens of the auspicious future Confucius hoped for from fulfillment of the Way), I am finished!"[89] This and other expressions are often taken to reflect Confucius's disappointment with his own failure to achieve high station, but such regrets might have arisen as much or more from the fate of the young men he had inspired with such world-changing zeal.

The Master and his legates were down but not out, however. Tian Chang's *cris de couer* in the early hours of his coup, "How can I act as if I have no ruler?" showed prescient insight. The coup had removed social and political impediments to the full operation of Tian Chang's power as a patron and employer, but it had not replaced those traditions with structures that would imbue his position with legitimacy and stability. If the position of a duke was not secure despite centuries of tradition and weighty spiritual authority, how secure could Tian clan leaders be in the loyalty of their clients, simply because those clients were rewarded (in sex or otherwise)? Such questions would not go away and would fuel the need for individuals who could think, speak, and write creatively about the problems facing the denizens of the Zhou domain. Subsequent decades and centuries would see the rise of more lords in the mold of Tian Chang, but it would also see the rise of many Masters following in the footsteps of Confucius.

Conditions in Qi and throughout the Zhou world after 481 BCE evoke the title and theme of Chinua Achebe's magnum opus, *Things Fall Apart*.[90]

Making the world less restrictive for lords and patrons was not the same as making the world safer for them (or anyone else). More strife and violence were sure to transpire in the absence of institutions capable of ordering this rapidly changing society, and it did not have long to wait after the death of the duke and Zai Wo to be roiled again. Events to the south of Qi would soon send a tremor through the political fabric of the entire Zhou world.

2

Song of the South
The States of Wu, Chu, and Yue,
527–473 BCE

Tian Chang's coup shocked the people of his day, but it took some time for the rulers and grandees throughout the Zhou states to fully understand just how profoundly his actions would reshape their society. It was, after all, far from the first time that a vassal had killed his lord and placed a pliant child on the ducal throne. Though (as we shall see in the next chapter) powerful aristocrats throughout the Zhou world eventually began to appreciate both *in what way* and *how much* Tian Chang had reshaped the state of Qi (and to attempt similar moves at home), this change set in over years and decades.

By contrast, an event that occurred eight years after Tian Chang's coup and 704 kilometers to the south instantly transformed perceptions of *inter*state (as opposed to *intra*-state) relations for all the nobles and rulers of the Zhou domain. The state of Wu was invaded by its neighbor, the state of Yue. Wu's capital was sacked, its sovereign forced to commit suicide, and the title held by Wu's defeated ruler in the name of the Zhou king transferred to Wu's conqueror. This cataclysm was the conclusion of a drama that had played out over several decades, and that immediately became the stuff of legend. Not only would the story be told and retold by literati during the Warring States, but it has provided fodder for poems, paintings, ballads, plays, novels, and movies ever since.[1] Most intriguingly, though both of the contending states in this saga were, at the time of their final showdown, full participants in Zhou society and politics, neither of them could in any meaningful sense of the word be called "Chinese."

These events in the South were driven by some of the same forces that had impelled the coup in Qi. Just as Tian Chang had exploited markets to buy loyalty and undermine his ruler's authority, accelerating trade upset the balance among the regions and states of the larger Zhou world, shifting wealth and power swiftly and unpredictably across the political terrain. In 473 BCE the South provided an object lesson shocking enough to make all aware just how volatile the affairs of this new world had become. The destruction of Wu shattered expectations throughout the Zhou realm. It was the most impossible event in a series of what had already seemed impossible events.

The city into which invaders marched that year, the capital of the state of Wu, was located on the site of the present-day city of Suzhou, a city that because of its many gorgeous mansions and gardens has been celebrated in Chinese travel lore as a "paradise on Earth."[2] In 473 BCE, however, though Wu possessed the same technology and its leaders affirmed most of the same religious and political traditions as the northern Zhou states, its people and rulers (and those of most of what is today "southern China") were ethnically quite distinct.[3] They did not speak a Sinitic language ancestral to modern Mandarin or Cantonese, but a form of Tai-Kadai or Hmong-Mien language ancestral to languages spoken in Southeast Asia and among non-Han[4] people of southern China.[5] They spurned silk in favor of dyed cloths made from plant fibers, cut their hair short, and tattooed their bodies with elaborate designs, all customs considered extremely foreign by the people of the North.[6] These customs were a response to the unique environment of the South. Short hair facilitated swimming, and the tattoo designs provided protection against dragons and other spirit-creatures that inhabited the rivers and marshes within and along which the people of Wu lived and worked.[7]

The neighboring state of Yue (or as the graph is pronounced in Vietnamese, "Viet," from which the modern-day state of Vietnam derives its name)[8] that had invaded Wu was inhabited by the same non-Sinitic people.[9] Fuchai (r. 495–473 BCE), the last ruler of Wu, died in abject disgrace. Wu's palaces and temples were destroyed; its territory was completely absorbed into the domain of the Yue invaders.

The destruction of a state and its annexation by a rival had become commonplace by 473 BCE. Why, then, would news of the destruction of such a distant and culturally alien state and the demise of a "barbaric"[10] ruler send waves of terror and disbelief through Zhou society? For several decades prior to its destruction Wu, a relatively new state with less than 100 years of recorded history,[11] had been growing rapidly in wealth and power. Just over 30 years before (during the reign of Fuchai's father), its armies had captured the capital of Chu, an ancient and vast imperial realm that had controlled much of the Yangzi River valley for centuries. This had made Wu an imposing regional power, and its expanding influence had continued to grow from there. For many years its armies ranged northward, progressively asserting Wu's dominance over the chieftains and states of the Zhou heartland in the Yellow River valley.

This ascendancy culminated in 482 BCE, the year before Tian Chang's coup in Qi. In that year Fuchai of Wu convened a meeting of the strongest Zhou vassal states at a town called "Yellow Pond" (*Huangchi*), where the collected chieftains of the Zhou domain swore allegiance to the ruler of Wu, acknowledging him as Lord Protector of the Zhou domain. This was a title, ratified by the Zhou king himself, that gave the vassal lord who held it authority over the military affairs of the entire Zhou domain. It had been held by legendary warlords of centuries past, such as Duke Jian of Qi's famous ancestor, Duke Huan (r. 685–643 BCE), history's first Lord Protector (as discussed in the preceding chapter).[12]

The title Lord Protector had for more than two centuries marked the ruler holding it as first of the regional lords, mightiest and most respected in all the civilized lands.[13] What transpired between Fuchai's assumption of the title in 482 BCE and his suicide in his own capital in 473 BCE confused and horrified elites throughout the Zhou world for two reasons. The first was that it should never have been possible for Fuchai to assume the title at all, because his state was a parvenu power and he himself was not a properly "civilized" ruler. But once Fuchai became Lord Protector in 482 BCE, his state should (according to conventional expectations) have been sure to remain powerful and secure for *at least* several generations. All of the states that had been ruled by past Lords Protector still survived at the time of Fuchai's death. That Wu was wiped off the map less than a decade after its ruler was named Lord Protector (during the reign of that same sovereign!) was nothing short of freakish.

This whole sequence of events defied all logic in the minds of Zhou social and political leaders. It undermined the most basic assumptions that for centuries had informed their understanding of interstate relations. In political terms, it was as if the very rules of gravity themselves had been suspended. To use a modern analogy: it was as if a nation in our own present-day world had become so wealthy and powerful that it had been granted a permanent seat on the United Nations Security Council, and then seven years later collapsed and was absorbed into the territory of a neighboring country, which was then rewarded by the UN with its victim's Security Council seat.

If Wu's rapid rise and fall were so improbable in the minds of Zhou elites, how and why did it happen? In order to understand the nature of this event and the reasons for its being so earth-shattering, we must take a detour into historical geography. Any schoolteacher who stands in front of a class today to give a "map class" on China will almost certainly begin by pointing out that China is crossed by two great rivers, the Yellow River to the north and the Yangzi River to the south. Both rivers have been firmly in the "Chinese" orbit for more than two millennia; together they have helped define the scope of Chinese civilization for untold generations. Indeed, if one searches on the globe for the densest concentration of Chinese speakers today, it is to be found on the banks of the Yangzi River and its tributaries and the regions south of it, stretching down to the Taiwan Strait and the shores of the South China Sea, where approximately six-tenths of the citizens of the People's Republic of China reside right now. The world's largest Chinese city, Shanghai, is at the mouth of the Yangzi River, where it spills into the Pacific Ocean, about 90 minutes by train from Suzhou, the modern city that marks the location of Fuchai's suicide when Wu was destroyed. Famous Chinese cities such as Guangzhou, Nanjing, Fuzhou, and Hong Kong (to name only a few) are all found in this southern clime.[14]

But the present-day state of Chinese geography did not prevail during the Zhou dynasty. The original Zhou states were concentrated along the Yellow River and its tributaries in what is now northern China, with the densest concentration of Zhou subjects along the lower reaches of the Yellow River, near where it spills into the Yellow Sea. In 473 BCE the population of the North China plain outnumbered that of the regions south of the Huai River (a major tributary of the Yangzi) by a factor of four to one.[15] This was the Zhou heartland, and from the perspective of Zhou elites there were strange peoples and alien terrains to be found in all directions moving out from this native soil.

Modern readers may be familiar with the northern frontier bordering on the Inner Asian steppe that was of so much concern to Chinese leaders during the long expanse of imperial history. Nomadic pastoral people such as the Huns, Turks, Khitans, Jurchens, and Mongols "traded and raided" along the territorial expanse that now houses the Great Wall, sometimes conquering large portions (or, in the case of the Mongols and the Manchus, the entirety) of the empire.[16] As we will see in later chapters, this frontier indeed posed challenges to Zhou elites from the time of the earliest kings through the Warring States.

Less well known is the extent to which, during early times, the South (that is, the general zone stretching from the area of the Yangzi River and its tributaries to the South China Sea) was a frontier region equally exotic and potentially threatening to the Zhou subjects of the Yellow River plain. The popular image of the South among northern Zhou elites was different than that of the far North. Where the northern steppe was seen as an arid and rugged terrain populated by fiercely hard-bitten peoples, the South was deemed a sultry, lushly overgrown expanse inhabited by exotic barbarians given to sensual license and material excess.[17]

Like most stereotypes, these images had a tenuous relationship to reality. It was true, though, that the ecology of the South was very different from that of the North. Where the Yellow River plain was flat, temperate, and relatively arid, the southern regions were warm, humid, and broken by a complex matrix of river valleys, salt marshes, swamps, and limestone mountain ranges. An old adage observes of China's geography: "In the South by boat, in the North by horse."[18]

The economic and demographic conditions of the South were thus distinct. A fraction of the number of people who lived in the North were dispersed over a larger area. This was in part because so much of the terrain was swamp or hills not suited to agriculture, in part because the prevalence of mosquito-borne illnesses such as malaria kept population density low.

The cultivated and built environment of the South was quite different from that found in the North. Where Northerners subsisted on arid-climate grains such as millet, wheat, barley, and sorghum, the humid conditions of the South allowed for the practice of wet-rice agriculture. Houses in the South were thus built on stilts to allow for the necessary flooding of the rice paddies during growing season.[19]

From the perspective of the Zhou kings and their subjects on the Yellow River plain, the South was generally divisible into two "zones." The more alien of these zones was the Lower Yangzi River delta region in modern-day Jiangsu Province, where the river spills into the Pacific Ocean. This region contains Lake Tai, near the shores of which stood the capital of the state of Wu. As late as the time of Confucius's birth in the mid-sixth century BCE, the Lower Yangzi was still largely wild and uncharted territory for Zhou leaders, an impenetrable terrain populated by strange and "uncivilized" inhabitants.[20] It was from this distant clime that the news of Fuchai's death would break (shortly after Confucius's death) in 473 BCE, sending shockwaves through the Zhou world. But in order to understand how the Lower Yangzi states of Wu and Yue came to have such an impact on the Zhou realm, we have to travel upriver, into the other "zone" that comprised the South as understood by the people of Confucius's time.

Still foreign, but more familiar to the Zhou rulers by the mid-sixth century BCE, was the zone comprised by the western reaches of the Yangzi River valley, those of its tributary, the Han River, and the region between the upper courses of the Huai and Yangzi rivers, an area situated in present-day Anhui, Hubei, and southern Henan provinces. At the time of Confucius's birth this Upper Yangzi region was under the consolidated control of the ruling clan of Chu.

The rulers of Chu had originally been vassals of the Zhou, from the time even before the Zhou ascended to the title of "king." An early ancestor of the Chu ruling clan is said to have been a sage advisor of King Wen, the founder of the Zhou dynasty.[21] Thus though Northerners were still disposed to view the denizens of the Upper Yangzi as strange and barbarous, the elites and rulers of this region were long well integrated into Zhou culture. They most likely spoke a Sino-Tibetan language ancestral to modern forms of "Chinese" (though a regional variant not intelligible to Northerners) and adhered to most of the religious and political norms maintained in the North.[22]

The Northerners' perception of the Upper Yangzi as "foreign" was not entirely a projection of their own prejudices, however. The geography and demographics of the South made the adaptation of pristine Zhou political institutions in that environment difficult. With lower population densities, rugged terrain, and sparse productivity, the territorial area drawn upon by regional chieftains to support the kind of ancestral temple complex that a Zhou regional vassal was expected to maintain had to be much bigger in the South than in the North. Competition over resources was intense and the ability of the Zhou kings to enforce a "king's peace" severely constrained. The Upper Yangzi thus underwent an early territorial consolidation that anticipated what would eventually transpire among the "central states" of the Yellow River plain, as states "devoured" one another through a process of rapid conquest and annexation. This is how the Upper Yangzi region came under the domination of the state of Chu.[23]

The Chu rulers were, in a sense, northern "émigrés" in the lush lands of the South. Their ancestors had originally operated from a northern city called Danyang, at the southern fringes of the terrain controlled by the earliest chieftains of the Zhou.[24] But relations between the early rulers of Chu and the new Zhou kings were intermittently rocky. In 957 BCE one of the Zhou kings drowned in the course of a campaign to discipline his ostensible Chu vassals.[25] Other Zhou-Chu wars followed.

After the move of the Zhou capital in 771 BCE the ruling clan of Chu took advantage of Zhou weakness to launch a campaign of expansion focused on the South. In 690 BCE they shifted their capital to a city named Ying, in the Han River valley, several hundred kilometers south of their original home base.²⁶ This new city eventually became a kind of Rome of the South. From here Chu embarked on an essentially colonial enterprise. Armed with the sophisticated bronze technology and cultural institutions of the Zhou world, they used a combination of hard and soft power to bring an ever-expanding territory under their sway. By the late sixth century BCE (while Confucius was gathering disciples in the North), Chu rulers had brought dozens of states and tribal groups under their dominion, forging a virtual empire in the Upper Yangzi region.²⁷

The practical requirements of power in this southern clime put the Chu rulers into an ambivalent relationship with their northern cousins. From a very early time, the success of rule in the South depended on trade. The brokenness of the southern terrain and the sparseness of its population isolated the peoples that Chu sought to tie into its expanding empire, both from the Chu court and from one another. Without something to offer its dispersed subjects, Chu hegemony would have depended on constant military coercion, which would have been unsustainable in the long term.

Instead, Chu rulers and their vassal lords established themselves as the guarantors of a burgeoning trade network. They issued safe transit passes to merchants over broadly drawn circuits navigable by the Yangzi and its tributaries, assuring traders unmolested passage between feudatories and tribal domains that otherwise would have been mutually suspicious of one another or altogether out of communication with the outside world. These circuits ended in major metropolitan centers like the capital city of Ying, where the wares of distant Upper Yangzi villages might be purchased by agents from as far away as the northern states of Lu or Qi.²⁸ Trade accelerated to such high volumes under Chu that the throne issued the first gold currency of the Zhou world, known as "*Yingcheng*" (weighed at Ying) plates. The importance of trade to the political economy of Chu is evinced in the fact that clay replicas of *Yingcheng* plates, along with balances and weights for measuring gold pieces, have been discovered in the tombs of many Chu elites.²⁹ Submission to Chu thus brought with it the advantage of access to markets that connected even the most remote denizens of the Upper Yangzi with the fertile Zhou heartland on the Yellow River plain.

Their position at the top of such a broad and internally diverse empire put the Chu rulers at odds with the Zhou. In order to solidify their status as guarantors of the peace between varied tribes and regions, the Chu rulers could not admit to being the vassals of any other potentate. They thus claimed the title "king," which was an egregious heresy among the aristocracy of the Zhou world. For the nobles of the Yellow River plain, only the true Son of Heaven could use the title "king," and the only true Son of Heaven (the ruler in possession of Heaven's "Mandate" to rule) was the Zhou monarch. Thus, though the Chu rulers were in virtually all other respects culturally aligned with Zhou society, their usurpation of the title "king" marked them as uncouth barbarians and enemies.[30] By the mid-seventh century BCE the Zhou kings no longer had the military force to defend the honor of their own title, but the Zhou vassal states of the North joined into coalition under the leadership of the state of Jin (the ruler of which claimed the title of Lord Protector) to punish Chu for its defiance. Wars between a northern coalition led by Jin and the southern empire of Chu began in 633 BCE, during the reign of Jin's most celebrated leader, Duke Wen, and continued for most of the following century.[31]

Though the allied power of the North was able to check the advance of Chu onto the Yellow River plain, it could not reverse the accelerating ascent of the Chu "kings" in the South. Chu's rise was an early sign, even before the spectacular career of a political operator like Tian Chang in Qi, that commerce was transforming the power dynamics of the Zhou world. The territory controlled by the Chu kings either produced or sat astride the route to the source of many luxury items highly prized by elites throughout the Zhou domain: cinnabar, lacquer, incense, kingfisher feathers, gold, ivory, rhinoceros horn, pearls, jade, and other rare goods. Chu thus effectively served as a brokerage for the transfer of these goods from South to North.[32] As trade intensified over the course of the seventh and sixth centuries BCE, the wealth that flowed to the Chu kings gave them increasingly formidable strategic power, which they used to threaten the Zhou states of the Yellow River plain.

It was this larger geopolitical struggle between North and South that first led the political leaders of the Yellow River plain to make contact with the chieftains of Wu in the Lower Yangzi region, and that set in motion the chain of events that would lead to the cataclysm of 473 BCE. The northern state of Jin and the southern kingdom of Chu were effectively the two "superpowers" of the sixth century BCE. As so often happens in such superpower conflicts, the combatants sought out allies and proxies in order to gain leverage that might turn the tide of competition.

To this end, military advisors from the northern state of Jin traveled to Wu in the Lower Yangzi in the year 584 BCE, to train its warriors in the technology and battle tactics of the North. The negotiations that forged this alliance had been brokered by an early defector from the Chu court. Prior to that year, Wu had been a tributary of Chu. After receiving northern aid and training, Wu embarked on a campaign of rebellion, attacking the vassal states along Chu's eastern frontier. In this way Wu was able to wrest away the allegiance of many tribal peoples that had previously paid court to Chu.[33]

From that point forward, Chu was no longer the unchallenged hegemonic power of the South. The ruler of Wu adopted the title "king," fabricated a genealogy by which he claimed descent from the ancestors of the Zhou house,[34] and defied Chu in offering the same guarantees of protection to merchants, villages, and tribal groups as had been customarily issued by the Chu king, focused in the Lower Yangzi but extending into the precincts of the Upper Yangzi region that had been the core of Chu's southern empire. A decades-long standoff ensued, in which the competing centers of Chu and Wu vied for supremacy over the trade networks of the Yangzi and its tributaries.[35] The stalemate only began to break in the final decades of the sixth century BCE, setting in motion the events that would become the stuff of legend.

A world controlled increasingly by markets is one in which power is difficult to contain, and in which the flow of power becomes progressively more difficult to predict. The more incentives and the fewer obstacles exist for elites to enter the open market in search of material profit, the more kinship, custom, and tradition erode as constraints upon political life. The coup in Qi (described in the last chapter) demonstrated how, in a single court, the forces of the market could overturn ancient traditions and undermine venerable institutions. The drama that unfolded in the South provides another example of this principle at work, but on an even grander scale.

How do we tell this story of the South? Where and when do we begin? There are many moments at which we could take up the tale, but the clearest "inception point" can be found in the biography of Wu Zixu (d. 484 BCE, hereafter referred to by his given name of "Zixu," to avoid confusion between his surname and the name of the state that he served, which are homophones in English), a Chu nobleman immortalized in countless chronicles, poems, and dramas, who for centuries down to the present day has been worshipped as a god in some parts of China.[36] For the people of the Warring States period and the many centuries since, Zixu's personal history was virtually synonymous with that of the saga that gripped the South and the larger Zhou world in the late sixth and early fifth centuries BCE. If any one person can be credited with breaking the decades-long stalemate that had ensued between the two great southern powers of Wu and Chu, Zixu is it.

Zixu's story begins in 527 BCE. Until that year, his family was highly placed in the ruling oligarchy of the great southern empire of Chu. Zixu's father was

Mentor of the Heir Apparent, charged with the welfare and education of the Crown Prince,[37] thus Zixu himself was virtually guaranteed a post in the court of the future King of Chu. But that year saw Zixu condemned and forced to flee, abandoning his father and brother to die. Like the "nail for which the kingdom was lost," the dislocation of Zixu would help set the entire South into crisis.

The manner in which Zixu became an exile is on one level a very personal morality play, but on another a very general example of how relationships within the Zhou world grew progressively more transactional. Zixu's father had an ambitious deputy, who in search of wealth and status hatched a scheme that undermined the peace of the entire court. He had been sent to escort from her home state to the Chu capital at Ying a bride for the Heir Apparent, a princess from the western state of Qin (about which we will learn much in subsequent chapters), and on seeing that she was exceptionally beautiful had hurried ahead of the cortege to urge the king to take the young princess for himself, which the king did.[38]

The king's gratitude for this bit of sycophancy earned the deputy a promotion, but once in his new post the former Junior Mentor began to worry what would befall him when the Heir Apparent came into his inheritance. Once the heir became king and had to see the still beautiful young princess cloistered among his widowed "stepmothers," would he be kind to the man who had robbed him of such a companion? The newly promoted ex-Junior Mentor thus embarked on a campaign of slander aimed at convincing the king to suspect and disinherit his son and heir. When Zixu's father upbraided the king for listening to the lies being told by the former deputy, the king did not pay heed, but condemned Zixu's father as a traitor and had him jailed to await the king's sentence.

Zixu and his brother were summoned to court, on the promise that if they appeared their father would be given mercy. Both brothers knew the summons was a ruse meant to forestall any chance they might avenge their father. It was a cruel stratagem. Answering the summons was suicide, but refusing to do so would brand the young men as "unfilial sons" who cared more for their own persons than the life of their father. Zixu's brother answered the summons out of devotion and died along with his father. Zixu, willing to exchange his good reputation for revenge, held the royal envoy who brought him the king's summons at arrow-point and fled, causing a large bounty to be offered for his capture. Told of his son's flight before being executed, Zixu's father expressed pleasure that the courtiers of Chu would have to "take their meals late" on account of his son (that is to say, they would be kept busy with court business by all the trouble Zixu would cause them).[39]

Zixu's world had been torn apart, and he was cast adrift. It must have been strange and terrifying for a young aristocrat, raised in the comforts of a palace, to be hounded into the river valleys and swamps of the South. Zixu sought out the entourage of the Heir Apparent that his father had served, but that prince was also hunted and eventually met death from intrigue in a foreign court.

Taking the Heir's son into his protection, Zixu fled eastward.[40] Circumstances became desperate. Zixu and his companion were reduced to penury and begging. At one point, having relied on the kindness of an old fisherman for transport across the Yangzi ahead of pursuers, Zixu offered the man his last possession as a reward: an heirloom sword bequeathed to Zixu by his father. The fisherman noted that the bounty on Zixu's head was much greater than the value of the sword. Offended that Zixu would try to "buy off" his silence, the fisherman redeemed his own honor and allayed Zixu's suspicions by throwing himself into the Yangzi to drown. Such stories are peppered throughout the accounts of Zixu's life and the struggles between the southern states of Wu, Chu, and Yue.[41] We might reasonably suspect that they are dramatic embellishments, but their point is not merely to entertain. By placing characters in the story who resist the transactional logic driving so much of the action, the literati who recorded these events registered their own dismay at the forces that were changing their world, and the direction in which it was moving.

In 522 BCE, after five grueling years as a fugitive, the political tide washed Zixu into the capital of the state of Wu. In this he was far from alone. Zixu found a sizeable and growing community of Chu and northern state émigrés in the Wu capital, some soldiers of fortune in search of opportunity, others refugees like him who had become *persona non grata* back home.[42] The atmosphere in Wu must have been analogous to what we read of "boomtowns" in the American "Wild West." The people of Wu were not (had never been, really) the "barbarians" that the denizens of the North thought them to be, but in 522 BCE they were only a few decades into the process of a total social transformation. The rulers and people of Wu were effectively rebuilding their polity as a Zhou-style "state" (*guo*).[43]

As mentioned in the last chapter, this was a process that frequently occurred along the periphery of the Zhou realm, and that we can see mirrored in the development of many civilizations across the ancient world. In the same way that the Romans had adopted many of the cultural and political traditions of the Greeks in order to accrue the benefits of trade and social integration with the Hellenic world, the people of Wu saw advantage in provisionally joining the regional order presided over by the Zhou Son of Heaven. The greatest obstacles to this goal were matters of "cultural literacy." Intercourse with the larger Zhou world required an elaborate infrastructure of architecturally distinct temples, precisely crafted material goods, and aristocrats deeply conversant with a dense web of rituals and protocols. It also demanded a cadre of scribes conversant in the script (ancestral to the modern Chinese writing system) in use throughout the Zhou world.

The project of "Zhou-ification" thus urgently impelled Wu rulers to recruit people with expertise that was in short supply among the non-Sinitic peoples of the Lower Yangzi region. This is why the Wu court exerted such a strong gravitational pull on Chu aristocrats like Zixu, cast adrift in the wider South. For someone who needed support and who had the requisite education and skills, there was high demand and lots of opportunity in Wu (in the same way that there was high demand for Greek scribes, artisans, and teachers in ancient Rome).[44]

Though the Wu court was at basis a "start-up enterprise," Zixu arrived at a moment of particular volatility. The reigning king was already the fifth ruler to claim that title, but he was only the grandson of the first king who had been enthroned in 584 BCE (during the early days in which Wu nobles and warriors were being cultivated by agents of the northern "superpower" of Jin). This was because the throne had passed laterally through a series of three brothers, the sons of the first king.

Why the royal throne had passed from brother to brother this way is an open question. It may have been a native tradition of the Wu people that dated to the time before they adopted Zhou political forms. Alternatively, as the written histories claim, the lateral succession may have been engineered deliberately to ensure that a fourth brother, the youngest son of the first king, would eventually inherit the throne. A rich body of lore celebrates the sage wisdom, upright moral character, cultural refinement, and diplomatic exploits of this youngest prince of the second royal generation. If there is any truth to these records, it may be that the fourth prince was being "groomed" for the Wu throne: sent out into the larger world to acquire the specialized knowledge and skills of the Zhou aristocracy while his brothers kept the throne warm for him. Whatever the actual case may have been, the fourth prince threw off the pattern by refusing to assume the throne when his third older brother died.[45]

Because of this youngest brother's intransigence, on his death the fourth king, unlike his two predecessors, was succeeded by his own son. This meant that the fifth king assumed the throne in a court chock-a-block full of first cousins, each of whose claim to the throne was just as strong as (or stronger than) that of the ruling sovereign. Such irregularities are profoundly destabilizing in the early stages of a new political enterprise.

Even more unfortunate for the new king, the most talented and dynamic among his cousins was Prince Guang, the first son and heir of the reigning king's late eldest uncle, the deceased second king. As a commander in the armies of Wu, Prince Guang had taken the initiative in the ongoing war of attrition against the rival power of Chu, leading Wu forces in successive campaigns against the western foe. Though he met with setbacks on these missions, he showed resolve and ingenuity. For example, when, in one battle, the forces of Chu captured the Wu royal barge, Prince Guang devised a ruse and reclaimed the vessel.[46]

At the same time that his skill, charisma, energy, and courage won him followers in the royal court, the prince harbored festering resentment against his cousin, the king. He told those in his inner circle that he considered the king illegitimately crowned. If the regular order of succession was to go from brother to brother, Prince Guang's and the king's youngest, and still surviving, uncle should have been crowned. If Wu was reverting to the rule of primogeniture, then Prince Guang, the heir of the second king, should have been next in line to the throne.[47]

This situation presented Zixu, newly arrived at the Wu court but consumed with the ambition to avenge his family, with an opportunity. He was given audience with the king after arriving in the Wu capital. At the time of his audience, Wu and Chu were at peace, and Zixu delivered a speech encouraging the launching of a punitive expedition against his home state of Chu. The king was impressed, but Prince Guang, who was in attendance, remonstrated against such a plan, noting that Zixu had an ulterior motive for urging war because of the murder of his father and brother. The king thus demurred.

To a naïve observer the audience would have seemed to put Zixu and Prince Guang at odds with one another. But in reality, it was a moment of mutual recognition between the two men. Perhaps even better than the king, Prince Guang could see and appreciate Zixu's intellect and energy. The prince had spoken out against Zixu's plan not because he was opposed to war, but to prevent the king from employing Zixu and profiting from the service of such a talented subordinate. For his part, Zixu was perceptive enough to recognize what was going on immediately. He could see that Prince Guang, who otherwise was enthusiastic to prosecute the war against Chu, had resisted in this case because he had ambitions for the throne. Moreover, Zixu recognized that if he was forced to choose between the king and the prince, the prince would prove a more able leader in executing any strategy that would enable Zixu to have his revenge on the King of Chu.

Zixu's next move demonstrated the political acumen and ruthless cunning that made him legendary. He recruited a strong knight of obvious courage and fighting skill and recommended him into the service of Prince Guang. Zixu then retired from court to take up the life of a farmer, knowing full well how the prince would employ the new retainer he had introduced into the prince's retinue.[48]

In 515 BCE the King of Chu who had murdered Zixu's father and brother died. Zixu was devastated by the word that he had missed his chance for vengeance. He fell to the floor sobbing in front of the young Chu prince (the son of the former Heir Apparent) that had followed Zixu into exile.[49] But events would eventually vindicate Zixu's strategic patience and discipline.

On hearing the news of his rival, the King of Chu's death, the King of Wu decided to take advantage of the moment. In the protocols of the Zhou world the death of the ruler was a very disruptive event. Everyone in the royal court and government (especially a king's son and successor) came under strict obligations of mourning. Austerities had to be observed in dress, food, and behavior. Public activities had to be curtailed. While the court of Chu was under these obligations of mourning, the kingdom's military preparedness was necessarily curtailed. Though traditionally it was considered dishonorable to launch a campaign during the initial phase of a foe's mourning, the King of Wu decided to throw tradition aside and attack Chu while it was vulnerable.

He sent two of his brothers as co-commanders of the invasion force. At the same time, he dispatched his famous uncle, the youngest brother who had been intended for the throne, as an ambassador to solicit the cooperation and support of the northern states in this campaign against Chu. Both decisions proved to be mistakes.

Chu rallied its forces under its new king, the son of the Qin princess on whose account Zixu's father had ultimately met his death. Chu armies surrounded the King of Wu's brothers, cutting off their retreat and forcing them to dig in and live under siege deep in enemy territory. The Wu-Chu rivalry had devolved into stalemate once again.

This moment of crisis, with the king's brothers trapped and his uncle abroad, provided Prince Guang with a golden opportunity. He invited the king to a banquet to be held in the prince's home. The king accepted the invitation, but he took precautions. He had the entire route from the royal palace to Prince Guang's abode lined with soldiers and entered his host's dwelling under armed escort made up of his most loyal supporters. The king was not a great leader or strategist, but he was no fool. He knew how dangerous his cousin was. But he also knew that Prince Guang was one of his most able military commanders, and thus he would need to cultivate the prince's cooperation if he wanted to rescue his brothers from the trap in which they were being held by Chu's armies.

Unfortunately for the king, he was no match for the combined tactical skill of Prince Guang and Zixu. When everyone at the banquet table was merry with wine, Prince Guang feigned a pain in his leg and excused himself. He then went into the cellar of his palace, where he had secreted a large party of armored warriors. Among them, dressed in servant's clothes, was the warrior who had been recommended to Prince Guang by Zixu. This man was sent back into the banquet bearing a platter with a huge fish, inside of which was concealed a dagger. Placing the platter before the king, the assassin ripped open the fish with strong hands and lunged at his target (see Fig. 3). The swordsmen guarding the king cut the assassin down, but not before he had fulfilled his orders to dispatch the king. As the king's attendants grappled with the shock and confusion of their lord's murder, Prince Guang's warriors poured out of the cellar with weapons drawn. In a rampage they killed all of the king's soldiers and supporters.

Prince Guang wasted no time. Before his uncle returned from abroad, the prince had already crowned himself King Helü of Wu (r. 514–496 BCE). The new king's famous uncle, on entering the capital, was characteristically diplomatic in his response to his nephew's coup, declaring that as long as the new king maintained the altars of the gods and ancestors, he was owed allegiance. The royal uncle would mourn his nephew the old king, but he would serve his other nephew, the new.[50]

The ascension of King Helü to the throne of Wu marked a turning point in the affairs of the South. The new king summoned Zixu out of retirement, appointed him Minister of Foreign Affairs, and consulted him in a reorganization of the government. Zixu oversaw a transformation of the Wu court from a narrowly familial affair, in which kings had been dependent on the support and talents of rival kinsmen, into a more open and efficient organization. He raised the most able among the foreign émigrés resident at court into positions of real power and responsibility. Among these appointments was the general Sun Wu, a native of Qi, who was given tactical field command of Wu's armies.

Fig. 3. The assassination of the ruler of Wu in 514 BCE. The assassin draws a dagger from a roasted fish in which it was concealed. This coup brought King Helü to power, who with the help of his foreign minister, Wu Zixu, and the commander Sun Wu forged the state of Wu into a major power. This depiction was carved onto the wall of the Wu Liang Shrine, a Han-era (203 BCE–220 CE) tomb. (Source: kknews.cc.)

He would achieve such success in his post that his name was eventually appropriated as that of the putative author of the famed text, *The Art of War by Master Sun* (*Sunzi bingfa* or *Sun Tzu*), which has been translated into dozens of languages and continues to be read at military academies around the world.

The situation facing the new king was initially very dire. On hearing of their brother's assassination, the two Wu princes being held under siege in enemy territory surrendered to the King of Chu, who enfeoffed them as vassals along the border between Wu and Chu.[51] This was a stratagem that might have spelled doom for Wu. Not only had the new King of Wu lost a large contingent of soldiers with his cousins' defection, but Chu, his mortal rival, now had the assistance of two princes who were strong contenders for the king's own throne.

But the new leadership that the King of Wu and Zixu had assembled demonstrated what could be done when the commercial wealth of Wu was employed by capable hands. In 512 BCE, just two years after he had taken the throne, the new King of Wu led his rapidly reinforced and refitted army, under the supervision of Zixu, Sun Wu, and other newly promoted émigré officers (in concert with some of the new king's brothers), in an invasion of the eastern marches of the Chu empire. He defeated and killed his renegade cousins, leaving the approaches to the Chu capital unguarded. In a consultation held on the battlefield, the king placed before his officers his desire to press on and take the Chu royal city of Ying. Sun Wu objected, observing that the army was tired and its supply lines overextended. The king assented to his general's advice and resolved to wait.[52]

A standoff ensued. At the advice of Zixu, King Helü adopted a strategy of attrition. Wu's armies probed the frontiers of Chu's empire and harassed its urban outposts. When the armies of Chu fell back, the soldiers of Wu pressed forward and seized territory. When the armies of Chu rallied to retaliate, the Wu invaders retreated. In this way the leaders of Wu patiently wore down the strength of Chu for five years.[53]

In 506 BCE the King of Wu summoned Zixu and Sun Wu to a war council and asked if the time was yet right to launch a final campaign aimed at the destruction of Chu. Zixu and Sun Wu had of course been monitoring the strategic situation carefully, and they gave the king their candid assessment. Spies told them that the Prime Minister of Chu had grown greedy. He had alienated two of Chu's key vassal states along the trade routes to the North. If those two states could be persuaded to defect from the Chu empire and join an assault on the Chu court, the balance of power would swing once and for all in Wu's favor and final victory could be achieved.

King Helü negotiated the alliance called for by his officials and took personal command of the invasion. The coalition army met the forces of Chu at a place called Cypress Rise (Boju) on the Han River and deployed for a decisive engagement. The Chu prime minister whose avarice had given Wu its opportunity had command over the Chu counter-invasion force. One of his subordinates proposed a plan to lead a detachment in a flanking maneuver to take advantage of the Wu invader's extended lines of operation. Another Chu officer, however, reminded the prime minister of how unpopular he had become at home. To redeem himself politically, the prime minister would need to perform some spectacular feat of battlefield mastery. Afraid of the risks of sharing credit for victory, the prime minister ordered a direct assault on the invaders. In the ensuing battle the Chu army was crushed so thoroughly that the prime minister was compelled to flee the kingdom in disgrace.

This time, unlike the invasion of six years previously, there was no hesitation. King Helü led the coalition army straight into the heart of the Chu empire, plotting a course toward the capital city of Ying. Chu rallied its remaining forces to resist, but the combined armies of the allied invasion force were too powerful, and the losses inflicted in the battle of Cypress Rise were too crippling. Chu commanders managed to regroup and challenge the King of Wu to five standing battles on his march to the capital, but were defeated each time.

As the defenses to the Chu capital of Ying crumbled, the King of Chu had no choice but to flee. The soldiers of Wu advanced so swiftly that only a desperate gambit saved the king from being captured. He ordered torches tied to the tails of the army's remaining war elephants so that they would stampede into the path of the onrushing Wu army. This slowed the enemy advance long enough to allow the king to cross the river to the north of the capital ahead of his pursuers, accompanied by his youngest sister. Even so, he was forced to abandon much of the royal household, including his mother the Queen Dowager (the very Qin princess whose marriage had set in motion the events that lead to Zixu's flight). Beyond the living hostages he left behind, the king abandoned the graves of his ancestors and all of the most sacred temples to the gods and spirits that were the foundation of his throne.[54]

Zixu, who had accompanied the army as a field commander, had returned to the city of his childhood after twenty-one years in exile, but it was not a happy homecoming. His first object was revenge. He broke open the tomb of the king who had murdered his father and brother, dragged the royal corpse above ground, and flogged it with 300 lashes of the whip.[55] This might seem like a futile gesture, but in the ancestral religion of the Zhou world it was a form of disgrace almost equal to the violation of a ruler's living person. The dead were said to inhabit an invisible yet materially tangible dimension of our own world, in which they continued to bear the status and honors that they held in life and commanded the austere service of the living.[56] For a dead king to be whipped like a common criminal instead of being feasted in a solemn and richly appointed temple banquet was a cataclysmic violation, especially since it signaled that the sovereign state over which he had once presided could no longer defend its most vital terrain or uphold its most sacred obligations.

Zixu did not stop at the indignities inflicted on the dead king's corpse. The seizure of Ying had been so rapid and the flight of the Chu court so precipitous that many of the most elite women of the kingdom were left in the hands of the invading army. Zixu led his comrades in an orchestrated rape of the wives of

Chu's leaders. He personally sought out and violated the Queen Dowager, the Qin princess on whose account the former King of Chu had disinherited his heir and murdered Zixu's father. King Helü, Sun Wu, and other Wu leaders raped the reigning Queen of Chu and the wives of the kingdom's high officials.

This act was shocking even to the people of the Zhou world. It was not uncommon for women to be made to suffer for their association with the men to whom they were tied by birth or marriage, but sexual assault was a form of cruelty ostensibly beneath the honor of a true aristocrat. Confucius is said to have praised Zixu's resolve to avenge his father, but deemed the harshness of his actions to be a product of having lived too long among the "barbarians" of Wu.

From our modern perspective this incident is of course irredeemably heinous and deplorable, even as we acknowledge that crimes like it (specifically, the use of sexual assault as a weapon of war) have been and are being committed all over the world. Even in the context of the hyper-patriarchal ethos of ancient times, literati were sensible of the depravity of Zixu's acts. The incident is elided from many chronicles, and cast in euphemistic terms where it appears, and had until recently largely been forgotten as a dimension of his historical persona (and that of his counterpart Sun Wu, the putative author of the *Sunzi bingfa*).[57]

The fever of war, the intensity of ethnic animosities, and passion for revenge may all have played a part in motivating this brutality. But the chronicles repeatedly note that these assaults were deliberately aimed at "humiliating" or "profaning" (*ru*) the King of Chu and his ministers. That goal was not (merely) personal, it had strategic dimensions. Zixu and the other leaders of Wu all understood that Chu was a multi-regional and multi-ethnic empire held together by the prestige of its ruling clan. An attack on the honor of the ruling clan and its allies was thus an attack on the coherence of the Chu empire itself. If the rulers of Chu could be sufficiently debased and degraded, perhaps the tribes and vassalages that formed the backbone of Chu's strategic strength could be shamed into relinquishing their allegiance to the ancient Xiong clan, and the Chu kingdom would fall apart. At the very least, the personal insults to the King of Chu might have had the effect of forcing him to turn and fight the pursuing Wu army, rather than fleeing ever deeper into the swamps and marshes of his realm, where he might gather his strength and wait out the inevitable erosion of the Wu army's strategic foothold so far from its home base.

The almost absurdly horrific nature of the moment embodied the entropic forces that were tearing the Zhou world apart. However pure Zixu's motives of revenge, the army that he helped lead into Chu was fighting to control trade in the South. The leaders of Wu were thus trying to use personal "honor" as a weapon in a conflict over commercial profits. Like many evil acts committed during times of rapid social and political change, its "logic" was head-spinningly self-contradictory, so much so that the literati who reflected upon this period in subsequent decades and centuries (and who produced the sources on which we rely today) were never quite able to make sense of it.[58] Many such moments would follow as the Warring States unfolded.

The sack of Ying might have ended with the total destruction of the state of Chu, an event that would have traumatized the Zhou world just as thoroughly as the debacle of 473 BCE did 33 years later. The Chu house had been regional lords for more than twice the length of the history of the United States and had ruled the Upper Yangzi region for almost two centuries. The ability of an upstart power to bring this southern empire to its knees was shocking.

But final victory eluded King Helü of Wu. The King of Chu fled into the marshes of the South with pursuers hot on his trail. He came close to death many times. At one place he stopped, he was set upon by bandits and only saved by the selfless act of a nephew who threw himself in the way of an arrow meant for the king. At the court of a vassal he would have been murdered by an aggrieved noble, except that the court's ruler, brother of the would-be murderer, caught wind of the plot and smuggled the king to safety. The king finally was trapped by his Wu pursuers in the walled capital of another Chu vassal. The Wu armies laid siege to the king's refuge and demanded that he be surrendered.

At this dire juncture the throne of Chu was saved by a combination of tradition and luck. The King of Chu's vassals maintained fealty and refused to surrender their lord to the soldiers of Wu. While the siege transpired, King Helü's position weakened.[59]

An old friend of Zixu's who had risen high in the Chu court escaped the sack of Ying and fled into the mountains outside of the city. He sent a message rebuking Zixu's disloyalty and exhorting him to restraint. On being rebuffed by Zixu ("Apologize to him for me," is as much conciliation as Zixu is said to have offered his friend's emissary), he journeyed to Qin and pleaded that an army be sent to rescue Chu from destruction. The records say that the Duke of Qin was moved to comply by this emissary's extreme display of loyalty: the man supposedly stood in the Qin court for seven days, wailing ceaselessly. In reality the Qin ruler might not have needed such inducements. The King of

Chu was his grandson, and Zixu had violated his daughter. Whatever the case may be, a force of 500 chariots was dispatched to assist Chu.[60]

At the same time that Chu received outside aid, divisions appeared in the Wu ranks. Some of the king's brothers had commanded elements of the invading army, and they squabbled over the spoils of war. Two of them set to fighting over which one would get to inhabit the abandoned palace of the Chu prime minister. The brother who finally claimed the prize at the point of a sword had been an especially effective field commander. He had led a decisive assault during the battle of Cypress Rise that had first broken the Chu counter-invasion force and sent the Prime Minister into ignominious exile. Living in the Prime Minister's luxurious palace did not placate his ambition, however. When the Qin rescue force joined up with the remnants of the Chu army and dealt King Helü a defeat on the battlefield, forcing him to fall back on the city of Ying, Helü's younger brother returned to Wu and declared himself king.

In the midst of all these crises yet another persistent source of trouble erupted within the Lower Yangzi region of the Wu homeland. Yue, a non-Sinitic vassal state whose capital was roughly one hundred kilometers south of Wu (on the site of present-day Shaoxing, famous for producing the Shaoxing wine that is a staple of Chinese culinary culture) took advantage of King Helü's predicament. As he had done in the past, the ruler of Yue launched an assault against the lightly defended territory of his Wu overlords.[61]

The Yue state was an even more novel polity than the kingdom of Wu. The first written record of the "Yue people" dates to 537 BCE, when they joined the army of Chu in a campaign against Wu during the reign of King Helü's second younger uncle, the father of the king whose assassination Helü himself had arranged. The emergence of Yue as a regional power was thus a product of the same geopolitical forces that had impelled the rise of Wu.[62]

In the same way that the northern superpower of Jin had cultivated the state of Wu as a proxy and ally, the Chu kings had encouraged the chieftains of Yue to assert themselves as an independent force in the Lower Yangzi region. From 537 BCE on the people of Yue had been a thorn in the side of Wu's ambitions. In successive campaigns, Wu rulers had enforced their hegemony over Yue. But as many times as Wu armies compelled Yue chieftains to give fealty to Wu, the rulers of Yue rebelled.

King Helü himself had already been forced to deal with this unruly vassal once before. In 510 BCE, during the interval in which he was resting and restoring his army in preparation for the final conquest of Chu, Helü had led an expedition to chastise Yue, and dealt them a defeat.[63] If he had imagined this would keep Yue docile, however, he had been mistaken.

Facing two rebellions at home and an assault from the northern state of Qin, Helü was forced to yield his ultimate goal of destroying the Chu kingdom. He abandoned the siege of the Chu king, decamped from the city of Ying, and led his armies eastward, toward home. It was a major setback and must have been demoralizing to his soldiers, but the retreat from Chu proceeded in good order. By the time Helü arrived back in his own territory the Yue assault had already been repelled by auxiliary forces, and he needed little time to defeat his younger brother and drive him into exile. That younger brother fled to Chu where, like his deceased cousins, he was enfeoffed as a vassal of the repatriated Chu throne.[64]

The campaign of 506 BCE had not succeeded in eliminating Chu, but it had effectively broken the stalemate that had prevailed in the South for many decades. Despite suffering so many disappointments, King Helü emerged from the campaign stronger than before. His position on the Wu throne was secure and the strategic balance of power in the Yangzi valley had shifted markedly in his favor.

This was made clear in 504 BCE, when Helü sent his son and chosen heir, Fuchai, to lead an invasion of Chu. This campaign scored a major naval victory in which many high-ranking Chu nobles were killed or captured. The King of Chu was so alarmed by this defeat that he abandoned the capital city of Ying and moved his government to a less vulnerable location seventy-five kilometers to the north.[65]

This was the beginning of Wu's "Golden Age." King Helü was not only a successful warrior, he also cultivated civil sources of power. He oversaw a relocation and major renovation of the Wu capital, constructing an elaborate complex of palaces, fortifications, ambassadorial residences, temples, and tombs. He settled the succession of his throne on his son Fuchai, further stabilizing the government within the norms of the Zhou states. As the fifth century BCE began, Wu was a rising power whose influence could be felt throughout the Zhou world. Rulers of the ancient northern states sought marriage alliances with King Helü and sent emissaries to foster good diplomatic relations.[66]

Helü was a robust and dynamic king and, like Phillip of Macedon in the Hellenic world, he might have achieved even greater power given more time. But fate intervened. In 496 BCE the ruler of Yue who had rebelled against Helü 10 years earlier died and was succeeded by his son. This was Goujian, who immediately demonstrated his determination to fulfill his father's vision of freeing Yue from the domination of Wu by claiming the title of king. King Helü of Wu responded by moving to take advantage of the mourning period for the deceased Yue ruler to deal once and for all with this upstart vassal. He led an invasion of Yue hoping to catch its new "king" by surprise, but was met with stiff resistance.

The young Goujian proved to be a ruthless and agile tactician. In the initial engagement with Wu he sent forward three ranks of soldiers drawn from among condemned criminals. These men, moving each rank in turn, advanced within sight of the Wu army, cried out in defiance, and slit their own throats. While the Wu soldiers were transfixed in horror by this gruesome spectacle, the main assault force of Yue emerged from hiding and descended upon Wu's flank. The Wu army broke, and in the ensuing melee King Helü was wounded, losing part of his foot.

The wound festered and ultimately proved mortal. As he lay dying, Helü enjoined his son Fuchai to vengeance, asking, "Will you forget that Goujian killed your father?" Fuchai swore that he would not and appointed attendants to repeat his father's dying admonition to him every time he passed through the main hall of the palace.[67]

Though Helü's death was a tragic shock, the smooth transition to the reign of King Fuchai was testimony to the new stability and power of the Wu kingdom. Fuchai continued his father's practice of relying on émigré talent in the upper councils of his court. He kept Zixu in his post as Minister of Foreign Affairs and raised another exiled Chu aristocrat named Bo Pi (whose father had been unjustly killed by the same king as had murdered Zixu's father) to the position of Grand Steward.[68] Together King Fuchai and his ministers reconstituted the military might of the Wu army.

In 494 BCE they invaded Yue again and dealt Goujian a crushing defeat. The Yue army was driven back deep into its own territory and finally chased up the slopes of Mount Kuaiji, the mountain overlooking the very capital of Yue itself (see Fig. 4). Trapped within sight of his own palace, Goujian called together a battlefield council of his officers to see whether any could devise a plan to stave off final destruction. Goujian and his father had emulated the rulers of Wu. They had recruited a staff of able émigrés, most of them from the Upper Yangzi kingdom of Chu. One of these men stepped forward and offered to parlay with the King of Wu.

Descending to the Wu camp, the emissary laid out terms of surrender to King Fuchai. If Fuchai would spare the Yue army, Goujian would pledge all the wealth and warriors of Yue to the service of Wu. Moreover, Goujian would personally lead a contingent of his nobles and palace ladies to Wu to serve as

Fig. 4. Excavations in modern Shaoxing have revealed the site of the original capital of the ancient state of Yue, which shocked the Zhou world by destroying its rival and former overlord, the state of Wu, in 473 BCE. (Source: canal44.com.)

attendants and concubines in Fuchai's court, thus repenting for the death of King Helü through ordeal of public disgrace. If King Fuchai would not grant this clemency, the emissary explained, Goujian would send a signal ordering the torch set to all the palaces and temples of Yue, its women put to the sword, and all its precious jades and metals cast into the Yangzi. Also, Goujian's encircled army would fight to the last man and take many of Fuchai's forces with them, leaving Wu with far fewer warriors than it could garner through mercy. King Fuchai was favorably impressed by this oration.

Zixu spoke up in strong opposition to any plan for clemency. Wu and Yue were too alike and too closely intertwined, he explained, to tolerate one another's existence; only one could survive. Goujian, moreover, was an exceptional character and a mortally dangerous foe. His capacity to weather adversity was virtually limitless; Wu would never be secure as long as he lived.

While the leaders of Wu were deliberating Yue's terms, Goujian worked behind the scenes to sway the outcome. He sent an emissary to Wu's Grand Steward escorting eight richly adorned beauties, promising that even more beautiful women would follow if Wu spared Yue. The Grand Steward, not coincidentally, then cast his support in favor of a brokered surrender. Goujian was spared and followed Fuchai back to Wu, where he was set to work as groom for Fuchai's mount while his wife became Fuchai's concubine. After several years of this humiliation, he was allowed to return to Yue to preside there as Fuchai's vassal.[69]

To all appearances, King Fuchai had brought Wu to a pinnacle of wealth and power greater than it had ever reached, and he made a key strategic decision. He diverted his kingdom's energies and strategic assets away from military campaigns against Chu and Yue (both of which he viewed as having been effectively neutralized) and launched a focused effort to extend and enlarge Wu's influence over the central Zhou states of the North China plain. The deliberate nature of this strategic campaign is exemplified by the long-range material investments Fuchai made in its support. He constructed a canal, for example, hundreds of kilometers long, connecting the Yangzi and Huai rivers, to aid the movement of men and equipment northward. He also built new fortifications in the far northern reaches of his realm.[70]

The prosecution of this northern strategy exacerbated divisions among Fuchai's advisors and officials. The general Sun Wu had passed away and could no longer offer the king tactical advice. Zixu, now an elder statesman honed through bitter experience, adamantly opposed a shift of focus to the North, and repeatedly urged his ruler to deal conclusively with the threat of Yue and its ruler Goujian. Zixu's colleague the Grand Steward affirmed King Fuchai's northern plans and enthusiastically participated in their design and execution.

The conflict between Zixu and the Grand Steward continued to escalate. During a famine in Yue, the Grand Steward, who continued to receive rich emoluments from the court of Yue, advocated the dispatch of food aid. Zixu urged the king to let Yue starve, warning that any move to aid Yue would lead to disaster.[71]

Zixu was right to warn his king. Goujian of Yue remained focused on the destruction of Wu. According to one account that became the source of a popular adage, Goujian suspended an acrid gall bladder on a long leather strap near his seat in the dining hall of his palace, which he would taste whenever he ate or drank, to remind himself that life was nothing but bitterness until he had revenged himself on Fuchai.[72]

He solicited stratagems for weakening Wu from his own stable of émigré officials. One of them proposed using sex as a weapon against Fuchai. A search was conducted throughout Yue which produced two women of exquisite beauty, Xi Shi and Zheng Dan. They were brought to the capital where they were clad in the most alluring garments and adorned with rich jewels. For three years they studied deportment and grace, learning the urbane ways of the court. After their studies were complete, they were presented as tribute to King Fuchai. Fuchai was greatly pleased with this "gift," viewing it as a sign of

Goujian's affection and loyalty. He accepted the new women into his harem, once again over the strenuous objections of Zixu.[73]

As had been the object of the Yue official's plan, Fuchai became besotted with the "kingdom-toppling beauty" Xi Shi. He neglected state affairs and grew estranged from his ministers while enjoying her company and exhausted vast sums of treasure to please her. He built her an immense new palace complex with ingeniously novel adornments and luxuries, and even constructed a canal from the palace to her favorite lake so that she would not have to endure a carriage ride to get there. So grateful was Fuchai for this great "boon" that he showed special favor to King Goujian of Yue.[74]

Why was Fuchai so blind to the threat posed by Goujian? From the vantage of more than two millennia the King of Wu appears either irredeemably naïve or obtuse, but this is an unfairly ahistorical judgment. Like many leaders living during a time of rapid change, Fuchai was receiving ambiguous lessons from his experiences and those of the people around him.

Fuchai's northern strategy seems to have stemmed from the lessons of his father King Helü's initially impactful, ultimately failed campaigns against the rival state of Chu. Why had Chu survived, despite being repeatedly outfought on the battlefield? Part of the answer lay in the prestige and mystique of Chu's ruling house. When the King of Chu had been reduced to a helpless refugee, his vassals kept faith with him because they believed in the abstract authority and legitimacy of the Chu throne, built through centuries of tradition and austere ritual. Helü's frustrations taught Fuchai that real security could not be purchased with the currency of warfare, but flowed from the more enduring symbolic power of prestige.

Fuchai knew that he could never fully replicate the centuries of tradition underpinning Chu's mystique, but he could tap into networks of tradition and ritual that enjoyed equivalent stature. This is why, through a combination of military engagements and diplomacy, he interceded in the affairs of the northern states with a single strategic aim: achieving the rank of Lord Protector that had been held by legendary rulers of past centuries. Past Lords Protector had been famed for keeping the peace between regional lords and protecting the hereditary prerogatives of the noble houses chartered by the founding Zhou kings.[75] King Fuchai set out to become a paragon of such values, moving aggressively to intervene in regional quarrels among and succession disputes within the northern states.

Fuchai's policy toward Yue followed naturally from this quest to become Lord Protector of the Zhou domain. By dealing mercifully with a recalcitrant vassal, Fuchai hoped to demonstrate to the rulers of the North (and the Zhou Son of Heaven himself) that he was committed to the traditional virtues of a Lord Protector. The King of Wu was prepared to use force if necessary, but he would not gratuitously exterminate a noble house that had been brought to heel. Those who submitted to Wu's authority would be dealt with fairly.

In regard to this last notion, the traditional values of the Zhou world (which most likely mirrored what had been the ethos of the non-Sinitic people of the Lower Yangzi region before their integration into Zhou society) left every reason for Fuchai to feel that Goujian had been neutralized as a threat. Goujian had allowed himself to be irredeemably disgraced in his surrender to Fuchai. He had done menial labor in service to Fuchai, he had let his wife share Fuchai's bed. Such abasements made it impossible to imagine Goujian challenging Fuchai's authority as long as anything approaching traditional conventions were in force: Goujian's own people (according to this way of thinking) would be too ashamed to obey any orders injurious to the man Goujian had so clearly acknowledged as superior and liege.

What Fuchai did not understand, and what Zixu persistently tried to warn him about, was that the old rules could no longer be consistently relied upon to apply. Tradition and protocol were powerful forces, but in the brave new world of the fifth century BCE they could be undermined by markets, wealth, and greed. Zixu had learned this lesson in the hardest way possible, through bereavement and exile. He knew that it did not matter how much personal honor Goujian had forfeited. As long as he could tap into and channel the copious material wealth that flowed through the territory of Yue, Goujian could purchase virtually anyone's complicity. Indeed, though Zixu may never have known (and could not have proven) it, Fuchai's own Grand Steward was a paid agent of Yue.

King Fuchai's campaign to exert influence over the Zhou states of the North reached a critical juncture in 485 BCE. In that year, as mentioned in the previous chapter, Fuchai led a coalition army northward to attack the state of Qi. Before embarking on this campaign, he was again admonished by Wu Zixu, who warned that the distraction of such northern adventures left Wu vulnerable to the ever-present threat from Yue. King Goujian was practicing severe austerities in his quest to be a model ruler; Wu should eliminate him before pursuing dreams of interregional dominance. Once again Zixu's advice was disregarded.

The northern campaign of 485 BCE achieved mixed results. The ruler of Qi, Duke Dao (the father of Duke Jian, whose ouster was the focus of the past chapter), had offended Fuchai,[76] and as Wu's armies approached, Duke Dao's own courtiers killed him in an attempt to placate the Wu king. Fuchai seized upon this opportunity to stage a bit of political theater, weeping disconsolately outside his tent for three days in mourning for his murdered "cousin" ruler. The campaign now became an expedition to punish the slayers of Duke Dao of Qi, harkening to the model of former Lords Protector that had enforced the hierarchical order of Zhou society. An amphibious assault was launched against the coast of Qi, but the state's warriors and nobles rallied to repulse the southern invaders.[77]

The following year (484 BCE), the newly crowned Duke Jian of Qi and his co-prime minister Zai Wo launched a campaign against Confucius's home state of Lu. Earlier Lu had acceded to Wu's demand that it enter into a sworn covenant, in which the Duke of Lu acknowledged King Fuchai as his superior and protector. Facing dire straits, the Duke of Lu sent one of Confucius's disciples as an envoy to call King Fuchai to honor his oath, and the king agreed.

On the word that another campaign was planned against Qi, a delegation from Yue arrived offering support for the imminent expedition. Rich gifts were dispensed to the king and his courtiers and were accepted with delight. This moved Zixu to deliver a grim speech of warning to the court at large: Yue was fattening Wu for the kill. For Wu, Yue was a disease "of the heart and vitals." If this sickness was not excised, Wu would certainly perish. Zixu urged King Fuchai to forego marching northward and turn Wu's swords on Yue instead.

The King of Wu was unmoved. He was much too deeply invested in his northern strategy to turn back at that point and forfeit so much hard-won credibility. He sent Zixu, in his capacity as Minister of Foreign Affairs, to Qi, to issue Wu's formal declaration of hostilities.

Contrary to Zixu's warnings, the campaign of 484 BCE was a triumph. In response to the challenge brought by Zixu, the Duke of Qi dispatched one of his most able commanders with a powerful force to meet the approach of Wu's armies. The combatants met at Mugwort Hill (Ailing) in present-day Shandong Province, where the Wu forces under the command of the Grand Steward crushed the army of Qi. The Qi commander and four other Qi nobles were captured, as well as 800 war chariots and 3,000 armored warriors.[78]

The battle of Mugwort Hill shocked the Zhou world as much as King Helü's sack of the Chu capital in 506 BCE. The army of Wu had achieved an uncommonly one-sided victory over one of the most time-tested and powerful military forces in the northern states. The military exploits of Wu could no longer be dismissed as a fluke or as an anomaly only pertaining to the strange circumstances of the "barbarian" South. Wu's military prowess was proven and deadly. The northern states were forced to pay heed.

While the campaign of 484 BCE brought King Fuchai's prestige to new heights, it brought his confidence in Zixu to a nadir. Zixu had taken his son with him on his embassy to the court of Qi. Convinced that in the long term Wu was doomed, he had entrusted his son to the care of one of Qi's noble houses.

That proved a fatal mistake. On his return to Wu, Zixu was denounced in court by the Grand Steward, who declared that he had sent spies to follow Zixu on his mission to Qi, and that they had witnessed Zixu give his son over to the care of the enemy. It was, in retrospect, an intensely ironic moment. The Grand Steward, a mole in the pay of Goujian of Yue, was accusing Zixu of disloyalty.

Irony notwithstanding, King Fuchai was appalled. In deference to his minister's long years of service he presented Zixu with a ceremonial sword and granted him the dignity of taking his own life. Zixu cut his own throat, but not before declaring that he wished his eyes to be mounted on the gates of the capital to watch the approach of Yue's armies and that his grave be planted with catalpa trees for use in making coffins for the dead. On hearing this, King Fuchai was so enraged that he had Zixu's corpse sewn into a leather wineskin and flung unceremoniously into the Yangzi. The people revered Zixu, however, and erected a shrine to him on the riverbank, where he was ever after worshipped as a god.[79]

King Fuchai's campaign to amplify his influence in the northern states progressed rapidly after the battle of Mugwort Hill. Only two years later, in 482 BCE, he was able to compel the rulers of the northern states to meet with him at a place called Yellow Pond (Huangchi), in present-day Henan Province, for a solemn covenant ceremony. An emissary of the Zhou Son of Heaven was present as witness, and the Duke of Jin, ruler of the state that had been patron of the earliest Wu kings and the last lineage to claim the rank of "Lord Protector," participated. As the Son of Heaven's representative watched, the northern rulers swore fealty to King Fuchai as "covenant lord" and Lord Protector of the Zhou realm.[80] It was the culmination of a strategy that Fuchai had been pursuing since his defeat of Yue in 494 BCE. In 12 short years he had achieved his objective. As he drained the cup of sacrificial blood that would be shared with his new vassals, Fuchai must have felt vindicated for having disregarded Zixu and blazed his own path to power.

In one of history's most poignant ironies, Fuchai's moment of greatest glory was also the turning point that prefigured his doom. Just as Zixu had tried to warn what was inevitable, Fuchai's nemesis Goujian, having held off until his advisors agreed that the timing was right, seized the opportunity that he had been waiting for so patiently. While Wu's army and king pursued ceremonial victories at Yellow Pond in the North, Yue's army crossed into Fuchai's territory in a full-scale invasion. Goujian overran the reserve force that marched out to meet him under the command of Fuchai's Heir Apparent. When that force had been crushed and the Wu Crown Prince captured, the army of Yue entered and sacked the Wu capital in which Goujian had once been compelled to work as a menial servant.

Word of the invasion reached Fuchai while he was still at Yellow Pond. From fear that the covenant would be undone if the other lords knew of his humiliation, Fuchai personally slit the throats of seven men present at the delivery of the news before anyone could leave the king's tent.[81] Returning to Wu, he found the capital empty of soldiers. His army was exhausted from its extended period on the march, so Fuchai resigned himself to passivity. Unable to take the offensive and vulnerable to attack, the King of Wu sued for peace from his former servant. He sent lavish gifts to Goujian to buy a cessation of hostilities, forfeiting the treasure that he had accepted in exchange for sparing Goujian's life 12 years prior.[82]

Wu had been humbled and Yue exalted. The rest of the Zhou world watched bemused as two rival kings, Fuchai and Goujian, contended for supremacy in the Lower Yangzi. After Tian Chang murdered his duke in 481 BCE (as we read about in the previous chapter) and was sending out emissaries to secure the complacency of the power brokers of the age, he made sure to dispatch missions to both Wu and Yue.

King Goujian did not make Fuchai's mistake of abdicating the initiative once it was his. He launched another expedition against Wu in 478 BCE,[83] and a third in 475 BCE. This last assault laid siege to the Wu capital. After two years of encirclement the capital was finally overrun and King Fuchai captured.

Fuchai pleaded to be spared and made a vassal of Yue, as he had done for Goujian when their positions had been reversed, but at the urging of one of his advisors, Goujian refused. Fuchai's life might be spared, but the state of Wu could not persist as a vassal: its temples and altars would all be destroyed and its ruling house made commoners. Too weak to bear such disgrace, Fuchai slit his own throat, asking that his corpse be blindfolded to spare him the shame of having to face Zixu in the afterlife. King Goujian destroyed all of the palaces and temples of Wu, effectively erasing the state from existence. Before returning to Yue, he executed his paid mole, the Grand Steward, to make an example of him for all ministers that would contemplate disloyalty to their sovereign.[84]

In the wake of the destruction of Wu, Goujian assumed the place previously held by Fuchai in the community of the Zhou states. He convened a meeting of vassal lords at Xuzhou, in present-day Jiangsu Province, where he was honored as covenant lord by an assembly including the rulers of both Qi and Jin, the two most powerful northern states. He sent a tribute mission directly to the Zhou king, and the Son of Heaven reciprocated with a gift of meat from the royal sacrificial altars, accompanied by an edict proclaiming Goujian Lord Protector of the Zhou realm.[85]

Goujian had achieved one of the most stunning strategic reversals in the history of East Asia, perhaps the world. However, though he has been remembered ever since as an icon of fortitude and determination, the political impact of his success was short-lived. Just as had occurred in the partnership between Fuchai and Zixu, in the wake of his final triumph Goujian became estranged from the foreign-born ministers that who had served him so well. They left his court, and Yue sank gradually back into obscurity. Goujian is one of the last Yue rulers for whom we have detailed records. The kingdom was ultimately broken up and subjugated by Chu in 306 BCE.[86]

The bizarre and erratic shifts of power between Wu, Yue, and Chu in the far South left the aristocracy of the Zhou world flabbergasted. On the one hand, the story was one of the immense potential of commercial wealth. Profits from trade had enabled Wu and Yue to develop seemingly irresistible military might with unnatural speed, and to leverage that influence through bribery and enticement. On the other hand, the power of markets had proven volatile and unstable. Like the nation-states of our own time that fall under the "resource curse," Wu's and Yue's prosperity had outpaced the elasticity and coherence of those states' political and social institutions.

Wu and Yue, each in turn, had seemed like new suns, only to be revealed as deceptively bright shooting stars. The spectacle of the Son of Heaven bestowing the rank of Lord Protector on Goujian, the tattooed barbarian who had served and murdered Fuchai, the barbarian last granted the same title, was a dissonant farce. What did it mean? The old values and institutions were obviously decadent, but the new sources of power were all unpredictable. For those entrusted with the leadership and security of a state, the world had become an intractably confusing place. All of the familiar signs for deciding where to seek cooperation and when to pursue quarrels, which states posed threats and which were benign, were no longer dependable.

The rules of power, if there were any, had to be rediscovered and reinvented. Confucius had died still preaching that the Mandate of the Zhou Son of Heaven could be revived, and relations between the many states rectified under the rejuvenated leadership of the Zhou royal house. The debacle of the South, in which the authority of the Zhou king had been so promiscuously dispensed, had suggested Confucius was wrong. Tian Chang had already begun reorganizing the great northern state of Qi in response to the changing conditions of the fifth century BCE even before Wu was destroyed. In the newly fluid world revealed by that cataclysm, the aristocracy of the other great northern state, Jin, maneuvered aggressively to radically reconfigure the political structure of their ancient home. That is the subject of the next chapter.

3

The Partition
The State of Jin, 472–453 BCE

The erasure of the kingdom of Wu by Goujian showed the people of the Zhou states that the political geography of their world was much more fluid than they had imagined. It would not take long for that lesson to be reinforced, and with a vengeance. Twenty years after the suicide of King Fuchai of Wu in the kingdom that would die with him, more seismic fissures opened in the territorial organization of the Zhou states. This cataclysmic change, moreover, did not take place in the "barbarian" South, but in the northern heartland, virtually in the backyard of the Son of Heaven himself.

In the reign of its thirty-ninth duke, the "superpower" of Jin, the geopolitical juggernaut whose machinations had helped produce the Frankenstein monster of Wu, was effectively split into three new states. Bizarrely, these individual parts proved, in the long term, to be more powerful than the sum of the whole. Like the state of Qi under the reorganizing leadership of the Tian clan, the three Jin successor states would each, over time, evolve into a new form of polity—a "Warring State." The dismemberment of Jin would thus change the course of history, for both the Zhou realm and all of East Asia.[1]

The significance of this change is difficult to overstate and operated on two levels: "macro" and "micro." On the macro level, the partition of Jin fundamentally reworked the power dynamics of the entire Zhou domain. To get a sense of this impact, one might imagine how destabilizing it would be to the politics of the United States if California were divided into three new states, each of which had *more* representation in Congress and the Electoral College than unified California had possessed originally, and each of which was controlled by a different political party. The analogy is imperfect, but conveys a central irony of the moment: though Jin had been a "superpower" of the Spring and Autumn era, through internal reform and reorganization the three states into which it was partitioned became economically and militarily more powerful than the unified domain out of which they had been formed.

On the micro level, the partition of Jin into three "Warring States" fundamentally restructured aristocratic society. Unified Jin had been honeycombed by dozens of aristocratic families, some stronger than others, but all of whom persisted in relative parity with the mean.[2] Partition "telescoped" the aristocracy, because it resulted from a devouring of the smaller families and a winnowing of the more powerful families until only three aristocratic clans were left standing. These three surviving clans, the ruling families of the new states, now had unprecedented power, wealth, and prestige.

The struggles in which the powerful clans were destroyed did not significantly decrease the population of individual aristocrats in the state of Jin, however. The many scions of the defeated clans simply became lowly knights without rank, title, or significant wealth. To whom these knights owed their allegiance; who were their friends; who their enemies; to what dignity they were entitled; in what way, for what service, and how much they would be remunerated: all of these were questions without clear answers in the post-partition world. It was a moment fraught with both possibility and peril. Only one thing was certain: restoring order to politics and society would be the work of generations, not just in the former territory of Jin but throughout the Zhou world.

The first Duke of Jin, who had assumed his throne almost six centuries before the suicide of King Fuchai of Wu, had been a younger brother of the second Zhou Son of Heaven. According to legend, the king, who had come to the throne as a child on the early death of his father, had been playing with his brother in the palace courtyard and jokingly presented him with a paulownia leaf cut into the shape of a jade investiture tablet, declaring, "With this I enfeoff you." On hearing him utter these words, the king's scribe compelled the king to establish his brother as one of the Lords of the Land (*zhuhou*),[3] insisting that the ruler can never speak such sentiments in jest.[4]

Whether or not the state of Jin really began so inadvertently, over time it became a central pillar of the Zhou regional order. Centered on the fertile plain watered by the Fen, a major tributary of the Yellow River, Jin occupied economically and strategically vital terrain. It guarded the lower reaches of the Yellow River from the approach of non-Sinitic people on the Inner Asian steppe, and sat astride major routes of communication and trade between the eastern and western regions of the Zhou domain.

Over decades and centuries Jin grew steadily in size, power, and importance. It did this by conquering other states on the North China plain, annihilating and annexing the territory of 17 states and subjugating the rulers of 38 others.[5] Many of the states thus absorbed by Jin were "cousins," courts led by rulers also belonging to the royal Ji clan. Others were states led by families other than the royal clan, who were subjugated as vassals of the court of Jin. Still others were states belonging to non-Sinitic peoples living on the periphery of the Zhou domain, which were annexed to the estates of existing Jin vassals or used to create new vassalages to reward successful military commanders.

By the turn of the fifth century BCE Jin was a mega-state by ancient standards, laying claim to a territory larger than the modern nation-state of Greece (which in the fifth century BCE housed dozens of city-states).[6] The geostrategic success of the state had not come without internal turmoil. Even as the Jin nobility warred to expand their patrimony (often, as mentioned above, with "kindred" states of the Zhou realm), they also fought incessantly with one another. Feuds between noble houses, rebellions against the ducal throne, and fighting within the ducal clan itself were almost constant facts of life in the Jin domain. For 60 years (from 739 until 679 BCE) an intermittent civil war persisted between the main branch of the ducal clan and a cadet branch that had been enfeoffed at a city called Crooked Ditch (Quwo). The war only ended when the cadet branch finally displaced the main line of the family as rulers of Jin.[7]

The fact that Jin continued to grow in size and power through all this strife shows, as we saw in Chapter 1 was the case in the state of Qi, the paradoxical and erratic nature of Zhou aristocratic society. Aristocrats' aggressive belligerence, easily offended honor, and extreme status-consciousness made internecine violence virtually constant in all the Zhou states. At the same time, their common devotion to family, ancestry, and tradition unified the Jin nobility enough to make them *collectively* a formidable military power on the North China plain.

In 632 BCE the most celebrated ruler of Jin, Duke Wen (the "Civil Duke," r. 636–628 BCE) became the second of the regional lords to be named Lord Protector by the Zhou Son of Heaven.[8] This marked Jin as one of the main power brokers of the Zhou territorial order. All through the sixth century BCE it was the court of Jin that took the initiative in defending the sovereignty of the Zhou king against the heretical challenge from the "barbarian" empire of Chu in the south. Successive Jin dukes claimed the position of Lord Protector as a hereditary entitlement and wielded it to assert precedence over the other vassal states of the Yellow River plain.[9]

Like Qi and Lu, though Jin was in theory the domain of a single ducal house, in practice each duke shared his realm with a coterie of grandee households honeycombed across the steadily expanding state. Some of these clans were offshoots of the ducal house, founded by the younger brother of a past duke that had been given permission to establish his own household (with a new clan name).[10] Others had been founded by warriors who had given good service to past dukes of Jin. Still others were families that had once been independent rulers in their own right, but had submitted and sworn allegiance to Jin.[11]

All of these families had their own ancestral temple halls and local shrines that were a mirror of those at the ducal court. Each had its own soldiers and collected revenue from the common farmers living in their territory. This patchwork framework of local warlords was inherently unstable and grew more unstable over time. As was true in virtually all the states of the Zhou domain to one degree or another, over the course of the sixth and early fifth centuries BCE the forces that produced internal division and conflict within the Jin state were growing stronger, while the forces that helped keep Jin (provisionally) integrated and united were weakening.

In theory every noble in the Zhou world was locked into a fixed relationship with every other from birth: upward or downward social mobility were only ever possible on the authority of someone of higher rank than oneself. In actual practice, with skill and luck an aristocrat could raise the fortunes of his clan, his family, or himself through coercion and conquest. Very often success depended on *both* loyalty to tradition *and* coercion and conquest. If the duke got angry at the head of a neighboring clan, for example, a grandee could see his lands increased and his title elevated by loyally executing the duke's order to kill his neighbor (who more often than not was also his kinsman, at least by marriage).[12]

The situation created perversely paradoxical incentives. Since new land could be won through campaigns against external foes, and victory in those enterprises would depend on preserving unified force, Jin nobles had an interest in respecting and cultivating good relations with fellow Jin nobles. But since their neighbors' land was conveniently near and accessible, the temptation was always present to find a way to undermine a neighbor's position in the state and maneuver him into the disfavor of the duke, or to simply attack that neighbor while the duke was otherwise distracted.

Though internal conflict was foreordained in this society, the cohesion of Jin deteriorated at an accelerating rate over the course of the seventh and sixth centuries BCE. As in other states such as Qi, the proliferation of noble scions from generation to generation created more and more pressure on available land for the support of temple cults. At the same time, the liquid wealth and market profits moving in ever higher quantities over intensifying trade networks that had given such immense power to upstart and alien states like Wu and Yue were progressively more enticing to the leaders of Jin society. The common bonds of tradition, kinship, and ritual grew weaker and weaker in the face of these corrosive forces.

The leaders of Jin were not blind to the problem. Over decades and centuries they improvised new institutions to try and bolster the traditional order. During the reign of the first Jin Lord Protector the court established a system of "three armies," in an attempt to formalize the hierarchical structure of the state oligarchy. The three most powerful families of the state were each given hereditary command of one "army," with the head of another powerful family ranked as "sub-commander." All six of these clan heads were installed as "Counselors" (*qing*) at the ducal court,[13] constituting a kind of "privy council" in charge of state affairs.[14]

Each "army" was in reality a confederation of noble clans, with the leader of one clan at the head, ostensibly empowered to demand the obedience of the lesser clans assigned to his "army." In theory this should have drawn clear lines between the separate spheres of influence of the lead families, as well as clarifying who was "up" and who was "down" in the organizational "flow chart" of the state. Fixing expectations this way was meant to deprive ambitious nobles of the opportunity for conflict and scheming.[15]

In practice this formalization did little to arrest strife between the houses. Over the next century the fortunes of the great families rose and fell erratically. As they warred with one another and the ducal house for power and influence, some families were destroyed and their place among the "Six Counselors" taken by others.

In 513 BCE a group of Jin Counselors, under the leadership of a dynamic and powerful aristocrat, Viscount Jian of Zhao (d. 475 BCE), forged an iron cauldron on which was inscribed a penal code. This was yet another attempt to arrest the accelerating disintegration of relations between the leaders of the Jin oligarchy. Unlike kinship, ritual, and tradition, which created varying obligations subject to shifting interpretation, the penal code was instituted to create consistent, clear, and universal rules to stabilize interactions between the noble clans. It was a measure that was adopted by other Zhou states at about this time, and which anticipated more intensive reforms that would be undertaken in the Warring States. Confucius, whose faith in kinship, ritual, and tradition was absolute, was aghast. He predicted that the Penal Cauldron was an omen of Jin's doom.[16]

Whether the cauldron contained too many laws (as Confucius claimed) or too few (as modern political scientists might insist), its stabilizing effects were short-lived. The clans that had cooperated in forging the Penal Cauldron were soon at war with one another. A set of remarkable documents discovered by archaeologists shows us how chaotic the situation had become some decades after the forging of the Penal Cauldron, in the early to mid-fifth century BCE.

These are "covenant texts," discovered in large burial pits at a site outside of what was once the ducal capital of the state of Jin. This site had been used for a number of years to convoke oath-swearing sacrifices. These ceremonies were modeled on the elite covenants sworn by the vassal lords to form alliances between states, such as the ceremonies at which rulers like Duke Wen of Jin or King Fuchai of Wu had been elevated to the position of Lord Protector.

Where those historic occasions had involved a handful of very high-ranking nobles, however, the ceremonies that produced the Jin pit burials typically involved dozens of warriors, most of them obscure knights otherwise unrecorded in the ancient chronicles. Each ceremony marked a high crisis point in an ongoing feud, in what appear in hindsight as "Hail Mary" acts of desperation to try and broker peace amid vicious and destructive fighting. Participants gathered for the ceremony and witnessed the offering of an animal as sacrificial victim over the pit.

Blood was collected in a vessel that was passed around to each celebrant. Each man in turn smeared some of the blood on his lips and read the words of an oath off of a stone tablet. Once the oath was recited, sacrificial blood was smeared on the written tablet, which was interred in the pit along with the tablets of all the other celebrants and the carcass of the sacrificial victim. In this way the spoken words of the oath (and notice of the obligations it entailed) were directed to the Heavenly spirits above, while the written words were kept on record with the Earthly spirits below.[17]

The texts of these oaths show how violent the aristocratic society of Jin had become. One such oath, for example, on pain of terrible retribution from the spirits, includes a promise not to harm the "covenant lord" (the noble who had convened the ceremony), a promise to avoid all contact with a long list of enemies, and a promise to kill certain enemies and their descendants if they should so much as be "met on the road." It also pledges the warrior who took the oath not to interfere with the sacrifices "to the former rulers of Jin in their ancestral temples."[18]

This last aspect of the ceremony shows how dangerously far the prestige of the Jin ducal house and its ancestral spirits had fallen. If lowly knights were not clamoring to be included in the sacrifices at the ducal temples, but had to be cajoled into swearing *not to interfere with them*, the traditional bonds tying Jin nobles to one another, always tenuous, were growing vanishingly weak. To understand the gravity of the situation, one might picture circumstances in the United States today in which citizens, rather than being eager to enter buildings like the White House or Capitol as elected officials or tourists, had to be asked to swear not to break in and interrupt the business being done there.

By the end of the second decade of the fifth century BCE, events in the South made the situation even worse. Foundational to the mystique of the Jin dukes was their claim to the hereditary title of Lord Protector. When the title was wrested away from the Duke of Jin by Fuchai of Wu, a tattooed "barbarian," at Yellow Pond in 482 BCE, the ducal house was humiliated. This humiliation was then compounded when the title passed to a second tattooed barbarian, Goujian of Yue, who won it through insurrection and betrayal less than 10 years later (an investiture that the new Duke of Jin was forced to acknowledge in a covenant meeting).[19] These debasements of tradition and ritual did not merely impact the dukes of Jin directly. They also radically eroded the moral and spiritual authority of the Zhou Son of Heaven, with which the prestige and cachet of the Jin ducal house was inextricably entwined.

By 472 BCE Jin had effectively become a "zombie state." The ducal throne had fallen to a low point of almost total impotence, the Counselors and grandees operated in a state of virtually complete mutual mistrust and antipathy, and yet the "state" soldiered on as a single territorial polity. A climate of expectancy prevailed. Everyone could perceive that a change was imminent, but few could anticipate how it would come about or what it would entail. In that year a leader emerged who would break the impasse, though few could have predicted exactly how his role took shape.

His name was Zhi Yao (d. 453 BCE), and in 472 BCE he had recently risen to become the head of his clan, one of six families claiming the rank of "Counselor" at that moment in the court of Jin.[20] Like the grandee clans of Qi discussed in Chapter 1, each of these families had been cultivating its power for decades, recruiting knights to its service with patronage and developing new ways to draw broadly and deeply upon the resources of the lands and people under their control. Each clan imposed a different system of land measurement and taxation within its territory, and each cultivated its own stable of "retained knights."[21]

Zhi Yao was the model aristocrat of Zhou times. He was, in the assessment of an older kinsman, exceptionally handsome, a fearsome warrior, an artful strategist, an eloquent speaker, and uncommonly resolute. That same kinsman urged Zhi Yao's father, the previous Viscount of Zhi, to set Zhi Yao aside in favor of his younger brother as heir to the clan headship. The viscount rejected this advice, complaining that Zhi Yao's brother was obstinate. The kinsman countered that while the younger brother's obstinacy showed on his face, Zhi Yao's was kept hidden in his heart, making him a far more dangerous character. Though Zhi Yao might have all the qualities prized in a high-ranking noble, he lacked humaneness. This weakness, in combination with his other virtues, was a recipe for disaster. When his advice was not heeded, the kinsman changed his surname and departed from Jin.[22]

In 472 BCE, having succeeded his father to become the new Viscount of Zhi,[23] Zhi Yao seized an opportunity to make his mark on the court. Tian Chang's coup of 481 BCE in Qi had thrown the always tense rivalry between that state and Jin, two major northern powers that had each held the title of Lord Protector, into open hostilities. In one armed exchange Qi had seized territory from Jin, and the honor of Jin required that it be recovered. An expeditionary force was raised, but the noble who had been in control of all military affairs in Jin for several decades, the cunning and charismatic Viscount Jian of Zhao (the leader of the group that had cast the Penal Cauldron in 513 BCE), had recently died.[24] A new leader was needed for this campaign, and the young Zhi Yao was chosen to be overall commander.

All eyes were on Zhi Yao. It was a chance for him to demonstrate whether his outward appearance of noble excellence was matched by internal substance. He understood the stakes were very high, and his ambition rose to meet them.

When the Jin expeditionary force was in sight of the Qi army, Zhi Yao went out personally to reconnoiter, taking position on a bluff overlooking the enemy position. As he surveyed the Qi soldiers from his chariot, his horses became frightened. This drew the attention of some of the enemy warriors, who could recognize him from the battle-standard that flew from his chariot. Zhi Yao knew that he was being watched on all sides, both by the warriors in his own army and those of the foe. Abashed that he would be thought a coward if he withdrew to calm his horses, he cracked his reins, urging the skittish animals forward. At breakneck speed he charged down the slope toward the enemy army below, turning when he reached the outer edges of their encampment. Only after this display of bravado and skillful charioteering did he wheel about and return from his reconnaissance, followed by the missiles of the enemy archers. It was the kind of moment that helped plant the seed of a warrior's legend, and Zhi Yao's grew from there.

Returning back to his own camp, Zhi Yao was approached by one of the Jin sub-commanders, who requested that they perform a divination ritual to see whether the auguries for battle were favorable. Zhi Yao laughed at the man. They had applied to the Son of Heaven for permission to launch this campaign, Zhi Yao explained. Auguries had been taken at the royal court. Beyond that, Jin had to be redeemed no matter what was divined. Qi had stolen territory, it had to be recovered. Their going into battle was foreordained by honor, nothing the spirits had to say could change that.

The battle was joined the next day at a place called Plough Hill (Liqiu). Zhi Yao threw himself into the thick of the fray and fought with great skill and courage. He personally captured one of the most renowned warriors in Qi, a right-hand aid of Tian Chang himself, who died of his wounds in the aftermath of the battle.[25]

These exploits vaulted Zhi Yao to a position of leadership among the Jin nobility. Four years after the battle at Plough Hill he was again given command of a Jin expeditionary force, this time to attack Jin's southern neighbor, the state of Zheng. Zhi Yao marched the Jin forces to within 60 kilometers of the Zheng capital, when the grandees of Zheng sent for help from Qi.

Tian Chang was still angry about the defeat at Plough Hill. He took personal command of the relief army that marched to Zheng's aid, and rewarded the sons of warriors who had fallen at Plough Hill with investiture for participation in the campaign. When the Qi army came within sight of Jin's forces they were delayed by rain. Tian Chang donned a rain cloak and assisted his men in getting their supply wagons and chariots moving again.

Zhi Yao caught sight of Tian Chang laboring alongside his soldiers and decided to abort the campaign rather than risk tangling with the combined forces of Zheng and Qi. He excused the decision to his own men, declaring that they had divined about going to war with Zheng, not Qi, and thus were forced to be prudent. He sent an insulting message taunting Tian Chang, inspiring the latter to predict that someone so fond of being rude could not last very long.[26]

However resentful Zhi Yao was of Tian Chang's meddling, he also clearly admired the Qi leader's drive and political acumen. He remarked to one of his aides that Tian Chang provided a good model of how to "take possession of a state."[27] This encounter with Tian Chang set Zhi Yao's mind moving along certain paths. What could be done in Qi, he thought, could be accomplished in

Jin. In the same way that Tian Chang had eliminated his rivals in the Qi aristocracy and wrested control of the state away from the ducal throne, Zhi Yao could similarly dispense with the rival Counselor-rank clans of Jin and make himself the state's sole effective ruler, controlling the duke as his puppet.

The failed campaign against Zheng in 468 BCE did not diminish Zhi Yao's influence at the Jin court. In 464 BCE he commanded another expeditionary force of Jin's military against neighboring Zheng. This time they penetrated into the heart of enemy territory and laid siege to the Zheng capital. As they were assaulting the southern gate of the city, Zhi Yao ordered one of his subcommanders, Zhao Wuxu (Viscount Xiang of Zhao, r. 475–425 BCE), to join the vanguard of the attack.[28]

Zhao Wuxu was the son and heir of Viscount Jian of Zhao, the famously brave and cunning warrior who had previously served as overall commander for Jin's forces and oversaw the forging of the Penal Cauldron. Zhao Wuxu's story was in many ways the mirror-inverse of Zhi Yao's. He had no reputation for being a great warrior or prime physical specimen. In fact, he had not originally been Viscount Jian's heir. He was a younger son born to one of the viscount's concubines, a captive woman taken in a raid against the Di, a Turkic people who lived to the north of Jin.

The previous viscount had presented his sons with a challenge: he told them that a precious talisman could be found on Mount Chang along the frontier of their terrain and promised a reward for anyone who could recover it. Zhao Wuxu's brothers searched in vain. On climbing the mountain, Wuxu saw that it overlooked the non-Sinitic state of Dai and understood that his father was instructing his successors to conquer that territory. When Wuxu reported to the viscount that he had solved the riddle, the viscount recognized his younger son's talent and invested him as heir.[29]

Zhi Yao's order to charge into the breach of the Zheng capital's southern gate was another challenge for Zhao Wuxu. Zhi Yao was in effect questioning whether Zhao Wuxu could live up to his father's grand name. It was also a gambit to get Zhao Wuxu killed by sending him into the thick of an assault on a fortified position. The young viscount of Zhao demurred, replying "You, my lord, are here." In other words: "After you."

Zhi Yao, displaying his usual tact, took the opportunity to heap scorn on his sub-commander. "How can someone as ugly and cowardly as you be your father's heir?" he asked, in plain hearing of the gathered leaders of Jin. It was more than a schoolyard taunt.

Physical beauty and courage were two of the sovereign markers of aristocratic birth. By slandering him as ugly and cowardly, Zhi Yao was casting aspersions on Zhao Wuxu's noble pedigree, implying that he was a commoner. This was both cruel and clever. All of the Jin nobility in earshot were aware that Zhao Wuxu's mother was a slave and a "barbarian."[30]

Zhi Yao must have expected that this insult would shame Zhao Wuxu into racing into the attack on the south gate of the city, to prove that he was in fact a brave noble. That, or Wuxu would draw his weapon and attack Zhi Yao, giving Zhi Yao the opportunity to kill Wuxu in self-defense. Either way, Zhi Yao might have eliminated the man who, because of the legacy of his famous father, was Zhi Yao's chief rival for leadership of the Jin court.

Zhi Yao had underestimated his target. Zhao Wuxu gave him none of his desired reactions, but calmly explained that he had been chosen to succeed his father because he "was able to endure humiliation, and thus would bring no harm to the ancestral altars of Zhao."[31] Translated into other words: "I am too smart to be drawn into a trap by the likes of you." It was a moment of mutual recognition like that between Prince Guang of Wu and Zixu many decades before, but instead of acknowledging one another as allies, each man knew he had discovered his arch enemy.

Despite the failure of Zhi Yao's stratagem aimed at eliminating Zhao Wuxu, the Zheng campaign was a great success. Zheng sued for peace and ceded nine towns to the control of Jin.[32] Zhi Yao returned to Jin covered in glory, having proven himself as a leader one more time.

Zhi Yao now stood unchallenged as the most powerful of the Jin grandee clan heads. He began operating independently to expand the wealth and power of his own court. He tried several ruses to win territory from the state of Wey.[33] He attempted to lull the Wey ruler into a false sense of security by sending him rich gifts, and when that did not work he tried to project a façade of weakness by sending his own son as a "fugitive" to the Wey court. The Wey ruler listened to good counsel from his advisors and avoided these traps.[34]

Others were less wise, or less lucky. Zhi Yao coveted the territory of Qiuyou, a non-Sinitic state that abutted his domain. Access for his army was blocked, however, by an impassable forest. He thus commissioned an enormous bronze ritual bell to be cast for the ruler of Qiuyou and presented it as a gift. The ruler accepted this boon gratefully, and in clearing a path while transporting the bell home, effectively constructed the road by which his own territory might be invaded and his state destroyed.[35]

While Zhi Yao engineered these opportunities to increase his wealth and power abroad, he invested resources in the cultivation of his security at home. In 462 BCE he built walls around Highbridge (Gaoliang), the city that housed his palace and ancestral temples. Fortifying his clan's cult complex in this way effectively established his court as a sovereign entity on par with that of the ducal house.[36]

By 458 BCE there were only six grandee clans that could claim parity with one another in terms of wealth and power in all the state of Jin. These clans had survived the power struggles of the sixth and early fifth centuries BCE, and could still collect revenue and field armies sufficiently to at least preserve their security in the face of an ever more hostile environment. Each clan claimed the rank of Counselor at the Jin court, and thus collectively (under the ostensible auspices of the duke) they constituted the ruling oligarchy of the unified Jin state.

In practical terms, the nominal parity of the Six Counselors masked underlying asymmetries and inequities. Zhi Yao's clan stood out as *primus inter pares* among the leading clans. Two of the six, the Fan and Zhonghang clans, though still viable, had been seriously weakened by power struggles at court during the time when Viscount Jian of Zhao was at the height of his power. In the civil struggles that erupted in the wake of the forging of the Penal Cauldron, the previous Viscounts of Fan and Zhonghang (both of whom had collaborated in the establishment of the Penal Cauldron code) were driven into exile.[37]

In 458 BCE Zhi Yao moved to finish the work that Viscount Jian of Zhao had begun. He negotiated secretly with his rival Zhao Wuxu and the heads of the remaining two leading clans of the Jin court, the Han and the Wei. The Fan and Zhonghang clans were allies and had the support of the reigning duke; no one clan (even that of Zhi Yao) could have displaced them. But Zhi Yao brokered an alliance that pitted four clans (the Zhi, Zhao, Han, and Wei) against two (Fan and Zhonghang). The four allied clans attacked and destroyed the palaces and temples of the Fan and Zhonghang clans, erasing them from the territorial fabric of the Jin state. In accordance with an agreement they had made prior to the assault, the four allied clans divided the territory of the Fan and Zhonghang clans evenly among themselves.[38]

This violation of sovereign prerogative infuriated the Duke of Jin. He sent an emissary to the states of Qi and Lu asking for assistance, hoping to field an army that could punish his delinquent vassals. This effectively forced an all-or-nothing standoff like that provoked by Duke Jian's appointment of Zai Wo to the co-premiership of Qi (that we read about in Chapter 1). In alarm the four allied clans of Jin combined forces in a swift preemptive attack on the ducal court, moving to unseat the duke before he could be reinforced by allies from abroad. The duke fled in advance of this assault and died while on the road to asylum in the state of Qi.[39]

Zhi Yao had maneuvered himself into a position of strategic superiority. He now had possession and control of the ducal court, and placed a child of his own choosing upon the ducal throne, making it possible for him to issue orders in the name of the duke himself. It is from this point that Zhi Yao is most often referred to in chronicles by the title of "Earl Zhi," which almost certainly reflects a deliberate practice on Zhi Yao's part. Earl (*bo*, literally "paternal elder uncle")[40] was a title rarely held by grandee vassals of one of the Lords of the Land; it generally applied to a regional chieftain who was at least nominally sovereign. By styling himself an "earl," Zhi Yao asserted his superiority to the heads of the other clans, who, like the Zhi clan head, traditionally held the rank of "viscount" (*zi*). Also, because the graph for "earl" was closely cognate with (and often used as a loan-word for) the title of "Lord Protector," by calling himself "Earl Zhi," Zhi Yao claimed to be "Lord Protector" of Jin, the chieftain who held permanent and formal leadership of the state's military forces.[41]

Having established himself as the supreme power in Jin, Zhi Yao rested his forces and gathered his strength for several years. In 455 BCE he pressed his advantage again. He sent an emissary to the head of the Wei clan, demanding that Wei surrender the territory it had acquired from the division of the Fan and Zhonghang lands to Zhi Yao. On consulting with his advisors, the Viscount of Wei decided that Zhi Yao had become too powerful to refuse and complied with the demand.

Zhi Yao next sent an emissary with the same demand to the Viscount of Han. The earl was maneuvering to consolidate his control over Jin in the same way that Tian Chang had made himself de facto Lord of Qi. If Zhi Yao could take possession of the lands and peoples that had belonged to two of the other Six Counselors, he would control half of the land of Jin, and thus effectively establish himself and his clan as the proprietors of the Jin state in perpetuity. The Viscount of Han likewise deemed the risk of refusal too high and surrendered the territory that Zhi Yao had demanded.

Predictably, Zhi Yao next pressed his archrival Zhao Wuxu to follow the example of his peers and surrender territory to the Zhi clan. Once again Zhi Yao had underestimated the Viscount of Zhao. Zhao Wuxu refused.

This may have been out of resentment for Zhi Yao's mistreatment of the past, but that would have been out of character for Zhao Wuxu. He had, after all, proven himself capable of "bearing humiliation" for the sake of his clan. More likely, he calculated that Zhi Yao's strategy could have only one end: the final destruction of all the grandee clans with which the earl was forced to share the lands and peoples of Jin. Refusing Zhi Yao would mean war, but since war was inevitable it was better to face the foe now than to buy time while making him stronger. Zhi Yao acted swiftly. He sent emissaries to the clans of Han and Wei, offering them a share of Zhao's territory if they would join an alliance against Zhao Wuxu.[42]

Zhao Wuxu knew an attack was imminent. He consulted his advisors about where they should make their stand, and one of the trusted men inherited from his father urged him to retreat to the city of Jinyang (on the site of present-day Taiyuan, in Shanxi Province), because Jinyang had been well governed in the past. The advice proved invaluable. Because it had been well managed, the city's resources were plentiful and its infrastructure sound. Zhao Wuxu and his commanders were able to make siege preparations quickly and thus be ready for the assault.[43]

The united armies of the Zhi, Han, and Wei clans surrounded Jinyang, trapping the Viscount of Zhao and his forces within. For three months they launched frontal assaults on Jinyang's walls and gates, with no success. At that point one of Zhi Yao's commanders had the idea to flood the city.

Jinyang was on the northwest bank of the Fen River, which like the Yellow River and most of its tributaries was kept in its course by a system of dikes. By building strategically placed new dikes and breaking some of the old, Zhi Yao's hydraulic engineers were able to divert the waters of the Fen into the city of Jinyang itself, flooding the streets so that the water reached to the third floor of all buildings. The city's inhabitants had to perch on roofs and suspend cooking pots from the eaves of buildings in order to feed themselves.[44]

The standoff persisted like this for another two years. By the end of that time hunger and disease were so rampant in the city that its people were desperate. Families sold their children to obtain scraps of food on which to survive.

Zhao Wuxu went back to his father's trusted advisor and asked if it was time to surrender. That he contemplated such a move showed courage. Whatever mercy Zhao might have been able to broker for his clan, he certainly must have known that he personally would die for having defied Zhi Yao.

Zhao Wuxu's loyal retainer brushed such talk aside. Instead, he asked permission to seek audience with the leaders of the Han and Wei clans, and was granted it. Slipping out of the city by night, he met with the Viscounts of Han and Wei in secret. "When the lips are gone, the teeth will be cold," the emissary said to the two leaders: if they allowed Zhao to be destroyed, Han and Wei would be next. The two viscounts conceded his point. They had no illusions about Zhi Yao's nature. But if word got out of their deliberations, they protested, Zhi Yao would destroy them instantly. Zhao Wuxu's advisor assured the two viscounts that no one needed to know about their plans. Together the three men made a pact and set a date for action.

Zhi Yao's kinsman observed a change in the demeanor of the clan heads of Han and Wei, and tried to warn Zhi Yao of imminent danger. Zhi Yao scoffed at these warnings, arguing that his allies would be foolish to give up on the potential profits of their campaign now that the Zhao stronghold was about to fall. Zhi Yao's kinsman pleaded with his lord to at least take the precaution of offering land to the key advisors of the Han and Wei clan leaders, to sway them to advocate for Zhi Yao's interests, following a strategy like that employed by Goujian of Yue, who used such bribes to procure the assistance of Wu's Grand Steward. Zhi Yao again refused this advice, complaining that dispensing such favors would take too steep a toll on his own profits in the venture.

On the night agreed to by the conspirators, the Zhi clan soldiers guarding the siege dikes were murdered, and the walls of the dikes breached, redirecting the waters of the Fen to flood the plain where Zhi Yao's forces were encamped. As the men of Zhi struggled to equip themselves and come to order, the combined armies of Han, Wei, and Zhao attacked. Zhi Yao's armies were slaughtered, and he himself fell in the fighting. In the aftermath of the battle all of the living scions of the Zhi clan were wiped out, its palaces and temples were razed.[45]

Zhao Wuxu made sure to identify Zhi Yao's corpse. He had it beheaded and the top of Zhi Yao's skull removed. Ordering the concave bone covered in lacquer and mounted on a metal base, Zhao transformed his foe's skull into a trophy goblet for use at banquet.[46]

With the extermination of the Zhi, the three clans of Zhao, Han, and Wei were the last grandee houses of Jin to retain their rank and status. They divided the Zhi clan's territory evenly and confined the ducal house to two cities: the capital of Feng and the ancestral home of the reigning lineage, Crooked Ditch. The duke was now a complete figurehead, his role in the conduct of state affairs purely ornamental.[47]

The unified state of Jin had effectively become three newly independent states of Han, Wei, and Zhao. The seeming simplicity of this political change (a tripartite partition) masked the very profound social transformation it brought to culmination. Though over the course of two centuries many grandee houses had been destroyed, the territory of Jin did not have any fewer individual aristocrats than before.

In earlier times the several hundred nobles of Jin had been embedded in an intricate three-dimensional web that separated them into different ranks and distributed powers and obligations in complex patterns, upward, downward, and laterally. As the grandee temples and palaces that provided the dozens of nodal points of that web were destroyed over time, the lower aristocracy became a much "flatter" field of basically equal knights, until eventually the sole allegiance of each and every one of these knights belonged to one of three houses. This created enormous opportunities for improved governance and strategic competition. Knights could be used much more flexibly and on the basis of merit, and rewards (or penalties) could be dispensed on the basis of performance rather than hereditary entitlement (we will read of these reforms in more detail in subsequent chapters).

But the new situation posed challenges too. Like King Fuchai of Wu, the leaders of Jin were caught between the opposing forces of wealth and power on the one hand and values and tradition on the other. King Fuchai of Wu had obviously placed too much faith in values and tradition. His successful quest to achieve the title of Lord Protector proved to be a fool's errand. Conversely, Zhi Yao had clearly placed too much faith in wealth and power. He operated under the assumption that, in a world where warriors lacked a complex web of obligations to constrain them, any problem could be solved by either a bribe or a blow (or both in timely succession, as he employed in conquering the state of Qiuyou). Though he achieved stunning success, his ultimate fate proved the old cliché about those who live by the sword.

A coda to Zhi Yao's story demonstrates how challenging this brave new world would be for leaders, and just how unstable the social order of the aristocracy had become, not only in Jin but throughout the Zhou realm. One of the men in Zhi Yao's retinue, a knight named Yurang who had previously served both the Fan and the Zhonghang clans, was deeply grieved by his lord's fate. Hearing of the insult done to Zhi Yao's remains, Yurang resolved to take revenge by assassinating Zhao Wuxu.

Changing his name and dressing as a convict laborer, he infiltrated the privy of Zhao Wuxu's palace working as a plasterer. He had sharpened his trowel to a knife's edge, intending to use it on his victim. On entering the privy, however, Zhao Wuxu could tell that something was not right. He had his guards question Yurang, and when they saw that Yurang was carrying a weapon, he confessed that he had come with the purpose of avenging Zhi Yao.

Zhao Wuxu's guards wanted to kill Yurang on the spot, but Wuxu would not allow it. He admired Yurang's loyalty. More than that, he could not help but respect Yurang's single-minded devotion to honor. Since Zhi Yao was dead and was not survived by any progeny who might reward Yurang or his family, there was no possibility of material emolument for his actions. His quest for vengeance was purely idealistic. "In future I will just be careful to avoid him," Zhao Wuxu declared.

Yurang did not give up. He realized that his disguise had not been complete enough. Though he had dressed like a common laborer, his general complexion and bearing were still those of an aristocrat. He thus spread caustic lacquer on his skin to raise sores that resembled those of a leper. He removed his hair and eyebrows, scarred his face, and went into the streets in rags to beg. He approached his wife, who expressed confusion over the fact that a beggar's voice sounded so much like that of her husband. This moved Yurang to swallow lumps of charcoal until his speaking voice became hoarse and unrecognizable.

On seeing the extreme lengths to which he was going, Yurang's friends expressed amazement. If he wanted to get close to Zhao Wuxu there was a much easier path. All three ruling clans were in desperate need of personnel. If Yurang applied for a position he would be employed, and a man of his talents would quickly rise to the inner circle of Zhao Wuxu's advisors. Then he would have a clear opening to his target.

Yurang berated his friends. What honor would there be in accepting the favor of one ruler to avenge another? More than being dishonorable, it was a scheme that defied basic logic. If all knights behaved that way, no one would ever be trusted again, and everyone, knights and rulers alike, would suffer.

Finally satisfied with his disguise, Yurang waited in ambush for Zhao Wuxu under a bridge outside of the viscount's palace. As Zhao Wuxu approached the bridge in his carriage, his horses were spooked and refused to cross. "This must be Yurang," he intuited, and ordered his guards to search for whomever might be waiting in ambush.

When Yurang was dragged before Zhao Wuxu, the viscount sighed and queried him in exasperation. "You served the Fan and Zhonghang clans," he observed, "both of which were destroyed by Zhi Yao. Why did you agree to serve Zhi Yao after he had harmed your former lords? Why do you persist in inflicting vengeance on me?"

Yurang's answer was simple but clear. The Fan and Zhonghang clans had employed him as a commoner, and thus he had repaid them with a commoner's

Fig. 5. The knight Yu Rang slices the cloak of Zhao Wuxu to avenge the death of the tyrant Zhi Yao. Such tales of assassins were fascinating to the literati of the Warring States era and continued to excite the imagination of the elites of imperial times. This depiction is also from the Han-era Wu Liang Shrine. (Source: kknews.cc.)

revenge. Zhi Yao had employed him as a "knight of the state," thus Yurang repaid him with the revenge that the honor of a man in such a station required.

Yurang asked that he be given Zhao Wuxu's cloak, so that he could strike it in fulfillment of his duty to his departed lord. The viscount granted him the boon. Slicing the cloak once, he expressed regret that this was the only vengeance he could give Zhi Yao (see Fig. 5) and fell upon his own sword. The knights of Zhao all wept for him on hearing the news.[48]

Yurang's story fascinated the people of the Warring States because it epitomized the existential situation of a growing majority of aristocrats. Yurang's forbears had been grandees with their own palaces and temples, which had been destroyed during the wars that ultimately culminated in the partition of Jin. By the time of his death his family had only produced knights (low-ranking nobles without their own ancestral temples) for several generations.

It was thus an open question to what degree he was entitled to the dignity and deference of a true aristocrat. His Fan and Zhonghang lords had made him feel that they did not view him as a peer. Zhi Yao, conversely, had employed him in a position of real responsibility and rewarded him as a knight of true merit. Avenging one's lord was an obligation borne by an aristocrat. Since only Zhi Yao had accorded Yurang the dignity of an aristocrat, he was the only lord that Yurang considered himself obligated to avenge.

In striving to fulfill that obligation, Yurang created a kind of paradox for the people of his time, especially rulers like Zhao Wuxu. The viscount's exasperated puzzlement at Yurang's actions arose in part from what he took to be very basic contradictions in Yurang's value system. Yurang's focus on revenge displayed a fastidious concern for aristocratic dignity, but his willingness to debase himself with common labor, the filth of the privy, self-mutilation, and the shame of begging were irredeemably vulgar. From the perspective of the Zhou-era aristocratic ethos, Yurang's conduct seemed analogous to jumping into a cesspool to wash some bird droppings off one's sleeve.

This aristocratic ethos presented knights like Yurang (and Confucius and his disciples, and many of the principal actors we will encounter in subsequent chapters) with a dilemma. In defending his aristocratic bona fides, Yurang was forced to choose among the conventional markers of noble status as his situation changed in response to political events. His unblemished appearance, respectable clothes, and avoidance of manual labor had not been enough to convince his Fan and Zhonghang lords to treat Yurang as a peer. He thus decided that those were not central to his position as a noble and could be sacrificed in service of the only values that mattered to his status: honor and courage.

Were honor and courage really the essential hallmarks of nobility? Some would have agreed, others not. They had worked well in the case of Yurang as an individual, but could they serve as guides for a whole family? A whole state? A whole society? At the very least, acknowledging honor and courage as sovereign qualities did not resolve the problem of their relationship to parentage and birth, which remained key foundations of social status.

These might seem like a quaint or outdated conundrums to our twenty-first-century sensibilities, but Yurang's dilemma posed a challenge to all the rulers of the changing Zhou world. The fate of Zhi Yao showed that the strategic use of wealth and power would not be enough; values and traditions would prove indispensable to rebuilding a functional political order. The story of Yurang's revenge showed that the values and traditions inherited from the founding ancestors of the Zhou had become at best problematic and mutually contradictory, at worst obsolete. If the world was going to be rescued from chaos, new traditions would have to be established and new values discovered.

Who was going to accomplish these tasks? Though Confucius had died, his disciples and latter-day disciples remained active and engaged these challenges with robust energy. They were not alone. Very quickly new Masters and groups of disciples arose to challenge Confucius's teachings and propose alternative value systems for the people of the Zhou realm.

One of the most mysterious, innovative, and influential of these new Masters was a man named Mo Di (ca. 480–ca. 390 BCE).[49] He began teaching in the state of Lu just as the civil wars that led to the partition of Jin were reaching a violent crescendo. As we will see in the next chapter, the movement that he founded would help set Zhou society and culture on a fundamentally new course.

4

Heaven's Whim versus Heaven's Will

The Extended Zhou Realm, 475–ca. 439 BCE

The successive crises of the early fifth century BCE acutely intensified the chaos of the Zhou world. Growing disorder in politics and social affairs had been evident for more than two centuries before the partition of Jin in 453 BCE, but in the decades following 481 BCE, the trifecta of Tian Chang's coup in Qi, the meteoric rise and cataclysmic destruction of Wu, and the brazen career of Zhi Yao in Jin had an effect analogous to puncturing a hole in the fuselage of a spacecraft. The very air of the political arena seemed to disappear, creating a void in which formerly unimaginable levels of entropy, iconoclasm, violence, and destruction became possible.

Amidst all this turmoil, faith in the core foundational concept of the Zhou political order, the Mandate of Heaven, was undermined. Modern readers who have some knowledge of Chinese history may be accustomed to reading about "the Mandate of Heaven" as an eternal and unchanging fixture of Chinese culture. It is true that the idea had a powerful mystique at the beginning of the Zhou dynasty (ca. 1045–254 BCE), and that from the late Han dynasty (206 BCE–220 CE) on, it was, in various forms, a touchstone of virtually all political discourse, at least among the classically educated elites who generally constituted the ruling class of imperial times.[1]

But as we will see in this chapter, beginning in the fifth century BCE and continuing throughout the Warring States, the idea of the Mandate of Heaven fell into general disrepute, especially among literati, and was reduced to being only one of several alternative perspectives whose advocates competed in the "marketplace of ideas."[2] Confucius and his latter-day followers remained staunch defenders of the "Mandate of Heaven." They insisted that, to the extent that it had lost persuasive power, it had been misunderstood. Interpreted correctly, in light of Confucius's "Way," they declared, the Mandate remained the only guide that could light the path back to political stability.[3]

This Confucian doctrine, however, was not by any measure a point of broad consensus during the Warring States. In the face of the crises of the fifth century BCE, many highborn aristocrats moved to discard the idea of the Mandate of Heaven entirely. As we will read below, they favored a more flexibly amoral vision of Heaven reflective of the *realpolitik* of the day.

Though this new theology was appealing to the increasingly powerful ruling families of the emerging Warring States,[4] it was met with stiff resistance by many of the knights who comprised the growing majority of aristocratic society (for reasons that will be discussed below). Some of these knights were among the latter-day followers of Confucius who continued to champion the "Mandate of Heaven." But by the latter half of the century a new group of literati emerged, led by a mysterious figure known as Mo Di (ca. 480–ca. 390 BCE).

In response to the spiraling violence of the political world and the amoral vision of Heaven promulgated by (what he deemed) the arrogant highborn aristocracy, Mo Di taught that the "Mandate of Heaven" was a misguided ideal. It was too vague and anemic to genuinely convey the moral wisdom of the ancient sages. He thus proposed to replace it altogether, with a more robust concept of Heaven's sentience and moral sovereignty: Heaven's Will. Mo Di gathered followers and organized them into a fellowship that competed directly with that of Confucius's latter-day disciples. In the mid-fifth century BCE this movement was still in its infancy, but as political conditions in the Zhou world steadily deteriorated, the appeal of Mo Di's doctrine grew, as did the size and influence of the fellowship he had founded. While the more powerful clans among the regional lords became ever more violently aggressive, Mo Di led his followers in progressively more audacious campaigns to alter the course of geopolitical events in a more moral direction.[5]

The practical state of affairs at mid-century was perhaps best exemplified by events at the Zhou court in 441 BCE, a "Year of Four Kings." The collapsing prestige of the Son of Heaven had undermined the peace and stability of the royal clan itself. On the death of the reigning king in 441 BCE, he was succeeded by his eldest son. Three months later that new king was assassinated by his younger brother, who had himself crowned. Eight months after his coronation, the usurper king was in turn killed by a younger brother, who likewise took the throne. Peace was only finally achieved when this fourth king agreed to enfeoff his younger brother as a new "Duke of Zhou" in a territory formed from a portion of the (already diminutive) Royal Domain, to the west of the royal capital, where his descendants would constitute a newly sovereign cadet branch of the royal clan.[6] If the coup in Qi, the debacle in the South, and the partition of Jin had not been enough to undermine faith in the Zhou house, the spectacle in 441 BCE of two princes marching to the throne through a pool of their brother's blood cast crippling doubt on the notion that the royal family held a unique mandate to rule granted by a moral Heaven.

The affairs of the regional states manifested the same rising climate of nihilism. Expansionism had been endemic since the founding of the Zhou dynasty, but over the course of the mid-fifth century BCE the aggressiveness of expanding states increased in scale, violence, and unscrupulousness. Virtually any pretense of deference to the traditions or ethos of the Zhou founders was abandoned, in favor of progressively more reliance on bribery, coercion, betrayal, and trickery in pursuit of wealth and power.

An example can be seen in the career of Zhao Wuxu, the viscount and clan head who defeated Zhi Yao and effectively established the Zhao domain as an independent state, free from its former Jin overlords. Zhao Wuxu had succeeded to the title of viscount because he alone among his brothers had understood his father's ambition to possess the lands of the Dai, a Turkic people whose home lay beyond a mountain to the north of Zhao territory. In 475 BCE, the same year that his father died and while he was still wearing mourning garb (a time when tradition demanded that he refrain from belligerent pursuits), Zhao Wuxu launched his conquest of Dai.

The viscount knew that the King of Dai was fond of beautiful women, so he gave his older sister to the king in marriage. From that point on Zhao Wuxu cultivated good relations with his new brother-in-law, purchasing finely bred horses for which the Dai people were renowned. When he knew that he had won the king's trust, Zhao Wuxu invited the King of Dai to a meet him for a banquet on the mountain that stood at the border between Zhao and Dai.

Before the banquet Zhao Wuxu had his artisans craft an especially heavy copper ladle. Wuxu himself used this ladle to serve his brother-in-law grain wine at banquet. When the merriment was at its height and everyone was tipsy with spirits, Zhao Wuxu made as if to serve the King of Dai some more wine, but instead smashed his unsuspecting brother-in-law in the head with the hefty ladle, splashing his brains upon the ground. At that signal the dancers that Zhao Wuxu had provided as entertainment drew the blades concealed in their feathered banners and slaughtered the courtiers and royal family members who had accompanied the King of Dai.

Having thus decapitated the Dai government, Zhao Wuxu gathered the assault force that he had ordered to follow him up the mountain. Descending from the high ground upon the leaderless people of Dai, Zhao Wuxu conquered the neighboring kingdom in a single stroke. He rode the Dai king's own chariot to the royal palace to retrieve his older sister, but when she heard of her husband's demise she committed suicide by stabbing herself with a sharpened hairpin. The people of Dai pitied her and named a mountain near the place of her death "Hairpin Mountain" in her memory. Zhao Wuxu enfeoffed a nephew (the son of a departed older brother) as the vassal "Lord of Dai," thus incorporating those lands into the emergent Zhao state.[7]

Even granting that the alien Dai were not deemed worthy of the same level of good-faith dealing as "civilized" people, behavior like that of Zhao Wuxu was shocking by the standards of earlier times. This no doubt played a role in the suicide of Zhao Wuxu's older sister. She may in fact have been very fond of her husband, but part of her motivation was almost certainly the shame of having to bear responsibility for her role, however unwitting, in the treacherous scheme that had brought on the King of Dai's annihilation.

Zhao Wuxu was far from alone in pioneering such tactics in pursuit of territorial ambitions. In 447 and 445 BCE the King of Chu, for example, annihilated the ancient states of Cai and Qii, whose rulers descended directly from the earliest generations of the Zhou founders.[8] Other states in the Zhou realm similarly expanded at the expense of ancient households whose ruling lines had survived since the time of the earliest sage kings.[9] We know fewer specific details about those conquests. Zhao Wuxu appears in a particularly draconian light because of an accident of history: more of the records of his activities survive than for most of the other potentates of the mid-fifth century.

It is for this same reason that we have more concrete knowledge of the cultural policies that Zhao Wuxu employed by way of rationalizing his tactics. He was very aware that his actions did not square well with traditional notions of the "Mandate of Heaven." According to Zhou ancestral teachings, Heaven had given the royal throne to the upright and benevolent founders of the Zhou because the last rulers of the preceding Shang dynasty had fallen into wickedness. Even then the Zhou had taken care to preserve the Shang lineage, by giving the descendants of the Shang kings their own state.[10]

Though Zhao Wuxu's conquest of the Dai suffered by comparison to the example set by the Zhou founders, he showed no remorse at that fact. He oversaw the affairs of Zhao until his death in 425 BCE, making him the steward of the clan's destiny for a full 50 years. In that time he made no overt act of contrition or shift in policy. Indeed, as his dealings with Zhi Yao demonstrated, he could be coldly realistic, even cynical in confronting the conditions of his time.

Realism did not preclude any and all concern for legitimacy, however. Though Zhao Wuxu and his descendants were not willing to be bound by the values and traditions of the Zhou founders, neither were they ready to do without values and traditions altogether. A ruler could not hope to achieve Zhao Wuxu's longevity through sole reliance on brute force and trickery. If the leaders of Zhao had ever doubted that, Zhi Yao's destruction would have taught them otherwise.

In this situation, as has been true so often in world history, necessity proved the mother of invention. Zhao leaders rose to the challenge of the moment by composing (or commissioning) doctrines that could make their policies and strategies at least understandable in the context of new times, if not quite "honorable." This can be seen in two surviving prophecies promulgated by the Zhao court, both preserved in the *Records of the Grand Historian* of the Han dynasty.

The first prophecy purports to come from the time of Zhao Wuxu's father, Viscount Jian of Zhao. According to the story, the viscount fell into a fever that lasted for seven days, during which time he remained unconscious. A famous physician was called and said that the viscount's case resembled one from more than a century before, involving the Duke of Qin. The physician predicted that, like that earlier ruler, the viscount would recover and have information to relate from the spirit world.

As predicted, the viscount regained consciousness and told a strange tale of his experience while comatose. He had been in Central Heaven and had been hosted with expansive hospitality by the High God Di, the king of the spirit realm. The spirits had played strange and beautiful music for him, and entertained him with an array of dances. At one point, a brown bear had clawed at him, and the High God had ordered the viscount to shoot and kill the animal with an arrow, which the viscount did. A grizzly bear also attacked him, and at the High God's order he killed that animal too.

The High God was very pleased with his marksmanship. Next to the High God the viscount saw a young boy, standing with a dog bred by the Turkic people of the steppes. The High God presented the dog to the viscount and told him to give it to the strongest of his sons.

Sometime after he recovered, the viscount was out traveling, and his carriage was blocked by a strange figure in the road who would not give way. The viscount's guards were ready to hack the man down, but the viscount sensed something was peculiar and ordered his attendants to stand down. Approaching the stranger, the viscount had the strong impression that he had met the man before and told him as much.

The stranger explained that he had been with the viscount during his time at the court of the High God. The viscount asked the stranger about the meaning of what had occurred there. The stranger explained that the two bears the High God had ordered the viscount to shoot were gods, the ancestral spirits of the Fan and Zhonghang clans (the clans that were ultimately destroyed by the fourfold alliance of the Zhao and three other Counselor-rank clans of Jin, which we read about in the previous chapter). As the High God had turned against their spirit ancestors, those clans were doomed on earth.

The boy that the viscount had seen with the High God was the spirit of his as yet unborn son, Zhao Wuxu. The dog with the boy was the ancestral spirit of the Dai people. The viscount had been given possession of this dog because that son would one day conquer the Dai.

The viscount offered the stranger a position in his court, but the man demurred, explaining that he had only come to transmit the High God's orders. On saying this, the man disappeared. The viscount ordered that everything about his illness and the words of the spirit emissary be written down and archived among the records of the Zhao clan.[11]

The second prophecy purports to date to the rule of Zhao Wuxu himself. In 455 BCE, when Zhao Wuxu had retreated to the city of Jinyang and was fortifying it against Zhi Yao's inevitable attack, one of his knights set out on the road to join his lord for the coming battle. Midway in the journey he encountered three mysterious men. They were only visible from the waist up and seemed to float in mid-air, being invisible from the waist down. They presented the traveling knight with a sealed bamboo tube, ordering that he deliver it to his lord at Jinyang.

On hearing his retainer's story, Zhao Wuxu knew that the tube contained a communication from the spirit world. He fasted for three days before personally breaking the seal on the tube and withdrawing the missive it contained, written in vermillion ink. The message identified the three spirits as the Heavenly emissaries of Marquis Sunnyside, the god of the Huotai mountains (in present-day Shanxi Province).

The spirits declared that on a specific day they would cause Zhao Wuxu to destroy his enemy Zhi Yao. The spirits instructed him to build a temple for them in the town of Baiyi, in return for which they would ensure that he conquered the territory of Forest Hu people. When events unfolded as the spirits had promised, Zhao Wuxu did as the message had instructed. A temple was established to the three spirits at Baiyi, and the knight who had brought the message was posted to oversee sacrifices to Marquis Sunnyside of the Huotai mountains.[12]

These prophecies, most likely in concert with others that no longer survive, sketched out a new theology for the leaders of Zhao in the decades after 453 BCE. The gods that Zhao Wuxu and his father are said to have interacted with expressed no concern for moral abstractions like the "Mandate of Heaven." Indeed, they provided no moral explanations whatsoever for their orders and deeds. The only logic that can be seen in their dealings with Zhao leaders is transactional, as when the three emissaries of Marquis Sunnyside rescued Zhao Wuxu from distress in exchange for the sacrifices from his subjects at Baiyi.

It is easy to understand, given the kind of tactics employed by Zhao Wuxu in his conquest of Dai, why Zhao leaders would not want to be held to a moral code of any rigor. But why would they want to publish these prophecies at all? Was their message really as simple as "the gods made us do it?"

Yes and no. The gods were still held in high enough esteem that claiming to act on their authority had some "public relations" value. In this way, the rulers of Zhao were declaring that their actions were not arbitrary or capricious. They broke with tradition and violated ethical norms only with the license of a higher power.

Beyond this, prophecies like these helped bolster the social position of Zhao leaders in the face of mounting threats. *All* of the noble clans of the Zhou era claimed to be descendants of the gods. When clans like the Fan, Zhonghang, and Zhi were destroyed, their scions murdered and their temples burned to the ground, it naturally raised questions in the minds of the common people witnessing such events: "What good is kinship with the gods, if this is where it leads?" Such questions could ultimately undo all of the noble clans, even those still possessing their own temples, if plausible answers could not be found.

Prophecies and the new theology they expressed helped provide such answers. The common people understood that there was a hierarchy among the gods just as there was a hierarchy among the aristocracy on earth. The prophecies demonstrated that when a noble clan was destroyed, it was because their ancestral spirits had been outranked and outmaneuvered in the realm of the gods. This likewise helped explain why the living did not have to fear retribution from the spirits of the dead for giving their allegiance to the murderers

Fig. 6. Bronze bells discovered in the tomb of Marquis Yi of Zeng 曾侯乙 (d. 433 BCE). All aristocratic courts in the Zhou world were equipped with sophisticated musical instruments and trained musicians. Music was indispensable to the ancestral religion, to court ritual, and to the leisure culture of the Zhou-era aristocracy. (Source: Wikimedia Commons.)

of departed nobility. As the prophecies showed, clans like the Zhao had powerful protectors among the gods.

We living in modern times might wonder at how these prophecies served as propaganda in a time when most people were illiterate. In exploring such a question, we should be aware that the perceived audience of these prophecies was very diverse. The rulers of Zhao almost certainly expected these prophecies to be read and interpreted by the literati knights who were becoming increasingly more important to state affairs. This can be seen in the details about the spirit world that the prophecies include. For example, the beautiful music that Viscount Jian was played by the High God (see Fig. 6), which he explicitly reported was "not like that of the sage kings." Such a report was a direct challenge to a Master like Confucius, who reportedly claimed to have discovered the "heights of music" in that of the ancient sage kings, or Mo Di, who claimed that Heaven's Will forbade music altogether.[13] Viscount Jian's encounter with the High God was a reminder to any literati who would moralize about the Zhao clan's activities that its highborn members were the favored kin of the gods, and thus had access to secret knowledge that superseded the claims of a humble knight like Confucius or Mo Di.

But literati were not the only potential audience of the Zhao clan prophecies. How did they reach the common people? Commoners could not generally read the texts of the prophecies stored in the Zhao state archives, most likely in the ancestral temples of Zhao rulers to whose lives they pertained. The prophecies themselves, however, contain hints at how they worked. The stories are tied to landmarks and monuments: the temple to the three spirit emissaries at Baiyi and to Marquis Sunnyside in the Huotai Mountains, a shrine to the departed shade of Zhao Wuxu's elder sister on Mount Hairpin. These places and the ceremonies held there provided occasions for the prophecy stories to be told orally and passed along as forms of "local lore."

Did everyone buy these ideas? No. The growing population of "knights," aristocratic descendants of families whose ancestral temple complexes had been destroyed in the intensifying civil wars of the sixth and fifth centuries BCE (figures, for example, like the aspiring assassin Yurang whom we read about in the previous chapter), had every reason to take offense at this new theology. If one followed the logic of the prophecies, the families of knights had effectively been cursed by the gods. This notion could do nothing to help knights' social status, which was already imperiled by their clans' loss of temples, territory, and wealth.

Though individually they operated at a disadvantage to the highborn aristocracy, collectively the knights were not without influence in the "culture wars" of the fifth century BCE. Leaders like Zhao Wuxu, though much wealthier and more powerful than the average knight, were nonetheless dependent on the service of knights as warriors, scribes, and officials. By forming fellowships and generating their own writings, knights promoted ideas to contest those being broadcast by the dukes, marquises, and viscounts of the Zhou world.

In the decades after the partition of Jin, many of Confucius's disciples were still active throughout the Zhou world (as we shall read in the next chapter). They defended the dignity of knights by expounding their Master's Way, which affirmed that the Mandate of Heaven was a living doctrine binding to all true aristocrats. Confucius never promised that Heaven could be relied upon to intercede consistently in human affairs: Heaven's moral purposes were veiled and often mysterious. But the Master taught that learning and practice of the Way could give individual leaders *de*, or "Potency" (often translated as "virtue"), a kind of moral charisma that partook of the material dynamism of Heaven, and which could sway others without coercion or trickery. When all else failed, learning gave one the wisdom and courage to see and do what was right, even when success was not possible. Such, according to Confucius, was the essence of true nobility.[14]

As conditions throughout the Zhou world became more chaotic, however, and the theological ideas broadcast by highborn leaders (like those embodied in the Zhao prophecy stories) more brazenly elitist, many literate knights found Confucius's teachings inadequate to meet crisis of the time. One such figure was the teacher Mo Di. Very little is known of his origins. He was most likely born in the state of Lu within a few years before or after Confucius's death, and as a young man may have studied with one or more of Confucius's disciples. Some modern scholars have speculated that he was a commoner, but he was almost certainly a knight.[15]

In his maturity Mo Di claimed the title of Master that had first been worn by Confucius. Like prior Masters, he gathered disciples and presented them with teachings he called "the Way," but his concepts were radically opposed to those of Confucius. The fellowship Master Mo formed, moreover, was organized and operated very differently than that of Confucius's latter-day followers.

Mo Di claimed to know, and be able to prove, that Heaven provided *and enforced* clear moral guidelines for human beings to follow. He rejected Confucius's notion that the "Mandate of Heaven" was a mystery that could only be approached through long study and deep pondering. With a few observations and some lucid reasoning, Mo Di proposed, the concrete rules that Heaven expected people to follow could be laid out for everyone to see and grasp.[16]

What does Heaven want? The answer, to Mo Di, was obvious. All we have to do is observe how Heaven acts in order to discover how we human beings should behave. Heaven is clearly impartial: it distributes sunlight and rain to all people no matter their parentage, language, region, or political allegiance. Heaven is also clearly benevolent: we can see its concern for humanity in the "benefit" (*li* 利, a graph which shows a knife 刀 cutting a stalk of grain 禾) it generates for all people. Everywhere Heaven provides the necessities for producing food, clothing, and shelter. We thus can be certain that Heaven wants us to aid in that task: as individuals and groups we must strive to provide as much *material* benefit as we can to as many people as we can reach.[17]

Though Mo Di agreed with Confucius about the importance of moral conduct, his methods of reasoning led him down different and sometimes surprising paths. Since Heaven's will could be seen in the material benefit it provided to humankind, the right and wrong of behaviors and institutions could likewise be measured in the material benefit such undertakings generated or maintained. Promoting men of worth, for example, was the right thing to do, as this would ultimately make everyone in the state more prosperous.[18] By contrast, mourning for one's father for a full three years (as was the convention among the aristocracy, and as Confucius affirmed was a moral imperative) was wasteful. If productive work had to be curtailed so long so frequently, everyone would suffer, and Heaven does not want that. Three months' mourning was deemed sufficient to show respect for parental authority.[19]

Among the most radical ideas promoted by Mo Di was "universal love." This was not a romantic or erotic notion, but a general call to impartiality. Like Heaven, we should be unselfish and unselfconscious in our dealings with others. We should not, for example, give special consideration to our own parents and family members. Each of us should strive as much to promote the welfare of *other people's* parents and families as we do for our own. For the followers of Confucius this was a rank heresy, as it negated what they understood to be a cardinal duty of filial piety to put one's own parents and family first.[20]

Another "Mohist" idea that Confucians condemned is one that is quite shocking even to our modern-day sensibilities. Mo Di's understanding of "Heaven's will" led him to propose a general and total ban on music. While he granted that listening to music was pleasing to the senses, Mo Di insisted that it produced nothing of tangible "benefit": it required expenditure of material resources but contributed nothing to the production of food, clothing, and shelter.[21]

In one respect Mo Di's perspective was closer to that of Zhao Wuxu and his courtiers than that of Confucius. For Mo Di, Heaven's will was not inscrutable or mysterious. It could be seen and measured all around us through very tangible signs. Those who practiced universal love and worked to benefit others would be rewarded directly by Heaven, those who did not would be punished. The most obvious form in which this Heavenly sanction could be seen was in the human lifespan. Heaven set the number of each person's days on earth—the more one pleased Heaven, the longer one had to live.[22]

But Heaven's intercession in human affairs could occasionally become even more visible. Mo Di agreed with the scribes of Zhao that Heavenly emissaries may often be seen interacting with human beings, especially the powerful. Unlike the spirits of the Zhao prophecies, however, Mo Di's ghosts and spirits always acted in enforcement of Heaven's will, with clear moral purpose. The text that conveys Mo Di's teachings contains many stories in evidence of that point. We are told of one early king who was slain by the ghost of an innocent subject he had murdered, a minister who perjured himself during a covenant oath and was butted to death by the revenant corpse of the sacrificial victim, and a temple officiant who was clubbed to death by a ghost in the ancestral temple because he had been negligent in preparing the sacrifices to the spirits.[23]

Mo Di himself did not leave the implementation of his ideas to Heaven, however. Though in certain respect the fellowship of his disciples resembled that of Confucius, in key ways it operated very differently. Mo Di imposed a kind of military discipline on his followers. He expected them to continue following his orders even after they had left the "gate" of his household in which he taught them.

This aspect of Mohist organization became most evident as Mo Di's students "graduated" to careers as government officials. Master Mo secured positions for his advanced disciples in the courts of various regional lords. When disciples took up these posts, they were expected to give good and loyal service to their new rulers, but they were also expected to continue to operate as "Mohists." If other disciples of Mo Di traveled through the state in which a disciple served, the serving disciple was expected to give them food, lodging, and whatever other assistance they might need in the completion of their mission. The lion's share of whatever salary a Mohist official received was expected to be sent to the Master, for use by the fellowship as a whole. Finally, if for any reason Master Mo became displeased with a disciple's service at a regional court, either because the ruler was violating Heaven's will, or because the disciple himself had dishonored the fellowship for some reason, the disciple was expected to resign his post on Mo Di's orders.[24]

A modern reader might well ask why the rulers and highborn aristocrats of the Warring States tolerated the existence of such an organization, and why they would ever defer to Mo Di's word in employing knights at their courts. But if we think for a moment about the existential situation of a ruler like Zhao Wuxu, we can understand why he might perceive that cooperation with a group like the Mohists offered some advantages. The knight Yurang, out of a sense of honor, had refrained from simply taking a post at Zhao Wuxu's court in order to have the opportunity to murder him. How many knights, however, could be counted upon to be so honorable, especially in a world in which the traditional values of the Zhou realm were eroding so quickly? As traditional honor became more scarce, what would protect Zhao Wuxu from his own ministers, apart from the stinginess of his enemies?

In this new climate, the Mohists offered a modicum of security. Their values might be strange, but they were at least consistent and predictable. When choosing between two knights, one of whom belonged to a group like the Mohists, the other of whom did not, the former would be more appealing. The group, after all, vouched for its member's good conduct, and *their collective reputation* was forfeit if he strayed. If your Mohist minister stabbed you in the back, his Mohist buddies were obliged to hunt him down and make him pay, at least in principle. It was not an ironclad guarantee, but it was better than nothing, which is all you had to depend on with most knights, apart from their word.

In this way the Mohist fellowship developed into a kind of hybrid between a religious cult, a trade union, and a political party. As the movement grew, its paramilitary structure split and branched. When Mo Di's disciples took disciples of their own, they remained part of a "chain of command" with Mo Di at the top as "Grand Master." When he died, he was succeeded as Grand Master by his chief disciple, who passed on the post in his turn. Like the Daoist Church or Communist Party of later eras, for successive generations the Mohist movement had its own personnel, hierarchy, income stream, and mission.

This last aspect of "mission" was not a theoretical abstraction. The tithes collected from serving members of the fellowship were pooled and invested in projects that furthered the goals of Mohist doctrine. The realm in which this was most tangible was military affairs. According to Mo Di, Heaven's will forbade the use of offensive warfare. Since all people belonged to and were cared for by Heaven, Heaven could only be angry when one state or people attacked another. Beyond this, if military aggression could be made to cease entirely, the material benefit to the world would be incalculable. Deterring offensive warfare was thus a key task in the effort to fulfill Heaven's will.[25]

Having established this ideal in principle, Mo Di and his disciples worked industriously to achieve it in reality. They devoted their collective talents, energies, and resources to developing the techniques of *defensive* warfare. Funds went into the research and development of counter-siege technology. Much of the text that bears Master Mo's name outlines the strategies and weapons that the movement developed for siege defense. For example, the text advises that commanders should take hostage the families of any scouts who are sent out to gather information for a city under siege, so that these operatives cannot be turned into double-agents if they are captured by the enemy.[26] It also contains schematics for the construction of trebuchets for use as defensive artillery and for the construction of furnace-and-bellows mechanisms to "smoke out" enemy engineers attempting to tunnel under city walls.[27]

During the Warring States the Mohist fellowship deployed at various points to assist in the defense of a state under attack. In about 439 BCE, for example, Mo Di himself learned that the King of Chu was planning to assault the capital of Song, the state whose rulers were descendants of the Shang kings of antiquity (and the ancestors of Confucius). The situation was especially urgent, because the Chu king had enlisted the aid of a famous siege engineer, Gongshu Ban, who had developed an ingenious "cloud ladder" that could nullify the defensive power of the city's walls.

Mo Di traveled to the Chu capital of Ying and procured an audience with Gongshu Ban. He surprised the engineer by leading with an indecent proposal: could Gongshu Ban murder someone on Mo Di's behalf for the price of 10 pieces of gold? When Gongshu Ban answered that his sense of rightness (*yi*) would not permit him to do such an act, he fell into Mo Di's logical trap. If murdering one innocent person for 10 gold pieces was wrong, what made murdering tens of thousands of innocents for a vastly larger sum right? Gongshu Ban agreed to procure an audience for Mo Di with the King of Chu.

In the presence of the king, Mo Di employed arguments similar to the one he had used on Gongshu Ban. Chu was vastly more wealthy than Song. Given that disparity, why was the moral harm that would be inflicted by a war a sensible trade against the meager profits Chu would derive? The king's reply reflected the latent cynicism engendered by the *realpolitik* of the times. He conceded that Mo Di had a point, but declared that since Gongshu Ban had already prepared the cloud ladders, the attack would have to go forward. In other words: "I would rather carry out an illogical plan than look weak."

Seeing that the king would not be moved by appeals to morality, Mo Di asked that Gongshu Ban be admitted to the audience, and the king agreed. When Gongshu Ban appeared, Mo Di removed his belt and placed it on a table in the audience hall, creating an extemporaneous model of the walls of the Song capital. A war game ensued between Mo Di and Gongshu Ban, in which each man used models improvised from scraps of wood to represent the siege engines and tactics that each would use in countering the moves of his opponent.

With every new offensive by Gongshu Ban, Mo Di was able to show how he would defeat it. After nine such exchanges, Gongshu Ban's devices were exhausted, but Mo Di still had techniques he had not yet deployed. Withdrawing from the table, Gongshu Ban declared cryptically that there was still one way that he could defeat Mo Di, but he would not say it out loud.

Matching his opponent's coyness, Mo Di declared that he knew what Gongshu Ban was planning, but likewise would not say. The king had no patience for this charade. If he was going to make a decision about the assault he would need to know all the facts openly. He demanded to know Mo Di's argument.

Mo Di explained that Gongshu Ban's thought process was easy to read. Since Mo Di himself was the problem, the king would only have to kill him here and now, and success could be secured. That would not work, however. Mo Di had shared all of his knowledge and strategies with his disciples, who were at that very moment unpacking their counter-siege engines and taking up battle stations on the walls of the Song capital. If Mo Di was killed, his chief disciple would assume command and was more than capable of mounting the same defense that had just been demonstrated to the King of Chu in his audience hall.

"Excellent!" the king declared, finally satisfied that he knew the entire situation. "Let us call off the attack on Song."

Mo Di departed Chu and went to rejoin his disciples in Song. As he approached the capital a storm began, and Mo Di hurried to the city gates in search of shelter from the rain. The gatekeeper did not recognize him, however, and would not let him pass. Mo Di remarked on the irony of the moment, which encapsulated the situation of knights throughout the Zhou domain. Although, through talent and courage, he had just frustrated the designs of one of the most powerful men in the world, Mo Di remained a "nobody" in the larger society of the Warring States.[28]

Mo Di's rescue of Song exemplified a dynamic that would persist for the rest of the Warring States (and beyond). Rulers like Zhao Wuxu and the King of Chu accrued progressively more wealth and power, but they were never able to unilaterally control events or shape affairs perfectly according to their will. An ever-more-complicated world required ever-more-sophisticated solutions. To succeed, rulers needed to draw upon as wide a variety of skills and abilities as possible, and that meant having to find ways of sharing power without compromising their own effectiveness or security.

It was a daunting challenge. Progress came over many generations, during which time many clever and able players in the political arena saw lives lost and fortunes destroyed. As the ingenuity of Zhao Wuxu and his court demonstrated, the Jin successor states, recently liberated from some of the dysfunctional bonds that had encumbered the aristocracy of that region, were well positioned to experiment with new institutions and progressive ideas.

As the fifth century BCE drew to a close, a leader emerged in one of the Jin successor states, Zhao's neighboring domain of Wei, who showed a talent for attracting worthy knights and fostering institutional innovation. In an era that produced few heroes, he came to enjoy a reputation as a wise and progressive ruler, almost an early "founding father" of the political order that would ultimately coalesce from the chaos of the Warring States. He is known to history as Marquis Wen of Wei (r. 445–396 BCE), and we will read about him in the next chapter.

5

The Prince
The State of Wei, 446–396 BCE

As the last chapter described, the Zhou realm of the fifth century BCE left an enduring black mark on the long annals of rulership in the Chinese-speaking world. Though there are heroes to be found among loyal ministers, brave literati, and stoic common folk, almost all rulers of the time come off in at best an ambivalent light in the surviving written records. In a time of expanding state power and widening gaps of wealth, status, and sheer might between rulers and ruled, virtually no sovereign leader of Zhou society cut a wholly sympathetic figure. On top of this, shifting values and accelerating chaos gave few clues as to what correct or effective lordly conduct could or should be. It is thus no wonder that almost no one possessed the vision or talent necessary to secure a positive written legacy from the vantage of a sovereign throne. There was one glaring exception to this rule.

In 446 BCE Viscount Huan of Wei, the Wei clan leader who had joined forces with the clan heads of Zhao and Han to bring down the ambitious Zhi Yao (see Chapter 3), died and was succeeded by his son Wei Si (d. 396 BCE).[1] Wei Si would lead his clan for the next five decades, and oversee both a burgeoning of its power and a radical restructuring of all aspects of social, political, and economic life within the territory that the Wei controlled. By the end of his life, he had won formal recognition of the position of "Marquis," a sovereign ruler whose authority could only be superseded by that of the Son of Heaven. His maneuvers secured this title not only for himself, but for the heads of the Zhao and Han clans with whom the Wei had partitioned the state of Jin. It was thus as a result of Wei Si's policies that Wei went from being a formal vassal of the Jin court to becoming one of (for a time the mightiest of) the Warring States, making him a "founding father" akin to George Washington or Simon Bolivar.[2]

All of that would have been remarkable even if Wei Si (like other leaders of the fifth century BCE, such as Tian Chang, who could boast comparable achievements) was remembered as a bloodthirsty tyrant, a rank opportunist, or a cunning cynic. But he is almost universally portrayed in the written records of the time as a paragon of conscientious leadership, an able statesman, and a moral exemplar. Of his many achievements, that is perhaps the most amazing.

Not all of Wei Si's glowing historical image was his own doing. We can see this in the very fabric of the written record itself. This is reflected in the posthumous title by which he is almost always referred to in sources, awarded to him by his surviving ministers of the Wei court: "Marquis *Wen* of Wei." I will refer to him as Wei Si throughout most of this chapter to avoid anachronism, his struggle to win the title of "Marquis" being so central to his role in the history of his time.

"Wen" ("Civil" or "Cultured") is the highest posthumous honor that could be accorded to a sovereign, marking him as uniquely excellent and accomplished. It was also heavily freighted with political significance.[3] The revered sage founder of the Zhou dynasty was posthumously titled "King Wen." By giving the first formally sovereign Wei ruler the posthumous designation "Marquis Wen," the ministers of the Wei court broadcast to the world that Wei's independence was as momentous an occasion as the founding of the Zhou dynasty itself, and was built upon equally grand foundations.[4] Such a message served the immediate political interests of a state that was seeking to gain advantage in competition against rivals. But, as we will see, this obviously self-serving bit of political propaganda was not wholly without basis in the evidence of Wei Si's life.

By 446 BCE the Wei clan was an ancient grandee family of Jin, though the surviving written record provides clues that their origins in the distant past may have been more humble than they claimed. According to the Wei clan's own version of their genealogy, they were descended from a son of King Wen of Zhou, one who had helped his brother King Wu defeat the wicked last Shang king in 1045 BCE. But that prince's family had fallen into disgrace and been scattered among the common folk, "some among the people of the central states, some among the Yi and Di barbarians."[5] So the man who was first given the Wei vassalage and title by the Duke of Jin in 662 BCE may have been a warrior from among the northern steppe people for whom a lofty pedigree was fabricated.[6] But in the subsequent two centuries the leaders of the Wei clan had risen to become Viscounts and Counselors, until finally their power had come to eclipse that of the ducal house itself.

Wei Si first took the headship of his clan less than a decade after the sudden, dramatic, and bloody death of the man who had briefly made himself dictator of Jin, Zhi Yao. The legacy of that larger-than-life ruffian still hung heavily over the Wei court, and the strategic dynamic between all the surviving vassals of Jin was unsure and unpredictable. Had Zhi Yao's death finally created stability, or would war between the three remaining clans of Wei, Han, and Zhao break forth again? What political path moving forward could replicate Zhi Yao's power without giving rise to the cruel malignancy that had brought him to ruin? These questions must have haunted the new chieftain, suddenly left without the father whose experience would have been most helpful in sorting out their answers. Given how long he ultimately reigned, Wei Si was almost certainly very young when he inherited his father's title, making his task even more challenging.

An anecdote about Wei Si gives some insight, both into the circumstances of his early reign and the qualities that would make him so successful. He was at a drinking party with some of his ministers, and at one point in the evening looked out over his goblet and sighed, "Why is it that I alone do not have a retainer like Yurang?" This mention of the famous would-be assassin and avenger of Zhi Yao, if it has any basis in fact, testifies to the degree to which the dramatic events of Zhi Yao's rise and fall continued to weigh on the minds of the Jin aristocracy long after the tyrant's demise. Over the space of millennia it is hard to guess in what sense Wei Si meant his remark. Was he making a joke, teasing his drinking companions for lacking the loyalty that Yurang had displayed in mutilating himself to avenge Zhi Yao? Had the wine made Wei Si maudlin about the fraught situation facing his court, so that he was feeling sorry for himself and thinking out loud?

Whatever the case may have been, one of Wei Si's companions immediately sprang up and, following the rules of a kind of running drinking game that was customary at such gatherings, ordered his lord to drink a cup of wine as "forfeit" for having spoken amiss. When Wei Si asked why, the minister answered, in effect: "Only bad parents are famous for having filial children, only bad rulers are famous for having loyal ministers. Besides, for all his loyalty Yurang didn't prevent his ruler from becoming someone else's wine goblet." Wei Si conceded the point and drank the penalty cup, saying, "It is only by lacking ministers like Guan Zhong (the famous prime minister who invented the title of Lord Protector and won it for his ruler, the Duke of Qi) that one acquires a Yurang."[7] In other words, "I may lack a minister who has the foolish courage of Yurang, but I have better than that—I have ministers like you gentleman here who can see when I am being stupid and have the wisdom to tell me so."

The story may be apocryphal, but it exemplifies an aspect of Wei Si's disposition that is borne out by the written record of his reign. He obviously intuitively understood that his success would depend upon the character and quality of the men in his retinue (as suggested by his longing for a figure "like Yurang"). But at some point he must have also come to understand that having worthy ministers alone would not be enough: the excellence of one's followers could only be harnessed if they were effectively employed. Talented ministers were wasted unless the government structure within which they worked empowered them to, and rewarded them for, making maximum use of their knowledge, virtues, and skills. Beyond this, as the anecdote about the drinking party demonstrates, having worthy ministers only makes a difference if you listen to their advice and admit when they are right and you are wrong.

Exactly when and how Wei Si learned these lessons, whether in a flash of insight at the drinking party depicted in the anecdote above, on some other occasion, or more gradually over time is impossible to know for sure. But that he eventually did absorb them and show real skill at carrying them into practice cannot be doubted.

To be sure, Wei Si was no saint. Like any effective political leader, he worked to burnish his own image. But even in this he demonstrated discernment, even genius.

This is shown in one of the early policies of his court, one which, while it might seem minor or purely cosmetic to our eyes, was in fact so daring a maneuver that it arguably served as the foundation on which all of Wei Si's subsequent success was built. In what year it happened we cannot know with any precision, but it had to have been early in Wei Si's long reign: Zixia (510–ca. 420 BCE), one of the youngest of the disciples who had studied at the feet of Confucius himself (and who was already 64 years old when Wei Si first took the headship of Wei), was persuaded to come to the Wei capital of Anyi to serve as Wei Si's teacher.[8]

We know little of the actual substance of this relationship, only that Zixia "taught Wei Si the classics." A text in Wei Si's name (The *Wei Wenhou*, or *Marquis Wen of Wei*) is recorded among the Confucian "Masters writings" held in the imperial library of the Han dynasty.[9] The text is now lost, and we cannot know if it contained anything written by Wei Si himself, or if it was compiled from material "ghost written" for him by literati serving at the Wei court, perhaps after Wei Si had already died.[10] The very existence of the text, however, is evidence that the Wei court very deliberately and aggressively cultivated Wei Si's image as a student of Zixia, and thus a latter-day disciple of Confucius. But even if, in the immediate instance, Zixia's installation as Wei Si's "teacher" was purely an act of political theater, it was inspired and effective theatrics. It was also a gamble that paid off handsomely in the long run.

To understand why Wei Si's decision was so daring and provocative, we must remember the condition of Confucius's fellowship at the end of the Master's life. As Confucius lay dying in 479 BCE, only two of his disciples had enjoyed any success at carrying his teachings into a position of real power and responsibility in the political realm. Zai Wo had risen to unimaginable heights, becoming Prime Minister of Qi, only to bring both himself and the ruler that had elevated him to that lofty perch to unprecedented ruin. Another disciple, Zilu, had died violently amid palace intrigues in the state of Wey. The summons from the Wei court was the first position of real responsibility that had been offered to any member of the fellowship since the Master's death. The reputation of the fellowship was in tatters; all that a ruler could seem to expect from employing one of the idealistic young men trained by Confucius was turmoil and collapse. Even among literati, the star of the Confucian fellowship was falling: a movement to challenge and contradict the teachings of Confucius had begun to coalesce around the leadership of Mo Di.

Add to all this the fact that most of the highborn aristocrats in the Zhou world must have viewed Confucius's disciples as upstarts and troublemakers, and it can become hard to understand why Wei Si would want to have been associated with them at all. If by the mid-fifth century BCE Confucius's band was down on its luck, that was, in the eyes of most sovereigns, all to the good. Rulers stood to gain from the humbling of Confucius's attempt to motivate and empower his fellow knights. Simply ignoring the fellowship at that juncture would have been an appealing and potentially very tactically effective policy to those who wished to see Confucius's posthumous influence wane.

In those circumstances, it is difficult to overestimate how much of and how timely a gift was Wei Si's enlistment of Zixia. It was a gesture of confidence in the Master's Way at a point when, challenged by the rise of Mo Di and his disciples, discredited by the public failures of some of its leaders, the Confucian fellowship faced a moment of profound insecurity. The choice of Zixia himself suggests that this bolstering effect was deliberate, a kind of "quid pro quo" offer of support from the Wei court. Though sources like the *Analects* show that Zixia's bona fides in the fellowship of Confucius's disciples were firm, there is little other evidence that he was a particularly prominent literatus of the mid-fifth century BCE.[11] Thus his personal connection to the Master seems to have been the main asset that made him appealing.

It might be hard at first to see what Wei Si and his government stood to gain, until we examine the situation from the perspective of the Wei court. Groping his way out of the fog created by Zhi Yao's brutal politics, Wei Si needed to chart a new path and set a distinct tone. Hitching together the wagons of the Wei court and the Confucian fellowship sent a clear message to the larger Zhou world: we in Wei are determined to do things differently. If one of Confucius's own disciples is willing to join our team, we cannot possibly be suspected of operating as ruthlessly and unscrupulously as Zhi Yao. Moreover, we are, in the spirit of Confucius's "Way," committed to offering opportunities to men of worth and learning, even those of relatively humble birth.

It was a daring gambit, and it yielded benefits in several ways. The three Jin successor states did not slip back into internecine fighting during Wei Si's reign, in part because his recruitment of Zixia lent credibility to the notion that Wei would respect formal commitments and keep the peace. Beyond this, because Confucius's latter-day disciples had disproportionate influence among literati, Wei Si helped ensure that his literary image would be a positive one, not only among the records transmitted to posterity, but in the written descriptions of courts and rulers that circulated among the states of the Zhou realm during Wei Si's own reign. Anything that cast the Wei court in a bad light would rebound to discredit the fellowship, thus the whole community of Confucius's latter-day disciples were motivated to portray Wei Si and his government in the most favorable light. In this sense, the recruitment of Zixia was one of the earliest recorded cases of successful "media manipulation" on the part of a political leader in world history.

Above and beyond these effects, Zixia's tenure opened an avenue of recruitment that drew talent to the Wei court. Even if Wei Si's studies with Zixia had been undertaken for appearances' sake, the relationship between the Wei court and the Confucian fellowship developed into a substantial partnership. At least three other prominent officials of Wei Si's court were drawn from the ranks of Confucius's known latter-day disciples.[12] Moreover, Wei Si skillfully utilized the traditions and symbols of Confucius's "Way" to amplify his reputation as a lord who understood the value of worthy knights. When, for example, one of Confucius's latter-day disciples settled in reclusion in the vicinity of Anyi, Wei Si made a grand public show of paying the man exaggerated courtesies. Driving past the disciple's gate, Wei Si bowed deeply over the crossbar of his chariot so that all could see the reverence in which the ruler of Wei held men of rectitude and learning.[13] From the perspective of today, this kind of gesture might appear superficial and contrived, but in the steeply hierarchical, highly ritualized, and obsessively status-conscious society of the fifth century BCE, such public displays were shocking enough to persuade low-ranking knights that Wei Si was willing to risk some of his own prestige and political capital by way of giving them a chance to prove themselves.

It is for this aspect of his reign, the opening of opportunity to "men of worth" (what political scientists would call a commitment to "meritocracy"), that Wei Si is most celebrated in the ancient historical writings. This should not surprise us. The people who wrote the ancient records tended to be knights (*shi*), relatively lowborn aristocrats. This was because during the Warring States era, the less you could rely on your ancestry to get ahead, the more you would have to rely on the development of skills like literacy and writing to make your way in the world. So almost all of the information we have about the period comes to us from people who had a stake in the question of whether or not talent and skill could win advancement and enrichment above and beyond what birth and ancestry could convey. If a ruler like Wei Si had not existed, the chroniclers of the Warring States would have had a strong motive to invent him.[14]

Thus, we have to be a bit skeptical about Wei Si's glowing reputation. We know, for example, that for a time he employed his own brother as his prime minister. Such nepotism was hardly unusual during the Zhou era, but it worked against what was generally considered Wei Si's "brand." The records themselves reflect this fact. Anecdotes preserved in various sources describe a kind of "competition" in which Wei Si's brother was weighed against another, lower-born candidate for the job of prime minister, and only won the post on the advice of knights who observed that Wei Si's brother had been exceptional in dispensing his wealth to the people and recruiting men of talent.[15] Were these stories fabricated by ancient scribes making biased excuses for Wei Si's lapse into nepotism? The likely answer is "yes."

But such justified skepticism aside, there is ample evidence that Wei Si really did promote men of talent, and that he relied on their advice in carrying bold and innovative policies into practice. We have more information about the officials that served in his court than we do for virtually any other ruler of the Warring States. His story is inseparable from theirs.

Among the many famous ministers who served Wei Si, Li Kui (ca. 455–395 BCE) is undeniably the one who had the greatest impact, both upon the state of Wei itself and the subsequent history of East Asia. As Prime Minister of Wei he oversaw a complete overhaul of the administrative and legal structures of the state. The policies that he pioneered became standard for governments stretching into the imperial era, and the legal code that he instituted exerted influence through successive ages and to regions as distant as Korea, Japan, and Vietnam.

For all of Li Kui's enduring influence, we know little of his background.[16] We know that he worked his way up through the ranks. Before he became prime minister, he served as prefect of a commandery on Wei's frontier. There he initially met with defeat at the hands of invaders, but after being given a chance by his superiors to regroup and change tactics, he dealt the enemy a serious defeat.[17] Li Kui himself thus testifies to the substance and success of Wei Si's commitment to cultivating "men of worth": the ruler did not discard Li Kui because of his mistakes born of inexperience, but gave him the opportunity to "learn on the job" and prove his ultimate capabilities.

Exactly when Li Kui became Wei Si's prime minister is impossible to know for certain, but logic dictates that it could not have been much more than about 20 years after the young prince ascended to his throne. In Wei Si's final 15 years in power, he oversaw a series of stunning military victories that greatly expanded the territory under Wei's control. Since the economic and strategic foundations for those conquests were almost certainly laid by Li Kui's reforms, and because those reforms would have needed a decade or more to yield real increases in Wei's military might, Li Kui's tenure as prime minister most likely began no later than the late 420s or early 410s BCE.

In his service as a regional official, Li Kui had seen that Wei was densely settled. This was a blessing in that it provided an abundant supply of conscripts for public works and military service, but it required careful husbanding of the state's agricultural economy. He calculated that the agricultural productivity of the state would have to be significantly augmented in order to keep pace with (and sustain) population growth. He thus oversaw an intensive program of state management of the farming economy.

He instructed regional officials to take an active hand in directing the farmers in their districts. To prevent harvest failure, in any given season crops would be diversified among wheat, millet, broomcorn, hemp, and soybeans. Farmers would be set to plowing and hoeing intensively to produce maximum yields, "responding to each harvest with the intensity of defending against a bandit raid." Within each farm, crops would be further diversified. On marginal or unused lands vegetables and melons would be cultivated or mulberry trees planted for the production of silk.

Li Kui had also observed that since farmers needed to purchase things like tools and clothing from the market economy, they were vulnerable to swings in the price of grain. If grain became too cheap, farmers would not have enough left after paying their taxes to purchase basic needs, and would be faced with a choice like that between going cold or going hungry. If grain became expensive, it was a boon to farmers, but it would cause deprivation among artisans, merchants, and other townspeople, who would have difficulty feeding themselves through their labor.

Li Kui thus decided to leverage the purchasing power of the state to stabilize the price of grain. He had regional officials assess each year's harvest as "good," "medial," or "poor." In good years cash would be used from state coffers to purchase grain and store it in state granaries, taking excess off the market and keeping the price afloat. In poor years grain would be sold out of state granaries to increase supply and prevent price inflation. This policy of price-stabilization spread from Wei throughout the Warring States, and eventually became a standard practice of all imperial governments.[18]

Together these policies fostered economic stability and growth. They encouraged and accelerated a trend in Wei that had been developing for more than a century throughout the North China plain, in which agricultural production shifted from being done mainly by bonded laborers and slaves to being done by small, independent farming families that owned or rented the land they worked. Li Kui recognized that accelerating this trend would vastly increase the power of the Wei state.

Independent farmers were more productive, more fit, and more available for (and more amenable to) other forms of state service, such as public works or military conscription. The encouragement of small freehold farming thus yielded benefits for the strength of Wei's armies and the quality of public infrastructure such as dikes, irrigation ditches, and roads (which in turn strengthened the economy, and so on, in a virtuous cycle). It also drew immigration from outside of Wei, which helped keep both the economy and the population growing.[19]

In addition to these forms of economic and social management, Li Kui set out to improve the administrative culture of the Wei state. He could see that Wei was evolving into a different kind of society and polity than the old state of Jin. Long-held traditions of personal fealty and ceremonial authority would not work well in this new world of ever-intensifying competition and increasing need for discipline. Wei would need a systematic and transparent legal code to coordinate the state's efforts at economic management and military strengthening.

To this end Li Kui reportedly wrote a text in six sections, the *Classic of Laws* (*Fa jing*). The text no longer survives, but we know about its structure, contents, and use through fragments and records preserved in later sources. Though the title makes it seem like a work of theory, it was in effect a comprehensive legal code for the state of Wei. Though, as we saw in the discussion of the "Penal Cauldron" in Chapter 3, there had been laws instituted in states throughout the Zhou realm in the centuries before Li Kui's tenure as Wei prime minister, and though he reportedly synthesized existing laws and statutes from across the Zhou domain in the composition of his text, his was the first comprehensive and systematic legal code promulgated in the Sinitic world.

The six chapters of Li Kui's *Classic of Laws* corresponded to six basic categories of law. The first, "Assault Law" (*Dao fa*), dealt with proscriptions against and penalties for violent crime. The next, "Theft Law" (*Zei fa*) outlined codes for crimes against property. "Prison Law" (*Jiu fa*) established rules for the incarceration of criminals. "Seizure Law" (*Bu fa*) laid down regulations for the arrest and apprehension of fugitives. "Miscellaneous Law" (*Za fa*) dealt with offenses such as gambling, trespassing, and official corruption. The last section, "Provisional Law" (*Ju fa*), dealt with mitigating factors and circumstances that might "increase or decrease" penalties imposed by other parts of the code.[20]

Li Kui's code was adopted and expanded upon in other Warring States, particularly, as we will read in Chapter 8, in the state of Qin, where it became the basis of a legal reform by the minister Shang Yang. The Qin code became the basis of the legal code of the Han dynasty, which in turn was transmitted and revised until it served as the foundation for the Tang Code of 653 CE. The Tang Code of 653 CE still survives in its entirety, and served as the basis for the legal code of every subsequent dynastic regime of the imperial period, as well as the laws promulgated by regimes in Korea, Vietnam, and Japan.[21] Its preface credits the *Classic of Laws* as a source, thus Li Kui's legislation was one of the most durable and broadly influential achievements of the Warring States.

Li Kui's economic policies and legal reforms were part of a general restructuring of the relationship between state and society in the Wei domain. In earlier eras, local power throughout the Zhou lands had been deeply rooted in heredity and tradition. The warrior-priests of the Bronze Age treated the land and the people living on it as their personal patrimony. In making decisions and exercising authority, they cared as much (or more) about their family honor and the appeasement of the ancestors and gods as they did about increasing productivity or improving efficiency.

That had begun to change as the Warring States began. We saw in Chapter 1 that competition had motivated aristocratic families like the Tian clan in Qi to begin managing their lands as a public trust and to buy the loyalty of the local populace through sharing wealth. Many of the larger and more powerful states of the Zhou domain had, over the course of the sixth and early fifth centuries BCE, established "commanderies" (*jun*) and "districts" (*xian*) in strategically sensitive territories. These were regions that were not held in the hereditary possession of a grandee clan, but were overseen and defended by a leader appointed by and answering directly to the ducal court.[22]

In the wake of the civil wars that had destroyed the privileges and cult complexes of all but three of the grandee houses of the old Jin state, the Wei court had a unique opportunity to develop these new methods and institutions of local rule. The majority of Wei's territory was organized as "commanderies" and "districts," and local management by a centrally appointed prefect or magistrate became the norm throughout the Wei domain. The other policies of Wei Si's government worked in tandem with this restructuring of local rule.

Recruiting men of worth provided a cadre of able literati to rotate through local Magistracies. At the same time, the reorganization of localities into "districts" provided a tempting incentive for ambitious knights to enlist in Wei, where they might be given powers and responsibilities that only grandees enjoyed elsewhere. Since magistrates generally took a percentage of the tax revenues collected from their districts as salary, they were highly motivated to implement Li Kui's wealth-expanding economic policies. The promulgation of a state-wide legal code helped ensure that as magistrates rotated in and out of district postings, the local populace would not be left wondering what to expect in the transition from one official to the next.

The institution of the District Magistrate was developed to such a high degree under Wei Si's rule that some of the men who served him in that capacity became folk heroes. The most famous was Ximen Bao. Like Li Kui, we do not have a detailed sense of Ximen Bao's background. The only information preserved about him concerns his service to Wei.

Stories of Ximen Bao's virtuosity are peppered throughout the surviving sources of the Warring States. This is probably, at least in part, a product of the efforts of the Wei court at self-promotion. In effect, Ximen Bao was made into a "poster boy" for the new type of government that Wei was establishing at the local level. That does not mean that his legend has no basis in fact, however, and even if it has been embellished to some degree, the kinds of messages that the Wei court was broadcasting about itself in its celebration of Ximen Bao tell us a great deal about how politics and society were changing in the Warring States.

Ximen Bao was appointed Magistrate of Ye, a key strategic district along the northern frontier of Wei's territory. One story says that at the end of Ximen Bao's first year as magistrate, when he returned to the capital to be assessed, he was asked to surrender his seal of office and step down. He protested that he now understood what he was expected to do as magistrate and declared that unless he could be given another chance in office, he would insist on being put to death.

Wei Si could not bear to see someone so earnest die, so he acceded to Ximen Bao's reappointment. The next year when Ximen Bao returned to be reassessed, Wei Si was so pleased with his performance that he bowed to him. Ximen Bao was not impressed.

"Last year I was scrupulously honest in my conduct of office and made no effort to ingratiate myself with your courtiers," Ximen Bao declared in reply to Wei Si's bow. "This year I taxed the people in my district heavily and worked hard to keep your courtiers happy. Last year I administered the district for you and was dismissed, this year I administered the district for your courtiers and was greeted with a bow. I cannot go on governing this way." He handed his seal of office over to Wei Si by way of resigning.

"Before I did not know you, now I do," Wei Si pleaded, refusing to accept the surrendered seal. "Please return to Ye and work to govern it on my behalf."[23]

Even if (as seems likely) this story is a fabricated piece of government propaganda, it tells us a great deal about the efforts the government of Wei made to reinvent itself, and to broadcast that new model to the world. The idea of a civil servant having to face a yearly review at the risk of losing his job is quite natural today, but in the fifth century BCE, when for centuries, if not millennia, local rule had been held by individual families for generations, the concept was shockingly innovative. The seal of office, without which Ximen Bao's orders bore no weight, concretely embodied the new nature of his authority. His power was invested in his office, not his person, and it came to him from the state, not his family legacy or inherent aristocratic superiority.

The drama that played out between Wei Si and Ximen Bao expressed the logic of this new power structure and its potential benefits. Even though the story is candid about the ways in which the new system was vulnerable to corruption, the anecdote deliberately illustrates the ways that devices like the seal of office and yearly assessment introduced new mechanisms of accountability that did not exist before. Venal courtiers and palace intrigue had always existed and would always be a problem, but at least institutions like the yearly assessment interview gave someone like Ximen Bao access to his ruler that could potentially fix current malpractice. Such hope was more than had existed under the previous system of hereditary entitlement.

Knights from other states who read this story would see that Wei had set up a system in which they had a real chance to exercise their talents and earn advancement. The dramatic resolution of the story of course sends a clear message: in Wei Si you would have a ruler who deals fairly with his officials and who sincerely wants them to succeed on behalf of the state. Not a bad recruitment pitch even today, much less in the fifth century BCE.

Another story about Ximen Bao expresses similarly provocative ideas. On arriving in Ye, Ximen Bao gathered the elders of the district and inquired about what might be most troubling them. They replied that they were being impoverished by the ceremonies to betroth a wife to the River God. It had become the custom of the region's knights and local headmen to take a yearly levy of the common people of several hundred thousand cash. Twenty or thirty thousand would then be spent on a ritual in honor of the River God, the rest would be split among the knights, headmen, and a local female shaman.

The ceremony itself was a form of human sacrifice. A beautiful young woman would be chosen from among the daughters of the common people. She would be bathed, clothed in fine silks, housed in a yellow tented pavilion by the riverside, and set to fasting for a period of time, after which she was plied with wine and rich food. After 10 days or so she would be brought to the riverbank, adorned as a bride, and set upon a raft. The raft would float a few kilometers downstream, then sink, taking the young woman with it to join her "husband." Families with young daughters fled the district in fear, leaving the area underpopulated and poor.

Ximen Bao asked the local elders to invite him the next time the marriage ceremony for the River God would be held. On the day itself he came down to see thousands gathered at the river. When the head shaman arrived with her entourage of 10 disciples, Ximen Bao asked to see the girl chosen as bride.

On seeing the "bride," Ximen Bao declared that she was too ugly. "Go ask the River God if he would like us to change brides," Ximen Bao told the head shaman, and ordered some of his guards to throw her into the river, where she sank. After the crowd had stood in shocked silence for a while, Ximen Bao declared, "What's taking so long? Have one of the head shaman's disciples hurry her along!" The guards obediently tossed a screaming disciple into the murk. After two more disciples drowned the same way, Ximen Bao declared that they must have gotten the message wrong and had the local headmen thrown into the water all at once.

When Ximen Bao turned toward the district knights, they fell to their knees and began to beg for mercy, banging their heads against the ground until blood flowed. "I guess the River God is busy entertaining his guests," Ximen Bao announced. "Let's all go home." No one in the district spoke of betrothing a woman to the River God ever again.[24]

To our twenty-first-century sensibilities this might seem like an expression of simple authoritarianism or paternalism, but it would be a mistake to dismiss it so easily. Long-entrenched and abusive local forces like the knights, headmen, and shamans depicted in the story had been an inescapable burden for the farmers of the North China plain for centuries. The tale of Ximen Bao deliberately demonstrates how, under the right circumstances, the new type of local administrative structure being built by the Wei court could serve as a rare check on the power of those oppressive elements. By offering to share some (small amount of) power with the common people of the local districts, the Wei court was maneuvering to increase the total reservoir of power at its disposal for the pursuit of political and military goals.

This can be seen in Ximen Bao's stewardship of the economy of his district. The soil in Ye was poor, so that taxes on land were assessed at half the rate of other districts in the state. Over the resistance of the local populace, who chafed at being enlisted for intensive public work, Ximen Bao built a system of irrigation canals to bring water from the Zhang River, vastly increasing the agricultural yield of his district's fields. His administration was thus a model of the kind of benefits that could be achieved through Li Kui's policies of state management of agriculture. The irrigation works built in Ximen Bao's tenure were still being used and maintained during the Han dynasty.[25]

By the third decade of Wei Si's reign his court's reorganization of the administrative and fiscal system of the state had begun to pay dividends in terms of military power. The reforms in Wei were adapted to take maximum advantage of changes that had been transpiring for almost three centuries. At the founding of the Zhou the main battlefield weapon had still been the war chariot, which largely restricted warfare to being an aristocratic affair. Only nobles possessed of significant landholdings could produce and maintain war chariots, and only they had the leisure time necessary to master the skills required to operate one effectively in combat.

As the competition between noble houses intensified over the seventh and sixth centuries BCE, combatants began to experiment with new deployments that would give them a battlefield edge. The composite bow in the hands of groups of archers could nullify the combat power of the war chariot. Since the bow did not require as much training as a chariot (especially if it was being used in mass formations, which decreased the need for accuracy on the part of individual bowmen), the move to make effective use of archers brought more and more commoners onto the battlefield as conscript infantrymen.[26]

In an infantryman's world the administrative and legal reforms instituted by the Wei court produced bigger and better-equipped armies (see Fig. 7). Increased food production freed more men from agricultural work for military service, and produced better nourished, more fit recruits. Surplus wealth circulating in the market economy helped generate resources for better provisions, weapons, armor, and gear. The active hand that wardens and magistrates took in the local economy gave them increased leverage for mobilizing the manpower of commanderies and districts. Li Kui's legal code provided clear "carrots and sticks" to enforce compliance with conscription quotas: farmers knew that they would be rewarded for appearing for duty, severely punished for failing to do so. Finally, the occasional use of state power in the interest of local farmers (exemplified by Ximen Bao's suppression of the River God marriage cult) helped secure some "buy-in" from local populations. Since the state could be an ally, coercion was not always necessary to get local farmers to answer the call to arms.

Fig. 7. Armor like this, made up of joined leather panels, was standard equipment for the infantry soldiers of the Warring States. (Source: news.artnet.com.)

These systematic enhancements of Wei's armed forces fueled an expansion of the state's power under Wei Si's rule. In 419 BCE, Wei began building a series of fortifications at the city of Shaoliang along its western frontier. This was seen as a threat by the neighboring state of Qin, which had expanded to make the Yellow River its eastern boundary during the reign of a particularly powerful Qin ruler in the seventh century BCE. Qin attacked Shaoliang, beginning more than a decade of hostilities.[27] In successive engagements the balance swung between the two combatants, until in 409 BCE Wei dispatched the fabled commander Wu Qi (d. 381 BCE, whom we shall read about in more detail in the next chapter) to serve as military governor along the western frontier. In a series of campaigns in which Wei's forces were joined by those of Zhao and Han, Wu Qi drove the armies of Qin back across the Yellow River, forcing them by 408 BCE to fall back to the Luo River as a defensive barrier. As a result the entire terrain "West of the Yellow River" was annexed to Wei, adding approximately 9,000 square kilometers of fertile farmland to its territorial domain.[28]

This victory made Wei undisputedly the most powerful of the three Jin successor states. It was most likely at around this time that Wei Si was able to achieve peacefully what Zhi Yao had tried to do through coercion: provisionally unite the whole Jin domain. Nominally, the territory of the three states of Wei, Han, and Zhao was still under the authority of the Duke of Jin. During the reign of Duke You (r. 433–416 BCE), the sitting duke had given up all pretense of being overlord and had begun to pay court to the three clans as if he were their vassal. In 416 BCE Duke You left his palace surreptitiously to meet a woman with whom he was having an affair and was waylaid and killed by bandits. Wei Si intervened to save the situation (and keep the peace) by avenging the dead duke and setting one of his sons up on the ducal throne.[29]

The efficiency of his administration, the obvious strength of his military, the courtesy he showed to worthy knights, and the good faith with which he handled crises like the duke's murder earned Wei Si the respect of the clan heads of Zhao and Han. Wei Si cultivated and capitalized upon that good will. During a dispute between Zhao and Han, both states came to Wei seeking soldiers to use against the other. Wei Si refused both requests, declaring that all three clans were "brothers." This persuaded Zhao and Han leaders to join Wei Si in a trilateral defensive covenant, with Wei as the "covenant lord."[30] In effect, Jin had been reunified, with the independent states of Zhao and Han accepting Wei's leadership as *primes inter pares*.

This new defensive covenant was put to the test in 408 BCE. In that year Wei Si launched his most ambitious campaign of conquest yet. He dispatched the general Yue Yang in command of an expeditionary force to cross the neighboring state of Zhao and attack the state of Zhongshan.[31]

The state of Zhongshan was exemplary of the dynamism and diversity of the society of the north China plain. It had been founded in a region settled by an Inner Asian people known as the "White Turks," and the elite culture of its ruling class combined elements of Zhou customs and those of the steppe.[32] Wei Si's invasion was thus an extension of the kind of expansionist policy pursued by many of the Zhou states against their "foreign" neighbors over the course of the fifth century BCE, such as, for example, Zhao Wuxu's conquest of the Dai more than 60 years previously.

The logistically complex campaign, undertaken in the immediate aftermath of Wei Si's triumph over Qin to the west, was a sign of profound self-confidence. Wei Si dispatched his own son and heir as Yue Yang's second-in-command.[33] He thus could not have anticipated that the risks of this venture would be very high.

However confident Wei Si may have been at the outset, the war was hard-fought and extended over two years. Yue Yang's forces eventually reached the walls of the Zhongshan capital and he put the city under siege. While Yue Yang drew up his siege lines, his son was held hostage inside the city. The reason for this situation is not recorded. Perhaps the younger Yue had been dispatched by the Wei court before hostilities began, in an attempt to end the conflict through diplomacy. Perhaps Yue Yang had sent him as a negotiator, and the Zhongshan court had refused to respect his status as an envoy.

Whatever the reason, the young man fell victim to the vicious intensity of the conflict. In a uniquely cruel maneuver of psychological warfare, the Zhongshan defenders cooked Yue Yang's son into a stew and sent the steaming pot out to the siege lines to be presented to the Wei commander. Resolved not to show weakness, Yue Yang had a table set in full view of the defensive walls of the city and ate the stew in sight of the city's defenders.[34]

That extreme force of will perhaps explains why, at the end of two years' fighting, in 406 BCE, the Wei forces completely annihilated the state of Zhongshan. Yue Yang was given the Zhongshan capital as his personal fief. Wei Si's son was made Lord of Zhongshan and thus given the entire state to rule on behalf of the Wei court. One of Zixia's disciples was dispatched to serve him as prime minister of his new vassalage.[35]

By 406 BCE Wei Si had not only reordered the politics and society of Wei, but of the entire former Jin domain. His influence would continue to expand to take in the whole North China plain and the Zhou realm in its entirety. In 405 BCE the head of the Tian clan died, setting off a succession crisis in Qi that spilled over borders and afforded Wei Si a political opportunity (we will revisit these events in Chapter 7). A grandee of the Tian clan who fell on to the losing side of the succession struggle defected with the frontier city of Linqiu (Granary Hill) to the neighboring state of Zhao. The Tian clan dispatched armies to besiege its wayward son, activating the trilateral covenant that had been brokered by Wei Si some time before.

The united armies of Wei, Han, and Zhao dealt the Qi force a crushing defeat, forcing them to fall back on the city of Pingyin, which controlled a gateway through the defensive walls guarding Qi's western frontier.[36] After a siege the city was taken, allowing Wei Si's coalition force to break through Qi's defensive barrier in 404 BCE and threaten the state's capital.[37] The Tian leaders were forced to sue for peace, and Wei Si wrested a concession from them that was an ingenious stroke of political strategy.

The nominally reigning Duke of Qi (the scion of the Lü clan who still held the formal title of "duke") was surrendered to the Jin coalition forces. He was forced to accompany a group of emissaries from the three Jin successor states of Wei, Zhao, and Han to the court of the Zhou Son of Heaven.[38] There, he presented a formal petition as the "sovereign" head of the Lü clan, one of the oldest and most prestigious families in the realm and one of the most ancient and closest allies of the Zhou royal house. The petition pleaded that the leaders of the Wei, Zhao, and Han clans all be given the title of "Marquis" and recognized as "Lords of the Land," thus transferring formal sovereignty over the territory of Jin away from the ducal house (cousins of the Zhou Son of Heaven) and to the families of the Jin dukes' former vassals.

Wei Si had presented the Son of Heaven with an offer he could not refuse. On the one hand, the proven military might of the Wei-Zhao-Han coalition was more than capable of inflicting terrible pain on the Zhou royal house. On the other hand, the expertly manipulated symbolism engineered by Wei Si gave the king every pretext to accede to the coalition's desires.

In 403 BCE the king capitulated to Wei Si's demands, ceremonially raising him and the leaders of his "brother" clans of Han and Zhao to the sovereign rank of Marquis.[39] It was a momentous decision, the last one of true geopolitical significance that the Zhou royal house would ever make. Though the formal hierarchy established by the Zhou founders had been under disfiguring strain for many centuries, with ancient houses destroyed or pragmatically humbled before the rising power of upstart clans like the Tian, this was the first time that the Zhou king had ceremonially ratified the loss of authority of one of his duly appointed vassals, one of his own kin.

The Nine Tripods, the massive ritual bronzes that were the most sacred regalia of the Zhou house, reportedly quaked at the moment that the investiture rite for Wei, Zhao, and Han was performed.[40] Heaven itself recognized that a threshold had been crossed. Almost 1,500 years later, when Sima Guang (1019–86 CE), the great scholar of the Song dynasty (960–1279 CE), wrote his masterpiece which charted the course of human history up to his own time, the *Comprehensive Mirror for the Aid of Government*, he began his study with the investiture of Wei, Zhao, and Han in 403 BCE. In his eyes, it was a date after which civilization was never the same again.[41]

When Wei Si died in 396 BCE to become, for all time, Marquis Wen of Wei, he could look back on a life of almost unalloyed forward motion and achievement. In his long 50-year reign he had successfully overseen a complete transformation of the government and society of Wei. On the strength of that accomplishment he had conducted a military and diplomatic policy that had brought infighting within the former Jin domain to an end and reunited its regional leaders into a powerful allied force. Through his partnership with the latter-day disciples of Confucius and his employment of innovators like Li Kui, he had helped reshape the very basis of politics and sovereign authority for a world in search of guiding values.

This can be seen in the evolution of the Confucian fellowship, which was forever altered by its interaction with Marquis Wen's court. Where Confucius himself had unequivocally condemned Tian Chang's usurpation of power in Qi, his latter-day disciples had partnered closely with the man who for good and all brought down the equally ancient ducal house of Jin. As calculating as this shift may seem, it was not entirely cynical.

For all of Wei Si's obvious skill at playing the game of power politics, he had not been completely contemptuous of Confucius's Way. Whatever else can be said of Wei Si, one must concede that he brought the conduct of politics back from the brink of a very dark and nihilistic place that it had reached by the mid-fifth century BCE. Zhi Yao's success had been based entirely on the use of coercion, deception, and brutality; Wei Si, though not above using trickery or violence, invented a new politics that created opportunities to foster trust and cooperation. Although the administrative system his court established operated on very different principles than the forms of ritual and tradition favored by Confucius, its effectiveness derived in part from its potential to (at least occasionally, as in the case of Ximen Bao's move against the River God cult) serve moral values that Confucius cherished such as "humaneness."

In his dealings with the leaders of Zhao and Han, we can perhaps see where Wei Si drew the most inspiration from Confucius's teachings. Zhi Yao's playbook would have required that Wei Si destroy the other clans so that he could rule unopposed. Wei Si, by contrast, in acknowledging the Zhao and Han clan leaders as "brothers" and engineering their elevation to the rank of Marquis simultaneously with his own, committed himself and his court to a future of coexistence and cooperation between the "three Jin." That ongoing relationship between "brother states," ideally, would have been conducted through the rituals and traditions of kinship so cherished by Confucius.

We should not underestimate the degree of self-conscious planning that went into these arrangements. In effect, Wei Si had deliberately set up a kind of "two-mode" system. Within the state of Wei itself the regional aristocracy had been largely eliminated and replaced by centrally appointed bureaucrats like Ximen Bao. But in the larger Jin domain that Wei Si still considered his natural sphere of action, power would continue to be shared between three aristocratic courts. In his dealings with Wei's ministers and magistrates, Wei Si would adhere to routine principles and rules like those embodied in Li Kui's legal code. In his dealings with the rulers of Zhao and Han, he would follow the traditions and rituals prescribed by Confucius that shaped the relationship of an "older brother" to his "younger brothers."

This arrangement was obviously, in some sense, a bow to strategic necessity (the choice between a destructive war and a prosperous peace), but it was not entirely without logic. The stories recorded about Wei Si's court show that his ministers understood the vulnerabilities of the power-sharing mechanisms they had built. The power of local elites needed to be checked by that of civil magistrates, but the power of such magistrates (and the potential of all officials to be corrupted by wealth and power) also needed to be held in check, and that job fell mainly to the court of the ruler from whom their authority was received.

This last fact of course raised the question of scale. How many magistrates could a single court efficiently oversee? How many courts would be necessary, in any given terrain, to monitor the civil officials holding power in that region? For the former state of Jin, Wei Si (for reasons that perhaps had as much to do with practical power dynamics as principle) accepted that the answer to this last question was "three" (Wei, Han, and Zhao).

It was a novel and inspired conceptual model, and during Wei Si's reign it yielded spectacular success, as we have seen. As Wei Si was succeeded by his son (who, in keeping with the symbolism applied to his father, would posthumously be titled "Marquis Wu"), a smart gambler would have bet that the state of Wei and the trilateral coalition Wei Si had forged would continue to grow in power. For many years such a bet would have paid off.

But as is true of any model, the one developed under Wei Si's leadership could be emulated. This is what happened in the case of the Warring States, and that process unfolded very rapidly. The ideas and methods developed at Wei Si's court began to spread to other parts of the Zhou domain even during his own lifetime, and quickly caused dramatic and unpredictable shifts in the power dynamics of the realm that would last for almost two centuries.

6

Wanderers

The Extended Zhou Realm, 402–381 BCE

As the fifth century BCE gave way to the fourth, the Zhou realm experienced a surge of mobility. People, goods, and ideas were all increasingly on the move. In the case of people, especially those who could claim the status of "knight," this new range of motion was both "vertical" and "lateral."

Vertically, knights saw a steep increase in what political scientists call "social mobility." A knight could begin life as a poor, humble rustic and rise to become an urbane figure of immense wealth and power. "Up," however, was not the only direction that one could travel. It was increasingly frequent for a knight to begin life as an aristocrat (albeit a low-ranking one) and be buried a commoner.

Laterally, geographic mobility reached new heights. This was true even for many commoners, but the opportunities and incentives for knights to relocate were even greater. A knight born in Han could find himself living hundreds of kilometers to the east in Qi. A knight born in Wey could end as a courtier hundreds of kilometers to the south, in Chu.

From about the mid-sixth century BCE on, as commerce intensified and became more important to the economy of the Zhou world and as more and more commoners became independent farmers rather than slaves or bonded laborers, both geographic and social mobility had grown steadily. But the late fifth and early fourth centuries BCE saw a rapid acceleration of this trend. As the previous chapters demonstrated, for the growing community of knights two forces were generally responsible for this development.

Working from the "top down," Marquis Wen of Wei (a.k.a. Wei Si) and his court made a commitment to opening up pathways of both vertical and lateral mobility, by "honoring the worthy" and by recruiting such men from beyond the state of Wei. The Wei court's obvious success inspired other courts to emulate their methods. As rival states competed to recruit talented personnel, a fluid "interstate market" for knightly service emerged.

Working from the "bottom up," groups like the fellowship of Confucius's latter-day disciples and the order of Mo Di's followers promoted and facilitated the mobility of their members. By vouching for one another's credentials and good conduct, these associations gave rulers a higher degree of confidence and security in recruiting personnel from below and far afield. As the unique conditions of the Warring States continued to develop, the raw fact of this ever-more-frequent movement up and down the social scale and across the political map itself became a force shaping the destiny of the Zhou realm.

A series of events in Wei's "brother state" of Han demonstrates this situation very clearly. Early in his reign, Marquis Lie of Han (r. 399–387 BCE), the second ruler of the independent state of Han, enlisted a close family member as his prime minister, his uncle Han Gui.[1] As Wei Si's use of his own brother in this capacity showed (as discussed in the previous chapter), this was far from unusual.

But by the accession of the second marquis in 399 BCE, the Han court had begun implementing the same kinds of meritocratic policies that had enjoyed so much success in Wei. A talented knight named Yan Sui rose to become one of the new marquis's high courtiers and close confidants. Han Gui resented the favor Yan enjoyed and was contemptuous of his low birth. Relations between the two men worsened until one day, when Yan Sui criticized a policy of Han Gui's during a discussion at court, the prime minister became furious and shouted rudely at his subordinate. For Yan Sui, this was a kind of inescapable trap.

Only a commoner could be shouted at insultingly; an aristocrat could not tolerate being bellowed at by anyone, even another aristocrat. Han Gui's outburst was done in the same spirit as the cliché scene often depicted in novels or movies about early modern Europe, where one noble slaps the other across the face with a silk glove. For a social group that considered themselves inviolable, such an offense could not be borne.[2] The target of Han Gui's verbal assault, moreover, was socially much more vulnerable than his attacker. Yan Sui lacked the prime minister's unimpeachable credentials of high birth. Like that of most knights, Yan's family would not have had their own ancestral temple, and without that form of monumental evidence to his family status, a knight could come under suspicion of being a commoner that was shamming aristocratic ancestry.

If Yan Sui did not defend himself, it would be a sign that doubts about his pedigree were justified, and he would be shunned as vulgar and cowardly by everyone, even the marquis. On the other hand, the regular chain of command set up by the new structure of the Han court did not leave Yan Sui free to treat Han Gui as a peer: you could not get away with hitting the boss in fourth-century BCE Han any more than you may in twenty-first-century CE New York. Any fittingly aristocratic response to Han Gui's insult would be unforgivably insubordinate from the perspective of the state and its rules.

It was an increasingly typical dilemma for knights who enjoyed success in a world controlled by both new forms of routine authority and venerably traditional aristocratic values. Yan Sui was forced to choose between being a loyal official and forsaking his noble status, or being a credible aristocrat and betraying the state. Either way, his position at the Han court would become completely untenable.

Yan Sui chose to defend his honor. He drew his sword and attacked Han Gui, knowing full well that the consequences would be catastrophic. His choice might seem surprising from our twenty-first-century CE perspective, but it made sense in the context of Zhou society. Though Yan was almost certain to die, and the law might have implicated Yan Sui's family in any crime he committed against the person of the prime minister, that was not guaranteed: there was a chance that the favor of the marquis might have spared at least Yan Sui's family. Disgrace, on the other hand, would have inescapably dragged down Yan and his entire family, barring them all from the ranks of the aristocracy from that time on. Events as they actually transpired vindicated Yan Sui's choice. Perhaps because the other ministers of the court were reluctant to offend the marquis, Yan Sui and Han Gui were both restrained and separated from one another before anyone could be hurt.

Yan Sui fled Han and headed east. For a time he drifted, because the unavenged insult dealt to him by Han Gui made him a figure of ostracism. As long as the man who had challenged his standing remained breathing, Yan would have to suffer petty slights and condescension from other aristocrats, especially members of the titled nobility (scions of the few remaining clans, like that of Han Gui, who enjoyed ranks like viscount or marquis and continued to operate their own ancestral temples). He thus wandered in search of someone who could secure him vengeance.

In the state of Qi, Yan Sui learned of someone who might help. His name was Nie Zheng. He was a fellow native of Han, a knight from one of the state's rural districts. He had a reputation as a brave warrior, but had suffered some disgrace and had settled in Qi as a commoner, where he plied the trade of a dog butcher.

Nie Zheng's story closely paralleled that of Yan Sui, demonstrating just how common the dilemma that had trapped Yan Sui was for the knights serving in the courts of the Warring States. Nie had served the Han clan, though we do not know in exactly what capacity. His position was much lower on the political ladder than that of Yan Sui and much less richly remunerated; otherwise he would have departed Han with more wealth.

As was the case with Yan Sui, a superior had insulted Nie during his term of service in Han. Nie refrained from avenging the insult to avoid the likelihood of being killed, not because he was afraid to die, but because he was the sole source of support for his elderly mother. The situation left Nie with a stark choice between death and disgrace. He chose to accept disgrace and go into self-imposed exile so that he could continue to care for his mother.

He took what he had saved from his service to Han and set himself up as a dog butcher in Qi. This was a wise choice economically, but a drastic one socially. Dog meat was a delicacy in Zhou cuisine (and remains one in many forms of Chinese cuisine today), so that a dog butcher was guaranteed to earn a steady income. But the life of a dog butcher violated multiple taboos of the Zhou aristocracy. Not only was Nie Zheng selling his services to common patrons, he was coming into repeated contact with blood and raw dead flesh, incurring regular pollution that the warrior-priesthood of the aristocracy were careful to avoid. Aristocrats naturally (and relatively infrequently) incurred pollution in the honorable contexts of warfare and sacrifice, and were careful to perform rites of purification whenever necessary. Commoners, especially ones engaged in labor such as butchery, came into contact with impure substances in the course of vulgar labor so frequently that they did not generally have the resources or leisure to purify themselves as often as would be necessary, thus being consigned to a constant state of pollution.[3] Though Nie Zheng had ensured that he would be able to support his mother, like Yurang (the knight who 50 years previously had mutilated himself and worked in a privy in his attempt to avenge his lord Zhi Yao), he had made his status as a knight and his position in the aristocracy utterly irredeemable.

An expression of the time declared that "a knight will die for one who recognizes him."[4] This was the principle that Yurang had sacrificed himself to uphold. As the highborn, titled aristocrats of the age increasingly looked upon knights with contempt, it became ever more imperative for the members of the lower aristocracy to focus their highest loyalty on those nobles and rulers who acknowledged knights as peers. Yan Sui understood this situation and saw in it an opportunity. Knowing that he and Nie Zheng faced common problems and thus might be kindred spirits, Yan Sui sought out the dog butcher and offered him courtesies Nie Zheng had long been denied.

Nie Zheng must have been surprised when Yan Sui, dressed in his courtly splendor, first entered Nie's humble butcher shop and introduced himself as a fellow native of Han. Yan made overtures of friendship, hosting Nie Zheng to banquets and drinking parties. Nie knew right away that Yan wanted some service of him, but that would not have necessarily made him suspicious or resentful. This was because Yan Sui was taking real risks by associating himself with Nie Zheng.

This risk did not hold true on Nie's side. Quite the contrary, seeing them together Nie's common neighbors would have viewed Nie Zheng in a new light: his disgrace could not be total if an obviously great man was still willing to treat him as a peer. By associating with Nie, Yan Sui was declaring to the world that there was a nobility in his new friend that could not be erased by his paid labor or exposure to pollution.

But just as the two men's friendship brought real benefits to Nie Zheng in the common society he now inhabited, the relationship would have cost Yan Sui in scorn from the titled aristocracy: "There goes the knight from Han who pals around with butchers." However transparently self-serving his motives, in exposing himself to further ostracism Yan Sui was paying Nie Zheng a real compliment. Yan obviously wanted something important done, and equally obviously was convinced that Nie Zheng had the character and ability to do it.

The other shoe finally dropped during a dinner party at which Yan Sui hosted Nie Zheng and his mother together. After toasting Nie's mother, Yan had servants bring in and present a gift of 100 gold ingots to "wish Nie's mother longevity." Nie was amazed at such generosity and finally forced to decline, declaring that, as much as he appreciated Yan Sui's friendship, he could not accept such a lavish gift.

Yan dismissed the servants and asked that Nie's mother be escorted home, so that the two men could talk alone. Once they had privacy, Yan Sui finally came clean to Nie Zheng. Without revealing the exact identity of the man who had insulted him, Yan explained his situation and pleaded for assistance in avenging himself. The poorer knight sympathized with his friend, but refused his request. Though Yan's offer of gold would have supported Nie Zheng's mother quite comfortably, it would not really replace having the protection and companionship of her only son. While his mother lived, Nie Zheng was not free to put his own life at risk. Yan Sui accepted his friend's refusal, and on parting graciously performed the full rites of "host and guest" in seeing Nie Zheng off. Thus one last time (and finally with no strings attached) Yan did his friend the honor of treating him as a fellow knight instead of a common dog butcher.

Sometime later, in 397 BCE, Nie Zheng's mother died. After attending to her funeral, he was filled with regret about the way that he had parted with Yan Sui. Yan, out of admiration for his friend's integrity and courage, was now virtually the only person who truly acknowledged and respected Nie Zheng's knightly birthright and honor. Nie felt obligated to repay Yan Sui with loyalty.

Selling off his shop, he traveled to see Yan Sui, who had taken refuge in the capital of the state of Wey. Yan welcomed his friend and fully revealed the nature of his vendetta: his enemy was the Primer Minister of Han. The butcher accepted the mission, and Yan offered to send Nie Zheng off with a troop of soldiers and war chariots to carry out the errand of revenge. Nie Zheng refused. He knew that a lone assassin would have the only chance of reaching Han Gui undetected and accomplishing the task.

Nie Zheng set out with nothing but his sword. Serendipitously, the Marquis of Han came to attend a covenant ceremony in the state of Wey, accompanied by his prime minister, Han Gui. Nie Zheng stormed onto the ceremonial platform, sword drawn, as the rite was getting underway (see Fig. 8). There were numerous soldiers on the scene, and Nie Zheng dispatched several guards in his determination to reach his target. As the assassin approached, Han Gui fled in terror, wrapping his arms around the Marquis of Han in panic. Nie Zheng ran Han Gui through, wounding the marquis as his sword passed through the prime minister's body.

Having secured Yan Sui revenge, Nie Zheng's first thought was to protect his friend. Since the assassination had taken place within the state of Wey at a time when Han Gui was being received as a guest, if Yan Sui was linked to the attack he would be punished by the Wey court that had given him refuge. Nie Zheng was thus determined that no one should discover his identity. He used his own sword to mutilate his face, cutting deep scars and gouging out one of his own eyes. Finally he opened up his own belly and let his entrails spill out, so that he would die before he could be questioned.

The Han court brought Nie Zheng's body back to Han and displayed it in the marketplace of the capital, in the hopes that his corpse might be identified in exchange for a reward of 1,000 gold ingots. His role in the affair might have been forgotten, except that his younger sister wondered at losing contact with her brother and suspected that the dead assassin might be Nie

Fig. 8. The assassin Nie Zheng assaults Prime Minister Han Kui to avenge the honor of his friend Yan Sui. This depiction was also included in the wall murals of the Wu Liang Shrine, along with other assassin tales. (Source: kknews.cc.)

Zheng. She went to see for herself, and finding that the body in the marketplace was indeed that of her brother, knelt weeping beside the corpse. "This is my brother, Nie Zheng!" she cried out to the stunned onlookers. Having guaranteed that her brother would be remembered for his courage, she took her own life, both to avoid collective punishment for Nie's crime and to prevent any possible suspicion that she sought to profit from her brother's death.[5]

Nie Zheng's saga electrified the Zhou realm, making him an instant hero to knights everywhere. His extraordinary courage and selfless devotion to his friend belied the gratuitous contempt in which he had been held by elite society, and by extension vindicated all knights everywhere who had been forced to suffer the arbitrary condescension of nobles who were their superiors in birth, wealth, and power. But like many events in the Warring States, the assassination of Han Gui created more heat than light. The newly emerging structure of the state in the early fourth century BCE both created and depended upon expanded social and geographic mobility, but that mobility was fraught with as much peril as promise. Though the rules and methods of the new state rewarded merit and demanded that the market for knightly service be open and fluid, the traditional position and values of the aristocracy were stubbornly resistant to change.

Even the case of Nie Zheng, for example, left open questions about the relationship between birth and honor. Though his integrity was manifest in Nie's actions, the fact that his sister shared his exceptional courage suggested that their merit was not acquired but inherited, that in fact theirs was an extraordinary bloodline that had been humbled in error. Questions about the true nature of nobility and the meaning of meritocracy in an aristocratic world would remain unresolved until long after the Warring States ended.

The deeds of Nie Zheng created shock waves that resonated far and long, but the contemporary case of another knight who likewise roamed broadly throughout the Zhou realm had an even greater and more durable impact on the shape of the Warring States. We encountered this knight, Wu Qi, in Chapter 5, which recounted some of the great deeds he accomplished in his early career, in the service of Marquis Wen of Wei. Wu Qi's story demonstrates, perhaps better than any other, the ways in which the intensifying mobility of the Zhou world reworked every aspect of its politics and social life.[6]

Wu Qi had been born in Wey, the small state that had given Yan Sui refuge after his disgrace in Han. Being the native of a small state conferred social advantages on a person of knightly birth. The smaller the state, the greater the likelihood that a knight lived near and had some kinship ties with the ruling family and some ceremonial role in the cult of its ancestral temples. Such ties were the best support that a knightly family (which lacked its own ancestral temples) had for its claims of aristocratic birth. Wey was a small state whose ruling family had a very prestigious ancestry: its founding duke had been the son of King Wen of Zhou and the younger brother of the famous Duke of Zhou (founder of Confucius's home state of Lu) by the same mother. The knights of Wey thus enjoyed association with a beacon of elite pedigree, which gave them an edge in the status competition of the Warring States.

Wu Qi combined these advantages of geography with benefits of inherited wealth. His family had managed to store up a sizable sum of money, which it entrusted to him to secure and improve the family's position. As a young man, Wu Qi squandered these advantages. He spent through the funds his family had given him without securing an office of significant power or responsibility.

This attracted the ridicule of other members of Wey elite society. It is a measure of just how insecure the position of knights was at this time that, even though he was ensconced in a small state and possessed significant wealth, Wu Qi felt compelled to fight repeated duels to defend his status in the face of derision. Eventually he had killed so many men in these duels that he was forced to depart Wey for its neighboring "brother state" of Lu.

In Lu, the home state of Confucius, Wu Qi joined the fellowship of the Master's latter-day disciples. He became the student of Master Zeng Shen (b. 505 BCE), one of the youngest of Confucius's original disciples and an outstanding intellectual leader among the first generation of the Confucian fellowship.[7] After leaving the circle of Master Zeng's disciples, he settled in the capital of Lu, where he studied the military arts.

At this time the state of Qi attacked Lu in another of the quarrels that had frequently incited war between those neighbors.[8] The Duke of Lu, having heard of Wu Qi's reputation as a learned strategist and tactician, wanted to enlist him to command Lu's armies in defense of the state. Ministers of the court objected, noting that Wu Qi's wife was a native of Qi, and that he thus might be a spy for the enemy state. Hearing these doubts about him being voiced, Wu Qi killed his wife to demonstrate his total loyalty to Lu.[9] He was given command of the defensive armies and led the soldiers of Lu to victory, crushing the invaders.

In the aftermath of his triumph the duke wanted to promote Wu Qi and make further use of his talents. Jealous ministers at the court once more spoke against him, however. They reminded the duke of the men Wu Qi had killed in his home state of Wey, neighbor and close kin of Lu. They declared, moreover, that Wu Qi was too selfishly proud. On leaving Wey he had sworn an impassioned oath. Biting his own arm to draw blood as a sacramental "seal," he vowed not to return to his home state until he had attained high office. He had kept that oath to the extreme extent of refusing to return to attend the funeral of his own mother when she had passed away. This was why, so they said, Wu Qi had been ejected from the circle of Master Zeng's disciples. To reward such behavior would bring disgrace on the Lu court.

Wu Qi was thus dismissed from the service of Lu and set out on the road once again. By this time Marquis Wen of Wei had become famous for giving opportunity to knights of proven worth; thus Wu Qi went to the capital of Wei. He became a commander in Wei's armies and led the conquest of the territory west of the Yellow River that was acquired from the state of Qin. By the time of Marquis Wen's death in 396 BCE, Wu Qi had risen to the post of Prefect of the Hexi (west of the Yellow River) region that he had conquered on Wei's behalf.

Wu Qi became renowned throughout the Zhou world as a brilliant and innovative commander. The new infantry armies of the Warring States required a new style of command and a new strategic outlook, and Wu Qi rose to meet these challenges. He was known to eat the same food as his soldiers and wear the same clothes that had been issued to them while on campaign. On the march he would travel on foot rather than by carriage or on horseback, and at night he would sleep on the open ground with his men without so much as a mat for comfort.

All of these actions might seem merely theatrical (or prosaically ordinary) to our twenty-first-century sensibilities, but they expressed a solid understanding of just how much military affairs had changed since the founding of the Zhou dynasty. Traditionally battlefield service had been considered an aristocratic privilege, so commanders had made a great show of their superiority in all realms: in courage, but also in birth, wealth, and status. They would not have traveled with their troops, for example, except in a richly adorned carriage, wearing elaborately decorated clothes and armor.[10] When armies had been made up mainly of aristocratic warriors, this style of command had worked well. It reminded everyone of what was at stake: of the disgrace that could be incurred from cowardice or failure and the glory that could be won through resolve.

But in an army made of up conscripted farmers none of the aristocratic traditions of command made any sense. A story told about Wu Qi illustrates the situation well. On one campaign Wu Qi came across a soldier who was incapacitated by an infected abscess. Kneeling down beside the soldier, Wu Qi sucked the abscess clean of pus, incurring pollution to which a traditional aristocratic commander would never have willingly exposed himself. Word of this reached the soldier's mother, who on hearing the news began to weep and wail uncontrollably. When those around her asked why the general's extraordinarily magnanimous kindness should make her so upset, she replied, "Last year Wu Qi sucked the abscess of my husband clean, and my husband fought bravely until he died. Having taken my husband, now Wu Qi is taking my son!"[11]

The story is clearly apocryphal, but it embodies the wholesale changes that were reshaping military affairs during Wu Qi's lifetime. The conscript soldiers of the new army had none of the social motivations of the old warrior-aristocrats. Farmers lived at the very bottom of the social scale; they had no status to lose from displays of cowardice. The mother's horror at anything that might motivate her son to fight bravely would be a freakish anomaly among the aristocracy, but it made perfect sense among the common farmers from whom the new army was being drawn.

This new army required a commander who found new ways of consolidating and motivating his soldiers. Wu Qi's approach to command, his determined efforts to demonstrate solidarity with rather than superiority over his soldiers, was a radical innovation that was well adapted to changing times. He was among the first generals to understand the evolving situation and respond to it effectively, achieving spectacular results on the field of battle. A text that bears his name (the *Wuzi,* or *Master Wu*) still survives, and purports to express his wisdom concerning military affairs. It is doubtful that he had any part in the actual writing and compiling of the text,[12] and it was never as highly regarded as the *Sunzi bingfa* (*The Military Methods of Master Sun,* sometimes known in English as *The Art of War,* which, like the *Wuzi,* was composed and compiled decades after Wu Qi's death, and which will be discussed in the next chapter), but it was no accident that Wu Qi served as the eponym of one of the "military classics." In life he pioneered techniques and elucidated principles that would eventually form the basis of texts like the one that bears his name.

By the time of Marquis Wen's death, Wu Qi was one of the most powerful and trusted ministers of Wei, and in time he might have served as prime minister. But again he fell prey to the jealousy of his peers, though this time his foe used Wu Qi's own pride to help secure his downfall. Marquis Wu of Wei (r. 395–370 BCE), Marquis Wen's successor, showed high regard for Wu Qi, but passed over Wu Qi twice in selecting his prime minister.

The second man who served Marquis Wu as prime minister worried that Wu Qi would supplant him; thus, on the advice of an aide he concocted a plan to eliminate his rival. The prime minister's own wife was a princess of the Wei ruling clan. The prime minister invited Wu Qi to dine at his residence and arranged for a drama to unfold before the unwitting guest. During dinner the prime minister's wife, following her husband's instructions, put on haughty airs and insulted her husband arrogantly.

Some days after this piece of "dinner theater," during a private moment with Marquis Wu, the prime minister made a show of speculating about whether or not Wu Qi could really be relied on to stay in the state of Wei, or whether he was eager to move on and sell his talents elsewhere. When the marquis took the bait and asked how they might be able to test Wu Qi's intentions, the prime minister "happened upon" the idea of offering Wu Qi the hand of a princess from the ruling clan in marriage. If he intended to stay, so the prime minister claimed, Wu Qi would be honored and accept the union, but if he intended to leave he would decline.

The trap was set nicely. Not realizing that the scene at the prime minister's dinner table had been play-acted for his benefit, Wu Qi was horrified by the prospect of marrying an arrogant princess from the ruling clan. This was the man, after all, who had won exile from his home state by defending himself in repeated duels against slights to his dignity. As the prime minister had counted on him doing, Wu Qi refused the marquis's offer of a marriage alliance.

Wu Qi experienced a repeat of what had happened to him in the state of Lu. Marquis Wu, fooled by the maneuvers of his prime minister, came to distrust Wu Qi. Seeing that he had come under suspicion and fearing what might befall him if he stayed too long in Wei, Wu Qi departed and traveled to the great southern kingdom of Chu.

Wu Qi arrived in Chu roughly 110 years after that state had nearly been destroyed by the rampaging armies of King Helü of Wu (as discussed in Chapter 2). In that time Chu had recovered much of its former power. The state that had been Chu's nemesis, Wu, had been annihilated by its former vassal, Yue. In the wake of that stroke of good luck, the resurgent Chu military machine had destroyed several small southern states that had resisted Chu's control for many centuries, some of which had lent support to King Helü's campaign of conquest. The Chu court had been able to move back to its former capital at Ying, closer to the heart of the Chu domain.[13]

But the position of the Chu kingdom remained precarious. To the southeast it faced the challenge of Yue. Though Yue had stagnated after the death of King Goujian, never developing into the urgent threat once posed by Wu, in the early decades of the fourth century it remained a robust force in the Lower Yangzi region.[14]

To the north Chu was menaced by the rising power of the Jin successor states of Wei, Han, and Zhao. In successive campaigns Chu had lost ground to the northern powers. The central state of Zheng, which had once been vulnerable to intimidation by the Chu court (we read of one of the frequent north-south struggles in this geopolitical contest in the account of Zhi Yao's career, in Chapter 3), sank steadily under the domination of its northern neighbors, especially the state of Han. Eventually the state of Zheng would be absorbed by Han entirely, a conquest so thorough that the Han rulers confidently moved their court into the capital of the former Zheng domain in 375 BCE.[15]

Wu Qi thus entered a kingdom balanced on the knife's edge. On the one hand, Chu's survival and recovery gave cause for optimism. On the other hand, absent some policy to engage the challenges of the moment, Chu faced a future of inevitable decline.

It was a moment in which a knight of talent could make his mark, and Wu Qi's reputation had preceded him. He was enlisted immediately in a position of trust, made Warden of Wan Commandery, which bordered the state of Wei where Wu Qi had previously served. His performance in this post so impressed the king that after one year Wu Qi was promoted to become prime minister of the Chu court.[16] It was a meteoric rise the likes of which the Zhou world had not seen since the ill-fated rise of Zai Wo to the premiership of Qi nearly a century earlier.

Wu Qi's time in Wei had given him firsthand experience of the reforms of Li Kui. He had seen the ways that the reorganization of the structures of state could yield dramatic improvements in economic prosperity and military power. As Prime Minister of Chu, Wu Qi set out to reorganize the ancient, sprawling southern kingdom.[17]

The social and political order that Wu Qi had seen work so well in Wei was radically different from what he encountered in Chu. Decades of infighting in Wei and the other Jin successor states had destroyed most of the aristocratic clans that had once existed in the north. The ruling clan of the Wei marquis was the last great house remaining in that state. Virtually no other nobles held hereditary titles such as "viscount" or "earl," possessed their own temples, or drew income from their own estates. Outside of the ruling clan, the vast majority of aristocrats held the rank of knight.

The aristocrats of Wei were thus collectively dependent upon state service for both wealth *and* status. By Wu Qi's time, the aristocratic society of Wei was well along in the process of being transformed from a body of freestanding landed elites into a labor pool from which the state drew paid servitors. Aristocratic rank did not disappear, but, as we will see in subsequent chapters, the dispensation of titles and estates came progressively under the control of the state.[18] This is why it had been possible to achieve the degree of discipline and coordination necessary for Li Kui's economic policies to succeed, and for the military campaigns that Yue Yang and Wu Qi led at the head of Wei's armies to triumph.

Little of this social leveling experienced in the Jin successor states had occurred in Chu by the early fourth century BCE. Though competition and infighting had driven many renegades like Wu Zixu into exile (as described in Chapter 2), such conflicts had not led to the destruction of most of the great clans. The South was too sparsely populated and the terrain too fragmented. Aristocratic clans had an incentive to join into the larger royal commonwealth in order to enjoy the benefits of interregional trade (explaining why the "kingdom" had grown so large in area), but each clan's home territory was protected by steep ridges and impassable marshes. The destruction and absorption of one clan by another was a much more difficult strategic task in the South than in the North, thus the ruling oligarchy had survived much more intact in Chu than in Wei at the time that Wu Qi rose to become the Chu court's chief minister.[19]

These facts did not deter Wu Qi, who was determined to reproduce the power and efficiency in Chu that he had witnessed in Wei. He laid ambitious plans before the king to reform Chu's laws and to reshape its government. He eliminated excess offices and sinecures, focusing personnel and resources on those offices that would encourage economic production and strengthen the military. In imitation of Li Kui's policies to encourage agricultural production, Wu Qi ordered the regional clans to clear and settle uninhabited areas of their domains, in an attempt to foster and sustain population growth.[20]

A key problem upon which Wu Qi focused was the "top heavy" nature of the Chu state. The aristocratic oligarchy was too big and its share of the state's resources too ponderous. Wu Qi set out to mandate a reduction in the number of noble clans, and to slow or reverse the growth of the aristocratic clans that continued to exist. He instituted a rule that noble scions could only hold rank and salary for three generations of removal from the main "trunk" of their family tree. If one's great-grandfather, for example, had been a marquis, one would still rank among the aristocracy, but one's sons would become commoners.[21]

Records of the exact legal reforms undertaken by Wu Qi do not survive, but we know that he took a close interest in affairs of state at all levels. He incurred public ire, for example, by mandating changes to construction methods in the capital city of Ying.[22] His changes to the recruitment and training of Chu's military bore fruit in the South as they had in Wei.

Before he had been in office for a decade, Wu Qi achieved a marked increase in Chu's military power. He led a campaign of conquest along the southwestern frontiers of Chu's empire, into a region inhabited by non-Sinitic tribal peoples known to the denizens of the Zhou realm as the "Hundred Yue" (Viet). These campaigns added thousands of square kilometers to Chu's territory in the area of what are now Hunan and Guangxi Provinces.[23]

Even more significantly, Wu Qi turned the tide of the geopolitical contest on the Yellow River plain. Marquis Wen of Wei had united the Jin successor states and made Wei the preeminent power of the Zhou realm, pressuring Chu to relinquish the influence it once had over the people of the North. Under Marquis Wen's successor, Marquis Wu (whose government Wu Qi had left under a cloud of suspicion), the unity forged by Marquis Wen of Wei between the "brother states" of Wei, Han, and Zhao broke down.

Marquis Wen (Wei Si) had made his state of Wei the leader of a trilateral coalition including the states ruled by the other two surviving vassal clans of Jin, Han and Zhao. For virtually all of Marquis Wen's long reign of five decades, peace and cooperation had prevailed between the three states. The situation held for more than a decade under Marquis Wen's heir, Marquis Wu. But trust between the three states gradually eroded. Wei and Han expanded by conquering the territory of neighboring states. As stated above, the formerly powerful state of Zheng was destroyed, with Han receiving the lion's share of its former terrain and Wei annexing the rest. The rulers of Zhao feared that the balance of power between the three states would be upset, and they decided to encroach upon the territory of their neighbor, Wu Qi's home state of Wey. In 383 BCE Zhao fortified the city of Gangping along its frontier with Wey, and then launched an assault, eventually laying siege to the Wey capital.

Wey sent a delegation to Marquis Wu begging for help. Though Zhao and Wei were historically "brother states," their ruling clans were from different families. The Zhao was a branch of the Ying clan that ruled in Qin. The Wei and Wey ruling lines were both descended from the royal Ji clan and were thus distantly "kin." Marquis Wu sent an army to halt Zhao's assault.

The clash between Wei and Zhao was bloody but indecisive. After a year of fighting, the Wei ruler enlisted the aid of Qi to repel Zhao's assault. The Zhao army was driven back, and Wey took advantage of Zhao's distress to capture the recently fortified city of Gangping. With its frontier defenses breached, Wey was able to march into the interior of Zhao in reprisal for Zhao's aggression.[24]

In 381 BCE Zhao, now fighting a defensive war and fearful for its own security, sent a delegation to Chu requesting assistance. This crack in the coalition formed by Marquis Wen was a rare strategic opportunity. Wu Qi responded by leading Chu's armies north against his former Wei rulers. Wei had been weakened by almost three years of bloody fighting with Zhao, and the new military that Wu Qi had built in Chu performed as well as the Wei troops Wu Qi had previously commanded in his wars against Qin. The Chu army met and defeated the forces of Wei at a battlefield in present-day Henan Province, then poured through a mountain pass into the interior of the state, finally pushing so far north that they "watered their horses in the Yellow River" itself. It was the farthest north that a southern army had penetrated in the former Jin domain, and it cut off the Wei capital from the eastern districts of the state, giving the armies of Zhao an opportunity to advance, driving back the troops that had penetrated its interior and destroying key Wei fortifications.[25]

It was a moment of existential peril for the state of Wei. Though the state survived and remained robust, the steady rise in power and influence it had enjoyed since the reign of Marquis Wen was arrested. Wei would not recover the initiative during the reign of Marquis Wu. Like the defection of Wu Zixu from Chu to the state of Wu more than a century before, the defection of Wu Qi from Wei to Chu had altered the course of history for the entire Zhou realm. Since by the early fourth century BCE Wu Qi was only one of hundreds of knights on the move between states, his case was an object lesson in just how volatile the Zhou world had increasingly become and would remain.

Wu Qi's own life was a study in capricious fortune. At the moment of what was perhaps his greatest vindication, when he had proven to his former masters just how foolish they had been to let him go, the floor of his own position in Chu collapsed beneath him. The King of Chu died suddenly and unexpectedly, setting in motion a coup d'etat at the Chu court.

The high courtiers had chafed intensely under the impact of Wu Qi's reforms. Though Wu Qi had increased the power of Chu, he had done so at the expense of the wealth and influence of titled aristocrats who felt entitled to a position in the ruling oligarchy of the state. The heads of the aristocratic clans resented having to clear and resettle lands, relinquish sinecures and emoluments, and accede to the demotion of their kinsmen in the interest of government efficiency.

Wu Qi's enemies did not wait to act upon their grievances. When he entered the royal palace in Ying to attend the funeral of his king, Wu Qi was assaulted by a mob of nobles and their armed escorts. Even hopelessly cornered, Wu Qi lost none of the tactical brilliance for which he had become famous. He ran into the ceremonial hall in which the body of the king had been laid out in state and flung himself over the corpse, as if pleading for sanctuary. His pursuers, emboldened by rage and what they perceived to be Wu Qi's cowardice, fired a volley of arrows at their prone target. Wu Qi was killed. The nobles who had slain him were determined to humiliate him. They took his corpse and dismembered it.

Wu Qi had already defeated his enemies before they dismembered his corpse, however. Some stray arrows among those with which he had been killed had pierced the body of the king. The new legal code that Wu Qi had instituted made such profanation of the body of the king a capital offense. In dispatching the prime minister they so hated, the plotters had thus made themselves outlaws. The new king, seizing upon this legal pretext and the sense of outrage engendered by the disrespect done to the former king's corpse, rallied supporters of reform to launch a counter-coup against the plotters. The new armies that Wu Qi had built and which, flush with victory, felt loyalty and gratitude to their slain commander, began to round up the nobles who had betrayed him.[26]

The widening gyre of strife set in motion by Wu Qi's murder engulfed another group of wanderers whose story embodies the unpredictable dynamism of the era. One of the leaders of the plot against Wu Qi, the Lord of Yangcheng, had employed the Grand Master of the Mohist order, Meng Sheng, as a member of his retinue. As the Lord left for the Chu capital upon hearing of the king's death, he broke a jade disc in half to serve as a tally. Giving one half to Meng Sheng, he appointed the Grand Master custodian of Yangcheng, and instructed that no orders coming from the capital should be obeyed unless the bearer of those orders presented the matching half of the jade disc.

Meng Sheng agreed and bid his Lord farewell. When the coup plotters were condemned, the Lord fled the state to escape punishment, taking his half of the jade disc with him. A regiment of the royal army arrived in Yangcheng to confiscate the Lord's domain in punishment for his treason. Grand Master Meng Sheng demanded to see the jade tally authorizing him to accept the orders of the regiment's commander, but of course his request could not be fulfilled.

The situation was hopeless. Though the Mohists were famed for their skill in defensive warfare, Meng Sheng did not have the forces necessary to hold off an assault. His chief disciple urged him to surrender, stressing the great loss that Meng Sheng's death would mean for the Mohist order. Meng Sheng countered that his surrender would be much more damaging to the Mohist cause than his death. Meng Sheng had been the Lord of Yangcheng's teacher, friend, subject, and minister. If now he handed the Lord's palace over to the armies of Chu without a fight, who would trust the Mohists ever again? The chief disciple declared that if the Grand Master was determined to die, his disciple would pave the way for him. He draw a knife and cut his own throat, dying in front of Meng Sheng to show his devotion.

Meng Sheng had 180 Mohist disciples with him in the palace of Yangcheng. He ordered two of his followers to travel to the state of Song, to report what was happening to the Mohist Master Tian Xiang, and to inform Tian Xiang that the title of Grand Master now belonged to him. The two disciples made the journey and delivered their message. As their superior, the newly elevated Grand Master Tian Xiang ordered the two disciples to stay in Song, declaring that they were more useful to the Mohist order alive than dead. The two disciples, most likely fearing that they would be scorned as disloyal and cowardly if they did not, sneaked away from Song and returned to Yangcheng so that they could die with their Master Meng Sheng.[27]

All of the events surrounding Wu Qi's death, like those involving Han Gui, Yan Sui, and Nie Zheng, demonstrated the ways in which new institutions and old traditions continued to mix together and roil the politics and social affairs of the Zhou realm. Leaders like Li Kui and Wu Qi pioneered forms of routine authority and regular order to increase the power, wealth, and efficient operation of the state. But venerable traditions of personal entitlement, honor, and allegiance remained resilient through decades and centuries of political and social reform. Even attempts by knights to organize *themselves*, like the division of the Mohist order into a routine hierarchy of Grand Masters, Masters, and disciples, was prone to distortion by the forces of tradition. When push came to shove, knights such as the two Mohist disciples who insisted on dying in Yangcheng against orders were more compelled by the values and customs of personal loyalty and aristocratic honor than by abstract ideals like the authority of the Grand Master or the Mohist Way.

These oil-and-water collisions between clashing social forces created a turbulent and unpredictable political dynamic in the larger Zhou world as the fourth century BCE progressed. The rising power of Wei, which had so dominated strategic affairs since the reign of Marquis Wen, had been obstructed, at least temporarily. A multipolar world was dawning.

Though Wu Qi's death disrupted the growth of Chu's strength, it did not bring the process of reform in that kingdom to an end. The fate of plotters like the Lord of Yangcheng showed that the cause of reform had strong support at the Chu court.[28] The struggle over the structure of the Chu kingdom's government, social order, and economy continued after Wu Qi's death, and Chu remained a robust player in the geopolitical struggles of the Zhou realm. But the South was not the only power center outside the Jin successor states in the emerging multipolar order of the fourth century BCE.

To the west and east of the Yellow River plain were the states of Qi and Qin, each of which was abundantly endowed with people, land, and resources. During the reign of Marquis Wen, both Qi and Qin had yielded territory and political capital to the premier power of Wei. In the decades after Marquis Wen's death, however, both Qi and Qin pursued reforms in their bids to survive and advance in the increasingly violent order of the Warring States.

Though much of the inspiration for these policies was drawn from the innovations pioneered in Wei, the Qi and Qin courts each explored new ideas and developed new institutions by way of exploiting the economic and human potential of their states. By the late fourth century, these respective reform efforts in the East and the West had radically reshaped the power dynamic of the Zhou domain, creating a world in which the regional courts were ever more sophisticated and powerful, but in which the competition between these power centers was ever more violent, unpredictable, and high-stakes.

7

The Altars of the Soil and Grain are Closer than Kin

The State of Qi, 389–345 BCE

By the middle of the fourth century BCE it had become obvious to the people of the Zhou domain that their world was on the verge of a radical transformation. Elites throughout what is now much of northern and central China had lived with at least the cultural tradition of Zhou rule for almost seven centuries. The Zhou kings had become like the moon in the sky: a fixture of the environment that was easy to ignore, but the absence of which was unfathomable.

But now it was clear that the accelerating chaos of the world would eventually consume the Zhou court itself. Every filament of the Zhou order had snapped, every value or concept upon which Zhou legitimacy rested had been strained to the breaking point and beyond. The onset of violent conflicts between and within regional states, and the destructiveness of such conflicts when they occurred, had become virtually impossible to predict. Social and political norms that had held for centuries were no longer reliable. The eventual demise of the Zhou themselves was a foregone conclusion. When and how it would happen and who or what could possibly take the place of the Zhou dynasty, however, were impossible questions to answer from the vantage of the mid-fourth century BCE.

As we saw in Chapter 5, during the rule of Wei Si (a.k.a. Marquis Wen of Wei, r. 445–396 BCE) the Wei court had become a major center of institutional innovation and, for a while, a dominant power broker in the interregional politics of the Zhou world. Marquis Wen's reorganization of the court and territorial administration of Wei according to the policies of Prime Minister Li Kui, his conquest of vast terrain from the neighboring state of Qin, his forging of an effective alliance between the three "Jin successor states" (Wei, Han and Zhao), and his successful maneuvering to elevate himself and his allies to the sovereign rank of marquis, all opened up new political possibilities for a world struggling to cope with rapid change. For a time it must have seemed clear that the leaders of Wei would be the authors of the future: whatever interregional political order that eventually replaced the Zhou dynasty would be invented in Wei. But the campaigns of Wu Qi as commander of the armies of Chu, and his damaging incursion deep into the Wei heartland, undermined any such certainty.

After the troops led by Wu Qi returned home and peace was restored, though Wei remained very powerful, anyone trying to predict where the lynchpin of a future "new world order" would be situated would be forced to consider alternative centers of power beyond the Wei court. By about 350 BCE or so the person doing such an assessment would naturally have looked 490 kilometers to the northeast of the Wei capital, to the city of Linzi, capital of the state of Qi. Since the coup of 481 BCE with which this book opened, Qi had been weakened by internal divisions. But in 374 BCE, seven years after the death of Wu Qi, a new generation of leadership emerged in Qi that charted a unique and progressively more successful course.

If the coup of 481 BCE had constituted a first revolution by which the Tian clan had consolidated permanent control over the Qi court, the program of reform begun after 374 BCE constituted a second and equally transformative revolution, an effective "second birth" of the Tian-Qi state. Many of the policies of these new rulers were done in emulation of the successful reforms instituted in Wei by Marquis Wen. The "second wave" Tian leaders of Qi, however, also developed distinctive approaches to the challenges of the Warring States that not only exerted enormous influence throughout the Zhou world in their own time, but established enduring norms for successive governments of the imperial era.

The ruler who can be credited with turning the tide in Qi was named Tian Wu (r. 374–357 BCE). He was the seventh Tian clan patriarch to rule the state of Qi since Tian Chang first seized control of the state. Until Tian Wu's tenure, the Tian clan regime had sat on shaky foundations. During Tian Wu's reign and that of his son Tian Yinqi (r. 356–320 BCE),[1] a new and sustainable identity was forged for the ruling house of Qi and the government over which it presided. This required a remarkable political and cultural transformation of a kind that had never been achieved before in the ancient world, and that was rarely if ever rivaled in subsequent eras.

At first glance it may seem surprising that it took more than seven generations for the Tian to develop the state of Qi into a power center that could contend to lead the Zhou world. Situated on the fertile spillway of the great Yellow River, Qi was not only large and well endowed with natural resources; it was also one of the most densely populated states in the Zhou realm. Like the neighboring state of Jin to the west, Qi had been a dominant power within the larger territorial order of the Zhou vassal states during the Spring and Autumn period, and in the seventh century BCE, during the reign of the Lü clan that held the charter to rule Qi for more than five centuries, the Duke of Qi had served as the first "Lord Protector," the vassal deputized by the Zhou king to exercise command of the military forces of the entire realm.

Unlike Jin, which had ultimately been partitioned into the three new states of Wei, Zhao, and Han, Qi had remained united through the turmoil of the fifth century BCE. Beyond this, the grandee clan that had risen to predominance in Qi, the Tian, had for many generations before taking total control of their state been master players of the grand game of power-politics, and early pioneers of new mechanisms of social and political control. Tian clan patriarchs, for example, had begun offering "tax rebates" and market subsidies to their common clients and tenants beginning in the six century BCE, in a bid to cultivate loyalty and good service. The first Tian ruler of Qi, Tian Chang, had built a large stable of client knights by offering generous emoluments and terms of favorable treatment to the cast-off scions of other noble clans, even ones that had been long-time enemies of the Tian. Rising clans like the Wei, Han, and Zhao had in large part followed a path already blazed by the Tian in Qi. It thus might seem intuitive that Qi should have been perceived early on as the leading power of a coming "post-Zhou" world.

But the very audacity of the Tian success limited the degree to which Qi could exert influence beyond its frontiers in the first generations of their rule. The Tian maneuvered artfully to eliminate, subdue, or co-opt all of their rivals for power among the other grandee clans of Qi, and to overpower the ducal Lü clan, but that process was tumultuous and fraught with danger. The peril that Tian leaders had courted can be seen in the fate of the Zhi clan of Jin that under the leadership of the rashly aggressive Zhi Yao, had met with annihilation in attempting to similarly consolidate control over their native state. During most of the fifth and much of the early fourth centuries BCE the leaders of the Tian clan were too preoccupied with the internal affairs of their state to have much force left to spare for conquests and intrigues in the greater Zhou domain.

Instability was engendered as much by doubts and confusion within the Tian clan itself as threats from external enemies. There had been a foreshadowing of this tension during the coup of 481 BCE. As recounted in Chapter 1, at one point Tian Chang had expressed doubts about defying his ruler Lü Ren, and one of his own kinsmen had threatened to kill him unless he pressed ahead with the plan, declaring that anyone who did otherwise was "not a true member of the Tian clan."[2]

This attitude from one of Tian Chang's own kinsmen was a sign of change that would deepen over time. Through their success in rising to control the government of Qi, the Tian clan progressively evolved into a new type of "super-elite" corporate body, one whose binding ties were a mix of ancient hereditary loyalties and newfangled transactional bonds of patronage and employment. When Tian Chang's son took over as clan head and prime minister, for example, he filled the Qi court in Linzi with his own cousins, brothers, and nephews, named as "Capital Grandees," titled aristocrats who did not have their own estates but who were given stipends out of the revenues collected by the court.[3] The family ties of these Capital Grandees to the clan head gave them preference, but their lack of lands and common clients made them more like government employees than true titled nobility. Thus even as the government of Qi became a Tian family affair, it also became, ironically, more impersonal and centralized.

Though such a process fostered efficiency, it could not help but create resentments. As this new system evolved it was difficult to distinguish where ties of kinship and tradition ended and those of pecuniary self-interest began. The supply of sinecures and salaried positions did not grow as fast as the spreading branches of the Tian clan family tree, and a balance always had to be struck between consolidating wealth in the hands of the ruling clan and sharing just enough wealth with allies and subordinates to keep them loyal and complacent. How the growing wealth of the clan would be managed, to which clan members it would be dispensed and in what amounts, and how much would be shared with clients and allies were open and often intractable questions. As the clan grew and penetrated into ever more aspects of government activity, the need to allocate tasks and the openings this created for talented or assertive members to rise in power and prestige, fostered opportunism and ambition.

Strife was inevitable. We know of several high-level defections from the Tian oligarchy and instances of bloody infighting, and there were almost certainly others of which we are unaware because they were expunged from the written record by Tian clan leaders. Though the official chronicles were sanitized, the dangers of the political climate are literally preserved in stone in the archaeological record. Excavations have shown that as Tian leaders consolidated their control over the government of Qi, they radically reworked the architectural layout of the capital city of Linzi (see Fig. 9). Palaces and government offices were concentrated in a sequestered "forbidden city," fortified against attack from *within Linzi itself* by walls twice as thick as those that defended the city as a whole from outside invaders.[4] The Tian leaders feared the internal enemies they had made among the elite of their own state during their rise to power as much or more than they feared the threat of invasion from other states.

Complicating the situation even further during the first century of Tian rule was the continuing existence of the ducal house. True executive authority in Qi was exercised by the Tian clan patriarchs, who for five generations held the title "prime minister" as an effectively hereditary prerogative. But though reduced to being figureheads, the Lü dukes remained the nominal sovereigns of Qi for almost a century after the coup of 481 BCE. This was a bow to necessity on the part of the Tian clan leadership.

During the Spring and Autumn period the state of Qi had (similarly to other large states such as Jin and Chu) grown expansively by absorbing myriad

Fig. 9. Archaeological excavations have revealed that Linzi, the capital of the ancient kingdom of Qi, was among the largest and most prosperous cities in the pre-industrial world. These are the remains of a sophisticated drainage system that allowed water runoff to flow out of the city underneath its massive defensive walls. (Source: erenow.org.)

surrounding states, some of which were allowed to retain their "sovereign" rank of "marquis" though compelled to pledge fealty to the Lü dukes.[5] In the absence of the traditional ducal house these Qi vassal "marquises" would be free to offer allegiance to other powerful states. Thus Tian control was not secure or stable enough to allow the Tian clan to rule in their own name. The Tian still needed the imprimatur of the hereditary dukes in order to keep the intricate political machine they had hijacked intact and operational.

The situation of the Tian clan had improved marginally by the time Tian Wu came to power in 374 BCE. The clan was finally able to come out from under the shadow of the Lü dukes in 386 BCE, during the tenure of Tian Wu's father, the fifth ruling Tian clan patriarch, Tian He (r. 404–384 BCE). Like so many aspects of the career of the Tian clan, the process by which Tian He broke free from dependence on the Lü dukes was complex and violent.

Tian He had come to power during the bloody succession struggle of 405 BCE (described in Chapter 5), through the ouster of his own brother. The facts of this coup are murky. We do not even know the given name of Tian He's predecessor, because Tian He expunged his brother's tenure as prime minister from the annals of the state of Qi. We know of his existence only from records kept in the neighboring state of Wei, where he is called by a posthumous title "The Mournful Viscount Tian" (Tian Daozi), suggesting he died by violence.[6]

Whatever the case may have been, in the chaos surrounding that transition one of Tian He's kinsmen defected, surrendering the territory over which he had control to the state of Zhao.[7] When Tian He launched a campaign in 405 BCE to recover that territory, he triggered a disastrous war with the triple alliance of Wei, Han, and Zhao, and was forced to surrender custody of the Duke of Qi to Wei Si. It was the petition (under duress) of the Duke of Qi to the Zhou Son of Heaven that finally raised Wei Si and his allied rulers to the rank of marquis, formalizing their control over the territory of the partitioned state of Jin where they had previously been vassals.

Though the whole episode had been humiliating for the Tian clan and exposed the relative weakness of Qi in the face of the coalition formed under the leadership of Wei, the deft political strategy of Wei Si served as an object lesson to Tian He. Wei Si had demonstrated that the ancient hereditary order of the Zhou states was no longer immutable. The Tian clan, like the Wei, Han, and Zhao clans of neighboring Jin, could potentially come out from under the shadow of the Lü ducal house and rule Qi in its own name.

Tian He spent almost two decades maneuvering to emulate Wei Si's stratagem. He rebuilt the economic and military might of Qi after the damaging defeat of 405 BCE. In 392 BCE he internally exiled the duke, who had fallen into drink and indulged in indiscrete sexual affairs, to a small fief along the coast of Qi, where he was allowed to maintain the sacrifices to his venerable Lü ancestors using the revenue from his own territory.[8] It was the first stage of a more fundamental shift. Technically Tian He was still only the "Prime Minister" of Qi, but with the "duke" out of sight and mind, Tian He was the sole personage of supreme power and status in the capital. He was preparing the people and aristocracy of Qi for a coming new order.

By 390 BCE Tian He was confident enough to challenge the might of Wei. He waged war on Wei Si's son and successor, Marquis Wu of Wei. On this campaign the armies of Qi triumphed, capturing the city of Highmount (Xiangling).[9] In negotiations during the peace covenant, Marquis Wu agreed to reciprocate what Qi had done for Wei in 405 BCE. He personally petitioned the Son of Heaven to raise Tian He to the rank of marquis.

Though Tian He's maneuver was unoriginal, it worked. In 386 BCE the Zhou king granted Wei's petition, and Tian He became the first head of his clan to rule over Qi in both fact and title.[10] He was posthumously honored by the denizens of Qi as "the Supreme Duke" (Duke Tai), acknowledging that in his person a new ruling line had begun. To broadcast the new order, in the calendrical system of the state of Qi the year was changed from being reckoned as the nineteenth year of the reign of the debauched duke Lü Dai (d. 379 BCE), internally exiled last scion of the old ruling house, to being first year of Tian He's reign as "duke."[11]

It was an extraordinary moment. The histories of the Zhou era are full of usurpations, but in every other case when one family replaced another it was compelled to rule under a new title. This was because a state title like "Qi" did not only signify a geographic territory; it also stood for a religious cult that intimately joined the local gods of the fields, forests, rivers, and mountains with the ancestral spirits of the ruling clan. The "state" belonged to its ruling clan and their ancestors (and vice versa), one could not exist without the other. A change of ruling clan would invariably compel the establishment of a new "state" (as had happened in the case of Jin's partition into Wei, Han, and Zhao). The successful appropriation of the "Qi" state title by the Tian clan was unprecedented, and subsequently virtually unparalleled.

Though Tian He's feat would have profound long-term effects, its initial impact was blunted by his death in 385 BCE,[12] less than two years after his accession to the rank of marquis and the ducal throne. Such a short tenure as duke was not enough time to acclimate elites to the sea change that had occurred.

Neighboring states continued to record events in Qi using the reign years of the exiled Lü Dai (who despite his decadent ways outlived Tian He by seven years, dying in 379 BCE).[13] Inside Qi the general instability that had characterized Tian rule over the court of Linzi continued.

Tian He was succeeded by his son, Tian Wu's half-brother, Tian Yan (r. 384–375 BCE). We know very little about Tian Yan, because his reign, like that of his uncle the "Mournful Viscount," was eventually also expunged from the records of the state of Qi.[14] His reign is remembered only because it is recorded in the chronicles of Wei, which gives no posthumous title for him (suggesting he never received one).

Tian Yan ruled Qi for 10 years, and was obviously an energetic and ambitious leader. On the one hand he was emboldened by the startling success of his father in maneuvering to seize the Qi throne. On the other hand, he must have felt pressure to prove himself a worthy heir of his father's legacy. Whichever of those two impulses drove him more, he overplayed his hand.

In his first year as duke (384 BCE) he launched a campaign to recover the city that had been lost due to the defection of a Tian prince in 405 BCE, but that gambit was defeated by the combined armies of Wei and Zhao. He endeavored several similar military campaigns over the course of his reign, with consistently bad results.[15] In this way he steadily depleted his political capital so as to make himself vulnerable to the machinations of his half-brother, Tian Wu.

Since Tian Wu was careful to expunge the record of his brother's reign from the chronicles of Qi, we do not know the exact circumstances that initiated his coup. In 379 BCE, Lü Dai, the last exiled duke of the old ruling clan, died without leaving an heir, thus ending that ancient lineage.[16] The death of Lü Dai should have made the climate in Linzi more stable and secure. Without any scion of the Lü clan to rally behind, enemies of Tian rule would face difficulty coordinating their opposition. But Tian Yan had obviously lost the confidence of the ruling oligarchy. His wars were expensive and unprofitable. In the political culture of Linzi, where elites expected that compliance with the throne would come with a share in the profits of rule, Tian Yan was too disappointing.

In 375 BCE, following the example of his father, the "Supreme Duke," Tian Wu killed his half-brother and took the throne. The coup was very violent. Tian Wu did not stop at eliminating Tian Yan, but made sure to kill his half-brother's infant son and Heir Apparent.[17] Tian Wu then became the first member of his family to be enthroned as "Duke of Qi" without any competing claimant from outside the Tian clan.

Though he was free of any challenge from the Lü ducal clan, Tian Wu came to the throne under a cloud of illegitimacy. Even in a state accustomed to ruthless politics, his ascent over the bodies of his half-brother and nephew, the latter a young child, was shockingly profane. As had happened after Tian He's coup of 406 BCE, neighboring states took advantage of the disorder inside Qi. The states of Wei, Zhao, Yan, Wey, and Lu all launched expeditions to punish Tian Wu as a usurper. For the first years of his reign Tian Wu fought defensive wars on all sides. Though he survived, he did so only at the cost of territory and resources.[18] The mood of the court was one of anxiety and insecurity.

Affairs reached a nadir in 364 BCE. In that year Tian Wu killed his father's primary wife, the mother of Tian Yan. This was almost certainly the violent end of yet another attempted palace coup.[19] The Dowager was most likely maneuvering behind the scenes to oust Tian Wu (perhaps in favor of one of Wu's surviving half-brothers). That he took the drastic step of killing her evinces the depth of his insecurity and the volatility of the political climate.

It was a dark moment. Older courtiers must have heaved deep sighs in private, expecting that the turbulence which had marked Tian rule for the whole of their lifetimes would continue indefinitely. But, perhaps driven by extremity to explore creative means, Tian Wu launched a political campaign in the wake of the Dowager's death that would not only turn the tide in his own reign, but lay a new foundation for his son and grandsons.

Like many rulers in history who have had trouble living down political transgressions, Tian Wu sought shelter in religion. He needed to protect himself from allegations that his succession to the throne was illegitimate, and he needed to whitewash his complicity in the death of his stepmother. Seeking a remedy to these woes, he turned toward the ancestral sacrifices to his own mother.

Tian Wu's mother was a secondary wife of his father, the "Supreme Duke." We do not know what part she played (if any) in the violent plots that brought her son to and kept him in power. The fact that she was a secondary wife may have contributed to Tian Wu's decision to kill the Dowager: being the son of a secondary wife would have weakened Tian Wu's claim to succeed his father as ruler.

On one level, the ancestral sacrifices to his own mother were a natural venue in which Tian Wu would seek rehabilitation. Only the mother of a ruler was accorded a place in the state ancestral temples, so underscoring the dignity of his mother's spirit was a way to broadcast the legitimacy of Tian Wu's own claim to the throne. But Tian Wu went further than simply exalting his mother. He innovated upon the traditions of the ancestral religion in serving his mother's spirit. These innovations were audacious and creative, and give us the first evidence of the ways in which Tian Wu and his successors redefined the state of Qi.

In 361 BCE (just over two years after his execution of his stepmother) Tian Wu held sacrifices to his mother in the capital.[20] These ceremonies would have been attended by the most powerful elites of Qi, including members of the Tian clan, its aristocratic allies, and their most prominent clients among the knights. Tian Wu reconfigured these ceremonies to make them more than just an austere religious occasion. They were, in effect, the first step in building a new political order.

First, Tian Wu collected bronze from his courtiers and vassals for use in forging the ritual vessels that would be used in perpetuity for his mother's cult. Such bronze vessels were equivalent to the crown jewels or sacred regalia (such as the "Stone of Scone") that traditionally symbolized and embodied the sovereignty of European monarchs from medieval times onward (see Fig. 10).

Fig. 10. Inscribed bronze vessel from the Western Zhou period (ca. 1045–771 BCE). Bronze vessels were essential ritual implements of the ancestral cult. Inscribing bronze vessels provided a means by which new relationships or agreements could be memorialized and maintained over generations. The bronze vessel pictured here commemorates the resolution of a land dispute between two of the regional states of the Zhou realm. Inscribed vessels were in frequent use throughout the Warring States, to the very end of the Warring States era. (Source: National Palace Museum.)

All high-ranking aristocrats of the Zhou realm had a set of bronze vessels. They were cast in the form of utensils for cooking and for the consumption of food and drink, but where ordinary versions of such implements were made of ceramic or wood, the sacred vessels used in preparing meals for the ancestral spirits were made of exquisitely crafted bronze, elaborately formed into evocative shapes and decorated with intricate geometric patterns covering virtually every inch of surface area. Such vessels were not merely prohibitively expensive, they represented an enormous investment of any state's total economic resources.[21]

By enlisting his vassals to provide the bronze with which his mother would be served, Tian Wu made them party to his rule. If, as enemies would have asserted, Tian Wu had been a usurper who murdered the rightful Dowager (his father's principal wife), then the sacrifices to Tian Wu's mother in the state temple would be sacrilege. By providing the bronze to make such sacrifices possible, the vassal lords thus committed themselves to the legitimacy of Tian Wu's ascension to the throne and (implicitly) the justness of the punishment of his stepmother.

The ingenuity of Tian Wu's maneuver was not confined to cleverly co-opting his courtiers, however. He did not strong-arm them into compliance without offering them anything in return. The bronze vessels that Tian Wu had cast were inscribed to mark the occasion, and the inscriptions would have been read aloud at the sacrificial rite. The inscriptions treat Tian Wu's courtiers as his peers: they are referred to as the "many marquises," and Tian Wu himself is referred to as "Marquis of Chen" (the extinct state from which Tian Wu's ancestors had migrated), rather than as the ruler of Qi.

In the context of the rite, Tian Wu and his courtiers thus became equals. All of them stood before the spirit of Tian Wu's mother and offered her food and drink to sustain her in the afterlife. In return, they begged her not to bless and shelter Tian Wu himself (as was traditional), but to "protect the state of Qi."

All of the individual elements of the ceremonies Tian Wu held for his mother in 361 BCE had precedent in the ancient practice of the ancestral cult. But taken altogether they made a bold and innovative statement. It was not unheard of, for example, to use bronze gifted by another aristocrat in the casting of vessels to serve one's own ancestors. Such a gift a formed a bond of kinship between two nobles: if you help me to feed my ancestors, we become "like family." But in Tian Wu's ceremony a family bond was not being formed. The courtiers who contributed the bronze are not named in the inscription: their personal relationship to Tian Wu is not what was at stake. *Everyone* in the ceremony, including the spirit of Tian Wu's mother herself, was being dedicated to the service *of the state of Qi*.

With these ceremonies, Tian Wu surrendered the proprietary claim of the Tian clan to the state of Qi. He ushered in a new era and a new cultural universe, in which Qi became an abstract and lofty ideal that transcended all the individuals and families which might be gathered in its service. This is what made Tian Wu and his courtiers truly equal: with respect to their relationship to the state of Qi, they were all equally close, equally distant.

That these changes were very deliberate is demonstrated by the fact that the principle on which they were based was ultimately summed up very succinctly by literati serving the Qi state: "The Altars of the Soil and Grain are closer than kin."[22] The Altars of the Soil and Grain were a fixture of the ancient state cult: they were used to serve the gods who held sway over the particular territory in which a state resided. By stating that these altars were "closer than kin," Qi literati declared that the state should be given even more reverence than family in all questions of value and duty.[23]

This was a radically novel idea in the fourth century BCE. In the traditional Zhou world, a state like Qi was the natural patrimony of the family whose ancestral temples were joined to its "Altars of the Soil and Grain," and an individual's honor was inseparable from the dense and complicated network of familial and personal obligations in which he or she was embedded. Every new crisis or dilemma forced a person to choose which of those many imperatives had first claim on their allegiance. One's duty to the state was always contingent upon one's personal relationship to the ruler, and one's relationship to the ruler was refracted through the varying degrees of kinship and intimacy created by heredity, marriage ties, and oaths of allegiance.

In the new world being invented at Tian Wu's court, the state was a common bequest held in trust for all its people by the ruling family, and *any* individual's loyalty to the state (from that of the highest-born courtier down to the lowliest commoner) superseded all others: to one's family, to one's parents, even to one's ruler. The common people and elite of Qi (up to and including the ruler himself) were being told that their moral path had been radically simplified. Come what may, they should live and die, first and foremost, in service to the state of Qi.

It can be difficult for us, looking back from the perspective of the twenty-first century CE, to appreciate just how revolutionary this new concept of state and society was in the early fourth century BCE. Abstract ideals that make claims on our loyalty are no novelty for us jaded postmoderns. People have been called upon to die for God or country for so long that the notion has become passé; the idea of asking people to "serve Qi" can seem unimaginative or even regressive.

But in the fourth century BCE the idea of a duty that did not entail a personal relationship to a particular individual (a kinsman, a friend, a parent, one's sworn lord) was so new as to be shocking. Why then would Tian Wu promote such notions? It is not difficult, if we think about the potential applications of these new ideas in the context of what had been happening in the state of Qi and the Zhou realm more generally, to see how they fostered new dynamism and political success for Tian Wu's court.

Firstly, the new ideology helped untangle some of the confusions of Tian clan oligarchy. If everyone, even members of the Tian clan themselves, were being measured by how well they served the state of Qi in the abstract, it was less difficult to explain why some clan scions were rewarded more richly than others, and why Tian clan members would have to share the generosity of the throne with those outside the clan. If as the ruler two people's loyalty is to me personally, and I reward one of them more richly than the other, they will both assume that my affections and personal loyalties guided my decision. This can easily cause resentment, especially if the person given the "short straw" feels he or she is more intimate with me (through kinship or personal history). If, however, all of us are being judged by how we serve a cause that stands outside our group, I can claim that I was forced to decide as I did, despite what my personal feelings might have been. Meritocracy was a trend that was transforming the entire Zhou world. The new ideology gave the Qi court leverage to accelerate and stabilize its implementation of meritocratic policies.

Beyond this, making the basis of all political allegiance less personal facilitated the process of making political organization less personal. Moving people into and out of offices became easier to explain: the office itself was not a personal prerogative, but existed to serve the state of Qi. If it was best for the state of Qi that Official A be replaced with Official B, who could question the legitimacy of that policy? The same principle applied in the case of territories that had been the hereditary possession of a particular family for several generations. If it served the interests of Qi for such a fief to be converted into a district overseen by a centrally appointed magistrate, that was the correct choice. The scions of the displaced family (and their ancestral spirits) had nothing to fear from such a change. If they had talents with which they could serve Qi, the coffers of the state would provide for them as amply as had been the case before (or more so).

Finally, the new ideology gave the Qi court important new ways to communicate with and engage the rapidly expanding and evolving literati society of the larger Zhou world. Tian Wu and his son Tian Yinqi clearly took the reform program of Marquis Wen of Wei (i.e. Wei Si) as a model and understood that one of the key elements of Marquis Wen's success was his ability to recruit literati knights from beyond the state of Wei. As "wanderers" like Wu Qi proliferated along the pathways that linked the competing states of the Zhou world, and as the changing nature of government made literate personnel ever more essential, the fitness and even survival of the state increasingly hinged on the ability to recruit such personnel from abroad (and retain literati at home).

But, as noted above, the Tian rulers of Qi were faced with severe challenges in emulating Marquis Wen's success. Marquis Wen had not needed to reinvent the state of Wei as an abstract ideal, because he was able to import an abstract ideal that could (at least in theory) serve as the lynchpin of meritocratic policies: the Way as taught by Confucius. By inviting Zixia to be his teacher and employing several of Zixia's disciples in positions of high authority, Marquis Wen fostered the idea that the court of Wei had a higher mission, the fulfillment of "the Way" as Confucius had understood it, that others, both inside the state of Wei and from without, could join, and in so doing give scope to talents that had as yet gone unrecognized.

Tian Wu could not easily emulate Marquis Wen in this regard. Any attempt Tian Wu made to "partner" with one of the existing fellowships of literati "Masters and disciples" was virtually doomed to fail. The latter-day disciples of Confucius still considered the state of Lu a kind of ideological "home," and the constant geopolitical rivalry between neighboring Qi and Lu made any cooperation between the Qi court and the Confucian fellowship difficult to achieve.[24]

Beyond this, the irreducibly transactional nature of Tian power was almost impossible to reconcile to the teachings of Confucius's Way. Confucius taught that knights should not serve rulers in the expectation of emolument, but out of a sense of duty to the Way. Conversely, rulers should not "pay" knights for their services, but should give knights the material support to which they were ritually entitled (which was itself dictated by the Way).[25] This was a very inspirational ideal in the abstract (and served well to bolster the dignity of knights, who were increasingly held in disdain by the ever-wealthier and more powerful rulers of expanding states), but unworkable even as a fiction in the political life of the Qi court. The Tian clan had been paying for people's loyalty for nine generations by the time that Tian Wu took the throne. It was far too late for them to pretend that they were doing anything else.

The tenets of Mo Di's Way (discussed in Chapter 4) were, on first consideration, more amenable to the political economy of Qi as the Tian rulers had established it. The Mohists taught that the rightness of society could be measured in the quantity of material benefit (food, clothing, and shelter) it produced for its people, and that everyone was equally motivated by the desire for profit and the fear of loss, pain, or death. Mo Di thus taught that government servants would have to be well remunerated for good work to harness their natural motivations for the greater good.

Though this teaching lined up well with established practice in Qi, other aspects of the Mohist Way were incompatible with the norms of Qi political life. The Mohists insisted on a policy of "universal love": the impartial dispensation of favor to individuals purely on the basis of need or merit, without any consideration for ties of kinship or intimacy.[26] This could never be squared with the privileged position that the Tian clan would continue to hold in Qi, or the preference (however slight) that Tian clan members would necessarily receive in the disbursement of emoluments. "Universal love" likewise required that officials show no partiality for their own state over others, which undermined efforts to elevate "Qi" as a common focus of loyalty within the Tian realm. Moreover, the Mohists had organized themselves into a corporate paramilitary body, and insisted that members of the fellowship tithe from their official salaries into the coffers controlled by the Masters and Grand Master who led the order. A partnership with the Mohist fellowship thus meant taking on extra mouths to feed and sharing power with forces whose interests could not always be guaranteed to align with those of the ruling clan.

Tian Wu (or some clever courtiers to whom he delegated the problem, and whose names, for reasons that will be suggested below, are now lost to us) realized that in order to have the same kind of success that Marquis Wen had cultivated in recruiting literati in Wei, the court of Linzi would need to develop a "third way" (or Way), an alternative set of teachings that would enable literate knights serving Qi to explain their place in the world and their role in the politics of Zhou society. The nucleus of this new Way can be seen in the principle underpinning the sacrifices to Tian Wu's mother: "the Altars of the Soil and Grain are closer than kin." As a vehicle for these new teachings, Tian Wu and his ministers created new Masters ("new" in the sense of their being figures who had not previously been considered "Masters," though they were generally based on historical personages). Of these, the most prominent was Master Guan.[27]

Master Guan was built on the historical memory of Guan Zhong (d. 645 BCE), a famed minister of the state of Qi during the reign of the overthrown Lü dukes. As prime minister, Guan Zhong had been the architect of the rise of the first Duke Huan (r. 685–643 BCE), who was universally acknowledged as the greatest former ruler of Qi. The historical Guan Zhong devised the title of "Lord Protector" and persuaded the Zhou king to grant the title to Duke Huan of Qi, making him a proxy leader among the regional lords. In his capacity as "Lord Protector" (the vassal deputized by the Zhou king to lead the combined armies of the regional states in defense of the realm), Duke Huan had curbed the aggression of nomadic peoples beyond the frontiers of Zhou rule and had re-established regional states that had been wiped out by "barbarian" invasions. Duke Huan's reign, at least while Guan Zhong was alive to guide him, was generally remembered as a period of relative peace and prosperity, not only for Qi but for the whole Zhou realm.[28]

During Tian Wu's reign teachings began circulating in the name of Guan Zhong, now given the title of "Master Guan." Many of these teachings survive in a large compendium known eponymously as the *Guanzi*, or *Master Guan* (the suffix "zi" appended to a teacher's surname is a shortening of the title "*fuzi*," or "Master"). The *Guanzi* as it is organized today probably did not exist during the Warring States; it was compiled by scholars who collected, transcribed, and redacted all of the versions of "Master Guan's" teachings that were extant during the Former Han dynasty (203 BCE–9 CE). But though the material in the *Guanzi* may have circulated in different forms (written and oral) than we encounter it in the transmitted Han compendium, most of what we find in the *Guanzi* was produced in Linzi by literati in the service (or at least living under the patronage) of the Tian rulers of Qi.[29]

The creation and promotion of Master Guan was a very creative and audacious campaign of state propaganda. Master Guan was most likely the first (though definitely not the last) Master of his kind. In our present time the title "Master" conjures a stereotypical image in the public imagination, not just here in "the West," but in China as well. We are inclined to picture a Master seated among a circle of his disciples, imparting personal wisdom. But that was never the case with Master Guan, in either "reality" or theory. The historical figure of Guan Zhong certainly never gathered young men for instruction, and to the extent that he "taught" anything it was indirectly, in the context of his activities as a minister of state.

The figure of Master Guan the teacher was thus entirely an invention of Qi literati working in the fourth century BCE, almost three centuries after Guan

Zhong's death. In the hands of the literati who brought him to life, Master Guan became a potent symbol, a mythic persona who embodied the identity and mission of Qi, its rulers, and its officials. Like the partnership forged by Wei Si almost a century earlier with Zixia and the latter-day disciples of Confucius, the initial construction of Master Guan at the court of Tian Wu was an early instance of successful government "media manipulation." This latter case, however, arguably brought the art of state propaganda to a new and even higher level of sophistication.

What was so ingenious about the invention of Master Guan? The choice of Guan Zhong himself, though perhaps "pre-ordained" to an extent by the established fame of the historical man himself, was perfectly adapted to the needs of Tian Wu and his court. Guan Zhong had died almost a century before Confucius was born. His "teachings" could thus be presented to the world of Zhou-era literati as being "older" and therefore (in a world that revered tradition and ancestral authority) more authentic than those of Confucius himself.

The literati who composed Master Guan's teachings appropriated and utilized all of the terms and ideas that the latter-day disciples of Confucius and Mo Di had made common parlance. Master Guan taught about "the Way," "ritual," "humaneness," etc. Wherever Master Guan presented these ideas with a different slant or meaning than was given to them by the disciples of Confucius or Mo Di (as, we shall see, was often the case), the literati of Qi could claim that since Master Guan's teachings were older, his understanding of (for example) "the Way" was more original and correct.

Master Guan's place in the chronology of the Zhou realm did not only serve the purpose of legitimizing his teachings among literati. It also helped Tian Wu and his officials promote the new ideas embodied in the sacrifices to Tian Wu's mother. Master Guan, after all, had been the loyal minister of the *previous* ruling house of Qi, the Lü clan. By broadcasting that "we today" (the people of Tian Wu's time) were going to follow the teachings that once guided the Lü dukes who had been overthrown by the present ruling clan, Tian Wu's court underscored the idea that they were no longer calling upon officials and aristocrats to serve a particular dynasty or lord. The eminence and honor of the ruler or his family was not what mattered. What mattered was the prestige, power, and security of the state of Qi. Since Master Guan had served those ends, it did not matter that he had done so out of loyalty to a different ruling clan.

All of these ideas were made explicit in the teachings attributed to Master Guan himself. These teachings were added to and elaborated upon for more than a century and a half. It is thus very difficult to date the material that is collected in the transmitted text of the *Guanzi*. The first chapter of the *Guanzi*, "Shepherding the People," however, is (on stylistic and linguistic criteria) likely to have been among the oldest, and gives us a sense of the form the teachings of Master Guan would have taken during Tian Wu's reign.[30]

"Shepherding the People" begins with a long poem, the "Hymn to the State," which systematically lays out the rationale for raising the state (in this particular case the state of Qi) to be an ultimate concern and a total focus of loyalty. For example, the hymn declares that "when the state has an abundance of wealth, people will come from afar" and also that "the essential component in reducing punishments is to prohibit luxury and artfulness."[31] This might seem like a paradox: why would people be attracted to a wealthy state that frowns on luxury? But the coherent logic becomes apparent if one thinks about "Shepherding the People" as a message being broadcast by Tian Wu and his court: "We understand that to be strong, a state has to have wealth to share, and to ensure that the state has wealth to share we the ruler, his courtiers, and officials cannot spend too much on *ourselves*." All will be well if the state is well, and in order for the state to be well, all of us have to begin rethinking our interests in terms of how they align with the welfare of the state.

It was a new and versatile message, one that could be understood in terms familiar to the latter-day disciples of Confucius and Mo Di, but which would be distinct and amenable to the institutional culture of Qi. The "Hymn of the State," for example, declares that "the standard for preserving the state is the promotion of the four cardinal values" (ritual, rightness, integrity, a sense of shame).[32] Thus Master Guan, in common with Confucius and Mo Di, drew an intimate connection between the state and morality. But in the teaching of Master Guan the relationship between the moral "Way" and "the state" proposed by both Confucius and Mo Di is reversed. Though Confucius and Mo Di disagreed with one another as to how "the Way" could be defined, they both agreed that the state existed to fulfill the moral Way. The "Hymn of the State" turns this model on its head. For Master Guan, the moral Way (the "four cardinal values") exists in order to protect and preserve the state.

These ideas were given concrete form in the construction of Master Guan's legend. The *Guanzi* records that Master Guan did not begin his political career in the service of Duke Huan, but was originally in the retinue of Duke Huan's older brother. When their father died, the two brothers warred over the throne, and Master Guan fought tenaciously for his sworn lord, going as far as to shoot an arrow at Duke Huan which would have killed him but for the fact that it lodged in the heavy buckle of the duke's belt.[33]

When the duke, on taking the throne after the death of his brother, was advised to employ Master Guan as his prime minister, he was shocked. How could such a man as Master Guan be credible? Why had he not died along with the duke's brother, the lord that he served (as conventional notions of aristocratic honor required)? How could Master Guan ever expect to enjoy the trust of the duke himself, the man he had tried to kill with an arrow?

The basic principle was explained to the duke: Master Guan had acted as he did on behalf of the state of Qi. He had tried his best to kill Duke Huan because Qi needed one ruler and could not sustain two claimants to the throne. When the duke's brother had died, Master Guan remained alive because he knew the state of Qi would need his talents, and that concern overrode any personal loyalty he owed to the duke's brother.[34]

Master Guan's legend embodied the principles that "the Way" existed to support the state and that "the Altars of the Soil and Grain are closer than kin." Confucius and Mo Di, for example, would both have insisted that to kill one brother on behalf of another was a violation of "the Way." However, according to the teachings of Master Guan, the needs of the Altars of the Soil and Grain supersede the bonds of kinship, thus Master Guan had displayed wisdom and virtue in shooting Duke Huan at the order of the duke's brother. It could not have been lost on Tian Wu and his officials, moreover, that much of the behavior displayed by Master Guan in such stories mapped out well onto the record of past Tian clan leaders. Generations of Tian clan patriarchs, after all, had killed one ruler in favor of another, sometimes (like Tian Wu and his father) going as far as to kill their own kinsmen. The teachings and life of Master Guan thus provided a robust rationale to explain why these clan patriarchs had consistently been in the right: they had been acting in the interests of the state of Qi, according to which the Way (correctly understood, contra both Confucius and Mo Di) could be defined and understood.

We cannot know how much of the narrative recorded in the *Guanzi*, if any of it, corresponds to the facts of the historical Guan Zhong's life. There are no contemporary records from the seventh century BCE to corroborate or deny much of the account of in that text. It is certain, however, that the life of "Master Guan" as the *Guanzi* presents it served as a powerful "charter myth" for the new political order being forged in Qi by Tian Wu and his successors.

As noted above, one key respect in which Master Guan differed from the Masters that had preceded his appearance is in his lack of disciples. In the stories of his life preserved in the *Guanzi*, Master Guan has only one "student," Duke Huan, and Guan's role as "teacher" is inseparable from his role as prime minister. This was deliberate on the part of the literati who formulated Master Guan's teachings. Tian Wu and his officials were not inclined to tolerate the existence of a fellowship of knights, like those of the latter-day disciples of Confucius and Mo Di, outside of the court. As an official of Qi, a knight could be celebrated as an individual, but as a thinker or theorist he was expected to remain anonymous, and to present his ideas to the broader literati community under the rubric of a "culture hero" like Master Guan.

This was modeled for literati in Qi in the form of another "new" Master, Master Yan. Master Yan, like Master Guan, was based on a historical figure: Yan Ying (d. 500 BCE), an aristocrat who had served loyally and effectively as minister in the court of three dukes of the Lü clan.[35] His putative teachings were compiled by imperial officials during the Han dynasty in a compendium known as the *Yanzi chunqiu*, the *Annals of Master Yan*.

Yan Ying was useful for the purposes of the Tian rulers because he had been an older contemporary of Confucius.[36] It was thus possible (where it was not in the case of Master Guan) to craft stories in which Master Yan interacted with Confucius and Confucius's disciples. Unsurprisingly, in all such stories Master Yan is depicted as being Confucius's superior in wisdom and skill.

In one anecdote, for example, Master Yan goes on embassy to the court of Lu. Curious to know about Master Yan's character, Confucius sends two of his disciples to see Master Yan's first audience with the Duke of Lu and report back. On returning from the court, the disciples report that Master Yan seems totally ignorant of ritual. He moved too fast and knelt when he was supposed to stand.

Soon after hearing his disciples' report, Confucius receives a visit from Master Yan and confronts Master Yan with the mistakes made at the audience with the Duke of Lu. Master Yan explains that the mistakes were not his, but the duke's. The duke hurried forward and held the gift that he presented to Master Yan too low, thus Master Yan had to mirror the duke's movements rather than make the duke look like a fool.

Confucius is forced to apologize to Master Yan, and the reader takes away a clear message: the kinds of fellowships that Confucius and his disciples formed do the world very little good. Yes, Confucius's disciples knew ritual well. But they had not taught what they knew to the Duke of Lu, and were so focused on their own learning (and that of other literati like Master Yan) that they did not realize the depth of their own ruler's ignorance. This was obviously a recipe for

THE ALTARS OF THE SOIL AND GRAIN ARE CLOSER THAN KIN 169

disaster. Better to do one's learning and teaching in the employ of the court, where it will have some practical effect.[37]

The success of Tian Wu's cultural program can be measured in the stability that he brought to the Qi court. Tian Wu ruled for 18 years, 10 years longer than his predecessor and 12 years longer than his uncle, the "Mournful Viscount" who had been slain by Tian Wu's father.[38] When Tian Wu died, he was succeeded peacefully by his own son Tian Yinqi (r. 356–320 BCE), who would go on to reign for an incredible 37 years.[39] Tian Yinqi passed on his throne peacefully to Tian Wu's grandson, who succeeded in passing it peacefully to Tian Wu's great-grandson. Tian Wu's reign thus initiated a period of more than 70 years of stability, prosperity, and increasing power for the state of Qi.

Tian Yinqi, on taking the throne in 356 BCE, continued the cultural program of his father. He installed Tian Wu in the ancestral state temple under the posthumous title "Duke Huan," the same posthumous title as the duke who had ruled during the life of Master Guan and had served as the first "Lord Protector." The message this broadcast to the elites and people of Qi was clear: "My father brought back the glory days of Duke Huan. We are now ready to embark on a second 'Golden Age' of Qi—never mind that the ruling family is no longer the same."

Tian Yinqi continued and expanded the religious reforms initiated by Tian Wu. In sacrificing to the spirit of Tian Wu, Tian Yinqi followed the pattern that Tian Wu had established in the sacrifices to Tian Yinqi's grandmother. Tian Yinqi collected bronze from courtiers and officials to cast the vessels used to sacrifice to Tian Wu, and collectively led the Qi court in pleading with the spirit of Tian Wu to "protect the state of Qi." The inscription that records these prayers declares Tian Yinqi's resolve to continue the legacy of the Lords Protector, thus broadcasting Tian Yinqi's commitment to the teachings of Master Guan.[40]

In his 37 years in power Tian Yinqi oversaw a robust reform of the government and society of Qi. Many of these reforms were patterned on the example of Marquis Wen of Wei. For example, where Marquis Wen had relied on the talents of his prime minister Li Kui, Tian Yinqi invested enormous trust in his prime minister Zou Ji.[41]

The appointment of Zou Ji itself was a sign of the changes that were transpiring in Qi. Zou was a figure whose status mirrored that of Zai Wo, whose appointment to the same office in 481 BCE (as described in Chapter 1) had brought on rebellion and personal ruin. The rise of Zou Ji to become Prime

Minister of Qi was thus a measure of just how far the efforts to reorganize Qi along meritocratic and bureaucratic lines had succeeded by the reign of Tian Yinqi.

Many stories survive about the interactions between Tian Yinqi and his ministers and courtiers, far exceeding the anecdotes we have about any of the Tian clan leaders who preceded him (including his own father, Tian Wu). This is a sign of another way in which Tian Yinqi emulated Marquis Wen. He enlisted the literati at his court to record and circulate accounts of his reign. In this way he cultivated a reputation for wisdom and integrity, in hopes of recruiting personnel and persuading the literati officials of other states that he (and his court) should be respected. These stories also served to broadcast the progressively well-articulated ideology of Tian rule, and the policies that Tian Yinqi's court adopted on its basis.

For example, one of the most famous stories of Tian Yinqi's reign is his first encounter with Zou Ji. In one version of this story, Zou Ji brought a zither to his first audience with Tian Yinqi and played it for the ruler. Tian Yinqi enjoyed the performance, and when it was over Zou Ji explained that the art of the zither was the model for the art of government. Tian Yinqi was intrigued, and spent the next three days listening to Zou Ji's explanations about what the zither could teach about government and the affairs of Lords Protector and kings. After the three days had passed, he appointed Zou Ji as prime minister.[42]

The story was crafted to send several messages to the literati of Tian Yinqi's time. The first was that Tian Yinqi was a ruler who was open-minded and receptive to the ways that literati thought. He would not discount a man for doing something unusual like playing a zither at a court audience, and was ready to give three days of his time to someone who had interesting and worthwhile things to say. Moreover, Tian Yinqi was a good judge of talent, both artistic and political. Finally, the anecdote broadcast Qi's embrace and promotion of the "third Way" articulated in the teachings of Master Guan and Master Yan. Zou Ji's use of the zither demonstrated that he was not a follower of Mo Di (whose teachings declared that "making music is wrong!"), but his celebration of the "Lords Protector" likewise showed that he was not among the puritanical followers of Confucius, who viewed the Lords Protector as violent coercers deficient by the standards of the true Way. The example of Zou Ji thus showed that in Qi, knights would find a court that welcomed and appreciated literati, but that was not dogmatically aligned with either the Confucians or Mohists, and thus would accept all comers, as long as they were loyal to Qi first and foremost.

Another anecdote, which closely models themes in the stories about Marquis Wen of Wei and his famed minister, Ximen Bao (recounted in Chapter 5), illustrates the kind of meritocratic and bureaucratic reforms that the Qi court committed to under Tian Yinqi's rule. In 348 BCE Tian Yinqi summoned two of his regional magistrates to court, the first of whom had been criticized severely by the officials at court, the second of whom had been praised lavishly by courtiers.

In the first interview, Tian Yinqi noted that though he had persistently heard the magistrate disparaged, an envoy sent by Tian Yinqi to inspect the district had found that fields had been cleared, the people were prospering, and the magistrate's subordinates were all diligent in their work. Tian Yinqi concluded from this report that the magistrate had used the revenue from the district to improve conditions there rather than buying the favor of the courtiers in the capital. Tian Yinqi rewarded the magistrate with the income from 10,000 households.

In his interview with the second magistrate Tian Yinqi declared that though the man had been widely praised, an envoy sent to his district had found fields left wild and the people impoverished. Moreover, the magistrate had failed to rally the people of his district to defend against an incursion from Zhao and had lost territory to the state of Wey. Tian Yinqi inferred that the magistrate had used the revenue he collected to bribe officials at the capital rather than attending to the needs of his own district. He had the magistrate boiled alive, along with the courtiers who had praised him.[43]

This anecdote demonstrated that Tian Yinqi was committed to the same kinds of bureaucratic and meritocratic reforms that had animated the career of Marquis Wen of Wei. It deliberately parallels the story about Marquis Wen's first and second interview with Ximen Bao (in which Ximen Bao demonstrated for Marquis Wen the different reports he would receive when a magistrate serves the people of his district rather than the powerful officials at the capital—see Chapter 5). But the differences between the story about Tian Yinqi and that about Marquis Wen of Wei are more than merely literary. They convey a concrete message.

The fate of the two magistrates models for the literati of Tian Yinqi's time that he would apply the most current statecraft theory of his day. During Tian Yinqi's reign a famous prime minister of the state of Han, Shen Buhai (d. 337 BCE), had formulated and promoted a doctrine of "forms and names" (*xing-ming*): the principle that a government should always collect empirical data about actual performance (the "form") to confirm that each official was fulfilling the duties of his office (the "name"). This information would then be used to dispense rewards and punishments. Such sanctions had to be both certain and weighty, in order to foster discipline and promote efficiency.[44] The story about Tian Yinqi and the two magistrates broadcast that his court had absorbed this lesson and would carry it out in policy. An ancillary message was that the court at Linzi was open to good ideas no matter where they came from (in this case, from the Prime Minister of Han), as long as they could be used to promote and defend the state of Qi.

His father, Tian Wu, had successfully set Qi on a new course, but Tian Yinqi deserves credit for following through on his father's policies and making the state a leading power. Ironically, among the clearest evidence of this success can be found in a policy that was forced upon Tian Yinqi as a compromise. As noted above, the teachings of Master Guan and Master Yan show that the rulers of Qi were at best ambivalent about supporting the fellowships of "Masters and disciples" modeled on the groups which had formed around Confucius and Mo Di. Tian Yinqi and his officials would have preferred that literati only compose and disseminate doctrine under the imprimatur of the "Masters" sanctioned by the state (in other words, by contributing to the ever-growing body of teachings attributed to Master Guan, Master Yan, and other culture heroes of the state of Qi), leaving their own identities anonymous. This, however, was an increasingly unworkable ideal in the social climate of the fourth century BCE.

The basic problem pressuring Tian Yinqi to compromise was the deepening social dilemma of the knights. Not all knights were literate, and not all who were literate became sufficiently learned to navigate the world of the Masters and their disciples. But as the number of aristocratic families who possessed titles and temples of their own steadily decreased, more and more noble scions needed a way to distinguish themselves in order to retain purchase, however tenuous, in the ruling oligarchy. Meritocratic reforms like those pursued by Marquis Wen in Wei and Tian Yinqi in Qi gave knights ever-increasingly powerful incentives to become deeply learned in courtly ritual, literary composition, and statecraft theory, so as to earn a spot as one of the new appointive officials who manned the bureaucracies of emergent mega-states.

But at the same time that knights found opportunity as literati in the courts of progressive rulers, they encountered a social climate in which elevated birth was still the supreme mark of honor and respect. Fewer and fewer knights could substantiate their claims of noble birth, and the disparity of wealth and power between rulers, their close kin, and the expanding sea of knights grew ever wider. As this process continued, the kinds of status pressures that had driven wanderers like Yan Sui, Nie Zheng, and Wu Qi into self-imposed exile (as described in the previous chapter) grew progressively more intense. For knights, fighting to defend their dignity against the bigotry and (sometimes lethal) scorn of titled aristocrats was a matter of survival.

These pressures made literati gravitate in ever larger numbers into the expanding fellowships of Masters and their disciples. Such fellowships created an alternate universe of status. At court, knights had no control over their social profile. If the ruler favored them they could win respect, but when that favor was withdrawn the respect that came with it evaporated. Within the Master-disciple fellowship, by contrast, knights themselves decided who was "high" and who was "low." Disciples revered their Master not because of his parentage but because of the learning that they recognized in him, and they rose or fell in one another's esteem on the strength of their own efforts and according to criteria they had a hand in creating (or at least enforcing).

It was a world over which titled aristocrats, even rulers, had no control, and it armed literati with tools to demand dignity and fair treatment. All Masters, even those who disagreed with one another, claimed to possess and serve "the Way," and because the Way was, according to the Masters, what gave meaning and function to everything else (including the titles of which rulers and their kin were so proud), Masters and the disciples they taught were entitled to stand alongside highborn courtiers in the palaces and ancestral temples of the powerful. Word of a slight by a ruler against a widely respected Master would spread far and wide, and would make other literate knights reticent to answer calls of recruitment ("If the ruler treats even a Master that way, what kind of treatment can I expect?"). In this way, the collective community of Masters and disciples served as a kind of sprawling, fractious "trade union" for literati.

The kind of dilemma this created for an ambitious ruler like Tian Yinqi is well illustrated by many anecdotes that depict the relationship between rulers and literati of the fourth century BCE. Some of the best examples of these undoubtedly concern Chunyu Kun (ca. 385–ca. 305 BCE), a native of Qi and a Master who became such a celebrity that he received two biographical notices in the *Records of the Historian*, the long historical compendium that provides much of our information about the Warring States.[45] Chunyu Kun was one of the most colorful characters of the Qi court during Tian Yinqi's reign. His fame as a gadfly, a humorist, and spinner of riddles spread throughout the Zhou realm, as evidenced by the dozens of stories about his antics which survive to this day.

Chunyu Kun was a kind of "poster child" for the Masters and what their prestige meant to literati knights. His clan name suggests that he was from an old family, but his household had obviously fallen on hard times. His second biography in the *Records of the Historian* describes him first as a "useless son-in-law," a man so poor he was forced to move into the lodging of his wife's family (a great disgrace in the patriarchal society of the Zhou era). Beyond this, he was exceedingly short, "not fully five feet three inches tall."[46] Both of these traits would have made him a very vulgar character among Zhou-era aristocrats, who were expected to be wealthy and well formed ("fit for battle," never mind that progressively more of the fighting was being done by common recruits). The fact that Chunyu Kun was celebrated as such a lofty figure among literati when he was such an object of scorn among the nobility demonstrated for the world that Masters and their disciples were operating according to their own rules and in alignment with their own priorities.

One of the most characteristic stories about Chunyu Kun concerns a trip that he made to neighboring Wei. One of the courtiers in Wei was reportedly a great admirer of Chunyu Kun's and, claiming that Chunyu Kun's wisdom exceeded even that of Master Guan and Master Yan, recommended him to Wei's powerful and driven ruler, Wei Ying (whom we will discuss at great length in Chapter 9). On the strength of this recommendation Wei Ying granted Chunyu Kun two private audiences, barring all others from the chamber as ruler and Master sat in conference. Despite being treated with such high regard, Chunyu Kun never spoke a word during his private time with Wei Ying. In frustration Wei Ying queried the official who had recommended Chunyu Kun about this strange behavior, who in turn put the question to Chunyu Kun.

Chunyu Kun explained that he had not spoken with Wei's ruler during their first audience because he could see that Wei Ying's mind was on the hunt, and that he had remained silent during the second audience because he could see that his mind was on music and song. When this was reported to Wei Ying, the ruler was amazed. He remembered clearly that he had been presented a hunting stallion before the first audience and a singer before the second. Though outwardly he had made a great show of giving Chunyu Kun his full attention, inwardly his mind had been on other pursuits.

Chunyu Kun's third audience with Wei's ruler lasted for three days without interruption, in which ruler and Master talked at great length. At the end of that time Wei Ying wanted to employ Chunyu Kun as a court minister, but the

Master refused. Wei Ying thus sent him off with gifts of silk, jade, and 100 catties (*jin*, about 880 ounces) of gold.⁴⁷

This story would have communicated a great deal to the literati of the time. Though the account was most likely recorded and disseminated by the court, it portrays Chunyu Kun as a Master in the terms of literati themselves: Chunyu Kun can see what is hidden to others, through reading subtle clues that only a Master can understand. The fact that the ruler of Wei was ready to confirm Chunyu Kun's superior wisdom, even at the cost of embarrassing himself, showed that he respected a Master's natural authority. The fact that he rewarded Chunyu Kun so richly even though Chuny Kun refused an offer of official position showed that the court of Wei understood the value of literati *even if they do not serve in government*. This was a concession to the world view of a Master like Confucius: learning entitles a person to support as much as (or more than) elevated parentage.

Finally, the ruler of Wei displayed humility in his encounter with Chunyu Kun that would have been gratifying to any knights, literati or not. For a highborn Zhou aristocrat to think about hunting or music was wholly commonplace, only to be expected. The fact that Wei Ying was ready to apologize for such natural aristocratic behavior to someone as lowly as Chunyu Kun broadcast the message that rulers must be ready to meet all knights on their own terms.

In a world in which literati jealously guarded the few remaining privileges of their rank and station, rulers had no choice but to indulge Masters such as Chunyu Kun if they wanted their courts to remain at all competitive in the market to recruit literate personnel. This was a problem, moreover, which was too big to handle with a public relations campaign alone. By the middle of the fourth century BCE all of the regional courts of the Zhou realm were competing intensely to create an atmosphere and generate institutions that would attract and retain literati. This imperative ultimately motivated the Qi court to initiate one of its most celebrated and distinctive policies: the founding of the patronage community of Jixia. We do not know the exact year in which Jixia was founded, but by the end of the fourth century BCE, Jixia had become one of the most vibrant intellectual centers of the Warring States, indeed in the history of all of East Asia.⁴⁸

One of the gates of the capital city of Linzi was labeled the "Ji Gate" (the Gate of the Altar of the Grain), for its proximity to the altar after which it was named. Beginning in Tian Yinqi's reign a set of residences were set aside within the city walls in the proximity of the Ji Gate. These residences were given to select

Masters, along with a noble rank among the "grandees" of Qi and a large stipend sufficient to support a retinue of as many as 100 disciples. None of the Masters or their disciples held formal posts in the government of Qi, but were at leisure to teach and study as the "guests" of the Qi ruler and his court.[49]

The Jixia Masters were not chosen for their allegiance to a particular doctrine, only on the basis of their broad reputation for wisdom and learning. Many of the Masters who resided together at Jixia vehemently (and openly) disagreed with one another. The Masters were free to teach their disciples and interact with one another as they saw fit, and were under no obligation to provide regular service to the ruler or the state. The one expectation placed upon them was that they would gather for a yearly sacrifice at the Altar of the Grain to give thanks for the patronage that they enjoyed from the ruler and people of Qi. This was the implication of the name "Jixia," which translates literally as "Beneath the Altar of the Grain." In both geographic and existential terms, the Masters of Jixia lived "under" the Altar of the Grain of the state of Qi.

Jixia became famous throughout the Zhou realm and attracted some of the most influential Masters of the Warring States. It persisted in various forms for more than a century and a half, and was celebrated ever afterward as a golden moment in the long civilization of the empire. The famed scholar and historian of the Song dynasty (960–1279 CE) Sima Guang (1019–86 CE), for example, who found mostly cause for lament in the annals of the Warring States, wrote a long poem in praise of Jixia.[50]

For all its glory, Jixia was from the beginning a source of tension within the larger framework of Qi state and society. The Masters held raucous debates in which subversive and at times even profane ideas were given voice. The lavish patronage given to the Masters was a cause of resentment among the working officials of the Qi government. The relationship between the Jixia Masters themselves and the government personnel of Qi could be strained.

This last situation is illustrated by a story about Zou Ji and Chunyu Kun. Chunyu Kun was among Jixia's earliest and most famous Masters. When Zou Ji was appointed prime minister, Jixia was abuzz with expressions of amusement and contempt. Chunyu Kun led a delegation of seventy-two Jixia residents to have an audience with Zou Ji, intending to make him look foolish and drive him from office. Zou Ji greeted them courteously, Chunyu Kun assumed an arrogant and disrespectful air.

"What should be done about a coat made of fox fur patched with lambskin?" Chunyu Kun asked. It was one of his famous riddles. He was challenging Zou Ji to figure out what the "real" point of the question was.

"One should never let the unworthy mix with the worthy" (in other words, one should employ only worthy men at court), Zou Ji answered, unfazed.

"If the house is square but the lamp is circular, what should be done?" Chunyu Kun riddled again.

"One must be careful what guests one allows to stay" (in other words, one must be careful that only those loyal to Qi should be employed from outside the court), Zou Ji replied.

"If three men are tending a single sheep, and the sheep does not get to eat, even though the shepherds get no rest, what should be done?" Chunyu Kun queried a final time.

"The number of officials should be trimmed, so as not to disturb the people," Zou Ji answered.[51]

The game Chunyu Kun had been playing was as clever as it was insulting. His three questions all contained veiled criticisms of Zou Ji himself: he was unworthy, he was a suspicious interloper, and his salary was an unnecessary drain on state coffers. Chunyu Kun had planned to prove his point by posing these three criticisms in the form of riddles. When Zou Ji failed to guess at what the riddles meant, he would have proven that he was indeed unworthy of the great trust Tian Yinqi had invested in him. Zou Ji, however, passed the test (so the story records). Chunyu Kun and the other Jixia Masters were mollified and did not challenge Zou Ji again.

This kind of tension between the literati community and government officials should not be surprising. Or rather, what is surprising about this story is the degree to which the situation in fourth-century BCE Qi so closely paralleled conditions all over the world today. A day rarely passes in our present world in which the newspapers do not record some conflict between government and the intelligentsia. The way we see figures like Zou Ji and Chunyu Kun butting heads is not a sign that the court of Qi was dysfunctional, but that it was ahead of its time.

The conditions at Jixia are testimony to the success of the political program initiated by Tian Wu and continued by Tian Yinqi. Any liabilities that the Masters of Jixia foisted upon the court of Qi were more than outweighed by the advantages it garnered from fostering Jixia as an intellectual center. An increasingly bureaucratic government required a steady stream of literate personnel. Though the Masters and disciples at Jixia did not hold posts in the government of Qi, they provided a kind of "bullpen" of potential recruits. They would also have been available for occasional ad hoc commissions and informal terms of service. Chunyu Kun, for example, is said to have served as an emissary of the Qi court on several occasions.[52] Many of the writings of "Master Guan" and "Master Yan" may have been contributed by literati resident at Jixia, who could have served as a kind of "brain trust" available to be consulted on questions of theory.

Apart from the direct contributions of Jixia literati to state affairs, the ancillary benefits of Jixia were significant. At any given time, the Masters and disciples resident at Jixia typically numbered more than 1,000 people. This alone was a sign for the whole world to see of Qi's power and wealth: an early example of what modern political scientists call "soft power." Rulers of the time would have paused to wonder—if Qi could support that many idle literati, how many soldiers could they field? For those living outside of Qi, the reputation of Jixia was a constant reminder that Linzi was a capital where literate knights were taken seriously, which must have created a powerful siren call for many officials unhappy in their home court and wondering whether there was a better opportunity for employment out there somewhere.

When Tian Yinqi's father, Tian Wu, first took the throne, Qi had been embroiled in two years of defensive military engagements. After fending off those challenges, Tian Wu had largely refrained from military adventures for much of the rest of his reign, focusing on rebuilding the economy of Qi and strengthening its civil institutions. As the stories above demonstrate, Tian Yinqi continued to strengthen and reform the civil government of Qi when his turn came to rule.

But as Qi grew wealthier and its civil administration became more sophisticated and efficient, the military power of the state likewise grew, and its military policy became progressively more assertive and ambitious. This change was not merely quantitative. By the mid-fourth century BCE Qi not only had more men under arms but its military had been thoroughly reorganized and, most importantly, its military doctrine and culture had been completely transformed.

This transformation of both the material form and the conceptual understanding of military force was one of the many profoundly significant dimensions of the revolution of the Warring States. It fundamentally changed the nature of state and society throughout the Zhou world (and indeed, eventually, its impact spread throughout East Asia), thus its origins and scope cannot be confined to the state of Qi. In both subtle and overt ways this change was already long ongoing when Tian Yinqi came to throne in 356 BCE. We saw in Chapter 5, for example, that Wu Qi, in his service to the state of Wei, had pioneered a new style of command more suited to the armies of common conscript infantry that had evolved over the course of the fifth century BCE.

But much evidence shows that, in tandem with the intellectual edifice built around the "teachings of Master Guan and Master Yan" and the Jixia patronage community, the Qi court became an enthusiastic patron and driving engine of the larger process of military reform. Tian Yinqi, for example, issued an edict ordering the grandees at his court (perhaps the "grandees" of the Jixia patronage community, though this is not specified) to "find and arrange the military methods of the Marshals of Horse, and include those of Marshal Rangju among them. This [collection of teachings] was called *The Military Methods of Marshal Rangju*."[53] This is the only clear record that we have of any Warring States ruler ordering the creation of a "text," and it demonstrates how embedded Tian Yinqi's court had become in the ongoing discourse about military reform.

"Marshal of Horse" was an antiquated title that for many centuries had been dispensed to highborn courtiers, giving them general authority over military affairs and defense of the realm. Like most such "offices" its powers and duties were never formally regulated during the early centuries of the Zhou dynasty. The lore surrounding "Marshal Rangju" shows that the literary project initiated by Tian Yinqi was part of a move to establish new standards and regulations for military service and military organization, to shift from an old aristocratic understanding of military leadership to a new concept more aligned with changing times. Marshal Rangju was, in effect, a culture hero like Master Guan or Master Yan, around whom a set of doctrines and teachings were built to serve as the guidelines for new policies.

According to the *Records of the Historian* (the account of which was almost certainly based on records first generated in Qi during the Warring States), Marshal Rangju was an ancestor of the Tian rulers (his full name was Tian Rangju) who had served as Marshal of Horse during the reign of Duke Jing (r. 547–490 BCE), one of the last Lü dukes to reign independently of the control of the Tian clan. Tian Rangju was purportedly a lowborn member of the clan (i.e. a knight without title or land), but because of his great talent was recommended for the post of Marshal of Horse by the wise Master Yan at a moment of great crisis, when Qi was being invaded on two sides. Rangju accepted the title on the condition that he was given a deputy from among the titled nobility, explaining that the soldiers would not obey his authority unless they could see that even highborn aristocrats were subject to it.

Tian Rangju issued orders for the army to assemble at a specific time and sat in camp with a water clock to check that everyone reported to duty promptly. His highborn deputy was late and explained that he had been delayed because he was being ceremonially sent off by his friends and family at a feast. This kind of send-off was the natural prerogative of an aristocrat, and Rangju's deputy expected no trouble. He was shocked when Rangju, citing the military code, ordered that his deputy be seized and beheaded. The deputy sent a servant to plead for mercy from the duke, but the plea was denied. The deputy was killed, and Rangju, who now had the full obedience of his soldiers, went on to repel the invaders.[54]

These events almost certainly did not happen exactly as the *Records of the Historian* reports them, but their historical accuracy is less important than the message they were meant to convey to the people and leaders of Qi in the mid-fourth century BCE, a full century and a half after the purported life of Tian Rangju. The story depicts a world in which military service is not only no longer an aristocratic affair, but is becoming one in which an entirely different set of values than those revered by the aristocracy hold sway. For nobles, the privileges of birth are sacrosanct and always trump other obligations. If my rank entitles me to be ceremonially sent off by family and peers, everything else has to wait until that is done before I can be expected to do anything else.

The new state and society being envisioned in Qi (in which "the Altars of the Soil and Grain are closer than kin") was one in which the military was a new form of social organization, one which existed apart from and above the distinction between commoner and noble. The military existed to serve the state, thus the only "rank" that a man had while serving in the military was the one that placed him in the chain of command. Though Tian Rangju was only a knight and his deputy a grandee, and though that would ordinarily have meant that Rangju would be forced to defer to the privileges of his deputy, in the army Rangju's office as commander gave him the power of life and death over everyone below him, no matter where they stood relative to him on the social scale.

Like the other ideas expressed in the teachings promulgated at and by the Qi court, these new concepts of military organization may seem ordinary from our twenty-first-century perspective, but they were revolutionary in the context of the ancient world. Their implications, moreover, were not confined to the internal organization of the military and the social relationships of its personnel. Literati reformers in Qi and elsewhere were not only fighting to get rulers and highborn courtiers to think differently about what military service meant, but to change their basic understanding of why military power existed at all, and how it could be used.[55]

THE ALTARS OF THE SOIL AND GRAIN ARE CLOSER THAN KIN 181

These arguments can best be seen in one of the most famous sources produced during the Warring States, the *Sunzi bingfa*, or the *Military Methods of Master Sun* (often translated in English as *The Art of War by Master Sun*). The *Sunzi bingfa* purports to have been written by Sun Wu (fl. ca. 510 BCE), a native of Qi and older contemporary of Confucius (see Fig. 11). As described in Chapter 2, Sun Wu had served as military commander for King Helü of Wu and had overseen that ruler's spectacular victories over his enemies in Chu.

Most modern scholars would agree that the attribution of the *Sunzi bingfa* to Sun Wu was a rhetorical fiction. The text refers to conditions and technology (for example, the crossbow) that did not exist during the lifetime of Sun Wu. Moreover, the ideas of the *Sunzi bingfa* are perfectly congruent with the arguments expressed in the lore surrounding Marshal Rangju (Marshal Rangju's

Fig. 11. Master Sun, the putative author of the *Sunzi bingfa* (*The Art of War by Master Sun*) is revered throughout East Asia as an authority on military affairs and all aspects of strategy. This statue of him stands in modern-day Yurihama, Japan. In his right hand he is holding a scrolled bundle of bamboo strips, presumably containing his eponymous text. (Source: Wikimedia Commons.)

biography in the *Records of the Historian*, indeed, has the marshal himself make proclamations that closely parallel those of the *Sunzi bingfa*). The teachings of "Master Sun" were thus most likely a product of the same milieu as that which gave us the legend of Marshal Rangju: the state of Qi, during the fourth century BCE.[56]

This inference is corroborated by the fact that one of the most legendary commanders of Tian Yinqi's court, Commandant Sun Bin (about whom more will be said), is purported to have been a descendant of Sun Wu and to have authored his own collection of teachings, the *Sun Bin bingfa*. The *Sun Bin bingfa* was lost for many centuries, but a manuscript of the work was recovered from a tomb at Yinqueshan, a location near the ancient capital of Qi. Its contents express ideas that echo those in the more famous *Sunzi bingfa*.[57]

The *Sunzi bingfa* is admired by military leaders around the world today as a timeless guide to strategy and tactics, and is still studied in military academies of many nations by officers-in-training who plan to apply its principles to the modern battlefield. The fact that advice that was useful in the Zhou world can still be applied today is testimony to how rapidly the world was changing during the Warring States, and how sophisticated the combat technology and military organization of the fourth century BCE had become. But along with its timeless strategic and tactical wisdom, the teachings of Master Sun were so influential in their own time because they forcefully laid out arguments explaining to Zhou-era rulers and elites why they would have to fundamentally change their thinking about military power.[58]

What were these arguments? Firstly, Master Sun argued that rulers could no longer think of military operations as an affair of honor or a religious rite, as aristocrats had for many centuries. As Wu Qi had realized, the new military was now made up mostly of common infantrymen, for whom aristocratic honor was not an effective motivation.[59] More importantly, military competition was now happening on such a grand scale and with such high stakes that honor and the pleasure of the spirits could no longer be a factor in one's planning Combat plans had to be formulated and their results predicted on the basis of "force (*shi*)," a gauge of the raw combat power of contending opponents. Military outcomes had to be measured solely in terms of how they impacted the material power of the state. Fielding a huge army of conscript farmers did not require refinement or chivalry, but it did require tons of supplies and armaments, resources which began to be expended as soon as the troops left the barracks and which would be lost *whether any battles were won or not*. A campaign that resulted in the death of tens of thousands of the enemy and left the granaries of our own state empty was not, in fact, a victory, but a defeat, especially when one considered that even the enemy dead were lost as potential recruits to our army.[60]

In contemplating any use of the military, so argued Master Sun, a ruler should ask, "Will this make my state more powerful?" If the answer is "no," the ruler should refrain, no matter how angry he is about a perceived insult or how much of his personal honor he may feel is at stake.[61] Very often, when one decides how to use the military on the basis of what will make the state more powerful, the best use of the military is no use at all. Fighting, what aristocrats were disposed to view as their highest purpose in life, is the most inefficient use of the military, because it wastes resources on our end and destroys enemy resources that we might otherwise capture or exploit through trickery.[62]

If we absolutely have to fight, we should do so in the most cowardly and devious way possible. Any advantage that we can acquire through lies or cunning should be exploited. The best situation on the battlefield itself is one that requires no courage or skill whatsoever: the "attack by fire," in which we kill the enemy indiscriminately by lighting them on fire, but make sure that the wind is not blowing in our direction so that our soldiers are never in danger.[63] In this new world, none of the old aristocratic virtues of honor, strength, courage, skill-at-arms, or stylish bravado were useful in a military commander.

The *Sunzi*'s ideal commander approaches his task as an intellectual enterprise. He is the antithesis of the aristocratic commander of earlier eras. He makes no display of power or status. He keeps hidden away, denying enemy spies any knowledge of his movements, while he gathers information, makes liberal use of spies, and secures victory through careful analysis, timely planning, and shameless deception.[64] As the text itself advises: "Stay strictly to the upper hall of the temple in prosecuting the affair. When the enemy opens a breach, you must quickly enter it.... [B]e like a virgin girl at the outset..., be like a darting rabbit in the end. [In this way] the enemy will not be able to grasp you."[65]

The efficacy of this new military doctrine was tested in the third year of Tian Yinqi's reign. In 354 BCE Zhao once again sought to expand its territory at the expense of neighboring Wey, as it had in 383 BCE. Marquis Wu of Wei's successor, Wei Ying, followed the same policy as his father had 29 years before. He attacked Zhao to block its expansionist ambitions and laid siege to the Zhao capital of Handan. In dire straits, Zhao sent an emissary to Qi begging for assistance.

The chronicles contain many different versions of what happened next, thus it is difficult to ascertain with any certainty the exact historical facts. What is clear, however, is that Qi's response to the siege of Handan made a deep impression on observers throughout the Zhou world. In an era when military campaigns were virtually constant, it is significant that Qi's campaigns of 353 BCE should be so often referenced and depicted in ancient sources. In their tactics and strategy on this occasion, Qi leaders showed the rest of the Zhou world something new.

Debates were held at the Qi court about whether to answer Zhao's call for aid. Prime Minister Zou Ji argued that Qi should remain neutral, but arguments by other courtiers to the effect that Qi had too much to lose if Handan fell to Wei prevailed. An expeditionary force was raised.[66]

Tian Yinqi purportedly favored giving command of the campaign force to Sun Bin, the descendant of Master Sun Wu. Sun Bin had studied military arts with a mysterious teacher named the "Venerable of Ghost Gorge" (*Guigu*), during which time he had befriended a fellow disciple, Pang Juan. Pang Juan had taken up a position at the Wei court and had invited his former "brother disciple" to come to Wei, promising that his talents would be employed. Unfortunately, all of Pang Juan's overtures of "brotherly" good will were false. He was fearful of Sun Bin's genius and determined to eliminate him as a rival. He trumped up a false charge of treason against Sun Bin, who was punished with amputation of both his feet.

Sun Bin returned to his native state of Qi, where Pang Juan was confident that he could no longer pose a threat. According to the traditional ethos of the aristocracy, Sun Bin had been irredeemably disgraced. His mutilation, in the ethos of the Zhou nobility, made him less than human, not fit to mingle even among commoners, much less to engage in the austere rituals and protocols of the court aristocracy. But Tian Yinqi was aware of his reputation as a brilliant strategist and tactician, and as Qi prepared to undergo a major offensive campaign for the first time in decades, Tian Yinqi summoned Sun Bin to serve the state.

Sun Bin declined overall command of the expeditionary force, explaining that it was not appropriate for someone who was crippled to take the position of leading authority. Command was given to one of Tian Yinqi's kinsmen, Tian Ji, with Sun Bin serving as "Commandant" (*shuai*), or chief strategist. Sun Bin accompanied the army in a covered wagon where he analyzed intelligence that was brought to him, drew up plans, and issued directives.

Tian Ji proposed, following conventional military wisdom, that the Qi force should march directly to the suburbs of Handan and engage the army of Wei to lift the siege. Sun Bin disagreed. He argued that while the main force of Wei's army was invested at Handan, the Qi troops should strike out in the direction of Wei's capital, taking them unawares and ill-prepared. It was a strategy drawn directly from the teachings of Master Sun (as recorded in the *Sunzi bingfa*): rejecting traditional aristocratic notions of honor which demand that one's opponent should be engaged in a "fair fight," we should attack the enemy where they are weakly defended.[67]

On the campaign trail itself, Sun Bin engaged in a series of feints and deceptions aimed at misdirecting his old nemesis, Pang Juan. He sent his two worst subcommanders to attack a well-fortified town along Wei's frontier, knowing that both men would be killed. He dispatched a force of light chariots to rush in the direction of Daliang, the Wei capital, and divided the rest of his infantry forces into small contingents, to make his numbers look weaker than they actually were.

Believing that the Qi expeditionary force was being incompetently commanded and would be easy prey, Pang Juan broke off the siege of Handan, abandoned his heavy armaments and supplies, and force-marched his troops toward Daliang, expecting to make quick work of the ineptly led Qi army. This was exactly the move that Sun Bin had maneuvered him into making. Sun Bin quickly re-concentrated his forces and intercepted the exhausted Wei army at a place called Cassia Hill (Guiling). Wei's forces were routed, and the Wei commander Pang Juan himself was taken prisoner. In what was perhaps the most cunning stratagem of the campaign, Sun Bin did not kill his old fellow disciple once he had him in his power, but left him alive, his perspective now beclouded by humiliation and vengefulness, to fight another day.[68]

The battle of Cassia Hill was a major turning point in the strategic dynamic of the Warring States. It did not end the war that had begun in 354 BCE. Despite the loss of its commander, Wei continued to fight. It renewed the siege of Handan and captured the city. In 352 BCE Wei allied with Han, and together the two states defeated a combined army comprised of forces from Qi, Song, and Wey (which had been persuaded to ally with Qi by its victory at Cassia Hill). The threat that Chu would then enter the war finally brought hostilities to an end, and Handan was returned to Zhao only after it entered a formal peace covenant with Wei in 351 BCE.[69]

Though the larger war ended inconclusively, Qi's victory at the battle of Cassia Hill marked the state's re-emergence as a military power that could stand on a par with the state of Wei. It also showcased the new military doctrine that had been embraced at the Qi court, one which eschewed traditional considerations of aristocratic honor and was centered purely on the material interests of the state, embracing the use of spies, deception, and the craven exploitation of any and every "unfair" advantage in pursuit of victory. This new concept of military affairs quickly became hegemonic throughout the Warring States and would be the foundation of military doctrine through successive dynasties of the imperial era.

Though the campaigns of 354–351 BCE did not permanently change the strategic disposition of the Warring States, by the end of Tian Yinqi's reign the military might of Qi would reshape the power dynamics of the entire Zhou domain. To explore and understand the military achievements of Tian Yinqi's court and their impact on the larger history of the Warring States, however, we must venture beyond Qi, to the powerful states with which Tian Yinqi and his ministers had to contend. As the dust from the mid-century war settled, Qi was one of three states that stood on a par with one another as "superpowers" of the Warring States. Wei, the persistent strategic juggernaut, was the second.

The third state that could claim a place as a leading power of the latter half of the fourth century BCE was Qin, a relatively young state of dubious pedigree that had previously been overshadowed by its neighbors. During the reign of Marquis Wen of Wei, in the fifth century BCE, Qin had lost hundreds of square kilometers of territory to its eastern neighbor. In the fourth century BCE, however, the state of Qin embarked on a program of reform and rebuilding that quickly expanded its power and influence. Time would ultimately prove that the growing influence of Qin had few limits.

8

The West's Awake
The State of Qin, 385–338 BCE

Qin presents the modern historian with a mystery. In 221 BCE the armies of Qin would destroy the last of the great Warring States and found a united empire. As best we can tell, by creating the unified empire, the state of Qin thus gave us the origins of the English name "China."[1] But as the fourth century BCE dawned, Qin was a mediocre power among the larger community of Zhou vassal states.

In pre-fourth century writings of the eastern Zhou states, Qin was generally ignored or mocked. The land of Qin was described as wild and underdeveloped, its people as alien and uncivilized.[2] One chronicle predicted (ironically, as it turned out) that after a brief effervescence of Qin power in the seventh century BCE, Qin would "never march east again."[3]

The unusual speed of Qin's rise has been fodder for much controversy. Though much ink has been spilled in these debates, the evidence of Qin history raises many questions without offering clear answers.[4] Something about the social and cultural conditions of Qin was unique, but determining what those factors were is difficult, virtually impossible with any high degree of specificity and exactitude.

One flashpoint of debate among modern historians, for example, has been the question of ethnicity. Given that Qin likely gave us the very name "Chinese," it is ironic that modern historians are divided over the question of whether the leaders of Qin were originally "Chinese" at all. This controversy between "eastern origin" and "western origin" theories concerning the founding Qin elite stems from the history of the region in which Qin resided.

Qin was centered in the far western reaches of the Zhou realm, in the Wei River valley. The Wei is a major tributary of the great Yellow River and blessed Qin with an abundance of arable land and exploitable forest. The valley is screened from the south by the Qingling Mountains and from the east by a spur of the Qingling range through which the Wei River flows, creating a pass. The fertile basin was thus known to the people of the Yellow River plain as Guanzhong, "The Land within the Passes," a terrain naturally fortified against military threats from great states of the East (Han, Wei, Zhao, Qi, and Yan) and South (Chu).[5]

Before 771 BCE, the Wei River valley had been the homeland and base of the founding Zhou kings. The protected resources of the Guanzhong region had been foundational to the power of the early Zhou rulers, giving them the wherewithal to first conquer their Shang overlords and then exert their authority over the vassal states established on the eastern Yellow River plain. But the geography of the Wei River valley had also proven a liability to the Zhou. Though Guanzhong is protected from incursions to the east and south, it is open and relatively vulnerable to attack from non-Zhou people living to the west and north. The dual challenge of keeping the peace among their vassals in the east and south while defending against incursions by alien people from the west and north placed a constant strain on Zhou leadership. In 771 BCE the dam broke, and the Zhou were driven from their western capital by a combined force of rebellious vassals and "barbarian" invaders.[6]

The cataclysm of Western Zhou collapse was the context for the founding of Qin. The *Records of the Historian* preserves an extraordinarily long, elaborate genealogy of the Ying clan, undoubtedly based on one produced at the Qin court, which purports to explain how the Ying clan patriarchs came into possession of the Wei River valley and the state of Qin. As was conventional among Zhou aristocrats, the story begins in the very distant past, with a highborn matriarch who, one day while she was weaving, was visited by the High God in the form of a black bird. The bird laid an egg, which the woman ate. This made her pregnant, so that she bore the first human male ancestor of the Ying clan.

For more than a millennium after that miraculous event, so the story continues, leaders of the Ying clan served in the court of every Son of Heaven, from the legendary rulers of high antiquity through the Shang and Zhou dynasties. During the reign of the tenth Zhou king (known posthumously as King Xiao, "The Filial King," r. 872–866 BCE), a virtuous scion of the Ying clan was enfeoffed at Qin, which was "at the confluence of the rivers Qian and Wei," about 175 kilometers west of where the tomb of the First Emperor lies today. Since the Ying ancestors had tended animals for the sage kings of high antiquity, the vassalage at Qin was established to breed horses for the Zhou house.

In 771 BCE, according to the account of the *Records of the Historian*, when the Zhou capital was overrun by an alien people known as the Xianyun or Rong, the Duke of Qin led forces to guard the retreat of the Zhou court as it moved to its new home east of the Wei River pass. The newly installed Zhou king, out of gratitude for and admiration of the martial prowess of Qin, ordered the duke to re-conquer the Wei River valley. Over decades this is what the duke and his descendants did, re-establishing their capital at the site where the Ying clan had originally been enfeoffed by the Filial King.[7]

The story above (which is much more complicated and riddled with internal contradictions in the account of the *Records of the Historian*) has long been suspected by scholars. The heavily embroidered genealogy of the Ying clan ancestors gives an impression that its compilers "protest too much," that there was a perceived need to construct an impressive pedigree to cover deficits or blemishes.[8] The proposition that the Duke of Qin re-conquered the Wei River valley and then *kept it for himself* flies in the face of logic. If the Ying had always perceived themselves as such faithful vassals of successive Sons of Heaven, why would their tradition not have compelled them to return the Wei River valley to their sworn lords?

If the Qin court's account of its own history is a fiction, what might be the truth? An alternative explanation is ready at hand, because we have clear evidence of analogous cases that happened in other parts of the Zhou realm. It is entirely possible that the Ying clan were never originally subjects of the Zhou or any preceding dynasty, but were chieftains of the Xianyun people who drove the Zhou from their original capital. Over decades and centuries in the aftermath of that conquest, the Ying rulers then adopted the culture, religious traditions, language, and political customs of their Zhou adversaries, transforming themselves and their subjects into the court and state of Qin.

If this latter hypothesis were true, the case of Qin would be analogous to that of the states of Wu and Yue, about which we read in Chapter 2. Wu and Yue had been founded by people who spoke an ancient non-Sinitic language and whose cultural traditions diverged sharply in many respects from that of the Zhou states on the Yellow River plain. But through trade and diplomacy the leaders of Wu and Yue became convinced of the advantages of joining the Zhou realm and deliberately reconstructed their societies along the lines of a traditional Zhou "state."

Did this happen in Qin? In the absence of contemporary written records, it is difficult to completely prove one account of Qin origins or another. The state of the evidence is very different in the case of Qin than that of Wu and

Yue. Contact between the Zhou states and the leaders of Wu and Yue transpired well into the fifth (and even, in the case of Yue, the fourth century BCE), when literati society was burgeoning and a denser body of written records was being produced. The officials, scribes, and other intellectuals of the Warring States provided us with ethnographic information about the people of Wu and Yue that does not exist for the Xianyun and Rong tribes who warred with the Zhou in the tenth through the eighth centuries BCE. No one attempted, for example, to transcribe words from the Xianyun language into the Zhou script (or if they did, that document does not survive). We are thus entirely dependent on the archaeological record to answer questions about the cultural identity of the Qin rulers and their subjects.[9]

Archaeology shows us that the culture of the Qin state was, in many ways, distinct from that of the Yellow River plain. The Qin rulers followed different mortuary customs. They buried the dead in a "flexed" position rather than lying supine, as was conventional in the other Zhou states. The tombs of the Qin rulers were built on an enormous scale, perhaps a harbinger of the giant mausoleum of the First Emperor (which will be discussed in later chapters). Moreover, the Qin continued a practice of mass human sacrifice on the burial of a ruler long past the time when it had become moribund in the rest of the Zhou world.[10] Duke Mu of Qin (r. 659–621 BCE), whose victories against the neighboring state of Jin during the seventh century BCE made him the only Qin ruler to merit mention in the chronicles composed in the eastern states, is said to have been followed in death by 170 people, including three of his most meritorious courtiers.[11] This written account is corroborated by excavations that reveal mass burials on a comparable scale in the tombs of Qin rulers.

War and diplomacy between the Qin court and the leaders of the "Rong" and other non-Zhou polities was constant through the Spring and Autumn period and well into the Warring States.[12] How should we view these conflicts? Were they the struggles of "Chinese" leaders to subjugate "non-Chinese" people? Alternatively, were they the struggles of an originally "non-Chinese" Ying clan to force other "non-Chinese" people to follow them in a program of "Sinification?"

The complexity of the evidence reveals the choice outlined above as a false dichotomy.[13] Though the Qin rulers followed different mortuary customs than their neighbors to the east, these may have been a regional cultural variation, perhaps inspired by the perceived need of Qin rulers to accommodate the sensibilities of their non-Zhou subjects. The burial practices of Qin do not prove conclusively that they originally spoke a different language than the Zhou kings or were descended from ancestors that had migrated into the Wei River valley from the west.

In the final analysis, to ask whether the Qin were "really Chinese" is an anachronism. There is no doubt that the leaders of Qin perceived their own realm as culturally diverse. In rare surviving bronze inscriptions, a Qin ruler boasts that his ancestors "cautiously cared for" both the alien "Man" people and the "Xia" people who practiced the customs of the Zhou kings.[14] But though the people of the Zhou era perceived a distinction between the "Man" and "Xia" communities, these labels do not translate neatly today as "non-Chinese" and "Chinese." Ancient people did not think about ethnicity or nationality in the terms that we do. A question like "were the Qin really Chinese?" would not be meaningful to them.

Thus there is much about the internal divisions of Qin society that we should not assume and cannot know for certain. We do know on good evidence, however, that as the fourth century BCE began, Qin was culturally and socially distinct from the rest of the Zhou world. The flight of the Zhou kings from their capital in 771 BCE left a power vacuum that was only gradually redressed by the rise of the Qin court and expansion of its sphere of control. A mass movement of people who did not share the traditions and cultural assumptions of the Zhou subjects into the Wei River valley faced Qin leaders, whatever their origins, with the challenge of integrating newly mingled communities that did not share a common social foundation.

This unique history explains why few political observers would have considered Qin a major power in the first century of the Warring States, and may (as will be discussed below) help explain why the development of Qin state and society in the fourth century BCE transpired so differently than had occurred in other Zhou states. Qin culture and society was unusually conservative during the Spring and Autumn period, and no evidence exists to show that Qin leaders were moved to change their ways in the decades after the cataclysms in Qi, Wu, and Jin sent such shock waves through the rest of the Zhou world. But in the final decades of the fifth century BCE the leaders of Qin were given a wake-up call by the state of Wei, their neighbor to the east.

The success that Marquis Wen achieved in harnessing the economic and human resources of Wei and in coordinating its strategic efforts with those of Wei's "brother states" Han and Zhao could not be ignored in Qin. When Wei in 419 BCE began fortifying the border town of Shaoliang, Qin rulers sensed a threat to their territorial security. They launched a war to push Wei out of Shaoliang that ended in defeat after years of bloody conflict.[15]

The greatest shock came in 408 BCE, when Wei armies under the command of Wu Qi captured the territory on the West Bank of the Yellow River (as discussed in Chapter 5).[16] That "Hexi" territory had been the legacy of Qin's greatest past ruler, Duke Mu, who had captured it from Jin in the seventh century BCE. Its loss deprived Qin of a key defensive buffer against incursion from the east. Leaders in Qin could see that if the power differential between Wei and Qin were allowed to continue to grow, the internal dynamics of the Guanzhong region and the existence of the Qin court itself would eventually have been threatened.

Qin was thus, like all of Wei's neighbors, eventually compelled to rise to the challenge posed by the successful reforms initiated by Marquis Wen. As we saw happen in Qi on Wei's eastern frontier (during the reigns of Tian Wu and his successor Tian Yinqi, as discussed in the previous chapter); a program of reform built the power of Qin over the reigns of two rulers, father and son, during the almost five decades between 385 and 338 BCE. Though Wei and Qi had both been engaged in reform for more than a century before Qin's efforts began, by 338 BCE Qin had developed into a force that could stand on a par with the two other "superpowers" of the Zhou world.

The first of Qin's reformist rulers, Ying Lian, was known posthumously as Duke Xian (r. 384–362 BCE). Duke Xian came to the throne after a period of extended turmoil at the Qin court. The young prince did not merely experience this disorder as "background noise" to an otherwise placid life. His own existence was shaped by the violence that roiled the palace and his family.

In 425 BCE Duke Xian's great-grandfather had committed suicide while under siege by his own courtiers. Because his Heir Apparent had died, the throne passed to Duke Xian's father. When Duke Xian's father died in 415 BCE, another coup drove Duke Xian himself into exile and placed Duke Xian's great uncle on the throne.[17]

Duke Xian spent 30 years in exile in neighboring Wei, where he was able to observe firsthand the policies of Marquis Wen and his prime minister Li Kui, by which state and society in Wei were reorganized to enhance the court's economic and military power. He was residing in Wei during some of Marquis Wen's greatest moments of triumph, including his capture of Qin's territory on the west bank of the Yellow River. Duke Xian's term of exile was thus a class in the urgency of reform, and time would show he learned its lessons well.

In 399 BCE Duke Xian's great uncle died and was succeeded by Duke Xian's cousin. That cousin died in 387 BCE, passing the throne to a one-year-old infant.[18] Power at court thus fell into the hands of the Dowager, who ruled in the name of her infant son. She relied heavily on palace eunuchs in her conduct of state affairs, which angered her court and subjects. In 385 BCE a rebellion broke out that Duke Xian took as his signal to return from exile.

Duke Xian's first attempt to return home was frustrated. A warden at the frontier pass recognized him and dutifully turned him away, understanding the threat he posed to the ruling court. Duke Xian thus traveled a circuitous route to another crossing, where he was met and admitted into Qin by a high palace official who was ready to turn on the Dowager.

When the Dowager heard of Duke Xian's return, she dispatched an army to deal with this incursion from a "bandit." The soldiers accepted her orders, but en route they decided that their mission was no longer to "repel bandits" but to "welcome the ruler." They escorted Duke Xian back to the capital, where he was enthroned. The Dowager and her son were both put to death, their bodies cast unceremoniously into a deep pond.[19]

The first official year of Duke Xian's reign began in 384 BCE, five years after that of his counterpart Tian Wu (Duke Huan) in Qi (as discussed in the previous chapter). Duke Xian wasted no time in placing his mark on the court of Qin. Given the degree to which the ducal throne had been weakened in the years since his father's accession, Duke Xian must have possessed remarkable qualities of leadership and persuasion. Within two years of assuming the throne, he oversaw a move of the capital of Qin from Yong, where it had been sited since 677 BCE, to Yueyang, a site more than 220 kilometers east.[20]

This shift of capital was a recognition of Qin's strategic peril. For centuries Qin's capital had been in the westernmost reaches of the Wei River valley, because the rulers of Qin perceived the non-Zhou people of the west as the greatest threat to the security of their state. The rising power of Wei had changed that dynamic. The move to Yueyang was the first step in reorienting the strategic policy of Qin to focus upon the Yellow River plain and the role of Qin among the larger community of Zhou states. Under Duke Xian's rule Yueyang grew to be an enormous city by the standards of the time, larger than the prior capital it had replaced. The deliberately aggressive posture of Duke Xian's strategic policy was made manifest in the site and architecture of Yueyang. The previous capital, Yong, being so distant from any of the other Zhou states, had required no defensive wall. Yueyang was in such easy reach of the western frontier of Wei that it was fortified with a defensive wall nine kilometers in circumference.[21]

Duke Xian was obviously a leader of insight and vision. Moving the capital alone would have been a profound legacy, but beyond this he acted assertively to reshape the political culture and the political economy of Qin. In these measures he showed that his thinking was not confined to tactics and strategy. He did not only focus on the ways in which the military might of Qin would have to be redeployed, but also on how the court and its relationship to the rest of society would have to be transformed. We can see this in the first of his major edicts, issued immediately upon his assuming power: a ban on the practice of "following in death," the burial of human sacrifices to accompany a leader in the grave.[22]

From our twenty-first-century perspective the choice to ban such a "barbaric" practice might seem intuitively obvious. But the "barbarity" of the practice would not have been as obvious to the people of the fourth century BCE, and for centuries the burial of victims to accompany the ruler in death had been a hallmark of the power of the Qin throne. Making such a dramatic change in the religious customs of the state was taking a real risk. In doing so, Duke Xian was very deliberately following trends that he had observed in exile, and that previous chapters have described in other states such as Wei and Qi: measures aimed at making government work in the interests of a broader section of the populace. The logic of Duke Xian's ban on "following in death" was the same, for example, as that of Ximen Bao's ban on the cult of the River God's bride in Wei (discussed in Chapter 5). If you make people feel that the court will side with them against magnates or bullies that have exploited them in the past, they may be better disposed to serve in the military and on public works such as roads and canals.

Another of Duke Xian's early policies shows his determination to align the interests of the court with that of a broader segment of society. The *Records of the Historian* reports that in 378 BCE Qin "first operated markets."[23] What this entailed exactly is not specified, but it is included in a list of reformist policies by which successive rulers cultivated the power of Qin. It is unlikely that no markets of any kind had existed in Qin prior to 378 BCE, so the markets in question must have been operated or at least regulated by the state. If this was another of the policies that Duke Xian imported from his time in exile in Wei, this date might mark the beginning of grain price regulation in Qin like that first established in Wei under Prime Minister Li Kui (as discussed in Chapter 5), in which the court bought up grain when it was too cheap to keep the price from dropping too low, and sold it out of government granaries during lean years to prevent the price from getting too high.

One of the most dramatic policy initiatives undertaken by Duke Xian occurred in 379 BCE, three years after the move of the capital. In that year the new duke instituted a territorial reorganization of part of the Qin domain along the lines of what he had observed during his years of exile. He converted three regions into "districts" of the kind that had been established in Wei under appointed magistrates like Ximen Bao (as described in Chapter 5).[24] As we saw in the case of Ximen Bao, conversion of regions into districts could help align the interests of the court with rural farmers, because centrally appointed magistrates would often have incentives to side with local commoners against elites who might exploit them. Wei and other eastern states had enjoyed much success in using this kind of reorganization to draw more deeply on the human resources and productivity of the rural economy, enhancing the military power at the disposal of the court.

In 375 BCE Duke Xian extended these measures, ordering a registration of households into "mutual responsibility" groups of five.[25] This was an organizational measure pioneered in Wei and Qi. An infantry squadron was composed of five soldiers, thus households were organized into groups of five for the purpose of military recruitment and corvée labor duties. Each group was responsible for providing five able-bodied men at regular intervals (theoretically one man from each household, though the actual burden could be shared between the families in whatever ratio they agreed, as long as the state got its quota in each conscription), either for labor on public works or for military service. If the group failed to meet its quota of conscripts, all the families would be punished. This might seem like a draconian policy, but by eliminating the hereditary aristocracy as "middlemen" for the purpose of recruitment, the state actually lightened the burden put on common farmers.

The fact that Duke Xian was able to undertake all of these dramatic policy initiatives within a few years of returning from exile is so remarkable as to be puzzling, deepening the mystery that the case of Qin presents us in the annals of the Warring States. In Wei, for example, where Duke Xian had lived in exile, reorganization into "districts" had only become possible gradually and after long decades of civil conflict. The ruling Wei clan had been hereditary vassals of the large state of Jin, all of the territory of which had been divided between the hereditary fiefs of dozens of grandee clans that shared power with the ducal house. The Wei clan had had to conquer rival clans like the Fan and Zhonghang before it had spare land to divide up and portion out to appointed magistrates. The hereditary privileges of the grandee clans themselves had to be systematically destroyed, their temples and palaces razed, their lands seized, to create a sufficiently large pool of knights humble enough to accept a salary from the court, but possessed of the skills needed to staff the bureaucracy of a burgeoning fiscal-military state.

One of the mysteries posed by Qin is that the evidence of this internal social restructuring is largely absent. We know there was turmoil in Qin. Palace intrigues had driven the young Duke Xian into exile, after all. But there is no clear record that the conflicts that rocked the Qin court in the fifth century BCE were caused by "upstart" grandee clans like the Tian in Qi or the Han, Zhao, and Wei in Jin. They may, instead, have been the result of fighting between factions at court that coalesced around different members of the ruling family.

If clans like the Tian of Qi or the Wei of Jin ever existed in Qin, no clear recorded evidence of them survives. It is possible that such grandee clans had been present in Qin and that their memory was later expunged from the written record by the centralizing Qin court. But this would still leave questions about Duke Xian's policies that are difficult to answer. If there were still such clans in Qin when Duke Xian began his conversion of territory into centrally administered "districts," why did they not resist the appropriation of their land and the dismantling of their temples? If the grandee clans had already been eliminated by Duke Xian's time, when did this happen, and how had the ruling Ying clan managed to triumph over its obstreperous grandee clans, where virtually all of the other ruling clans of the Zhou realm had failed in that task (many of them meeting with destruction in the attempt)?

Archaeologists have discovered the tombs of Qin aristocrats, so we know that Qin was not a society in which everyone but the ruler was considered a commoner. But in the absence of written records or inscribed artifacts, though we can know that there were aristocrats in Qin, we cannot be sure that there were aristocratic clans of the kind that characterized Zhou society beyond the Guanzhong region. All the evidence taken together suggests that the structure of elite society in Qin had evolved differently than that of eastern states like Wei and Qi.

Aristocrats outside of the ducal family in Qin did not, as was the custom in the other Zhou states, organize themselves into hierarchical clans under the headship of a single patriarch, whose authority within the clan itself was identical to that that of the duke over the whole state. This may have been a consequence of Qin's internal cultural diversity. The excavated tombs of Qin aristocrats show that some followed the customs of the Zhou, others did not. An aristocracy in which some members spoke a different language and practiced different religious traditions than others would be less conducive to the formation of strongly cohesive clans like those found in the eastern Zhou states.[26]

Whatever the underlying reasons, there do not seem to have been aristocratic clans in Qin who could challenge the ruling Ying clan for hegemony. The court thus faced less disciplined competition and resistance from entrenched interests in elite society at large, a situation which an ambitious and deliberate reformer like Duke Xian was able to exploit (and which would be further exploited by his son's government, as we will read later). This would explain why the extreme disorder of the fifth century BCE had not resulted in the Ying clan suffering the same fate as the ruling clans of Jin and Qi, and why a castoff prince like Duke Xian could return from 30 years of exile to wield enough power not only to shift the state capital in two short years, but to successfully implement an array of ideas and policies he had seen at work in neighboring Wei.

The reforms undertaken by Duke Xian paid dividends. The duke had obviously spent his days in exile mourning the relative weakness of his native state and planning how its fortunes could be revived. Perhaps the best explanation for his swift success was that he inspired his courtiers with a vision of a new path. After decades of internal division and decline, a demoralized court was ready to follow a ruler who could lead them to new strength. That is, in fact, what Duke Xian did.

In 366 BCE Wei once again fortified a city along its western frontier, threatening Qin. A similar move by Wei five decades prior, while the young Duke Xian had been living in exile, had set off a series of wars that had ended in the disastrous loss of Qin's territory on the West Bank of the Yellow River. Duke Xian felt confident that the new political and military machinery he had painstakingly built since taking the throne could match forces with Wei. He attacked the new fortifications. Wei joined forces with Han to repel the Qin expeditionary force, but the allied defenders were defeated.[27]

It was the first serious challenge that Qin had issued to the power of Wei in 50 years. Wei had a new young ruler, Wei Ying (whom we will read about in the next chapter), the grandson of Wei's "founding father," Marquis Wen (Wei Si). Wei Ying had come to the throne after a bloody succession struggle with his brother. Perhaps because of the pressure to prove that he was the "right brother," he was determined to revive the glories of his grandfather's reign. He mobilized a massive force to punish Qin for its assertiveness.

Duke Xian was not cowed. The armies of Qin crossed the Yellow River in response to Wei's mobilization and marched deep into the Wei heartland. Battle was joined at a place called Stone Gate, just over 20 kilometers southwest of the Wei capital. The day ended in disaster for Wei. The Qin chronicles claim that its soldiers took the heads of 60,000 enemies. That may be an exaggeration, but there can be little doubt that in the immediate aftermath of the battle Wei was in profound peril. Wei was only saved from having its capital overrun by the arrival of an army from Zhao, which helped drive Qin's forces back beyond the Yellow River. Qin's victory was so extraordinary that the Zhou king, who was by tradition obligated to acknowledge any outstanding feat of martial skill on the part of his vassals (and who was also no doubt intimidated by this new sign of Qin's power), sent Duke Xian a richly embroidered ceremonial garment as a token of congratulations.[28]

The following year Qin assaulted Wei's frontier fortifications again, and Wei was forced to rely on the assistance of Zhao to repel the attack.[29] Qin attacked again in 362 BCE and on this campaign captured the commander of Wei's defenses, a member of the ruling Wei clan.[30] This pressure on Wei's western region contributed to Wei Ying's decision in 361 BCE to move his capital, re-establishing his court in a city known as Daliang (Greatbridge), 360 kilometers east of Wei's original capital of Anyi.

It was the beginning of a new world. Wei was so powerful that its young ruler continued to pursue lofty ambitions even after the debacle at Stone Gate (as we will read in the next chapter). But the strategic situation of the Zhou domain had changed. One could not have foreseen even then that Qin would become an overwhelmingly dominant force. But Qin, at least as a military power, could never again be mocked, or ignored.

In 362 BCE Duke Xian died and was peacefully succeeded by his son Ying Quliang, known posthumously as Duke Xiao, "the Filial Duke" (r. 362–338 BCE). As Duke Xiao's posthumous title suggests, he came to the throne determined to continue the legacy of his father. One of his first acts was to issue a general edict that served as a kind of "mission statement" for his reign. The text of the edict is preserved in the *Records of the Historian*, and it shows that Duke Xiao, like his father, was a keen observer of the political trends of his day.

In emulation of Tian Wu and Tian Yinqi in the eastern state of Qi, Duke Xiao appealed to the past glory of Qin. In the same way that the Tian rulers of Qi proposed to bring back the golden days of Guan Zhong and Duke Huan, Duke Xiao promised that he would revive the splendor and triumph of the reign of Duke Mu, who in the seventh century BCE (roughly contemporary with the careers of Guan Zhong and Duke Huan in Qi) had conquered the territory on the West Bank of the Yellow River, wresting it away from the state of Jin.

Duke Xiao's edict noted that Qin had been weak under successive rulers whose courts had fallen into turmoil, and that this had led to the loss to Wei of the territory conquered by Duke Mu. It was now the mission of the throne to restore the might of Qin and retake the land on the West Bank of the Yellow River. This, according to Duke Xiao, had been his father's primary objective all along. Duke Xiao expressed pain that his father had died before his ultimate ambition had been realized, but swore to fulfill his father's wishes. He called on any men of talent who had plans that could aid in the restoration of Qin to come forward, offering them employment and reward.[31]

In this last aspect of his inaugural edict Duke Xiao showed again that he, like his father before him, was aware of the emerging political trends in the Zhou world. The flow of people across state frontiers, especially the flow of literate knights, "wanderers" in search of employment and the opportunity to advance, had become a permanent fixture of social and political life. Duke Xiao could see that if it was to stand against powers like Wei and Qi, Qin would have to be able to compete in the "interstate" market for political talent. His edict, which so carefully emulated the historical imagery and rhetoric that had successfully attracted many literati to Qi and its Jixia patronage community, was effectively an "ad campaign" designed to sell Qin as a prospective employer to the literati who formed groups of "Masters and disciples" throughout the eastern states, and who had been inclined to think of Qin as an isolated and uncultured backwater. As it turned out, it was among the most successful ad campaigns in history.

The man most famous for answering Duke Xiao's call is known by various names, though he is most often referred to in literature as Shang Yang (ca. 390–338 BCE), after a title he received from the Qin court (the "Lord of Shang"). He would eventually become the most powerful official in the state of Qin and oversee one of the most profound and consequential programs of reform ever executed. Though he had not been born in Qin, Qin would both make Shang Yang immortal and destroy him.[32]

He was a native of the state of Wey (he is thus sometimes known as Wey Yang), the same state that had produced the famous Wu Qi a generation before. Shang Yang was a scion of the ruling family of Wey (ergo another of his monikers: Gongsun Yang, which literally means "ducal grandson" Yang), but because his mother was a concubine instead of a principal wife, his ambitions in his home state were limited. As a youth he studied, reportedly favoring writings on statecraft in his scholarship.

Like Wu Qi before him, starting out from his home state of Wey the young Shang Yang first gravitated to the Wei court, which was still a premier power and a center of meritocratic recruitment and thus a natural destination for ambitious literati. The young Shang Yang was clearly talented. In Wei he secured a position as deputy to the state's prime minister.

In 360 BCE (the year after Duke Xiao took the throne in Qin and issued his inaugural edict), the Prime Minister of Wei fell ill. Wei Ying, the ruler who had been defeated by Duke Xian of Qin at Stone Gate, came to visit the prime minister on his sickbed and asked the ailing official to recommend someone who might replace him should he not recover from his illness. The prime minister purportedly urged Wei Ying to make Shang Yang the next Prime Minister of Wei, warning that if Wei Ying did not employ him in that high post, he must have Shang Yang killed. If Shang Yang was not to be trusted with the state, he should not be trusted at all. Allowing any other state to have the benefits of Shang Yang's talent would spell disaster for Wei.

Emerging from the sickroom, Wei Ying remarked to his entourage that his prime minister's illness was much more serious than the ruler had previously imagined. Only his being deranged by sickness could, in Wei Ying's opinion, make the prime minister so grievously overestimate the talents of a mediocrity like Shang Yang. When the ailing official finally did die, Shang Yang was passed over for the post of prime minister. Seeing that he was not valued in Wei, and hearing of Duke Xiao's edict pleading for talent, Shang Yang headed west to Qin.[33] In Qin, Shang Yang made the acquaintance of an influential palace eunuch, who was impressed, and recommended him to Duke Xiao, who took him on as a courtier.

In 359 BCE Shang Yang presented a set of reform proposals to Duke Xiao.[34] They met with opposition from the other advisors at court, who warned in debate before the duke that Shang Yang's plans were too much of a departure from tradition. Shang Yang countered that those of ordinary talent took comfort in tradition and that such people, though mediocre, could be trusted to administer policy. But, he continued, people of extraordinary vision transformed tradition, and by setting new policies changed the world.

Shang Yang's argument was patronizing to his fellow courtiers, arrogantly self-promoting, and obsequiously flattering to the ruler. He had, however, read the room correctly. Duke Xiao had been born after his father returned from exile in Wei. He thus had not seen the results of the reforms in Wei directly. But he had obviously absorbed his father's trust of progressive policy, and he earnestly desired to build upon his father's legacy. He was a receptive audience for Shang Yang's urgings to the effect that "fortune favors the bold." Shang Yang was promoted to the rank of "Left Chief of Staff."

The court embarked on a set of reforms under Shang Yang's guidance. Shang understood that his proposals were novel and that (as exemplified by the attitude of his fellow courtiers in response to his ideas) the political culture of Qin was conservative. He thus designed some theatrics by way of broadcasting the nature and seriousness of his plans. He set up a pole at the southern gateway of the market in the Qin capital and had an announcement made that anyone who moved the pole to the northern gateway would receive 10 gold ingots. This was a ridiculous sum to be offered for such a simple task, so no one responded, assuming it must be some kind of trick. Shang Yang had been counting on this reaction and ordered a second announcement that the reward for moving the pole had been increased to 50 gold ingots.

This was enough temptation to overcome one man's suspicion. After he moved the pole, Shang Yang made a very public display of giving the man the promised reward, though it had gone from being ridiculous to being unthinkable. It was a grandiose gesture, but it established the principle that Shang Yang hoped to convey: if the government tells you that there will be consequences for an action (whether that entails reward *or punishment*), no matter how unreasonable those consequences may seem to you, you can count on them being real.

It was a basic principle of Shang Yang's reform program: in order to quickly coordinate the efforts of a large number of people spread out over a broad terrain, the rewards and punishments that backed government policies would have to be heavy. The government could not be everywhere at once. Some rewards and punishments would be delayed. Some meritorious subjects might be overlooked; some perpetrators might slip the surveillance net. The only way to cultivate obedience to government regulations was to make the sanctions so weighty that to risk punishment, even if some people did get away with infractions, or to forgo the opportunity of reward, even though some people got short-changed, was a real gamble that could end very badly.

Once his "public service announcement" stunt was done, Shang Yang put his plans into effect. Many of his reforms were modeled on the institutions that had been established in Wei. Shang promulgated a legal code outlining infractions, punishments, and methods of enforcement based on the code of Marquis Wen of Wei's Prime Minister Li Kui.[35]

Shang Yang departed from the precedents set in Wei, however, by attuning his statutes and methods to what he perceived as the urgent strategic needs of Qin. He viewed the two sources of Qin's strength as farming and military service,

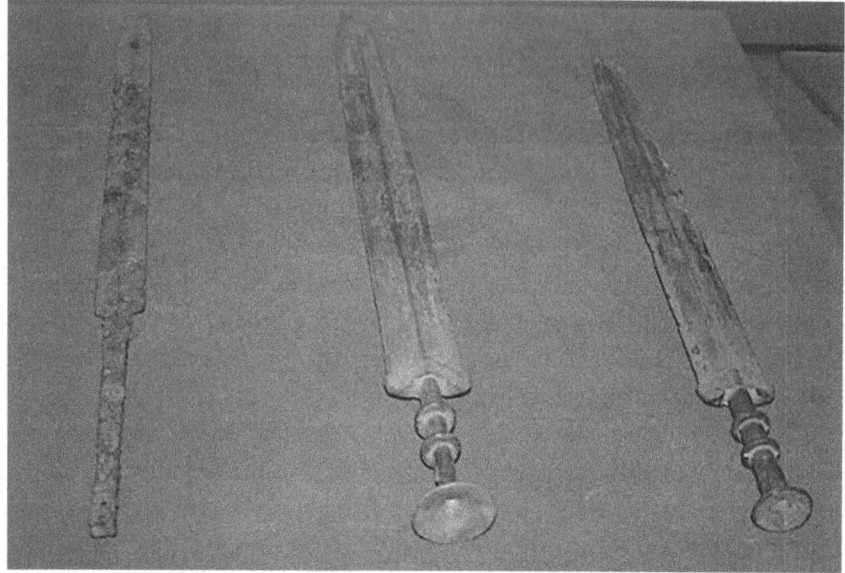

Fig. 12. Expertly forged swords made of bronze or iron were standard armaments issued to infantry soldiers during the Warring States Era. (Source: www.worldhistory.org.)

and established a system of generous rewards and harsh punishments to channel the people's energies into these two domains. Soldiers were rewarded for each enemy head they could present as evidence of a kill, punished severely for fleeing in the face of the enemy or disobeying orders (see Fig. 12). Similar punishments were established for those who committed violent acts in private feuds rather than saving those energies for the service of the state. Farmers were rewarded for high yields of grain and woven textiles, and were punished for engaging in profiteering and "secondary pursuits" such as peddling. Those who "became poor through laziness" (who failed to be productive on their own initiative) were taken as bondservants of the state.

Some of the mechanisms that Shang Yang employed to enforce these policies had become conventional by the time his program went into effect and had been employed beyond the state of Qin. He expanded and intensified the network of "mutual responsibility" groups that had been established during the time of Duke Xian. Members of these household groupings became responsible for reporting noncompliance with the new regulations. Anyone who reported an infraction within his or her mutual responsibility group would be rewarded equivalently with taking the head of an enemy in battle, anyone who failed to do so would be cut in half at the waist.

The most unique aspect of Shang Yang's program was his use of social status as incentive. A system of 20 ranks was established for assessing the relative status of all male subjects, from commoners to members of the ruling clan. The lowest eight ranks were all dispensed on the basis of military merit, though ranks could be purchased by wealthy commoners. Men moved up or down in rank on the basis of service to the state. It was not generally possible for a commoner to advance beyond the eighth rank, but even men at the very top of the social ladder were not exempt from the demands of the rank system.

Shang Yang understood that in order for any rank system to provide real incentives, it would have to be universal. People always assess their own status relative to all others in the society in which they live, so if the rank system was confined to a part of the community, it would not be as motivating. If I know that any rank I earn can be dismissed as meaningless by someone who is not subject to the rules and demands of the system as a whole, the rank's value to me is undermined. Thus in the new system even members of the ruling clan were assessed within the merit rank system. Any member of the ruling clan who failed to provide meritorious military service, for example, would not be registered as a member of the clan and would thus enter the ranking system as a commoner.[36]

This dimension of Shang Yang's program was in line with trends going on in the rest of the Zhou world. In states like Qi and Wei, rulers and courts were accumulating ever greater power over determining social status in the community at large. The second Tian ruler of Qi, for example, had elevated some of his kinsmen to become "Capital Grandees," solidifying the position of the Tian clan at the top of Qi's social pyramid. Successful generals like Yue Yang in Wei (who had shocked the enemy and the world by eating a stew made of the flesh of his own son) were rewarded with titles and fiefs, and civil ministers who performed meritorious service were given similar remuneration. As the fourth century BCE drew to a close, governments throughout the Zhou domain were actively campaigning to take control over the determination of social status within their terrain. But Shang Yang's ranking system was the most audaciously systematic and comprehensive program to institutionalize state control of social status in the Zhou world.

These facts suggest once again that the pre-fourth-century BCE society of Qin had been distinct from that of the rest of the Zhou world. It cannot have been the case that Qin lacked aristocratic families. In order for status to be so motivating, Qin had to, from its origins, have been as intensely hierarchical and status-conscious as the rest of the Zhou states. But the aristocrats of Qin clearly had less organization and collective power than the grandee clans of the eastern Zhou states. The eastern nobility resisted moves by the states to control status; they persisted in insisting that their privileges were Heaven-ordained, and thus had to be respected even if they conflicted with the interests of the ruler and his court.

Whatever the preconditions were that made it possible in Qin, Shang Yang's ranking system's function as a means to micromanage status mobility made it a very powerful and efficient mechanism of control. Using status as a reward (or a punishment) cost the state very little, only what had to be spent on personnel and materials for the purpose of recordkeeping. The ranks themselves did not come with income or stipends; they merely conveyed privileges (such as exemption from corvée labor service) and opportunities to be promoted to higher office. Much of the value that the ranks conveyed came in the form of respect from and influence within the community in which one lived, which cost the state nothing.

The ranking system thus subtly motivated people to spontaneously align themselves with the interests of the state. Take, for example, the hypothetical case of a recruit who fought bravely and took enemy heads and was thus raised to a rank that would allow him to become an officer or military prefect. He would no doubt feel he had been exceptionally well rewarded. But from another perspective, one could say that his reward for working hard for the government was the chance to work even harder for the government. It is little wonder that the rank system was one of the most durable elements of Shang Yang's reforms. Even after the first imperial Qin dynasty had fallen, the Han dynasty which succeeded it maintained a ranking system closely based on that of the Qin.[37]

A test of Shang Yang's reforms came in the early stages of their implementation, when Duke Xiao's son, the Heir Apparent, violated the regulations that were put into effect. The histories do not preserve the nature of the prince's offense. Perhaps he simply refused to do the military service that was required even of members of the ruling clan. Shang Yang believed that the whole program would fail if the example being set by the heir were allowed to stand; no one would obey the laws if they could be spurned even by someone as powerful as the ruler's son.

As the history of Qin and many other states had clearly demonstrated, fiddling with the line of succession in a dynastic system is always an invitation to disaster. It was thus impossible for the heir to be subjected to the heavy corporal punishments demanded by the law. Shang Yang devised a solution to this dilemma. He declared that the heir's malfeasance was the responsibility of those entrusted with educating him. He had the Heir's Tutor punished by the removal of his foot, and his Preceptor sanctioned by the incision of a tattoo on the face (both standard penalties for infractions of the law).

Shang Yang's program was implemented over the course of seven years, during which time the economic and military power of the state grew rapidly. In 352 BCE Duke Xiao put Shang's policies to the test. War once again broke out with Wei. Shang Yang was given the command of an expeditionary force. He led it into Wei's home territory and surrounded the former capital of Anyi, compelling it to surrender after a siege.[38]

This proof of success caused Shang Yang's star to rise even further. He was named "Great Excellent Charioteer," the title within the Qin system equivalent to prime minister.[39] In this position and on the strength of his victories against Wei, Shang embarked on a second round of reform.

He converted all of Qin universally into "commanderies and districts," extending the territorial reorganization begun during the reign of Duke Xiao's father. This was accompanied by a general reassessment and redistribution of land to break up manorial estates and establish privately owned, single-family farms as the norm.[40] In theory, every able-bodied man was guaranteed at least 100 *mu* (about 16.5 acres) of land under the new system, and taxes would be levied on a per capita basis. If individual farmers did not divide their land between all of their sons, each individual's tax burden was doubled. This measure gave people incentive to clear new lands and develop fallow areas for farming, so as to keep productivity growing ahead of population.[41]

To manage this new system of territorial administration and taxation, a network of literate personnel was required. In 349 BCE the court first mandated that "official scribes" would be established in all of the commanderies and prefectures.[42] We do not know what form this staff originally took in the time of Shang Yang, but archaeologically recovered records from a bit more than a century after Shang's death (dating to between 222 and 208 BCE) show that this scribal bureaucracy would, over time, grow extraordinarily extensive and sophisticated. The records of Qin government on the eve of unification show that the local scribes were part of a network that administered justice, surveyed land, regulated the populace, and oversaw all manner of economic activity according to a set of intricate yet highly systematic rules and protocols.[43]

In 350 BCE Shang Yang moved the capital of Qin once again, establishing the city of Xianyang. Xianyang was on the west bank of the Jing River, a tributary of the Wei River that formed the valley in which Qin was centered. The Jing

River thus formed a natural moat against threats from the eastern states. Though Xianyang was close enough to the neighboring state of Wei to facilitate keeping military pressure on Qin's rival, the screen of the Jing River precluded the need for expensive walls to secure the capital.[44]

A final aspect of Shang Yang's "second wave" reforms provides us with some of the most interesting evidence of his influence. In 344 BCE Shang ordered the standardization of all weights and measures throughout the Qin domain, a prerequisite for the success of his new system of per capita taxation. To ensure that the tax burden was being allocated fairly and impartially, metallic grain measures were crafted in the capital and sent to the officials responsible for collecting taxes (which were levied in grain) in the outlying districts. One such measure survives and is housed at the Shanghai Museum. The inscriptions on its surface declare that its dimensions were mandated by "Great Excellent Charioteer Yang."[45]

This invocation of Shang Yang's name on artifacts that were so widely disseminated throughout the countryside demonstrates that even in his own lifetime Shang Yang had achieved a level of celebrity that few people other than rulers did anywhere in the ancient world. For each of the Warring States one can name a "reforming prime minister" who is credited in the sources with having overseen an overhaul of the machinery of state. Historians have pointed out that this may be less of a hard fact than a reflection of the world view of the literati who produced our sources.[46] The knights who wrote the annals on which we rely were motivated to depict a world that was being reshaped by "men of learning" (in other words, men like them). But the case of Shang Yang seems to be one in which we can genuinely "believe the hype." If the awe induced by Shang's name was thought to ensure that official grain measures would be obediently employed, it suggests that many of the reforms undertaken in Qin during his life really were impelled by his initiative and personal prestige.

The power of Qin was visibly growing, and the rest of the Zhou world took notice. In 343 BCE the Zhou king conferred the title of "Lord Protector" on Duke Xiao.[47] This was largely ceremonial; the title had not conferred effective authority since the demise of Fu Chai. But the gesture conveyed prestige, and was a sign that the Zhou court was intimidated by the burgeoning strength of Qin, and felt the need to cultivate the good will of its ruler. The following year the rulers of the other Zhou states sent their congratulations to Qin, and Duke Xiao, in fulfillment of his role as "Lord Protector," dispatched his son and heir to lead a delegation of 92 defeated chieftains from among the Rong and Di people to pay tribute to the Son of Heaven.[48] It was a public relations campaign aimed to convey the message that Qin had arrived as a force with which to contend.

The Zhou world did not have long to wait before the message was driven home. In 341 BCE Wei suffered a grievous defeat at the hands of Qi (which will be discussed further in the following chapter). Shang Yang thus proposed to Duke Xiao that Qin should take advantage of Wei's momentary weakness to strike. The duke agreed and in 340 BCE dispatched Shang Yang with an army to attack Wei.

When Qin's army encamped within sight of the enemy, Shang Yang learned that the enemy commander was a scion of the Wei ruling clan with whom Shang Yang had been on good terms when he served in Wei. Shang Yang sent a messenger to his counterpart, proposing that they meet to perform a covenant ritual and part ways without bloodshed.

The Wei general accepted Shang Yang's invitation, and the two men met to perform the rite. When the formalities were over, they shared a drink, and Shang Yang saw his friend off. On his way back to his army, the Wei commander fell into the ambush that Shang Yang had set in waiting. With the enemy general a prisoner, Shang Yang ordered the attack and took the Wei force by complete surprise, destroying them.[49]

In 338 BCE another invading army from Qin clashed with the forces of Wei and took its commander, Wei Cuo, prisoner.[50] Defeated on all sides and fatally vulnerable, the Wei ruler was desperate. He sent an envoy to Qin suing for peace. He offered the only terms that he knew could appease Duke Xiao and Shang Yang: cession of some of the territory on the West Bank of the Yellow River that had been ruled by Wei for three generations.[51]

Shang Yang's campaigns had partially achieved the goals set out in Duke Xiao's inaugural edict two decades prior. They thus not only procured military victory, but a highly symbolic political triumph as well, comparable in the national memory of the United States to the battle of Trenton during the American Revolution or the Liberation of Paris during World War II: a sign that the tide might be turning in what had been a long, hard, and existentially fateful struggle. Shang Yang, already one of the most famous and powerful men in Qin, instantly became one of its immortal heroes. He was given a fief that conferred lordship over 15 towns, and the title "Lord of Shang."

In another eerie parallel with his fellow Wey native Wu Qi, Shang Yang's moment of greatest triumph was followed by a swift downfall. In 338 BCE, right after Shang Yang's great victory over Wei, Duke Xiao died. He was succeeded by his son Ying Si (r. 337–311 BCE), the same Heir Apparent who had been made an example of by Shang Yang at the beginning of the program of legal reforms. Ying Si had never forgiven Shang Yang for the cruel punishments that had been visited upon his Tutor and Preceptor, and his animosity was shared by other members of the ruling family who chafed at having lost privileges to Shang Yang's program of reform.

Courtiers accused Shang Yang of plotting rebellion, and Shang fled the capital ahead of the soldiers sent to arrest him. He headed to the Hangu Pass, intending to flee. An inn at which he tried to stop while traveling incognito refused him lodging, reminding him that the laws of Lord Shang forbade taking in anyone who was traveling without an official pass.

Shang Yang eventually slipped through to Wei, but met a cold welcome there on account of his treachery during the invasion of 340 BCE. He pleaded to be allowed to pass through Wei to travel on to another state, but was refused. The frontier guards ultimately drove him back through the pass into the territory of Qin.

Back in Qin, Shang Yang took refuge in his fief. There he was able to rally followers into a military force and raised the banner of rebellion against Ying Si and his court. It was a last desperate gamble. Shang Yang must have known that he stood little chance of success, but he hoped that his famous name would draw followers to his side. Perhaps, he reasoned, the people of Qin would feel that he was too indispensable, and would rally to replace Ying Si with a ducal scion who would work with rather than against the Great Excellent Charioteer.

Shang Yang and his followers headed toward the capital, striking at the district along the northern border of his fief. He was met by a force of Qin troops. In the ensuing battle Shang Yang's band of insurgents was defeated and he was killed. His body was taken to the capital, where the new ruler had it publicly torn apart by chariots as a warning to anyone who would rebel against the court.[52]

Shang Yang was a larger-than-life figure, and like so many of the outstanding leaders of the Warring States his legacy was extraordinarily complicated. Though he was ignominiously killed and his body desecrated as that of a traitor, within the state of Qin that he had shaped so profoundly his works and his memory could never wholly be repudiated. The *Book of Lord Shang* attributed to him was most likely not written by Shang Yang himself, but it reflects many of the principles behind his reforms, and its contents were most likely composed under Qin state patronage as a way of elevating "Lord Shang" to the status of a Master who could stand on a par with those figures, like Guan Zhong or Confucius, who were revered in the eastern states.[53]

In the rest of the Zhou world Shang Yang's legacy was even more ambivalent. For most of the century after Shang Yang died, the gravitational center of literati life remained in the east. As the power of Qin grew, it was obvious to outside observers that Shang Yang had made an enormous impact on the evolving balance of power. This presented literati with a dilemma. On the one hand, to celebrate Shang Yang was to promote the interests of Qin, a state that increasingly threatened the security, and ultimately the existence, of the eastern states that most literati called home. On the other hand, to denigrate Shang Yang was to devalue the achievements of one of the most successful literati in the Zhou world, and by extension the worth of the literati community as a whole. Almost all of what we read about Shang Yang's life in the surviving sources is colored by these tensions. It is difficult, sometimes impossible, to separate factual testimony from propaganda and rhetoric.

For example, there are several versions of the story of Duke Xiao's first audience with Shang Yang. We have seen in the case of figures like Prime Minister Zou Ji of Qi (discussed in the previous chapter) that such "first audience" stories became a kind of fixed genre in the historical writings of the Warring States era.[54] These initial moments of contact between ruler and minister were considered profoundly significant. The stories recounting them were thought to crystallize a comprehensive comment on the nature of an entire era.

The version of Shang Yang's "first audience" story in the *Records of the Historian* uses a narrative device familiar from the legend of Chunyu Kun (discussed in the previous chapter): "three first audiences." On the recommendation of Duke Xiao's trusted palace eunuch, Shang Yang was presented to the throne for a private interview with the ruler. Though Shang Yang talked passionately and in great detail, the duke was unimpressed. He grew bored and frequently fell asleep. After Shang Yang had been dismissed, Duke Xiao scolded his palace eunuch for recommending such a fool.

The eunuch angrily upbraided Shang Yang, demanding to know why the interview had gone so badly. Shang Yang explained that he had presented the duke with the principles and policies that had guided the "Thearchs" of high antiquity, such as the sage rulers Yao and Shun. Such lofty material had obviously not held the attention of the duke. Shang Yang pleaded for a second audience.

The second audience went almost as badly as the first, and the duke scolded the eunuch once more. Shang Yang explained that he had tried to present the duke with the principles of the Former Kings, the founders of the Shang and Zhou dynasties, but these teachings were also too elevated for the duke's tastes. He pleaded for a third audience.

In the third audience Shang Yang presented the duke with the principles and policies of the Lords Protector, like Duke Huan of Qi, who had made his state into a military powerhouse under the guidance of Guan Zhong. These teachings were of great interest to Duke Xiao, who finally began to see the worth that his eunuch perceived in Shang Yang. He invited Shang Yang back for a fourth interview, and became so absorbed in the discussion that he forgot all decorum, leaning forward to focus on Shang Yang's words until his knees protruded beyond his mat and touched the floor. The discussion went on for three days, at the end of which Shang Yang was installed as a "Chief of the Left."[55]

As is true for so many of the stories in our sources, we cannot trust the historical veracity of this account. Whether it actually happened or not, however, it speaks volumes about how the literati of the Warring States perceived the rise of Qin, and of their relationship to power more generally. On the one hand, Shang's contribution to Qin's strength proved how powerful and effective literati could be. Why then, if literati had so much of value to offer, did Qin become so much more powerful than the eastern states where most literati lived? The answer to this conundrum expressed in the tale of Shang Yang's "first audience" was elegant.

In effect, the story argues that the Masters and their disciples had held the key to rescuing civilization all along. This is embodied in the person of Shang Yang, who was obviously a paragon of learning, being able to discourse on three completely different sets of teachings with equal mastery. The fact that Qin's employment of Shang Yang was the key to the state's rise thus proves the efficacy of the Masters and their teachings, since Shang Yang had such superior command of the larger body of learning on which the Masters' teachings were based.

Why did Qin become so powerful without (in the estimation of literati) becoming more civilized? The fault lay with the characters of Shang Yang and Duke Xiao, respectively. Duke Xiao was too benighted to adopt the best and purest of the Masters' teachings drawn from high antiquity, but instead insisted on using the debased dregs of latter eras. Shang Yang, for all his brilliance, was a rank cynic. His willingness to keep "changing key" until he found a tune that Duke Xiao liked was a betrayal of the values he had professed to learn. The problem was thus not that the Masters and their literati followers had no pearls to offer, but that the rulers of the world were swine, and in Shang Yang one of the swine had found an exceptionally talented but wholly unscrupulous enabler.

This was a consoling story and an elegant apology for the literati chroniclers of the Warring States. Even as late as 100 BCE, the approximate date of the composition of the *Records of the Historian*, Shang Yang's legacy remained an intellectual problem with which Sima Qian (b. 145 BCE), the Grand Historian of the Han court, was compelled to wrestle. Shang Yang's biography is among the longest in the *Records of the Historian* as a whole, and much of it is taken up by a long dialogue between Shang Yang and a remonstrating scholar, in which Shang Yang's critic explains why his term as minister was far inferior when compared with the glory days of the earlier famed ruler, Duke Mu of Qin.[56]

Though the earliest record we have of this defamatory dialogue is found in a Han dynasty text, it was almost certainly composed during the Warring States by eastern literati trying to grapple with the burgeoning power of Qin. Long after Shang Yang's demise, literati throughout the Zhou world continued to champion Marquis Wen of Wei (Wei Si) as a paragon of effective rulership, and to denigrate Qin and its leaders as "semi-barbarian." Decades of subtle logic and ingenious literary rhetoric, however, would not be enough to determine the material trajectory of the larger Zhou world.

On Qin's eastern frontier, Marquis Wen's grandson Wei Ying had (with some difficulty) ascended a throne possessed of profound economic, human, and cultural resources. Like his grandfather, who ruled Wei for 50 years, Wei Ying enjoyed extraordinary longevity, presiding over the Wei court for a remarkable 51 years. Also like his grandfather, Wei Ying was a leader of vision and vast ambition.

This, however, is where the similarity ends. Marquis Wen's five decades of rule had ended at the pinnacle of his political success, after he had built the power of his state and expanded its influence. Wei Ying was the legate of that success, and when he ascended the throne, Wei was still the most powerful state in the Zhou domain.

Unlike that of his grandfather, Wei Ying's long reign did not end in unequivocal triumph. By the end of his life, Wei was in rapid decline and would never recover. This should not be taken to mean that he did not shape history, however. The creativity and ingenuity of his ambitions were such that, even in failure, he had a lasting influence on the political culture and social evolution of the Warring States. We cannot understand the history of the era without exploring the nature of his political agenda, the way he adapted to the challenges and setbacks with which he was confronted, and the means by which his policies transformed the political and strategic dynamic of the entire Zhou world.

9

The Marquis Who Would Be King

The State of Wei, 369–334 BCE

In 370 BCE, during the fifth year of Tian Wu's reign in Qi and the fifteenth year of Duke Xian's reign in Qin, the second ruler of the independent state of Wei, Marquis Wu (Wei Ji, r. 395–370 BCE), died.[1] His posthumous title, "the Martial Marquis," was given to him, as was customary, by ministers under the direction of his son and successor, Wei Ying. The title conveys enormous honor: it likens Marquis Wu to King Wu, "the Martial King," the warrior-sage who had defeated the wicked last king of the Shang dynasty and thus founded the reigning Zhou dynasty.

We do not know exactly what kind of relationship Wei Ying had with his father, but the grand posthumous title was almost certainly not awarded purely out of filial affection. It was an early sign that Wei Ying had very grand ambitions, so great that he was willing to "airbrush" the history of his father's reign at his own expense. Wei Ying himself had real cause to doubt the image of his father implicit in the title "Marquis Wu." But Wei Ying, as time would reveal, had purposes of his own for which he needed his father to be commemorated as a "sage founder."

Marquis Wu's legacy was a mixed bag at best, and perhaps his greatest failing as a leader had impacted Wei Ying (r. 369–319 BCE) quite personally. The Wei clan had, until Marquis Wu's death, avoided the internal discord that had marked the long careers of the Tian clan in Qi and the ruling Ying clan of Qin. The first imperative of the kind of bureaucratized dynastic state that had been deliberately built in Wei during the reigns of Marquis Wu and his father Marquis Wen (Wei Si) before him was to provide for the orderly transfer of power. The records do not survive that would tell us exactly why or how

Marquis Wu failed in this regard,[2] but after ruling for 25 years he left a court divided between the claims of two of his sons to succeed him as Marquis of Wei. Civil war erupted between Marquis Wu's elder son Wei Ying and Wei Ying's younger brother, Wei Huan (also known in the chronicles as Gongzhong Huan, "Second Ducal Scion Huan").

The internal turmoil in Wei quickly attracted outsiders eager to exploit the situation. Han and Zhao had been Wei's "brother states" during the reign of Wei Ying's celebrated grandfather, Marquis Wen (described in Chapter 5). But since Wei Ying's father had broken the peace between the "three Jin" successor states in 383 BCE (as described in Chapter 6), both Zhao and Han had been suspicious of their more powerful "brother state" in the best of times, hostile to it otherwise. They saw an opportunity in the crisis following Marquis Wu's death to weaken Wei. Supporting the claims of a younger brother during the succession struggles of a rival is always the most efficient way to sow chaos. Thus in 369 BCE a joint army fielded by both Han and Zhao invaded Wei in support of its young prince and pretender, Wei Huan.[3]

Wei Ying had control of Ximen Bao's old magistracy of Ye and the support of one of Wei's most competent prefects in another district, giving him effective control over half of Wei's territory. He met the combined armies of Han and Zhao at a place called Muddy Marsh (Zhuoze), and was defeated. Retreating, he was besieged by the armies of Han and Zhao.[4]

At this juncture the rulers of Han and Zhao met to discuss strategy. Marquis Cheng of Zhao (r. 374–350 BCE) proposed that the siege should be pressed until Wei Ying could be killed. Wei Huan could then be set upon the throne and forced to cede territory to both Han and Zhao.

It was a deeply ironic moment. The situation of Wei Ying was strikingly parallel to that of Marquis Cheng of Zhao's great-great-grandfather Zhao Wuxu, who, because he had refused to cede territory, had been besieged by the combined forces of Han, Wei, and the tyrant Zhi Yao (as described in Chapters 3 and 4). What Marquis Cheng of Zhao was proposing to do to Wei Ying in 369 BCE was almost exactly what Zhi Yao had attempted to do to Marquis Cheng's great-great-grandfather in 453 BCE.

The irony of the moment was not lost on Marquis Cheng's ally, Marquis Yi of Han (r. 373–363 BCE). He rejected Zhao's plan as politically infeasible. Killing the rightful ruler of Wei would be deemed sadistic cruelty by the wider Zhou world; taking advantage of the moment to seize territory would be viewed as rapacious greed. The long-term political damage of such acts would, in Han's view, far offset any short-term material benefit: rulers could no longer get away with behaving as Zhi Yao had done. Instead, the Marquis of Han proposed that the coalition should simply divide Wei into two states, one under each brother, and thus terminate Wei's status as the most powerful of the three Jin successor states. Han's hesitation to follow Zhao in murdering Wei Ying was testimony to the enduring influence, despite the dissolution of the alliance between the "three Jin" successor states, of Marquis Wen of Wei's efforts to establish new and less ruthless political norms in the wake of the bloody days of Zhi Yao.

The rulers of Han and Zhao could not come to consensus on a strategy, and overnight Han withdrew, giving Wei Ying the chance to break the siege and escape. He rallied his forces and attacked the Zhao invaders, defeating them at Pingyang, just south of the frontier between Wei and Zhao. Wei Huan was killed, and before the year was out Wei Ying had been formally installed as the unchallenged Marquis of Wei.[5]

Wei Ying would hold the throne of Wei from 369 BCE until his death in 319. He was the longest-reigning ruler of Wei (and the third-longest reigning ruler in all of the Warring States),[6] exceeding the tenure of even his famed grandfather Marquis Wen by one year. Like his rival contemporaries Duke Xiao in Qin and Tian Yinqi in Qi, Wei Ying inherited a legacy of achievement upon which he was eager to build. Unlike those of his rivals, Wei Ying's ambitions were persistently thwarted.

His reign has a quality of Shakespearean tragedy. He was a forceful and dynamic leader, unafraid to undertake ambitious projects or pioneer bold new strategies. He possessed incredible reserves of ingenuity and resilience, demonstrating a capacity to adapt and persevere even in the face of crushing adversity. His legacy does not conform to conventional measures of "failure" and "success." He undoubtedly left the state of Wei weaker than it was upon his accession to the throne. But in the space of his 51-year reign, Wei Ying arguably did as much to remake the political culture of the Zhou world as had his celebrated grandfather.

The sheer scope of Wei Ying's ambition, in retrospect, is quite astounding. The political program that he put into effect began so early in his reign and had so many different moving parts that he must have begun planning it long before the death of his father in 370 BCE. He clearly had a sophisticated grasp of the strategic situation of the Zhou world. He understood that power flowed from multiple sources and had various aspects. Military force was of course key, but political, economic, and cultural resources were equally important, and had to be harnessed by any ruler who wished to exert a broad impact. Wei Ying obviously hoped that his impact would be virtually limitless.

Reconstructing the history of Wei Ying's long reign is a frustrating task. There was a general purge of written records of all the Warring States in the wake of the Qin unification, but because Wei Ying had been an especially intense adversary of early Qin reformers (as we read in the previous chapter), the records of his court were clearly singled out for special diligence by Qin censors. In some cases, Qin chroniclers altered their account of the past to give Qin rulers credit for inspiring, or actually accomplishing, projects undertaken by Wei Ying. Wei Ying was so active, however, that no purge of the record, no matter how thorough, was able to completely efface the evidence of his influence and ambition.

What was Wei Ying trying to do? We noted at the beginning of Chapter 7 that by the mid-fourth century BCE the eventual demise of the Zhou kings was clear. Rulers and elites throughout the Warring States anticipated that the reign of the Zhou kings would end: that, in the terms of the Zhou's own professed doctrine, the Zhou dynasty would lose the "Mandate of Heaven." This left open the question of what order would replace that of the Zhou and who would lead it. Wei Ying obviously understood the situation and began his reign determined that the new order would be forged in and led by Wei.

This might sound like a megalomaniacal ambition, but in fairness to Wei Ying, his actions suggest that he did not embrace it gratuitously or out of mere vanity. Though he obviously believed that, in 369 BCE, Wei had an opportunity to bring the crisis of the Warring States to a close, he likewise understood that any such opportunity was provisional and eroding quickly. Wei had been the most powerful of the Zhou states since the reign of Wei Ying's grandfather Marquis Wen, whose achievements could not have been matched by any of his contemporaries, and would not be eclipsed until long after Marquis Wen's death in 396 BCE. But by the time that Wei Ying took the throne in 369 BCE, though Wei remained the most powerful state in absolute terms (i.e. arable land, tax revenues, population, soldiers-in-arms), in relative terms it was already in decline.

Wei's "brother states" of Zhao and Han had not only slipped the bonds of the triple alliance formed by Marquis Wen, but had also emulated the reforms that had made Wei so economically wealthy and militarily powerful.[7] Wei's neighboring states of Qi to the east and Qin in the west had (as discussed in Chapters 7 and 8, respectively) likewise joined the common wave of reform, and done much to close the gap between themselves and mighty Wei. Even the sprawling confederation of Chu to the south had become a threat under the leadership of Wu Qi, poached from the Wei court during the reign of Wei Ying's father.

If any of the Warring States had a window of opportunity to forge a new pan-political order in 369 BCE, it was Wei, but that window was closing rapidly. Any attempt to leverage Wei's power would require both careful planning and bold action. Wei Ying showed himself capable of both.

Most of the surviving transmitted sources produced after Wei Ying's accession to the throne make mention of him, and several describe him as "fond of war."[8] There is some truth to this characterization. Within his first decade in power, he had embroiled Wei in more than half a dozen military campaigns, with mixed success, and for almost his entire reign Wei remained periodically on the warpath.[9] But Wei Ying's military operations, while they were a cornerstone of his overall policy of rule, were carried out in coordination with a strategy of diplomacy, propaganda, economic stewardship, and public works.

Wei Ying undeniably focused much attention on military preparedness. He initiated a recruitment program that became famous throughout the Warring States. A series of endurance and skills tests were established for potential soldiers in the armies of Wei. They had to demonstrate mastery of the crossbow (see Fig. 13), and complete a forced march of 100 *li* (about 40 kilometers) wearing heavy armor and carrying a sword, heavy crossbow, halberd, quiver of 50 bolts, and three days' provisions by noon in a single day. Men who completed these tests were enlisted into an elite force of "warrior troops" (*wuzu*) and won special tax exemptions and property privileges for their families. These elite forces were feared and respected by the rulers and military leaders of the other states.[10]

Wei Ying paid as much attention to defensive infrastructure as he did to strengthening his state's offensive capabilities. In 366 BCE he began fortifying the aptly named city of Martial Fortress (Wucheng), on the western frontier of the territories Wei had captured from Qin. This prompted Duke Xian of Qin to attack Wei, and started the series of campaigns that ended with Wei's disastrous defeat at Stone Gate in 364 BCE, from which Wei Ying had to rely on rescue by the armies of Zhao.

Duke Xian of Qin may have interpreted the fortification of Martial Fortress as an act of aggression, or he may merely have disliked the obstacle it would pose to the recovery of Qin's lost territory on the West Bank of the Yellow River. Whatever the case may have been, the subsequent course of Wei Ying's actions shows that the project at Martial Fortress was part of a much larger plan, the direct, immediate object of which was not aggression against the state of Qin.

In the same year as his attempt to fortify Wucheng, Wei Ying met with the ruler of Han for a conference at a city close to the fortified boundary between

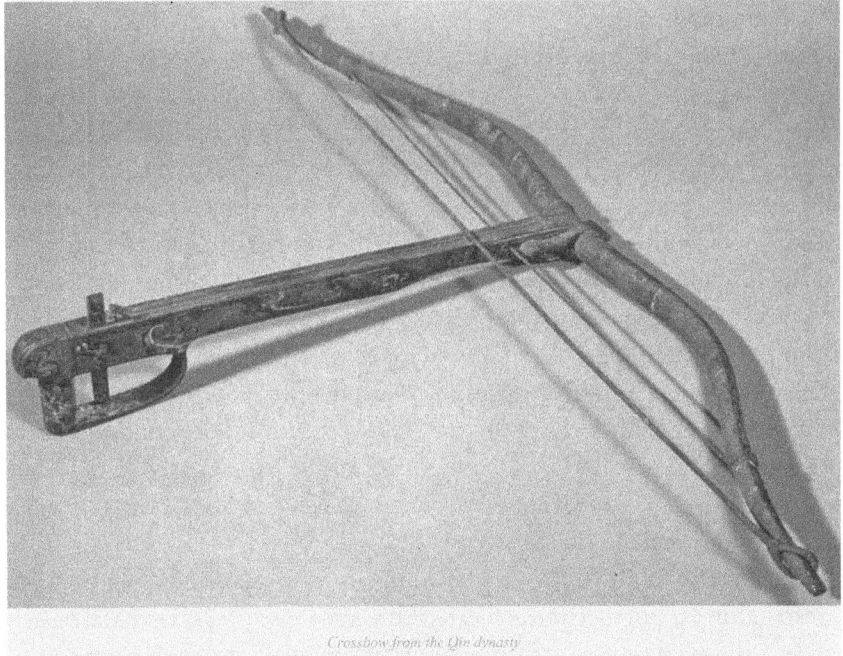

Crossbow from the Qin dynasty

Fig. 13. The crossbow was the main weapon issued to infantry soldiers in the army of the Warring States period. Massed columns of crossbowmen were the backbone of any military force, much like the musketeers of early modern Europe. This crossbow was manufactured for the arsenal of ancient Qin and was discovered among the terra cotta warriors that guarded the First Emperor's tomb. (Source: worldhistoryedu.com.)

Han and Wei's eastern "Henei" territories.[11] This was the opening of a combined campaign of military aggression and diplomacy that would reshape relations between the "Three Jin" successor states over the next half decade. In 365 BCE, despite the setback at Stone Gate, Wei Ying managed to capture territory from the neighboring state of Song.[12] In 362 BCE he defeated the combined forces of Zhao and Han, capturing the Zhao commander in the process. Wei pressed the attack, and by the time the fighting had ended Zhao had lost three cities to Wei.[13]

This campaign of aggression was matched by a corresponding "diplomatic offensive." The challenge that Wei Ying was grappling with most concretely in these operations was that of geography. In the partition that had created the "three Jin" successor states, Wei had come into possession of a territory shaped like a south-pointing magnet or horseshoe, consisting of a "Hedong" arm in the west and a "Henei" arm in the east connected by a narrow adjoining territory. This had made Wei vulnerable at several points, as when Wu Qi's armies had effectively cut the territorial bridge joining Hedong and Henei, or when

Han had proposed simply giving one part of the Wei domain to Wei Ying and the other to his brother, Wei Huan.

Wei Ying set out to redress these vulnerabilities through strategic exchanges of territory. In 361 BCE, working off the momentum gained from his string of victories against Song, Zhao, and Han, Wei Ying met with the ruler of Zhao and agreed to exchange two cities in northern Wei for a single city of southern Zhao.[14] Shortly after, Wei Ying negotiated the exchange of Zhao's former capital city of Zhongmou for the city of Fanyang, about 80 kilometers northeast.[15] In 357 BCE Wei Ying received an emissary from the ruler of Han who brokered a comparable agreement. In exchange for several cities, most likely in Wei's Hedong region, Han ceded a line of cities extending south from the vitally strategic White Horse Ford on the Yellow River in present-day Henan Province.[16] This gave Wei a much more defensible frontier against Qi to the east, and created a much wider strategic buffer between Wei's eastern frontier and its new capital of Daliang.

The overall effect of Wei Ying's early military campaigns and diplomacy was to expand and strengthen the Henei region as the strategic center of Wei power, while at the same time re-enforcing his defensive fortifications along the western frontier of the Hedong region. By pushing the boundaries of the Henei region eastward and northward and going on the defensive in the west, he sought to make the key economic and demographic assets of Wei more easily defensible and the projection of Wei power eastward less costly in labor and resources. This was the logic of his integrated campaigns of conquest and diplomatic negotiations in the first decade of his rule.

In 361 BCE Wei Ying moved into the new capital of Daliang (Greatbridge) on the site of the present-day city of Kaifeng. From that point forward Wei was referred to alternatively as Liang ("Bridge," the second word in the name of Wei's new capital). The shift of the capital is often interpreted as a defensive measure, but that was almost certainly not the case. The threats to Wei from the east were as substantial as those from the west. Wei Ying was moving the capital to the Henei region to put his base of operations closer to the economic and demographic center of the Zhou world, at the intersection of the major trade routes along which the wealth of an increasingly prosperous society was moving. The system of western fortifications that he began in 366 BCE was an attempt to mitigate the threat posed by Qin, so that he would have spare power to apply in his efforts to rework the geopolitical dynamics of the larger Zhou world from his new capital. In other words, he was defending his rear in the west so that he could go on the offensive in the east.

The new capital was a major project of urban planning and civil engineering, one that must have begun almost as soon as Wei Ying took the throne of Wei. Palaces, gardens, and monumental multistoried wooden towers adorned the new city. In a gesture of magnanimity, Wei Ying granted a hunting park on the outskirts of the capital, Welcome Pond (*Fengze*), "to the people," giving common farmers permission to hunt and fish in what had previously been an elite preserve.[17]

In 360 BCE a series of hydraulic engineering projects was completed around the capital. A system of irrigation ditches brought water from the Yellow River to the farmlands surrounding Daliang, increasing agricultural productivity. At the same time, canals were dug to facilitate the movement of goods in and out of the capital by riverboat, tying Daliang securely into the ever-accelerating networks of trade driving economic growth throughout the Warring States. The canals also served as a defensive moat to protect the approaches of the capital from overland attack.[18]

The Stone Gate campaign, in which Wei's armies had been badly defeated by the forces of Qin (as discussed in the previous chapter) had set back Wei Ying's plans to bolster his defenses in the West, but in 358 BCE Wei Ying sent one of his most trusted generals to re-initiate the fortification of the western frontier. Over several years an extensive series of defensive walls were built, precursors (along with other fortification systems built by other Warring States) of the famous "Great Wall" visited by tourists today (see Fig. 14). This system screened Wei from the approach of Qin armies through the mountain passes on Qin's eastern frontier. By the end of Wei Ying's reign the fortifications would stretch more than 150 kilometers, in an arc extending from the city of Shaoliang (Lesserbridge) in the north to the foothills of Mount Hua in the south, past the southern bank of the Wei River.[19]

In 356 BCE Wei Ying hosted an event in his new capital that gave advance notice of his ultimate ambitions. The rulers of the small states of Wey, Song, Confucius's home state of Lu, and Wei's "brother state" Han came to "pay court" to Wei Ying, playing the role of his "vassals" in attending him as "lord."[20] The summit included a mixture of austere sacrificial rights and gala festivities. One drinking party that Wei Ying used to showcase the grand architecture of his new capital is commemorated in an anecdote that will be discussed in more detail, shortly.

The summit was noteworthy because it served as a kind of "dry run" for more ambitious meetings that Wei Ying would host later in his reign. In these moments we can see how Wei Ying alternated between different aspects of an

Fig. 14. The Qin empire (221–206 BCE) used corvée labor enlisted from all parts of its extensive realm to extend and link together pre-existing systems of fortifications that had been erected by the contending Warring States, establishing the first Great Wall. These are the remains of the Qin Great Wall still visible in Guyang County, Inner Mongolia. (Source: chinadailyhk.com.)

integrated strategy. He would first exert effort toward "changing the facts on the ground," expanding his territory (through conquest and/or diplomacy) and developing key infrastructure like irrigation works, canals, roads, and defensive walls. He would then seek to secure those material gains by formalizing his new position among the larger community of Zhou states through symbolic and ceremonial actions like the summit of 356 BCE.

These ceremonial dimensions of Wei Ying's program might seem frivolous or misguided from our twenty-first-century perspective, but they were not without strategic logic. Extrapolating from the reports of early sources, during Wei Ying's reign the state of Wei had almost as many men under arms as the states of Han, Zhao, and Qi combined.[21] This was made possible by the very dense population of Wei's fertile lands and the efficiency of the bureaucratic institutions that had been built to draw upon the material and human resources of Wei's territory. But sheer numbers would not be enough to restore the position of dominance that Wei had enjoyed in the time of Marquis Wen.

The paradox of Wei Ying's situation was that he (in all likelihood) had more soldiers and revenue than his grandfather had commanded, but was less powerful in relative terms. Marquis Wen had been the most powerful ruler of his time, able to force his will upon the Son of Heaven himself, because he had forged an effective coalition between the "three Jin" successor states. As long as Wei, Han, and Zhao were pursuing coordinated goals, they were unstoppable.

The breakdown of this unity during the time of Wei Ying's father, Marquis Wu, had been the chief (though not the only) cause of Wei's relative decline. The effects on Wei's power had been almost immediate. During the reign of Marquis Wen, for example, Wei had conquered and annexed the state of Zhongshan (as described in Chapter 5). Wei's hegemony over the territories of former Zhongshan, however, required total cooperation with Zhao, which stood between Wei's northern frontier and the southern limits of Zhongshan. The Wei armies that had conquered Zhongshan had crossed through Zhao, and all communication between the Wei court and its agents in the former Zhongshan lands likewise had to pass through Zhao's territory. We do not know in what precise year it occurred, but some time shortly after war broke out between Zhao and Wei in 381 BCE, the people of Zhongshan threw off the yoke of their Wei conquerors and revived the independent ruling line of the Zhongshan state.[22]

If so much had been at stake for Wei in the maintenance of the "three-Jin" coalition, why had its rulers allowed it to fall apart? The chronicles attribute the cause to Marquis Wu's personal failings, but that is at least partly an expression of the social interests of the literati who composed the chronicles. They were highly motivated to depict a world in which all problems could be fixed by individual learning and the building of personal character: the more traction that message gained, the more opportunity would be available to literati like themselves for political and social advancement.

The disintegration of the Wei-Han-Zhao coalition was more concretely driven by what social scientists call the "prisoner's dilemma." Very often, when acting as a group, people can achieve more by restraining their immediate pursuit of their own self-interest, but they will only do so if they are confident that the other members of the group will accept the same constraints (the "prisoner's dilemma" refers to the hypothetical scenario in which a group of prisoners, being questioned separately, will all go free if none of them accepts the offer of reduced jail time for testifying against their accomplices).[23]

Wei Ying's Father, Marquis Wu, breached trust in 381 BCE, when he had intervened on Wey's behalf against his "brother state" of Zhao. One might question his judgment in that decision, but the breakdown of the peace had probably been inevitable. Zhi Yao had come close to wiping out all three ruling clans of Wei, Han, and Zhao through sheer ruthlessness before his death in 453 BCE, and he had never controlled anything like the bureaucratized war machines developed through the reforms of leaders like Li Kui. As Han and Zhao emulated Wei's program of reform and all three states became increasingly more powerful, each state posed an ever more potentially lethal threat to the other two. As the stakes grew progressively higher, any shift in the balance of power could cause suspicion to win out over trust and the informal compact binding the three states together to unravel. Zhao's move to expand its territory at the expense of Wey (which itself was a product of Zhao's fear of having fallen behind Wei and Han in those states' wars of conquest against weaker neighbors such as Zheng and Song) had been the triggering event, but even if Marquis Wu had not broken the peace in that instance, some other crisis would probably have come along in time.

Wei Ying's use of ceremonial occasions like the summit of 356 BCE was an effort to escape the "prisoner's dilemma" and re-establish the trust that had held the coalition of Han, Zhao, and Wei together during the reign of Marquis Wen of Wei. If Wei's position as leader could be formally institutionalized, so that its authority could be depended upon to keep the peace, the pressures driving the individual states to compete for more power might be allayed. In the same way that all the prisoners in the hypothetical dilemma would stay silent if someone that they trusted assured them that everyone else was doing the same, individual states like Zhao would feel more secure within their current borders if there was a force they trusted to have both the power and the effective authority to deter any external threats. Wei Ying's coordinated military, economic, and political strategy aimed at developing Wei into just such a force.

The ruling elites of the wider Zhou world all clearly understood what Wei Ying was attempting and offered him resistance. The Zhou king had little material power to obstruct Wei Ying's plans, but he still had symbolic cards to play. Wey was one of the only vassal states in the Zhou realm whose ruler held the formal rank and title of "duke" (*gong*); all of the other regional courts used the title for their own rulers as a ceremonial courtesy (analogous to a lieutenant who commands a warship being addressed as "captain" by his crew). In response to the ruler of Wey "paying court" to Wei Ying as overlord, the Zhou king demoted the ruling lineage of Wey's title from "duke" to "marquis."[24] Wei Ying, after all, still only held the rank of marquis, so if the ruler of Wey was to be Wei's vassal, Wey could not hold a higher rank under the auspices of the Zhou king. It was a somewhat empty gesture, but it was a way of signaling to all the regional lords that there would be a political price for abetting Wei Ying's ambitions.

Wei's "brother states" also understood the implications of Wei Ying's ceremonial maneuvers, and Zhao moved to counter. Though Han attended the summit of 356 BCE, Zhao, which had almost certainly been invited to attend, did not. Moreover, in the same year that Wei Ying convened his "guests" in Daliang, Zhao met with the rulers of Song and Qi in one summit held in Qi territory and hosted the ruler of the northeastern state of Yan in another summit held in Zhao.[25] These were a clear signal that Zhao would resist any attempt by Wei to formally establish its authority and would continue to conduct its relations with other states independently of Wei.

Tension between Zhao and Wei had broken the "three Jin" coalition during the days of Wei Ying's father, when Zhao invaded the state of Wey in 381 BCE. At mid-century it was Zhao that once again produced the first serious test of Wei Ying's attempt to formalize Wei's supremacy. The later challenge, moreover, took the same shape as the former. Perhaps emboldened by the king's demotion of Wey, Zhao invaded its smaller neighbor once again in 354 BCE, taking two cities and threatening Wey's capital. Wei Ying dispatched an army to rescue his "vassal" Wey and laid siege to Handan, the capital of Zhao.[26]

As we read in Chapter 7, Wei Ying's assertion of his authority was obstructed by the intercession of Qi, under the tactical leadership of Sun Bin. As Wei's army besieged Handan, Qi launched an assault against Daliang. When Pang Juan, the Wei commander, rushed his forces back from the siege of Handan, having been fooled by the stratagems of his old "brother disciple" Sun Bin into believing that the Qi army was ineptly led and would be easily dispatched, he was ambushed at Cassia Hill and taken prisoner.

This defeat took the Zhou world by surprise. It had been several decades since Qi had exerted its military might beyond its borders and achieved such a decisive victory. The states of Song and Wey, which had just sworn allegiance to Wei at the summit of 356 BCE, were intimidated into joining a coalition with Qi to besiege Wei's city of Highmount (Xiangling). While Highmount was under siege, Shang Yang, who had previously served as deputy for Wei Ying's prime minister (as described in the previous chapter), led an army from Qin that managed to temporarily capture the former Wei capital of Anyi.

The defeats at Cassia Hill and Anyi were a severe blow to Wei Ying's prestige, but militarily he was not significantly incapacitated. His armies regrouped, broke the siege of Highmount, forced Shang Yang to withdraw back to Qin, and captured Zhao's capital of Handan. Qi was compelled to appeal to the southern state of Chu for aid, and only when he was threatened with the prospect of fighting six states at once (the smaller states of Wey and Song, along with the large states of Qi, Qin, Chu, and Zhao) did Wei Ying agree to an armistice with Qi, Wey, and Song. In 351 BCE Wei Ying met separately with the ruler of Zhao. After brokering the return of Handan to Zhao, the two rulers performed a covenant rite to seal the peace.[27]

The battle of Cassia Hill helped establish the legend of Sun Bin and the prestige of the putative teachings of his fabled ancestor, Sun Wu ("Master Sun" of the *Sunzi bingfa*). The fall of Anyi propelled Shang Yang to the effective post of Prime Minister of Qin, where his transformation of that state into a newly powerful force intensified. It thus might seem illogical that Wei Ying emerged from the campaigns of 354–351 BCE with his ambition to lead the Zhou world undeterred.

But the significance of the defeats suffered by Wei Ying during the mid-fourth-century BCE wars only became clear in hindsight (and was inflated by embellishments in repeated recounts by later chroniclers). Viewing his situation from the perspective of the moment, in 350 BCE Wei Ying had reason to believe that his plans remained viable. A powerful coalition had risen to obstruct him, and had only managed to do minimal damage to his actual capacity to make war. He had lost no territory, and despite all of the setbacks he had suffered he had provisionally achieved the object for which he had initially mobilized: Zhao's encroachment on Wey was thwarted, and Zhao's rulers had been forced to humble themselves to Wei to recover their own capital.

Over the course of the next decade, Wei Ying pressed ahead with his plans to reorder the Zhou world. He was a ruler in quest of more power, and like so many of the other rulers of the Warring States he understood that a key dimension of power in the evolving Zhou political realm flowed from the growing community of literati knights. The *Records of the Historian* notes that Wei Ying was famed in his time for being "humbly courteous and materially generous" in his efforts to attract "worthies."[28] As the story of Wei Ying's interview with "superstar" Master Chunyu Kun (recounted in Chapter 7) suggests, Wei Ying's deliberately cultivated reputation succeeded in attracting literati. The most famous Masters of the day all at least passed through his court, and some of them were enlisted to realize his grand dreams.

Unlike his revered grandfather, Marquis Wen, who is praised even today for his commitment to "cultivating worthies," Wei Ying generally receives little credit for the patronage that he lavished upon the learned Masters of his day. The *Records of the Historian*, for example, suggests that he sought the aid of literati only after being weakened by military defeats. His loss of the talents of Shang Yang to Qin, and his failure to secure the service of other famous literati, is taken as evidence that he himself was unlettered, or that he did not have his grandfather's ability to recognize true merit.

We should be suspicious, however, of how neatly the sources draw this negative picture of Wei Ying. As noted above, the literati chroniclers who recounted Wei Ying's story had a concrete interest in promoting the idea that a failure to recognize or retain talent could result in doom. The more traction the concept achieved, the more they would benefit in terms of opportunity and emolument. The fact that Wei Ying had more difficulty retaining personnel than his grandfather is almost certainly a product of changing times: lateral mobility is the natural product of a labor market that becomes more competitive—ask any Wall Street broker or professional athlete.

If we "read against" the biases of the sources, it is clear that Wei Ying faithfully emulated his grandfather's policy of cultivating and utilizing literati talents in his development of Wei's power. There was no pretense or insincerity in Wei Ying's patronage of literati; he engaged the teachings of the Masters knowledgeably and seriously, and treated their contribution as vital to his larger political program. Under his rule the Wei court became a leading intellectual center of its day.

Though the records of Wei Ying's reign were intensively purged, much evidence survives of his court's engagement with the intellectual currents of the day. An example can be found in an account of the summit of 356 BCE, at which Wei Ying hosted the rulers of Han, Lu, Wey, and Song. A surviving anecdote describes a drinking party held during that summit at the "Fan Pavilion," a monumental tower adorning the Wei capital of Daliang.[29]

During the drinking party the visiting Duke of Lu is said to have risen and offered a speech by way of a toast. The duke recounted stories of four wise rulers of old. The first was of the sage King Yu, who employed a brewer so skilled that he had produced the most enchanting wine ever tasted. On sampling the wine, Yu dismissed the brewer, explaining that he did so as a warning to future leaders: "Someday, there will be rulers who lose their states because of wine." The second story concerned a ruler whose chef produced the most delicious food ever tasted; the third story told of a ruler whose consorts were the most alluring ever seen; and the last story recalled a ruler whose terraces and pavilions were the grandest ever built. Each of these rulers had relinquished the pleasure of such luxuries, warning that "someday there will be rulers" who suffer disasters on account of such indulgences.

When his stories were finished, the Duke of Lu pointed around him to the scene in which Wei Ying's drinking party was being held. The wine, food, women, and architecture of Wei Ying's court all matched the grandeur of those former rulers' luxuries. If even one of those vices could bring a ruler catastrophe, concluded the Duke of Lu, what must Wei Ying expect from indulging in all four? Wei Ying was duly alarmed by this warning and repeatedly praised the Duke of Lu's words as "Excellent!"[30]

This might seem like an innocuously quaint parable, but it was a carefully crafted polemic designed to deliver provocative and partisan arguments. The Duke of Lu almost certainly did not make a speech remotely resembling the one recorded in the anecdote; he was appropriated as the mouthpiece of a doctrine that was growing in popularity and influence among literati in the mid-fourth century BCE. The existence of this doctrine is well evidenced, but the exact nature of the group that promoted it is somewhat mysterious.

The doctrine in question is most often associated with the figure of Yang Zhu (ca. 395–ca. 335 BCE) or "Master Yang," the concrete facts of whose life are virtually completely unknown. The crux of Yang Zhu's teachings, to the best that we can reconstruct them using available evidence, was rooted in "valuing life." Yang Zhu proposed that any search for "the Way" must begin with the question, "what will make a person (particularly, the ruler) healthy and long-lived?"[31]

On this basis the followers of Yang Zhu claimed that they had formulated a political doctrine more consistently reliable than those of both Confucius and Mo Di. From the perspective of the followers of Confucius, for example, Mo Di's denigration of music was venally materialistic. Conversely, from the perspective of Mo Di's followers, Confucius's infatuation with music was foolishly idealistic. The disciples of Yang Zhu declared that both Confucius and Mo Di had missed the point entirely. Too much music (or, as the anecdote set at Fan Pavilion showcased—wine, food, sex, or living space) would wreck your health and shorten your life, but too little music (or wine, etc.) would have the same effect. The right course was thus neither to ban music or fetishize it, but to find the engagement with music that would be most conducive to health and longevity. If only literati would get their priorities straight, all the questions that had vexed so many misguided "Masters" could be resolved and the state set to rights.[32]

We cannot know how much actual traction Yang Zhu's teachings got at the court of Wei Ying. If scribes at the Wei court composed and disseminated the anecdote about the drinking party at Fan Pavilion, then Wei Ying and his officials were obviously broadcasting the message that they appreciated Yang Zhu's teachings and were open to employing his followers. Conversely, if the anecdote was produced outside the Wei court by the followers of Yang Zhu themselves, by setting their teachings into a scene that flatteringly showcased Wei Ying's power they were making a plea for patronage. Either way, we can be sure that the Wei court was a milieu of sufficient intellectual sophistication to put it "into play" for groups of literati with doctrines and agendas as elaborate and robust as that espoused by Yang Zhu.

We see more evidence of the intellectual ferment at Wei Ying's court in the sources concerning Mencius (Meng Ke or Mengzi, "Master Meng," ca. 390–ca. 305 BCE), the most famous Master of the fourth century BCE and a vehement opponent of Yang Zhu.[33] Mencius was a native of Zou, the small vassalage ruled by Confucius's home state of Lu. He had studied under a disciple of Confucius's grandson Zisi, so he represented the fourth generation of the fellowship that had first formed around Confucius himself. In his early career as a Master he was based in the capital of Lu, where Confucius's descendants continued to live and revere his memory, and which was still the effective (though informal) "headquarters" of the extended Confucian fellowship spread throughout the Zhou states. In Lu, Mencius gathered disciples and acquired a broad reputation for learning and wisdom. From there, sometime in the late fourth century BCE, he set out with a group of his disciples in search of a ruler who would enlist him as an official. His first destination on this journey was Wei Ying's court, where he arrived in the final years of Wei Ying's reign.[34]

The first book of the *Mencius* is named after Wei Ying and recounts several interviews between the two men during Mencius's sojourn in the Wei capital of Daliang. The encounter as depicted in the *Mencius* was contentious, perhaps because ruler and Master were so much alike. Mencius (if the testimony of the *Mencius* is accurate) believed himself to have a great destiny. He claimed to have the power to transform a ruler into the figure who could reunite the world and revive the Mandate of Heaven. As impressive as that feat sounds, it was not the outer limit of what Mencius saw as his destiny. The stakes of his mission were higher than the mere establishment of a new royal dynasty; he was fighting to save human civilization itself from destruction.[35]

The crisis, from Mencius's perspective, stemmed from the surging popularity of the teachings of Mo Di and Yang Zhu. If those doctrines prevailed, the true Way as taught by Confucius would be forever lost, and the people of the world consigned to living in bestial turmoil.[36] Mencius traveled the Warring

States in search of a ruler who would submit to his instruction and lend him a broad platform for the propagation of the sages' Way.

Like Confucius before him, Mencius claimed only to transmit what he had been bequeathed from earlier generations, but his formulation of Confucius's teachings was quite innovative, crafted to meet the challenge being posed by Mo Di and Yang Zhu. Both Mo Di and Yang Zhu claimed to be able to provide perfectly consistent and objective standards of value by which ethical choices could be made and moral outcomes measured. They also asserted that external forces such as rewards and punishments would be sufficient to reorder society and make the state serve just ends, rendering forms of personal cultivation like Confucius's program of "learning" meaningless.

Mencius set out to prove that Confucius had been right. He argued that moral truths could not be realized using purely objective reasoning as Mo Di and Yang Zhu proposed, but could only be apprehended and carried out in practice through the shaping and activation of our subjective inborn "nature." His most famous illustration involved a child about to fall into a well. The fate of the child will not impact an observer's health and longevity, nor can the tragic poignancy of the situation really be explained in terms of what material "benefit" might be gained or lost. Thus neither the teachings of Mo Di (who "valued benefit") or Yang Zhu (who "valued life"), according to Mencius, can capture the moral truth of the moment. That truth can only be found in the instantaneous emotional response that any person, no matter how venal or callous, would experience on seeing the child about to fall: a pang of pain and terror that had nothing to do with any thought of reward or punishment, but that was purely an expression of empathy for the plight of an innocent human being.[37]

This pang of empathy was, Mencius claimed, one of the "seeds" from which the Way grew. Human nature contained four such "seeds" when a person was born: the heart that could not stand the suffering of others (activated by the endangered child), the heart of shame, the heart of modesty, and the heart of right and wrong. Each of these "seeds," though present in every human being from birth, was quite faint and weak. They needed to be developed to produce the mature virtues of the Way: humaneness, rightness, ritual propriety, and wisdom. The means to developing these four "seeds" was the program of learning advocated by Confucius: an intensely personal engagement with the poetry, prose, ritual, and music of the ancient sages, in the company and with the support of fellow seekers and under the guidance of a wise and learned Master.

Mencius taught that if a ruler of even a state as small as "100 *li* (about 40 kilometers) square" learned assiduously and became a true "gentleman" possessed of humaneness, rightness, ritual propriety, and wisdom, the whole world would gravitate to him like water running downhill, and he would inevitably become the founder of a new royal dynasty possessed of the Mandate of Heaven. More importantly, the advent of a True King would finally choke off the toxic teachings of deceivers like Mo Di and Yang Zhu, and restore the rightful authority of the authentic Way of the sages. This was the only hope for humanity, and thus everything depended on the success of Mencius, who (according to Mencius himself) was the steward of the Way in his generation.[38]

Wei Ying obviously possessed much more than the requisite territory to fulfill Mencius's vision. That alone, however, does not explain why Mencius journeyed to Wei Ying's court. Many states that fit Mencius's criteria did not entice the Master to visit, so his choice to travel to Wei was a sign that during Wei Ying's rule his court was perceived as an intellectual hub where an ambitious Master like Mencius would find an informed audience. Beyond this, it would have been clear to Mencius that Wei Ying (as we shall read in more detail below) had shared Mencius's dream of founding a new royal dynasty. Mencius perhaps calculated on that basis that Wei Ying would be especially receptive to his message.

The encounter did not transpire as Mencius might have hoped. The opening lines of the *Mencius* depict Wei Ying and Mencius meeting for the first time across a virtually unbridgeable philosophical gulf. Wei Ying's first words to Mencius were reportedly, "Sir! Showing no reluctance to travel 1,000 *li*, you have come. Surely you must have something to benefit my state?" The mention of "benefit," the cardinal value of Mo Di, to Mencius, was the equivalent of waving a red cloth in front of a bull. Mencius launched into a long speech about why Wei Ying should "speak only of humaneness and rightness, what need is there to speak of benefit?"[39]

Relations between the two men went downhill from there. At one point in the *Mencius* the Master is shown offering consolation to his host,[40] but the text's final assessment of Wei Ying is quite harsh. He is deemed especially "inhumane" (the exact opposite of the quality developed from the "heart that cannot bear the suffering of others"), because the harm that he meted out to his enemies eventually impacted even those he loved.[41]

The condemnation of the *Mencius* has helped solidify Wei Ying's image as one of the most benighted rulers in East Asian history, but this judgment is arguably biased. Wei Ying's relations with the Confucian fellowship were more strained than those of his grandfather, Marquis Wen, had been, but that divergence almost certainly did not stem from any great difference in attitude or education between grandfather and grandson. Rather, the change did not flow from Wei Ying's mindset or character, but from the nature of the larger literati community. The intellectual culture of the literati world had become vastly more complex and pluralistic in Wei Ying's time as compared with that of Marquis Wen almost a century prior. Groups like the followers of Yang Zhu and eclectic figures such as Chunyu Kun had not existed (or to the extent that they did, did not wield much influence) during Marquis Wen's days. If Wei Ying had been able to achieve the same high degree of prestige and popularity among literati as had Marquis Wen by becoming the "disciple" of Zixia, Wei Ying might have embraced a Confucian Master such as Mencius as his "teacher."

But the literati world had moved on. Taking the same kind of partisan stance adopted earlier by Marquis Wen would not have yielded the same results in the diversified and contentious literati community post-350 BCE. There was no longer a single doctrine or model of rulership that had broad enough currency among literati to achieve what Wei Ying desired in his recruitment of personnel. He was thus compelled to take a more ecumenical and open-ended posture in doctrinally engaging with the Masters and disciples of his own time.

When Wei Ying asked Mencius about "benefit," for example, it is unlikely that he was either wholly ignorant of the term's implications or deliberately trying to offend the Master from Zou. Rather, he knew that "benefit" had become a broadly used term of art among various groups of Masters and disciples (including both the latter-day disciples of Mo Di and Yang Zhu), and was making a good-faith effort to speak with a "Master" in his own language. Mencius's desire to see Wei Ying commit overtly and exclusively to a narrowly orthodox "Confucian Way" was too far out of step with the ruler's deep-seated instincts and strategic outlook to ever have had much chance of success. After a brief sojourn at Wei Ying's court, Mencius departed for the state of Qi, where his efforts achieved (slightly) more traction.

As the saga of Mencius (from the perspective of the Wei court, a mere footnote) demonstrates, the history of Wei Ying's relations with the literati community over his long 51-year reign is complex and fascinating, and much more could be said about the figures who came through his court. Zhuang Zhou (i.e. Zhuangzi or "Master Zhuang"), for example, famous for having dreamed that he was a butterfly and awakening to wonder whether he was a butterfly dreaming about being a man,[42] is said to have visited Wei Ying's court and been considered for the post of prime minister.[43] We will defer discussing Zhuang Zhou's putative teachings for a later exploration of the origins of the "Daoist" movement.

It is important, however, to mention one other Master associated with Wei Ying's court, because his teachings were not only durably influential in the cultural history of the Warring States and later empire, but also played an important role in Wei Ying's strategic policies during the decade after the defeat at Cassia Hill. This was Master Zou Yan.

Zou Yan was a native of Qi, and most likely a kinsman of Tian Yinqi's prime minister, Zou Ji. Though Zou Yan is less well known (especially outside of East Asia) today, in his own lifetime he achieved much wider fame and much greater material success than Mencius.

Zou Yan's putative writings are for the most part lost (though fragments still survive and have been collected by late imperial scholars),[44] but in his lifetime they supposedly constituted more than 100,000 characters on subjects as diverse as astronomy, geography, calendrics, meteorology, and history. His teachings centered on what in modern English parlance is called "correlative cosmology," the body of theory which (in East Asia) centers on concepts of yin, yang, and the "five phases of *qi*" (wood, fire, earth, metal, water) that give rise to and control all matter and all phenomena.[45]

"*Qi*" is a concept that has become familiar to some readers in Europe and America through the popular literature on traditions grounded in early Chinese cosmological thought. "*Qi*" originally denoted steam or vapor. By the Warring States period the word had been taken to represent the fundamental matter/energy out of which all objects are composed and by which all dynamic processes are animated. In its original and most ethereal form *qi* is a gas so insubstantial that it is invisible and undetectable by the senses, and so dynamic that it is responsible for phenomena like lightning and magnetism.[46] The body of theory surrounding the operation and uses of *qi* is foundational to many cultural traditions that have become well known in global popular culture, such as *fengshui* (the art of designing the built environment to take maximum advantage of the flow of *qi* through space and time), acupuncture (the art of controlling the flow of *qi* through the body to foster health, by nurturing of the viscera in which the body generates different forms of *qi* and manipulation of the meridians through which it moves), and the divinatory practices based on the *Yi jing* (or *Classic of Change*).

Zou Yan did not invent these concepts, they had been current for centuries by the time he became active as a Master. But he was, according to our best evidence, among the most prominent thinkers to attempt to systematize ideas about yin, yang, and the "five phases of qi" and work them into a framework that could be consistently applied to practical affairs.[47] He can thus be credited as one of the ancestral "founding fathers" of cultural traditions that have become well known outside of East Asia today.

Zou Yan is said to have traveled broadly throughout the Warring States, and have been met with lavish courtesy and showered with rich emoluments at every court he visited.[48] When Zou Yan arrived in Greatbridge, for example, Wei Ying is said to have welcomed him with exaggerated pomp and courtesy. He did not wait for Zou Yan to arrive at court, but went out personally to meet the Master and his entourage in the suburbs of the capital. On meeting Zou Yan, Wei Ying himself performed the welcoming rite of "host" to "guest."[49] This was a radical humbling of Wei Ying's position of privilege and power, equivalent to the President of the United States serving as "doorman" to honor a guest's visit to the White House.

The story of Zou Yan's visit to Greatbridge is most likely apocryphal,[50] but it is exemplary of a fact about Wei Ying that would have become widely known throughout the Warring States. Wei Ying took an early interest in teachings about correlative cosmology and promoted them through some of the most prominent policies of his court. These ideas were foundational to one of his most cherished ambitions. It was thus natural that the "grandaddy of correlative cosmology" (Zou Yan) would become associated with Wei Ying in the popular imagination of the Warring States.

For Wei Ying one dimension of correlative cosmological teachings had special significance: the proposition that no events in either the natural or the human realm were wholly arbitrary, and that all processes bore the mark of the ordering patterns of the qi that makes up the cosmos. This included the very broadest movements of human history. The cyclical replacement of one dynasty by another (for example, of the Shang by the Zhou) was, like the changes in season over the course of the calendar year, accompanied and driven by cyclical changes in the prevailing qi of the cosmos. Someone who understood the patterns by which qi evolved could predict when and how the next change of dynasty would come, and could even harness cosmic energies to direct and hasten the transition from the current dynastic regime to the next.

The political stratagem for which Wei Ying harnessed the developing traditions of correlative cosmological thought occurred in 344 BCE. In that year Wei Ying gathered the rulers of 12 states outside his capital of Greatbridge, at the same Welcome Pond (Fengze) he had gifted to the common people of Wei when the capital had first been established. The use of Welcome Pond as a venue had almost certainly been conditioned by cosmological criteria, but its "public" nature was likewise a factor. Wei Ying was showing his people how much prestige he enjoyed among the other Zhou lords, and at the same time was showing the other Zhou lords what affectionate terms he was on with the common people.

The choice of Welcome Pond for this particular occasion was an especially magnanimous gesture, because the event that Wei Ying chose to share so intimately with his people was no less than his ascension to the position of king. Like the summit of 356 BCE, when the rulers of Han, Song, Wey, and Lu had paid court to Wei Ying as their overlord, in 344 BCE Wei Ying gathered the rulers of 12 states to give their fealty to him.[51] This time, however, the stakes had been raised. The 12 rulers gathered were not simply offering their submission to Wei Ying as liege, but were acknowledging him as the new Son of Heaven.

This might seem like facile political theater from our present-day perspective, but it was deadly serious, and exquisitely difficult to manage. The Zhou dynasty had held the Mandate of Heaven for 700 years. The last change of dynasty was so far out of collective memory that it was almost impossible to formulate the signs that would make such a transition even recognizable, much less credibly authentic. Wei Ying was setting out to shock the world, but to do so he had to find a way of committing a "transgression" (crowning oneself king in place of the still-reigning Zhou monarch) that everyone understood, but that no one had ever seen or could even imagine. This is why Wei Ying so desperately needed the services of literati schooled in the teachings of correlative cosmology.

The easy part was the semantics of the occasion. Wei Ying himself took the title king and compelled the lords in attendance to address him by that rank. This was unprecedented: none of the Zhou vassals on the Yellow River plain had ever trespassed upon the title of the Zhou Son of Heaven. But usurpation of the title would not be enough to carry the point of a dynastic transition across. "Barbarian" rulers in Chu, Wu, and Yue had deemed themselves "king," as had the leaders of non-Sinitic people like the Dai. If Wei Ying had simply begun using the title "king" he would have made himself appear boorishly grandiose rather than boldly progressive.

Wei Ying needed to craft a duly majestic occasion with unequivocally clear rituals and symbols. He had to show the world that the die was cast, the Rubicon had been crossed. That he succeeded in these tasks is perhaps best evinced by the fact that the records of what happened at Welcome Pond are so fragmentary and distorted.

The few surviving accounts of Welcome Pond give a hazy picture. One set of records claim that it was not Wei, but Qin that convened the meeting.[52] Another source admits that Wei was host, but claims that Wei Ying was "tricked" into convening the summit and declaring himself "Son of Heaven" by the clever Shang Yang.[53] These were almost certainly fabrications by Qin literati aimed at denigrating and debasing the political prestige of rival Wei. Since the Qin victors oversaw the final purge of the chronicles of the Warring States, their distorted records make up much of what we must rely on in reconstructing the events at Welcome Pond and their political rationale.

Even with such fragmentary evidence, however, the general shape of the conclave at Welcome Pond can be discerned. Long deliberations undoubtedly transpired at the Wei court, and intense planning sessions out of public view. Copious resources were expended. The few details we possess give us a sense of the concept that Wei Ying's court developed using correlative cosmological ideas.

The palaces in Greatbridge were remodeled and expanded to align with Wei Ying's new "royal" station. A new set of regalia were adopted: "cinnabar robes," a flag with nine silk tassels, a "falcon banner" with seven stars. Most significantly, Wei Ying commissioned a carriage in the style of the Xia dynasty in which to ride and styled himself "King of Xia."[54]

All of these paraphernalia and dimensions of the Welcome Pond conclave reflect the use of teachings like those of Zou Yan. These teachings underpinned the cosmological principles that necessitated, for example, the adoption of a "nine-tasseled" flag and a "seven-starred" banner, as well as the design of a "Xia dynasty carriage." The Xia dynasty had purportedly ended more than a millennium previously (and was almost certainly legendary in any case),[55] no one in Wei Ying's time could possibly have known what a "Xia dynasty" carriage looked like. However, using an understanding of the types of cosmic energies that had prevailed in the time of Xia, one would have been able (in theory, at least) to "reverse engineer" what the coloring, design, and iconography of a Xia carriage "must have been."

The reversion to the dynastic era of Xia was a hallmark of the kind of cosmological thinking associated with Zou Yan. According to these teachings, the universe moved in natural cycles akin to the change of the seasons. There were five basic "phases" of *qi*: wood, fire, earth, metal, and water. One type of *qi* transformed into another in regular sequence, producing the observable changes that we see in the world around us. As wood transforms into fire, for example, spring gives way to summer, and so on, until we cycle back to spring as water transforms into wood. The cycles of dynastic rule worked the same way: this was why one could "work back" through the pattern of time to reconstruct the institutes of the Xia. Xia had given way to Shang, Shang had given way to Zhou, and now Zhou was cycling back to Xia, each transition embodying a change in the prevailing phase of *qi*. There had most likely been subdivisions within that sequence, so that the cycle from Xia back to Xia corresponded to the five-stage pattern of the "phases" of *qi*, but that rationale was lost in the purge that destroyed most of the records of the Wei court.[56]

The conclave at Welcome Pond was, in its own time, "the greatest show on earth." It was as richly staged and elaborately planned as it was flagrantly audacious. Wei Ying may have been disappointed by the attendance. Though we know that Qin sent a prince of the ducal house to give the state's obeisance to Wei Ying,[57] none of the other large and powerful states of the Zhou world participated (in other words, the other 11 states that attended were all "small fry" such as Wey, Lu, and Song). A surviving anecdote describes a minister of the Han court pleading with his ruler not to comply with Wei Ying's summons, because "large states hate having a Son of Heaven, only small states benefit from it."[58]

The Zhou king, as he had done after the conclave of 356 BCE (when he had demoted the "Duke" of Wey to punish him for giving allegiance to Wei Ying), used his cachet to undermine Wei Ying's pageant at Welcome Pond. In 343 BCE (as discussed in Chapter 8), the Zhou king conferred the title of "Lord Protector" on Duke Xiao of Qin. The wholly symbolic title of "Lord Protector" was both a bribe to get Qin to repudiate the "allegiance" it had offered to Wei through its princely envoy and a pretext for the states that had not attended Welcome Pond to register their defiance of Wei Ying by sending their "congratulations" to Duke Xiao of Qin.[59] This move on the part of the Zhou court lent fuel to the later efforts of Qin scribes to distort and obscure the record of Wei Ying's ceremonial policies.

Though Wei Ying would no doubt have liked to have met with more compliance from the large states, he cannot have been totally disappointed in the outcome of his plans. He had successfully staged a rite of dynastic transition and thereby "thrown down the gauntlet." He had done so in the full knowledge that his claims would be militarily challenged and would have to be affirmed by a test of arms. He did not wait long before initiating that test himself.

In late 342 BCE Wei Ying sent an army to attack Han. Though the immediate casus belli is not recorded, Wei Ying was clearly punishing Han for its failure to attend the conclave at Welcome Pond. The armies of Wei and Han met at Southbridge (Nanliang), and Han was badly defeated.[60] As the armies of Wei advanced on the Han capital, Han sent a delegation to the court of Qi begging for assistance. It was a repetition of the strategic dynamic of 354 BCE, but with Han calling for rescue from Qi instead of Zhao.

Wei Ying's object was probably not the outright annexation of Han. He almost certainly would have been satisfied with a declaration from Han accepting Wei Ying's new status as king, and pledging allegiance to the new dynasty. Having achieved that, Wei Ying would then have joined forces with Han to compel Zhao to likewise acknowledge him as king. Having thus reconstituted the "three-Jin" alliance under his coordinated command, Wei Ying would then have been an unstoppable force. With all three "brother states" reunited in the cause of his new dynasty, Wei Ying would have had the power to compel all the (former) Zhou states to accept the new order.

As Tian Yinqi and his officials debated the merits of answering Han's call for aid, they knew exactly what was at stake. Some of Qi's courtiers, afraid of the potential consequences of Han's defeat, urged a rapid response. Others warned that a precipitous attack while Wei was still strong would cause casualties and cost resources that would weaken Qi's defenses, putting it at the mercy of Han and other powerful states. It would be better, so these officials argued, to allow Han and Wei to weaken one another before committing Qi's forces to the fray.

The argument for delay won out. Han's envoys were sent home with assurances that Qi's assistance would be forthcoming. As the fighting continued, however, Qi's armies remained safely in their barracks. Only after Han had been defeated in five separate engagements were Qi's forces ordered to mobilize.[61] The Qi expeditionary force was once again put under the overall command of Tian Yinqi's kinsman, Tian Ji, with Sun Bin as Commandant and chief strategist. As they had done in the campaigns of 354 BCE, the Qi commanders led their soldiers directly toward Wei's capital.

Wei Ying sent out an army under the command of his son and Heir Apparent to defend Daliang. As the Heir Apparent's forces mobilized, a Wei army under Pang Juan was besieging the Han capital of Xinzheng. Wei Ying ordered Pang Juan to withdraw from Xinzheng and join the Heir Apparent to repel the Qi invaders.

Once the Qi army had crossed into Wei territory and made contact with the enemy, Sun Bin embarked upon a subterfuge. Knowing that Qi's soldiers had a general reputation for cowardice, he ordered that on the first night campfires should be lit for 100,000 men. The next day he withdrew in the face of the oncoming Wei army, and on the second night ordered that the number of campfires be decreased to serve 50,000 men. The following day he withdrew again, and decreased the number of campfires to serve 30,000 men.

Pang Juan believed what he saw. When the Qi forces withdrew the next morning, Pang Juan was convinced that more than half of Qi's soldiers had deserted, and that the army was retreating in disarray. He took off in hot pursuit of the enemy, leaving his regular troops in the rear and deploying only the elite forces that could keep up the pace of a forced march. At dusk they reached a place called Horse Hill (Maling) where the road narrowed and ran along the bottom of a wooded ravine. One of his advance scouts reported that a strange tree had been found on which the bark had been stripped and into which writing had been carved. Pang Juan approached and ordered a torch lit, on which he read: "Pang Juan dies under this tree." At that moment the crossbowmen that had been set by Sun Bin to lie in ambush along the sides of the ravine and wait for the lighting of a torch opened fire, and a general slaughter of the Wei army began. Seeing that he had been beaten, Pang Juan cried out, "I have made the bastard's name for him!" In shame and rage, he cut his own throat.[62]

The dramatic story of the rivalry between Sun Bin and Pang Juan may have been a later embellishment, but the outcome for Wei of the battle of Horse Hill was verifiably catastrophic. The Heir Apparent who had been in overall command was taken prisoner, and thousands of Wei soldiers fell as casualties.[63] Wei was critically weakened, and its rival states exploited its distress. Qi and Zhao joined forces in invading Wei from the east, while Qin scored successive victories against Wei armies invading from the west.[64] Wei Ying's dreams of dynastic splendor were in free fall.

Though Wei had very clearly failed the military test of its claim to the Mandate of Heaven, the immediate consequences might have been far more grave but for a combination of quick action on Wei Ying's part and quirks of chance. Wei Ying ceded part of the territories on the West Bank of the Yellow River to Qin to buy peace. This would probably have only slowed the belligerent encroachment of Qin on Wei's western frontier, except for the fact that Duke Xiao of Qin died suddenly, casting his dynamic prime minister Shang Yang into the radical disfavor of the court and the Qin state into internal turmoil.[65]

In the east, the pressure against Greatbridge was similarly eased by divisions that appeared in the leadership of Qi. The overall commander of the forces that had beaten Wei at Horse Hill, Tian Ji, was disliked by Tian Yinqi's prime minister, Zou Ji. While the armies were still on campaign, Zou Ji's deputy hired a man to seek a prediction from a fortune teller in the public marketplace of the Qi capital of Linzi. The man approached the diviner and in a loud voice asked if the omens showed that General Tian Ji, who had won such great victories for Qi, could "do the great deed" (i.e. overthrow his kinsman, Tian Yinqi). The diviner was not foolish enough to offer a clear prediction, and reported the matter to the court.

Sun Bin had anticipated such a stratagem from Zou Ji and had earlier warned Tian Ji that he had no choice but to preemptively stage a coup. Sun Bin gave his commander a plan of how their forces might be deployed to force Tian Yinqi to abdicate. Otherwise, he warned, Tian Ji would never be able to return home. Tian Ji had ignored the warning, and when news reached him of the suspicions that had been raised by the marketplace diviner, he fled to seek asylum in Chu.[66]

These internal conflicts among his foes bought Wei Ying some breathing room, but he remained in profound peril. His military strength had been so badly deteriorated that recovery, if it was ever possible, would require many years. He needed a political strategy that could compensate for his military vulnerability. This was one of several moments in Wei Ying's long reign that belies his image as a boorish warmonger. If that conventional picture were true, it would be difficult to fathom how or why he responded to the aftermath of Horse Hill with the ingenuity, imagination, and daring that he displayed.

In the midst of his via dolorosa, Wei Ying sought help among the Masters and disciples that he had cultivated for more than three decades in power. If Wei Ying's credibility among literati had rested on shallow foundations, intellectuals would almost certainly have completely abandoned him at this low point of humiliation. Conversely, if Wei Ying himself had lacked genuine respect for literati, the decision that he made in this moment could not be logically explained. Facing direst need, Wei Ying turned to one of the most notoriously eclectic and quixotic intellectuals of the Warring States: Master Hui Shi (ca. 380–310 BCE).[67]

Hui Shi was a native of Song (the state ruled by the descendants of the Shang kings, and whose ruling line had produced Confucius's ancestors), where he earned a reputation as a Master of superlative intelligence and subtle logic. His writings, now lost, at one time were said to have been voluminous enough to fill four carts. Among Masters he was a maverick. His teachings did not conform to those of any particular fellowship, and it is not clear whether he ever had a formal group of disciples. The one concrete report we have of his interactions with other literati before his arrival in Wei are the stories of his friendship with his fellow Song native Zhuangzi (of the butterfly dream, mentioned above). The two Masters are said to have engaged in heated but amicable debates, and it was on a visit to see Hui Shi in Wei that Zhuangzi, much to his own disgust, was supposedly considered for the post of prime minister.[68]

Hui Shi was as controversial as he was famous. Many anecdotes about him are spread through the chronicles and compendia of the Warring States. Some of them cast him as unconventionally brilliant, others as hopelessly effete. Two essays written to "summarize the field" of Masters' teachings during the Warring States give him prominent place, though both criticize his teachings as "fantastic" and "impractical."[69] From this we can see that whatever literati might have thought of him, none was ready to write him off as an intellectual who could be ignored. He was, in certain respects, a "Master's Master," a teacher so deeply and cogently engaged with the fundamental problems being explored by the literati community that even those who vehemently disagreed with him were compelled to give him a modicum of respect.

What is preserved of his teachings in the essays that summarize his contribution to the Masters' discourse shows that he was fascinated by abstruse logical problems. For example, one of his tersely phrased dicta was reportedly, "I go to Yue today and arrive there yesterday."[70] Here Hui Shi was playing with the categories that human beings use to classify time and space. If a person goes to the exact point at which Chu becomes neighboring Yue and steps forward at precisely the moment that today becomes tomorrow, one can logically claim to have "gone to Yue today and arrived yesterday." He had hit upon the observation made by the philosopher Kurt Gödel more than two millennia later, that any sufficiently complex system of signification will generate paradox.[71] Hui Shi carried these observations to the conclusion that all categorical distinctions were ultimately arbitrary, and thus that "concern should spread to all things"[72] equally. In practical terms, Hui Shi seems to have drawn the inference from this principle that, for example, all weapons should be banned and the military thereby abolished.[73]

Much more could be said about Hui Shi as Master among other Masters,[74] but what is important to underscore is that nothing about his intellectual profile made Wei Ying's choice, in the aftermath of Horse Hill, to seek out Hui Shi's political assistance, at all intuitively obvious. Quite the contrary, Wei Ying's decision to recruit Hui Shi was, even in its own day, as counterintuitive as a hypothetical scenario in which the American president Lyndon Johnson, despairing over the negative blowback from the Vietnam War, offered a cabinet post to Jean-Paul Sartre, or perhaps Timothy Leary. The fact that Wei Ying not only risked this gambit, but that it worked, makes the conventional "wisdom" that Wei Ying was a bad judge of political ability rather bizarre.

Hui Shi was enlisted as Wei's prime minister.[75] His first task was to tend to the imminent threat of invasion and military cataclysm. He presented a plan to Wei Ying that ran counter to all of the ruler's political instincts: Wei Ying should halt all military operations, don the cloth robes and hat of a commoner, and go to Qi pleading to be accepted as a vassal. Doing this might only appease Qi momentarily, but it would also anger Chu. Once Chu and Qi were in conflict, Wei could sit safely on the sidelines and recover from its recent defeats.

If Wei Ying's belief that Hui Shi would make a good prime minister despite all appearances to the contrary showed a high degree of confidence in Hui Shi, his choice to implement Hui Shi's plan showed even more. Hui Shi had baldly told Wei Ying that he should not only completely abase himself, but do so in a way that totally abandoned and deconstructed everything that Wei Ying had been attempting to achieve for decades. To do as Hui Shi proposed would constitute a complete and irretrievable forfeiture of any claim to the Mandate of Heaven. The fact that Hui Shi had the courage to offer this advice to Wei Ying, and that Wei Ying had the personal fortitude to take it, speaks highly of both men.

The plan worked, perhaps because Wei Ying's actions were so astonishing to the leaders of Qi and the other Zhou states as to be disorienting. In 336 BCE Wei Ying groveled before Tian Yinqi in commoner's garb and begged to be his vassal. The enormity of the shame that Wei Ying was accepting, the sheer scale of the failure he was acknowledging, was so shocking as to momentarily distract Wei's enemies from its position of military vulnerability.

Events transpired as Hui Shi had predicted. Angered by the presumption of Qi's ruler and egged on by Tian Ji, the disgraced Qi commander who had taken refuge at his court, the ruler of Chu attacked Qi. Wei was given a respite to recover from its political and military overreach.[76]

Service in high office seemingly did not change Hui Shi's basic nature, at least not sufficiently to alter his reputation. One story, for example, recounts what happened when he attempted to draw up a legal code for the state of Wei. On asking one of the experienced courtiers if the code was well written, Hui Shi was pleased to be told that it was. He was vexed, though, when he asked if the code should then be implemented. It should not, the courtier explained, because Hui Shi's code was so overly sophisticated that using it would be like asking some workers who were lifting a log to sing one of the airs of the ancient sages rather than simply chanting "heave-ho!"[77]

Despite his over-cerebral approach to the job, Hui Shi continued to give good service. He did not merely save Wei Ying from the worst consequences of his actions, but actually managed to redeem some of Wei Ying's dignity and recapture some of the political initiative on behalf of his sovereign. He did this by brokering a summit with the ruler of Qi, held at Xuzhou in 334 BCE.

The ceremonies at Xuzhou mirrored the conclave at Welcome Pond a decade earlier. A number of smaller states were in attendance to witness the solemnities as Wei Ying and Tian Yinqi met to ritually acknowledge one another as "king."[78] From this point forward Tian Yinqi and his descendants styled themselves "kings" of Qi, and the same would be true of the rulers of Wei. Unlike the attempt at Welcome Pond to initiate a new dynasty, the titles adopted at Xuzhou in 334 BCE proved durable. Wei Ying is generally known in all Chinese chronicles by his posthumous title of King Hui of Liang, and Tian Yinqi is memorialized consistently as King Wei of Qi.

Wei Ying consummated the moment by establishing it as a new "origin": he reset the calendars of the state of Wei to count 334 BCE as the new "year one" of his reign as "king."[79] This was at least partly a face-saving measure. It implied that his first assumption of the title at Welcome Pond in 344 BCE "did not count," and that the summit of Xuzhou marked the "real" beginning of his reign as king. The long-term implications of the ascension to "kingship," however, went far beyond saving face, and justified the austerities of the occasion.

For those of us in the twenty-first century the very radical implications of Wei Ying's meeting with Tian Yingqi may not be immediately clear, but they are very difficult to overstate. It effectively constituted a distinct "sub-revolution" within the long revolution of the Warring States as a whole. Prior to 334 BCE, the elites of the North China plain would have decried as heresy and barbarism the idea of a world with more than one legitimate "king." The profane audacity of Hui Shi's plan, moreover, was exacerbated by the fact that the two rulers crowning one another "king" were both from clans that had only recently achieved the rank of marquis (relative to the oldest families in the Zhou realm). Regardless of such controversy and outrage, however, by the time Wei Ying died and passed his royal throne on to his son and successor, all of the major states had emulated Wei and Qi in adopting the royal title.

In his new "first year" Wei Ying still had 15 more years left on the throne of Wei. Though by 334 BCE it was already obvious that any chance for Wei to unite the Warring States had been lost, Wei Ying would see his state even more diminished in size and weakened before he was through. He might have taken some solace, however, in having forged a path out of adversity that not only rescued Wei from worse disaster, but fundamentally changed the historical trajectory of all the Warring States. The novel political order he had helped to initiate (with the guidance and help of Hui Shi) was completely transformed from the one in which Wei Ying had first assumed the throne of Wei, and he lived to see some of the effects of what he had wrought. The next chapter will explore the ways in which this brave new world of "many kings" reshaped the society and politics of the Warring States.

10

We Kings

The Extended Zhou Realm, 334–310 BCE

The meeting between Tian Yinqi and Wei Ying (the rulers of Qi and Wei, respectively) at Xuzhou in 334 BCE, in which both men acknowledged one another as "kings," ushered in a new era for the Zhou world, a sub-revolution within the larger revolution of the Warring States. In the decades after the Xuzhou summit, all of the rulers of the strongest states acquired the title of king. These changes of title might seem purely semantic, but the "royal revolution" substantively transformed the political, social, and strategic dynamics of the Warring States in unexpected and at times violently destabilizing ways.

The rank of king had become radically dysfunctional among elites on the North China plain by the fourth century BCE, because though it still conveyed prestige and cultural influence, it was exclusively held by a man (the Zhou Son of Heaven) who wielded virtually no material power, in relative terms. Wei Ying had initially tried to rationalize the situation by claiming the sole and unique title of "king," thereby reuniting the formal position of social and cultural leader of the world (the "Son of Heaven") with the person of its most economically and militarily powerful ruler (Wei Ying himself, at that moment lord of by far the most powerful state). When Wei Ying's original plan did not work, he settled (following the inspiration of his prime minister, Hui Shi) for the next best thing. If the world could not have one king, it would at least create a more logical situation if it had many kings.

Though "a world of many kings" might seem quite unremarkable to someone accustomed to the patterns of European, Middle Eastern, or Indian history, it was a profane absurdity to elites throughout the northern Zhou world until Hui Shi conceived of it. In retrospect, it is unsurprising that it took a figure as unconventional and iconoclastic as Hui Shi to both imagine such a world and plot the path by which to arrive at it. For centuries the aristocracy of the Yellow River plain had insisted that the civilized realm could have only one true king, and that all the potentates on the periphery of the Zhou domain (like the "kings" of Chu or Yue) who affected that title were heretics and/or barbarians. When Hui Shi first proposed the plan (and for many years after) it of course, like most radical new ideas, elicited widespread disbelief, mockery, and outright revulsion.

In one of history's many ironies, the plan of 334 BCE contradicted even the professed ideals of Hui Shi, the Master of Paradox, himself. At the Xuzhou summit, one of Qi's generals confronted Hui Shi, reminding him that his teachings of "equal concern" precluded honoring status and rank of any kind. Was it not hypocritical of the Master, who claimed that ranks and titles were vainly arbitrary, to bow down to the ruler of Qi as a "king"?

Hui Shi, always able to think on his feet, compared the situation to one in which a man had gone mad and was about to beat his innocent son's head. In that instance, would it not be wise, if one could, to put a rock in place of the son's head, so that the madman beat the rock instead of injuring his son? The principle in the case of the Xuzhou summit was, according to Hui, the same. Convincing people that a man should be called a king rather than a marquis might, in the logical abstract, be just as arbitrary as convincing a madman that a rock was his son's head, but if it would save the lives of thousands of common people it was worth doing nonetheless.[1]

One might argue, in retrospect, that Hui Shi exaggerated the beneficial effects of the royal revolution he helped initiate. Whether or not a world of many kings really saved the lives of so many common people is open to debate. There can be no doubt, however, that his plan had revolutionary impact. Hui understood that a title like king only exists because people believe in it (that it is, in the parlance of modern cultural theory, a "social construct"). The fact that it is a purely conceptual reality, however, does not preclude its having very profound material effects in the "actual world." It was obvious to everyone in 334 BCE that the role of the king had become (like the actions of the madman in Hui's parable) increasingly irrational, when it was not irrelevant. If, however, you could reconstruct what kingship meant (swap a rock for a head), the institution could perhaps be made more functional.

Hui Shi's tactical ingenuity is evident when one compares the maneuver he engineered at Xuzhou to what his ruler, Wei Ying, had originally attempted to accomplish at the conclave of Welcome Pond in 344 BCE. If all had gone to plan after Welcome Pond (at which Wei Ying had his 12 "guests" honor him as

"King of Xia"), Wei Ying would eventually have convened a summit in which the Zhou king would have been expected (compelled) to abdicate the throne and the Mandate in favor of Wei Ying. The extraordinary difficulty of getting to that goal, however, lay in the necessarily unilateral strategy by which it had to be reached. Wei Ying's claim of sole kingship, even though it had been buttressed by the elaborate rituals and symbols that literati experts on cosmology helped devise, was open to immediate challenge by any and all (and any combination of two or more) of the powerful states of the Zhou realm. If Wei Ying had been able to compel his "brother states" of Han and Zhao to join him in his gambit, he might have consolidated the power necessary to defend his regal claim, but the fact that his armies were so badly weakened by Qi (at the battle of Horse Hill in 341 BCE) before he could bring even Han to heel undermined any chance he might have had of success. The deck had been stacked against Wei Ying from the outset.

Hui Shi understood, however, that a more limited goal could be salvaged from Wei Ying's ruined ambitions, if it were pursued in bilateral fashion. Any combination of states could attack Wei to prevent its sole consolidation of regal authority. But if *two* powerful states acknowledged one another as kings, *both* would have to be attacked and defeated simultaneously in order to undermine their claims of royal status. Fighting the combined might of Qi and Wei was a daunting proposition; it was not likely that the most powerful states of the Zhou realm would be tempted to risk it in 334 BCE, even in conjunction with allies. Unlike Wei Ying's self-proclaimed title of "King of Xia," the kingships bestowed by Tian Yinqi and Wei Ying on one another at Xuzhou were likely to stick—and did. In the chronicles both men are consistently referred to by their posthumous regal titles: King Wei of Qi and King Hui of Wei (or Liang).

Modern readers might be confused by the idea of rulers "making one another" kings. How could they do that? Were there no rules? The answer, of course, is that in politics there are no rules until someone invents and begins enforcing them, and that 334 BCE saw the inception of a new set of rules. If the rules seem strange, it is only because the mechanisms for determining "sovereignty" in almost any era are limited and never completely escape a degree of arbitrariness. In our own present day, for example, if one asks why Kiribati, a group of Pacific islands with a population of 121,000 people, is a sovereign nation-state (having first been conceived as such shortly before its independence in 1979)[2] while Kurdistan, a homeland which has been dreamed of by 30–45 million Kurds and their forbears for generations, is not,[3] the only answer one can offer is that "other nations recognize the existence of Kiribati, but not

Kurdistan." In the same way, one became a king in the Warring States (following the convention invented and established by Hui Shi) through being recognized as one by other kings.

The Xuzhou summit set off a domino effect that soon spread to encompass the entire Zhou domain. In just over a decade following 334 BCE, most of the powerful rulers of the Yellow River plain followed suit in acquiring the title of king. In 325 BCE the rulers of Wei and Han met with the ruler of Qin, and all three leaders hailed one another as monarchs.[4] Two years later the five rulers of Wei, Han, Zhongshan, Zhao, and Yan all met (over the objections of the King of Qi, who did not deem Zhongshan powerful enough to merit the title) to recognize one another as fellow kings.[5] The rulers of Chu, who had been ostracized for profaning the title of king for generations, found their customs normalized by the shift in the North. The ninth and last ruler to join the "kings club" was the lord of Song, who declared himself king in 318 BCE.[6]

The rapid shift confirmed Hui Shi's intuition that a "royal revolution" would have profound material impact. Though a rose by any other name might not smell any different, a ruler who went from being a marquis to being a king during the Warring States found that he possessed significant new powers. These new powers had many complex forms and ramifications, but they generally fell into two discrete realms.

The first of these was the realm of social status. As kings, the rulers of the Warring States asserted novel control over the whole range of the status hierarchy, from bottom to top. Where previously the final word on an aristocrat's status had rested with the Zhou Son of Heaven, once the regional lords became the Zhou king's peers, they could institute ranks and titles that stood on a par with the highest of those established by the Son of Heaven, and which could not be gainsaid by a "royal decree." In a world in which status privilege was virtually equivalent to (and could often be converted into) military force or economic wealth, this dimension of kingship enhanced the power of the regional lords enormously.

A king's ability, in particular, to make an individual into a "marquis" was motivating to a degree that is difficult to exaggerate in the context of Warring States society. Long after 334 BCE, rulers of states such as Lu and Wey, who were powerful enough to remain autonomous but not powerful enough to win recognition as kings from other rulers, remained stuck at the rank of marquis. Thus when, as happened more frequently over the course of the late Warring States, a king made one of his subjects, perhaps a lowly knight who might not know the name, much less the rank, of his great-great-grandfather, into a "marquis," he was giving that man the same rank as rulers who could count marquises among their direct line of forebears going back dozens of generations, to the founding sages of the Zhou dynasty. The award of such a rank conveyed prestige and influence that land or wealth literally could not buy.[7] We will see in subsequent chapters that the exercise by kings of their status imprimatur reshaped the internal dynamics of the court and the state in profound ways.

The other dimension in which the new and vastly expanded power of regional kings was materially institutionalized was in the realm of diplomacy. Diplomacy had been a fixture of political life in the Zhou states for many centuries before 334 BCE. But the royal revolution that transpired in the decades after the Xuzhou summit completely transformed the nature and practice of diplomacy, with effects that reverberated through all dimensions of social, political, economic, and even cultural life.

Even before the Zhou kings moved to their eastern capital in 771 BCE, the regional lords had regularly exchanged emissaries and engaged in various forms of courtly communication. The social and political realities of the Spring and Autumn period (and earlier eras), however, had placed severe constraints on the strategic potential of diplomacy. The movement of aristocrats from one court to another was done in accord with strict protocols and in deference to a densely complex web of status privileges and kinship obligations. Most such communications transpired in the context of a ceremonial event such as a funeral or wedding, and thus were bound by the ritual imperatives of the occasion.[8]

Such diplomacy did not favor secrecy, speed, or efficiency. Protocol and custom entitled many non-participants to know of most exchanges. It was customary, for example, to notify the Zhou royal court about all important interactions between states. Even in the infrequent moments when emissaries were free enough from ritual duties to negotiate strategic interests, the segmented nature of pre-Warring States Zhou society made it difficult to arrive at clear bilateral agreements that would be meaningful and binding.

The limitations of diplomacy under such conditions were extreme. If I was the Marquis of X, hypothetically, attending the wedding of the Marquis of Y during the Spring and Autumn period, and hoped to use the occasion to settle a territorial dispute, it would be difficult to find a space of time to discuss the matter that was not filled with ceremonial obligations. When I did, any territorial trade I proposed with the Marquis of Y would then face me with the problem of compensating my own cousins or in-laws (the grandees whose territory included the traded land) for the loss of part of their estate. Most diplomatic agreements of any significance thus required the participation of many parties, and could only be effected by large conclaves of aristocrats in which all swore covenant oaths. This kind of diplomacy could be effective in ameliorating conflict, but obviously required time and did not admit to a high degree of tactical flexibility or nuance.

The fourth century BCE saw the diplomatic realm change radically, in ways that would impact the entirety of political and social life throughout the Zhou world. Though this change was vastly accelerated by the summit of 334 BCE, by that time it had been building gradually for many decades. We saw in Chapter 9 that Wei Ying and the other rulers of the Yellow River plain had begun to engage in frequent ruler-to-ruler meetings to discuss matters of state. This trend was a byproduct of the political transformations that had been sweeping the Zhou world. The extensive internal reorganization of states in commanderies and districts made newly robust forms of diplomacy possible. Soldiers under routine command could be deployed and demobilized more rapidly and assuredly than warriors who swore allegiance to a particular regional lord. If I as ruler no longer had to secure the compliance of the hereditary nobles of a region in order to cede it to another ruler, I could confidently offer that land "in trade" in exchange for something I wanted.

New mechanisms of regulated, routine authority further facilitated this new wave of diplomacy. The use of seals and tallies to discipline centrally appointed magistrates gave the ruler and his court a degree of control that could be leveraged in service of diplomacy. Once local administrators became habituated to following orders that came bearing the ruler's official seal (and/or accompanied by an authorized tally), swift exchanges of territory or deployment of resources could be confidently negotiated. If the ruler of Zhao, for example, knew that the magistrate in district X would surrender his headquarters, yield up revenue, or mobilize his soldiers if he received the order to do so under the royal seal, the ruler could offer that land or those assets in trade, knowing that the deal could be swiftly executed and could not be undermined by rogue vassals or local elites.[9]

After 334 BCE the Zhou world moved from being the domain of a single king into one populated by many, and the nature of interstate relations rapidly transformed, accelerating developments that had been in process for decades. It is at this point that the most powerful of the Warring States can accurately be called "kingdoms," because they openly, explicitly, and consistently assumed fully sovereign control over geopolitical and social policy. Kings no longer acknowledged any obligation to inform the Zhou Son of Heaven (who was now their peer) of matters of state. They could negotiate swiftly and in secret, with no fear that any counterpart (king or not) could invoke the authority of "the king" to back out of a deal.

With these new powers in hand, kings began very quickly to embark on aggressive programs of strategic diplomacy, which in turn radically reshaped the institutional form of interstate relations. Royal courts began to regularly exchange "tallies" to establish sovereign channels of rapid communication. Tallies were simple devices that had long already been in use for verifying orders from the court to regional officials. Usually made of bronze, they were small figurines (depicting dragons, tigers, or other creatures) that were broken to produce two uniquely fitted halves. If an emissary arrived in Zhao, for example, claiming to offer a deal from the King of Qi, the Zhao court only had to collect the envoy's tally and search among the official tallies that had been provided to them by Qi. If one of them could be joined flush with the envoy's tally to form a complete figurine, they knew that the envoy was fully authorized to cede land or mobilize resources on the King of Qi's behalf. Very often the envoy would come equipped with other, domestic tallies and seals enabling him to issue immediate orders to officials in the state that had dispatched him, so as to begin fulfilling the terms of any deal and leaving no question about compliance.[10] At times diplomatic agreements were secured by hostages: the sons of rulers given into the custody of another state to ensure fulfillment of or continuing compliance with a deal.[11]

These establishments facilitated the emergence of a new type of political literati. They functioned in a way analogous to the "diplomats" of our present day, but the norms that controlled their activities were very different from those that inform the conduct of politics in the twenty-first century. These new literati are identified in the chronicles by various labels, but perhaps the clearest conventional designation for them was "wandering persuaders." They inhabited a traveling circuit that developed between the royal courts of the Warring States, and over which an increasingly high volume of itinerant literati moved from 334 BCE until the end of the era in 221 BCE.

What distinguished wandering persuaders most from today's diplomats is that they did not generally give their permanent allegiance to any one court. None of the Warring States generally established a "foreign ministry" or a regular "diplomatic corps." They employed envoys on an ad hoc basis from among the wandering persuaders, who operated as free agents, and who would travel from court to court in search of an opportune commission. When they were provided with credentials at one capital, they would travel to another and try to persuade that ruler of accepting whatever deal was being offered by the king who had commissioned them.[12]

Very often such persuaders would propose policy on their own initiative. They would procure an audience with a king for the purpose of laying out a plan of alliance or exchange. If the king was convinced, he might enlist the envoy on the spot and send him on the road, equipped with tallies and resources, to try to execute that envoy's own plan.[13]

It might seem strange, from our current-day perspective, that rulers generally preferred wandering persuaders for such sensitive duty, but it was logical in the social context of the Warring States. If a king used one of his own courtiers on an important (and secret) diplomatic mission, he was likely employing a kinsman, whose own dignity and ambitions (the king's brother or cousin is only ever a heartbeat from the throne, potentially) might conflict with the object of the mission itself. A king was free to choose a nobody from among the knights sojourning at his court, give him rank and emolument, and credential him to negotiate a deal with another ruler. Since the new status of the envoy flowed entirely from the gift of the ruler whose tally he now carried (rather than from a family connection that he shared with the ruler, as was true for many courtiers), the envoy was strongly motivated to fulfill his mission and protect the credibility of his new rank. Moreover, as the community of wandering persuaders grew and circulated between states, it became advantageous to draw from its members, since they were familiar with the environments and protocols of the various courts and developed knowledge of and relationships with the key players, all of which could aid the success of diplomacy.

Kings and officials throughout the Warring States quickly caught on to the fact that this newly versatile diplomacy was a vital constituent of power, on a par with economic wealth and military force, and could be leveraged in pursuit of a wide variety of strategic goals. Territory or treasure that might otherwise only be acquired through bloody warfare could be won through skillful negotiation. The military maneuvers of one's enemies could be foiled before they began. Before long, the (justified) perception took broad hold that any resolution of the crisis of the Warring States would depend as much on diplomacy as anything else (or even more so).[14]

Stories about Warring States diplomacy recorded in the sources abound. One anecdote set in the early days of the royal revolution, though perhaps apocryphal, exemplifies the mystique that quickly developed around the wandering persuaders and their work. In 323 BCE, when the rulers of Wei, Han, Zhao, Yan, and Zhongshan (see Fig. 15) planned to meet to acknowledge one

Fig. 15. This bronze dragon was recovered from a tomb in the ancient state of Zhongshan, a kingdom founded by a non-Sinitic people known as the "White Turks" who adopted the political norms of the Zhou realm. (Source: erenow.org.)

another as kings, the King of Qi was furious. He was ashamed to share the rank of king with a ruler whose army was one tenth of his own (and, as we will soon read, had strategic reasons to want Zhongshan excluded from the community of "kingdoms"). He offered territory to the rulers of Yan and Zhao in exchange for refusing to recognize Zhongshan's kingship and joining an assault on Zhongshan.

The Prime Minister of Zhongshan was terrified. A persuader named Zhang Deng offered to fix the situation if he was given a commission. The prime minister agreed to play the role of the King of Qi in a rehearsal of Zhang Deng's persuasion, to test whether it would work. Zhang Deng then argued (as if he were at the Qi court) that the plan to cede land to Yan and Zhao was too costly and risky. There was a much safer and more frugal way for the King of Qi to get what he wanted.

If the king sent an envoy to Zhongshan, Zhang explained, inviting its ruler to come to Qi to be recognized as king (giving the excuse that Qi had only objected to the title because Qi had not initially been consulted), the ruler of Zhongshan would certainly come, looking for the patronage of the most powerful state. This would infuriate Yan and Zhao who, feeling slighted, would break off relations with Zhongshan. When Qi, perhaps with mock regret, refused to unilaterally endorse Zhongshan's royal title, its ruler, now isolated and alone, would be forced to abandon it. This way the King of Qi could block Zhongshan's kingship without losing land or risking troops.

At this pause in the rehearsal, the Prime Minister of Zhongshan conceded that the King of Qi would accept that plan, but complained that though it avoided an invasion, it also forced the ruler of Zhongshan to give up the title of king, which was almost as bad. "Not so!" explained Zhang Deng. When the King of Qi's envoy arrived in Zhongshan, rather than accepting his invitation to journey to Qi, the ruler of Zhongshan should instead send envoys with rich gifts to Yan and Zhao, informing those rulers of Qi's invitation. The rulers of Yan and Zhao would then suspect Qi of trying to double cross them, believing that the offer of land from Qi was never really about Zhongshan's kingship, but about alienating Zhongshan from Yan and Zhao and pulling it into Qi's orbit. They would then refuse Qi's offer of land and move swiftly to recognize Zhongshan as a kingdom.

Once the rehearsal was done, the prime minister saw the merit of the plan. He gave Zhang Deng credentials and sent him as an envoy to the King of Qi. Everything transpired as Zhang Deng predicted: Zhongshan was spared invasion, and its ruler ascended to the rank of king with the recognition of Yan and Zhao.[15]

The convoluted plot of this story perhaps raises doubts about its veracity, but it conveys a truth about the new realm of diplomacy that was a source of fascination and terror to elites of the late Warring States. Because diplomatic intercourse had been accelerated to such high speeds with such potentially profound effects, it created a playing field on which exquisitely complex maneuvers became possible. As in the game of chess, everyone could see the competitive potential of the diplomatic game, but not everyone was equally well equipped to exploit it. In the story above, for example, Zhang Deng knows that he can entrap the King of Qi, because the basic logic of using diplomacy to get what you want is easy to understand. But the King of Qi is ultimately out of his depth, because he cannot think as many moves ahead as Zhang Deng.

One can see why the wandering persuaders quickly achieved folk hero status among the literati of the Warring States. To be successful, a wandering persuader had to be consummately learned. Beyond being merely literate and well spoken, he had to be broadly conversant in history and ritual, so that he could both conduct himself with proper etiquette among highborn nobles in many varying regions and argue cogently on the basis of solid precedents. Such qualities, however, had been displayed by some literati long before 334 BCE. What made the wandering persuaders so uniquely awe-inspiring was the possibility, however rare, that like Zhang Deng they could outsmart a king. The royal revolution had finally created a realm, long dreamed of in the moral theorizing of Masters such as Confucius and Mo Di, in which knowledge truly was power.

Given the sheer force with which the personae of the wandering persuaders could be used to promote and defend the status and dignity of literati like those who composed our sources, it should be obvious why the history of the wandering persuaders' activities is difficult to reconstruct. The baroquely epic folk hero tales of the most prominent wandering persuaders are thickly laden with dramatic embellishments, anachronisms, and internal contradictions. Using them to assemble an empirically "verified" account of the political and strategic dynamic of the late Warring States requires careful reading, and even then can only afford provisional confidence.

By the Han dynasty (206 BCE–220 CE), when virtually all of the transmitted sources on which we depend were compiled, the most famous of the wandering persuaders was a native of the tiny state of East Zhou (created from a portion of the Zhou Royal Domain) named Su Qin (d. 284 BCE). He had achieved legendary status, and is the first of the wandering persuaders given his own biography in the *Records of the Historian*, the account of which makes him a major player in the diplomatic intrigues of the Warring States from the very earliest days of the "royal revolution." That is hyperbole, however—an embellishment most likely inspired by the fact that the deeds for which Su Qin eventually did become famous contributed to a catastrophic disruption in the balance of power.[16] But those events transpired much later than those of the royal revolution and will be discussed in the following chapters.

Evidence demonstrates that the most influential persuaders who first pioneered the new strategic world created by the Xuzhou summit were, again unsurprisingly, two knights native to the trendsetting state of Wei: Zhang Yi (d. 310 BCE) and Gongsun Yan (ca. 360–ca. 300 BCE). Both men were born in similarly humble circumstances and rose to dizzying heights of wealth and authority, surpassing all but the crowned heads of the Warring States in power and influence. Both men embodied the restless dynamism of their time. Their success was built on wanderings that traversed many states and brought them into negotiations with many kings. Their careers also exemplify the fluidity and ambiguity of political identities and allegiances in a world undergoing rapid change. Though both men were at times united in the service of a common ruler, in the long breadth of their careers they were vehement rivals, and each respectively became the key architect and leading practitioner of a strategic orientation diametrically opposed to that of the other.

Zhang Yi had become the more celebrated figure by the Han dynasty, when most of our sources were compiled. He was given his own lengthy biography in the *Records of the Historian,* within which Gongsun Yan's biography was included as an appendix.[17] Two factors contributed to this disparity.

The first, as we shall see, was that Gongsun Yan did not initially earn fame as a "wandering persuader," but as a military leader. He made his early reputation as a commander in the armies of Wei, where he held the title of *xishou*, literally "Rhinoceros-head [General]" (perhaps so named because of a distinctive helmet that identified the rank).[18] His victories in that post were so impressive that the sobriquet followed him throughout his career, and he is often referred to as "the Xishou" in the sources that record his later life.

This military pedigree perhaps contributed to the second reason for Gongsun Yan's relative obscurity: his historical role as Zhang Yi's great rival in the game of diplomacy was eventually displaced in lore (as reflected in the *Records of the Historian*) by Su Qin, who in historical reality became most active only after Zhang Yi had died. A legend developed that made Zhang Yi and Su Qin simultaneous disciples of the mysterious Venerable of Ghost Gorge, the Master who had purportedly been the teacher of both Sun Bin and Pang Juan (as discussed in Chapter 7).[19] The co-discipleship of Zhang Yi and Su Qin is pure myth, however: a literary device conceived by literati who were fascinated by the idea of a pair of "civil antagonists" to match the martial rivalry of Sun Bin and Pang Juan.

Though Gongsun Yan embraced diplomacy as a strategic weapon later than Zhang Yi, he was the first to reach the peak of power. He was born in Yinjin, a town very close to the defensive frontier between Qin and Wei. His clan name (literally "Ducal Grandson") suggests that his family descended from either the ruling house of Jin or Wei (or perhaps Qin, if his noble ancestry was very distant), but he was born a humble knight.

As stated above, Gongsun Yan had made a name for himself as a commander in Wei's army early in his career, but after the Xuzhou summit he left Wei. We do not know what particular obstacle or disappointment moved Gongsun Yan to depart, which is unusual in the context of the early chronicles. The historians who produced our sources were, like virtually all knights during the Warring States, preoccupied with the vicissitudes of fellow knights who were trying to make their way in a world ruled by condescending and bigoted highborn nobles. The compelling allure of figures like Zhang Yi, Gongsun Yan, and Su Qin for literati chroniclers was that these wandering persuaders represented the ultimate vindication of knightly dignity: the enormous power that they were able to accrue and wield so effectively proved that having more titled ancestors did not make one person superior to another. The sources provide ample details about insults that Zhang Yi and Su Qin were forced to endure from highborn aristocrats in early life, and that spurred them on to the pursuit of power. But we are left in the dark about what specific frustrations (and there *must* have been some) made Gongsun Yan seek opportunity beyond his native state.

Whatever the case may have been, like Shang Yang before him, Gongsun Yan found that his knowledge of and experience in the sophisticated fiscal-military bureaucracy of Wei was welcome and well rewarded in neighboring Qin. In 333 BCE he was employed by the Qin court as "Great Excellent Charioteer" (*daliangzao*), the same office (equivalent to "prime minister") in which Shang Yang had served before his death five years earlier.[20] In that post (and congruent with his previous service in the armies of Wei) Gongsun Yan continued the same strategy that Shang Yang had pursued: placing relentless military pressure on Wei's western frontier.

On assuming office in Qin, Gongsun Yan immediately took Qin's army on the offensive against his home state, resuming Qin's campaign to regain its lost territory on the west bank of the Yellow River. He defeated Wei at a town along the Luo River in the Upper Commandery, the far northwestern reach of Wei's territory.[21] By way of suing for peace, King Hui of Wei (the title by which Wei Ying would be known to history after the Xuzhou summit) ceded Gongsun Yan's native town of Yinjin to Qin. The ruler of Qin was pleased and renamed the town "Appeasing Qin" (Ning Qin) to humiliate his rival ruler.[22]

Gongsun Yan kept Qin's forces on the offensive. In 330 BCE he assaulted Wei in a two-pronged attack. He personally led an army to strike Wei at the Upper Commandery in the north, while the Qin ruler's younger half-brother led an army through the Hangu Pass in the south and assaulted the town of Crooked Ditch (Quwo), in the southern reaches of Wei's territory on the west bank of the Yellow River.

Both campaigns were victorious. Gongsun Yan captured one of Wei Ying's most trusted generals, the commander who had overseen the construction of Wei's massive complex of western defensive fortifications and guarded the frontier for decades. The casualties endured by Wei's armies were catastrophic, as many of 80,000 of Wei's soldiers were reportedly killed. It was the greatest defeat that Wei had ever suffered at the hands of Qin, surpassing even the blows dealt to Wei by the fabled Shang Yang. As a result, Wei was finally forced to return all of the territory on the west bank of the Yellow River that it had conquered from Qin during the time of Marquis Wen and Wu Qi.[23]

In early 329 BCE Gongsun Yan remained on the offensive against Wei. He crossed into Wei's commandery on the east bank of the Yellow River and defeated all of the armies sent against him. King Hui of Wei met in a summit with the ruler of Qin to seek peace, and ceded three key cities in the territory occupied by Gongsun Yan's forces.[24]

It is at this point that the rivalry between Zhang Yi and Gongsun Yan began. If we discount the legend of Ghost Gorge, we do not know much about Zhang Yi's early life and education. The broad knowledge and honed eloquence that won him such fame, however, must have been developed during his early life in Wei. He was formed during the years in which Wei was at the height of its power, and he would have had the benefit of seeing all of the progressive institutions that state had established at work, as well as exposure to the intellectual richness of the scene during the days when the greatest Masters of the age were drawn to Greatbridge by Wei Ying's patronage.

Zhang's ancestors belonged to the ruling clan of Wei, but had been established as a separate cadet branch, with its own clan name, some unknown number of generations before Zhang's birth.[25] In the affluent circles of the high aristocracy he was deemed poor and lowborn. This was made clear to him during an early sojourn in Chu, where he had traveled in search of patronage and employment.

After a drinking party attended by both the Prime Minister of Chu and Zhang Yi, the prime minister found that a precious jade disc he had been wearing was missing. The prime minister's entourage assumed that the impoverished Zhang Yi must have stolen it. They seized Zhang Yi and beat him with a bamboo cane, demanding the disc's return. Zhang Yi adamantly maintained his innocence and was eventually released.

As we saw in the case of Yan Sui and Nie Zheng, such an insult was potentially catastrophic for an ambitious knight. The person of a true aristocrat was thought to be inviolable, only a commoner could be beaten with impunity. If a knight let the violation of his person go unavenged, he cast doubt on his pedigree and status, and risked being shunned from court circles.

Zhang Yi's wife was furious with him for allowing them to fall into such straits. She berated him, asking what value all the books he had read as a young man would be to him in the wake of this disaster. In reply, Zhang Yi pointed at his open mouth, and then asked his wife whether she saw that his tongue was still intact. It was, she acknowledged. Since that was true, Zhang explained, all would be well. As long as he still had a tongue, he would be able to make something of himself.[26]

Events bore out Zhang's confidence. Zhang departed Chu and made his way to Qin. There he managed to procure a position as a counselor at the Qin court, where he was serving in 329 BCE, when Gongsun Yan's invasion of Wei's East Bank Commandery forced the King of Wei to agree to a summit at which he ceded three cities to Qin.

Shortly after the summit between Wei and Qin, news arrived that the King of Wei's southern neighbor, Chu, had died. Wei took this opportunity (a state was always vulnerable during the mourning rites for its departed ruler) to attack Chu, hoping to strengthen its southern frontier from attack.[27] Zhang Yi seized this occasion to deliver a persuasive speech during court debate in Qin. He argued that Gongsun Yan's army, which was then occupying the newly ceded cities formerly of Wei's East Bank Commandery, should be offered to Wei in support of its campaign against Chu.

This was, Zhang Yi argued, a "win-win" proposition. If the joint campaign against Chu failed, Wei would be forced to recognize that the threat posed by Chu to the south was so severe that Wei could not afford to anger Qin. If the campaign succeeded, Wei would be taught that its security was much easier to guarantee when it was cooperating with Qin, rather than fighting against it. In either case, Wei would ultimately be compelled to cede territory adjacent to the West Bank Commandery.

Zhang Yi's persuasion succeeded in convincing the ruler of Qin. Gongsun Yan thus joined his forces with those of Wei, and together they were able to capture a strategic mountain along the boundary between Wei and Chu. Events transpired as Zhang Yi had predicted. Wei was initially reluctant to give up the territory beyond what it had already ceded on the west bank of the Yellow River, but when it appeared as if Qin might join into an alliance with Chu if its aid to Wei was not repaid, King Hui of Wei finally accepted the necessity of ceding the territory to Qin, and did so without a fight.[28]

It was an object lesson in the strategic potential of interstate diplomacy. By joining into alliance with Wei and threatening alliance with Chu, Qin had achieved strategic goals at much lower cost in blood and treasure than it had been expending through unilateral military action. In effect, Zhang Yi was advocating a broadening of the horizons of strategic thinking in Qin. Shang Yang had (understandably, given the circumstances in which he took office) focused on the development of Qin's wealth and power (agriculture and warfare) in the pursuit of its goals through principally military means. Gongsun Yan had continued Shang Yang's basic tactics, using the increased military might of Qin to ratchet up the pressure on its neighbor and chief rival.

Zhang Yi perceived that in the "new world order" that had been initiated by the royal revolution, interstate diplomacy could be used to leverage a state's power, and thus attain levels of influence unachievable by the employment of military force alone. He was, moreover, urging the ruler of Qin to recognize the needs of this new moment. While the conventional goals of building armies and filling state coffers were always necessary, they would no longer be enough to guarantee strategic success. Victory in this new climate would ultimately depend on configuring the relationships *between* states in whatever way gave one's own state the most power and authority.

In simple terms, Zhang Yi stood for the principle that (in the long run) Qin would need allies, and that the first place Qin should look for one was in Wei. From the moment he was given office in Qin until his death, he advocated for a strategic partnership between Wei and Qin. It was an audacious idea.

For more than a century, Wei had been pursuing a partnership with its "brother states" Han and Zhao, and had been locked in bitter rivalry with Qin. Under Shang Yang and then Gongsun Yan, Qin had relentlessly and brutally eaten away at the foundations of Wei's power. Looking backward from 329 BCE, the idea that Qin and Wei should join their fates together was wildly counterintuitive.

Even so, viewed in the abstract, the concept was inspired. Wei had been the most powerful state in the Zhou world, but in 329 BCE it was in steep decline. Qin had been a middling outback power, but was swiftly on the rise. Joining them together at this "mid-point" where both states met along their respective trajectories was a potentially brilliant idea. Together, at that moment, Wei and Qin might have become invincible.

The fact that he had correctly predicted the outcome of Qin's assistance to Wei in 329 BCE, and that his plan had yielded such impressive results, gave Zhang Yi enormous credibility. In 328 BCE, having been converted to Zhang Yi's new strategic vision, the ruler of Qin removed Gongsun Yan from his position at the head of Qin's government. In his place Zhang Yi was installed as "prime minister" (*xiangbang*), bringing the formal title of Qin's top official into conformity with the usage of the other Warring States.[29]

Gongsun Yan deeply resented being cast aside in favor of Zhang Yi, and from that point forward the two men were enemies, working tirelessly and at every opportunity against one another for the rest of their lives. In the short term, however, Gongsun Yan harbored his grievance quietly. He returned to Wei, where the court was not too proud to re-enlist him as a military commander and put his talents to use once more. In 325 BCE he brokered an alliance between Wei and Qi that inflicted a defeat on Zhao.[30]

Zhang Yi spent the next decade using hard and soft power to realize his vision of a strategic union between Qin and Wei. In his first year as prime minister, Zhang personally took command of an invasion force along with a Qin prince, and besieged a strategic town deep inside Wei's East Bank Commandery. When the town surrendered, King Hui of Wei, realizing that his supply chains were no longer sustainable, was compelled to cede 15 districts from its Upper Commandery, directly to the west of the East Bank Commandery, to Qin.[31]

The following year, in a gesture of magnanimity meant to court Wei's good will, Zhang Yi returned two of Wei's cities that had been captured in the campaigns led by Gongsun Yan.[32] At the same time that he was wooing friends abroad, he was consolidating Qin's control within its home territory of the Wei River valley. In 327 BCE the ruler of Yiqu, a non-Sinitic, Rong principality on Qin's northwestern frontier, formally submitted to Qin as a vassal. The next year the Qin court instituted an annual "Winter Feast" at a location known as Dragon Gate. At the first such gathering the Qin ruler received the tributes of chieftains of the Rong and Di people who lived on Qin's borders, and established that they would gather regularly at this festival to affirm their allegiance to the Qin throne.[33]

In 325 BCE Zhang Yi brought Qin into the royal revolution. He convened a conclave with the rulers of Han and Wei at which all three rulers recognized one another as kings. The following year was thus declared a new "year one," and the Qin ruler under whom Zhang Yi served (Ying Si, the son of Duke Xiao of Qin) is thus known to history by his posthumous title, King Huiwen of Qin (r. 337–311 BCE).[34]

After brokering Qin's ascension to "kinship" Zhang Yi kept up relentless pressure on Wei, using a combination of military coercion and diplomatic maneuvering. He captured more territory on Wei's western frontier, and built a system of fortifications in the Upper Commandery territory that Wei had ceded to Qin in 328 BCE.[35] He kept the olive branch extended to Wei, but at the same time made threatening overtures of alliance to Wei's neighbors.

During this period Gongsun Yan worked diligently to frustrate Zhang Yi's plans. Though his previous distinction had been earned as a military leader, he learned the diplomatic game quickly (perhaps because in these early days of the royal revolution its rules were just being invented). It was he, as Wei's envoy, who negotiated the meeting of five rulers in 323 BCE at which Wei, Han, Yan, Zhao, and Zhongshan all recognized one another as kings.[36]

This meeting of "five kings," which Qi opposed, was a step toward the building of a strategic coalition that could serve as an alternative to the "Qin-Wei" axis being promoted by Zhang Yi. Though Wei was in decline, it still possessed a critical mass of economic and military might, enough to give it a determinative role in setting the balance of power. Whichever side Wei "invited to the dance" would have the advantage. While Hui Shi remained Prime Minister of Wei, it resisted Zhang Yi's overtures of strategic alliance from Qin and sought to forge a partnership with states in the east.

These two basic approaches to geopolitical strategy were eventually given figurative labels in the deliberations of Warring States literati. Zhang Yi's concept of an alliance between Qin and Wei was termed "the Horizontal [Alliance]" (the term eventually expanded to include any alliance between Qin and any of the eastern states). This label had two significances. The first was geographic: virtually any alliance entered into by the far-western kingdom of Qin would, if plotted on a map, form a horizontal east-west line. The second meaning of "Horizontal" was strategic. Because at the time Qin and Wei were on a relative par, militarily and economically, a "Horizontal" plan was generally taken to be an alliance between strategic peers, a partnership between strong states to assert their hegemony.

The type of coalition between eastern states that Gongsun Yan (as Hui Shi's deputy) labored to realize was designated a "Vertical [Alliance]." The same two basic forms of meaning applied in the case of this term. The geographic sense of the label derived from the fact that any group of two or more eastern states joined together would form a north-south row on standard maps. The strategic significance of the term derived from the fact that a coalition of eastern states would necessarily bring together stronger and weaker powers. It thus entailed a partnership in which weak states were seeking protection from the strong, or in which a group of relatively weak states was attempting to leverage their combined power to strategic advantage.[37]

Over the span of the century following the Xuzhou summit, the sources record various figures who advocated either the Vertical or the Horizontal Alliance, respectively. One anecdote recounts an occasion on which Chunyu Kun, in one of his quixotic fits and determined to demonstrate his rhetorical brilliance, presented a ruler first with an ironclad argument in favor of joining a Vertical Alliance, followed immediately by an equally cogent persuasion in favor of the Horizontal Alliance.[38] The two labels became so current that they were eventually joined to create a compound expression, *zongheng* (literally, "vertical-horizontal"),[39] which is among the earliest terms used in the Chinese script to designate the realm and practice of diplomacy more generally.

The permutations of Vertical and Horizontal alliances would mix and shift over time. As Wei steadily declined in power and influence, it eventually lost its status as the "indispensable kingdom" in any coalition plan. But during the decade of the 320s BCE Wei still held the determinative "swing vote" as to which plan would control the geopolitics of the Zhou states. Zhang Yi was the leading advocate of the Horizontal Alliance, and his nemesis, Gongsun Yan, became the champion of the Vertical Alliance.

Of the two models, the Horizontal Alliance was the easier of the two to pursue, strategically. This was entirely a product of geography. Because Qin inhabited the distant and sheltered Wei valley, it was only bordered by three states other than Wei (Zhao, Han, and Chu) and had strong natural defenses against incursions from its neighbors.

If Qin found just one sufficiently powerful ally in the east it would be secure enough to pursue a very assertive policy. Wei and Qin alone might not be powerful enough to bring the rest of the Zhou states to heel, but they could defend against all aggressors. Meanwhile, by keeping pressure on the other individual states to submit to their leadership and join their coalition, they might eventually, like a snowball picking up momentum and mass on the downhill run, roll the whole world up into one.

By contrast, a stable and defensible Vertical Alliance was more difficult to form. During the last decades of the fourth century BCE the next most powerful state (after Wei and Qin) in the eastern Zhou world was Qi, and thus was the indispensable partner for Wei in the formation of any alliance ex-Qin. This had almost certainly contributed to Hui Shi's logic in choosing Qi as the partner with which to hold the Xuzhou summit in 334 BCE. But unlike Qin, Qi was neighbored by six states other than Wei (Yan, Zhao, Song, Lu, Chu, and Yue), and had few natural defenses against any of its neighbors. Forming a Vertical coalition that had defensible boundaries thus required bringing three or more states into alignment, and realistically required the participation of at least five or six separate powers. Piecing such a complex multiparty coalition together was akin to "herding cats."

This can be seen in the difficulties that beset Gongsun Yan's mission of 323 BCE to arrange the meeting of "five kings" between Wei, Han, Zhao, Yan, and Zhongshan. The inclusion of Zhongshan in the "kingly circle" was most likely done at the behest of the rulers of Zhao and Yan. Both rulers shared borders with Zhongshan, and would have wanted to secure guarantees of Zhongshan's non-belligerence before embarking on any potentially risky multistate strategic venture.

As we saw in the story about the persuader Zhang Deng cited above, the King of Qi objected to the recognition of Zhongshan as a kingdom. This opposition was not purely an expression of vanity. The King of Qi had to worry about how the precedent set by Zhongshan would affect his relations with his neighbors, particularly Confucius's home state of Lu, which had been a bitter rival of Qi for many centuries. By 323 BCE the threat of Lu had largely been neutralized, because Qi had become so much more wealthy and powerful, and could treat Lu as a "quasi-vassal" in many affairs. But if, citing the precedent of Zhongshan (which though larger in area was comparable in population, wealth, and military might to more densely populated Lu),[40] the Duke of Lu won recognition (perhaps from another of Qi's rivals, such as Chu) as a peer "king," Qi's strategic position would be threatened.

Gongsun Yan's ultimate success in brokering the five-king meeting incurred the resentment of Qi, and made the formation of a cohesive Vertical Alliance untenable, at least temporarily. Prime Minister Hui Shi undertook intense diplomatic efforts on the part of Wei to try and form a "Vertical Alliance." He sent royal Wei princes to Qi and Chu, respectively, as hostages, and brokered a meeting between the kings of Wei, Han, and Qi in 324 BCE and again between the kings of Wei and Qi in 322 BCE.[41] Despite these initiatives, Qi could not be persuaded to ally with Wei.

All this while, the political pressure on the Wei court intensified. In 323 BCE Zhang Yi successfully brokered a meeting on behalf of Qin with the high ministers of Qi and Chu.[42] No clear strategic partnership emerged from that meeting, but the very fact that it took place was disconcerting to the leaders of Wei, who had exerted such effort to enlist Qi's help against Qin.

Along with its increasing political distress, the military pressure on the Wei court escalated. In late 323 BCE Chu went on the offensive against Wei and captured eight cities.[43] The following year Wei sent an army to retaliate against Chu under Gongsun Yan, but it too was defeated.[44]

In that year King Hui of Wei agreed to receive Zhang Yi as an envoy of the Qin court and hear his proposals for a Horizontal Alliance. Prime Minister Hui Shi argued firmly in favor of the Vertical Alliance. In Hui's assessment, the interests of Qin and Wei at that moment did not align. Qin, blessed by geography, did not need allies for the purpose of defense. Its only motive for seeking allies in the east was thus to go on the offensive. Wei, by contrast, had been economically and militarily exhausted by decades of war. It needed to "rest its military" in order to regain its strength, and thus needed allies that would join it in a defensive pact. For that purpose, Wei had to look east and south, to Qi and Chu.[45]

Zhang Yi pressed the case that events were moving too fast for Hui Shi's plan to be feasible. As long as the many states were locked in strategic conflict, Wei would not know peace for very long, no matter what allies it acquired. Wei could never achieve a "defensive pause" long enough to build up its military strength to sufficient levels. To be truly secure, Wei had to choose the shortest path toward a final resolution of the strategic deadlock of the Warring States, and that road went through Qin. He proposed that Wei enter into an offensive alliance with Han and Qin.[46]

The matter was debated at the Wei court, and King Hui gave consideration to both sides. Virtually all of his officials urged him to accept Qin's offer of an alliance. According to Hui Shi this was because Zhang Yi had engaged in coercive factionalism and intimidation. Zhang's techniques of persuasion no doubt played a role in swaying the Wei court, but the obvious hostility of Qi and Chu as contrasted with Qin's friendly overtures in 322 BCE must have also been a factor.

King Hui of Wei followed the consensus of his court and agreed to join into a Horizontal Alliance with Qin. As part of the terms of the alliance, Zhang Yi stayed in Greatbridge. He formally resigned his post as Prime Minister of Qin and was made Prime Minister of Wei. One of his first acts was to exile the faithful and innovative Hui Shi.[47]

The idea of one kingdom sealing a diplomatic deal with another by appointing its counterpart's prime minister is very strange to our present-day perspective. What Qin succeeded in negotiating from Wei is analogous to if, during the Paris Peace Accords, the United States had asked North Vietnam to accept Henry Kissinger as its prime minister by way of securing an armistice. That such an arrangement was possible in the case of Qin and Wei of course underscores how differently the ancient Warring States operated from the nation-states of today. But even in the fourth century BCE, though it would not be the last such agreement between states, the ascension of Zhang Yi to the prime ministership of Wei at Qin's behest was surprising. The rulers of Qi and Chu were reportedly prepared to go to war in protest of the influence Qin had exerted over Wei, and were only dissuaded by the argument that to do so would drive Wei further into Qin's orbit.[48]

Like most such precedent-setting political maneuvers in history, Zhang Yi's tenure as Prime Minister of Wei held the promise of high reward and came with the threat of high risk. The power that had been consolidated through allying Wei and Qin was truly formidable, and potentially put very audacious goals in reach. At the same time, the hostility to Zhang Yi both outside and inside the Wei court was predictably very intense and placed obstacles in his path at every turn.

Zhang Yi's strategy was simple but bold. He sought to capitalize on the combined power of Wei and Qin as quickly as possible and at the least possible cost in blood and treasure. To this end he sought further allies to join the Horizontal Alliance, while at the same time exerting pressure on the Zhou king to abdicate the title of Son of Heaven.

These deeds were easier said than done. In 321 BCE, for example, Zhang Yi tried to negotiate a territorial exchange with neighboring Han that would have given Han twice as much territory as it was ceding, but that would extend the frontiers of Wei so that it completely surrounded the Zhou Royal Domain. The object of this deal was obvious. Once Wei controlled all travel and commerce going into or out of the Royal Domain, Zhang Yi would have enormous leverage to extort concessions from the Zhou king. Eventually he would be able to force the king to surrender the famed Nine Tripods that were the supreme regalia of the Zhou house, effectively abdicating the Mandate and title of "Son of Heaven." The Zhou king was able to block Zhang Yi's move, however, by sending envoys to secure the intercession of Chu and Zhao.[49]

The resistance to Zhang from inside the Wei court was equally confounding of his designs. The Horizontal Alliance had brought Zhang Yi and Gongsun Yan (who remained an official of Wei) together again in the service of a single ruler. Both men seem to have had a grudging respect for one another, but their rivalry never flagged. As Zhang Yi departed on a high-stakes diplomatic mission to Qi during his first year as Prime Minister of Wei, Gongsun Yan used the opportunity to frustrate his competitor's plans.

Gongsun Yan knew that Zhang Yi's cortege would pass through Wey. He thus asked the ruler of Wey to help arrange an occasion at which he might be reconciled with Zhang Yi, explaining that he had no enmity for Zhang, but only held different ideas about matters of state. The ruler of Wey passed this request along to Zhang Yi, who agreed to see Gongsun Yan. During the banquet at which Zhang was entertained by the ruler of Wey, Gongsun Yan crawled forward before Zhang on his knees, offering wishes that Zhang enjoy "one thousand autumns" of long life.

The next day, as Zhang set off, Gongsun Yan saw him as far as the border of Qi. The King of Qi, still angry about Gongsun Yan's role in securing the kingship of Zhongshan, was furious when he heard of the gross display of affection between Zhang Yi and Gongsun Yan. He refused to listen to Zhang, whose hopes of bringing Qi into the Horizontal Alliance through diplomacy (and thereby, potentially, securing a bloodless end to the crisis of the Warring States) were dashed.[50]

This anecdote might seem too neatly constructed to be plausible, but if we think about it in the context of the time, there is a real chance that events transpired just as the source reports. Zhang Yi's position at the Wei court was tenuous from the outset, especially since he had found it necessary to exile Hui Shi, a figure who commanded enormous affection and loyalty among Wei's officials and courtiers. With Hui Shi's departure, Gongsun Yan was one of the few individuals left at the Wei court who could command equivalent respect. Zhang Yi knew that any dealings with Gongsun Yan entailed risk, but in a society where honor and ceremonial recognition were real currency, Gongsun Yan's willingness to crawl on his knees before Zhang Yi was very literally too good an offer to refuse. If Zhang Yi had rebuffed Gongsun Yan and word had spread, Zhang's position among the resentful and suspicious ministers of the Wei court would have become worse than it already was. Gongsun Yan had thus not duped Zhang Yi, so much as he had set a trap from which Zhang Yi could not escape.

Impediments to Zhang Yi's program came from the very top of Wei's political establishment. Since the partnership between Qin and Wei was fundamentally offensive in nature, it required the determination of a leader. The object of the Horizontal Alliance from the outset was to establish a new Son of Heaven. Zhang Yi had never been in any doubt that the ruler who would ascend to that role when the Horizontal Alliance prevailed was King Huiwen of Qin, and he thus expected King Hui of Wei to formally subordinate himself to his ally.

It was perhaps understandable for Zhang Yi to expect that King Hui of Wei would comply with this plan. Wei Ying had, after all, been willing to abase himself before the ruler of Qi when Hui Shi had urged that expedient upon him to avoid military disaster in 336 BCE. But whether it was because Wei Ying had grown more stubborn and proud in old age, or because he did not trust Zhang Yi as thoroughly as he did Hui Shi, or because he simply did not respect the power of Qin, the King of Wei refused to formally swear himself as a vassal of Qin. This led to the strange circumstance of Qin going to war against the very king whose prime minister it had chosen. Qin's armies poured across the western frontier and seized two cities that Zhang Yi had returned to Wei while he still served in Qin.[51]

The meaning of the lesson was clear, and King Hui of Wei understood: the good will of Qin could not be taken for granted. The Horizontal Alliance held together through this crisis, but its terms became more explicitly coercive. Archaeologically discovered artifacts show that in 321 BCE Zhang Yi formally resumed his post as Prime Minister of Qin, giving him the ministerial seals of both courts simultaneously.⁵² This made it easier for Zhang Yi to coordinate the economic and military assets of Wei and Qin in tandem, but it effectively foreclosed his hopes of reaching his goals through diplomacy. The cost in terms of a kingdom's autonomy of joining the Horizontal Alliance had been raised too high for any of the eastern states to find the prospect tempting. Zhang Yi would be forced to employ significant military force in pursuit of his ultimate ambitions.

In 320 BCE Zhang Yi went on the offensive. He mobilized an army from Qin that crossed the territory of Han and Wei to assault Qi. Having failed to secure Qi's cooperation with diplomacy, Zhang had no choice but to try military coercion. It was a bold gambit. If Qi could have been forced to join the Horizontal Alliance, the coalition would have been made effectively invincible. No combination of other states could have stood against the combined might of Qin, Wei, and Qi.

If Zhang had been able to mobilize the full strength of Qin and Wei, he might have succeeded, but he could not. The sources tell us that Han and Wei "lent the road" to Qin. In other words, the contribution of Han and Wei to this offensive was largely limited to allowing Qin's soldiers through their territory unmolested. Wei, even under the newly constrictive terms of the Horizontal Alliance, was still a reluctant partner. Though Qin was steadily growing in power, it was not yet sufficiently strong, either to coerce Wei into fully supporting a long-range offensive, or to score a victory operating alone and with such extremely extended supply lines. Qin's invasion force was beaten in Qi, and returned home in defeat.⁵³ Having failed its first serious military test, the first successfully negotiated Horizontal Alliance collapsed. Zhang Yi returned to Qin.

In the immediate aftermath of Zhang Yi's departure, King Hui of Wei had passed over Gongsun Yan and chosen a man named Tian Xu as prime minister to replace Zhang Yi. The sources do not tell us what was behind King Hui's decision. Perhaps he was distrustful because Gongsun Yan had done so much damage to Wei as an official of Qin. Perhaps the frenetic politics of Zhang Yi's tenure had wearied King Hui of brilliant and ambitious officials.

A fellow persuader who was passing through Wei to Qi on a mission for the Qin court tried to call upon Gongsun Yan, and eventually found him idly indulging in drink. When confronted, Gongsun Yan rationalized that he might as well drink, because he had little work. His companion offered a plan which, he predicted, would get Gongsun Yan as much work as he could possibly want.

King Hui of Wei had sent the new prime minister Tian Xu on a mission to Chu, in an attempt to find new allies now that Qin was again a threat. The visiting persuader suggested that Gongsun Yan, pleading idleness, request a small entourage to visit "old acquaintances" in Yan and Zhao, on the off chance that something of benefit to Wei might be negotiated. The king was likely to grant this request, seeing no harm in it. When he had the king's permission, Gongsun Yan should then let his carriages be visibly prepared, announce his destination to all and sundry, and wait.

The plan worked as its designer intended. When the wandering persuaders living at the Wei court saw that carriages were being prepared to send Gongsun Yan to Zhao and Yan, the news spread like wildfire. Everyone assumed, on the basis of Gongsun Yan's reputation, that the prime minister's mission to Chu had been a decoy, and that whatever policy Wei was really planning to pursue would be entrusted to the wily Gongsun Yan. Persuaders rushed to return to their home states and inform their rulers of Gongsun Yan's movements.

When the news reached the capitals of the other eastern kingdoms, a general speculative panic ensued. Each ruler who heard of Gongsun Yan's mission was convinced that Gongsun Yan must have a clever plan, and that anyone who was late to join it would at best lose out on its potential profits, at worst be among those who paid out whatever dividends Gongsun Yan intended to collect. As Gongsun Yan dallied, purposefully delaying his departure, envoys arrived in the Wei capital from Han, Zhao, and Yan requesting to join whatever alliance Gongsun Yan was negotiating. The King of Qi that Gongsun Yan had angered had died. His son, not harboring a grudge against Gongsun Yan and angry about Qin's attempt to assault Qi in 320 BCE, sent an envoy inquiring about Gongsun Yan's plans. Even the King of Chu, who had received an actual offer of alliance from the hands of King Hui of Wei's chosen prime minister, sent an envoy insisting that he be allowed to treat with Gongsun Yan, convinced that the first offer he had received could not be in earnest. King Hui of Wei was left with little choice but to appoint Gongsun Yan prime minister.[54]

The chain reaction illustrated a key dynamic set in motion by the royal revolution. Since before the coup in Qi of 481 BCE, leaders throughout the Zhou world had worked to depersonalize and bureaucratize state power. In the progressively more rule-bound and routinized governments of the Warring States, individual charisma and personal reputation should ideally not have been a factor. Such a principle was even given voice by a famous theorist of the time, Master Shen Dao (ca. 350–274 BCE), who described the way that civil officials, like their military counterparts at the head of troops on the battlefield, could be said to have "force" (*shi*, sometimes translated as "strategic advantage"—see the discussion in Chapter 7). Ideally, according to Shen Dao, an official should only have the political "force" allotted to him by the formal powers and authority of his office. It was a great danger to the state when a minister, because of his reputation or the result of clever factional scheming, acquired more political force than his office conveyed. Such ministers could sometimes become even more powerful than their rulers, which was potentially a recipe for disaster.[55]

The wisdom of Master Shen's teachings was broadly acknowledged, in the abstract. But raising the rulers of the Warring States to the position of "king" had widened the already yawning gap in wealth and status between rulers and the knights who made up the bulk of officialdom. The social pressures on knights, who were now even more humble by contrast to the highest rungs of the status ladder in each individual state, became even more severe. This made it imperative for them to protect themselves and one another from the depredations of highborn aristocrats.

In the face of increasing insecurity, ordinary officials were spontaneously inclined to seek out the leadership and sheltering patronage of knights, like Gongsun Yan, whose manifest talent and meritorious service gave them unimpeachable credibility and inviolable authority. Such individuals could not fail to accrue "political force" and exercise influence far exceeding the formal parameters of their offices. Gongsun Yan had traded upon his political force to entrap Zhang Yi during the banquet at the court of Wey, and in the wake of Zhang Yi's departure he further parlayed his political force to engineer his own ascension to the post of prime minister. Thus, though the rise of rulers like Wei Ying to the height of kingship had imbued their thrones with new and greater powers, it had also set into motion social dynamics that forced kings to share power with the collected officials of their respective courts in unexpected ways.

One of Gongsun Yan's first acts as prime minister was to recall Hui Shi and re-employ him as a counselor at the Wei court. The Master's return was fortuitous. In 319 BCE, during the first winter after Gongsun Yan became prime minister, King Hui of Wei died after 51 years on the throne.[56] It was the end of an era. Wei Ying had made Wei into a kingdom, and had presided over the period in which his state was, in both absolute and relative terms, the most powerful it had ever been, surpassing even the era of his fabled grandfather, Marquis Wen.

As if in cosmic response to the event, on the day planned for Wei Ying's funeral a freakishly intense storm settled on the Wei capital of Greatbridge, burying the city in snow "up to a cow's eye." Wei Ying's son King Xiang was intent on going through with the funeral ceremony, convinced that to do otherwise would be a breach of filial duty. None of his ministers could dissuade him, they thus called upon Hui Shi to help make the king see reason.

In audience, Hui Shi presented the king a story about how King Wen, the sage founder of the Zhou dynasty, had been faced with similar circumstances. The Luan River had flooded the tomb prepared for King Wen's father on the day planned for his funeral. King Wen declared that his father's spirit must have commanded the River God to flood the tomb out of a desire for more time to say farewell to his people. King Wen thus delayed the funeral for several days, and had his father laid in state to receive homage until the flood waters subsided. Having recounted the story, Hui Shi declared that it would be arrogant of King Xiang of Wei to refuse to follow the model of the great sage King Wen. King Xiang was persuaded, and delayed the funeral of his father until the snow could be cleared.[57]

The moment revealed latent forces that had undermined Zhang Yi's Horizontal Alliance. The fact that the Wei court spontaneously turned to Hui Shi to resolve the crisis of Wei Ying's funeral demonstrated that Hui Shi's political force exceeded even that of Gongsun Yan. This is why Zhang Yi had only ever been able to imperfectly wield the power of Wei, and (in part) why Hui Shi's protégé Gongsun Yan had risen to the prime minister's seat despite the preferences of Wei's king. Even in exile, Hui Shi had exerted a restraining influence on the Wei court that made it impossible for either Zhang Yi or Wei Ying to fully realize their designs.

The combined political force of Gongsun Yan and Hui Shi had been enough to unravel the Horizontal Alliance and knit together a Vertical coalition. Even their influence, however, had limited power in the fractious and volatile world of the Warring States. The dubious cohesion of the Vertical Alliance was demonstrated by the fact that it mobilized against Qin in 318 BCE, less than a year after Gongsun Yan had become Prime Minister of Wei and scandalously long before the mourning rites for King Hui of Wei had concluded. The haste with which the Vertical allies set out on campaign (impelled in part, perhaps, by the haste with which the coalition had initially formed during the "chain reaction" set off by Gongsun Yan's ruse) suggests that political tensions threatened to shake the coalition apart if it did not strike quickly.

A "Five Kingdom" alliance consisting of Wei, Han, Zhao, Yan, and Chu attacked Qin in 318 BCE. Qi did not join the assault, and Yan and Chu likewise did not provide significant forces. The latter two kingdoms' contribution to the alliance consisted mainly of a pledge to refrain from hostilities against the Three Jin successor states for the duration of the war. The Qin army met the invaders at the Hangu Pass and defeated them soundly, sending them into retreat.[58] The next year Qin forces sallied forth from the Hangu Pass and engaged the armies of the coalition at a location deep within the territory of Han, just west of the defensive wall that divided Han from Wei's eastern Henei region. The battle ended in complete victory for Qin. Two of Han's top commanders were captured, and 82,000 soldiers of Han, Zhao, and Wei were killed.[59]

The coalition sued for peace.[60] The war might have continued longer, at greater cost to Wei and its allies, except that back through the Hangu Pass, Qin was faced with a rebellion by the Rong state of Yiqu that threatened its home territory. This was at least partly thanks to the machinations of Gongsun Yan. The Lord of Yiqu, who had only recently sworn himself a vassal of Qin, had visited the Wei court while Zhang Yi was prime minister. Gongsun Yan, knowing he would not get many chances to communicate with the Yiqu leader, offered him the advice that if ever the King of Qin should present him with exceptionally lavish gifts, it would be a sign that he was engaged in a war with the states in the east (and was trying to ensure the passivity of the Yiqu state). That, Gongsun Yan noted, would be an opportune time for rebellion. As Gongsun Yan had intuited would be the case, the Qin court did send lavish gifts to the Yiqu lord during the war with the Vertical coalition, and bought a rebellion instead of peace.[61]

The failed invasion of Qin did not completely undermine Gongsun Yan's authority, but it did make Wei increasingly vulnerable, and it weakened Gongsun Yan's hold on the Wei court. In 317 BCE, the King of Qi took advantage of Wei's distress and attacked from the east, defeating the coalition army at a place called Overlook Marsh (Guanze).[62] This prompted Gongsun Yan to complain to King Xiang of Wei that the former prime minister, Tian Xu (whom Gongsun Yan himself had ousted with the ruse of his "mission to Yan and Zhao"), had been undermining him. He requested that Tian Xu be exiled or killed, so that Gongsun Yan could pursue his policies free of interference.

The interference by Tian Xu (to the extent that Gongsun Yan had been correct in his accusations) was another example of the distortions of "political force" that Master Shen Dao had warned about. The fact that Gongsun Yan had to request Tian Xu's exile rather than simply ordering it (as Zhang Yi had done to his predecessor Hui Shi) demonstrated how much Gongsun Yan's position had softened as a result of the defeats incurred by Wei and its allies on his watch. The king would not grant Gongsun Yan's request outright, complaining that the former prime minister was as close to him as his own arms and legs. To exile or kill such a trusted official would, according to the king, completely undermine his own credibility in the eyes of the world. He would not allow Tian Xu to be molested, but promised that the former prime minister would be watched closely and would be prevented from doing anything to undermine Gongsun Yan's authority.[63]

Gongsun Yan saw that his position at the Wei court was tenuous, and that the threat of Qi had to be neutralized if the Vertical coalition were to have any hope of resisting Qin. He thus approached Tian Ying, a kinsman of the Qi king whom had been enfeoffed as Lord Jingguo and had served as Qi's prime minister, and struck a deal with him to secure peace between Wei and Qi. In accordance with this deal, Gongsun Yan resigned as Wei's prime minister and took up the post of Prime Minister of Han.

In Gongsun Yan's place, the Lord Jingguo's young son, Tian Wen, was appointed as Prime Minister of Wei. Tian Wen would eventually go on to have a fabled career, becoming one of the most powerful men in the Warring States.[64] This tenure as Wei's prime minister was a brief tutelage in politics by way of preparing him for bigger things. We will have much more to say about him in the next chapter.

Gongsun Yan's ability to shuffle the high offices of Han and Wei showed that he had not entirely lost the confidence of leaders in the eastern states. From his vantage as Prime Minister of Han, Gongsun Yan hoped to mobilize the armies of the Vertical coalition for a second assault on Qin. Before he could do so, in 315 BCE Qin attacked preemptively, penetrating deep into Han territory and defeating its army at a location named Muddy Marsh (Zhuoze), just southwest of the Han capital. This prompted the King of Han to send an emissary seeking peace with Qin.

When news reached Chu that Han might ally with Qin, its king was alarmed. He sought advice on how to respond, and a trusted knight among the wandering persuaders counseled him to mobilize his forces as if he were coming to Han's rescue. That would persuade the King of Han to break off peace talks with Qin. Once that goal was achieved, the soldiers of Chu could return to their barracks.

The King of Chu did as he was advised. The King of Han was warned that Chu's mobilization could not be trusted, but he fell for the ruse. Confident that Chu's soldiers could be relied upon to support him against the invaders, the King of Han broke off peace talks with Qin. In 314 BCE Qin's army, which had remained at Muddy Marsh, pressed forward and engaged the Han army again at a place known as Rivergate (Anmen). Chu's army did not arrive to support them, and the soldiers of Han were badly defeated, losing ten thousand men. Gongsun Yan, who had been in overall command, was forced to flee the battlefield.[65]

This put an end to Gongsun Yan's vision of a Vertical Alliance, and he himself sank into obscurity after the debacle at Rivergate. He returned to Wei, where his reputation was still formidable enough to secure him a post as a military commander. His old enemy Tian Xu became prime minister again, however, and finally succeeded in plotting Gongsun Yan's ultimate downfall, framing him for the murder of a fellow official.[66]

While Gongsun Yan floundered in the east, his rival Zhang Yi, once again Prime Minister of Qin,[67] continued to pursue his ambition of making the King of Qin the new Son of Heaven. In the wake of Qin's victory at Rivergate he successfully pressured Han and Wei to join in coalition once again with Qin. To vouchsafe the alliance, the King of Han sent his Heir Apparent as a hostage to reside in the custody of the Qin court.[68] King Xiang of Wei met with King Huiwen of Qin in a summit near the frontier between the two kingdoms, and agreed to declare one of his sons who had lived as a hostage in Qin as his Heir Apparent, to seal the bond of friendship between the two states.[69]

This second formation of the Horizontal Alliance raised alarm in the east. The states of Qi and Chu, which had known almost nothing but mutual hostility for most of their history, formed an alliance to meet the new threat. With Qi's assistance Chu struck north and captured the city of Crooked Ditch (Quwo), which controlled the approach to the strategic Hangu Pass. King Huiwen of Qin set Zhang Yi the task of not only recovering Crooked Ditch, but of pushing Qin's frontier farther south into the Han River valley.

Zhang Yi made an embassy to Chu. He delivered a speech at the Chu court declaring that the King of Qin was angriest at the King of Qi, who had thwarted the efforts of the first Horizontal Alliance. Qin was willing to buy peace from Chu so that it would be free to punish Qi. Zhang Yi offered to cede "six hundred square *li* of the land of Shang and Wu," territory that Qin had conquered from Chu and that had contained the fief of the famous Shang Yang (giving him his title of Lord Shang). All that the King of Chu would have to do in order to receive this land was to break off his alliance with Qi and leave that state isolated.

Though the King of Chu was warned not to trust Zhang Yi, he was drawn in by the tempting offer of land. Chu broke off its alliance with Qi. When the King of Chu sent an envoy to receive the promised territory, Zhang Yi declared, as if this had been the terms of the agreement all along, that Chu would now receive *six* square *li* of territory (rather than the six hundred actually promised).

It was a dish of revenge served very, very cold: repayment for the beating that Zhang had received at the hands of Chu's prime minister and his entourage almost three decades earlier. Back when he was a humble knight, the aristocracy of Chu had beaten Zhang Yi on the presumption that he was a liar. Honor thus did not compel him to deal truthfully with the leaders of Chu now that he was a titled lord. Quite the contrary.

The King of Chu was furious, and mobilized the full might of his military to punish Qin's treachery and seize the promised territory. Without allies, however, Chu's military was poorly matched against the combined forces of the Horizontal Alliance. The Alliance army met the Chu force on the north bank of the Dan River, as it entered the territory with which Zhang Yi had baited the King of Chu. Chu was routed, and one of its most famed generals captured. The Qin force drove across the Dan River and into Chu's Hanzhong Commandery. It was the final move of a classic shell game. In the hopes of getting something for nothing, the King of Chu had instead gambled away his own territory at the cost of some of his best soldiers.[70]

The story of Zhang Yi's revenge has such an air of folklore that we are justified in reading it skeptically. We of course can never be sure if the beating that Zhang Yi is said to have received in Chu as a young man actually took place, or whether it was created retrospectively by literati to add heightened drama and moral import to this instance in which a king had been humbled by the strategies of a man born as a knight. But there is good evidence to corroborate the record that Zhang Yi did employ a ruse to bait the King of Chu into breaking off his alliance with Qi.

During the Song dynasty, farmers living in what had been the Qin state discovered several inscribed stone steles that had been erected by the order of King Huiwen of Qin. These monuments bore inscriptions of curses called down upon the King of Chu by the Ancestral Supplicator (*zongzhu*, the chief priest and ritual expert employed by the court)[71] of Qin. The curses were transcribed by Song literati and have survived in transmitted manuscripts.

The texts describe the general wickedness of the King of Chu, which (according to the words of the Ancestral Supplicant) had been made even worse by the fact that Chu was trying to seize the "territory of Shang and Wu" in violation of an oath. The recorded prayers call upon the ancestral spirits of the Qin house and the protective gods of the Qin kingdom to bring calamity upon the King of Chu and his armies, in repayment of his transgressions. The curses themselves had been cast during sacrifices performed as the Chu armies advanced in 313 BCE.[72]

Cursing one's enemies like this was an occasional practice during the Warring States. There are records of other such instances in the sources.[73] But the particulars of the "Qin-Chu curse texts" jibe so closely with what the historical chronicles report about the *casus belli* of the campaigns of 313 BCE as to be suggestive. It would have been quite in character for elites of the fourth century BCE to seek spiritual protection through sacrifice and invocations when they knew they had done or said something (like Zhang Yi's bait-and-switch about the "six hundred/six square *li* of territory") that might offend the gods and ancestors (even those of an enemy, who could be formidable even if they lacked jurisdiction in one's own kingdom).

Though the second incarnation of the Horizontal Alliance had achieved more of strategic significance than the first, the most durable legacy of Zhang Yi's service to Qin came from a policy that he opposed. In 316 BCE a fugitive arrived at the Qin court from the kingdom of Shu, a non-Sinitic state situated in the Sichuan basin.[74] Today Sichuan Province is known as the "rice bowl of China." The Sichuan basin is ringed by impassable mountains, and has provided shelter to besieged regimes at many turning points in history, over more than two millenia.[75] By the Warring States the Sichuan basin had been home to vibrant and distinctive cultures for many centuries. Twentieth-century archaeologists began revealing the richness of that cultural legacy with the discoveries at Sanxingdui, a village near the modern-day provincial capital of Chengdu.[76]

These discoveries embody an artistic tradition of unique sophistication and haunting beauty. Bronze statues of human figurines, some life size, adorned with startlingly oversized eyes, resemble nothing ever before seen by modern observers of the cultural history of East Asia (see Fig. 16).[77] They have been admired throughout the world as hallmarks of a distinctive ancient Sichuanese aesthetic.

In 316 BCE, the two most prominent political regions of the Sichuan basin were the kingdom of Shu in the west and the confederation of a people known to the Zhou world as the Ba, in the east. The Ba people spoke a different language and practiced different customs than those of Shu. They had a reputation for being very fierce and warlike, and were known for carrying bronze drums known as *chunyu* into battle with which to frighten the enemy.[78]

Fig. 16. Bronze statues with these characteristically exaggerated features have been discovered in abundance at Sanxingdui, site of the capital of an ancient non-Sinitic civilization that once inhabited the Sichuan basin, and which was ancestral to the kingdom of Shu. (Source: blog.hmns.org.)

The Ba people had originally lived in the Han River valley and the region east of the Jialing River in Sichuan, but they had been pushed west, into the territory of Shu, by the encroachment of the kingdom of Chu during the fourth century BCE. As Chu reconsolidated its power in the aftermath of wars with Wu and Yue, its soldiers and merchants ventured upstream along the Yangzi River and established an expanding foothold for Chu in the eastern reaches of the Sichuan basin. This encounter between the polities of Shu, Ba, and Chu facilitated trade and fertile cultural exchange. But, predictably, it also bred conflict, and destabilized the social and political institutions that had patterned life for the people of the Sichuan basin for many centuries.[79]

The people of Shu had interacted with those of the Yellow River plain for many centuries, but that contact had been limited and intermittent. The founding kings of the Zhou dynasty had the support of Shu's rulers in their rebellion against the Shang dynasty.[80] The Qinling and Daba mountain ranges, traversable only with difficulty and in small numbers, divided the territory of Qin from that of Shu, but the two states had engaged in occasional communication, trade, and conflict since Qin's initial founding. In 337 BCE, the year that

King Huiwen of Qin first ascended the ducal throne after the death of his father, the ruler of Shu had paid court to the new ruler.[81]

Prior to 316 BCE, interaction between Qin and Shu had been intensified by the construction of the Stone Cattle road, a narrow artery cut through the Qinling and Daba mountain ranges, connecting the source of the Han River with the upper Jialing River valley. The road was a marvel of ancient engineering. Its route has been reconstructed by modern archaeologists, who have documented the many places where work crews burrowed through mountain ridges and reinforced tunnels with wooden beams and struts. In order to provide purchase to vehicles and footholds to pack animals, many kilometers of the road were paved with hardened wooden planks.[82]

According to legend, a group of envoys from Shu to the Qin court had been shown a group of stone statues of cattle, below the tails of which had been placed "droppings" made of solid gold. The gullible envoys had been told that the stone cows were magic beasts, and had been providing gold to the Qin court for many years. When he heard report of this wonder, the King of Shu asked that he might be given some of the stone cows as a gift, and in this way was duped into assisting with the construction of the road that gave Qin access to his kingdom, thereafter known as the Stone Cattle road.[83]

This legend is surely ethnocentric Qin propaganda, expressing contempt for a people that Qin elites deemed "barbarians." It is almost certain, given the time and resources invested in the project and the improbability of its having been accomplished in the face of hostile opposition, that the road had been constructed by mutual agreement between the Qin and Shu courts, for the purpose of facilitating trade. The work must have required many years; thus, it is very possible that it had first been negotiated in 337 BCE, the year that the King of Shu visited the Qin court on the future King Huiwen's ascension to the Qin throne.

In 316 BCE the King of Shu faced a rebellion by his younger brother, the Marquis of Zu. Zu had been established as a vassalage on the Jialing River at the point close to where it met the Stone Cattle road. This territory had been settled by large numbers of the Ba people, and the King of Shu had given his brother the task of pacifying it. The Marquis of Zu was thus caught between the court of Shu in the west and ruler of the Ba in the east, who was himself under constant pressure from the encroaching forces of Chu. Once the destabilizing forces of accelerating trade over the Stone Cattle road were added to this mix, the potential for conflict was limitless.

In 316 BCE the Marquis of Zu took the side of Ba in a conflict between its ruler and the Shu court. The King of Shu thus marched against his brother and seized Zu's capital on the Jialing River. The marquis fled along the Stone Cattle road, and arrived at the Qin court in search of aid, followed closely by the envoys of the King of Shu, who likewise asked that Qin send troops to help put down the remaining forces loyal to the marquis and his Ba allies.[84] King Huiwen of Qin consulted his ministers on the question of how to respond to these requests. A debate ensued, and the king received conflicting opinions.

Zhang Yi argued against any involvement in the affairs of the Sichuan basin. At the moment Qin was still engaged with Gongsun Yan's Vertical Alliance to the east. The people of Shu and Ba, Zhang noted, were aliens, and did not figure in to the political dynamics of the Zhou world. Qin should remain focused on the struggle with Han and Wei. Once those states were brought to heel, pressure could be placed on the Zhou king to surrender the Nine Tripods. When that was accomplished, the other states would all be forced to submit to Qin as the new Son of Heaven.

A minister named Sima Cuo stood forward to argue against Zhang Yi. Symbols like the Nine Tripods, he declared, were too easily manipulated and commodified. If he ever truly felt that Qin was closing in on its goal of becoming the new Son of Heaven, the Zhou king could offer the Nine Tripods to some other ruler (for example, the King of Wei), in exchange for help fending off whatever pressure Qin was trying to exert on the Zhou court.

By contrast, the potential profit that Shu had to offer was securely attainable. The Sichuan basin had some of the most fertile lands in the world, and was densely populated with potential recruits for Qin's armies. Much wealth moved along its rivers and roads in trade. Geographically, occupying Shu would give Qin's armies another gateway (moving along the Yangzi River that formed a pass through the mountains ringing the Sichuan basin) through which to assault the southern kingdom of Chu. Precisely because they were alien cultures, Qin could conquer and subjugate the people of Shu and Ba without earning a reputation for cruelty or immorality among the other Zhou states. Qin should take advantage of this moment of internal strife within the kingdom of Shu to do just that.[85]

It was the distillation of a more general debate that would transpire among officials and literati of the Warring States for most of the next century. A resolution of the crisis of the era would depend on success in two basic dimensions. On the one hand, victory would hinge on fiscal-military factors: the recruitment, training, and arming of powerful armies and the production and extraction of wealth to support that enterprise. On the other hand, as strategic leaders like Zhang Yi and Gongsun Yan had demonstrated, because the contending military forces of the Warring States were too evenly matched, arriving at peace would ultimately require skillful political leadership and manipulation of the symbols and institutions at the basis of power (for example, getting the Zhou king to abdicate in favor of a ruler who would be accepted by the other leaders of the Warring States as a new Son of Heaven). The question that underpinned the debate between Zhang Yi and Sima Cuo (and that would occupy literati throughout the Warring States from that time forward) was whether one of these dimensions of power was more essential than the other. Would success rely more on the development (and tactical use) of economic and military resources, or on the cultivation of political consensus and cultural legitimacy?

Fiscal-military goals won out in the debate of 316 BCE. King Huiwen authorized an expeditionary force under the joint command of Sima Cuo and Zhang Yi to escort the Marquis of Zu back along the Stone Cattle road.[86] The Qin troops met and fought the army led by the King of Shu at the capital of Zu, along the banks of the Jialing River. With the help of soldiers of Ba, the Qin expeditionary force defeated the King of Shu and set him to flight. He beat a long retreat, and only regrouped to stand against the Qin invaders at a location 59 kilometers southwest of his own capital of Chengdu. There he was defeated again, and was captured and killed. His Heir Apparent and Chancellor fled with the remnants of their forces up the slopes of White Deer Mountain, but they were pursued and annihilated by the Qin invaders.

Having achieved their ostensible objective, Sima Cuo and Zhang Yi did not cease military operations. They turned on the Marquis of Zu and destroyed his court, and pressed on past Zu into the heartland of the Ba confederation, likewise taking its king captive. By 314 BCE Qin had established military supremacy over most of the Sichuan basin.[87]

One of the King of Shu's surviving sons was established as the new ruler of Shu in the capital of Chengdu, his title now demoted by royal fiat of King Huiwen of Qin to that of marquis. As Marquis of Shu, the new ruler was a vassal of and held his title under the auspices of Qin. An aristocrat of Qin was appointed by King Huiwen to be Shu's prime minister, and another Qin official became Prefect of Shu's military defenses.[88]

It was an awkward power-sharing arrangement between the indigenous elites of the former Shu kingdom and their Qin conquerors, and it would be tested over time by conflict and strife. In one form or another, however, Shu remained under Qin rule for the next century. During this time Shu's people were progressively pressured to conform to the norms and customs of Qin, and thousands of families were transplanted from Qin to colonize the Sichuan basin. Thus began a long process by which the culture and society of the Sichuan basin were transformed, and the legacy of its indigenous civilizations largely forgotten.[89]

From being a land considered distant and alien during the Warring States, Sichuan eventually, over many centuries, became what the people of China today think of as the home of one of the most celebrated regional varieties of Chinese cuisine.[90] That shift began with the debate between Sima Cuo and Zhang Yi in 316 BCE. The events of subsequent decades would ultimately prove that Sima Cuo had been arguing the better case in that dispute. Successive attempts to arrive at a political resolution of the Warring States would fail. Qin would (as we will read in Chapter 14) eventually go on to militarily defeat and destroy the other Warring States, a feat of conquest that arguably dwarfs the deeds of figures like Alexander the Great or Napoleon.

That achievement was largely underwritten by the surplus agricultural wealth and human resources provided by Qin's conquered lands in Sichuan. As Sima Cuo had predicted, the extraordinary fertility and productivity of Sichuan, once it could be harnessed, gave Qin an overwhelming advantage in the fiscal-military competition against its rivals.[91] That insight, however, was prescient on Sima Cuo's part from the vantage of 316 BCE. As the fourth century BCE came to a close, though Qin was obviously rising in power, it would not have been obvious to any politically literate observers that Qin was destined to become a juggernaut with the power to conquer the whole Zhou world.

Though the conquest of Sichuan was, with the power of 20/20 hindsight, a world-altering event, it did not (as Zhang Yi's dismissal of Sichuan as an irrelevant backwater in his debate with Sima Cuo anticipated) land with immediate impact on the perspective of Warring States leaders. Another incident that began in 318 BCE, approximately 1,800 kilometers from the Shu capital of Chengdu, made a much stronger impression on the elite of the Zhou world. This world-shaking moment transpired in the northeastern state of Yan, the capital of which was located on the site of the present-day city of Beijing.

Yan was, by the standards of the late fourth century BCE, a middling power. It was vast in area, comprising part of modern-day Hebei and most of Liaoning Province, extending at its easternmost point into what is now Korea, but more sparsely populated than the states better watered by the Yellow River and its tributaries. It could not field armies to rival those of Qi, Wei, or Qin. It had a venerable pedigree, however. The title of Yan had been given to the descendants of the Duke of Shao (fl. ca. 1050 BCE), one of the sons of the sage King Wen and a founding father of the Zhou house. Moreover, Yan benefited from geographic isolation. It had to defend itself from non-Sinitic people to the north and east, but it only shared borders with three of the other Zhou states: Qi, Zhongshan, and Zhao.[92]

Yan's previous ruler, King Yi (r. 332–321 BCE) had assumed the rank of king in 323 BCE, during the summit of "Five Kings" brokered by Gongsun Yan. His son officially succeeded him in 320 BCE, but was never given a posthumous title. Thus in breach of custom, historical sources generally refer to him by his given name, "King Kuai" (r. 320–318 BCE, d. 314 BCE).[93]

This distinction reflects the fact that in 318 BCE,[94] King Kuai shocked the Zhou world by abdicating his throne in favor of his prime minister, a man known to history only as Zizhi (d. 312 BCE). The act did not come completely "from out of the blue." According to accounts of high antiquity generally accepted by the literati community, including the latter-day disciples of both Confucius and Mo Di (among others), two of the greatest sage-kings of ancient times, Yao and Shun, had refused to pass the royal throne to their own sons, but had each sought out and abdicated in favor of the wisest and most worthy man in the realm.

By 318 BCE these stories had taken on the status of "charter myths" in the elite society of the Warring States.[95] The urgency of finding a leader with sufficient Potency[96] was so great, these examples demonstrated, that the sage kings of high antiquity had passed over their own children in order to ensure that the necessary conditions of proper rule were fulfilled. The abdication stories were not generally viewed as practical models to be followed, but as unique cases from the distant past that proved an abstract truth: earned merit surpassed elevated birth as a credential of leadership.

In 318 BCE King Kuai of Yan took these tales of ancient times and used them as a blueprint for current policy, emulating the great sage kings Yao and Shun. In doing so he was obviously motivated, at least in part, by the great reverence in which those rulers were held. But this still forces us to ask why him, why then? In the two thousand years since the purported reigns of Yao and Shun, no ruler had followed their example. Why did King Kuai break this trend? The sources give us different explanations of his reasons for doing so.

In virtually all accounts of the abdication affair, King Kuai is portrayed as either naïvely foolish or fecklessly gullible. Some sources give the credit for what happened to the cleverness of Prime Minister Zizhi, who is said to have used flattery, eloquence, and lies to persuade King Kuai to abdicate.[97] Other sources claim that the abdication affair was a piece of political theater gone wrong.

According to these latter accounts, King Kuai did not intend to give up his throne, at least initially. In some accounts of the abdication affair of 318 BCE, a wandering persuader outlines for King Kuai a plan by which he can enhance his prestige and that of his court at no cost in either blood or treasure. Among the abdication legends of high antiquity were stories of wise hermits who so disdained the corrupting influence of politics that they refused to accept the throne when it was offered to them. Before Yao abdicated to Shun, for example, he is said to have offered the throne to the enlightened recluse Xu You, who was so offended by the prospect that he washed his ears to clear them of impurity.[98]

In emulation of the legend of Yao and Xu You, all King Kuai would have to do was to *offer* to abdicate the throne to Prime Minister Zizhi, in the sure confidence that the prime minister would decline. In this way the king would earn the reputation of being a "latter-day Yao," and his prime minister would be deemed as enlightened and pure as Xu You. The king was convinced by this scheme, and was effectively trapped when his prime minister accepted the offer of the throne rather than playing the part of Xu You.[99]

Other dimensions of the written record give King Kuai a much more deliberate role. In some sources, the king is told that his plan to abdicate is flawed, because so many of the officials at court were clients and protégés of the Heir Apparent. King Kuai thus recalled the ministerial seals of all officials with an income over "3,000 measures [of grain]," so that Zizhi, on assuming the throne, could fill those posts with men loyal to him.[100]

If we resist the temptation to caricaturize King Kuai, we can see that there was obvious "method to his madness" in the context of the royal revolution. We have seen that one of the most versatile and robust new powers that the ascension to kingship conveyed upon the rulers of the Warring States was magnified control of the status hierarchy. King Kuai was effectively testing the boundaries of this new power. The royal revolution had implicitly raised the question: now that they had become kings, how high could a ruler of one of the Warring States raise one of his subjects? The abdication affair was an attempt to establish that the status imprimatur of a king was unlimited, and that the boundaries of aristocratic status were completely elastic. King Kuai set out to prove, in other words, that like an alchemist who could turn lead into gold, a king could turn a knight into a king.

Why would he want to do that? The history that we have been reviewing above provides an answer. Unless we truly believe that not only King Kuai, but virtually everyone around him, were either irredeemably foolish or incurably insane, there must have been a general awareness at the Yan court that the abdication plan posed very dangerous risks. When we see rational people taking dangerous risks, we must try to understand what benefit they were pursuing. In the case of Yan one potential benefit is clear: the Yan court was trying to establish itself as the single government of the Warring States where the dignity and status of knights was most respected, where the learning and value of literati were most revered, and where individuals of talent faced the fewest limits to the rewards they could potentially receive for their service to the state.

If these benefits seem, to our perspective, to be too insubstantial to merit the risks that King Kuai and his court took, then it is perhaps because we are looking at their situation through an anachronistic lens. If we try to understand their position on their terms, we can see the logic of what they attempted to do. The competition between the Warring States was, by the late fourth century BCE, becoming increasingly more violent and zero-sum. Survival in that destructive game was uncertain. The lesson to be drawn from the rapid decline of Wei and the equally meteoric rise of Qin was that as one state bled talented personnel to another (in the case of Wei to Qin, first Shang Yang, then Gongsun Yan, then Zhang Yi, among others) power likewise was transferred, with seismic results.

If the leaders of Yan, quite understandably, viewed the recruitment of able literati as vital to the state's survival, they had to find something knights wanted that Yan could afford to offer them. The ambitious talents of the Warring States, like those of virtually any time and place, desired wealth and power, but Yan could not compete with wealthier states such as Qin and Qi in offering such emoluments to entice potential officials. As we have seen above, however, the royal revolution had exacerbated the already severely dysfunctional social dynamics of the aristocratic community, and further undermined the position of literati at court. Literati thus placed ever increasingly high value on status, dignity, and security.

In this regard, the power and popularity of the "abdication myths" (that is, the stories about the sages Yao and Shun) among literati and other knights was on vivid display for all to see in the late fourth century BCE. By then some knights who were militating to assert and defend their collective dignity, like the famous Master Chen Zhong (ca. 350–ca. 260 BCE) in Qi (a member, albeit a low-ranking one, of the royal clan of that state), had begun openly emulating the hermit Xu You. Chen Zhongzi vowed to avoid any taint of the culture of the royal court, to the extent of running outside to vomit up a goose that had been prepared for him by his own mother, when he heard that it was a gift of the (from Chen's perspective) irredeemably corrupt king.[101] Other knights had begun to emulate the sage king Shun. They claimed, on the authority of the ancient sage Shen Nong (the "Divine Farmer"). that farming was the only redeeming occupation, and that all true gentlemen (*junzi*, a category that would include all aristocrats up to and including the king) must till the fields like common farmers if they hoped to develop the Potency that would make them fit to lead (or rule).[102]

The abdication affair in Yan, if it had succeeded in some form, would have established a revolutionary precedent that resounded throughout the Zhou world. It would have broadcast the message that Yan was the state where knights were most respected and secure, compared to any other state of the Zhou domain. It is important to note that this would have been the case *whether King Kuai ultimately stepped down from the throne or not.* It is possible that, as some of the sources claim, the original plan had never envisioned an actual change of monarch. A scenario in which King Kuai had ostensibly "attempted" to abdicate to Zizhi would still have made Yan a place where (in theory, at least), no man born a knight could ever be scorned, because if he became learned and wise enough, he might someday become a king. By entertaining abdication to any degree, King Kuai had thus perhaps made himself vulnerable to a trap set by disloyal members of his court. But, whatever the actual facts of the affair (which we may never know), King Kuai and (at least some of) his advisors were almost certainly operating on the principle that the potential benefits of an "abdication plan" for the long-term power and security of Yan far outweighed its obvious risks.

Though King Kuai surely had a more logical plan than the sources give him credit for; the results of the abdication affair proved his strategy catastrophically misguided. As we have seen in other cases (such as the violent accession of Wei Ying to the throne of Wei in 369 BCE), nothing was more destabilizing to the operation of a "Warring State" than a disruption of the line of succession. In earlier eras, when courtiers belonged to well-established aristocratic clans possessed of their own temples and estates, succession crises had been less cataclysmic. If I as an aristocrat knew that I could seek the protection of my own clan and estates and enjoy the privileges of my rank no matter who was in power, I had less to fear from a sudden change of Heir Apparent.

But when, over the course of the fifth and fourth centuries BCE, court officials became effective employees of the throne, a succession crisis became an existential threat to virtually all government personnel. The only guarantee that an official had of long-term job (and personal) security in any of the Warring States was the knowledge of where one stood with the Heir Apparent. The fate of an official like Shang Yang demonstrated that no amount of merit or power could protect one from the displeasure of the Crown Prince. Conversely, if one made sure to cultivate the trust and favor of the Heir, one's position in the bureaucracy should have been secure (or at least as secure as such positions ever could be, given the fraught social and political dynamics of a typical court).

The ascension of Zizhi to the throne of Yan threw the government of the kingdom into chaos. Reports of famine and tyrannical depredations must be viewed skeptically. But a large group of officials who had planned the future trajectory of their careers around the eventual coronation of Yan's Crown Prince were radically antagonized by the abdication of King Kuai.

In 315 BCE the resentments roiling below the surface of the Yan court broke out into open bloodshed. King Kuai's son, the Crown Prince, with the support of one of Yan's most respected military commanders, rose up in rebellion against the "pretender" Zizhi. Together they assaulted the royal palace, but were repulsed. The following year Zizhi's forces counter-attacked, and the Crown Prince and his commander were both killed.

At this juncture the turmoil in Yan drew a response from its neighbors. In 314 BCE King Xuan of Qi, with the encouragement of Mencius (who had taken up a post in the Qi court), mobilized his armies to punish Zizhi as a usurper.[103] His armies were supported by a force from Zhongshan, led by that state's prime minister Sima Zhou.[104]

The invasion of 314 BCE tested the legitimacy of Zizhi's regime in Yan, and found it lacking. According to the sources, the defensive gates in Yan were not closed, and its soldiers refused to fight. That may be an exaggeration, but even so they convey a grain of truth. The invading armies tore through Yan's territory at unprecedented speed, suggesting that they must have been assisted by the kingdom's common people and elites. Within fifty days all the armies of Yan had been defeated and its territory occupied.[105] King Kuai died in an assault on the royal palace in the kingdom's capital. Zizhi was captured alive. The severity of his crimes was made manifest by the fact that he was not merely killed, but subjected to the extreme sanction of having his body "minced," so that he could not be properly buried or attended by his descendants.[106]

The speed with which Yan fell to his armies tempted King Xuan of Qi into overreach. He announced that Yan would be annexed, and its territory converted into centrally administered districts of Qi.[107] The King of Yan's neighboring kingdom, Zhao, was predictably furious at the prospect of having two of his neighbors merge into an even more powerful "super-state." He sought out one of King Kuai's sons who was living in Han. Inviting him to Zhao, he sent him into Yan with funds and supplies under the escort of a wandering persuader who had been deputized by the Zhao court.[108]

The prince raised a rebellion among the people of Yan to expel the Qi conquerors.[109] Qi's rule of Yan had been too exploitative, and the Yan royal family still held the loyalty of a critical mass of Yan's people and elites. The returning prince was able to form an army and drive Qi's soldiers from Yan, and the autonomous state of Yan was revived. The returning prince was enthroned[110] and ruled until 279 BCE. He was known posthumously as King Zhao of Yan (r. 312–279 BCE), and we will have more to say about him in the next chapter.

The abdication affair brought the royal revolution to a culmination, in the sense that it settled one of the urgent questions that had remained open about the power of the Warring States kings since the Xuzhou summit of 334 BCE. By making their rulers kings, the courts of the Warring States had claimed greater control over the social hierarchy that determined power and wealth throughout the Zhou world. What the absolute limits of that control were had not been made clear until King Kuai of Yan set out to test them. Could aristocratic status become purely an expression of state power? Did the court and its ruler have absolute authority to determine each person's rank relative to everyone else?

The resolution of the abdication affair proved that the answer to both of these questions was provisionally, but perhaps unsurprisingly, "no."[111] Both rulers and knights had reasons to want to see status become purely tied to merit and service to the state. But to do that in 318 BCE, as King Kuai attempted, would have brought the whole house of cards that leaders throughout the Warring States had been trying to build tumbling down. If every ruler had to worry about which of his ministers might force him to abdicate, and each minister had to worry about which of his rival co-ministers might become king, functional court politics would become impossible.

This was the dimension of the abdication affair that made it so intractable for the literati chroniclers who produced our sources. On the one hand, they were broadly and profoundly committed to the ideals and doctrines that had animated King Kuai's actions ("A knight can be worthy enough to become a king!"). On the other hand, they did not want to be perceived as endorsing or sharing responsibility for those actions' predictably catastrophic results. The abdication affair and its outcome illuminated a "dead zone" in the larger ideological perspective of Warring States literati, a terrain in which the abstract logic of their world view and the pragmatic necessities of the actual political realm could never be fully reconciled.

This conflict between conceptual logic and political reality is illustrated in many of the circumstances surrounding the abdication affair, but perhaps none more so than the fate of Prime Minister Sima Zhou (d. 314 BCE) of Zhongshan. He is known to historians from stories about him that are recorded in transmitted texts.[112] But the facts of Sima Zhou's demise were not known until, in 1973, archaeologists discovered a group of bronzes interred in the tomb of Zhongshan's King Cuo (d. ca. 308 BCE).

Several of the bronzes include lengthy inscriptions that detail Sima Zhou's actions leading up to and in the face of the abdication affair in Yan.[113] The prime minister himself is extolled as a model minister, a figure of abundant Potency whose conduct in all respects conformed to the Way. The inscriptions describe how Sima Zhou had served as regent of the Zhongshan court when King Cuo was a child. As King Cuo grew to manhood, he continued to rely on the prime minister to oversee the court, while the king indulged in leisure, traveled the kingdom, and took advantage of Sima Zhou's trustworthiness and talent.

When the wicked Zizhi stole the throne of Yan, Sima Zhou was seized with righteous anger. He led an army from Zhongshan to punish the usurper, and scored great victories. On the campaign trail, however, Sima Zhou received orders from the court that he disregarded in his haste to defeat the enemy.

What Sima Zhou had done was (according to the inscriptions) in the best interests of the Altars of the Soil and Grain of the kingdom of Zhongshan. It was also sanctioned by the teachings of Master Sun (preserved in the *Sunzi bingfa*), who declared that the commander on campaign is not bound to follow orders that come from the ruler if they conflict with the needs of the battlefield.[114] But when Sima Zhou returned from campaign he insisted that he had committed a capital offense.

King Cuo had no desire to punish his prime minister, he claimed to be willing to pardon him virtually any transgression, even one that would have required the execution of his family to within three generations. Sima Zhou, however, was adamant. He insisted that the rightness inherent in the relationship between ruler and minister could only be upheld if he himself was punished. He insisted on being put to death.

It is remarkable that no record of this event survives in the transmitted records of the Warring States. That very fact, however, helps demonstrate the degree to which the abdication affair upset and challenged political elites throughout the Warring States. So many aspects of this event were dissonant; it would have been difficult for the literati of the age to keep track of them all. The abdication affair fell outside of any manageable framework, and left rulers and their ministers at sea in search of functional responses.

We can see this in the inscriptions concerning Sima Zhou. Did he really submit to death willingly? We cannot know. All we can be sure of is the paradox the inscriptions present us with: on the one hand he was a model minister, a paragon of service and merit, and on the other hand he had to die.

It is perhaps easiest to understand the reasons why Sima Zhou had to die. He was a prime minister who had accrued extraordinary power and had defied the orders of his ruler, in a world where the prime minister of the neighboring state had just replaced his own king. In a strange sense, Sima Zhou's death might have been considered less urgently necessary if he was a more mediocre official. Sima Zhou had to die to prove that King Kuai and Prime Minister Zizhi of Yan had been wrong: no matter how much learning, wisdom, and merit an individual minister developed and displayed, the line between king and minister could *never* be crossed.

What is perhaps more difficult to understand is why, given that Sima Zhou was executed, he was yet memorialized with such high praise, for many years after he had been put to death. If he was ultimately a criminal, why gild his image? The dilemma posed by Prime Minister Sima Zhou's fate was the same as that raised by the abdication affair itself. The hereditary prerogatives of the sovereign had to be affirmed and defended, but in doing so one had to avoid denigrating or debasing the value of merit and service.

The competition for talent between the Warring States was too steep. If a kingdom like Zhongshan got the reputation of being a court that callously and carelessly put to death men of the caliber of Sima Zhou, the state was doomed. Whatever the actual circumstances of his death may have been (he might, for all we know, have gone to the executioner kicking, screaming, and cursing Zhongshan's name), it was vital that the rulers of Zhongshan project the message that he had been executed reluctantly, and that the memory of his excellence and service was cherished and honored.

The abdication affair of 318–314 BCE bracketed the royal revolution that had begun at the Xuzhou summit in 334 BCE. Over the course of twenty years, new norms had been negotiated that would inform the conduct of court politics and interstate diplomacy for much of the following century and beyond. As the fourth century BCE came to a close, the people of the Zhou world settled into the new rhythms of a world with many kings.

Zhang Yi, like Shang Yang before him, had his career in Qin cut short at the moment of his greatest triumph, having just achieved so much at the helm of the second Horizontal Alliance. King Huiwen of Qin died in 311 BCE. Huiwen's successor, King Wu (r. 310–307 BCE), did not like or trust Zhang Yi, and the Qin royal princes who had served as Zhang Yi's subordinates had resented his high position. The princes slandered Zhang Yi to the new king, who needed little convincing to remove Zhang Yi from office.[115] Perhaps the echoes of the abdication affair played a role in King Wu's decision: it was not a good time to be a famous and powerful prime minister anywhere in the Zhou realm. Zhang Yi returned to Wei, where he died within the year.[116]

The initial tests of the strategic potential of the Horizontal and Vertical Alliances, respectively, thus ended inconclusively. After Zhang Yi's death in 310 BCE neither strategy had been definitively discredited or assuredly vindicated. For almost all of the following near-century until the crisis of the Warring States would finally be resolved, variations on both the Horizontal and Vertical models remained current, and were advocated by strategists who deliberated political affairs.

Long after Zhang Yi died and Gongsun Yan faded from prominence, debates over whether fiscal-military or political factors would be most important in bringing the Warring States to a close persisted. Sources such as the *Book of Lord Shang*, eponymously attributed to the fabled Shang Yang, contain implicit arguments that the crisis of the Warring States would primarily be resolved by economic and military means. But teachings as diverse in outlook as those in the *Mencius* and the *Daode jing* (which will be discussed in the next chapter) envisioned and argued for a political solution of the strategic deadlock faced by the Warring States.[117]

Many literati expected that a stable new order would only be arrived at through a voluntary association of states that formed through some permutation of the Vertical or Horizontal alliances, and that would finally put its authoritative imprimatur on a sustainably harmonious but still pluralistic world order.[118] In other words, as the fourth century BCE came to a close, few literati could have expected or felt it wise to openly advocate for one kingdom's conquest of all the others. The phoenix-like revival of Yan (and before it, Zhongshan) from the ashes of conquest made it clear that the annihilation of a state over the objections of its people and leaders was not easily accomplished. Most literati thus envisioned that the "next world" would be one in which peace reigned, but in which many states still divided the territory of the former Zhou domain (and its surrounding environs). How that peace would be achieved, and what would enable those future states to coexist harmoniously, were open questions.

Would there be a Son of Heaven in that future world order? Most of the sources imply there would be, though almost all are vague about how exactly that Son of Heaven would establish his rule. An informed political observer looking at the world in the wake of Zhang Yi's death, would not have been able to confidently predict which of the newly minted royal houses (if any) would produce next the universal dynasty.

Wei's decline had been so steep that its path to final supremacy had been foreclosed. Qin had become a great power, and would certainly have been picked as a serious contender to found the next dynasty in 310 BCE, but it did not yet stand alone as strategically dominant. Zhao and Chu remained powerful, and in conjunction with allies could exert broad influence.

Alongside Qin, one other state stood out as a power that could potentially impose its will on the other Warring States. That was Qi. Over the course of the fourth century BCE Qi had steadily grown in power and wealth, and had developed a unique political culture that increasingly set the pace for the rest of the Zhou world. By 310 BCE the power of Qi had not yet reached its peak.

11

Better to Give

The State of Qi and the Greater Zhou Realm, 320–294 BCE

In 320 BCE Tian Yinqi, posthumously named King Wei of Qi, died. His son Tian Pijiang was enthroned, and is known to history as King Xuan of Qi (r. 319–301 BCE).[1] King Xuan's coronation marked the second peaceful transfer of power in Qi since King Xuan's grandfather Duke Huan of Qi (Tian Wu) had violently seized the throne in 374 BCE. The accession of the new king in 320 BCE thus came at the end of five decades of persistent stability and growing prosperity for the state of Qi. While Wei to the west had been embroiled in constant wars and dangerous political gambits, the leaders of Qi had picked their battles, bided their time, and nurtured their kingdom's strength.

King Xuan thus inherited a throne that was secure and growing in power. The sense of expectancy that attended his reign is reflected in his very identity. His personal name, "Pijiang," literally means "expanding the frontiers." From earliest childhood he had been made the embodiment of his dynasty's ambition to lead Qi to grandeur.

As King Xuan's rule began there was every reason to expect that he would live up to the promise of his name. Though it is difficult to know precise population figures for the Warring States, Qi was certainly the first- or second-most populous kingdom among the Zhou states (matched or surpassed only by Wei).[2] Its farms grew abundant surplus; its workshops and markets produced wealth and luxuries on an unprecedented scale.

Qi's capital, Linzi, was a metropolis virtually without rival for size and sophistication in the Zhou world. Under King Xuan's reign its population grew to approximately 350,000 people. This not only made it the largest city of the Warring States, but among the largest cities on the planet Earth during all of premodern history.[3] Archeological excavations reveal that Linzi was an urban center of diverse complexity. Its many wards housed workshops where skilled artisans fashioned silk, lacquer, bronze, iron, silver, gold, jade, and other materials into sophisticated jewelry, textiles, clothing, furniture, tools, utensils, armor, and weapons. Throughout the city were dispersed specialized bazaars dealing in a vast array of goods. Commercial kitchens produced delicacies for sale to the urban elite.[4] Contemporary descriptions of Linzi make clear that it was a hub of cultural cosmopolitanism. Its denizens were renowned for their accomplishments playing the flute and zither, and their leisured enjoyment of cock-fighting, dog-racing, board games, and kickball.[5]

King Xuan's father, King Wei, had successfully sabotaged Wei Ying's attempt to found a new dynastic order by defeating Wei's armies at the battles of Cassia Hill and Horse Hill. He had then showed daring by joining Wei Ying in launching the royal revolution at the Xuzhou summit of 334 BCE. From that point on, Qi had followed a largely defensive policy as the changes set in motion by the royal revolution unfolded. The one occasion on which King Wei adopted an aggressive stance was when Gongsun Yan negotiated the meeting of five kings in 323 BCE. Qi had tried to intervene, unsuccessfully, to prevent the ruler of Zhongshan being recognized as a king.

King Wei had otherwise resisted all attempts to be drawn into the strategic games of wandering persuaders such as Zhang Yi and Gongsun Yan. He met with representatives of both Wei and Qin in the last decade of his reign, but he was coy with anyone who brought him overtures of alliance. He seems to have anticipated a future point when the powers to the west of Qi would have exhausted themselves in mutual competition, and Qi would be in a position to dictate the terms on which the crisis of the Warring States would be resolved.

King Wei's last act as ruler was to successfully defend against the attack by Qin's armies in 320 BCE, with which Zhang Yi had hoped to finally strong-arm Qi into joining in coalition with Qin and Wei. That defeat had caused the first Horizontal Alliance to disintegrate, yet again frustrating the attempts of outsiders to impose a place upon Qi in some new political order. As King Xuan succeeded to the throne at the end of the year, Qi rested, secure and powerful, facing an increasingly troubled and uncertain world.

King Xuan began his reign with confidence and audacity. The Confucian Master Mencius journeyed to Qi during the early days of King Xuan's rule, coming from his unsuccessful attempt to enlist King Hui of Wei to the teachings of a True King, and met with a warmer reception in Linzi. The dialogues with King Xuan recorded in the *Mencius* reveal that King Xuan harbored grand ambitions. On one occasion the king asked Mencius if, as many of the king's officials urged him to do, the "Bright Hall" should be torn down. The Bright Hall was a temple within the territory of Qi that had been used by the Zhou kings to worship the gods of Mount Tai, the most sacred mountain in the Zhou realm.[6] It was long unused, because the Zhou kings no longer had the means to maintain the sacrifices there. To tear it down would have asserted the end of the Zhou Mandate of Heaven, and the anticipation of a new dynasty that would rebuild it and use it once more.

Mencius was being baited. If he said "no," then he was contradicting the regal authority implicit in King Xuan's title. A king should be able to dispose of buildings on his own territory however he likes. But if Mencius said "yes," he was implicitly conceding that King Xuan had the authority to decide whether the Mandate of Heaven had already been lost, which Mencius would only (hypothetically) grant to a ruler of profound learning and proven devotion to the Way as taught by Confucius. In this instance Mencius characteristically refused to play by King Xuan's rules. He told the king that the smart thing to do would be to begin practicing the government of a True King, so that someday he could use the Bright Hall himself.[7]

We don't know what the fate of the Bright Hall ultimately was, but the exchange bears witness to the atmosphere of anticipation at King Xuan's court. As the stability and sophistication of Qi's political culture had grown during the years of Tian Wu and King Wei, so had the economic and military power of the kingdom as a whole. By 320 BCE Qi was in a position to challenge any of the most powerful states of the Zhou realm for geopolitical preeminence.

King Xuan did not have long to wait for an opportunity to bid for power. The abdication affair in neighboring Yan began two years after King Xuan was crowned. When war broke out between Yan's Crown Prince and the pretender Zizhi, King Xuan seized the chance to launch a full-scale invasion of Yan.

The speed with which Qi's armies overran Yan, seized its capital, and meted out punishment to Zizhi was a vindication of the state-building policies that had been pursued by Qi's leaders since the time of Tian Wu (Duke Huan). Qi had become a disciplined and effective power. It possessed a well-organized government, a united and loyal cadre of officials, a well-trained and ably led military, and the robust means to provide logistical support to its soldiers on campaign.

The relative lack of opposition Qi encountered to its invasion tempted King Xuan into a common political miscalculation made by victors throughout history. Because they had welcomed Qi's conquest, King Xuan wrongly concluded that the people (and elites) of Yan would welcome Qi's rule. Rather than finding a member of Yan's royal family to rule Yan by proxy, as King

Huiwen of Qin did in his conquest of Sichuan two years earlier, King Xuan decided to annex all of Yan's vast territory as centrally administered commanderies and districts of Qi.[8]

If it had worked, it may well have turned the tide of the larger crisis of the Warring States permanently in Qi's favor. Yan did not have agricultural and commercial wealth in the same abundance as Qi. It was more sparsely populated, and large parts of its territory were arid.[9] But it was nonetheless a large and powerful state by the terms of the Zhou world. Adding its human and material resources to the already considerable might of Qi would have created a megastate of unprecedented power.

Mencius, according to the text that bears his name, warned King Xuan against the annexation plan. His objections were moral and religious. Because the rulers of Yan were an ancient family with a venerable mandate to serve the gods and spirits, it would take some clear sign of Heaven's favor (the most important being the love and compliance of Yan's people) to terminate the Yan royal line and put its land and people under the aegis of Qi's Tian clan rulers.[10] We of course do not know when Mencius's warning was first written down, thus it may have been composed with the benefit of hindsight.

Beyond moral and religious concerns, there were real practical challenges that any observer could have anticipated in Qi's plan to annex Yan. Zhao, a state whose power was considerable and in the process of growing (as we will read about in the next chapter), shared a long and largely open border with Yan, and viewed Yan's annexation by Qi as an existential threat. Zhao worked tirelessly to dislodge Qi's forces from Yan, a contingency that was easy to foresee. By contrast the kingdom of Chu, the only one of the Zhou states that could interfere with Qin's conquest of Shu and Ba in Sichuan, faced long supply lines and obstructed terrain in trying to aid the local resistance to Qin's armies.

In the case of Yan, the resistance of Yan's people and elites to annexation was likewise predictable. Yan's elites resisted Qi for the same reason that they had aided Qi's invading armies to dislodge "King" Zizhi. In theory much of Yan had been put under the routine authority of centrally appointed magistrates, thus it should not have mattered whether the magistrate in any given locality was appointed out of the Qi capital of Linzi or the Yan capital of Ji. But in reality the whole structure of Yan's society, like that of all of the Warring States, was pervaded by a complex network of informal personal and kinship relationships, the central spokes of which had radiated from the Yan royal family prior to the abdication affair.[11]

Too many people of wealth and influence, at all levels of Yan's social hierarchy, had a stake in the restoration of the Yan royal family for King Xuan's annexation plan to be feasible. Some extraordinary effort would have had to be made to woo Yan's elites over to the new order, and clearly was not. Though reports of Qi soldiers and officials inflicting suffering on Yan may be exaggerated, it is probable that a bevy of Qi "carpetbaggers" descended on Yan and alienated its traditional elites.

When Zhao sent Prince Yan Zhi, one of the late King Kuai of Yan's sons, into Yan under escort, the prince found the state ripe for rebellion. With military and material support from Zhao, Prince Zhi was able to raise an army and expel all of Qi's forces from Yan. In 311 BCE he was formally crowned, and is known posthumously as King Zhao of Yan.[12] To the end of his life he harbored resentment against Qi for its attempt to annihilate his state.

King Xuan of Qi reportedly confessed his shame for having refused to heed Mencius's warning.[13] If the account of the *Mencius* can be believed, King Xuan felt respect and affection for Mencius, and awarded him rank and office among Qi's court grandees. The rapport between the two men was a sign of how well the leaders of Qi had succeeded in raising their state's prestige and rehabilitating their clan's reputation among the literati of the Zhou world. Mencius was a renowned leader in the fellowship to which Zai Wo had belonged almost two centuries prior, and King Xuan was a descendant of the man (Tian Chang) who had humiliated and killed Confucius's most successful disciple (and the duke that both Zai Wo and Tian Chang served). The fact that Mencius could envision a rapprochement between the Tian clan and the Confucian fellowship was tribute to the efforts by Tian rulers to engage literati on their own terms.

Mencius, however, expected that his learning and stewardship of the Way entitled him to the post of Qi's prime minister. King Xuan was not prepared to go that far to be reconciled with the latter-day disciples of Confucius. When it became clear that Mencius's ultimate ambitions would never be fulfilled, and that King Xuan would never be wholly converted to the Way of a True King, Mencius departed Qi reluctantly and in sorrow. King Xuan tried to convince Mencius to stay as one of the Masters who accepted patronage at Jixia, which would have afforded him the means to support himself and 100 disciples. Mencius, however, declined. The stipend at Jixia was a fraction of what the prime minister's salary would have been; thus, Mencius felt compelled to refuse, lest he give the world a false measure of the value of the Way.[14]

In his search for means to repair the political damage of the adventure in Yan and fulfill what he perceived to be his great destiny, King Xuan turned to a figure whose character and world view were vastly different than that of Mencius. This was the king's cousin Tian Wen (fl. ca. 300 BCE). Tian Wen is known most frequently in historical sources by his title, the Lord Mengchang.

Tian Wen was one of those remarkable figures whose insight and dynamism helped shape an age. He was born to privilege, but was clearly a person of talent and vision. His father, Tian Ying, had served as prime minister under King Xuan's father, King Wei. Tian Ying had negotiated on Qi's behalf in arranging the summit at Xuzhou, at which the rulers of Qi and Wei had recognized one-another as kings.[15] For this and other meritorious service, Tian Ying had been rewarded with the title "Lord Jingguo" and a sizeable fief, the formerly autonomous state of Xue in conquered lands along Qi's southwest frontier.[16]

Tian Wen is said to have had more than 40 brothers, and to have been the son of one of the lowest-ranking women in Tian Ying's harem. He was born on the fifth day of the fifth month, which his father deemed gravely inauspicious. Tian Ying ordered Tian Wen's mother to dispose of her baby. She disobeyed and raised Tian Wen in secret. When he had grown into an obviously bright child, Tian Wen's mother risked scheduling an audience at which she revealed her living son to Tian Ying.

Tian Ying was furious that he had been disobeyed. Tian Wen knelt and asked why his father had not wanted to see him raised. Tian Ying explained that, according to conventional wisdom, when a child born on the fifth day of the fifth month grows as tall as the head of the door frame, he will bring calamity on his parents. Tian Wen then asked whether fate was determined by Heaven or by door frames. If by Heaven, then Tian Ying had nothing to fear from his son. If by door frames, the answer was simple. Raise all of the door frames in the house and calamity could be averted.[17]

It was an early sign that Tian Wen would supplement his natural advantages of birth with a sharp wit and a forceful nature. Tian Ying was obviously impressed, because among his many sons he began to groom Tian Wen for power as a young man. Tian Ying, in a familiar pattern, had stepped down as Qi's prime minister after the death of King Wei and the accession of King Xuan. He had parted with King Xuan on good terms, however, and retained influence over court policy. Thus in 316 BCE when Gongsun Yan approached Tian Ying seeking a deal that would secure peace with Qi while the Vertical Alliance continued to assault Qin (as discussed in the previous chapter), Tian Ying chose Tian Wen to be the agent of Qi's interests in the deal. In return for Qi's promise to remain neutral while Gongsun Yan's Vertical Alliance made war on Qin, Tian Wen was appointed Prime Minister of Wei, while Gongsun

Yan withdrew to become Prime Minister of Han. The Vertical Alliance failed, and Tian Wen's tenure as Prime Minister of Wei proved short-lived, but it was far from the last time that Tian Wen would hold high office.

Tian Wen ultimately far surpassed his father in fame and influence, because he more subtly understood the implications of the royal revolution that his father had helped set in motion. As Tian Ying's impulse to dispose of Tian Wen because he was born on an inauspicious day indicated, Tian Ying was inclined to view affairs within a traditional framework. He cherished the fief that he had been awarded by the throne, for example, but measured its value as an asset in outmoded terms.

This was made clear when Tian Ying decided to build a defensive wall around the capital of his fief. Such fortification had been, for many centuries during the Western Zhou and Spring and Autumn periods, a clear sign (and material foundation) of power. It would have enhanced Tian Ying's raw military force, but at the same time, because it threatened the royal court and would arouse the fear and animosity of the king, would ironically have made Tian Ying's overall political position much more precarious. His advisors all pleaded with him to abort the plan, but Tian Ying stubbornly clung to his design. He finally became so furious that he declared the next person to speak on the matter would be put to death.

One of Tian Ying's advisors begged and was granted permission to speak three words. "Great ocean fish," he said. Tian Ying took the bait: he asked to know what those three words meant. The advisor demurred, complaining that he was not willing to gamble his life. Only after Tian Ying promised there would be no punishment did the advisor explain: Tian Ying was the great fish, Qi was his ocean. As long as there was Qi, what need would Tian Ying have for a wall? If the ocean dried up, Tian Ying could build walls as high as Heaven and they would do no good.[18]

Tian Ying again proved persuadable on that occasion. Perhaps because Tian Wen had witnessed such interactions at his father's court, he became convinced that the assets of their family were being wasted. True power did not come from walls or hoarded wealth, but from human talent. Tian Wen correctly perceived that the royal revolution had produced a new social dynamic that enabled well-placed leaders to gather and utilize large funds of human talent, if only they were skillful enough to exploit the situation.

The consolidation of immense power and control of the status hierarchy in the king had, ironically, created opportunities for men like Tian Ying and Tian Wen. As we saw in the last chapter, the social position of knights, who did most of the daily work of political, economic, and military management in the Warring States, had been made even more insecure by their relative baseness now that the apex of regional society was a king rather than a mere marquis. Knights thus sought the protection and patronage of securely elite individuals, those possessed of wealth and whose status credentials could not be challenged.

With his title of "Lord Jingguo" and the resources of Xue at his disposal, Tian Ying was perfectly positioned to offer the knights of Qi patronage and protection. Tian Wen urged his father to stop investing in defensive walls and stockpiling wealth, and to throw his doors open to the wandering literati and itinerant knights of the realm. If he offered knights protection and support without demanding an explicit *quid pro quo*, Tian Ying would find his prestige, influence, and power vastly more enhanced than could be garnered from a walled city or massive stores of grain and cloth.

Tian Ying began to act on his son's advice toward the end of his life, which is perhaps why he retained enough influence after stepping down as Prime Minister of Qi to engineer his son's appointment as Prime Minister of Wei. When Tian Wen succeeded his father as Marquis of Xue, he intensified the policy of offering patronage to knights. He expanded his retinue of clients to include thousands of men.

As was commonly the case during Zhou times, many of the knights who sought Tian Wen's patronage were outlaws, fleeing feuds or indiscretions that had driven them from their home communities or states. Tian Wen turned no one away.[19] He developed protocols for life in his expansive household that were eventually widely emulated by other great patrons elsewhere in the Warring States. Retainers were divided into three ranks: Senior, Regular, and Junior (*shang*, *zhong*, and *xia*). Privileges in the household were distributed by rank. Senior retainers ate meat, Regular retainers ate fish, and Junior retainers ate vegetables.[20] Retainers were given audience with their patron on a rotating schedule, the Senior retainers having the most frequent access to Tian Wen, the Junior retainers the least.[21]

Stories about Tian Wen's magnanimity as a patron abound. He frequently took meals in a large dining hall with his retainers. At one such gathering, one of the retainers, suspicious because someone had blocked off the torchlight and dimmed the dining area, leapt up and loudly accused Tian Wen of feasting on delicacies while his guests ate ordinary fare. Tian Wen brought his bowl over to show the man and demonstrated that he was eating the same food as everyone else. The knight was so ashamed that he drew his sword and slit his own throat in the presence of the assembled guests, to acknowledge his mistake and atone for insulting his patron.[22]

The story is most likely apocryphal, but it demonstrates the basic logic at the heart of Tian Wen's position of leadership. The knights of the era all sought employment and material support, but status recognition was in a sense even more valuable to them than food, clothing, and shelter. Being given a meal would feed a knight for a day. Being treated as a peer by a man of Tian Wen's rank, wealth, and power, however, was a guarantee of security that no amount of wealth could buy. Tian Wen intuitively understood this and exploited that dynamic to make himself one of the most influential power brokers of his day.

In his second decade on the throne, King Xuan enlisted Tian Wen to be his prime minister.[23] From the vantage of first his father's court, then the office of Prime Minister of Wei, and finally as head of his own large household of retainers drawn from across the Zhou world, Tian Wen had become a seasoned observer of interstate politics. He was convinced that the future supremacy of Qi rested in allying with the central states of Wei and Han, and required the subjugation or cooptation of Qin and Chu.

Securing a coalition with Wei and Han was not difficult. After the departure of Zhang Yi from Qin, the second Horizontal Alliance had disintegrated, and Qin resumed a policy of persistent aggression against Han and Wei. Tian Wen had established his credibility with the central states during his time as Prime Minister of Wei, and the leaders of Han and Wei were in any case desperate for allies to fend off Qin. But for Tian Wen's purposes the combined power of Han, Wei, and Qi was not sufficient to securely challenge both Qin and Chu simultaneously.

In 306 BCE Tian Wen thus wrote a letter to the King of Chu on behalf of King Xuan of Qi. In the letter he outlined the dangers posed by the rising power of Qin and proposed that Chu should join into alliance with Qi, Han, and Wei to meet the threat. Once Qin had been defeated, Chu could regain the Hanzhong Commandery that had been lost to Qin during Zhang Yi's final campaigns as prime minister, and from there could launch operations to take possession of Qin's conquests in Sichuan.[24]

The King of Chu had just annihilated Chu's old rival of Yue, finally reducing that once powerful kingdom to a commandery along the eastern reaches of the Yangzi River.[25] With that threat to the east eliminated, the King of Chu assented to Tian Wen's offer of an alliance against Qin.

Before this new coalition could mobilize, however, events unfolded in Qin that changed the incentives for Chu. King Huiwen of Qin had died in 311 BCE and been succeeded by his son, known posthumously as King Wu (r. 310–307 BCE). King Wu did not share his father's vision for the governance of Qin. He thought of himself as a warrior (hence his posthumous title, "The Martial King"), and did not have patience for the diplomatic stratagems of a literatus like Zhang Yi. He also was seemingly nostalgic for a time when the court and government of Qin had been more exclusively an affair of the Qin royal clan. He dismissed Zhang Yi and other personnel not native to Qin and appointed two of his uncles, each famous as a military commander, as co-Chancellors.[26]

As part of his martial ethos, King Wu of Qin was fond of wrestling and feats of strength. He also harbored an intense fascination with the Zhou royal court, having told his uncle on one occasion that if he could travel incognito in a woman's carriage to the Zhou court and steal even a peek at its solemnity, he would die happy.[27] In 307 BCE he was able to pressure the Zhou Son of Heaven into granting him a special audience at which he would be able to see the Nine Tripods, the ancient ritual bronzes that were sacred regalia of the Son of Heaven. Each tripod was large and enormously heavy.

On striding into the hall in which the Nine Tripods were held, King Wu of Qin challenged one of his officials, who had been chosen because he was likewise renowned as a man of great strength. The contest was to see which man could lift one of the tripods. The king chose to lift the "Scarlet Tripod with Dragon Writing." This was of course a very profane and theatrical act, but one with enormous potential value as propaganda. If he had succeeded, King Wu would not only have demonstrated enormous strength but, like Arthur drawing the sword from the stone, would have broadcast to the world an unmistakable omen that he was destined to be the next Son of Heaven.

What reportedly happened was exactly the opposite of what King Wu of Qin had intended. King Wu exerted so much effort to lift the tripod that blood began to run from both of his eyes. Finally, the bones of his shins snapped under the pressure and strain, and he fell to the floor, dead.[28]

King Wu's sudden death, in combination with his reconsolidation of power back in the hands of the royal clan, destabilized the Qin court. A succession struggle erupted, with different factions backing different claimants to the throne. King Wu left behind no sons, so the contest was between groups aligned with different contenders for the throne among his brothers. The chaos in the Qin capital persisted for two years.

As was often the case in Zhou times, the leading factions of the succession struggle were led by powerful women in the royal palace. King Wu's mother and his own queen were aligned in support of one of his mature younger brothers. One of the late King Huiwen's concubines, a woman known as Mi Bazi (d. 265 BCE, "*bazi*" is a title, denoting her status as eighth in rank of the royal harem),[29] led an opposing faction in support of her own son (King Wu's half-brother), a 17-year-old youth who was at the time of King Wu's death living as a hostage in Yan. Events (some of which will be recounted in the next chapter) would prove her to be an extraordinarily formidable figure.

Before her husband had died, Mi Bazi had used her influence with King Huiwen to have her own brothers given positions in the Qin government and military. Her half-brother, Wei Ran, was a commander in the defensive garrisons around the Qin capital.[30] This gave her faction a powerful advantage. The Queen Dowager and queen held a ceremony to crown their favored prince, but his authority did not bear up under pressure. Wei Ran's forces put down the "rebellion" by this "Third Lord" (so-called because he was the third-born of King Huiwen's sons). The prince and Queen Dowager were both killed, as were any of King Wu's brothers who had offered resistance to Mi Bazi and her brothers. King Wu's queen was sent back to her home state of Wei.[31] Mi Bazi's son was brought home from Yan and crowned. He was known posthumously as King Zhao (or alternately Zhaoxiang, r. 306–251 BCE) of Qin, and he would ultimately be the longest-reigning ruler of the Warring States.[32]

Mi Bazi was given the title Queen Dowager Xuan. She and her brothers were children of the extended royal clan of Chu, and were thus inclined, having taken effective control of the Qin court, to seek advantage from allying with Chu. They sent an envoy to the King of Chu making overtures of cooperation.

Tian Wen's efforts to use Chu as a cudgel with which to beat Qin were thus thwarted. The King of Chu decided that he would treat with Mi Bazi and her brothers, and withdrew from the coalition with Qi, deciding instead to ally with Qin.[33] Tian Wen was undeterred in his plans to secure Qi's supremacy. If he could not use Peter to club Paul, he would first beat Peter into submission and then deal with Paul at leisure. He mobilized the allied forces of Qi, Wei, and Han in an invasion of Chu in 303 BCE, beginning a series of campaigns that would have Qi on a war footing for the next several years.[34]

The King of Chu appealed to Qin for help. Mi Bazi and her brothers were not sentimental about their connection to Chu; they asked for and received the Crown Prince of Chu as a hostage to secure their assistance against the coalition formed by Tian Wen. The Qin court then sent an army to aid Chu in repulsing the invaders, forcing Tian Wen and his allies to withdraw.[35]

At the same time that Tian Wen was pressing his military campaign against Chu, he switched tack with respect to Qin and made diplomatic overtures to the new leaders of that state. At the suggestion of one of his many guest clients, he sent the man as an envoy to the Qin court, to sound out the new Qin king and report back on what he was like. When the young King of Qin heard that an embassy had arrived from Tian Wen, he was determined to humiliate the envoy. He began his audience with Tian Wen's client by insolently declaring that since Qin was 10 times larger than his fief of Xue, it was foolish of Tian Wen to imagine that he was worth the King of Qin's notice.

The emissary, unfazed, declared that Tian Wen's power did not come from land, but from the extent to which he valued knights. This intrigued the king, who asked for an explanation. The envoy explained that Tian Wen's extraordinary courtesy to knights had attracted a retinue so large that it contained three men too proud to serve as a minister to the Son of Heaven or befriend any of the regional lords, five men learned enough to teach Guan Zhong or Shang Yang, and seven men, including himself, who upon hearing their lord insulted by a king, would slit their own throats and splash blood over the finery of the royal in question.

King Zhao understood the implicit threat and was impressed. He laughed, urged the envoy not to take offense, and asked him to convey his admiration to Tian Wen.[36] The story may be embellished, but Tian Wen's embassies to Qin clearly made an impression on that state's leaders. His diplomacy began to pay dividends almost immediately, and may have led ultimately to one of the most unique episodes of Tian Wen's exceptional career, some years later.

A combination of diplomacy and chance changed the strategic position of Tian Wen's coalition. In 302 BCE the Crown Prince of Chu, who had taken up residence in the Qin capital to secure the pact between those two states, got into a quarrel with one of the grandees of the Qin court. He killed the man and fled home to avoid punishment. The alliance between Qin and Chu was thus broken.

Conversely, Tian Wen's "charm offensive" managed to produce a period of entente between Qin and its eastern neighbors. In the same year that the Chu prince fled Qin, the young King Zhao of Qin met with the rulers of Han and Wei. As a result of those meetings, Qin returned some of the territory that it had taken during recent campaigns of aggression.[37]

In 301 BCE Tian Wen pressed the attack against Chu again. Qi, Wei, and Han each sent one of its most able commanders at the head of an invasion force. Thanks to Tian Wen's diplomacy, and the cooling of relations between Qin and Chu (because of the Chu Crown Prince's vendetta), Qin remained neutral during this campaign. The coalition forces attacked the region within Chu's "Square Great Wall," a system of fortifications, shaped as a south-pointing horseshoe with square corners, that protected vital terrain against approach from the north. The territory was adjacent to the Hanzhong Commandery, which had been largely conquered from Chu by Qin during the tenure of Zhang Yi, and that Tian Wen had offered the King of Chu help in recovering. Thus this campaign was a very pointed rebuke to Chu for having pulled out of Tian Wen's original plan of alliance.

The coalition army met the forces of Chu at the Bi River. The two armies were on opposite banks of the river, and the coalition did not know which points were shallow enough to ford. All attempts to sound the river failed because Chu's archers would rain lethal fire on any coalition soldiers that approached the river's bank.

The armies remained deadlocked for six months. King Xuan sent an envoy to the Qi commander, the same general who had conquered Yan in 50 days, demanding that he order an assault. The general replied that the king could dismiss him, kill him, or order the extermination of his family, but the king could not force him to give battle when that was not possible.

The deadlock was broken by a local woodcutter who witnessed one of the coalition force's attempts to reconnoiter the riverbank. He approached the soldiers as they retreated again from Chu's arrows and told them that it would be easy to know where to ford the river. When the soldiers brought him before the Qi commander, the woodcutter explained that the Chu army had made the mistake of concentrating their forces at the shallow points of the river to defend against attack. The coalition scouts only had to mark the places where there were the most Chu soldiers on the opposite bank of the river; those were the convenient fords.

The Qi commander picked out a force of his most elite soldiers and sent them in a night assault across the river at a place called Hanging Sands (Chuisha). They smashed through the Chu lines and led the rest of the coalition army in totally routing the Chu defenders. The Chu commander, who was famed as a scholar of the astronomical arts, was killed in the assault.[38]

As a result of that campaign Chu lost most of its territory within the precincts of the Square Great Wall. All of this territory was annexed to Han and Wei. Qi took nothing from its allies by way of compensation for its expenditure of blood and treasure. In this way Tian Wen showed that under his stewardship Qi would follow the same policy of magnanimity that he personally had pursued as a patron of his guest knights. Friendship and loyalty would be requited with material generosity, without expectation of future obligation.

It was a subtle but distinct departure from the approach of former strategists like Zhang Yi and the wisdom that had been enshrined in the teachings of Master Sun (as transmitted in the *Sunzi bingfa*). That earlier perspective had held that a state should make no move with its military that did not increase its own power, in which regard success could be measured in the acquisition of land, people, and wealth. Tian Wen basically agreed that all military policy should be geared toward increasing the power of Qi, but his experience as a patron had confirmed him in the belief that a state's power could sometimes be enhanced more by what it *gave away* than what it acquired. He had set out to show the rest of the Zhou world that Qi would be a stern and unforgiving opponent, but a liberal and generous patron of those who accepted Qi's leadership.

The novelty and audacity of this new strategy had immediate and broad impact. The King of Chu sent his Heir Apparent as hostage to Qi to secure a cease of hostilities.[39] Even Qin was impressed. In the wake of the coalition's victory at Hanging Sands the Qin court sent one of King Zhao's younger brothers, another of Mi Bazi's sons, as a hostage to reside in Linzi, by way of courting good relations with Qi.[40]

The Hanging Sands campaign made Tian Wen the man of the hour. He achieved a kind of celebrity status throughout the Warring States rivaled only by legendary figures such as Confucius or Marquis Wen of Wei. Some of this fame flowed from his unique approach to interstate diplomacy. The sheer bravado of yielding up the fruits of Hanging Sands to Han and Wei, no strings attached (ostensibly), made an impression on jaded political elites. But some of Tian Wen's fame was the product of his unique persona. He was a man of pedigree, wealth, and power who displayed erudition, eloquence, generosity, and political genius. Like the young Alcibiades in the fifth-century Mediterranean world, Tian Wen embodied the full gamut of ideal qualities toward which elites aspired.

This mystique that developed around Tian Wen contributed to a strange turn in the politics of the Zhou world that unfolded in the aftermath of Hanging Sands. The internal stability of Chu was undermined by a continuing series of military setbacks. A scion of a noble family of Chu, Zhuang Qiao (fl. ca. 300 BCE), went bandit, raising a rebellion that threatened the Chu capital and effectively divided the kingdom into four separate "zones" of control.[41] At the same time, the armies of Qin mobilized to take advantage of

Chu's weakness and to avenge the insult inflicted upon Qin by Chu's Heir Apparent. An invasion force captured New Fortress (Xincheng), east of the Square Great Wall, inflicting heavy casualties and killing another of Chu's top commanders.[42]

King Zhao of Qin wrote a letter to King Huai of Chu, inviting him to a summit at the Wu Pass that had traditionally been a point of travel and commerce between Qin and Chu. King Huai, under pressure on many fronts, agreed to the meeting. In 299 BCE he traveled through the gate at the Wu Pass into Qin territory, where he was met by a Qin general masquerading as the King of Qin. Before King Huai realized that anything was amiss, the gate had been closed and barred behind his entourage. He was escorted to the capital of Qin, where he was compelled to meet with King Zhao of Qin using the ceremonies of a vassal meeting his lord. At the negotiations the King of Chu was given an ultimatum: he must cede the two commanderies of Chu bordering on the Shu (Sichuan) region to Qin. This would have brought the boundaries of Qin control hundreds of kilometers closer to the Chu capital at Ying.

It was a strange moment. Since the Xuzhou summit 35 years prior (the beginning of the royal revolution), such king-to-king meetings had become standard fixtures of interstate diplomacy. It is difficult to see why the Qin court felt this plan would advance their strategic interests in the long term. Even if they felt that there was a chance that coercion would work on King Huai of Chu, the damage that Qin's leaders did to their own credibility in the face of future negotiations with other monarchs was a very steep price to pay. This was one of several moments that suggest that the court culture of Qin had been disrupted by King Wu's reversal of his father's policies and erratic behavior, and that the young King Zhao and the faction who brought him to the throne (his mother and uncles, Mi Bazi and her brothers) were, at least in his early years on the throne, facing a steep learning curve in the use of diplomacy for strategic ends.

King Huai, predictably, did not capitulate to the demands of his captors. He was held in the Qin capital and would never return to Chu again. In 297 BCE he escaped confinement and fled as far as the frontier with Zhao, hoping to obtain aid in returning home. The ruler of Zhao, however, feared angering Qin, and would not give him permission to enter the kingdom. His pursuers from Qin caught up to him and escorted him back to the Qin capital, where he became ill and died soon thereafter.[43] Long before King Huai perished, however, his confinement proved of no benefit for his Qin captors. Officials at the court of Chu refused to capitulate to extortion and determined immediately that a new ruler would have to be enthroned.

Even with a consensus on the need to replace the king, however, the leaders of Chu were faced with difficult choices. The Heir Apparent was still hostage in Qi. Many of the court ministers advocated that a younger son of King Huai's who was still resident in the Chu capital should be enthroned, so that Qi could not use the situation as leverage to extract concessions from Chu. The Prime Minister of Chu refused to heed such advice. Bad enough, he declared, that we are abandoning our king to captivity in Qin. If we refuse to even respect his orders as to the succession, we will lose all credibility as officials of the throne. To forestall any resistance to his plan, he falsely announced the death of King Huai to the people of Chu, creating an urgency to settle the succession that precluded deliberating about someone to replace the Heir Apparent.

When the news came to Qi about the succession crisis in Chu, many of the officials at the Qi court responded as their counterparts in Chu feared would be the case. Advisors advocated that Chu be forced to cede the territory directly south of Qi's boundary with Chu as the price for the Heir Apparent's release. Tian Wen opposed any plan to use the Heir Apparent to leverage predatory concessions from Chu. Such a move would undo all of the work that the Hanging Sands campaign had done to establish Qi's reputation as a "magnanimous power." He pointed out that if Qi made harsh demands of Chu, the Chu court would simply respond as they did to Qin's initial seizure of King Huai. Chu would enthrone a different prince, and all Qi would have earned for its pains was a reputation for being cruel and unscrupulous (as Qin already had).

Tian Wen's critics brushed this objection aside. If Chu enthroned a different prince, they argued, Qi could then send an envoy offering to kill the Heir Apparent in return for the ceded territory. The new king would see the value in that trade, and if he did not, Qi could simply march south with its allies and the Heir Apparent in tow, join forces with whoever in Chu was still loyal to the Heir, and install the Heir as the new King of Chu. Then Qi would be in a position to demand territory in repayment of its service (and, presumably, as the price for withdrawing its armies once the new king was enthroned).

Tian Wen held firm to his convictions against the cynical plans of his critics. It was a test of his influence, and it came at a crucial moment. In 301 BCE King Xuan had died and been succeeded by his son Tian Di known posthumously as King Min of Qi (r. 300–284 BCE). Prime ministers, we have seen, often lost their office on the accession of a new king. The relationship between a crown prince and his father's prime minister was often combative, and even if it was not, on assuming the throne a new king might naturally want to work with someone who had not already become accustomed to the habits and authority of another ruler. The fact that Tian Wen had become such a celebrated figure throughout the Zhou world made the situation more fraught. A king does not generally like to share the spotlight with anyone else, much less his prime minister.

By 299 BCE Tian Wen had retained his post as prime minister for almost two years since King Xuan's death. The succession crisis in Chu was thus a test of whether Tian Wen fully held the new king's confidence. The sources are ambivalent about the outcome of this struggle at the Qi court. Some report that the king followed Tian Wen's advice and released the Heir Apparent without preconditions, while others indicate that the king wrested concessions from the heir (ultimately unfulfilled) before allowing him to depart. In any case the heir did return to Chu, where he was crowned king. He is known posthumously as King Qingxiang of Chu (r. 298–263 BCE).[44]

The strange phase in the politics of the Zhou world, however, continued in the immediate aftermath of the succession crisis induced by Qin's seizure of King Huai of Chu. In the kingdom of Zhao, King Wuling (r. 325–299 BCE) abdicated in favor of his son, but retained a title and remained active in government. He was officially known thereafter as "Father of the Ruler" (*zhufu*) and retained command of military operations on Zhao's frontier.[45] The former king's aim seems to have been twofold: to secure the succession against disruptions (including the kind that Qin had just foisted on Chu), and to free himself to focus on wars of conquest. It was not a policy entirely without precedent or logic, but it was unusual, and as events would prove (as will be discussed in the next chapter), it was very risky.

Even more extraordinary, in that same year Tian Wen himself traveled to the Qin court. The circumstances that initiated this journey are hazy. The young King of Qin had reportedly sent word of his admiration of Tian Wen through the mission that brought one of his younger brothers to Qi as a hostage. Tian Wen is said to have been interested in answering these overtures by traveling to meet the king in person.[46]

Why would he have wanted to do so? He may have seen an opportunity to finally "close the deal" on a grand "Horizontal Alliance" between Qin and Qi, creating a real opportunity to end the crisis of the age. He may have been curious and encouraged by what he perceived to be the malleability of the Qin king and his court. Finally, like many successful and ambitious people throughout history, Tian Wen may have begun to believe his own hype and thus been confident that a journey to Qin could only be to his advantage.

Whatever the case, Tian Wen's journey was a radical and surprising move. However much relations had improved between Qin and Qi, they were still intense rivals. His clients all pleaded against doing so, for understandable reasons. King Huai of Chu had learned the hard way how dangerous an invitation from Qin could be. The wandering persuader Su Qin was reportedly one of Tian Wen's guests at the time, and on coming to dine with Tian Wen said that on the way to dinner he had overheard a pair of mortuary figures, one made of mud and the other of wood, arguing. The wooden figure mocked the clay, saying that when it rained he would melt. The clay figure shrugged off this insult, noting that he himself was made of earth and would be happy to return to it in the case of rain. The wooden figure, however (so rejoined the clay), would be washed who-knew-where by the rain and would never get back. Su Qin concluded by wondering whether by going to Qin, Tian Wen was risking the clay figurine's mockery.[47]

Accounts suggest that Tian Wen was inclined to heed Su Qin's advice, but was finally pushed to make the journey by an order from King Min, dispatching him as a royal envoy to the Qin court. This was a sign that the succession crisis in Chu (and the debates at the Qi court over how to respond) had obviously strained relations between King Min and his prime minister. Sending him to Qin afforded a way for the king to "demote without demoting" Tian Wen. In practical reality Tian Wen was being removed from the center of power for an extended period (perhaps indefinitely), but in theory King Min could claim that he was only sending Tian Wen away temporarily, acting to take advantage of the good will that his prime minister had cultivated at the Qin court. If Tian Wen, following the advice of his retainers, had resisted, he could have avoided leaving for Qin, if only by resigning his post and withdrawing to private life. But in the end he accepted the commission.

Whatever ambitions or pressures moved him to do so, Tian Wen traveled to Qin in 299 BCE with a retinue of his client knights. What happened next is perhaps the most surprising dimension of the whole affair. Within a short time after arriving in Qin, Tian Wen had so impressed its king that he was appointed Qin's prime minister. As Qin's prime minister, Tian Wen continued his aggression against Chu, sending an army out through the Wu Pass and capturing 15 cities to the southwest of the Square Great Wall. The new King of Chu was so alarmed by this aggression that he offered his Crown Prince as a hostage to Qin to secure peace.[48]

Despite this promising start, Tian Wen's career as Prime Minister of Qin was short-lived. The rulers of neighboring Zhao were alarmed by the developing partnership between Qin and Qi. A knight dispatched by the Prime Minister of Zhao made a persuasion to the King of Qin, pleading that Tian Wen could not be trusted. Being a member of the Qi royal clan, Tian Wen's first loyalty, claimed the envoy, was to Qi. He would always put Qi's interests first and Qin's last. As an alternative, Zhao offered to broker a new coalition. If Qin would accept a prime minister of Zhao's choosing, Zhao could enlist Song into alliance. This new partnership, the Zhao envoy promised, would be even more powerful and would be pledged to benefit Qin.[49]

King Zhao of Qin was won over by the Zhao envoy. He not only dismissed Tian Wen, but had him arrested and thrown in prison, intending to execute him. Su Qin's warning was coming true. The clay figurine was laughing.

At this juncture Tian Wen displayed his tactical ingenuity and skill at court politics. He sent one of his clients as an envoy to King Zhao's favorite concubine, asking her to intervene on his behalf to have him released. She agreed to do so, but in return she asked to be given a priceless white fox-fur coat that Tian Wen had worn on first being presented at court.

This posed a problem, because Tian Wen had already presented the coat as a gift to the king, and it was housed in the palace treasury. One of Tian Wen's lowest-ranking clients, a diminutive knight known as the "dog thief" because of his stealth and his ability to masquerade as a dog, volunteered to procure the coat. At night, true to his reputation, the dog-thief dressed as a canine and broke into the royal vault. On being given the coat, the concubine spoke to the king on Tian Wen's behalf and secured his release.

Immediately upon his release, Tian Wen hastened to leave Qin, traveling under an assumed identity. As he fled, the king once again changed his mind and sent carriages to retrieve Tian Wen and return him to prison. Tian Wen and his retinue arrived at the gate of the Hangu Pass while it was still dark and were told that the law did not allow for the gate to be opened until the cock crowed. Fearing that pursuers were hot on their trail, Tian Wen turned again to his knights for a solution. One of the lowest ranking retainers had a special knack for imitating the crow of a cock. He performed this trick, and the gate wardens, believing that they were indeed obligated to open the gate, let Tian Wen and his knights pass. When the Qin soldiers arrived at the gate and realized that Tian Wen had a whole morning's head start on them, they turned back to the capital.[50]

The basic facts of Tian Wen's brief tenure as Qin's prime minister (that he was appointed at all, and that he was dismissed in favor of someone chosen by Zhao after less than a year at his post) are so odd as to make the entire event's veracity suspect, as if the whole episode had been woven out of whole cloth to glorify Tian Wen himself and denigrate Qin. But testimony of the events appears at too many different points in too many different sources to make such an outright fabrication likely.

Why did this happen? The normal patterns of the Qin court had been disrupted by King Wu's erratic behavior and the inexperience of Qin's new rulers. But we cannot understand the event without considering the factors that had produced a figure like Tian Wen himself. Tian Wen was among the first to discover (though far from the last, as we will see in subsequent chapters) that the evolving political economy and social dynamic of the Warring States created the perfect conditions for a person of sufficient status and wealth to use patronage to become an autonomous force.

This can be seen in the aspects of the tale of Tian Wen's sojourn in Qin that show obvious embellishment. The stories of the "dog thief" and the "cock-crow knight" are not meant to be believable, they are meant to register a point: a knight is born special, but the world may not be able to see that in the case of any individual knight until a man of vision like Tian Wen comes along who sees his true worth. These stories (and others) about Tian Wen must have been produced and disseminated by the knights in Tian Wen's retinue themselves, at the behest of and under the direction of Tian Wen himself. Tian Wen had, in effect, forged his retinue into a corporate body with its own organizational structure, mission, culture, and public relations operation. In this respect, his retinue took on some of the social dimensions and political functionality of a fellowship like that of the Confucians or the Mohists: "join us, and we will take you places you could not get on your own."

The sophistication of the operation Tian Wen built around himself helps explain, at least in part, the otherwise odd nature of his tenure as Prime Minister of Qin. The success that Tian Wen and his retinue had enjoyed in establishing his broad reputation as a uniquely perceptive judge and reverent appreciator of knightly talent made him strongly appealing to the rulers of Qin (and elsewhere), because royal courts were always on the lookout for anything that could give them an edge in personnel recruitment. But when he took up post in Qin, the fact that Tian Wen effectively came as a "package deal" with a moveable organization of client knights ("Tian Wen Inc.") may have soured him on his erstwhile Qin admirers very quickly. When Zhao approached Qin offering to swap out Tian Wen for a prime minister of their choosing, the plan may have been appealing simply because a single official, even one who was tied to the interests of a foreign royal court, was still less of a loose cannon than Tian Wen, who traveled with his own personal political machine.

Tian Wen was produced by (or perhaps, produced himself by exploiting) the clash between the bureaucratic principles underpinning the newly evolved government forms of the Warring States and the stubbornly elitist and aristocratic logic of Zhou society. He was a force that the royal courts of the time literally could not live with, but likewise could not live without. The organic nature of his rise is attested to by the frequency with which it was repeated over the course of the last century of the Warring States. He was the first of the "great patrons" of the Warring States, but he was far from the last. His working model would be emulated and elaborated upon by many who followed in his footsteps (and whom we will encounter in subsequent chapters), even in the state of Qin where Tian Wen himself met with such frustration.

In 298 BCE Tian Wen was welcomed back to Qi and reinstated as prime minister. He displayed no sense of humor about his misadventure in Qin. From the moment Tian Wen arrived home, Qi and its allies were at war with the West, and would remain so for several years. A joint army made up of soldiers from Qi, Wei, and Han marched into the Hangu Pass and dug itself in to a fortified encampment, blocking all traffic in or out of Qin.[51]

Battle lines between Qin and the new Vertical coalition remained static for more than a year. One story claims that Tian Wen was convinced not to press the attack against Qin because to add yet more territory to Han and Wei would shift the balance of power too much in those states' favor.[52] That is not likely the explanation for Tian Wen's caution, however. Tian Wen had the precedents of Qin's assault on Qi in 320 BCE and Qi's conquest of Yan in 314 BCE to guide him. The Qin assault of 320 BCE demonstrated that operating over supply lines as extended as the ones that would face Tian Wen if he crossed through the Hangu Pass into the Wei River valley was a dangerous proposition. The Qi conquest of Yan in 314 BCE demonstrated that even if all went well and Tian Wen conquered all or part of Qin, holding on to it was going to be difficult, if not impossible. If Qi could not occupy the bordering kingdom of Yan, could it expect to successfully occupy Qin, hundreds of kilometers to the west? Moreover, Tian Wen had to be cautious of Zhao and Song, which had joined into tentative alliance with Qin. If Tian Wen's army entered the Hangu Pass, Zhao and Song might assault them from the rear.

Forgoing these military risks, Tian Wen elected for economic warfare. He set up a blockade at the Hangu Pass and effectively cut Qin off from all commerce with the heartland of the Zhou world. He would force Qin to accept Qi's leadership as the price for rejoining the community of states.

The standoff persisted, with intermittent fighting, for more than a year. In 296 BCE the coalition forces broke camp and marched toward the Qin capital of Xianyang from the Hangu Pass, overcoming all resistance. Seeing Qi, Han, and Wei successfully on the attack, Zhao and Song broke their alliance with Qin and opportunistically marched on Qin's conquered territories east of the Yellow River. Alarmed, the Qin court sued for peace, and agreed to return three cities on the East Bank of the Yellow River to Han and Wei to secure the withdrawal of the coalition army from the home territory of Qin.[53]

Later in the same year war broke out again between Qi and Yan. The immediate cause of the conflict is not recorded, but its outcome was a resounding victory for Qi. Ten thousand of Yan's soldiers were killed and two of its generals captured. Qi was only prevented from wresting large territorial concessions from Yan by the intercession of Zhao.[54]

Qi was at the peak of its power. Though Tian Wen's approach to conflict had not been as aggressive as that of recent strategists such as Zhang Yi and Gongsun Yan, it had been effective. Qin had been on the offensive for decades before the coalition led by Qi had entered the Hangu Pass. Tian Wen had enjoyed the most success in rolling back Qin's power of anyone since the days of Marquis Wen of Wei and his general, Wu Qi, more than a century prior.

The rising wave of Qi's military influence coincided with a surge in the kingdom's soft power and cultural leadership. The reign of King Min of Qi corresponded to the golden age of the Jixia patronage community. The leading Masters of the age all gathered at Jixia, which developed a reputation as a hotbed of radical thinking.

One story gives a sense of the climate at Jixia. A wandering persuader came to Jixia from Song and issued a general challenge to any and all of its residents to debate the proposition that "a white horse is not a horse" with him. This was a paradox (similar to those proposed by Hui Shi) made famous by Master Gongsun Long (ca. 320–ca. 250 BCE), a native of Zhao, who proposed that any qualifier applied to an object changes its identity, thus one cannot speak of "white horses" and "horses" as being the same things.[55] Many of Jixia's literati accepted the challenge, but none could defeat the persuader from Song. Replete with bragging rights, the scholar from Song road home on horseback. On arriving at the pass gate between Qi and Song, the man found that an extra toll was being levied on those traveling by horse, and though the horse he was riding was white, he could not convince the gate wardens that, because "a white horse is not a horse," he should not have to pay the toll.[56]

The prevalence of propositions like "a white horse is not a horse" embodies the level of self-referential complexity that literati culture had reached as the fourth century BCE gave way to the third. It had become increasingly common for Masters advocating mutually incommensurate versions of "the Way" to meet one another in open debate at forums like Jixia. Even within the confines of a single fellowship, points of doctrine and ethical questions were ever more frequently the focus of intramural deliberation. This lent ever-escalating urgency to "meta-questions" about the principles that underpin logical debate and rhetorical persuasion. Progressively more interest was paid to problems of how the rules of debate should be configured and what the successful strategies of logical contention might be. The transmitted *Mozi*, for example, contains several late chapters dating from this period that outline a complex system of logic, complete with definitions of key terms and modular examples of "permissible" and "impermissible" forms of argumentation.[57]

Looked at from the outside, this culture of Masters-and-disciples was increasingly lampooned by court officials as unrealistically "ivory tower," as the above story of Jixia's defeat in the "white horse" debates shows. But such satire notwithstanding, the community of the Masters was flourishing, and with it the prestige and reputation of Jixia. The evolving culture at Jixia demonstrates this trend. Though the questions being pursued and argued among the Masters at Jixia grew further and further removed from the practical concerns of the Tian kings, the patronage lavished upon Jixia continued to increase over time.

The wisdom and success of this policy can be seen in the career of one of Jixia's most famous residents of the time: Xun Kuang (ca. 340–ca. 245 BCE), or Master Xun (Xunzi). Xun Kuang was a native of Zhao, but had dedicated his life to following the Way of Confucius. Xunzi spent two periods of his life at Jixia. His early stay at Jixia transpired during the reign of King Min, when he was young man in the early phase of his studies. He returned to Jixia later as a mature Master, when he was well on his way to becoming the most famous Confucian teacher of his time, occupying the informal position of leadership in the Confucian fellowship once held by Mencius during the reign of King Xuan of Qi.[58]

Mencius had served in the court of Qi and had cultivated good relations with its king, but he had not been sufficiently reconciled to the new political culture of the Qi court and the legitimacy of its Tian rulers to accept a residency among the Jixia Masters. Xun Kuang, by contrast, had no compunction about lending his cachet to Jixia, and in his later years in Linzi he accepted the distinction of being Jixia's "Libationer," the Master who had the honor of leading the whole Jixia community in the annual sacrifices of thanksgiving held at Qi's Altar of the Grain. Xun Kuang demonstrated that the Tian rulers had finally "made it": they had legitimized themselves to the point that they could partner with the Confucian fellowship (and other groups of Masters) in the same manner that Marquis Wen of Wei had done more than a century earlier.

Xun Kuang's reconciliation with the new world embodied by the Tian kings was more than merely instrumental. At the level of doctrine, Xun Kuang reinterpreted Confucius's teachings to align them with the new political, social, and cultural realities of the late Warring States. Xun Kuang is sometimes called "the Aristotle (384–324 BCE) of China," and the analogy is apt in the sense that both Xun Kuang and Aristotle lived in and worked to engage with increasingly pluralistic intellectual cultures.

The emerging Hellenistic world of Aristotle was raucously multivocal, with many different philosophers advocating radically different visions of *logos* and *praxis*, and he set out to prove that a single Truth could be discovered among those contending doctrines. Similarly, the late Warring States world that Xun Kuang encountered had produced a proliferation of mutually contradictory teachings of "the Way." Xun Kuang studied and engaged with the whole panoply of thought current during his life. He not only set out to show that the Way as taught by Confucius was superior, but to demonstrate that Confucius's true Way in fact contained and integrated all of the doctrines of the other contending Masters, if one could only understand where those other teachers had erred through misperception or partial understanding.[59]

An example of this syncretism can be seen in a chapter of the transmitted text that bears Xun Kuang's name, the *Xunzi*. In "The Institutions of a King," the text describes what the government of a True King looks like. Of course, a True King is distinguished from other types of rulers by the fact that he is deeply learned in the Way and has developed profound personal moral Potency (*de*). He rules through the example of his own ethical character and through ritual, and serves no purposes higher than the realization of values such as humaneness and rightness. But the chapter concedes that there are two other types of rulers who could be provisionally successful and legitimate in the context of the Warring States.

A Lord Protector (according to the *Xunzi*) does not have the learning or Potency of a True King, but uses a combination of diplomacy, military power (to defend other states that are under threat), and economic suasion (the provision of grain or other essential wealth to states experiencing hardship) to assert his authority and maintain order. As long as there is no True King and a Lord Protector does nothing to violate the values of the Way (such as humaneness and rightness), he will be able to lead a harmonious world.

Below a Lord Protector, the *Xunzi* acknowledges that there is yet a third type of legitimate ruler. That is the ruler who (rightfully) depends on material strength. This ruler maintains strong armies and is wise in all the principles of tactics and strategy. As long as there is no True King or Lord Protector in the world and a ruler who depends on strength does nothing to violate the values of the Way, he will be able to preserve his state and safeguard his people's prosperity.[60]

This three-stage model was a departure from the teachings of earlier Confucian Masters like Mencius, who essentially insisted that a ruler could only be redeemed by at least making a good faith effort to follow the pristine Way of a True King. What is especially interesting about the *Xunzi*'s vision is that it folds the teachings of other Masters into the true Way as taught by Confucius. The *Xunzi*'s Lord Protector is basically guided by the teachings of Master Guan and Master Yan as they were formulated by the literati of the Qi court (and as they are transmitted in the *Guanzi* and *Yanzi*, the eponymous texts attributed to those Masters). The *Xunzi*'s "ruler who depends on material strength" embodies the wisdom of Master Sun (as transmitted in the *Sunzi bingfa*). The True King does not lack the tools or skills of those two types of rulers below him, but merely adds to those faculties the incomparable Potency that comes from learning. The teachings of other Masters are thus no longer completely incommensurate or irreconcilable with the teachings of the true Way; they are only flawed in giving expression to partial truths that are viable in contingent contexts.

The practical implications of this new vision tallied nicely with the evolving social circumstances of the late Warring States. The number of literati was proliferating, and literati themselves were becoming more indispensable to the function of government, even as the community of Masters and disciples became more Balkanized between different contending teachings. This posed a problem from the perspective of kings. On the one hand, there was great appeal in endorsing the vision of a particular Master or fellowship, to enhance one's ability to recruit among literati committed to that particular vision. On the other hand, taking such a partisan stance invited the open hostility of opposed literati and cut off avenues of recruitment. If you followed Mencius, for example, how could you employ any of the Mohists, who according to Mencius were the fatal enemies of civilization itself?

The teachings of Xun Kuang neatly circumvented this problem.[61] Xun Kuang's vision of the Way allowed for more flexibility. It was of course preferable, from Master Xun's perspective, for a ruler to employ only the latter-day followers of Confucius, and ideally only they would be given authority as government officials. But since the "heretical Masters" had correctly identified some of the underlying principles of effective government, a king who had no other choice could usefully employ the followers of Master Mo, Master Guan, or Master Sun, so long as they were governed and controlled by a ruler who understood and embodied the teachings of the true Way.

One of the ways in which Xun Kuang broke with Mencius most concretely tells us interesting things about the state of literati culture and the eclectic climate of Jixia. Mencius had taught that human nature was good: the task of learning was to nurture the "four germs" housed in the human heart from birth, until they developed into the fully mature virtues of humaneness, rightness, propriety (or reverence for ritual), and wisdom. Xun Kuang, by contrast, taught that human nature was evil.[62]

This did not mean that Xun Kuang claimed human beings to be born with malignant qualities wholly absent from Mencius's model of human nature. Instead, Xun simply denied that the "four germs" existed. Human beings, according to Xun Kuang, are born only with the emotions and desires that he and Mencius both agreed are hard-wired into the human animal. In the absence of anything like Mencius's "heart that cannot bear the suffering of others" (or any of the other three germs), a person has no inborn internal mechanisms to restrain his or her impulses from being expressed in immoral and destructive ways.

Learning, for Xun Kuang, was thus exclusively a process of looking outside of ourselves for the means to transform our natures.[63] If we mindfully, earnestly, and persistently submit to the positive influence of the ancient sage's rites, music, and literature, we can rework our basic internal emotional and perceptual impulses so that we can lead ethically productive and fulfilling lives. In practical terms Xun Kuang and Mencius agreed about what learning looked like: it involved a great deal of reading, thinking, and discussion with fellow seekers and with those more learned than ourselves, along with mindful appreciation of music and performance of ritual. They also agreed about the practical implications of learning: a learned person was for both Masters a natural leader whom should be entrusted with governmental authority.[64]

But Xun Kuang vehemently denied that learning could involve any amount of internal "soul searching." If one looked inside, all that one would find is the source of our trouble. Everything that could help us become our best potential selves was "out there," in the tradition bequeathed by the sages.

Why did Xun Kuang turn in this direction? Many interpreters attribute Xun Kuang's teachings about human nature to the worsening political climate of the Warring States. Indeed, if one wanted empirical evidence that human nature was brutal and violent on the Yellow River plain circa 285 BCE, one did not have to wait long or travel far. But the writings in which we encounter Xun Kuang's teachings are not dour or pessimistic in tone. Nor is the practical perspective of his doctrine. The *Xunzi* tells its readers that the object of their learning (though they may never reach it) should be to become a sage, a goal that even Mencius is never reported to have lain before his disciples as a target. Giving people such lofty ideals for which to aim is not the act of a pessimist.

Why then did Xun Kuang teach that human nature is evil? Since the writings attributed to him show that he was conversant with all the major trends of thought of his day, we can examine them to get a sense of the doctrinal context to which he was responding. Many of the essays collected in the *Xunzi* show the influence of a new tendency in the teachings of some of the Masters, one which we know was well-represented among the Masters resident at Jixia. Like Mencius, these Masters taught that the resources human beings can and must access lie within our hearts and minds. Unlike Mencius, these Masters did not teach that learning played any role in that personal transformation. Indeed, according to this perspective, learning could only obstruct what a person needed to do to fully realize his or her ultimate potential.

We have already encountered one of the most famous Masters associated with this perspective in Chapter 9, Zhuang Zhou, or Zhuangzi. Zhuang Zhou may not have been the first proponent of these types of ideas, but he is among the earliest figures associated with them that we can situate in time and place with relative confidence. Zhuang was a native of Song and a friend and occasional intellectual sparring partner of Hui Shi, who served consequentially as Prime Minister of Wei (see Fig. 17).[65] No record suggests that Zhuang Zhou himself was resident at Jixia, but his putative teachings were well known there. Much evidence suggests that Xun Kuang was conversant with teachings attributed to Master Zhuang. The *Xunzi* weaves some of Zhuang's insights into its own discussion of human consciousness, and at other points vehemently criticizes teachings like Zhuang's as harmfully nihilistic.[66]

Like Xun Kuang, Zhuang Zhou (if, as many scholars have contended, and I would agree, his perspective can be reconstructed from the "Inner Chapters"

Fig. 17. A modern depiction of a debate between Master Zhuang (Zhuangzi) and his friend Hui Shi, who became prime minister of the state of Wei. (Source: wapbaike.baidu.com.)

of the text that bears his name, the *Zhuangzi*)[67] was broadly conversant with the teachings of all the major Masters of his time. Unlike Xun Kuang, Zhuang Zhou made no attempt to redeem other Masters' teachings or reconcile them with his own. His putative writings display a caustic wit and deploy brutal satire. He lampoons virtually all of the other Masters as peddling "dregs and leavings" by comparison with an authentic understanding of the Way.[68]

Zhuang's critique of the other Masters begins with an exploration of what they claim to mean by "the Way." Confucius and Mo Di, for example, both claim that the Way expresses ultimate truth and is the measure of ultimate value (the basis of what is right and wrong, good and bad). Why is it, then, Zhuang asks, that these two Masters have such different understandings of the Way? For Zhuang the answer was simple: "truth" and "value" are always a matter of context and perspective. What from the perspective of a human being is a group of wood shavings floating in a puddle on the floor is a flotilla of boats sailing on a lake from the perspective of an ant. When the glamorous consort of a ruler strolled by the side of a river, she was simultaneously "beautiful" from the perspective of the people standing along its banks, "ugly" from the perspective of the fish looking up from the water.[69]

Zhuang Zhou did not conclude from these observations that there could be no "Way" at all. But he did insist that if "the Way" was to encompass ultimate truth and ultimate value it could not be reduced in the manner that Masters such as Confucius and Mo Di proposed. "The Way" would have to simultaneously encompass the "beauty" and "ugliness" of the ruler's consort, the grandness and minuteness of the flotilla/wood shavings. It would have to include all perspectives and all contingent contexts at once. "The Way" thus could no longer be captured in language or contained in human culture. Even to label it "the Way" is to distort it, since in language to label something "the Way" immediately implies the existence of something that is "not the Way," which is impossible.[70]

Zhuang Zhou's Way is not a human construct. It preceded the existence of all time, generated and contains all matter, and pervades all space. A person cannot relate to it as an object any more than an eye can look at itself without the aid of a mirror.

A human being can, however, access the power and dynamism of the Way. Since all things come from and are within the Way, it is the ultimate and most authentic core of a human being's identity: the part of a person that will remain unchanged when, long after she dies, she is transformed into a pile of dirt. If a person strips away the learned concepts and habits of thought (such as fear of death) that make up the sense of "self," what is left is the Way. Since the Way is the dynamic force that spontaneously drives cosmic transformation (the changes of day to night, autumn to winter, etc.), once a person has relinquished "self" and merged with the Way, she can unlock profound potential within her body and mind and become an agent of extraordinary power, able to respond with marvelously spontaneous efficacy to virtually any situation.

Zhuang Zhou's teachings thus, like those of Confucius and his latter-day disciples, envisioned a path of personal transformation that would enable the individual to fulfill their potential by means of the Way. But the methods envisioned by Zhuang Zhou were diametrically opposed to the learning advocated by Confucius, Mencius, and Xun Kuang. Zhuang Zhou even uses a satirical scene between Confucius and his star disciple, Yan Hui, to illustrate his methods of personal transformation. In a series of meetings Yan Hui tells Confucius "I am improving!" In each case, Yan has improved not because he had learned, but because he was able to "sit and forget." First he forgets humaneness and rightness, then rites and music, and finally forgets the existence of his body and mind altogether, merging completely with the "Great Thoroughfare" (i.e. the Way).[71]

Scholars have debated what the meaning of "sitting and forgetting" is, but much evidence suggests that Zhuang Zhou and those who shared his perspective were devotees of various forms of sitting meditation and macrobiotic yoga. Through focusing on the breath and aligning the energies of the mind-body system, the practitioners of these "arts of the mind" (sometimes called "arts of the Way") sought to still the constituent elements of ordinary consciousness and experience unmediated merger with the Way. Through the sustained practice of such methods, it was proposed, a person could develop insight, wisdom, and liberation from the coercive power of fear or deprivation.[72]

Zhuang Zhou was exceptional among the Masters of the Warring States in that his teachings do not address the political realm except by way of mockery and satire. It is very difficult to discern any form of political program in the teachings outlined in the "Inner Chapters" of the *Zhuangzi*. To the extent that they offered anyone political advice it was to warn his fellow knights to steer clear of the court if possible, do what they could to stay alive if not.[73] Within the "Inner Chapters" of the *Zhuangzi* the most urgent concerns of human beings in relation to the "Way" are intensely personal. Politics only ever impinge on the "arts of the Way" indirectly or tangentially.[74]

Other Masters who shared his vision of the Way and embraced common methods of personal cultivation, however, proposed that these concepts and practices could all be applied to politics. The basic idea was simple: a government would become most functional and positively transformative if its ruler and officials practiced the methods of personal cultivation aimed at merger with the Way. If the people who composed the government partook of the dynamism of the Way, then so would the government as a whole, and the operations of the state would become as spontaneously harmonious and effective as the movements of the cosmos.

This basic idea is expressed in many different surviving writings that date to the Warring States. None is more famous or has had more broad or enduring influence, however, than the *Daodejing* (*The Classic of the Way and Potency*). The *Daodejing* has been traditionally read as the written teachings of Lao Dan, or Master Lao (Laozi). The text is thus often referred to by the eponymous title of *Laozi*.

According to legend, Lao Dan was an older contemporary of Confucius who served as the archivist of the royal Zhou court. On his visit to the Zhou court Confucius is said to have met Lao Dan and become his disciple. Later,

Lao Dan became utterly disgusted with the decadent state of Zhou civilization and decided to depart for "the West." At the westernmost gate of the realm the gate warden recognized him as a man of great wisdom and would not let him depart unless he wrote down his teachings. Otherwise, we would not possess the *Daodejing*.[75]

The lore surrounding the *Daodejing* is fiction. We cannot be sure that Lao Dan existed at all, but if he did, he was assuredly not the author of the *Daodejing*. No mention of the *Daodejing* appears in any source that can confidently be dated to before 300 BCE or so. "Master Lao" is thus a construction similar to "Master Guan" or "Master Sun." Some person or group of people appropriated the figure of Lao Dan to be the "mouthpiece" of the ideas transmitted in the *Daodejing*.[76]

Why did his inventors create Master Lao? Some of their motives were the same as those anonymous literati who constructed Master Sun or Master Guan. Since Master Lao was (purportedly) older than and had even taught Confucius, Lao Dan's teachings showed that the concept of an ineffable cosmic Way he professed, and the practices of macrobiotic personal cultivation he advocated, were more original and authentic than the "human Way" and program of learning advocated by Confucius. Establishing the authenticity and efficacy of these concepts and practices, moreover, lent cogency to the political agenda animating Master Lao's teachings. The *Daodejing* reads as an extended political manifesto: if government could be made to align with and harness the Potency of the true cosmic Way, so the text promises, human society could be restored to a state of peace and harmony.[77]

We do not know precisely who began associating the teachings contained in the *Daodejing* with the figure of Lao Dan, but as an exercise in messaging it succeeded brilliantly. The teachings of Master Lao were distinct from those of other Masters, in that they were transmitted in laconic and often hauntingly beautiful poetry. The *Daodejing* addresses the reader directly and speaks in intensely personal terms ("I alone remain still! Waiting for the situation to reveal itself. Like a babe who has not yet smiled...."[78]), conveying the sense that one is communing with a sage.

The teachings of Master Lao did not begin circulating before the second decade of King Min of Qi's reign at the earliest, but they made an immediate impact on the culture of Zhou literati. Xun Kuang, for example, seems to have been aware of these ideas, and to have drawn inspiration from them in his own discussions of cosmology.[79] The influence of the *Daodejing* would grow over time. It helped popularize the use of "the Way" to refer to the cosmic ultimate rather than to a product of human sages, so that this cosmic understanding of "the Way" has inflected the common usage of the word ever since.

The word "Way" (*Dao*) became so closely associated with Master Lao and others (like Zhuang Zhou) whose perspective overlapped with his that these figures became grouped together in imperial times under the label "Daoist."[80] It was a neat instance of "cultural theft." Though Confucius had coined the term "Dao" as a signifier of ultimate truth and value, the group that eventually became labeled "Daoists" were among his most vehement critics.

By the second half of the Han dynasty (203–220 BCE) the *Daodejing* had acquired the status of a sacred scripture among some of its readers, and it became a seminal text in the formation of the organized Daoist Church, which has existed and continues to evolve in various forms down to the present day.[81] Many modern scholars have drawn a sharp distinction between the "religious Daoism" of Han and later times and the "philosophical Daoism" of the Warring States, but such a division has little organic basis in the historical evidence provided by the sources.[82] Though the Daoist Church was demographically and socially very distinct from any movement that existed in the pre-imperial era, it was pursuing political goals commensurate with those articulated in the *Daodejing* and other sources from the late Warring States: a government led by individuals cultivated through meditative and yogic practices aimed at merger with the Way. Though no self-identified movement of "Daoists" had formed during the Warring States (the label "Daoist" itself would not exist, to our best evidence, until about 100 BCE), the ideals that would eventually inspire the formation of the Daoist Church had already been given robust expression by the early third century BCE.[83]

The fact that these ideals had achieved broad traction among literati is evinced by the reaction they evoked in an oppositional figure like Xun Kuang. By the time Xun Kuang was active at Jixia, the forms of meditative personal cultivation aimed at merger with the cosmic Way had achieved the status of a robust alternative to the more conventional forms of Confucian learning among some literati. Several figures resident at Jixia, such as the Tian clan member Tian Pian (ca. 350–ca. 275 BCE), were advocates of the "arts of the Way," and several of the writings anthologized into the transmitted *Guanzi* demonstrate that notions like the cosmic Way and the meditative arts aimed at merger with it had adherents among Jixia's Masters and disciples.[84] Xun Kuang viewed this tendency as a dangerous heresy, and configured his doctrine to establish that only the forms of learning advocated by Confucius, which oriented the individual toward engagement with the objective world, the larger society, and the human Way articulated by the ancient sages (rather than the internal exploration of subjective consciousness) could legitimately develop the Potency that would transform an individual into a gentleman and a leader.

The doctrinal divisions between Masters at Jixia ran deep, and were not limited to the conflict between a Confucian like Xun Kuang and an advocate of the "arts of the Way" like Tian Pian. Virtually the whole gamut of ideas and practices current among the literati of the late Warring States was represented among the Masters resident at Jixia during the reign of King Min of Qi. It was not merely one of the most diverse and vibrant intellectual milieus of the Warring States, but could arguably be described as such for the entire history of the premodern world. Literati who resided in or visited Linzi might have seen in the sophisticated culture of Jixia a sign that Qi was destined to rise to the leadership of the Zhou world. If so, as it turned out, they would have been wrong.

12

The Harder They Fall
The State of Qi, 294–278 BCE

The victory against Yan in 296 BCE was the high-water mark of Tian Wen's influence at the Qi court. In 294 BCE a dramatic incident occurred that caused a radical shift in the leadership of Qi. A member of the royal clan "kidnapped" King Min.[1] The particulars of the incident are not recorded in any surviving sources. We do not know what motivated the kidnapper or how King Min ultimately survived this threat. But in its aftermath, relations between King Min and Tian Wen finally collapsed. King Min suspected his prime minister of complicity in the plot.

Tian Wen fled Qi. He remained too ambitious, and had become independently much too powerful, to exit the public stage quietly. He quickly achieved purchase as prime minister of neighboring Wei, where his career in public life had begun two decades earlier.[2] Though Tian Wen would never again be as broadly influential as he had been at the helm of Qi, he would continue to play an active role in the affairs of the Warring States for the rest of his life.

The first effect of Tian Wen's exile was to break the tripartite alliance between Qi, Wei, and Han that had been driving the geopolitical dynamics of the Zhou world for most of a decade. The immediate beneficiary of this shift was Qin. The partnership between Qin and Zhao that had ejected Tian Wen from Qin dissolved in 295 BCE, and King Zhao of Qin's uncle (Mi Bazi's half-brother) Wei Ran had consolidated control over the Qin court as that kingdom's new prime minister (replacing the Zhao native appointed to cement the Qin-Zhao alliance).[3] Wei Ran took quick advantage of the break between Qi and Wei. In 293 BCE he dispatched Bai Qi (d. 257 BCE), who would prove to be one of Qi's most brilliant commanders, to attack Han and Wei in the east. The combined armies of the two eastern states were crushed, losing more than 20,000 men and suffering the capture of Wei's commanding general.[4]

Over the next several years Qin remained relentlessly on the offensive against Han and Wei. In successive campaigns Bai Qi and other Qin commanders captured enormous swaths of territory from Qin's neighboring states, effectively undoing everything that Tian Wen's three-kingdom alliance had accomplished. Even the southern territories of Chu that Qi had won on behalf of Han and Wei were overrun by Qin and given to Qin princes (King Zhao of Qin's uncles and younger brothers) as fiefs.[5]

During this period of Qin aggression the strategic policy of King Min's court drifted. Because of lingering animosity between King Min and Tian Wen, Qi did not seek to negotiate any sort of defensive alliance that would check Qin's advance, which would have aided Tian Wen, now prime minister of the embattled state of Wei. Instead, King Min became focused on the conquest of the neighboring state of Song.

According to many sources, the inspiration for King Min's ambition to conquer Song came from the wandering persuader Su Qin. Su Qin, as we read in the previous chapter, became the most famous wandering persuader of the Warring States. The stories about him are so numerous and so elaborate as to make the historical reality of his life difficult (if not impossible) to recover with any confidence. But a persistent theme that recurs in the sources concerns his work as a "double-agent" in the service of King Zhao of Yan.

King Zhao of Yan harbored a vendetta against Qi because of the occupation of his kingdom under King Xuan and the humiliating defeat of his armies under King Min. In 295 BCE, one year after Yan's army had been dealt a crushing defeat by Qi in which thousands of its soldiers had died and two of its commanders had been captured, King Zhao of Yan enlisted Su Qin as an emissary to the Qi court to sue for peace. To establish that Su Qin was fully empowered to treat on behalf of the Yan throne, King Zhao raised Su to the rank of "Counsellor" and enfeoffed him as "Lord Wu'an" (Martial Pacification). The message that Su Qin conveyed to King Min's court was a straightforward proposition: if Qi would cease hostilities against Yan, the two kingdoms could join into alliance to pursue the conquest of Song.

Though on the surface Su Qin's commission was typical for the wandering persuaders of the time, at a deeper level the emissary had agreed with the King of Yan to carry out a long-term plan that went far beyond the scope of his immediate mission. Su Qin promised to use all of his skill for elegantly plausible rhetoric not only to convince King Min to accept Yan's help in launching a campaign against Song, but to persistently do everything he could to distract and weaken Qi. He would work from inside the Qi court over months and years to derange King Min's policies and isolate his government, until such time as Yan could join in alliance with other states to destroy Qin.[6]

Why would Su Qin undertake such a mission? The *Records of the Historian* records that Su Qin had an affair with the mother of the King of Yan, and that this relationship moved him to act as a spy for Yan.[7] Another source reports that King Zhao of Yan agreed to award Su Qin a sizable fief from the conquered territory of Qi once the great deed had been accomplished.[8] Both of these explanations are unlikely, given the enormous risks Su Qin is said to have undertaken and how difficult his goals would have been to achieve.

Perhaps the most plausible explanation for Su Qin's motives might be found in a particular group of sources, some preserved in the transmitted *Zhanguoce*, others among the silk manuscripts discovered in the Han-era tomb at Mawangdui. They recount a conversation in which Su Qin told King Zhao of Yan that he would serve the king more faithfully than famous ancient paragons of filial piety and faithfulness had been true to their parents and lovers, even though the outward appearances of his service might *seem* disloyal, and make all of the ministers at the Yan court speak against Su Qin.[9]

That would well describe the conditions under which a mole like Su Qin would have worked, but why would Su Qin have been moved to offer the King of Yan such service? In a letter purporting to be from Su Qin to the King of Yan preserved among the silk manuscripts at Mawangdui, Su Qin recounts having been enfeoffed by the king and expresses his determination to repay the king's magnanimity.[10] This is the best explanation for why Su Qin would go into "deep cover" for Yan over many years: he had reportedly been born in very poor and humble circumstances, and incurred the scorn of his family.[11] He would have felt obligated by the great faith that King Zhao of Yan had demonstrated in the worth and talent of the poor knight from East Zhou. "A knight will die for one who recognizes his worth."[12] It had been the creed of knights like Yurang and Nie Zheng, and would inspire knights to acts of self-sacrifice to the very end of the Warring State and beyond.

King Min did ultimately join into alliance with Yan for the purposes of conquering Song. There were reasons that Song made a tempting target. Though it was a small state, its land was densely populated and fertile. Moreover, the kingdom sat astride some of the most profitable trade routes in the Zhou world. The city of Tao, situated at the confluence of the Ji and He rivers, boasted the most profitable markets of any city in the Warring States. An enormous share of the goods traded between all the Zhou kingdoms flowed through Tao.[13]

Song, moreover, was vulnerable. Its King Yan (r. 328–286 BCE)[14] had come to the throne through the murder of his own brother and had pursued a policy of aggression. Though he had conquered territory from his neighbors, he had done so at a steep cost of blood and treasure, and had courted enmity from surrounding states.[15] The king's son had risen in rebellion against his father and briefly taken over the court. Though he had been driven into exile, he still had loyal followers who remained behind in Song.[16]

Beyond these vulnerabilities, King Yan reportedly indulged in manic profanity and rude arrogance directed against his fellow sovereigns. He would use leather bags filled with blood as target practice for his bow, calling this "shooting at Heaven" (the bag was meant to be the High God of Heaven in effigy). He had figurines of all the other kings of the Warring States carved, then placed in the privy upon which to urinate.[17] With such erratic and insulting behavior he became ever more isolated in an era when diplomacy had become key to survival.

Even given these conditions, King Min of Qi's aggression against Song represented a departure from the course that Qi had followed successfully during the tenure of Tian Wen as prime minister. Tian Wen had been careful to act in concert with as many allies as possible and to refrain from creating the impression that Qi was solely interested in enriching itself. By contrast, King Min was transparent in his desire to profit from the conquest of Song. He engaged in horse-trading over the potential spoils of war in an attempt to secure the support of Zhao's prime minister, and was ultimately frustrated in his initial attempt at conquest by Tian Wen, who as Prime Minister of Wei joined forces with a senior commander of Zhao to block Qi's invasion of Song.[18]

The geopolitical tide had shifted from the trajectory previously established by Tian Wen. Qi remained powerful, but complacent in the face of Qin's aggressive expansion. In response to these new conditions, in late 288 BCE Wei Ran, the King of Qin's uncle and Qin's new prime minister, made overtures to King Min of Qi. He sent an emissary with a plan to initiate a "next phase" in the politics of the Warring States, a diplomatic maneuver akin to the "royal revolution" set in motion by the Xuzhou summit of 334 BCE.

In the same way that King Hui of Wei and King Wei of Qi had recognized each other as "kings" at Xuzhou, Wei Ran proposed that King Zhao of Qin and King Min of Qi should certify the emerging territorial order of the Warring States by granting new and more exclusively elevated titles to one another. This was the rank of *di*, which in other contexts literally referred to the High God and ruler of the spirit world (the same deity who had entertained Viscount Jian of Zhao during his near-death experience, as described in the prophesy discussed in Chapter 4). No human ruler in living memory had assumed that rank.[19] In 288 BCE it would have been understood to mean something like "Divine Ruler" or "Thearch" by the aristocracy and literati of the Warring States. The plan proposed by Wei Ran entailed Qin recognizing King Min of Qi as "Thearch of the East" while Qi recognized King Zhao of Qin as "Thearch of the West."[20]

It was a bold ("arrogant" might be more apt) and profane gesture, but it sent clear and pragmatic signals to all of the political elites of the Zhou world. By ordaining one another as "Thearchs," the rulers of Qin and Qi were each committing to respect the "sphere of influence" of the other. Qin would continue to engulf the land of its eastern neighbors. Qi would be free to conquer Song and parts east (the states of Lu and Yan, for example). Both states would cease playing the "diplomatic game" pioneered by leaders such as Zhang Yi in attempts to stymie the other, and would instead cooperate in subjugating Zhao, which was the only state that had sufficient power to seriously challenge this "partition plan."

It is at this juncture that Su Qin began to make an indelible mark on the political history of the Warring States. All of the states of the Zhou world were horrified and enraged by the effective partition plan set in motion by Wei Ran. Su Qin came once again to the Qi court as the envoy of Yan. He delivered a persuasion to King Min, arguing that the plan proposed by Wei Ran was not in the interests of Qi, but that it gave Qi an opportunity that it should not miss.

The plan proposed by Wei Ran, according to Su Qin, was not in Qi's interests because any benefit that could come of it would go disproportionately to Qin. The other Zhou states were all angered by the presumption and irreverence of the title "Thearch," and Qi would receive the same disdain as Qin in that regard. To the extent that the aggressiveness of this move won anyone's respect, most of it would go to Qin, because Qin had initiated this plan, while Qi was being led.

Qi was thus caught in a foolish move, but the moment, according to Su Qin, gave King Min a chance to do something cunning. If he unilaterally (and without informing Qin or seeking its approval) discarded the title of Thearch and reverted to the rank of "king," repenting of the profanity of the prior title, Qin would be hung out to dry. All of the anger of the many states would be focused on Qin, and Qi would have won their affection.

This would give Qi a chance to finally ascend to a position of supremacy. If King Min went along with Wei Ran's plan, he might eventually conquer Song, but that could only be accomplished after Qin and Qi had gone to war with Zhao, which would be a costly affair. The final outcome of such a strategy would (as Wei Ran proposed) necessarily be a world divided between the two powers of Qin and Qi.

But if King Min followed Su Qin's advice, he could set Zhao and all of the other states against Qin. When Qin was thus weakened and Qi had added Song's wealth to its own assets, Qi would become the unchallengeable power of the Warring States. This, said Su Qin, was "the work of the sage kings Tang and Wu" (founders of the Shang and Zhou dynasties, respectively). In other words, if King Min double-crossed Qin as Su Qin proposed, he could become the next Son of Heaven.[21]

King Min was won over by this persuasion. He put Su Qin's plan into effect immediately. Before the year 288 BCE had ended, King Min had backed out of Wei Ran's "mutual recognition" compact, ending the agreement almost as soon as it had been struck.

Su Qin departed Qi on a mission to build an anti-Qin alliance.[22] He traveled to the courts of Han, Wei, and Zhao, enlisting those states to join Qi in punishing Qin for its arrogant presumption. He was received favorably at each court, and was able to broker a meeting between the kings of Qi and Zhao at which an alliance was formed for the purpose of forcing Qin to renounce the title of *di*.[23] By the end of 288 BCE Su Qin had been simultaneously invested with the prime minister's seals of Qi and Yan, and was leading a five-state coalition that included Zhao, Han, and Wei.

In 287 BCE the coalition mobilized to assault Qin. Bad weather and poor coordination impeded the operation. The coalition armies stalled at Full Marsh (Chenggao), a city far to the east of the Hangu Pass that marked the gateway to Qin's home terrain and deep within territory that Qin had seized during its recent campaigns of conquest.[24]

While the campaign was in full swing (albeit bogged down), King Min of Qi tried to exploit the moment. He launched an invasion of Song, hoping to conquer that neighboring state while Zhao and Qi's other allies were distracted by the campaign in the west. This provoked immediate anger and resistance among the allied states, who began to withdraw troops from the western battle front to redeploy to Song, so that Qi would not have the chance to swallow that rich prize whole.[25]

Qin took advantage of the discord among the five-kingdom coalition. It renounced the title of *di* and returned conquered territories to Wei and Zhao in exchange for peace. By the end of 287 BCE the new Vertical Alliance had thus dissolved, and Qi was forced to withdraw from Song under pressure from its erstwhile allies.[26]

Su Qin's plan had backfired badly for King Min of Qi. Instead of vaulting Qi to a position of unchallenged leadership, through its transparently venal pursuit of its own interests Qi had earned the mistrust and enmity of leaders throughout the Warring States. This may have been Su Qin's intention all along if, in fact, he was operating as an agent of Yan.

The negative consequences for Qi were immediate. Zhao sent one of its top commanders to assault Qi, to punish Qi's bad faith. In the west, the collapse of Qi's credibility and the dissolution of the Vertical Alliance put Qin back on the offensive, conquering new territories from its eastern neighbors to replace those it had ceded to buy peace, and forcibly displacing the people of its conquered territory to make way for settlers from Qin.[27]

In response King Min did nothing to win back the trust of his allies and mobilize to block Qin's aggression. Instead, he set out once again to conquer Song by way of enriching his own state. In 286 BCE armies from Qi poured into Song. Qin threatened to mobilize to block Qi, but King Min was so bent on plunder that he negotiated to secure Qin's complacency. He agreed to offer no resistance as Qin conquered Wei's former capital of Peace (Anyi) in return for Qin's acquiescence to Qi's conquest of Song.[28]

This third invasion of Song finally achieved King Min's object. His armies overran the Song capital. King Yan of Song fled to neighboring Wei, where he died.[29]

Though King Min had won a rich prize in material terms, he had done so at a steep political cost. Qi was more isolated than it had been since the days of Tian Chang's coup of 481 BCE. A series of diplomatic meetings between the leaders of Qin, Zhao, Yan, Han, and Wei quickly formed a five-state coalition allied for the purpose of punishing Kin Min of Qi's perceived duplicity and greed.[30] Tian Wen, as Prime Minister of Wei, was one of the chief advocates of the punitive alliance aimed at his native state.[31]

In a bid to secure the success of the alliance, Qin yielded command of the five-state coalition. It recommended Yue Yi, a native of Zhao and the scion of an illustrious military family who was serving in Yan, to be the joint commander of the assault force. Yue Yi was simultaneously invested with the prime minister's seal of Yan and Zhao and took command of both states' forces.[32]

At this juncture Su Qin, who had retained the confidence of King Min of Qi and was serving as prime minister in Linzi, was exposed as a double-agent in the service of Yan. Among the silk manuscripts discovered in a Han tomb are texts that purport to be letters sent by Su Qin to King Zhao of Yan, reporting on the progress of his mission to destroy Qi. If Su Qin himself had actually been engaged in such correspondence, perhaps one such letter was intercepted, finally exposing Su Qin's true loyalties. Su Qin was seized and publicly torn to pieces by chariots, an especially undignified end meant to requite his total lack of honor.[33]

In 285 BCE the assault on Qi began with a long-range attack by Qin, whose armies were granted passage by Han and Wei, and seized nine cities in the "Hedong" (east of the Yellow River) region of Qi.[34] Shortly afterward, Yue Yi led a joint force of coalition soldiers against the strategic town of Divine Hill (*Lingqiu*), which defended the crossing of the Yellow River, Qi's main natural defense on the western approach to its capital. King Min dispatched the bulk of Qi's armies to mount the defense of Divine Hill, threatening the commander with the extermination of his clan and the desecration of the graves of his ancestors if he did not offer battle. This so offended the Qi commander that he signaled the retreat in the face of the coalition armies and departed the battlefield in a single chariot, never to be seen again. Yue Yi took advantage of the enemy's retreat and captured the key ford, thus opening the gateway to Qi's heartland and capital.[35]

The following year Yue Yi advanced from Divine Hill at the head of the five-kingdom army, marching in the direction of Linzi. The remnants of Qi's armies, under a new commander, met the coalition at Qinzhou, a town that controlled the road toward the capital. The new Qi commander pleaded with King Min to issue an edict mandating generous rewards for soldiers who fought successfully in the defense of the capital, but King Min refused. The resulting battle was again a total rout of Qi's forces. The new commander himself died in the fighting.[36]

The defeat at Qinzhou left Linzi defenseless. The city was sacked. The soldiers of Yan rampaged through the streets of one of the greatest metropolises on earth, plundering in revenge for Qi's occupation of their home state. For the urbane residents of Linzi and the erudite scholars of Jixia it must have seemed like the unthinkable was transpiring and the world was ending. It was the most radical reversal of fortunes suffered by any state since the armies of Yue had overrun the capital of Wu in 473 BCE.

While the armies of Yan sacked Linzi, Yue Yi led the soldiers of Zhao on a march to the eastern coast of the Shandong peninsula, where they seized the city of Langya. Langya was the eastern anchor of Qi's Great Wall, a system of fortifications that was Qi's only substantial defense against an assault on Qi's heartland from the south. With its capital sacked and the Qi Great Wall occupied, the kingdom of Qi had effectively been erased in strategic terms.[37]

King Min successfully fled the capital and headed initially to the small neighboring state of Wey. The Lord of Wey gave him asylum and engaged King Min using the protocol of a courtier serving his ruler. But King Min behaved so arrogantly that he was eventually driven from Wey. He fled from there to Lu, where he was again driven out.[38]

He finally was given shelter in the city of Ju, south of Qi's Great Wall, which had continued to hold out against the invading armies of Yue Yi and the coalition. King Min was met there by an army dispatched by Chu to "rescue" Qi, led by a commander named Nao Chi. King Min set up a "court in exile" at Ju, with Nao Chi as his prime minister. But relations between the two men quickly went sour, and Nao Chi executed King Min in grisly fashion, drawing out his tendons and suspending him by them from a beam in the ancestral temple, where he lingered all night before dying.[39]

Nao Chi sought an agreement with the armies of Yan, attempting to trade his murder of King Min against being granted Ju as a fief by the new rulers of Qi. The people of Ju, however, rose up and expelled Nao Chi and continued to resist the occupying armies. They found King Min's son Tian Fazhang hiding as a groom in the household of the Grand Scribe of Ju, and crowned him King of Qi. He was known posthumously as King Xiang of Qi (r. 283–265 BCE).[40]

Qi was on the brink of annihilation. Only two cities continued to offer allegiance to the Tian clan: Ju in the south and Jimo in the northeast. The defenses of Jimo were led and organized by a low-ranking member of the Tian clan named Tian Dan. Tian Dan had been a government clerk in charge of monitoring markets in Linzi. During the sack of the capital he had organized the flight of his extended family. Thanks to his foresight and ingenuity they made it safely to Jimo, where they became the core of the resistance that fortified the city against the coalition invaders.

In the face of war, Tian Dan revealed a genius for command. He used espionage and psychological warfare to awe his own soldiers and beguile the enemy. By ordering sacrifices done outside, for example, he caused birds to hover over the city, which he then put out to be a "sign" that he had been contacted by the gods. He chose an ordinary young man from among the soldiers defending Jimo and established him as "Divine Teacher," claiming that through the young soldier he was receiving special instructions from the spirit world.

Tian Dan sent an agent to Yan to circulate the rumor that General Yue Yi was being lenient toward Jimo and that the people of that city only feared he would be replaced. This got Yue Yi sacked by the King of Yan, and effectively drove a wedge between Yan and Zhao (which retained Yue Yi as commander), causing Zhao to withdraw its forces from the siege of Jimo. Tian Dan then collected gold from the rich families of Jimo and offered it as a bribe to the new Yan commander, pleading that he should be merciful with the people of Jimo when the city finally capitulated.

Having thus lulled his enemies into a state of complacency, in 279 BCE Tian Dan launched a breakout assault against the Yan invaders. He gathered 1,000 cattle from within the city of Jimo and decorated them with red silk and bright paint. Tying knives to their horns, he gathered them at breaches in the city wall at night and set fire to grease-soaked bundles of reeds tied to their tails. This terrifyingly demonic-looking (and sounding, as the cows made unnatural sounds of fear and pain) stampede took the Yan army by complete surprise, and was followed by the emboldened soldiers of Tian Dan's Qi loyalist army.

The siege of Jimo was broken and the Yan army routed, its commander killed. Tian Dan marched forth to engage all the occupying forces throughout Qi, gathering more soldiers to his banner as he advanced, and eventually joining with forces loyal to King Xiang of Qi emanating from Ju. Within a year, all the invading armies had been expelled from Qi. The kingdom was restored and the throne of the Tian Kings re-established at Linzi. Tian Dan was raised to the title of Lord Anping.[41]

During the occupation of Qi, Tian Wen returned to take possession of his fief of Xue. He was able to maintain its autonomy even after the restoration of Qi and pass the throne of Xue on to his sons. His sons squabbled among one another and indulged in fraternal strife, however, and before the throne of Xue could be passed to a third generation the state had been destroyed.[42]

One of the most remarkable figures involved in the revival of Qi was King Xiang's queen (known as Queen Jun), the daughter of the Grand Scribe of Ju. She had recognized that the future King Xiang, who was hiding among her father's servants after King Min had been gruesomely slain, was no ordinary commoner. She began a relationship with the prince, and his love and admiration for her made him take her as his queen and one of his chief advisors. Though her father was furious at her, and disowned her for taking a husband without seeking paternal permission or following the correct protocol, she remained faithful and attentive to her father his whole life.

King Xiang relied on his queen's counsel frequently, and after he had died and her young son assumed the throne, the officials at the Qi court continued to seek her guidance. One day they received an emissary from King Zhao of Qin bearing a set of ingeniously linked jade rings. According to the Qin envoy, only a person of great intelligence could separate the rings. He challenged the literati of the Qi court to do so.

The learned men of the court worked on the puzzle for some time, but could not solve it. Finally, the queen (now the Queen Dowager) ordered the ministers to step aside and smashed the rings with a mallet. Setting the mallet down next to the jade shards, she instructed the Qin envoy to report to King Zhao that she had separated the rings.

On her deathbed she summoned her son and bade him to remember a list of ministers who could be trusted. Her son excused himself and went to fetch a brush and bamboo tablet to write the list down. When he returned the Queen Dowager sighed and told her son that she could not remember the names anymore.[43]

The Queen Dowager's frustration with the men by whom she was surrounded neatly embodied the existential situation of the Qi throne in the wake of the sack of Linzi. Qi remained rich in people, land, and commercial wealth, but its strategic position had been forever compromised by the cataclysmic collapse of its civil and military institutions and the plundering of its infrastructure. Qi could never hope to regain the initiative as a leader among the Zhou states, and could only hope to survive if it conducted itself with extreme diligence and strategic wisdom.

The Queen Dowager embodied the two central pillars of such wisdom. The first was that a ruler had to keep faith with the values and people that were truly fundamental. Even though her father had disowned her, for example, the Queen Dowager remained faithful to him, because she knew that if people saw that her own father could not depend on her, no one else would trust her.

This contrasted starkly with the behavior of the Queen Dowager's late father-in-law, King Min. After he had cast off the guidance of Tian Wen, King Min kept faith with others only when it was in the most venal material interests of himself and his throne. He broke faith with allies and subjects whenever he saw some advantage in doing so. In this way he had burned through his credibility until Qi was completely isolated, and went from being one of the most powerful states in the Zhou world to being a cautionary tale.

The second great pillar that the Queen Dowager embodied was especially urgent in the face of Qi's weakness. To keep faith with what is most fundamental, a leader must know when to obey the rules and when to break them. Breaking one's word to an ally in the middle of a war, as King Min had done, was grossly foolish. But waiting for a matchmaker to form a union with a hunted prince who was obviously in need of help, as her father would have desired, was just as foolish. Keeping to the rules of a game set up by a stronger and clearly predatory enemy, as her officials had in the face of the challenge from King Zhao of Qin to solve his puzzle of linked jade rings, was more foolish still.

When the Queen Dowager, as she lay dying, saw that her son was foolish enough to *write down* a list of "trusted officials" that could be used to confound or destroy him if it fell into the wrong hands, she finally gave up the struggle. Trying to give him advice that would protect him in her absence was a losing battle.

Even before the Queen Dowager's death, it was clear to all observers that Qi would never again be in a position to lead the Warring States or produce a new Son of Heaven. With Qi thus neutralized, there were only two kingdoms among the Warring States that could contend to lead the Zhou world. One was Qin, which had been expanding in size, wealth, and power since the days of Shang Yang. The other was Zhao, one of the "three Jin" successor states. Under the leadership of its first king, the Zhao court had embarked on a program of military reform and territorial expansion that had given it the power to challenge any of the other states, including Qin. The two decades after the sack of Linzi would witness a contest for dominance between Zhao and Qin.

13

The Duel

The States of Zhao and Qin, 307–260 BCE

In the wake of the cataclysmic implosion of Qi, the strategic dynamics of the Zhou world were reduced to a simple polarity. By 284 BCE, of the "Seven Titans" (*qi xiong*,[1] a phrase coined by imperial-era historians to denote the seven greatest Warring States), five had suffered disasters which crippled or at least severely curtailed their military power. Wei had been exhausted by King Hui's campaigns of conquest. Han had suffered successive invasions and lost territory to all of its stronger neighbors. Chu had been wracked by internal division and was losing ground to Qin in its Yangzi basin heartland. Yan had been torn apart by civil war and invasion in the wake of the abdication affair. Qi had lost its potential position as leader of the eastern states and suffered ruinous defeat due to the callousness and arrogance of King Min. Only the northwestern, neighboring kingdoms of Zhao and Qin had preserved sufficient economic and military power to project force beyond their own frontiers and pursue aggressive agendas in the arena of interstate politics. They had been allies in the war to humble Qi, but in that conflict's aftermath it was clear to all observers that the fate of the Zhou world awaited a reckoning between Zhao and Qin.

Though Zhao was one of the "Three Jin" successor states and had been the "brother" of Wei and Han for more than a century since the time of Marquis Wen of Wei, there were old affinities between Zhao and Qin. The rulers of Zhao claimed descent from the same Ying clan that produced the royal line of Qin,[2] thus all of the same questions about "Chinese" origins that apply to the Qin royal family (as discussed in Chapter 8) hold force in the case of Zhao. The founders of the Zhao line may have been indigenous aristocratic vassals of the Zhou (as the genealogy provided for them in the *Records of the Historian* claims), or they may have been warriors of one of the northern Rong tribes who joined the retinue of the Duke of Jin sometime in the seventh century BCE, and for whom was fabricated a pedigree by appropriating the "origin myth" of the Ying clan.

Moreover, the territory of Zhao (like that of Qin to the west and Yan to the east) backed on to the great open Inner Asian steppe. In the same way that the rulers of Qin had labored intensively to integrate the various Rong people who lived within and adjacent to their terrain under consolidated Qin rule, Zhao leaders had been intensively engaged with the non-Sinitic people of the North since the earliest days of the clan. Zhao Wuxu, the first independent ruler of a Zhao "state," had been the son of a woman captured by his father in campaigns against the Turkic-speaking peoples of the steppe. He, in turn, had married his sister to the alien King of Dai, as part of a ruse in which he seized the Dai lands in a surprise attack. The former Dai "kingdom" (and its people) was then appended as a separate domain within the territory of Zhao, and given to Zhao Wuxu's son and Heir Apparent as a fief.

This engagement with steppe culture and steppe peoples had been a hallmark of politics in both Qin and Zhao during the first centuries of the Warring States era. In assuming the royal title, the first King of Qin had initiated a "Winter Feast" at which to receive the yearly submission of the chieftains of the Rong people living under Qin rule. From the earliest establishment of the Qin state its rulers had contended with the challenge of Yiqu, a kingdom established by non-Sinitic people along the northwest frontier of Qin's Wei River heartland. Wars between Qin and Yiqu were endemic throughout the fifth and fourth centuries BCE.[3] Even after Yiqu had been subjugated as a vassal state in 327 BCE it remained a liability, as will be discussed later.[4]

All of these events and conditions taken together (among many others that could be listed) are again exemplary of the larger truth that applying modern categories such as "Chinese" and "non-Chinese" to the people and traditions of the various Warring States is anachronistic. Though Yan, Zhao, and Qin were distinct in being intensely engaged with the people of the steppe, all of the largest Warring States incorporated non-Sinitic peoples within their social and political fabrics. One of the remarkable achievements of Warring States leaders was the creation and implementation of institutions that could integrate peoples who spoke diverse languages and adhered to varying cultural traditions within a common matrix of rule.

This particular dimension of political life drove the rise of Zhao, from having been a junior partner among the three "brother states" formed from the partition of Jin, to a position of preeminent strategic power in the wake of Qi's collapse. Though the leaders of Zhao had been working to integrate steppe peoples into their domain by way of growing the power of the state since its earliest inception, that process was radically intensified and accelerated during the reign of the eighth independent leader of Zhao, Zhao Yong. Zhao Yong was the first ruler of Zhao to assume the title "king," and is known to history by the posthumous title of King Wuling (the "Martial and Numinous" King, r. 325–299 BCE). The power that Zhao had consolidated by the second decade of the fourth century BCE can largely be attributed to his efforts at reform and to his aggressive engagement with the steppe peoples and polities on Zhao's borders.

During the reign of King Wuling's father, Zhao had defied Wei's attempts to reunite the "brother states" of Han, Wei, and Zhao. Though Zhao had successfully asserted its independence, Wuling's father had focused his attention on the central Zhou realm, seeking to conquer agrarian lands from neighboring states such as Wey. Watching such conquests yield ambivalent results, and the failure of successive attempts by leaders such as Zhang Yi or Gongsun Yan to forge a new interstate order through diplomacy, King Wuling became convinced that the strategic dilemma of Zhao compelled its leaders to seek power in unconventional directions, and that the natural place to turn for such resources was to the pastoral people living along Zhao's northern frontier.

In 307 BCE King Wuling held deliberations at his court over a new policy proposal. He argued to his chief advisors that the combined threat of Yan and Zhongshan to the east, Qin to the west, and the various non-Sinitic peoples who roamed the northern frontiers of Zhao was too grave to be ignored. Drastic measures were required to vouchsafe the long-term security of the kingdom. To meet the challenge, the king proposed that army, court, and kingdom should adopt "barbarian dress" (*hu fu*). In place of the long tunic belted with a cloth slash and sandals favored by Zhou tradition, King Wuling would have the men of Zhao wear short jackets, trousers fastened with a leather belt, and leather boots.[5]

The fact that this proposal was so radical is evidence of just how stringent the status conventions that controlled Zhou social life really were. Clothing was a vital marker of a person's place in the social hierarchy; Zhou elites invested enormous resources into competing with one another in sartorial display. We know how absolutely determining clothing was of social position from the dozens of stories included in the writings of Warring States literati that recount moments in which knights were made to feel humiliated or inferior because of their deficiencies of dress in the company of highborn aristocrats.[6] Any change in the customary patterns of dress would force the wealthiest and most powerful figures in the kingdom to expend huge sums of wealth "retooling" their wardrobes. These expenditures would be especially punishing for "new men" who were working their way up through the ranks of the meritocracy, and racing to invest rising incomes into clothes fashionable enough to keep pace with the elevation in their status.

Despite these problems, the adoption of "barbarian dress" could (and ultimately did) secure Zhao military, social, and political advantages. In strictly tactical terms, the clothing designs favored by steppe peoples were perfectly adapted for cavalry warfare (see Fig. 18). Shorter jackets and trousers allowed riders to sit comfortably in the saddle on long rides and at high speeds, and gave riders the freedom to direct their mounts using pressure from their legs when their hands were occupied with a bow and could not hold reins. Leather belts fastened with metal buckles allowed for the carrying of weapons and equipment without the use of the rider's hands (which needed to be free to hold reins or fire a bow) while a horse was in motion, even at the gallop. The stirrup had not yet been invented, so the combat power of cavalry was still somewhat limited. But using the equipment and techniques they had developed, steppe people could field disciplined units of well-mounted archers capable of firing arrows from horseback, giving them a deadly advantage during Iron Age warfare.

King Wuling wanted to match and counter this threat from the northern frontier. He was also particularly sensible of the strategic challenge posed by Zhongshan, to the east. The revived kingdom of Zhongshan was ruled by a clan that openly acknowledged its roots in the tribal society of the "White Turks" (*bai di*), and whose elite culture mixed elements of Zhou tradition with aspects of steppe custom.[7] In the debates he held among his courtiers, King Wuling emphasized that "Zhongshan is our belly and heart".[8] Zhao enveloped Zhongshan in such a way that the southern Zhongshan frontier had close access to the Zhao capital of Handan. For Zhao to be secure, Zhongshan had to be destroyed, and to accomplish that end Zhao would need to counter the strength that Zhongshan derived from its ties to the steppe.

The conversion to "barbarian dress" facilitated the training and outfitting of cavalry that could achieve King Wuling's strategic goals. This was not merely a matter of equipping archers to fight on horseback. Much of the advantage of mounted archers derived from their ability to travel speedily into position, where they might be asked to dismount and fight on foot. The commanders who led such units would thus also have to be mounted and would be forced to adopt the same kit as the men they led. These leaders would be drawn from the elite ranks of Zhao society, but many of them would be upwardly aspiring

Fig. 18. The people of the Inner Asian steppe developed cavalry warfare to a high level of sophistication and combat power. Zhou tradition favored the chariot over the mounted warrior, but over the course of the Warring States period many armies developed and deployed cavalry units in emulation of those among the steppe peoples, often with the aid of or by enlisting steppe warriors themselves. This figurine was discovered in a Qin tomb. Northern states such as Qin, Zhao, Zhongshan, and Yan exerted particular effort at the development of cavalry forces. (Source: Wikimedia Commons.)

knights who had much to lose from being forced to dress differently than higher-born aristocrats. If King Wuling wanted to make leadership in the new cavalry corps a coveted promotion rather than a punishment, he had to remove the potential stigma inherent in the necessary cavalry uniform. He thus mandated that all elite men had to adopt the style of "barbarian dress," and provided the example of formally holding court while dressed according to steppe custom.[9]

The adoption of "barbarian dress" served broader strategic goals above and beyond its tactical and social applications. Like all struggles, the campaign to extend Zhao's control into the northern steppe had political as well as military dimensions. To truly develop cavalry power, Zhao would need the help of steppe people to provide horses and training for Zhao conscripts, as well as to serve as mounted auxiliary forces within the larger army of the kingdom. The adoption of "barbarian dress" was thus an olive branch extended to steppe elites: "Make peace with us, pledge fealty to the Zhao throne, and you can enjoy a position of privilege within our society. Where custom is concerned, we are ready to meet you halfway." In this way King Wuling hoped to both decrease pressure along Zhao's northern frontier and draw new power from the steppe that could be used in the fight against Zhongshan. This political dimension of Zhao's policy was evinced by the creation of cavalry units distinguished by purely ornamental elements of "barbarian dress" like bird plumage and belts decorate with cowrie shells.[10]

King Wuling was a forceful and dynamic leader. He successfully effected the transition to "barbarian dress" over the resistance of his more conservative courtiers and officials. The sources suggest that he was very strategic in the implementation of this policy. For example, in the same ceremony in which he promoted a knight to be the Crown Prince's tutor, he gifted the man with a set of "barbarian clothes."[11] This move sent an unequivocal message to all Zhao elites: the new policy and the values it expressed had such high priority that they were going to be incorporated into the education of the next king, and every official should understand that not only current favor but future career success at the Zhao court would depend on how compliant they were with the new order of things.

King Wuling's efforts to develop cavalry power quickly bore fruit. In 306 BCE Zhao assaulted the "Forest Hu" people along the kingdom's northwest frontier, and in the negotiated truce that followed, the Forest Hu agreed to supply horses to Zhao and to place their mounted archers under the command of a member of the Zhao royal clan. That same year Zhao invaded Zhongshan and conquered a strategic defensive position along its western frontier. The following year Zhao invaded Zhongshan again and forced the cession of four cities to secure an armistice.

Over most of the next decade King Wuling pressed this simultaneous campaign against both the kingdom of Zhongshan and the tribal confederations of the steppe. By 302 BCE he had consolidated enough control of the frontier region to establish two new commanderies along the steppe lands to Zhao's northwest, adding new steppe cavalry units to his army in the process. Increasingly the king took personal command of part or all of Zhao's forces, so that his focus was drawn progressively more into military affairs and away from the court. In 299 BCE he thus formally abdicated the throne to a younger son, Zhao He, known posthumously as King Huiwen of Zhao (r. 298–266 BCE).

The newly crowned King Huiwen was only 10 years old at the time, so Wuling sought mainly to relieve himself of civil ceremonial duties. He retained the formal title of "Ruling Father" (*zhu fu*) and continued to command Zhao's armies in the long strategic struggle along the northern frontier. One of his first acts after abdication was to enter Qin in his military "barbarian dress," pretending to be an emissary, for the purpose of military reconnaissance. Finding his garb offensive when Wuling appeared at the Qin court, the King of Qin summarily dismissed Wuling from the audience hall and had him ejected from Qin, realizing only belatedly that he had held the effective ruler of Zhao in his grasp.

Like the transition to "barbarian dress," Wuling's redoubled focus on military affairs proved effective. In 297 BCE he conquered and absorbed a large tribal confederation to Zhao's west. The following year he achieved his final object of eradicating the kingdom of Zhongshan (for the second and last time). The King of Zhongshan was captured and internally exiled. On returning to Zhao, Wuling declared a general amnesty and initiated five days of feasting with wine to celebrate the great victory. He dispensed rewards to meritorious courtiers, in the course of which he enfeoffed his older son Zhao Zhang as a regional lord, assigning one of his own trusted officials to be Zhao Zhang's prime minister.[12]

In more than two decades of rule Wuling had proven himself a bold and competent strategist. With audacious policies and assertive leadership he had vastly increased the territorial scope, economic wealth, and sheer military power of the kingdom of Zhao, establishing Zhao as one of the leading powers of the Zhou states. By any metric he was among the rulers of the Warring States who exerted the greatest personal impact on the course of historical affairs.

But his brilliance as a military strategist was starkly contrasted by his failings as a family patriarch. His meddling with the traditions of primogeniture was inherently risky and difficult to explain. The *Records of the Historian* records that Wuling invested his younger son Zhao He as Heir Apparent, setting aside the older half-brother Zhao Zhang, because Wuling had fallen so deeply in love with Zhao He's mother, a famed beauty. After Zhao He's mother died, King Wuling, seeing the elder son humbling himself before the younger, began to feel sorry for Zhao Zhang and elevated him in station to make amends.[13] While such personal feelings may have provided some of Wuling's motivations, it is difficult to believe that such a calculating figure acted purely from sentimental impulse. He clearly abdicated the throne to focus on leadership of the army, but in doing so he may have deliberately chosen one of his younger sons (who despite being a child could perform all of the civil ceremonial duties required of a king) so that he could retain control over the administration of government. In this light, his decision to grant his older son Zhao Zhang a fief after the destruction of Zhongshan was perhaps an attempt to play his two sons against one another, and thus retain supreme power to determine state policy in his own hands.

If the latter was Wuling's intention, in this instance his maneuver did not work out as he planned. Zhao Zhang was not content to serve his younger brother as vassal, and coveted the royal throne for himself. In 295 BCE, while Wuling and Zhao He were on an excursion together outside the capital, Zhao Zhang rose in rebellion. He killed his brother's prime minister and tried to seize control of the court, but met resistance from one of his uncles and another powerful courtier. Their forces reclaimed the royal palace and pursued Zhao Zhang, who fled to join his father, Wuling, in his retreat outside the capital. Zhao Zhang and his confederates were killed, but hostilities did not cease with the rebels' deaths. Royal forces kept Wuling besieged in his satellite palace for 100 days, at the end of which time he died of starvation. Since Zhao He (known to history as King Huiwen) was still only 14 years old, Wuling's death left Zhao He's uncle and allies effectively in control of the Zhao court.[14]

King Wuling's life was a study in just how cutthroat the politics of the Warring States had become. The brutal cruelty of his death posed no impediment to his successors' capitalizing upon the foundations that Wuling had laid in developing the basis of Zhao's power. In 284 BCE, just over a decade after Wuling's demise by starvation, under the reign of his son and heir King Huiwen, now 24 years old, the Zhao court helped orchestrate the allied invasion that broke the burgeoning power of Qi.

The humbling of Qi in 284 BCE represented a high point of Zhao's influence over the general affairs of the Zhou states. It also marked a turning point in the relations between the neighboring kingdoms of Zhao and Qin. During the decades of Qi's rise, Zhao and Qin had found as many occasions to cooperate as to compete. Both kingdoms were rising in power, but neither had special cause to view the other as a particular threat. But when Qi's power was finally effectively broken, a state of "cold war" settled over relations between Zhao and Qin.

This intensifying high-stakes rivalry influenced the domestic politics of both kingdoms. Though both Zhao and Qin had been growing steadily in economic and military might during the late fourth and early third centuries BCE, both states had likewise experienced crises of leadership. An existential struggle would require more than land, soldiers, and weapons. Those assets would have to be used to maximum advantage and with penetrating intelligence. It was incumbent upon the rulers of both Qin and Zhao to enlist and empower talented civil officials and strategically adept military commanders. The ultimate survival of each kingdom was at stake, and in the early decades of the third century BCE both courts underwent extensive reorganization, each motivated in part by the explicit aim of defeating the other.

By 284 BCE King Zhao of Qin had been on the throne for 23 years. His accession to the throne as a child (following the sudden death of his half-brother, King Wu, as discussed in Chapter 10) had been engineered by his mother, Mi Bazi (whose formal title was the Queen Dowager Xuan) and her two brothers. The king's mother and uncles took pains to consolidate their own family's power over the Qin court.

This "Mi-clan clique" was an interesting affair. Mi Bazi and her younger brother Mi Rong were natives of Chu. Their half-brother Wei Ran had been sired upon their mother by a prior husband, a member of the Wei ruling clan. Once this trio had eliminated rival claimants to the Qin throne, they fortified their position by giving themselves and their kin lucrative titles. Wei Ran was made a marquis, Mi Rong and the King's two younger brothers were all made lords of sizeable fiefs carved from conquered eastern territory. Together the revenues controlled by the family came to eclipse those under the direct control of the Qin court and its civil bureaucracy.

"Mi-clan" nepotism and transactionalism changed the tenor of Qin policy from what it had been in the days of King Huiwen of Qin (King Zhao's father) and Zhang Yi. An anecdote about Mi Bazi in her early days of controlling the Qin court gives a sense of her reputation and that of the governing culture she and her brothers fostered. The neighboring kingdom of Han was under attack by Chu and had been promised defensive reinforcements from Qin. Time passed and no troops materialized, so a Han envoy arrived in Xianyang to inquire of Mi Bazi why Qin had done so little to defend Han, when Han stood as a buffer between Qin and Chu. Mi Bazi praised the envoy's eloquence and explained that in the past she would speak the same way to her departed husband. When he would put his leg on her she found it too heavy, because that would be of no profit to anyone, but when he put his whole body on her she found it light, because the encounter might eventually produce a male child. The Han envoy wanted a similar escalation of engagement on the part of Qin. The problem was that sending troops through the passes was costly, so how could the encounter be made profitable to both Qin and Han?[15]

The message that Mi Bazi was sending was clear: the new rule of the Qin court was "pay to play." If Han wanted Qin to "put its whole body on" (i.e. send enough troops to rescue) Han, it would have to pay a premium on top of the troops' expenses. This tale is of course suspicious: powerful women in patriarchal societies are very conventionally depicted as vulgar and hypersexualized, so it is unlikely that Mi Bazi communicated with a royal envoy in such crass terms. But the story does give us a sense of the reputation of the Qin court during the time when Mi Bazi and her brothers had control. She was considered a very salient and powerful force in Qin court politics, and the government over which she and her brothers presided was viewed as pursuing a radically venal, transactional approach to policy. Even if we doubt the veracity of the anecdote, what it reports about the reputation of the Mi-clan clique and the Qin court is plausible. We know that episodes like the kidnapping of King Huai of Chu and the erratic treatment of Tian Wen (discussed in the previous chapter) had tarnished Qin's image in the last decade of the fourth and the early third century BCE.

Mi Bazi's half-brother Wei Ran served as prime minister for most of his nephew King Zhao's early reign. Wei Ran was very aggressive in pressing Qin's advantage against Wei, Chu, and the other eastern states,[16] and to that end he was not averse to employing talent from beyond the scope of his own relatives. He discovered and promoted one of the most brilliant military commanders of the Warring States, General Bai Qi, who led the campaigns that, in 279 BCE, captured Chu's ancient capital of Ying, forcing the southern kingdom to retrench and move its capital eastward.[17]

But like his half-sister Mi Bazi, Wei Ran consistently formulated policy with an eye toward what would best serve the interests of his family in its domination of the Qin court. It was at his initiative, for example, that the scheme to effectively partition the Zhou realm between Qi to the east and Qin to the west (as described in the previous chapter) was first proposed. Rather than pressing for a global solution of the geopolitical crisis that would honor the posthumous ambitions of past Qin kings, as Zhang Yi had attempted, Wei Ran was content to claim a "sphere of influence" in which he and his family could continue to broaden and deepen their wealth and control. The aggressive acquisitiveness of this policy had galvanized a five-state coalition to mobilize against Qin, which had only been saved from the consequences of Wei Ran's leadership by the fact that King Min of Qi had proven himself even more venal and grasping, thus causing the anti-Qin coalition to disintegrate (and a new anti-Qi coalition to form).

Mi-clan control of the Qin court only came under challenge during the fourth decade of King Zhao's reign. Following a pattern that had begun with Shang Yang almost a century prior (and that had continued through the careers of Gongsun Yan and Zhang Yi), once again the agent of dramatic change at the Qin court was a humble knight who came to Qin from the central state of Wei. This time the man who brought his talents west was named Fan Sui (d. 255 BCE).

Fan Sui had desired to serve the King of Wei, but despite having a reputation for brilliance he had only been able to obtain employment as the retainer of a highborn Wei courtier named Xu Jia (fl. ca. 275 BCE). During an embassy to Qi, the King of Qi tried to recruit Fan Sui by offering him gifts of gold, beef, and wine. Fan refused these overtures, but on account of them he was suspected of disloyalty. On returning to Wei, Xu Jia reported the incident to the prime minister, a scion of the Wei royal clan. The prime minister had Fan Sui seized and beaten during a drinking party. Thinking him dead, he had Fan Sui rolled into a mat and thrown into the privy, where drunken guests urinated on him throughout the night. The next morning he was discovered by one of the household servants, and Fan convinced the man to help him escape to the house of a friend.

Fan's friend, coincidentally, was approached by a visiting emissary from Qin, who inquired about any men of talent that he might recruit and bring back with him to Qin. Fan was thus introduced to the Qin emissary as "Zhang Lu," and under this assumed identity he made his way west to Qin. In the eastern districts of Qin they encountered Prime Minister Wei Ran, who was on an inspection tour.

Fan Sui had heard that Wei Ran disliked "eastern persuaders," so he stayed out of sight inside his wagon as the emissary exchanged greetings with the Qin prime minister. As Fan had expected, Wei Ran asked the emissary whether or not his entourage included any new recruits being brought from the east. Only on being assured that there were none did he bid the emissary farewell and continue on his inspection tour. Fan Sui deduced that though Wei Ran was not a fast thinker, he would eventually realize that it had been a mistake not to search the wagons to verify the emissary's statement. Fan thus dismounted from his wagon after they had traveled for a few kilometers and hid in the underbrush alongside the road. Indeed, some riders dispatched from Wei Ran did arrive with orders to inspect the wagons. Once they had departed after finding nothing, Fan remounted his wagon and the cortege continued on to the Qin capital of Xianyang.[18]

These stories of Fan's early life and entry into Qin are very dramatic, and may have been embellished by literati eager to add luster to Fan's mystique and use Fan's career as an example. But the very existence of these accounts testifies to a general tension in the Qin state and government. The dominant position of Wei Ran and his kin at the apex of power contradicted the established methods of meritocracy that had become the norm in Qin politics from the days of Shang Yang on. The Mi-clan clique had led the kingdom's armies to great victories, but they were reluctant to share power or wealth with talented officials from outside their small family circle. There was growing discontent among the knights who served the Qin state as salaried officials. They wanted to see an end to the nepotism of the ruling clique.

The key obstacle to these impulses was the king himself. He was acclimated to the power dynamics of the court as they had been established by his mother and uncles, and was inclined to share his family's suspicion of the wandering persuaders who flocked to Qin in search of employment. On first arriving in Qin, Fan Sui thus did not have any success attaining an audience with the king. He waited for more than a year in the Qin capital, hoping for an opportunity to discuss affairs with the king and demonstrate his talent.

The event that changed the situation was the "Yiqu Affair." As noted above, the non-Sinitic kingdom of Yiqu had been Qin's rival for several centuries, contending with Qin for control of the people and territory of the Wei River valley. In 327 BCE during the early reign of King Huiwen, Yiqu had finally acknowledged Qin's supremacy and accepted subordination as a vassal state. Yiqu retained regional autonomy, however, and continued to be administered by its own king.

Sometime after her ascent to a position over the Qin court, the Queen Dowager Mi Bazi had begun a romantic liaison with the reigning King of Yiqu. The affair went on for several years and produced two sons.[19] The testimony about this relationship is scanty, but there is no reason to doubt that it had both personal and political dimensions. The King of Yiqu and Mi Bazi were both figures in equivalently ambivalent positions. Though he was the leader of his people, as a Qin vassal he lacked true sovereign autonomy. Though she was the *de facto* ruler of Qin, she was not a native of the state she controlled, and was dependent upon a network of her male relatives, each of whom had his own political and economic interests in the ongoing exercise of power. Whatever forces of personal attraction brought the King of Yiqu and Mi Bazi together, there was advantage to both of them in an alliance. The fact that Mi Bazi had given birth to two of the King of Yiqu's sons made the alliance more tangible and gave the couple leverage that could be used in various ways as they navigated the labyrinth of court politics.

The tacit understanding that held this partnership together fell apart in 272 BCE, for reasons that are not recorded (in all likelihood, because they were embarrassing to the Qin throne and court). Perhaps the existence of Mi Bazi's sons by the King of Yiqu had been kept a secret and was only discovered belatedly by the king or one of his uncles. Perhaps some scheme planned by

Mi Bazi and the King of Yiqu had caused a rift in the family, forcing Mi Bazi to choose between her lover and her blood kin.

Whatever the case may have been, in 272 BCE the King of Yiqu arrived at the Sweet Spring Palace in the Qin capital, where he was presumably accustomed to meeting Mi Bazi for romantic trysts. On this occasion he was instead ambushed by Qin soldiers and killed,[20] breaking the peace between Qin and Yiqu and setting off another bloody war that would only end a year later, when the independent kingdom of Yiqu was finally destroyed and divided into three centrally administered commanderies under the direct rule of the Qin court.[21]

The ancient chronicles make note of how disruptive this war was to the affairs of Qin. Fan Sui was in the Qin capital for its duration and memorialized the throne in the hope of receiving an interview with the king. Accounts of their first meeting make special note of the king apologizing for the long delay in granting Fan Sui an audience on account of the "Yiqu Affair," explaining that the incident had forced him to be particularly attentive to his mother the Queen Dowager.[22] This strongly suggests that King Zhao had experienced a change of outlook. Where before he had been suspicious of "foreign" persuaders, the final Yiqu war (and his mother's hand in inciting it) had caused the king to rethink his perspective. As successful as the Mi-clan clique's management of the court had been in terms of conquest and plunder, their extremely instrumental and self-serving orientation created unnecessary friction and waste in the conduct of state affairs. The destruction and expense of the Yiqu crisis seem to have made the king realize that he could benefit from listening to the ideas of a man who was less entitled than his mother, uncles, and brothers, and who did not view his personal interests as being separate from those of Qin.

Fan Sui made a strong impression on King Zhao, and became his close confidant and advisor. The ancient chronicles record texts of memorials and speeches that Fan purportedly delivered to the king. We cannot know the veracity of such accounts. By the third century BCE a literary tradition had evolved among learned knights designed to prepare literati for a career in government service. Texts presented set speeches as examples of how to deliver persuasive advice or debate policy in an official setting. The career of famous figures such as Fan Sui was often the context of such speeches. Because students were expected to know the political history of the Zhou courts, the careers of influential officials provided convenient "stagings" for the composition of exemplary speeches. The reader would be familiar with the problems that had been faced by the figure in question, and would be given examples of how someone *in that situation* would use logic, rhetoric, literary allusion, and historical precedent to sway listeners to choose the right course of action.[23]

We thus cannot be sure whether the transmitted speeches and memorials of Fan Sui were actually delivered, or whether they represent later reconstructions by literati for the purpose of instruction. But we can be confident that over the course of months and years Fan Sui persuaded King Zhao to adopt a new set of priorities in the governance of Qin, and helped the king chart a course that ultimately won him independence from his mother, uncles, and brothers. Moreover, though the precise wording of the speeches attributed to Fan Sui may be embellished or imagined, the substance of their content almost certainly accurately reflects the general thrust of Fan's advice.

Fan extolled the inherent value of meritocracy: the potential effectiveness of a system in which officials are rewarded purely for the benefits they garner for the state, without regard to their personal status or intimacy with the ruler. He warned the king about the dangers of allowing individual officials to accrue too much power and influence, and of allowing the prestige of the throne to be eclipsed by the charismatic mystique of any of the king's subjects (such as his uncles and brothers). Finally, he pointed out to the king the ways in which his family's pursuit of its own interests had hamstrung the power of the state of Qin as a whole.

Fan showed the king that this last problem was especially egregious in the case of the king's elder uncle, Prime Minister Wei Ran. During the war with Qi, Wei Ran had managed to acquire the territory surrounding Tao (Ceramictown), which had been part of the destroyed kingdom of Song, as his personal fief. This was a particularly valuable prize, because Tao sat at the very center of the transport web that connected the many Zhou states and was the wealthiest trading entrepot of the Zhou world. The revenue from Tao that filled Wei Ran's personal coffers made him fabulously wealthy.

But the centrality of Tao to Wei Ran's personal economy created a divergence between his individual interests and those of the government of Qin that he ostensibly led. Wei Ran was persistently concerned for the security of his fief, because none of its territory was contiguous with the eastern frontier of Qin. His agents had to cross the states of Han and Wei to retrieve the revenue from Tao, and cross again on the way back to Qin with the wealth they had garnered, forcing Wei Ran to make concessions to Han and Wei so that he could continue to collect his profits. Wei Ran worried about the distant eastern state of Qi and planned campaigns to seize territory from Qi as a buffer to defend his fief of Tao. These campaigns entailed extraordinary expense, because they were conducted over such long supply lines and required the concession of free passage for Qin's armies from Han and Wei.

Fan Sui argued forcefully to King Zhao that Qin should not be pursuing the policy dictated by Wei Ran's pecuniary concerns. Since the days of King Xiao and Shang Yang, Qin had been engaged in a campaign to increase its power and influence over the Zhou states generally. That path, according to Fan, should, during King Zhao's reign, have led naturally to Qin becoming the new "Lord Protector" of the realm, but such an outcome would only be possible if the resources of the Qin government were used exclusively to strengthen the Qin state, not one of its officials or families. The logical strategy for Qin to pursue in the face of its current challenges was to cultivate the good will of far states like Qi and Yan, and to seek aggressive expansion at the expense of nearer states such as Han, Wei, Zhao, and Chu. Prime Minister Wei Ran's far-flung campaigns in support of his own fief were an extravagance that Qin could not afford.[24]

The relationship between King Zhao and Fan Sui did not lead immediately to a restructuring of the Qin court. Fan remained close to King Zhao for several years, continuing to confer with him and instruct him in matters of history and policy. In this endeavor he was almost certainly not alone. During the whole reign of the Mi-clan clique the power and scope of Qin rule continued to grow, and this is attributable in part to the self-sustaining durability and efficiency of the regular state institutions that had been developed in Qin since the tenure of Shang Yang. The fourth and third centuries BCE had seen the development throughout the many Zhou states (to varying degrees) of what is today (often disparagingly) called "the deep state": a matrix of meritocratically recruited, regularly organized, and routinely authorized officials with their own rationale and esprit de corps. Fan Sui became the point man of a quiet campaign on the part of these officials in Qin to win King Zhao over to the cause of political reform.

In 266 BCE, at least in part because of mounting tensions between Zhao and Qin, these efforts won out. In that year Fan Sui was raised to the rank of marquis and made prime minister. This was effectively a bloodless palace coup, ending the long rule of the Mi-clan clique. Wei Ran and the king's other uncle and brothers were sent out through the eastern Hangu Pass guarding the Qin heartland, to take up permanent residence in the conquered fiefs from which they had been drawing revenue for many years, and thus were removed from central court affairs. The gate warden who inspected Wei Ran's baggage train on his exit made note that the former prime minister's artistic treasures were more numerous than those of the king.²⁵ Wei Ran was ultimately buried in his fief of Tao. Upon his death it was converted into a centrally administered commandery under the direct rule of the Qin court.²⁶

Given how dramatic this shift in the power dynamics of the Qin court was, it is remarkable (and quite atypical in the annals of the time) that it transpired with so little violence. The chronicles do not, for example, clearly record what happened to the Queen Dowager Mi Bazi during this transition, or what role she might have played in brokering its resolution.²⁷ She died in 265 BCE and was buried with full state honors one month after her brother Wei Ran's departure from the home territory of Qin.²⁸ The coincidence might suggest that Mi Bazi met with foul play, but the sources suggest that she retained her power and influence to the very end of her life. On her deathbed she reportedly ordered that the new lover she had taken to replace the departed King of Yiqu should be buried with her. She was only persuaded not to carry through with the plan by the argument that if the dead have consciousness, her husband would object to her having a lover in the afterlife, and if they do not, there would be little point of having someone she cared for buried alive.²⁹ This of course does not prove that she met with no violence. She may have been quietly "disposed of," and the whole story could be a fabrication meant to slander her after her passing. Whatever the case may be, we can be sure that she was an imposing presence in Qin politics. It is a shame that the records do not give us a clearer picture of her life.

Though Fan Sui's ascent did not set off internecine violence within Qin, it was not without drama. During his tenure in Qin, Fan had continued to use the assumed identity of "Zhang Lu."³⁰ This was because the humiliation that Fan had been subjected to in Wei would have made him a figure of ridicule among the aristocrats in Qin. The fact that he had spent hours in a privy being urinated upon added the disgrace of bodily pollution to the raw insult done to his dignity.

Everyone in Wei thought "Fan Sui" was dead, but they knew that the new Prime Minister "Zhang Lu" of Qin had advocated for a policy of "befriending the far and attacking the near," and that, in a change from Wei Ran's tendency to cultivate good relations with Qin's eastern neighbors to maintain access to his fief at Tao, Zhang Lu would mobilize Qin's armies to assault Han and Wei. The King of Wei thus sent Fan Sui's old patron, Xu Jia, as an ambassador to try and negotiate peace with Qin.

When Xu Jia arrived in the Qin capital, Fan Sui donned tattered rags and went to visit the Wei ambassador in his guest hostel. Xu Jia was surprised to see

Fan Sui alive, but received him magnanimously. Fan claimed to be working as a laborer, which would have tallied with Xu Jia's expectations. Under ordinary circumstances, no knight who had suffered the indignities Fan Sui had endured could expect to ever mingle as a peer among those in elite society ever again. Xu Jia assumed that Fan Sui had capitulated to "social death," and since he was now living as a commoner posed no threat to anyone of Xu Jia's stature. He hosted Fan Sui to a "decent meal" and gifted him with one of his own silk robes so that he would not have to wear rags.

During dinner Xu Jia asked if Fan Sui knew anyone who could help him arrange an interview with Prime Minister Zhang Lu. Fan replied that the lord he served could arrange the meeting. Xu explained that he would need to borrow a carriage for the occasion, since his own team of horses had taken ill, and his carriage had broken an axle. Fan, continuing his ruse, offered to "borrow" a chariot from his lord and to serve as Xu's driver.

On the appointed day of the interview, Fan Sui drove Xu Jia to the palace gates and dismounted, explaining that he would precede his old patron into the audience hall and announce Xu Jia's arrival. Xu waited for a long while and finally asked the guards attending the gate why Fan Sui had not returned. The guards, of course, replied that they knew no Fan Sui, and when further questioned explained that Xu Jia's driver had been the Prime Minister Zhang Lu himself.

Xu Jia knew immediately that he was in mortal danger. As a commoner Fan Sui posed no threat to anyone, but as a marquis and a prime minister he would be compelled to take vengeance on anyone and everyone who had insulted him, to protect his own dignity and that of the state of Qin. Xu Jia stripped down to his bare torso and knelt before the palace gates, beseeching the guards to take a message to the prime minister, begging for forgiveness. He was led into the audience hall where, half-naked, he knelt before Fan Sui, who was now dressed in the splendor befitting his new rank and seated amidst the grandeur of the Qin court. Xu admitted that his offense against Fan Sui merited death, but Fan declared that he would spare Xu Jia's life on account of the kindness that his old patron had displayed in gifting "poor" Fan Sui with one of his own silk robes. He demanded, however, that Xu Jia return to Wei and deliver an ultimatum to its king. The Wei prime minister who had ordered Fan Sui beaten would have to be killed, and his head sent to Qin. Otherwise the armies of Qin would raze the Wei capital of Greatbridge to the ground.

On receiving this message the Prime Minister of Wei fled, seeking refuge in the palace of Lord Pingyuan (Zhao Sheng, d. 252 BCE), a powerful scion of the

Zhao ruling clan (whom we will speak more about later). He found no security there or anywhere else, however. The King of Qin himself took up Fan Sui's vendetta, and through cunning and coercion hounded the former Prime Minister of Wei until he was finally forced to commit suicide, angry and aggrieved.[31]

The lengths to which King Zhao of Qin went to avenge Fan Sui show how resilient the norms of aristocratic society remained in the last decades of the Warring States, despite their being in such tension with the values and logic of the new bureaucratic state. In the ethos that Fan Sui himself had championed, King Zhao's duty to his prime minister was discharged in heeding good advice and rewarding the prime minister fairly for his service. But in the worldview of the nobility, things could not be so simple. King Zhao had sided with Fan Sui against his own mother, brothers, and uncles. The king's own dignity was thus inextricably intertwined with that of Fan Sui: he had treated Fan Sui "as if he were family." This was one of the reasons that the king had raised Fan to the rank of marquis: it was unseemly of a king to take the part of a lowly knight against his own highborn relations. In that same light, when it became public knowledge that the Prime Minister of Wei had dealt such a terrible insult to Fan Sui, it became incumbent upon the king to move Heaven and Earth to expunge that stain. Otherwise, the king's own majesty would be profaned.[32]

At the same time that the court of Qin was being reorganized under the leadership of Fan Sui, new leadership took the fore in the rival kingdom of Zhao. The violent death of the "Ruling Father" had left the court in the effective control of a clique led by one of the adolescent King Huiwen of Zhao's great uncles. But as King Huiwen grew into his majority he, like his counterpart in Qin, invested authority in a group of officials chosen for skill and merit. As had been the case in Qin, in Zhao this process of reform was strained by tensions between the traditional ethos of the Zhou aristocracy and the needs of new bureaucratic and meritocratic political systems.

An initial significant appointment came as a result of the alliance against Qi. The man brought to prominence by this crisis was named Yue Yi (fl. ca. 290 BCE). Yue Yi was a humble knight with a lofty pedigree. He was a descendant of Yue Yang, the Wei commander who had initially conquered the state of Zhongshan. Yue Yang had been given a fief in Zhongshan, and his clan continued to reside there even after the kingdom had been revived. When King Wuling of Zhao finally destroyed Zhongshan, Yue Yi had migrated to Zhao and served among its officials, where he earned a reputation as a skilled strategist and capable military commander.

In the wake of King Wuling's death, Yue Yi, who had earned his good name under Wuling's patronage, left Zhao. His wanderings eventually brought him into the service of the King of Yan, who valued his counsel highly. During negotiations over the alliance against Qi, the courts of Zhao and Yan, in search of a means to secure their mutual cooperation, turned to Yue Yi as a man of proven worth who had roots in both states. He was made joint Prime Minister of Zhao and Yan and executed the plan that would lead ultimately to the sack of Qi's capital.[33]

During Yue Yi's tenure as prime minister the Zhao court enlisted several distinguished officials of exceptional merit. Among these was Lian Po (fl. ca. 275 BCE), who served as a field commander in Qi and helped secure major victories in the conquest and pacification of that state. In the wake of Qi's defeat, Lian Po led Zhao's forces to major victories over Wei and Han, establishing himself as one of the most consistently successful military leaders of the era.[34]

With Qi humbled, the rivalry between Qin and Zhao escalated, and the pressure to enlist talented civil leaders and diplomats in the Zhao court mounted. This climate of rising tension is exemplified by the career of Lin Xiangru (d. ca. 260 BCE), a poor knight who rose from among the ranks of Zhao's state servitors and became a leading policy strategist. He had served with only minor distinction on the staff of Zhao's Prefect of Eunuchs, but when a particularly sensitive diplomatic mission to Qin arose from which more senior officials shrank in fear, Lin's patron put him forward as the man whose talents were up to the task.

Zhao had come into possession of one of the prized regalia of the kingdom of Chu, the Circular Jade of the He Clan (*Heshi bi*).[35] The Circular Jade was a fabled treasure celebrated in many tales passed down from the Warring States. Such rare objects were a key dimension of "soft power" among the Zhou states (see Fig. 19). The acquisition and ritual display of uniquely beautiful and costly talismans were overt markers of a court's power, stability, and legitimacy, signs that its ruling dynasty was replete with Potency and favored by the gods and ancestral spirits.

In an attempt to intimidate his rival ruler, the King of Qin sent an envoy to Zhao offering the cession of 15 cities in exchange for the Circular Jade of the He Clan. Everyone at the Zhao court understood this as a test of will and power. The Qin court, in episodes like its kidnapping of the King of Chu, had proven itself unlikely to keep faith with the kind of bargain it was offering at that moment. If Zhao sent an emissary to Qin bearing the Jade and did not

Fig. 19. Exquisitely polished and carved jade *bi* discs such as this one were valued treasure objects throughout the Warring States. (Source: Wikimedia Commons.)

receive the promised cities, it would appear weak. Any emissary who took up the mission was likely doomed to failure. The best he could expect was to humiliate himself and his sovereign, the worst was to end up a prisoner in Qin or a corpse.

Lin Xiangru promised that he would return from the mission having either secured the cession of the promised cities or having retained the Circular Jade. On initially meeting with the King of Qin, Lin reverently handed over the treasured object, only to see the king pass it jovially among his wives and concubines for their amusement. From this flippancy Lin Xiangru could see that the King of Qin was not dealing in good faith. He thus pretended that the Jade had a flaw and asked for it to be handed back to him so that he could show it to the king. Once the Jade was in his hands again, Lin Xiangru backed up to a pillar and berated the King of Qin, threatening to smash the Jade against the pillar unless the king atoned for his rudeness and mendacity.

The king, convinced that Lin Xiangru did not make idle threats, agreed to fast for five days to purify himself for receiving the Jade in a formal ceremony. Lin Xiangru was not satisfied that the King of Qin could be trusted, so during the fasting period he ordered one of the knights in his retinue to don the coarse robes of a commoner and flee back to Zhao with the Circular Jade concealed on his person. On meeting with the King of Qin, Lin Xiangru did not try to conceal his actions. As a sign that Zhao had brave officials and would not be intimidated, he confessed having reneged on the offer of the Circular Jade and invited the king to boil him alive for his insolence. The courtiers of Qin were enraged and ready to put Lin Xiangru to death, but the King of Qin, perhaps understanding that martyring Lin Xiangru would only exacerbate relations with Zhao without making Qin look any stronger (quite the contrary), sent Lin home after performing the formal ceremonies of parting.

This success earned Lin Xiangru a promotion to Senior Grandee and a position on the permanent staff of the King of Zhao himself. In that capacity he accompanied the King of Zhao on another risky diplomatic trip to Qin. This time the King of Qin had invited King Huiwen of Zhao to negotiations inside Qin's territory. King Huiwen wanted to refuse the invitation, fearing what had happened to the King of Chu. On being advised that to refuse the invitation would make Zhao appear weak, King Huiwen undertook the journey to Qin, agreeing that his heir should be crowned king if he did not return in 30 days.

The King of Qin did not attempt to hold his royal guest hostage, but he did use the occasion of their meeting to intimidate and humiliate his fellow sovereign. During a banquet, the King of Qin became drunk and, noting that he had heard of his guest's fondness for music, asked to hear him play. The King of Zhao, perhaps not suspecting any hostile intent, strummed a zither that was provided for him. As soon as he did so, the official scribe of Qin who was on hand to record the events of the banquets came forward and announced that the record would show that the King of Qin had ordered the King of Zhao to play the zither.

This was a terrible insult to the dignity of Zhao. Lin Xiangru, who was part of Zhao's official retinue, responded quickly. He rose and declared that he had heard of the King of Qin's skill in playing the tunes of his own state. He wondered whether the king might strum out a rhythm on a clay pot for the assembly to hear. The King of Qin angrily refused, but Lin Xiangru picked up a clay pot and rushed to kneel before the king, holding the pot upside down for the king to strum. When the king still resisted, Lin Xiangru threatened to cut his own throat and splash blood over the king's robes. This kind of threat is recorded at many places in the ancient chronicles. It exhibited the willingness of brave knights to die in service of their states, even if it was only to achieve the object of polluting the robes of the powerful with human blood.[36] Qin courtiers rushed forward to intercede, but Lin Xiangru disoriented them by making his eyes wide and shouting loudly. Such uncourtly behavior brought them up short.

The King of Qin, unnerved, tapped once on the bottom of Lin's clay pot. Lin Xiangru turned to the Qin scribe and ordered him to record that the King of Qin had played the pot for the King of Zhao. The King of Qin tried to recover the initiative by demanding that Zhao cede 15 cities as a "gift" to Qin. Refusing to be intimidated, Lin Xiangru rejoined immediately that Qin should give its capital Xianyang as a gift to Zhao. The King of Qin's bluff had been called. He knew that Qin was not ready for all-out war with Zhao, so he returned to quietly drinking his wine and finished the banquet without revisiting the matter of exchanging "gifts."

For having so boldly saved the face of his king, Lin Xiangru was again promoted on his return to Zhao. This elevation gave him equal rank and precedence as Lian Po, the famed military commander of the wars against Qi. Lian felt that both his birth and his service entitled him to more formal honor than Lin Xiangru, who was of humbler parentage and whose service to Zhao bore no military distinction. Lian Po made it generally known that he would take the first opportunity to publicly insult Lin Xiangru. This would, in the unwritten code of the Zhou aristocracy, have necessitated a duel, and most likely led to the death of one or both men.

Lin Xiangru began to avoid Lian Po. He pleaded illness so that he would not have to attend court at the same time as Lian Po and could avoid an argument over ranking. One day as he was leaving home in his carriage, Lin Xiangru saw Lian Po in the distance and ordered his carriage to turn off the road so that he would not be seen. This prompted the men in Lin Xiangru's retinue to immediately offer their resignation. If Lin was going to show himself a coward he would eventually be cast out of elite society, and his subordinates would suffer the same disgrace. They told him as much when they pleaded to be released from his service.

In the face of this challenge Lin Xiangru demonstrated his usual coolness under fire. He asked his men how they would compare Lian Po to the King of Qin: which did they feel was more dangerous? All of them admitted that the King of Qin had many more means than Lian Po to do a body certain harm. Lin then asked his men why, having seen that Lin was not afraid to shout down the King of Qin, they would imagine that he avoided Lian Po out of cowardice? Lin explained that he was avoiding Lian Po out of a sense of duty to Zhao. Qin was a mighty opponent and Zhao would need the talents of both Lin Xiangru and Lian Po to withstand that threat. "When a pair of tigers fight, one of them cannot live." If Lin Xiangru allowed the quarrel between him and Lian Po to cause either man's death, it would injure Zhao. Lin had thus determined to risk being thought a coward so that he could keep the strength of Zhao whole.

When Lian Po heard about this conversation he was ashamed. He offered himself at Lin Xiangru's gate, naked to the waist and bearing a thorn branch, with which he begged to be lashed. Instead, Lin Xiangru greeted him as a friend, and the two men swore to die together as comrades.[37]

The abortive feud between Lian Po and Lin Xiangru, like the drama surrounding the King of Qin's efforts to avenge the insults done to Fan Sui, embodies some of the key forces driving the social, cultural, and political changes of the Warring States. The governments of the Zhou states were increasingly reorganizing along routine and impersonal lines, even as the ethos of the Bronze Age aristocracy continued to powerfully influence attitudes and behaviors among the members of elite society, especially as one approached the top of the status pyramid. These two trends remained in conflict to the end of the Warring States, but as the case of Zhao and Qin demonstrates, the sometimes slow but persistently steady shift towards bureaucracy and meritocracy was driven by the competition *between* states. The more urgent and zero-sum the contest between states became, the more consistently aristocratic norms gave way in favor of the needs of the new routinized fiscal-military state.

This pattern was evident once again in the career of another key player in the geopolitical rivalry between Zhao and Qin: Zhao She (fl. ca. 270 BCE). He was a scion of the Zhao ruling clan, but because the clan was so large Zhao She was, like Tian Dan in Qi, a person of humble circumstances, compelled to earn his living by his own efforts and talents. Zhao She served as a tax collector under King Huiwen of Zhao.

In that capacity Zhao She was mobilized in a campaign to strengthen the kingdom's treasury by reinforcing the collection of revenue. We do not know the particulars of this campaign, but it is another sign that the rivalry between Zhao and Qin was exerting pressure for reform on both kingdoms, one in response to the other. Just as Fan Sui led the Qin government in breaking the hold of the Mi-clan clique and clawing back some of the wealth that cabal had hoarded for itself, the Zhao court began to consolidate the wealth of the kingdom in the hands of the central government, rather than that of the princely houses. To that end Zhao She was assigned to collect from the estate of the king's brother, Lord Pingyuan. The lord's household officials would not comply with Zhao She's investigation of the estate, and in accordance with the laws of the kingdom, Zhao She put nine of them to death.

Lord Pingyuan was enraged at this insult and was prepared to execute the upstart tax collector who trespassed on his dignity. Zhao She rebuked him, explaining that if the treasury of Zhao were depleted, Lord Pingyuan himself would be taken down by the resulting disaster. Conversely, if someone as prestigious as Lord Pingyuan would make a good example of complying with the new tax policy, the policy itself would be greatly successful, the kingdom made strong, and Lord Pingyuan himself would feel much of the resulting benefit. Meanwhile, the short-term insult to Lord Pingyuan was not worth bothering about, since as the king's brother he had dignity to spare—no one would ever question his impeccable pedigree.

Lord Pingyuan was persuaded by this argument and impressed by Zhao She's courage and perspicacity. He not only spared Zhao She but recommended him to his brother the king, who promoted Zhao She to supervise the new tax policy for the entire kingdom. In this way Zhao She came to serve alongside Lian Po and Lin Xiangru as one of the chief councilors of state.

When the escalating cold war between Qin and Zhao broke finally into hot conflict, it was Zhao She who struck the first blow for Zhao. In 269 BCE Qin launched an invading army far from its eastern frontier, with the objective of capturing the strategic citadel of Eyu, which threatened the approaches to the Zhao capital of Handan. To reach the objective the Qin assault force had to cross the territory of both Wei and Han.[38]

The Qin court was waging war to "punish" Zhao for having reneged on a deal to swap land.[39] But the strategy and goals of this campaign were not a simple expression of the intensifying rivalry between Qin and Zhao. In 269 BCE Wei Ran was still Prime Minister of Qin, so his military operations were being done in support of the financial interests of himself and his kin. This is why the Qin court had taken such a keen interest in exchanging land with Zhao, and why its armies were operating along such extended supply lines so far from the kingdom's eastern frontier. The objective was not merely to punish Zhao, but to further open and secure the lines of communication between the Qin homeland and the fiefs that had been carved out of the eastern states for Wei Ran and the other members of the Mi-clan clique.

The initial stages of the Eyu campaign showed that Qin planners could be clever. The terrain around the city was rugged hill country, ill-suited to the use of the cavalry units which had become foundational to Zhao's power. When the Qin armies had invested the region, King Huiwen of Zhao summoned first Lian Po and then another minister and asked if the Qin forces could be dislodged. Both men declared in succession that the rough terrain made a counter-attack too risky. The king then summoned Zhao She and put the same question to him. Zhao She said that the terrain made any conflict around Eyu analogous to putting two rats in a hole to fight. In such cases boldness and aggression will take the day.

Zhao She was given overall command of the counter-attack and set out from Handan with a large force to repel the Qin invaders. At the outset of the campaign he assembled the army and announced that anyone who offered him any military advice during their operations would be put to death. When the army had marched less than 10 kilometers from Handan, Zhao She ordered it to make camp and to begin building fortifications.

One of his officers warned Zhao She that the Qin army had garrisoned Eyu and sent an assault force toward Handan. The drums of the assault force were loud enough to shake the roofs of every house in Wu'an, a city along the capital road. If Zhao She did not advance quickly, Wu'an would also fall to the Qin invasion force. Zhao She had the man beheaded on the spot.

Zhao She spent 28 days strengthening the fortifications of his camp. A Qin scout was caught in the encampment. Zhao She dined with the man, and afterwards released him to return to his own army, presumably bearing the message that the soldiers of Zhao were well dug-in and ready to repel the soldiers of Qin should they try to advance on Zhao's capital. The Qin commanders, on hearing the scout's report, celebrated the fact that Zhao had effectively ceded Eyu and its adjoining territory to Qin.

While the Qin army celebrated, Zhao She broke camp and ordered his best forces to rush forward, taking up position between the Qin garrison at Eyu and the advance force in Wu'an. The Zhao soldiers traversed more than 20 kilometers in a single overnight maneuver. Zhao She had thus, by lulling his Qin opponents into a false sense of security, reclaimed the advantage that Zhao enjoyed from the possession of its fine cavalry units. The terrain would not allow the soldiers of Zhao to fight from horseback, but they could be moved with blinding speed and take up positions that gave them the element of surprise.

When the Zhao forces arrived in the zone of conflict, one of Zhao She's subcommanders begged to incur a death sentence in order to offer some advice. Given leave to speak, the officer suggested that Zhao She take up position on a point of high ground that would give Zhao forces a critical advantage. The Qin leaders were disoriented and enraged; they could be counted on to join combat wherever the Zhao army offered battle. The man pleaded to be beheaded on the spot like his comrade, but Zhao She brushed the suggestion aside with a promise that the death sentence would be carried out later. The officer most likely guessed before speaking that he would be spared. The subterfuge that Zhao She had been building with his draconian measures had been exposed, there was no longer any need to "keep the genie in the bottle."

Zhao She once again rushed his mounted forces to the elevated position suggested by his subordinate. As that man had predicted, the Qin units speeding south from Eyu and north from Wu'an tried to dislodge Zhao's archers from the hill on which they had deployed, but successive attack waves failed to reach the summit. Zhao She counter-attacked downhill and routed the Qin army with heavy casualties. The Qin commanders were forced to abandon both Eyu and Wu'an and return home, having incurred heavy losses of men and equipment.

Zhao She had proven himself a paragon of the new ethos of military command articulated in the teachings of figures like "Master Sun." He had used a confusing combination of "orthodox" and "extraordinary" tactical maneuvers to disorient and misdirect the enemy, and had been able to force battle on his own terms, when victory was assured. He became instantly celebrated as a hero in Zhao and was enfeoffed as "Lord of Mafu."[40]

The next year the Qin court launched another long-distance expedition against the city of Ji, which stood along a trade route into Wei Ran's fief of Tao. Lian Po took command of the force sent to interdict that attack, and like Zhao She he succeeded at repulsing the Qin invaders with heavy casualties.[41] These expensive defeats, in combination with Queen Dowager Mi Bazi's role in setting off the costly war against Yiqu, contributed to the decision of King Zhao of Qin to enlist the talents of Fan Sui and take the reins of government away from his uncles, mother, and brothers. Fan Sui became prime minister less than three years after the debacle at Eyu, in 266 BCE.[42] He immediately reoriented Qin's strategy to focus its power on the expansion of its eastern frontiers, rather than on the maintenance of the complex set of compromises and accommodations that kept revenue flowing into the coffers of the ruling clan from their disparate detached fiefs.

The far-flung campaigns of Wei Ran had depleted Qin's military resources, but Fan Sui rebuilt the treasury and armed forces while at the same time remaining on the offensive in the east. On his orders, the armies of Qin steadily encroached upon the kingdom's eastern neighbors, winning territory from either Han, Wei or Zhao (or some combination of these states) in every year following his assumption of the prime minister's seat.[43]

The conflict between Zhao and Qin built toward a showdown. King Huiwen of Zhao died in 266 BCE and was succeeded by his son Zhao Dan, who was known posthumously as King Xiaocheng (The "Filially Accomplished" King, r. 265–245 BCE).[44] In 262 BCE King Xiaocheng had a strange dream. He was wearing clothes on which the embroidery had been turned inside-out and mounted a flying dragon. He flew up toward Heaven, but fell back down before reaching his objective. On the ground he found gold and jade piled as high as a mountain.

The next day the king summoned his diviners to interpret his dream. They explained that the inside-out embroidery was a sign of incompleteness. Falling before reaching Heaven showed that the king had ambition but not the means to fulfill it. Finally, the pile of gold and jade was a sign that the king was beset by worries.

Three days after his dream was explained the king received an extraordinary envoy. He was a messenger from the Prefect of the Upper Commandery of Zhao's "brother state" and neighbor, the kingdom of Han. Han had been invaded by Qin and had agreed to cede its Upper Commandery to Qin in order to make peace. Rather than obey his king's orders to surrender his territory to Qin, the Prefect had called the elders and elites of Upper Commandery together and proposed that rather than become the subjects of Qin, they should offer their allegiance to Zhao, with which the Upper Commandery also shared a border.[45]

It was an extraordinary moment, a gambit of a kind for which we do not have any parallel cases in the annals of the Warring States. Why did the Prefect act this way? His motives are easy to guess at: as the agent who delivered new territory to the King of Zhao, he could expect to be rewarded. What is less easy to understand is why the local elites of Upper Commandery went along with him. Their compliance would have been essential: once the order to surrender his post came from the Han capital under official seal, his formal authority over the local people was nullified. Without the "buy-in" of the local leaders of the Upper Commandery, the Prefect's plan would have been unworkable (were this not the case, such a maneuver would almost certainly have been attempted by some earlier ambitious regional magistrate). In this respect, the events of 262 BCE (like the story of Ximen Bao and the cult of the River God discussed in Chapter 5) give the lie to modern myths about the "oriental despotism" of Warring States society. The new institutions of bureaucratic local administration that had been developing throughout the Zhou world since even before the coup of 481 BCE entailed "power-sharing" as much as or more than "power-concentration."

The agency of the local leaders of Upper Commandery is easier to explain than their reasons for complying with the Prefect's plan, however. It is possible that the people of Upper Commandery preferred to join the Zhao commonwealth rather than that of Qin because of historical or cultural affinities (in other words, the long tradition of Han and Zhao having been "brother states," and the reputation of Qin as being "semi-barbarous"). But that explanation seems wanting. From the days of King Wuling the court culture of Zhao had been progressively incorporating more "barbarous" customs and traditions and, in the long view, the frequency of military hostilities between Zhao and Han was close to what had been the case between Han and Qin.

A more likely explanation, from the perspective of the particular circumstances of 262 BCE, resides in the rise of Fan Sui in 266 BCE to become Prime Minister of Qin. Qin's demand for the cession of Upper Commandery was in following with Fan Sui's resolution to adopt a new policy of "befriending the far and subjugating the near." Fan Sui's predecessors, Wei Ran and the other members of the Mi-clan clique, had most likely offered special concessions and inducements to the officials and local elites of Upper Commandery in order to secure access to their detached fiefs, such as Tao.

The change of regime in Qin had brought with it bad times for Upper Commandery. Where the old Qin rulers had viewed the leaders and elites of Upper Commandery as "partners" (of a kind), Fan Sui's government viewed (and would treat) them as conquered subjects who should be exploited for the good of the Qin state. This was all the more true because the revenues paid to them by the Mi-clan clique belonged, in the view of Fan Sui and his officials, in the coffers of the Qin treasury, and should be reclaimed. This most likely explains why the elites of Upper Commandery felt it was worthwhile to risk brokering a "new deal" for themselves with the rulers of Zhao.

Though the benefits sought by the leaders of Upper Commandery may have been substantial, the risks they incurred were likewise very real. King Xiaocheng of Zhao immediately recognized this as a situation fraught with both opportunity and danger. He called his ministers together to debate whether the Prefect's offer should be entertained. Resistance to doing so was strong. One minister warned that "the sages always greatly feared baseless profit."[46] Though the sentiment was expressed in abstract terms and cloaked in the prestige of antiquity, the principle at stake was quite urgent. The Prefect's plan was a complete break with the norms of interstate diplomacy that had evolved since the first "royal" summit of 334 BCE. If the King of Qin let a local official (even that of another kingdom) undo his own negotiations, his writ became void, and his capacity to use diplomacy as an instrument of power was nullified. For the Zhao court to accept the offer of the Prefect of Han's Upper Commandery meant certain and all-out war with Qin, and many of King Xiaocheng's officials doubted that Zhao was ready for such a confrontation.

King Xiaocheng was inclined to view the moment as one more of opportunity than peril. He argued that the profit he stood to gain was not baseless, but reflected the desire of the people of Upper Commandery for a ruler of true Potency. Perhaps he saw in his dream an omen that confirmed his inclination: where before he had only unfulfilled ambitions to expand the territory of Zhao, this offer from the Prefect of Upper Commandery was giving him the means to achieve that end.

Envoys were sent from Zhao accepting the offered fealty of the Prefect of Upper Commandery. The Prefect and his subordinate district magistrates were all given the hereditary rank of marquis. The Prefect was granted an estate comprising three cities that had the administration of 10,000 households each, his subordinates were given estates of three cities that controlled 5,000 households each. Upper Commandery itself was said to house 17 cities, so the offer of nine cities as fiefs is significant. King Xiaocheng had effectively agreed to split the revenue to be derived from Upper Commandery with the Prefect and his subordinates, 50/50.[47]

Qin mobilized for war. In 260 BCE an army under the command of a general named Wang He crossed into Upper Commandery, creating a wave of refugees that fled to Zhao. Lian Po was given command of the retaliatory force from Zhao. Both kingdoms committed the bulk of their armed forces to the conflict.

As the courtiers of Zhao had feared, Qin had the advantage in men and material. Beyond this, the terrain of Upper Commandery impeded the cavalry forces of Zhao. The region was mountainous and obstructed, even more ill-suited to cavalry warfare than the terrain on which Zhao She had waged his campaign to reclaim Eyu. The armies of Qin and Zhao met on the banks of the Dan River, which flowed through a valley bracketed by steep mountains. After a few bloody skirmishes between advance forces that made manifest the difficulty and danger of attempting mobile warfare in such constricted terrain, both armies dug in to fortified positions on high ground in the vicinity of a town ironically named Changping (Longpeace).[48]

The campaign congealed into a contest of attrition. The opposing armies, by ancient accounts (almost certainly exaggerated) amounting together to almost one million soldiers, faced each other along a battle front that stretched for 20 kilometers of earthworks and trenches, each side preparing multiple redundant lines of defense to repulse any attack from the enemy. In this way a stalemate persisted for months.

Lian Po, Zhao's veteran commander, remained committed to a strategy of caution. Given that the terrain favored infantry over cavalry, robbing Zhao of the one solid advantage it enjoyed over Qin, Lian Po calculated that attrition was Zhao's best chance at victory. The battle lines of Changping were much closer to the home territory of Zhao than they were to that of Qin. Given enough time, cold, hunger, illness, and desertion would take a greater toll on the forces of Qin than those of Zhao. Lian Po held his defensive lines and resisted any urge or encouragement to go on the attack.[49]

King Xiaocheng of Zhao became impatient with what he perceived to be Lian Po's lack of aggression. In this he was abetted by agents of Qin acting inside Zhao on the orders of Fan Sui. These were most likely what the *Sunzi bingfa* calls "turned spies":[50] officials of the Zhao court who had been enlisted to the service of Qin by bribes. They spread the rumor that the Qin court was relieved to know that Lian Po was in command and only feared that command of the Zhao army would be given to Zhao She's son Zhao Kuo.

By 261 BCE Zhao She, the hero of Eyu, had died, and his title of "Lord of Mafu" had been inherited by his son Zhao Kuo. Zhao Kuo had been trained by his father and had the reputation of being a brilliant student of military affairs. In 260 BCE, when the campaign at Changping had been dragging on for several months, King Xiaocheng of Zhao ordered that Lian Po be relieved of command and replaced by Zhao Kuo.[51]

When she heard of Zhao Kuo's new commission his mother remonstrated with the king. Zhao Kuo, she explained, was a brilliant theorist, but he lacked his father's wisdom and character. Zhao She had been a close comrade of his soldiers and shared their adversity on campaign. Zhao Kuo was aloof and selfish and thought only of his own ambition. If he was going to be given command, his mother pleaded that she be excused in advance for any collective responsibility for his malpractice that the law might place on his family. King Xiaocheng agreed to Zhao's mother's request for advance absolution, but ignored her warning against employing her son.[52]

When the news reached Qin that Lian Po had been replaced by Zhao Kuo, the Qin court secretly made a change of their own. They sent Bai Qi, the commander who had already helmed many of the greatest victories in the military annals of the Warring States, to replace Wang He, the general who had overseen

Qin's offensive for the many months since the invasion of Upper Commandery had begun. It was a classic subterfuge drawn directly from the new military doctrine of the age. The old aristocratic image of a commander had been a very visible and ostentatious paragon whose overt courage and grandiosity was thought to be an inspiration to his fellow noble warriors. The new commander was a quiet, virtually invisible functionary whose chief function was to gather, analyze, and devise tactical plans on the basis of intelligence. Because this new commander was (unlike the aristocratic warrior of old, who always had to defer to the prerogatives of his lieutenants, who were his noble peers) in complete and regular control of all aspects of the campaign, everything about him, even his identity, was a source of potential intelligence for the enemy.[53] The Qin court concealed the fact that Bai Qi had taken command because they did not want Zhao Kuo to know just what kind of exceptional genius his counterpart was.

The tactical plan Bai Qi devised was simple but elegant. In effect, he deployed a variant of the same strategy Zhao Kuo's father had used in the campaign for Eyu. He ordered a direct assault on a section of the Zhao fortified line. After a period of fierce fighting, the Qin forces broke and ran, fleeing back toward their own lines in feigned exhaustion and terror.

Zhao Kuo took the bait. Bai Qi had created the illusion of an opportunity to engage in the type of mobile warfare in which Zhao had the advantage. Zhao Kuo ordered his forces to follow the retreating Qin soldiers in hot pursuit, and he took personal command of a massed counter-attack. He chased the retreating enemy across the valley floor to the first line of Qin fortifications, where his counter-attack was bloodily repulsed.

While Zhao Kuo set off on his wild goose chase, Bai Qi sprang his trap. Two forces that Bai Qi had held in reserve emerged from the flanking ends of the Qin line. The first was a force of 5,000 cavalry, which Bai Qi employed for their speed just as Zhao Kuo's father had done. They were able to race behind the Zhao assault force and find the point in the Zhao defensive line that had been left weakly defended by the rush forward to pursue the retreating enemy. As the *Sunzi bingfa* says, "When an opening appears, be as fast as a racing hare."[54] The Qin cavalry began exploiting the weak point in the Zhao line and were followed quickly by Bai Qi's second reserve force of 25,000 elite infantry.

Together the two Qin assault forces were able to overrun Zhao's first line of fortified defenses. When Zhao Kuo and his soldiers finally gave up their attempt to breach the staunchly defended Qin front line and returned across the valley floor, they found their own trenches and barricades manned against them by

Qin soldiers. Bai Qi had effectively divided the Zhao army in two. Half of the Zhao force, with their commander among them, was trapped on the valley floor, hemmed in by fortified Qin soldiers on all sides.

When news of this victory reached the Qin court, King Zhao of Qin personally traveled to the region and issued a general call for recruits, promising that whoever joined the Qin assault would be rewarded with an elevation in "merit rank" of one grade. In this way Qin was able to recruit new forces that maneuvered behind the Zhao army as a whole, cutting off the routes through the mountainous terrain by which reinforcements and supplies might be sent even to the Zhao soldiers who were not trapped on the valley floor.

Both halves of the Zhao army dug into fortified positions and waited, hoping that relief would arrive. Zhao's best hope at this juncture was that other states such as Wei or Chu would send forces to lift the siege and help Zhao's army slip the noose. This was the point at which King Xiaocheng of Zhao's folly in ignoring the warnings of his own ministers became most plain. The other courts of the Warring States could not readily come to Zhao's aid, because the principle at stake in the Changping campaign worked too much against the interests of all kings. Any king who defended the power of a regional Prefect to disobey his own court was inviting catastrophe. If Zhao and the leaders of Han's Upper Commandery succeeded in setting a precedent, the territorial cohesion of every state was thrown into question, and the efficacy of all throne-to-throne diplomacy was potentially undermined.[55] King Xiaocheng's ministers had tried to warn him that this would be the case, and now it was too late.

Zhao Kuo and his trapped soldiers held their ground for 46 days. By the end of that time the Zhao army had begun to starve, and Zhao Kuo realized that if he waited much longer his soldiers would be too weak to defend themselves, much less mount an assault. He personally led an attack on the Qin line, hoping to punch a hole in the Qin fortifications that would enable the army to escape. The assault failed at the cost of thousands of casualties, among whom was Zhao Kuo himself.

Starving, demoralized, and without a commander, the Zhao army surrendered. Bai Qi (most likely with the explicit assent of the Fan Sui, King Zhao, and the rest of the Qin court) felt that the soldiers of Zhao could not be treated with the ordinary level of clemency that might be extended to defeated foes. Among the prisoners were some of the leaders of Upper Commandery whose presumption had first ignited the conflict. An example would have to be made to show the world that the throne of Qin would not be profaned in the manner that Zhao and the leaders of Upper Commandery had dared to attempt.

According to the ancient chronicles, all but 240 youths from among the defeated Zhao soldiers were buried alive. That small handful of survivors was hand-picked by Bai Qi to bring word of Zhao's punishment to the rest of the Zhou world. Many accounts put the number of Zhao dead at 450,000.[56] That figure is almost certainly an exaggeration. Such a large number of men would never have acquiesced to being buried alive, even if they had been forced to fight and die trying to save themselves with their bare hands. But the ancient histories are united in reporting that the Changping campaign ended with an act of terror committed by Qin of sufficient enormity to shock and awe the Zhou world. Modern archaeological excavations at the site of the battle of Changping do not confirm the enormous casualty figures reported in ancient sources. But mass graves have been discovered that corroborate testimony that the defeated soldiers of Zhao met a grisly end unprecedented in the annals of the Warring States (see Fig. 20).[57]

The Changping campaign was a major turning point in the geostrategic affairs of the Zhou states. It broke the power of Zhao, which we shall see in the next chapter was placed in peril of extinction in the immediate aftermath of the Changping catastrophe. From that point on, though the Zhou realm remained a multipolar world, there was no state that could contend with Qin as a leading power. It would be an exaggeration to assert that the conquest of the eastern states by Qin was foreordained by the events of 260 BCE, but any successful effort to resist the encroaching might of Qin would, from then on, require the coordinated initiative of two or more states that were effectively economic and military peers.

The bilateral contest between Zhao and Qin that transpired between the defeat of Qi in 284 BCE and the battle of Changping in 260 BCE presents a fascinating study of some of the social and political forces that were driving the greater dynamic of the whole Warring States in microcosm. Both kingdoms exerted pressure upon one another to break the dysfunctional restraints of aristocratic tradition and optimize the bureaucratic and meritocratic mechanisms of the emerging fiscal-military state. Both kingdoms worked aggressively to reorganize socially (by, for example, incorporating non-Sinitic peoples and elites into the larger matrix of rule) and economically in pursuit of maximum strategic power. Both kingdoms learned hard lessons about the necessity of not only drawing deeply upon the material resources of the fields, forests, rivers, and mountains, but also upon the human talents of their servitors.

At times the sources recording these events present such a clear picture of a world changing along particular lines that we might suspect scribal manipulation. The literati who composed and transmitted the ancient chronicles had a

Fig. 20. Excavations at the site of the battle of Changping (260 BCE) revealed several mass graves, suggesting that ancient reports of massive casualties inflicted on the defeated army of Zhao by Qin victors have some basis in fact. (Source: *Jingji guancha wang*, Beijing, https://www.eeo.com.)

stake in the continuing growth and viability of a bureaucratic and meritocratic order. Incidents like that of Zhao Kuo's mother pleading against his promotion to commander read like embellishments, conveying the sense that "the historian doth protest too much." The episode boldly underscores the fact that qualities of leadership are not hereditary, and that it would behoove us as a society to stop acting as if they were, even in the case of our own families.

But though the record may be embellished, these interventions are rhetorical flourishes rather than radical distortions. The bare facts of the conflict between Zhao and Qin do not require much embellishment to demonstrate that competition drives social and political reform. In the careers of remarkable figures like Fan Sui and Zhao She we can see personal embodiments of historical forces that would continue to resonate far beyond and long after the Warring States, and that indeed arguably continue to do so even today.

It would be wrong to assume, however, that the resolution of the conflict between Zhao and Qin settled all questions about the wisdom and necessity of political reform. The battle of Changping did not leave behind a world ruled exclusively by meritocratically chosen officials such as Fan Sui or talented military commanders such as Bai Qi. As the eastern states grappled with the challenge of responding to Zhao's massive defeat at the hands of Qin, several key figures emerged as outstanding leaders. These men resembled Fan Sui much less than they did Tian Wen, the Lord Mengchang, who had used his title and wealth to develop a huge retinue of knights that he crafted into a movable "political machine."

Three such "great patrons," one in Zhao, one in Wei, and a third in the kingdom of Chu, exerted a shaping influence on the political affairs of the Zhou states during the two decades after 260 BCE. These men had social and economic power that operated independently of any formal role they played in the governments of their respective states—often they exerted the most profound impact on affairs when they held no government post at all. Their story thus exemplifies the ways in which the tensions between the emerging bureaucratic order and the entrenched traditions of the Zhou aristocracy persisted throughout the Warring Staes in the aftermath of the battle of Changping, and the challenges this posed for leaders in the east who sought to oppose the growing predominance of Qin.

14

Gilded Age

The Various Zhou States, 260–238 BCE

The cataclysmic defeat of Zhao at Changping left Qin unchallenged as the predominant strategic power of the Warring States. The advantage that Qin enjoyed in soldiers and armaments was compounded by its steadily growing economic might. By 260 BCE the conquered territories of the Sichuan basin had been under the occupation of Qin forces for more than 50 years. In that time the Qin court had eliminated the proxy "Marquis of Shu" and put the entire region under the administration of centrally appointed Qin magistrates. Qin commanders had steadily expanded the area of the region under Qin control, and Qin officials had invested in the development of agriculture, commerce, and industry: establishing markets, draining wetlands, constructing roads and canals, and building facilities for the production of commodities such as salt. The wealth flowing into its coffers from Sichuan gave increasingly greater heft to the sheer combat power at the disposal of the Qin court and the fiscal-military state over which it presided.[1]

The irony of the mid-third century BCE is that though Qin enjoyed an advantage because of the expanding wealth of its domain, this was only an advantage in relative terms. In other words, it is not the case that Qin was getting wealthier while the rest of the Warring States were getting poorer. Despite endemic conflict and frequently destructive warfare, all of Zhou society was continuing to prosper and enjoy accelerating growth and advancing prosperity. Advances in technology, new methods of governance and management, and an efficient reorganization of the political sphere facilitated the burgeoning of agriculture, commerce, and industry throughout the Zhou states. The Dickensian line used to describe the fifth century BCE in Chapter 1 applies even more aptly to the mid-third century BCE: it was the best of times; it was the worst of times.[2]

This was especially true because the benefits of this gilded age were distributed intensely unevenly, in both horizontal and vertical senses. As noted above, looking across the Zhou map one would have seen that Qin was increasing in wealth at a faster rate than any of the other Zhou states, a trend that was exacerbated by the increasing ability of Qin to conquer land and wrest people away from its neighbors. But within each Zhou state one would have seen a similarly lopsided pattern at work. As each individual Warring State became wealthier, its society manifested ever-growing wealth inequality. The wealthiest individuals at the apex of the economic pyramid in each kingdom controlled astronomically more resources than those at the bottom, and as time passed that differential continued to widen.

Wealth inequality has been very common in agrarian and industrial societies for all of recorded history, and it has been more the rule than the exception that periods of rising wealth are likewise periods of widening inequality.[3] But this common phenomenon was exacerbated for the Warring States by the unique dimensions of Zhou sociocultural history discussed at several points in previous chapters: the nature and evolution of the Bronze Age aristocracy. As the whole community of Zhou aristocrats became progressively more steeply bifurcated between the seven lofty kings at the apex of the status pyramid and the vast sea of undifferentiated knights at the bottom, there were increasingly more opportunities for the few individuals (other than kings) who retained credibly elevated status bona fides, those who could claim that among their ancestors there were only "kings and marquises" going back to the beginning of recorded memory, and thence to the gods, to concentrate enormous wealth and power into their own hands.

Due to this massive concentration of wealth, power, and status into the hands of a few individuals, in the eastern states the two decades following the battle of Changping may fairly be called "the age of the great patrons." In the scramble to respond to the urgent and growing threat of Qin's power, the figures who set the agenda in the mid-third century BCE were neither crowned heads like King Xiaocheng of Zhao, technocrats such as Li Kui (author of the legal code discussed in Chapter 5), or literati such as Hui Shi (the idiosyncratic logician and Prime Minister of Wei). The movers and shakers of the 250s and 240s BCE were all cut from the same cloth as (and following deliberately in the footsteps of) Tian Wen, Lord Mengchang, the charismatic and dynamic patron who had made such waves throughout the Zhou world before he helped facilitate the near destruction of his home state of Qi in 284 BCE. In their engrossed estates and enormous retinues of dependent knights, the great patrons became autonomous powers within the larger political field of the Warring States, unbeholden to the writ of a particular government or sovereign. At times these individuals were able to mandate or even hijack the policy agenda of one or more of the Warring States, exercising influence that operated independently of and ran counter to the formal political structures of the time.

Patronage retinues had become a ubiquitous fixture of elite life throughout the many Zhou states by the mid-third century BCE, so any list of patrons about whom we have knowledge from the sources would be very long, and there were most likely many others whose names were not preserved in the written record.[4] But in the two decades of the mid-third century BCE, three figures stand out as having built extraordinarily large and politically influential patronage retinues. Two of them were the brothers of kings. Zhao Sheng (d. 252 BCE) was named the Lord of Pingyuan by his brother King Huiwen of Zhao. Wei Wuji (d. 243 BCE) was named the Lord of Xinling by his half-brother King Anxi of Wei (r. 276–243 BCE). The third great patron of the mid-third century BCE was an outlier. Huang Xie (d. 238 BCE) became a favorite of King Kaolie of Chu (r. 262–238 BCE) through extraordinary service and self-sacrifice, but after being enfeoffed as Lord of Chunshen he parlayed his estate into an extensive political operation that made him one of the most powerful men in the Zhou world.

As noted above, in charting a course through the political maze of their time, Zhao Sheng, Wei Wuji, and Huang Xie all very deliberately emulated the earlier example of Tian Wen, the Lord Mengchang. Like Tian Wen, the latter three "great patrons" invited knights from all over the Zhou world to come pledge fealty to them, in exchange for which these knights would be given protection, hospitality, and support without any reciprocal expectation of specific duties or service. Also in emulation of Tian Wen, the three made "informal" use of their retainers' talents, forging these clients into loosely organized corporate bodies that had their own sense of identity, esprit de corps, and carefully cultivated public image.

This pattern is evinced in many of the sources that record the deeds of the great patrons. A good example can be seen in a famous story about Zhao Sheng, the Lord of Pingyuan. The gate of the mansion in which Zhao Sheng resided in Handan, the capital of Zhao, faced a neighborhood in which poorer families lived. One day a lame man who lived across from Zhao Sheng's gate was limping on his way to draw water from the neighborhood well, and one of Zhao Sheng's beautiful concubines spotted him from one of the mansion's towers that overlooked the street. Finding his limp funny, she burst out laughing at him.

The next day the man sought and was granted an audience with Zhao Sheng, and reported to the lord what had happened, declaring, "I have heard that you are so fond of knights that they do not consider a journey of 1,000 *li* far to come to you. This is because you are able to value knights more than you do your concubines. I unfortunately have a malady that impairs me, yet one of your rear-palace women laughed at me. I would like her head." Zhao Sheng listened to the man's complaint and agreed to his request, but after the man had exited the audience hall Zhao Sheng turned to his courtiers and laughed, dismissing the man as unreasonable.

Soon after this incident Zhao Sheng's client knights began to leave. Within a year more than half of the knights in his retinue had departed his service. Zhao Sheng was upset by this trend, and resentfully queried a group of his remaining clients why it should be happening, when he had been such a courteous patron. One of the men explained that knights were taking their leave of Zhao Sheng because he had not kept his promise to give the lame petitioner his concubine's head. This was seen as a sign that Zhao Sheng did not value the dignity of his knights as much as he did female beauty, and for this reason knights were departing in large numbers. Realizing his error, Zhao Sheng had the offending concubine executed and personally brought her head to the lame man's humble dwelling, with his apologies. After that the knights who had left Zhao Sheng began to return.[5]

This story is quite offensive to our modern sensibilities, but it dramatically illustrates the social and cultural forces which underpinned the power and influence of the great patrons. The status of knights was so precarious that seeking the protection of an unimpeachably highborn and powerful patron was not enough. Above and beyond being a figure of clearly superior status, one's patron had to be seen to treat knights with pristine (even exaggerated) courtesy and to be zealously protective of his knights' dignity. Anything less, any sign that a patron's appreciation of his client knights was not perfectly sincere, could expose them to contempt and ridicule that might fatally undermine their social and political prospects.

The story of the lame man and the concubine was carefully crafted to deliver a message within that context. Concubines and knights were both dependent members of a lord's household, so the treatment of these two groups was always a particularly sensitive point of comparison within the discourse of the Warring States. Many sources contain stories that mark "good patrons" by illustrating the ways in which the lord in question took pains to differentiate the honor given to his knights from the favor shown to his palace women.[6]

Following the same logic, suffering from a physical disability was socially significant in Zhou society in ways that made it a fertile topic for discourse. Those who were lame or disfigured were generally excluded from elite society,[7] as exemplified by Yurang's efforts to camouflage his knightly status by applying lacquer to his skin and injuring his vocal chords with lumps of coal. The presumption of Zhao Sheng's concubine, who enjoyed her position of privilege because she had been born beautiful, in laughing at the lame man, who was forced to live among commoners because of his congenital disability, exemplified everything that knights found arbitrarily unfair about the society in which they lived. It paralleled the ridicule that knights had to suffer simply because they had not been lucky enough to be the son of a high-born father.

The story of Zhao Sheng's concubine thus elegantly broadcast a clear message to the knights of his time: "Zhao Sheng gets it. He understands what knights go through, and what kind of support they need from their patron. Those who join his household can expect to have the dignity they need to give full scope to their talents." The person who had the greatest interest in recording and disseminating a story with this kind of message was of course Zhao Sheng himself. Thus, though we cannot ever be sure if this story really happened, we can confidently infer that it was written down at Zhao Sheng's behest by some of the knights who had accepted his patronage for dissemination to the broader literati public, and that the harnessing of literati talent in this way was a standard feature of the general ethos that structured life in Zhao Sheng's retinue.

With their own income streams, personnel, structural hierarchies, missions, and public relations operations, the retinues of great patrons like Zhao Sheng developed into alternative power centers in Warring States society. Such patronage communities stood alongside and on a par (occasionally overlapping) with the military, the civil bureaucracy, and self-regulating fellowships of literati such as the Confucians and Mohists. In the confusion and panic that attended the aftermath of the battle of Changping, the political energy of the latter institutions of Warring States society reached a low ebb. The general trend for state institutions to become more coherent, efficient, and powerful relative to the influence of the hereditary aristocracy, which had been fostered by the competition between Qin and its geopolitical rivals, was brought up short by Qin's overwhelming victory at Changping. In the eastern states, the direction of this latter tide reversed. In the grips of general demoralization and malaise, the bureaucratic governments of the eastern states effectively disengaged from the political and strategic arenas, and the great patrons and their retinues stepped in to fill the resulting power vacuum.

By early imperial times Zhao Sheng, Wei Wuji, and Huang Xie had been recognized by historians as key leaders of their era. The *Records of the Historian* gives each man his own biography, and their three eponymous chapters are grouped together in the larger work, following directly upon the biography of their predecessor and the pioneer whose example had provided the template they emulated, Tian Wen.[8] The association of Zhao Sheng, Wei Wuji, and Huang Xie with one another was not merely literary, however. They interacted personally, and periodically collaborated. Indeed, one of the most seminal turning points of the mid-third century BCE, the siege of Handan in 258 BCE, brought all three men together in a concerted effort to thwart the power of Qin.

The battle of Changping had obliterated much of Zhao's military power. The Qin court saw an opportunity to destroy its rival completely. The *Records of the Historian* suggests that the ebbing of competition between Qin and Zhao made the personal, charismatic power of elite individuals begin to win out over the interests of the bureaucratic state almost immediately. In its telling, Fan Sui convinced King Zhao of Qin to demobilize Qin's forces after the battle of Changping because he feared how much the power of the Qin commander Bai Qi would grow if he successfully completed the conquest of Zhao.[9]

We cannot know whether that was really the case, or is a later embellishment expressing the bias of one group of literati or another. It would have been very out of character for Fan Sui to act in such venal self-interest (effectively emulating the Mi-clan clique leaders he had lobbied to replace), but it is possible that his actions proved the general principle that "power corrupts." Whatever Fan Sui's motives, it was true that the Qin army had been seriously taxed by the Changping campaign. It would have been remarkable if Qin had been able to mount a successful assault of Handan, one of the most heavily defended cities in the Zhou realm, before 258 BCE.

When the attack on Handan began the great commander Bai Qi refused the commission to command. The *Records of the Historian* reports that initially Bai Qi was incapacitated by illness, but that even after he recovered, he refused to serve out of resentment for Fan Sui's obstruction of his career. Whether the latter was true or not, even the *Records of the Historian* records that Bai Qi's reasons were not purely personal. In his judgement as a military commander, the attack was a foolish gambit.

The campaign was difficult, as Bai Qi had anticipated. The soldiers of Qin reached the walls of Handan, the Zhao capital, but were forced to dig in for a prolonged siege. The encirclement dragged on for many months. Bai Qi had foreseen this outcome: Qin's military power had not yet surpassed Zhao's sufficiently to make a swift, dynamic victory possible.

Beyond this, according to Bai Qi's analysis the overall strategic context of the campaign made victory virtually impossible. The stakes were different in 258 BCE than they had been in 260 BCE. The other Warring States had had reason not to defend Zhao's annexation of Han's Upper Commandery in 260 BCE (as discussed in the previous chapter). But Qin's attempt to destroy Zhao once and for all in 258 BCE threatened the vital interests of all the other Warring States. They were sure to come to Zhao's rescue eventually and inflict a costly defeat on Qin.

As the siege of Handan ground on, the Qin court put increasing pressure on Bai Qi to step in and take charge. He pleaded illness, convinced that the campaign was ill-fated, and refused repeated requests to take up the baton of command. Ultimately, he so angered the king that he was ordered to commit suicide.[10]

Though the logic of Bai Qi's analysis was sound, the response he predicted did not materialize swiftly or smoothly. By 258 BCE the demoralization of the royal courts of the eastern states had reached such heights that the political will to formulate a robust policy response to the emergency was lacking. As the siege of Handan dragged on and conditions within the city grew progressively more desperate, alarm climbed toward panic.

In this moment of imminent catastrophe, the power and influence of the great patrons was cast into stark relief. Zhao Sheng was besieged within the Zhao capital of Handan and saw that Zhao would be destroyed without the intervention of other states. His wife was the elder sister of Wei Wuji (and thus half-sister of the King of Wei), and Zhao Sheng prevailed upon her to write to her brothers and beg for help.

The King of Wei sent a senior general in command of a force of 100,000 men to relieve the siege of Handan. Before the Wei expeditionary force had arrived, however, the Qin court sent an envoy to Wei, declaring that Handan was sure to fall, and promising that if Wei did anything to try and prevent that, Qin would focus its wrath on Wei next. The King of Wei was cowed by this threat and ordered his army to halt its march toward Handan.[11]

Wei Wuji was distressed by this cowardice and felt honor-bound to help his sister and her husband. In this dire state of affairs, his past deeds and qualities as a patron proved pivotal. Like all of the other great patrons, Wei Wuji had very deliberately cultivated a reputation for honoring the talents of exceptional knights. One of the knights that he had labored most assiduously to recruit into his retinue was instrumental in his efforts to lift the siege of Handan.

The knight in question was named Hou Ying (d. 258 BCE). He was 70 years old, but drew a small income from a sinecure position as the watchman at one of the gates of Greatbridge, the capital of Wei. Hearing Hou Ying's reputation for great talent and wisdom, Wei Wuji paid a call on him bearing lavish gifts. Hou Ying refused the offered tribute, explaining effectively that though he was poor, his integrity was not for sale.

Wei Wuji next tried to recruit Hou Ying by throwing a banquet in his honor. He assembled all of his guest knights and royal kinsmen and seated them in front of a lavish feast, then personally drove his carriage to retrieve Hou Ying and escort him to the banquet. On the arrival of Wei Wuji at his dwelling, Hou Ying smoothed his worn cap and clothes and mounted without hesitation into the seat of honor in the carriage, deliberately testing to see what the prince's reaction would be to this presumption. In response, Wei Wuji simply straightened his posture and assumed the deferential air of a carriage driver. Hou Ying tested Wei Wuji's patience further, asking to be driven to the workplace of one of his own clients, a butcher named Zhu Hai.

Wei Wuji obediently drove into the marketplace and waited while Hou Ying dismounted from the carriage and greeted Zhu Hai. The gate watchman and the butcher chatted contentedly for some time as Wei Wuji sat at the reins and the assembled guests in the banquet hall waited for the wine to be served. The servants who had accompanied Wei Wuji began to curse under their breath, but when Hou Ying surreptitiously glanced at Wei Wuji, he saw that the prince's countenance remained cheerful and deferential. Finally, Hou Ying took his leave of Zhu Hai and returned to the carriage.

When they finally arrived at the banquet hall, Wei Wuji personally led the meanly dressed Hou Ying into the assembly and introduced him to each of the guests. The gathered knights and nobles watched astonished as Wei Wuji escorted the poor gate watchman to the seat of honor. When Hou Ying was seated Wei Wuji ordered the wine served and offered the first toast in honor of Hou Ying. When Wei Wuji's toast was done, Hou Ying rose and addressed the crowd, describing every aspect of the way that he had tested Wei Wuji and how the prince had responded. He bore witness to all present that Wei Wuji was truly a man of honor who treated knights with profound courtesy.

After this, Hou Ying became one of Wei Wuji's senior retainers. He told Wei Wuji that Zhu Hai, the butcher, was a man of true worth, but because he had not been able to support himself as a knight, he had withdrawn into the marketplace to work as a commoner. Wei Wuji called upon Zhu Hai several times to pay his respects, but his visits were never reciprocated.

When, during the siege of Handan, it became clear that the King of Wei would abandon Zhao to its fate, Wei Wuji was distraught. He called for volunteers from among his guest knights and set off with 100 chariots, having sworn an oath along with his men to die in the attempt to rescue Handan. Wei Wuji and his entourage passed through the gate attended by Hou Ying. On seeing his patron, Hou Ying bid him a casual farewell, expressing regret that his age would not allow him to join the expedition.

Hou Ying's blitheness troubled Wei Wuji, and before he had gotten many kilometers from Greatbridge he turned back to confront the gate watchman. Why, Wei Wuji asked, was Hou Ying so unphased by his lord's departure on such a dangerous mission? Had Wei Wuji done something to insult the older man, to keep him from offering more heartfelt words of parting? Hou Ying laughed and explained that he had deliberately offended the prince to get him to pause his rash undertaking. The plan for the present expedition was a suicide mission, which was as good as no plan at all.

When Wei Wuji heard this he understood that Hou Ying had counsel to offer. He knelt before Hou Ying and asked his advice. Hou Ying dismissed everyone else and spoke to Wei Wuji alone.

Hou Ying explained that Wei Wuji would need to mobilize the army of Wei that had been halted on its way to Handan, and that it was possible to do so. The royal military tally used for issuing orders to the commanding general was kept in the king's bedchamber. Fortunately for Wei Wuji, the king's current favorite bed companion was a palace woman named Concubine Ru, who was greatly indebted to Wei Wuji. Concubine Ru's father had been killed a number of years before, and when for three years no one else proved willing to avenge her father, Wei Wuji had sent one of his retainers to cut off the head of her father's slayer, which he then presented to Concubine Ru.

Hou Ying declared that Concubine Ru would acquire the royal military tally for him if Wei Wuji asked. He did so, and she complied. Once Wei Wuji had the military tally in hand and was about to set out to meet the army, Hou Ying advised him again. The general in command of the army was an able officer and might suspect that any orders that Wei Wuji delivered with the military tally should be disregarded. For this reason Wei Wuji should bring Zhu Hai along with him, as Zhu Hai was incredibly strong and could kill the general if needs be.

Wei Wuji wept to think that he would be forced to kill an honorable servant of Wei, but he accepted Hou Ying's advice. He asked Zhu Hai to accompany him. The butcher agreed, explaining that he had never returned the prince's visits because he had no material needs and would not want to be mistaken as seeking Wei Wuji's support. The courtesy that Wei Wuji had shown Zhu Hai, however, made the butcher honor-bound to serve the prince in his hour of need.

Wei Wuji and Zhu Hai set out in a single chariot so as to travel swiftly. Hou Ying saw them off, promising that he would calculate the days that it would take them to arrive at the army camp and would commit suicide by cutting his own throat on the day that they reached their goal. This, like Zhu Hai's obligation to serve Wei Wuji, was a debt of honor. Wei Wuji had publicly treated Hou Ying as a man of ultimate worth. To be deserving of such courtesy, Hou Ying had to show himself willing to give Wei Wuji the ultimate degree of service (the sacrifice of his own life). By killing himself at the precise moment that Wei Wuji arrived at the army camp, Hou Ying accepted responsibility and executed upon himself the punishment for the crimes that Wei Wuji would commit, and that he was doing on Hou Ying's advice.

Wei Wuji and Zhu Hai arrived at the army camp and were received in the command tent by the general. Wei Wuji claimed to have been given command of the army by order of the king and presented the stolen military tally as proof. The general matched the presented tally with his own and saw that they fit correctly.

This would ordinarily have confirmed Wei Wuji's authority. But, as Hou Ying had anticipated, the general intuited that something was amiss. It was odd for Wei Wuji to arrive for the purpose of taking command of such a large army in a single chariot. The general noted that this was too strange to ignore and refused to yield command to Wei Wuji. At this, Zhu Hai brandished a large war hammer that he had concealed beneath the billowy sleeve of his robe and stove in the general's skull. Wei Wuji took over the army and drilled it for war. After releasing the men in the force who were serving alongside their sons or younger brothers, or who were only sons, Wei Wuji took the remaining 80,000 men of the original 100,000-man army and marched to the relief of Handan.[12]

While Wei Wuji was working to mobilize the forces of Wei, Zhao Sheng had likewise been employed seeking other allies to come to the aid of Zhao. The King of Zhao ordered Zhao Sheng to brave a journey to Chu in search of an alliance. Zhao Sheng accepted the mission and sought out 20 men from among the bravest and ablest of his knights to serve as his entourage.

After some deliberation he had composed a force of 19 men and deemed none of his other knights fit for this mission. A knight named Mao Sui stepped forward and asked to be included as the twentieth man. Zhao Sheng refused, noting that a worthy knight was like a sharp nail placed in a sack, the tip of which will quickly emerge. Mao Sui had been in Zhao Sheng's service for three years without distinguishing himself; he could not possibly be worthy.

Mao Sui rejoined that he had never yet been placed in the sack. If Zhao Sheng did so now, he would see Mao Sui burst from the sack altogether. Zhao Sheng gave way before Mao's persistence and included him in the party.

On arriving in Chu, Zhao Sheng and his men met with a cold reception. The King of Chu admitted them into audience at dawn and listened half-attentively as Zhao Sheng spoke in favor of an alliance between Zhao and Chu. By noon the King of Chu had shown no signs of assent, so Zhao Sheng's retainers turned to Mao Sui, urging him to go forward and assist their lord.

Mao mounted the dais upon which Zhao Sheng and the king were deliberating, and interrupted them, noting that the case for an alliance could be put into two sentences and was ironclad. Why, he asked, were the discussions over such an easy decision taking so long? The King of Chu was furious at this presumption and shouted at Mao Sui, asking why he would not keep his place and withdraw?

In response to the king's wrath, Mao Sui put his hand on his sword and continued his verbal assault on the monarch. The king, Mao explained, presumed to know Mao's place, but he was mistaken. The king was only above Mao because he had command of such a huge army. But while Mao stood 10 paces away from the king, the army of Chu could not protect him. Since Mao was willing to die, he held the king's life in his hands. The question was not why Mao did not know his place; it was how the king would dare to shout at Mao?

Having thus seized the King of Chu's attention, Mao explained that the question of an alliance was not really worth debating. Chu had already lost its ancient capital and much of its western territory to Qin and would lose even more if and when Qin no longer had to contend with the strength of Zhao. The men of Zhao were not asking a favor of Chu, but offering their assistance in beginning to avenge the wrongs that Chu had already suffered at the hands of Qin.

The King of Chu assented to this logic, and on Mao Sui's orders the blood of three sacrificial animals was brought in for the swearing of a covenant of alliance. As Mao's fellow knights of Zhao smeared their lips with the sacrificial blood and swore the covenant oath, Mao Sui berated them as mediocrities who had rendered poor service to their common lord. Zhao Sheng conceded that he could not have been more wrong in his estimation of Mao and declared that he would never dare pronounce judgment on a knight's worth ever again.

The King of Chu sent an army under the command of the third great patron, Huang Xie, to help lift the siege of Handan. In 257 BCE the combined forces of Chu led by Huang Xie, Wei led by Wei Wuji, and a sallying party of Zhao knights led by one of Zhao Sheng's retainers, which Zhao Sheng had raised by ordering his own wives to act as servants to his knights, drove the armies of Qin back from the walls of Handan. As Bai Qi had predicted, the invasion was thwarted at great loss to Qin, and the independence of Zhao was preserved.[13]

This collaboration between Zhao Sheng, Wei Wuji, and Huang Xie in lifting the siege of Handan set the tone in the eastern states for the next two decades. The stories contained in the chronicles about this event convey such pointed morals and elaborately articulated messages that we would be justified in suspecting that the record had been embellished. But embellished or not, the chronicles provide clear evidence of the great patrons' power. Some accounts of the events surrounding the lifting of the siege of Handan, for example, highlight the respective roles of Yu Qing (ca. 305–ca. 235 BCE) and Luzhong Lian (ca. 305–ca. 245 BCE), two literati who served as the eponymous "authors" of Masters texts that were housed in the Han imperial library. Without their guidance and advice, these accounts suggest, the great patrons would have made critical mistakes in their response to the crisis of Handan. But even these stories that highlight the power and dignity of the "Masters" place the great patrons at the center of events.[14] Either Zhao Sheng, Wei Wuji, and Huang Xie were the three agents most responsible for the lifting of the siege of Handan, or they were powerful enough to ensure that in the aftermath of the event the written record would give them credit for it.

In the messages encoded by the stories surrounding the siege of Handan, we can see a general world view that underpinned and gave structure to the great patrons' pursuit and exercise of power. The relationship between the prince Wei Wuji, the watchman Hou Ying, and the butcher Zhu Hai, for example, demonstrated that the great patrons repudiated the transactional notions of service that were increasingly becoming the norm in the bureaucratic governments of the Warring States. The great patrons were not "paying" knights for their labor (as the court did its officials), but (in accordance with the traditional ethos of the Zhou founders) merely giving due tribute to knights' worth, in the trust that men of honor would reciprocate whatever courtesy was given to them. The story of Mao Sui's confrontation with the King of Chu demonstrated that the great patrons would testify to the inalienable dignity born of true merit. High birth might entitle a man such as Zhao Sheng or the King of Chu to more wealth or authority, but since every individual had only one life to give, a person of genuine courage was morally inferior to no one, no matter how highborn.

Though the three later great patrons were following a model established earlier by Tian Wen, the stories surrounding the siege of Handan suggest that they were self-consciously committed to an even more extreme ethos of "humbling themselves before knights." Where, for example, the cases of the "dog thief" and the "cock-crow knight" showed that Tian Wen could see the hidden value in knights, the exploits of Mao Sui forced Zhao Sheng to admit that he could not be trusted to pronounce on a knight's worth at all. Where the relationship of Tian Wen to his knights had shown that a patron was wise to tolerate his retainer's eccentricities, the relationship of Wei Wuji and Hou Ying demonstrated that a patron would be wise to allow his most trusted retainers to occasionally and very publicly humiliate him.

These dimensions of the great patrons' public personas and general world view evince the paradoxical forces transforming state and society in the mid-third century BCE. On the one hand, the era was one of extreme social mobility. The superheated atmosphere of competition between rival states made it possible for a figure like Fan Sui to emerge from a filthy privy and become one of the most powerful men in the world. On the other hand, power and wealth were concentrating ever more intensively into a few hands at the very top of the social and political hierarchies, the most numerous and secure of whom remained those who had been born to privilege. If you were of humble birth and rose high enough, the world was literally your oyster. If you did not, you found yourself increasingly subject to the arbitrary whims of your superiors in status, wealth, and/or power.

It is easy to understand why, in that milieu, knights would seek patronage and protection even as they competed for official positions and salaries. The great patrons, perhaps inadvertently, crafted their public personas and established the norms of the retinues over which they presided to accord with the general needs of the knights of their time. In this way they were able to capitalize upon the contradictions of late Zhou state and society, and become the premier power brokers of the mid-third century.

The stories about themselves sponsored by Zhao Sheng, Wei Wuji, and Huang Xie make it clear that they were aware of the political opportunities of the moment and determined to capitalize upon them. Take, for example, the accounts of the vigilante justice that Wei Wuji enacted for the wronged concubine in his brother's harem, or of Mao Sui compelling the King of Chu to do what was in his own kingdom's self-interest. Such narratives broadcast an unmistakable message about the changing political order: governments can no longer be relied on to do what is right, thus some other force must intervene. The lore that the great patrons formulated and disseminated about themselves in the mid-third century BCE was no longer a simple call for recruitment, but a kind of "manifesto" asserting their claims of leadership over state and society at large.

The trends and contradictions of the age were best embodied by the third great patron of the mid-third century BCE, Huang Xie. Huang was of extremely humble birth relative to the respective pedigrees of Zhao Sheng and Wei Wuji. The latter two men were born princes: each was the brother of a king. We know nothing of Huang's forbears. He began his public life as a knight, born to a family of only local prominence in Chu.

Though Huang's beginnings were modest, his rise took him to heights that made his wealth and power eclipse that of both Zhao Sheng and Wei Wuji. He devoted his youth to study and became an extraordinarily learned literatus and artful wordsmith. These skills earned him a commission from King Qingxiang of Chu to undertake an embassy to the Qin court on behalf of Chu.

The context of that embassy was fraught with danger. In 273 BCE the Qin commander Bai Qi had scored great victories against the "three Jin" successor states,[15] and secured an agreement from Han and Wei to follow Qin in a joint attack on Chu. King Qingxiang of Chu dispatched Huang Xie to plead for peace, and Huang arrived in the Qin capital before the planned invasion of Chu was launched. He wrote a long, richly detailed and elegantly structured memorial to King Zhao of Qin, arguing against the wisdom of Qin's new offensive coalition.

In this memorial, a version of which is preserved in historical chronicles, Huang invoked two historical precedents in particular: that of Zhi Yao (the ruthless leader who aspired to unite Jin under his rule, as discussed in Chapter 3) and King Fuchai (the doomed last ruler of Wu, discussed in Chapter 2). The implied message was far from subtle: if Qin trusted Han and Wei as partners, they would betray Qin just as they had Zhi Yao. On returning from its expedition south, Qin would find itself mortally threatened by a geographically close foe (Zhao!) just as Fu Chai had been assaulted by King Goujian of Yue when he returned from his foolish campaigns in the North. It would be better for Qin to accept the friendship of Chu and continue expanding its frontiers at the cost of the central states, with the aim of eventually reaching the sea and dividing the Zhou realm in two.

King Zhao of Qin was impressed by this argument and the eloquent terms in which it was cast. He offered his apologies to Han and Wei, and sent Huang Xie back to Chu with an offer of alliance. It was a singular moment in the history of Zhou interstate relations. "Wandering persuaders" in the role taken up by Huang Xie had been a ubiquitous fixture of political life in the Warring States for more than half a century, but in all that time no single "persuasion" delivered by a traveling literatus had surpassed Huang's in impact. Huang's memorial was a magisterial performance of the literati's craft. It made him instantaneously famous.

King Qingxiang of Chu was understandably delighted with Huang Xie's service. The terms of the alliance offered by Qin required that Chu send its Heir Apparent as hostage to reside at the Qin court. This was a standard feature of such peace compacts and could not have been unexpected in this instance. It is a measure of the confidence that Huang Xie had earned from him that the king dispatched Huang back to Qin to serve as chief retainer of the Heir Apparent. The king was literally trusting Huang Xie with his son's life. That trust would prove well justified.

Huang Xie spent almost 10 years in Qin, serving as the heir's chief of staff while the heir resided as a hostage. In 263 BCE reports reached Qin that King Qingxiang of Chu had fallen gravely ill and neared death. The Qin court, in following with its past practices of bad-faith dealing, would not release the heir to return to Chu. The heir had developed good relations with the new Prime Minister of Chu, Fan Sui. Huang Xie thus procured an audience with Fan Sui and argued for the wisdom of Qin allowing the heir to return home. It was better for Qin, Huang Xie explained, to ensure that the Chu throne was held by a ruler whom the prime minister knew and with whom he was friendly, than to risk the throne passing to some other member of the royal family who was an unknown quantity.

Fan Sui found this line of argument persuasive and took it to the King of Qin. The king listened to his prime minster's arguments, but was not completely convinced. He ordered that the heir's tutor should be allowed to travel to Chu and inquire about the King of Chu's health. If and when they received confirmation that the King of Chu was about to die, they could decide how to proceed from there.

Huang Xie conferred with the heir and warned him of the danger of his situation. The King of Chu could die at any time, and if he did so while the heir remained hostage in Qin, one of his cousins would surely be crowned king in his place. The risk of waiting for the heir's tutor to return from Chu was too high. Drastic measures were needed.

The heir agreed and complied with the plan that Huang Xie outlined. The heir changed clothes and hid himself in the cortege that made its way south toward Chu as a common carriage driver. While he was on the road, Huang Xie stayed behind in Qin and covered for the heir's absence. He supervised servants who brought food and clothes into and out of the heir's bedchamber as if he was still there, and deflected anyone who sought an audience with the heir by claiming that the heir was ill.

When enough time had passed that the heir was sure to have crossed through the border pass into Chu, Huang Xie confessed his actions directly to the King of Qin. He requested that he be able to take his own life in punishment for his offense against Qin. The King of Qin was furious and wanted Huang dead, but Fan Sui intervened. Punishing Huang Xie, the prime minister explained, would not be perceived as strength, but would only do damage to the general reputation of Qin. Huang Xie had merely been acting as a faithful vassal of his lord. Killing him would only prove that Qin feared men of good character. Beyond this, if they let him go, he would surely be employed by Chu's next king, and this would give Qin leverage with the future government of that southern kingdom. The king was ultimately persuaded by his prime minister's reasoning.

Huang Xie returned to Chu, and as Fan Sui anticipated, when the Heir Apparent that Huang had served so faithfully was crowned king (known to history as King Kaolie of Chu, r. 262–238 BCE), Huang Xie was appointed his prime minister. The bond of intimacy that had grown between Huang Xie and his future king was very close. They had lived together in adversity for years, and King Kaolie had effectively come into his birthright only through the willingness of Huang Xie to give his life in exchange for his king's freedom. Though the king and Huang Xie were not kin, they were in some respects closer than brothers. One can well understand why King Kaolie reposed such extraordinary trust in Huang Xie.

Such trust was a currency the reach and value of which had few limits. In the unique social and political conditions of the mid-third century BCE, Huang was able to parlay the king's confidence into the development of a patronage retinue the size and sheer power of which the world had not yet seen. Huang Xie was given the title "Lord of Chunshen," the name by which he is almost always known in the ancient chronicles, and granted a fief consisting of 12 districts north of the Huai River. He used the income from his fief to underwrite his retinue of followers.

Over time Huang's power became indispensable to the operation of the state system of Chu as a whole. When, for example, 15 years after being invested with his title, Huang's fief came under threat from a militarily resurgent Qi, this did nothing to undermine Huang's position. He simply surrendered his original fief to be made into a centrally administered commandery of the Chu throne and was granted the more sheltered territory of the former kingdom of Wu as his new domain. He built a walled city on the ruins of the old Wu capital (the site of the present-day city of Suzhou) and moved his expansive retinue of client knights into this new headquarters.[16]

Huang served as Prime Minister of Chu for more than two decades. His training as a literatus, his rise from obscurity, his longevity in office, all distinguish him from the other two great patrons of his time, Zhao Sheng and Wei Wuji. One might be tempted to argue that Huang Xie should not be classed as a "great patron" with the latter two princes at all, but rather should be viewed as having played a political role analogous to that of a literatus prime minister such as Fan Sui or Hui Shi.

The sources, however, make clear that Huang Xie deliberately constructed himself as a patron. One story, for example, describes an embassy sent from Zhao Sheng to Huang Xie's court. Zhao Sheng's emissary had brought an especially beautiful jade hairpin and a treasured sword encased in a pearl-crusted scabbard, and requested that a special assembly of Huang Xie's retainers be held for their presentation. Huang Xie, understanding that the emissary meant this to be a display of Zhao Sheng's wealth and power, held an assembly as requested. To the embarrassment and chagrin of the emissary, the reception was attended by 3,000 of Huang Xie's retainers, the most senior of whom attended wearing pearl-encrusted sandals.[17]

We of course cannot know whether the above event really took place. But the very existence of the story shows that Huang Xie wanted it generally known that knights who came seeking his protection could expect to be treated as lavishly as they would by any other patron in the Zhou world, or more so. By offering knights patronage and protection, he developed power that transcended and was separable from the formal authority of his office, and he wielded that power in pursuit of goals that, while they might have benefited the Chu state, were undertaken as much in his own interest as that of the throne.

In this light, it is perhaps the most paradoxical dimension of Huang's career, and an outstanding example of the extraordinary dynamic at work in the age of the great patrons more generally, that as his personal power grew, so too did the strength of Chu. Chu had been in a condition of advanced disintegration before Huang assumed the office of prime minister: losing territory on all sides, wracked by rebellion and internal division. Huang Xie was able, by lending the cohesive energy of his patronage retinue to the formal structures of the court, civil bureaucracy, and military, to restore vitality to the Chu state and throne.

This can be seen most clearly in one of the signature achievements of Huang's tenure as prime minister. In 255 BCE the armies of Chu marched north and conquered the ancient state of Lu, Confucius's birthplace and the home of his descendants.[18] Lu had not been a significant military power for more than two centuries, and it was a small state in terms of land. But it was densely populated and enjoyed enormous prestige throughout the Zhou world, both for the ancient pedigree of its ruling house and its continuing role as the geographic epicenter of the Confucian fellowship (even though the latter was largely in symbolic terms).

The invasion of 255 BCE terminated the rule of the Lu dukes, who were forcibly relocated and given a small fief with which to perpetuate the sacrifices to their revered ancestors. The territory of Lu itself was reorganized as a centrally administered commandery, newly named "Lanling," under the direct rule of the Chu throne and its appointed magistrates. This was a remarkable change in the political structure of the Zhou world. The dissolution of the Lu throne was comparable to the destruction of the kingdoms of Song and Zhongshan in geostrategic significance. Possession of a centrally administered district encompassing the former territory of Lu brought the writ of the southern, "barbarous" Chu court farther north than it had ever reached in recorded memory, into the very heartland of the ecumene established by the Zhou founders.

The conquest demonstrated Huang Xie's personal power in several ways. The conquest itself would arguably not have been possible with any other individual at the helm. It is certainly true that general conditions over which Huang had exerted no influence were instrumental in the operation's success: the wars of 284 BCE had crippled Qi's ability to contest Chu's ambition, and the campaigns of Bai Qi had similarly weakened Han, Wei, and Zhao. But even in the face of such circumstances, the passivity of the northern powers, who offered absolutely no resistance to the prospect of Lu's destruction, was very odd. In this light the timing of the invasion, which happened less than two years after the siege of Handan ended, strongly suggests that Huang's personal relationship with Wei Wuji and Zhao Sheng was an instrumental factor. The tolerance of the kingdoms of Wei and Zhao in the face of Chu's conquest of Lu was most likely, on some level, a quid pro quo on the part of Wei Wuji and Zhao Sheng for Huang Xie's assistance in lifting the siege of Handan.

Beyond the role of Huang Xie in personally engineering the conquest of Lu, the accommodations that he succeeded in making for its domestication under the power of the Chu throne were likewise testimony to his extraordinary influence and prestige. The most potentially vexing problem that the Chu court faced in pacifying Lu was in the outrage and resistance of the literati of the Confucian fellowship. The destruction of the ancestral temples of Lu and the subordination of its subjects to a "barbarous" sovereign would almost certainly have been seen to "pollute the shades of Confucius and his descendants," all of whose tombs are maintained in a mortuary park within the former Lu capital of Qufu to this very day.

Huang Xie's solution to this problem was elegant and wildly effective. He recruited the most revered Master among Confucius's latter-day disciples of the mid-third century BCE. In 255 BCE that distinction still belonged to Xun Kuang, whose tenure as "Libationer" of the Jixia patronage community was discussed in Chapter 11, and whose eponymous text contains some of the most brilliant and sophisticated examples of the Masters teachings of the Warring States. Xun Kuang (Xunzi) was most likely more than 60 years old when he was approached by Huang Xie, but he accepted the offered commission of Prefect of Lanling. He remained in the post for most of the next two decades.[19]

It was a brilliant maneuver on Huang Xie's part. Xun Kuang's willingness to serve as Prefect of Lanling silenced all questions about the legitimacy of Chu's campaign of conquest. If even the great Master had no objection to Chu's rule of what had once been the state of Lu, it could not ultimately be a transgression of "the Way" or a betrayal of the ancient sages.

The collaboration between Xun Kuang and Huang Xie exemplifies the ways in which the great patrons exerted influence not only on politics and society, but on the culture of the Zhou world as well. Xun Kuang's decision to coordinate the activities of the Confucian fellowship with the leadership of the great patrons was not merely a matter of pragmatic policy, but implicated questions of doctrine as well. Over the course of his life and travels, Xun Kuang interacted with all of the great patrons, and he accepted the support of both Zhao Sheng and Huang Xie at different times. If the mission of the Confucian fellowship could not be reconciled to the status and position of the great patrons, if their role in politics and society ran contrary to the Way, Xunzi's project in defense of Confucius's legacy was not sustainable.

All of the great patrons figure in the eponymous text putatively authored by Xun Kuang. One essay in particular, "On the Way of a Minister" (*Chen Dao*), engages questions raised by the careers of the great patrons in the realm of political ethics. Wei Wuji, for example, is especially praised as a type of "good minister" who, though he countermanded his ruler's orders (in his efforts to lift the siege of Handan, using a stolen military tally), did so for the purpose of bringing his ruler back into accord with the Way.[20] It was a neatly elegant solution to a knotty and potentially catastrophic problem. Xun Kuang did not go as far as declaring that the power exercised by the great patrons was necessarily *good*, but he demonstrated in clearly logical terms that the power of the great patrons was not necessarily *bad*.

Not all of the Masters of the mid-third century were so ready to reconcile with the presence of the great patrons, but virtually none could avoid responding to them in some way. An innovative voice among mid-third century literati, for example, was Master Han Fei, or Han Feizi (ca. 280–233 BCE). Han Fei's social origins were distinct from most of the men who entered the world of the literati fellowships. He was not born a knight, but was a high-ranking scion of the royal clan of Han. This would ordinarily have given him enough of an advantage in any competition to see his political ambitions fulfilled that he would not have needed any special period of study beyond the normal tutoring given to highborn boys. But he is said to have been born with a speech impediment, and it was perhaps this handicap that drove him, in an effort to distinguish himself from his royal siblings and cousins, to seek out the training and credentials that would earn him credibility and authority among literati.[21]

Han Fei is sometimes called a "Legalist," but that is an anachronistic label. Moreover, to reduce him to being the purveyor of a particular "ism" distorts and diminishes the importance of his insights and legacy.[22] Han Fei was one of the most original and provocative political thinkers of the Warring States.[23]

As a young man Han sought out Xun Kuang and was accepted as the great Master's disciple. Han was not won over to the Way as conceived of by Confucius, but was impressed by and emulated Xun Kuang's erudition and profound engagement with the broad field of Masters teachings. Though the formula is never repeated verbatim in the writings attributed to Han Fei, he does also seem to have agreed in principle with his Master Xun Kuang that "human nature is evil."

The teachings of Master Han Fei were eclectic and engaged many different topics, but were bound together by the common theme of the power of the ruler and the state. Han Fei expressed dismay over the degree to which the power of the throne had been diluted and dispersed in his own time. With the goal of establishing theories and practices that would enhance and preserve the power of the ruler, Han brought together and synthesized many of the teachings of earlier Masters such as Shen Dao, Shen Buhai, and Shang Yang. His work was not purely synthetic, however. He presented a new vision unlike anything found in the teachings of any prior Master, so groundbreaking and provocative that it would arguably not be paralleled in much of the rest of the world until early modern times.

All of the earlier Masters had observed and lamented the chaotic state of politics and the frequency of conflict and disorder. The various Masters had different explanations for this chaos and distinct prescriptions for how the situation might be fixed, but their teachings all had one common feature: every Master taught that conflict and disorder were a product of dysfunction and deficiency. Conflict arose because people were ignorant of the Way, lacking in moral character, or unequipped with the tools and guidelines that would be conducive to good order. When government was operating as it should, rulers and ministers related to one another like the members of an affectionate family. If they were at odds with one another, something was missing or wrong.

Han Fei rejected these basic premises of the earlier Masters. He taught that the court was naturally and inevitably a place of conflict. Ministers were constantly plotting against their ruler, the ruler had to continually be on guard against and ride herd over his ministers. To theorize as if this were not so was a fiction and a pretense.

Where both Confucius and Mo Di had agreed that violence is always a sign of failure within a properly functioning system, Han Fei taught that violence was a natural and inevitable byproduct of political life. Given the nature of human interaction, no system could eliminate violence completely. The best-case scenario was a situation in which violence happened infrequently and was confined to "the right people." In one essay, for example, Han Fei compares the court to an arboretum, and enjoins that a wise ruler must periodically "prune his trees" (i.e. kill or at least punish a few ambitious and untrustworthy ministers, or simply make an example of some conveniently expendable ones) to ensure that the court continues to operate properly.[24]

This dimension of Han Fei's thought describes what was most distinctive in his perspective, but this cursory exploration does not do justice to the breadth and complexity of the teachings to be found in his eponymous text. Its essays analyze all aspects of state power, social and economic interaction, and even cultural communication from the perspective of this unique world view. They posit insights and propose solutions that were not only challenging and often trenchant in their own time, but remain so even today.

What should be obvious even from this brief synopsis, however, is that Han Fei's perspective could not be reconciled with either the ideas being promoted by the great patrons and the retinues they led or the practical circumstances in which they operated. The idea that the worth of knights was too lofty or inscrutable to be assessed, for example, was ridiculous: everyone could be ranked and remunerated on the basis of their usefulness to the ruler and the state. For anyone outside of the ruler himself to have control over the "two handles" of reward and punishment (as the great patrons claimed entitlement to do) was a recipe for catastrophe: such dispersal of power could only lead ultimately to the assassination of the ruler and the destruction of the state.[25]

Though Han Fei's putative teachings implicitly condemn the role exercised by the great patrons, even the *Han Feizi* provides indirect testimony of the power and influence exercised in the mid-third century BCE by Wei Wuji, Zhao Sheng, and Huang Xie. As a royal prince of his home state, Han Fei needed no patron, and since he had broken ties with his Master he was not invested in the fortunes of any fellowship of literati. But though Master Han Fei was clearly hostile to them and their works, and though the writings attributed to him as a whole comment freely on virtually every major figure of the Zhou era about whom Han Fei would have had knowledge, none of the great patrons of Han Fei's time are mentioned by name anywhere in the surviving writings attributed to him.[26] In abstract theory the *Han Feizi* eviscerates the idea and condemns the practical reality of the great patrons, but as a matter of concrete policy the putative writings of Master Han Fei seem to have taken great pains not to offend any of them personally.

The cultural influence of the great patrons extended beyond the realm of the Masters' teachings into the domain of *belle lettres*. We know that the appreciation and composition of poetry was a feature of aristocratic life during the Warring States, but few examples of poetic compositions original to the era have been preserved in writing. It may be coincidental that some of the earliest extant examples of Warring States poetry date to the era of the great patrons, but it is likely that the interest figures like Huang Xie took in the poetic talents of their retainers contributed to this trend.

We can see evidence for this in the work attributed to Xun Kuang. That source contains two chapters devoted entirely to poetry, one of "working songs" and another of a genre that would become immensely popular in the early imperial period, "rhyme-prose" (*fu*). The last of the *fu* preserved in Xun

Kuang's eponymous text is a poem of remonstrance addressed directly to Huang Xie.

Huang Xie was at one point persuaded to dismiss Xunzi from his post as Prefect of Lanling, purportedly (as one transmitted anecdote suggests) out of a fear that to give such a virtuous man even so modest an amount of power might lead to his taking over the whole world as the sage kings of antiquity had done.[27] In response to being dismissed Xun Kuang wrote and disseminated a short satirical poem, which chides Huang Xie for being a poor judge of precious jewelry, fine clothes, and female beauty (all appropriated as allegories of official merit).[28] The poem had its intended effect. Huang Xie reappointed Xun Kuang, who would serve in Lanling until Huang Xie's death. It would be rash to infer that Xun Kuang and his disciples were drawn to poetry purely to impress the great patrons, but we can see that poetry was a language that Huang Xie and Xun Kuang shared. The fact that Xun Kuang chose to respond to his dismissal with a satirical *fu* shows that he knew poetry would add heft to his message.

What type of poetry did the great patrons value and promote? We do not have any direct examples that can be tied to the court of Huang Xie, but a suggestion of what the poetry appreciated by and produced in his court was like might be seen in an imperial-era anthology known as the *Chuci* (the "Verses of Chu"). That work was compiled by a series of Han-era redactors and contains poems spanning more than a century. The earliest of the compositions in the anthology are attributed to a poet named Qu Yuan, who is purported to have lived in the fourth century BCE and, out of frustration that his talents were not being employed by the Chu court because the king had heeded slander against him, committed suicide by plunging into the Yangzi River after composing his masterpiece, "Encountering Sorrow" (*Li sao*), the first poem of the *Chuci* anthology. The lore surrounding Qu Yuan has excited the imagination of countless generations, and he is honored every year at the Dragon Boat festival, during which celebrants throw sticky rice dumplings into a river in hopes that the fish will be appeased and refrain from eating Qu Yuan's corpse.[29]

Most historians today would agree that Qu Yuan was a legendary figure invented during the Han dynasty.[30] No source confidently datable to the Warring States mentions him. But at least some of the poetry collected in the *Chuci* may have been composed in the Warring States, albeit by poets whose identities have been lost.

If we look at "Encountering Sorrow," we see many dimensions and themes that resonate strongly with the social milieu that prevailed in the mid-third

Fig. 21. This elaborate wine vessel was discovered among the grave goods buried with Marquis Yi of Zeng (d. 433 BCE). It reflects the degree to which tastes became more baroque as the Warring States period progressed. (Source: the-past.com.)

century BCE, especially at the court of Huang Xie in Chu. The aesthetic expressed in the poem, paralleling the formal qualities that can be seen in the surviving craftsmanship and visual arts of the late Warring States, is extremely baroque (Fig. 21). "Encountering Sorrow" is densely embroidered with intense sensual imagery, exotic phrasings, and esoteric allusions. It displays an ornamental style in which "more is more," reminiscent of the pearl-studded sandals flaunted by Huang Xie to impress Zhao Sheng's emissary.

The themes of the poem also tally well with the interests of Huang Xie and his clients. The poem begins with the narrator's claims of high birth: he is a scion of the god Gao Yang from whom the kings of Chu claimed descent. Over the course of the poem the narrator embarks on a journey throughout the cosmos (often conducted on flying chariots yoked to soaring dragons) in search of a "mate," whom alternately can be read as a goddess the narrator is attempting to woo or a ruler that the narrator hopes to serve. At points on his quest the narrator beautifies himself with flowers, jewels, fine raiment, and sweet perfumes, but he meets with only aloofness, condescension, and contempt from the "Fair One" he pursues in vain. At the end of the poem the narrator flies away, seemingly leaving the material world in disgust.[31]

"Encountering Sorrow" is a richly complex poem open to many different readings, but it is easy to see why it might have been admired and emulated at the court of Huang Xie. The ironies of the poem parallel the paradoxes and contradictions confronted by Huang and his retainers. The poem depicts a world in which privilege of birth ostensibly reigns supreme, but in which even high birth cannot protect someone from arbitrary condescension and contempt. At the same time, the poem itself materially embodies an argument about the nature of true merit. Creativity, talent, skill, and learning are "adornments" that can never be taken away. Anyone who can compose or even appreciate a work of subtle beauty like "Encountering Sorrow" need not feel inferior to anyone. Quite the contrary.

Taken together, the poetry preserved in the *Xunzi* and that contained in the *Chuci* give us a sense of one way that literati culture was evolving in the mid-third century BCE. Poetry was a pursuit that was increasingly valuable to both patrons like Huang Xie and Masters like Xun Kuang, and that could be powerfully useful in making up for deficiencies of birth, though in slightly different ways for each man. Poetry provided a medium in which a Master like Xun Kuang could display the breadth and seriousness of his own personal cultivation. At the same time, poetry was an arena in which a great patron like Huang Xie could broadcast his taste, erudition, and refinement, as well as that of the knights he drew to his service. In both cases (and in the intersection between them) we can see that a dialectical process was at work, shaping both the social structures within which literati lived and the art that they created.

In the years after the lifting of the siege of Handan, the situation of the eastern states gradually stabilized. Qin's aggression slowed, especially in the wake of Fan Sui's death in 255 BCE.[32] At least some of the relative stability that settled over the Warring States in this period was facilitated by the leadership of the great patrons.

In the immediate aftermath of the siege, Wei Wuji was compelled to live in exile. His hijacking of the command of Wei's army and murder of its general understandably infuriated his half-brother, the King of Wei. Wei Wuji was not alone in exile, however. He was joined by his retinue of knights. The King of Zhao planned to grant Wei Wuji a fief of five cities, but one of Wei's retainers, on seeing how arrogant this news made the prince, warned him against accepting such a large bequest. In deference to his retainer's wisdom, Wei Wuji refused the fief and was instead given a single city to serve as his "bath town."

Despite this diminishment of his material means, Wei Wuji continued to increase his reputation as a noble patron. He sought out two knights of Zhao who had a reputation for great wisdom but who had secluded themselves among the gamblers and wine-sellers and cultivated their friendship. When Zhao Sheng berated his brother-in-law for this behavior, his own retainers began to leave his service in order to offer their allegiance to Wei Wuji, deeming that the latter prince had been the one to truly show an appreciation for the genuine dignity of knights.[33]

Given the kinds of tensions such rivalries must have engendered, it is a wonder that peace prevailed between Zhao Sheng and Wei Wuji while the latter sojourned in Zhao. Perhaps their being kin by marriage prevented overt hostilities. Friendly relations between the two great patrons persisted despite their living at such close quarters, however, lasting even until Zhao Sheng died in 252 BCE.[34]

In 251 BCE King Zhao of Qin died after a reign of 56 years. His death initiated a swift and dramatic transition of leadership in Qin, that will be discussed in more detail in the next chapter. The new regime that eventually settled into place in the western kingdom resumed an aggressive stance against its rivals to the east. In 249 BCE Qin invaded the small state of "East Zhou."[35] The feudatory of "West Zhou" had already been annexed by Qin in 256 BCE, and in that same year the last Zhou monarch, King Nan had died, without an heir to the Zhou throne being coronated. The conquest of "East Zhou" wiped out the last remnants of the Zhou house.[36] In that same campaign Qin took three cites from Han and combined them with the conquered terrain of "East Zhou" to form a new commandery along Qin's advancing eastern frontier.

In 248 BCE Qin captured 37 cities from Zhao. The following year Qin marched on Wei and took two cities. Qin's resurgent aggression raised alarm in Wei.[37] Distressed, the court turned to Wei Wuji for leadership. Emissaries were sent to Zhao pleading for Wei Wuji to return and take up the position of prime minister.

By this point Wei Wuji had been living in exile for 10 years and resented having been so ostracized by his homeland. He angrily ordered his gate guards that any of them who admitted an emissary sent by the King of Wei would be put to death. His two new retainers who lived as hermits among the gamblers and wine-sellers of Handan came to call on him. They reminded him that his prestige in the world still derived from his being a prince of Wei. If Wei were destroyed and the ancestral temples of his forbears destroyed, what dignity would he have left?

Wei Wuji was chastened by these words, and in 247 BCE he returned to Wei. On his arrival his brother the king embraced him, and the two men wept. When word spread that Wei Wuji had been given the seal of command in Wei, emissaries began arriving from other states with offers of alliance. Wei Wuji assembled a coalition of five states and led its armies west to meet the advancing forces of Qin. By the end of the year he had dislodged Qin's soldiers from all the territory they had conquered in their recent offensive and driven the army of Qin back through the Hangu Pass.[38]

It was the most serious setback Qin had suffered in its military operations since being defeated in the Eyu campaign by Zhao She in 269 BCE. Wei Wuji dug in to fortified lines and kept the Qin forces bottled up in the Hangu Pass. The coalition army rested, resupplied, and gathered reinforcements in preparation for an assault through the pass into Qin's home terrain.

The Qin court was alarmed. Qin spies sought a former retainer of the general who had been murdered by Wei Wuji when he used Wei's troops to lift the siege of Handan. They paid the man a large bribe to slander Wei Wuji to the King of Wei, claiming that Wuji's spreading popularity among the other states had convinced him he should be king. To lend credibility to these slanders, Qin sent agents into Wei Wuji's camp masquerading as well-wishers bearing congratulatory gifts, who wondered aloud, so as to be overheard by many witnesses, when Wei Wuji would be crowned King of Wei.

The king succumbed to these tactics. He sent a new general to the Hangu Pass to take Wei Wuji's place as overall commander. In the absence of its popular and charismatic leader, the coalition force soon broke up, and Qin went on the offensive through the Hangu Pass again.

Wei Wuji knew that he had been removed from command because of slander. He became deeply disenchanted, and though he remained in Wei, he stopped attending court. He withdrew to his palace, where he spent all of his time carousing with his retainers over strong wine and in the company of women. After four years of such debauchery he died in 243 BCE, the same year as his half-brother King Anxi of Wei.[39]

Wei Wuji's death left Huang Xie as the only remaining great patron. In 241 BCE Huang helped coordinate another attempt to rally the forces of the eastern states. He pledged Chu's forces to a coalition that included armies of Han, Zhao, Yan, and Wei. Overall tactical command was given to a general from

Zhao, but in deference to Huang Xie's influence in bringing the coalition together, the King of Chu was made the "covenant lord" of the alliance.

The coalition army reached the Hangu Pass, but was met there by a Qin counter-attack. The encounter was a military disaster. The allied force was defeated with heavy losses and its soldiers fled in panic.[40] It was the last time that the eastern states would rally to take the offensive against Qin. King Kaolie of Chu was bitterly upset by this catastrophe and blamed Huang Xie. From this point on relations between Huang Xie and the king cooled.[41]

Huang Xie was aging and no longer capable of the dynamic leadership he had exercised in his youth. His estrangement from the king worried him, as did the fact that the king, who was also aging, had thus far failed to produce an heir. In the midst of these concerns he was approached by a knight from Zhao named Li Yuan who desired to join Huang's household.

Li Yuan was traveling in the company of his sister, who was very beautiful. He had hoped to introduce her to the King of Chu, but when he heard that the king was infertile, he concluded that it would be foolish to present his sister at court, since only her becoming pregnant would guarantee that she received special favor from the king. Instead, he accepted patronage from Huang Xie and devised a plan to take advantage of his sister's charms.

First, Li Yuan aroused Huang Xie's curiosity by pretending that the King of Qi had sent an emissary to inquire about his sister as a concubine. When Huang believed that the King of Qi had been interested in Li Yuan's sister, he asked to meet her. On seeing that she was indeed very beautiful, Huang accepted her as a concubine. She soon became his favorite companion and was pregnant with child.

Before her pregnancy began to show, Li Yuan's sister approached Huang Xie with a proposal. She explained that though no one knew it, she was pregnant. This created a potential opportunity for Huang Xie. If King Kaolie died childless, the throne would pass to another member of the royal clan, and Huang Xie would lose the base of his power. If the king died and left an infant son on the throne, Huang could become Regent and remain in power indefinitely. To secure this outcome, Huang would only have to install Li Yuan's sister in the king's harem, so that her child could become heir.

Huang saw the logic of this proposal. He presented Li Yuan's sister to king, who like Huang was charmed by her beauty. He took her as a concubine and within a few months of entering the palace she had given the king a son.

In 238 BCE King Kaolie fell ill. By this time Li Yuan had become an official at the royal court and was no longer a member of Huang Xie's household. As the king neared death, one of his retainers named Zhu Ying approached Huang Xie and warned him that he was in danger. Li Yuan resented the fact that Huang knew the secret of the heir's parentage and did not want to share power with anyone when his sister became Queen Dowager. He would be sure to enter the king's chambers first with his own men when the king died and kill Huang Xie from ambush when Huang came to pay his respects to the departed king. To prepare against this threat, Huang Xie should install Zhu Ying as a palace attendant. Zhu would thus be in a position to know about the king's demise right away. He would be sure to enter the king's chamber first and would assassinate Li Yuan when Li came to set up his ambush.

Huang Xie brushed Zhu Ying's warnings aside. Li Yuan, Huang declared, was a weakling. Besides which, he had no reason to resent Huang Xie, who had always treated him well. Zhu Ying offered his apologies and departed Chu to avoid disaster.

Age and complacency born of power had clouded Huang Xie's judgment. Seventeen days after Zhu Ying issued his warning, King Kaolie died. Huang Xie was ambushed and killed by Li Yuan's forces as he entered the king's chamber. Li Yuan then led his men in an attack on Huang Xie's household and killed Huang's whole family. The child that Huang had fathered on Li Yuan's sister was enthroned as king. He is known by the posthumous title of King You (r. 237–228 BCE).[42]

The death of Huang Xie ended the age of the great patrons in the eastern states. No one in the eastern states would ever consolidate power to match that wielded by Zhao Sheng, Wei Wuji, and Huang Xie ever again. In the absence of such leadership in the east, the strategic dominance of Qin grew steadily greater.

Why was this? The legends generated by the great patrons themselves tempt us to fall back on the "great man" theory. The great patrons, by this view, were epochal talents. As they lived, so did the hope for the security of the eastern states. When they were gone, all was lost.

Temptingly dramatic as such an assessment might be, if we take a broader view of the age in which they lived, we can see that the great patrons were as much symptoms of the contradictory forces impelling Warring States society as drivers of its history. The governments of the Warring States were increasingly bureaucratized fiscal-military states, structured on principles of meritocracy and routine authority. The society that housed the governments of the Warring States, however, was dominated by an aristocracy deeply rooted in kinship and ritual and intensely committed to traditions of hereditary privilege and charismatic authority.

The great patrons lived at the point of contact between these two aspects of state and society, and exploited the resulting collision. The low-status functionaries who staffed the organs of state needed protection from their aristocratic superiors, and the great patrons possessed social and material assets that enabled them to provide such protection. The great patrons were literally "power brokers," lending some of the sheltering authority that flowed from aristocratic tradition to their retainers, so that the operation of the routinized state could be "deconflicted."

Though the career of the great patrons well illustrates the potential effectiveness of the informal structures and mechanisms they improvised and implemented, it also makes clear their limits. The great patrons were powerful and influential, but the best their efforts at resistance could produce was a temporarily effective policy of "containment" of Qin's power. "Rollback" of Qin's aggressive encroachment proved beyond their capabilities.

These limits of the great patron's power were predictable, because ultimately their existence did not serve to solve a problem, but depended upon the persistence of one. Indeed, one might venture that the great patrons lived at a fault line in Warring States society that eventually swallowed them whole. The contradictions and conflicts between the traditional aristocratic order and the new fiscal-military state did not end with the great patrons' deaths, but continued to impel the evolution of state and society through the end of the Warring States and beyond.

In 246 BCE, the year after Wei Wuji's coalition army reached the Hangu Pass, a new sovereign took the throne of Qin. His name was Ying Zheng, and he would eventually go on to take the title of First Emperor. As his court pressed Qin's strategic advantage, its leaders had to navigate the same contradictions between aristocratic tradition and bureaucratic organization as had impeded the efforts of their eastern counterparts to mount an effective resistance.

15

Unification

The Kingdom of Qin and the Former Zhou States, 256–221 BCE

In 256 BCE King Zhao of Qin felt confident enough in the unassailable power of his government and military to effectively bring the Zhou dynasty, which had held the title "Son of Heaven" for almost 800 years (a feat that would never be surpassed, or even matched by half, in the Chinese-speaking world), to an end. He annexed the territory of the state of West Zhou, terminating its line of "dukes" who had ruled the feudatory since the bloody "year of four kings" (441 BCE), and appropriating the regalia of the Zhou throne (which had taken up residence in West Zhou). When in the same year of 256 BCE King Nan of Zhou died after a reign of 59 years, no scion of the Ji clan was crowned in his place, finally and totally relinquishing the Zhou dynasty's claim to the Mandate of Heaven.[1] King Zhao of Qin's successors would mop up the last residual remnants of the Zhou house seven years later, destroying the tiny state of East Zhou that had been the last refuge of the Zhou king. In a truly multipolar world such profanations of ancient prerogative would have been impossible, as Wei Ying (a.k.a. King Hui of Liang), the last person to try to end the Zhou dynasty (as discussed in Chapter 9), had learned the hard way.

If these acts left any doubts about Qin's supremacy, the failure of the "Vertical Alliance" campaigns of 247 and 241 BCE (discussed in the conclusion of the preceding chapter) put those to rest. As the soldiers of the last coalition army to threaten Qin fled in panic in 241 BCE, it was clear to all informed observers that the eastern kingdoms would never again mount an effective resistance to Qin's power. The question of the formal capitulation of the states of Wei, Han, Zhao, Yan, Qi, and Chu to the King of Qin was not one of "if" but "when."

Despite the clear signs of inevitability in 241 BCE, Qin's final victory and the resolution of the crisis of the Warring States would take another 20 years. In retrospect, this should not be surprising. "When" was far from the only question confronting the people and leaders of the Warring States. "How" loomed just as large. Would the final victory of Qin be achieved militarily, politically, or by some combination of both these methods? What would be the fate of the eastern kingdoms and their royal families? Was it possible that the sophisticated, wealthy, still well-armed, and deeply rooted territorial systems they had established could be dismantled and displaced, or (as seemed more likely) would the eastern kingdoms persist as vassal-states within a new world order led by Qin? If the latter, by what process would that new system be formalized, and by what mechanisms would it be enforced?

If the only questions that awaited resolution concerned the relationship of Qin to the other powers, unification might not have taken so long. But all of the problems of internal social coherence and political dysfunction that beset the eastern kingdoms were present in Qin to varying degrees. King Zhao had overcome the problematic grip that his mother, uncles, and brothers had exerted over the court and government of Qin, and had put the organs of state under the steady guiding hands of Fan Sui. Fan Sui, in turn, had groomed a talented literatus (Cai Ze, a native of Yan) to take over for him as prime minister when he died in 255 BCE, creating a smooth transition of power from one civil administration to the next.[2]

But King Zhao's death in 251 BCE upset the court culture of Qin yet again. King Zhao had come to the throne very young and proven a physically robust and long-lived king. It had taken him a long time to come into his own as a monarch and shake free of the shackles of his maternal kin, but his partnership with Fan Sui had set a pattern of stable and effective leadership for a decade and a half.

King Zhao's longevity, however, which had been such a boon while he lived, created problems upon his demise. He had outlived one Heir Apparent,[3] and had lasted so long on the throne that the reign of his two immediate successors proved very short. In the wake of King Zhao's death, Qin would go on to have three kings in five years, the last of whom came to the throne as a 12-year-old boy. Qin had developed efficient institutions that were staffed by a disciplined and well-trained civil bureaucracy, but such jarring transitions of power inevitably create disruptions in any royal dynastic system, no matter how well led.

The years of transition following the death of King Zhao might have been marked by much more disturbance but for one man. His name was Lü Buwei

(d. 235 BCE), a native (like the famous Shang Yang of yore) of the state of Wey. He was a complex and dynamic figure, whose mark on the politics of Qin might be described as constructive in some cases, disruptive in others, but always substantial. Any account of the ultimate unification of the Warring States must begin with his story.

In certain respects Lü Buwei resembles figures we have encountered before in the annals of the Warring States. Like Fan Sui he became Prime Minister of Qin and proved an able administrator. Like Huang Xie, he rose from humble beginnings to become one of the most celebrated patrons in the world: he has, in fact, been called the fifth and last of the "great patrons," having emulated Huang Xie specifically, as we will see. But in the final analysis Lü Buwei defies being reduced to any pre-existing model or role. His career was so idiosyncratic, his approach to politics was so innovative and distinctive as to make him sui generis.

Lü began his public life as a merchant, and enjoyed such success at that vocation that it had made him fabulously wealthy before he first became involved with the royal family of Qin. Being a denizen of the markets and trade routes gave Lü a very cosmopolitan perspective. His travels taught him a great deal about how politics worked and how different forms of power could be cultivated and applied.

At the same time, Lü's experience as a merchant made him understand where real control of the wealth of the Warring States lay. One source records a purported conversation between the young Lü Buwei and his father:

> "How much profit can be made on farming fields?" asked the son.
> "Ten times [their cost]," answered the father.
> "How much profit can be made on pearls and jade?" the son asked again.
> "One hundred times [their cost]."
> "How much profit can be made from establishing the ruler of a kingdom?"
> "Unlimited."[4]

The conversation almost certainly never took place, but it expresses a truth of which Lü Buwei clearly became aware early on. Though merchants were increasingly indispensable to the economy and social life of the Warring States, the control and use of the era's wealth was concentrated in the hands of its political leaders and aristocratic overlords. Whatever heights of riches might be scaled among the most successful merchants of the age could not compare with those reachable by the most dominant among its government officials and the most elevated of its nobility.

This insight enabled Lü Buwei to recognize (or perhaps motivated him to seek) the opportunity that would change his life and the course of history. His travels brought him to Handan, the capital of Zhao, where he encountered a Qin prince who was residing there as a hostage to the Zhao court, Ying Yiren (d. 247 BCE). We do not know exactly when this encounter occurred, but it was during the years leading up to the fateful battle of Changping, when relations between Qin and Zhao had reached their nadir. The prince had already been residing in Zhao for many years, and because there was so much hostility between his home and his hosts, he had been forced to live in relative squalor.

Lü Buwei is said to have proposed that he could "enlarge the door" (i.e. improve the living situation) of the prince, to which the prince laughingly replied, "Enlarge your own door, sir." Lü rejoined that this was just what he planned to do, but it would require him to help the prince first. Lü was impressed by the prince's resilience; the prince was won over by Lü's candor. The two became friends, and Lü outlined a plan by which both men could raise one another's fortunes.

Lü's scheme was premised on what he knew about the political dynamics of the Qin royal family. Prince Yiren was the grandson of King Zhao and the son of the Lord of Anguo (d. 250 BCE), who had become Heir Apparent at the death of his older brother. Prince Yiren had been given over as a hostage to Zhao because he was one of more than 20 brothers, and his mother was not one of his father's favorites.

Among the Lord of Anguo's wives, he was most fond of the Lady of Huayang. She was in effect his "principal wife," except for the fact that she had not been able to bear him any children. The love the Lord of Anguo felt for her would guarantee that she would be named his queen when he took the throne, but since she could have no children, a son by one of the Lord of Anguo's other wives or concubines would become the next Heir Apparent.

That would place the Lady of Huayang in a very vulnerable position. However much influence she enjoyed because of her intimacy with the Lord of Anguo, once one of the other palace woman became known as the mother of the future king, that woman's power would be paramount, and the Lady of Huayang in danger. The situation would become even worse for the Lady of Huayang when the Lord of Anguo died, leaving her without either husband or son.

Lü Buwei proposed that Prince Yiren should campaign to become the Lady of Huayang's adopted son. This would ordinarily be impossible. The prince was trapped in Zhao and completely without resources. That is why he and Lü

Buwei could make such beautiful music together. As a merchant Lü Buwei was free to move between Qin and Zhao and could advance Prince Yiren the funds that he would need to conduct such a campaign. Prince Yiren agreed that the plan had merit, and promised that if all went as Lü Buwei proposed, the two men would "share the state of Qin" once the prince was king.

Lü Buwei gave Prince Yiren 500 catties (*jin*) of gold for the purpose of improving his residence and wardrobe and expanding his retinue of retainers, and spent another 500 catties in the markets of Handan on rare objects and novelties to present as gifts to the Lady of Huayang. He journeyed to the Qin capital, where he was able to obtain an audience with the Lady of Huayang's older sister.

On meeting the Lady of Huayang's sister, Lü presented the gifts that he had purchased in Zhao, asking that they be given to the Lady of Huayang with the compliments of Lü Buwei and his friend, Prince Yiren. The prince, Lü reported, was a man of extraordinary character, who had attracted a retinue of worthy retainers from far and wide. The prince looked up to the Lady of Huayang as he did Heaven, and was continually grieved that she and the Lord of Anguo had no children between them.

Lü's visit had its intended effect. Her sister reported on her meeting with Lü to the Lady of Huayang and urged the Lady to consider adopting Prince Yiren as her son. The Lady of Huayang saw the advantage of doing so immediately, and in turn pleaded with her husband that he should name Prince Yiren (whom she renamed "Zichu," or "Son of Chu," in commemoration of her being a native of Chu) as his principal son and Heir. He assented to her request, and the couple sent Lü Buwei back to Zhao loaded with gifts for the prince. They moreover enlisted Lü Buwei to be the prince's tutor.

Lü Buwei settled in Handan so that he could be near the prince. While there he took as a concubine a famed beauty who was a daughter of one of Handan's most prominent families. At a drinking party the prince caught a glance at Lü's new companion and was enamored of her. Rising to make a toast to her health, the prince begged that he be given the lady to have as his own concubine by Lü Buwei. Lü was angry at the prince's presumption, but he was loathe to jeopardize their partnership when he had already sunk so many funds into his plan. He acquiesced to the prince's request. When that lady gave birth to a son, the prince made her his principal wife, and her son, Ying Zheng (259–210 BCE), his heir.[5]

The child Ying Zheng would eventually become King of Qin and the First Emperor. The *Records of the Historian* reports that Lü Buwei's lady was already pregnant by Lü when she moved to the prince's household. This story is of course suspect; even if it were true there could have been no evidence on which the account in the *Record of the Historian* is based.

What is interesting to note here is the parallel that the story creates between the narrative of Lü Buwei's relationship with the prince and that of Huang Xie's relationship with King Kaolie of Chu. This parallel (one man being the father of the other's "child") is of course not the only correspondence between the story of Lü Buwei and that of Huang Xie. Both men built political careers by befriending a royal prince who was forced to live in exile.

This latter connection is not likely to have been coincidental. Lü Buwei would have been very aware of Huang Xie's history—the two men are likely to have met personally during Lü's travels. The commonly known facts of Huang's rise to become Prime Minister of Chu may well have provided the inspiration for Lü Buwei to cultivate his partnership with the prince, and the parallels between Lü's career and Huang Xie's did not end with Lü's activities in Zhao. In later life Lü continued to employ or elaborate upon strategies previously utilized by Huang Xie. Lü seems to have drawn a great deal of inspiration from Huang, and this lent credence to rumors (or perhaps deliberately fabricated myths) that Lü, like Huang, had committed fraud with regard to the paternity of a royal heir.[6]

The peace of the prince's household was broken by the siege of Handan in 258 BCE. As the armies of Qin surrounded the city, the Zhao court prepared to execute the prince. Lü Buwei dispensed immense bribes to guards and officials, and in this way was able to purchase transit for himself and the prince across the battle lines to join Qin forces, who provided passage for them to return to Qin. The Zhao court would have killed the prince's wife and son, but the lady's powerful family in Handan took the woman and her child in and gave them refuge.

When King Zhao died six years after the lifting of the siege of Handan, in 251 BCE, the Lord of Anguo was crowned king, known posthumously as King Xiaowen (the "Filial and Cultured" king). His beloved Lady of Huayang was enthroned as queen, and the prince, her adopted son, became Heir Apparent. On this transition, the prince's wife and son were finally returned to Qin by the Zhao court.

King Xiaowen of Qin reigned for one year before dying, only three days after the royal calendar had officially been changed to initiate the "year one" of his reign. In 250 BCE he was succeeded by his son, the former Prince Yiren, who is recorded in the histories as King Zhuangxiang of Qin (r. 249–247 BCE). True to his word, he appointed Lü Buwei as his prime minister. Lü was raised to the rank of Marquis Wenxin and given a fief consisting of 12 districts. In this way, in less time than Lü could have possibly imagined, his plan had made him one of the most powerful men in the Warring States, and his power would continue to grow from there.[7]

Lü's ascent to the head of Qin's civil administration caused controversy and tension (evidence of which we will see). Though figures like Fan Sui and Huang Xie had set a precedent for rapid social mobility in the former Zhou states, Lü's career as a merchant marked him with a social stigma. Trade was considered an unworthy occupation that bore the taint of pollution.

But controversy did not constrain Lü from exerting leadership. In his first year as prime minister, during 249 BCE, the lord of East Zhou, the tiny state that housed the last remnants of the Zhou house, colluded with Han, Wei, and Zhao in a plot against Qin. Lü went aggressively on the offensive, destroying and annexing East Zhou (as discussed above) and seizing three districts from the kingdom of Han, from which Lü ordered the creation of a new commandery. As a reward for these victories the king granted Lü the former Zhou capital of Luoyi, with 10,000 households, as an extension of his fief. The following year Lü continued to press the attack to the east, seizing territory from Zhao that was converted into another commandery extending Qin's eastern frontier.[8]

In 247 BCE King Zhuangxiang died, leaving his 12-year-old son Ying Zheng to inherit the throne. At the same time the eastern kingdoms, alarmed by the recent wave of Qin's aggression, formed a five-state coalition under the leadership of Wei Wuji (as discussed in the previous chapter). The coalition army drove Qin's forces back to the Hangu Pass, rolling back some of Qin's recent gains and cutting off many of its garrisons in the east from communication with the Qin court.[9]

It was a watershed moment, and an atmosphere of tense expectation must have hung over the Qin court. When the young Ying Zheng was crowned king, Lü Buwei was given the official title of "Second Father" (*zhongfu*, the same title that had been given many centuries before to the famed minister Guan Zhong, or Master Guan, in Qi), effectively becoming regent of Qin and wielding virtually all of the powers of both the throne and the prime ministerial seal.[10] This gave Lü Buwei some breathing room and political clout, but it could not have made him feel completely secure. If he had continued to lose ground in the east he would most likely have lost the confidence of the Qin court very quickly and come to a very bad end.

As discussed in the last chapter, however, Lü proved capable in a crisis. He orchestrated the campaign of espionage and disinformation that brought down Wei Wuji, and exploited the resulting division and demoralization within the eastern coalition to go back on the offensive. Qin's armies broke out of the Hangu Pass and advanced steadily. By the end of 246 BCE, Qin forces had occupied all of Han's Upper Commandery (the prize over which the Changping campaign had been fought) and had re-established its commandery carved from the territory of Zhao two years earlier.[11]

At the same time that Lü was prosecuting these campaigns against Qin's eastern neighbors, he was negotiating with more distant states, and taking advantage of the hostilities that continued to persist among the kingdoms to the east despite the common threat of Qin's growing power. In the aftermath of the battle of Changping, a period of extended conflict had ensued between Zhao and its neighbor to the northeast, Yan.[12] Lü Buwei sent Cai Ze, one of his predecessors as prime minister (the Yan native whom Fan Sui had chosen as his successor) as an emissary to the court of Yan (conveniently distancing Cai Ze from the Qin court he had once led), and in 244 BCE he was able to negotiate the surrender of Yan's Crown Prince Dan as a hostage to Qin, so as to secure peace and cooperation between the two courts.[13]

By such tactics Lü Buwei was effectively continuing Fan Sui's policy of "befriending the far and attacking the near," with measurable success. In 244 BCE Qin seized 13 more cities from Han and two districts from Wei. In 242 BCE Qin conquered enough territory from Wei to establish an "Eastern Commandery" that brought Qin's eastern frontier almost to the walls of the Wei capital of Greatbridge.[14]

By the beginning of 241 BCE Lü Buwei was arguably the most powerful leader ever to exercise power in Qin, and his strength continued to grow. In that year the last "Vertical Alliance" assault attempted by the eastern states was launched against Qin and repulsed easily (as discussed in the preceding chapter).[15] It was also in that year that he unveiled the fruits of one of his most ambitious cultural programs.

In the years after Lü took over as prime minister and then "Second Father," he used the enormous income flowing in from his estates to build a retinue of clients that rivaled those any of the previous great patrons. He is said to have had 3,000 knights in his service, and he gave special favor to literati.[16] We might be tempted to view this as gratuitous self-aggrandizement, but Lü was obviously a perceptive enough observer of current affairs to have realized that by 249 BCE patronage had become an indispensable element of both social and political power. We saw this in his early advice to Prince Yiren, whom he provided the funds with which to develop his own retinue of retainers. Without such a retinue the prince could not have made himself attractive as an adoptive son to the Lady of Huayang: if he had not shown that he could take knights under his protection, there was no reason for the Lady of Huayang to believe that he would be capable of protecting her.

Though Lü Buwei's enormous retinue of clients resembled that of Huang Xie in scale, Lü employed his retainers in radically new ways. Most significantly, he tasked them with an immensely ambitious literary commission: the construction of a text the likes of which had never been seen before. The text still survives today, and is one of the only sources that we can be confident was transmitted through the ages in something closely resembling the form that it originally took during the Warring States. It is known now by the title *Lüshi chunqiu*, or *The Annals of the House of Lü*, but we cannot be certain of what title it might have been given at the time of its production. Literati at that time may simply have designated it the *Lüzi* or *Master Lü* (as it is sometimes called in imperial-era sources).

In 241 BCE Lü Buwei unveiled this product of his retainers' work. The *Records of the Historian* reports that Lü had the entire text posted at the gates of the market in the Qin capital of Xianyang, and offered a reward of 1,000 catties of gold to any of the wandering knights or persuaders of the world who could improve the text in any way, by so much as adding or deleting one word from it. This story may be apocryphal. The entire text of the *Lüshi chunqiu* is huge. In its current redaction it comprises over 100,000 logographs. If it were written out on standard-size bamboo strips of the kind that were used to record texts during the Warring States (of about a half centimeter wide), the entire text laid end to end would have gone on for the length of a football field (see Fig. 22). If it were written in a much larger hand (as one would suspect would be necessary for such a public display) the text could easily stretch to a kilometer or more.[17]

Though the story may be embellished, it is congruent with what we can clearly perceive to have been the agenda of the project when we look at the text of the *Lüshi chunqiu* itself. The *Lüshi chunqiu* has been derided as overly eclectic or crudely derivative. The text does express an array of different viewpoints and shares much content with other sources that date to the same period. But dismissive criticisms of the *Lüshi chunqiu* miss the point of the work entirely. Any fair reading of the text must recognize that aside from being a work of authentic insight and originality within the larger field of the "Masters'

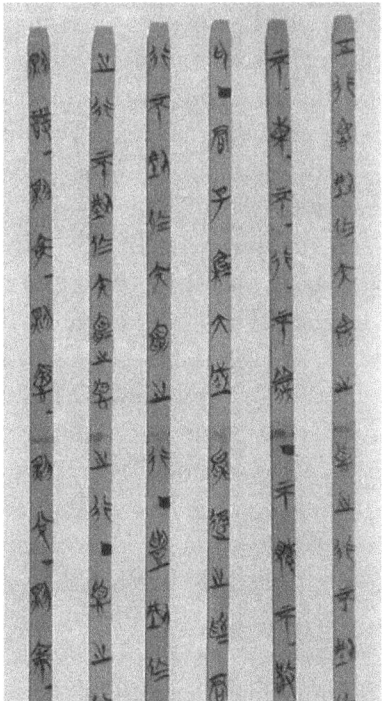

Fig. 22. The principal medium for the composition and transmission of writing during the Warring States period was bamboo strips like these. The bamboo was cut, specially cured and lacquered, and the written strips were bound together by leather strips into a "snow fence" structure that could be rolled up in a scroll. These strips were discovered in Tomb 1 of a Chu funerary park at a place named Guodian in Hubei Province. (Source: inf.news.)

teachings," it was one of the most creative and ingenious works of political messaging produced in the ancient world, bar none.[18]

What makes the story about the posting of the *Lüshi chunqiu* to the market gates of Xianyang most plausible is that the text marks the first time that we know of in the field of Chinese letters that the producers of a text used its organization into titled sections and chapters to encode part of the text's message. Virtually all of the other transmitted sources that contain Warring States material were collated and organized during the Han dynasty by imperial-era scholars. Their "sections and chapters" are thus anachronistic interventions. We can never really know, for example, what form the material we encounter in the *Analects* or the *Mozi* took when it was first written down and circulated during the Warring States.

But the *Lüshi chunqiu* is radically different. Its sections and chapters unfold in a clearly logical and thematically significant order, one which implicitly argues for the significance and message of the text as a whole. The central theme is articulated in a colophon appended to the end of the first of three sections of the text, the "Twelve Records." It records a dialogue between Lü Buwei and an unnamed questioner simply called the "good person." In response to the good person's general query, Lü Buwei answers that the work contains the teachings passed from the Yellow Thearch (sometimes translated as "Yellow Emperor"), the very first ancestral ruler at the beginning of human history, to his son and successor. The gist of that teaching is that to become "father and mother to the people" one must take the cosmos as one's model. There are three basic forces in the cosmos: Heaven above, Earth below, and human beings in the middle. If one impartially uses these cosmic structures as the basis of doctrine and practice, the world runs smoothly. This was how the "age of purity" was achieved in high antiquity, which was only lost in subsequent generations.[19]

The claim of having reconstituted the secret teachings of high antiquity is so grandiose as to perhaps seem absurd, but the content and structure of the *Lüshi chunqiu* lend heft to its assertions. The work as a whole divides into three sections, each of which divides into a number of "Books": "Twelve Records" (Books 1–12), "Eight Expositions" (Books 13–20), and "Six Discourses" (Books 21–26). Each of the three divisions of the text is thus correlated to one of the cosmic structures mentioned by Lü Buwei in the colophon: the first to Heaven, the second to Earth, and the third to human beings.[20]

The use of the organization of the text to mimic the structure of the cosmos would have been intriguing to the literati of 241 BCE, as evinced by Wei Ying's earlier appeal to correlative cosmological ideas. Basic to Zou Yan's doctrine was the idea of "cosmic resonance" (*ganying*, literally "stimulus and response").[21] Objects made of the same type of *qi* are sympathetically linked, they are constantly exchanging simultaneous "vibrations" with one another, unhindered by the separation of vast gulfs of space. A "stimulus" to an object made of "fire *qi*" in one part of the universe will instantaneously produce subtle vibrations in all other objects made of "fire *qi*."[22] Anyone who knows what to look for can thus reconstruct the situation of the entire cosmos from observing a very localized set of facts (for example, within the *Yi jing* divination system, from observing the fall of a group of yarrow stalks or coins), and thus predict the future on the basis of knowledge not otherwise available.

Knowledge of cosmic order could, according to Zou Yan, be used even more proactively. Human leaders could utilize the patterns of cosmic energy flow to benefit human society. For example, during the summer, when "fire *qi*" is ascendant and driving the changes of the season, human rulers could (and should) assist and nurture cosmic forces by sending sympathetic "vibrations" out into the universe through the use of "fire *qi*." Since fire *qi* is responsible for the color red (that is, everywhere we perceive red it is caused by the presence of fire *qi*), the ruler could align himself with the energies of the larger cosmos and send harmonizing vibrations out to the natural world by wearing red robes, driving in a red chariot, etc.[23]

The prospect that political leaders could harness cosmic forces made the task of governing on an ever more expansive territorial scale less daunting. But Lü Buwei and his retainers took this logic a step further. They proposed that cosmic models could be used to reconcile the mutually discordant teachings of the many Masters that had arisen since the time of Confucius.

Their methods in this regard can be best seen in the layout and content of the Twelve Records. From "The First Month of Spring," Book One, the section follows the order of the calendar through to Book Twelve, "The Third Month of Winter." In the earlier books of "spring" (the season of birth) one encounters teachings reminiscent of the Master Yang Zhu, with their emphasis on life and longevity. As one moves forward through the year into late spring and summer (the season of growth and maturity) one encounters first teachings about embodied personal cultivation like those attributed to Master Lao and Master Zhuang, then teachings about text-based learning corresponding to those of Confucius and his latter-day disciples. In autumn (the season of the harvest) one encounters teachings about warfare like those of Master Sun, and in winter (the season of death) one encounters teachings about "frugality in funerals" that echo the ideas of Master Mo.[24]

The overall rhetorical argument of the text is quite elegant: in the same way that the world would perish if all of the mutually opposing processes of the calendar year did not emerge in their proper times, the government of a rightly guided ruler could not function if it did not employ the teachings of all of these various Masters in their proper context. In effect, each of the Warring States Masters had discovered a fragment of the cosmic Way of high antiquity and mistaken that piece for a functional whole. Lü Buwei and his retainers realized the Masters' errors and reassembled the fragments to restore the pristine unity of the true Way of the ancient sages.

In purely intellectual terms this idea was intensely provocative, but as part of a program of political messaging it was brilliant. On a basic level, Lü had used his retainers to create a unique and virtually inimitable expression of "soft power." They could plausibly claim that with the creation of the *Lüshi chunqiu* they had reunified the fractured Way of high antiquity. In the terms of the Masters themselves, the importance and sheer majesty of such a feat could not be overstated. Who unified the Way unified the world. By unifying the world in the abstract, Lü declared powerfully and cogently that the concrete, material unification of the world by Qin was both inevitable and well justified.

Beyond these somewhat ideal (but nonetheless potent) claims, the *Lüshi chunqiu* spoke to the collected literati of the Warring States in a very instrumental, pragmatic vein. In contemplating any future new world order, the chief anxiety of knights throughout the former Zhou domain was the prospect of their future employability. This concern was especially poignant for literati, whose future career chances always hinged on the preferences and tastes of those in power. From the perspective of a literatus trained as a Mohist, for example, the possible ascent of a universal ruler who was a follower of Confucius was deeply troubling. Such a turn could render a knight's learning meaningless and condemn him to perpetual obscurity, or worse.

In that context, the *Lüshi chunqiu* broadcast a message with obvious appeal, crystallized by Lü Buwei's declaration (in the colophon to the "Twelve Records") that those who follow the true Way of high antiquity must be "impartial." Qin was promising that, in the wake of its final triumph, it would be unbiased and ecumenical in its employment of all the literati of the world. This claim was backed up by the structure and the contents of the *Lüshi chunqiu* itself, which showed that Lü and his retainers had discovered and were able to demonstrate to the world how the teachings of all the different Masters could be made to work in tandem. Thus, in the future new world order overseen by Qin, all literati could feel confident that their career prospects would be the same, no matter which tradition they had devoted themselves to learning. It was the kind of conciliatory message perfectly calibrated to overcome resistance and motivate compliance. If the literati of the world could be made to feel they had less to fear from Qin's victory, perhaps they could be dissuaded from advocating for armed defiance on the part of Qin's foes.

The conciliatory messages embedded in the *Lüshi chunqiu* were not confined to those aimed at literati. The same broad appeals aimed at expressing respect for the dignity of knights in general that animated the projected self-image of the great patrons (such as the story of Wei Wuji's courtship of Hou Ying) are spread thickly throughout the sections and chapters of the *Lüshi chunqiu*. The text as a whole promises that the future realm overseen by Qin is one in which knights will be valued and honored (as they were by Lü himself at his court).[25]

Another prominent theme of the *Lüshi chunqiu* involves the path toward future unification. A general ban on the military and a ban on offensive warfare (both of which had been proposed in the teachings of some Masters) were explicitly rejected by the text. The existence of destruction and violence in the workings of the cosmos is offered as proof that the existence and occasionally aggressive use of the military organs of the state are natural and correct.[26]

But the text does repudiate any ambition to unify the realm by purely military means. Long sections regarding the "righteous use of the military" denote that a ruler who follows the Way may use the military to "punish" a wicked or obstinate ruler, but that such campaigns may never end with the extinction of a duly constituted aristocratic lineage. A righteous king or Lord Protector may imprison or kill a wicked ruler, but that offender must be replaced by one of his kinsman, so that the court of the punished ruler will continue and the sacrifices to its ruling lineage will persist.[27] This was an all but overt offer of a negotiated peace to the courts of Wei, Zhao, Han, Yan, Qi, and Chu. If those states would surrender and accept subordination to Qin, their ruling houses could persist as vassals of the Qin king.

The *Lüshi chunqiu* landed in the cultural world of the former Zhou realm with enormous impact. The proof of that can be seen in the very survival of the text itself, which was faithfully transmitted for many centuries. Long after its specific political agenda (the unification of the Warring States under Qin) was no longer relevant. it continued to exert influence on the intellectual culture of China and East Asia more broadly.[28] The text boosted the spreading popularity of the correlative cosmological ideas it had drawn upon so deeply, so that by the end of the second century BCE the use of correlative categories and appeals to concepts like "cosmic resonance" had become virtually hegemonic among literati in the Han empire.

Apart from the intellectual and geopolitical impacts of the *Lüshi chunqiu*, the text brought to fulfillment a strategy that proved Lü Buwei a political operator of amazing ingenuity, and that arguably had made him, in 241 BCE, the single most powerful individual the Warring States had yet seen. As noted above, Lü Buwei had clearly taken some of the inspiration for his personally ambitious plans from the particular example set by Huang Xie. But the promulgation of the *Lüshi chunqiu* showed that Lü's vision was much more expansive. On the most basic level he had learned how important the generous patronage of knights was to the power and success of any politically ambitious figure. But he had also observed the benefits that the state of Qi had derived from the patronage of literati in the Jixia community, and the positive impact of promoting ideas that supported the power of Qi in the form of the teachings of "Master Guan." Finally, he had perceived how important the fellowships organized around the learning and realization of (various versions of) "the

Way" were to the self-identity and political orientation of so many literati, and the broad power and influence of men like Xun Kuang who became prestigious "Masters" within the precincts of that world.

In the construction and harnessing of his patronage retinue for the purpose of creating the *Lüshi chunqiu*, Lü Buwei effectively merged all three of those models of leadership and tapped into all three of those sources of power. All of his retainers had the same personal relationship with him as other knights had with figures such as Wei Wuji or Huang Xie, giving Lü the power of a conventional patron. But beyond this, the *Lüshi chunqiu* clearly served the interests of the Qin throne (as the teachings of "Master Guan" and "Master Yan" served the interests of Qi), thus all of Lü's clients could feel that they had rendered meritorious service to the Qin state and had a proprietary stake in its final triumph. Finally, by exerting himself, employing his wealth, and directing his clients in the exploration (and, by their telling, the resolution) of questions so central to the mission of the Masters, Lü Buwei had forged his retinue into a fellowship that paralleled that of the Confucians or Mohists, led by himself as "Master Lü." The esprit de corps and loyalty that this new hybrid "patronage retinue/state enterprise/literati fellowship" communal association fostered among his retainers was extraordinary and gave him power that vastly eclipsed that of his role models such as Huang Xie.[29]

The *Classic of Change* says that "When the sun is at noon, it begins to set."[30] With the promulgation of the *Lüshi chunqiu* and the defeat of the last Vertical Alliance attack on Qin, Lü Buwei reached the apex of his power. But as had happened with Tian Wen in Qi, Wei Wuji in Wei, and Huang Xie in Chu before him, the concentration of so much charismatic authority in a single individual created resentment against Lü Buwei in the bureaucracy and royal court of Qin. The resentments against Lü had most likely existed from his first rise to prominence, but had remained submerged below sight. In the wake of Lü's most visible triumphs, however, those forces bubbled to the surface.

In 240 BCE Qin went back on the offensive, capturing territory from both Zhao and Wei. In the same years inauspicious omens appeared. A comet appeared in different parts of the sky, lingering in the west for 16 days. The Queen Dowager Xia (grandmother of the reigning king) died, as well as a famous general who had scored major victories for Qin.[31]

The following year a Qin royal prince, Lord Changan Ying Chengjiao, younger brother of the king, Ying Zheng, was sent with an army to take the Upper Commandery of Zhao. Zhao's Upper Commandery shared a border with the Upper Commandery of Han, which had finally been annexed by Qin in 242 BCE. The invasion of 239 BCE was thus a culmination of the efforts exerted by Qin against Zhao since the victory at Changping 21 years previously.

The invasion did not go as planned. On entering Zhao's Upper Commandery, Lord Changan surrendered his army to the Zhao court and accepted a title and fief from the King of Zhao.[32] It was an extraordinary setback that must have shocked the whole Warring States, since the Lord Changan was abandoning a kingdom, his native home, which by all appearances was poised to conquer the entirety of the former Zhou realm. The sources do not provide details of Lord Changan's motives, but he can only have been driven by anger at the regime back home. Much of his anger may have been directed at his brother Ying Zheng, whose position on the throne the Lord Changan may have coveted for himself. But some of his rage was almost certainly focused on Lü Buwei, who had become more powerful and wealthy than any member of the Qin royal clan, even the king himself.

Whether or not Lord Changan had defected in part out of anger at Lü Buwei, the fallout on the prime minister was immediate and serious. This political rebuke from a member of the royal clan, following hard upon a "cosmic rebuke" in the form of a strange comet and the death of prominent elites, made Lü Buwei appear vulnerable. In 238 BCE a report was given to King Zheng that his mother, the Queen Dowager, who had been Lü Buwei's concubine before marrying King Zheng's father, had secretly given birth to two sons by a lover.[33]

The timing of this report is so perfect as to make its being a coincidence unlikely. Whoever told Ying Zheng about his secret half-brothers would have known that this incident would do damage to Lü Buwei, for reasons that will be discussed below. The events of 240–239 BCE had opened a chink in Lü Buwei's armor, and someone moved to exploit it. If the news of the Lord Changan's defection had exposed tensions in the royal family, that of the Queen Dowager's secret children exposed volcanic rifts.

Though Lü Buwei was not the father of the Queen Dowager's illegitimate sons, he was culpable for their births. On the death of King Zhuangxiang (the former Prince Yiren) and the enthronement of the 12-year-old Ying Zheng in 249 BCE, Lü Buwei and his former concubine, now the Queen Dowager, were thrown together again. The reins of government remained in Lü's hands as prime minister, but the formal Regency (control of the sovereign seal of the throne itself) was technically in the hands of the Queen Dowager, by virtue of her blood kinship to the new king. In those circumstances the former sexually intimate relationship between the Queen Dowager and Lü Buwei resumed.

Like the love affair between Mi Bazi and the King of Yiqu decades before, the affair between the Queen Dowager and Lü Buwei had both personal and political dimensions. The couple had a history, and we know for certain that the attraction had been very strong on Lü Buwei's side. The political motives are likewise easy to infer. Prince Yiren's death had left Lü and the Queen Dowager jointly in control of an enormously powerful kingdom of which neither was a native and in which both had only shallow roots. The Queen Dowager's position was particularly precarious: her husband was survived by not one but *two* mothers (his adoptive mother, the Lady of Huayang, and his birth mother), both of whose influence would have rivaled that of the Queen Dowager's. Lü Buwei and the Queen Dowager needed one another, and a love affair was one way of "sealing" the bond between them. In politics a common transgression and a shared secret can sometimes cultivate trust.

Over time, as Lü became more confident of his footing in Qin and increasingly worried about the growing maturity (and perceptiveness) of the king, he desired to extricate himself from the affair with the Queen Dowager. His plan was to distract the Queen Dowager by finding her a new lover. The man that he ultimately found to fill that role is known to history as "Lao Ai."

"Lao Ai," as his story is recounted in the ancient chronicles, is a figure of some mystery and no little salacious fascination. His name literally translates as "Lustful Misdeed," so it is unlikely that the written record has preserved his real identity. The designation "Lao Ai" seems to have been coined by some clever scribe to posthumously punish the man.[34] There is good reason to believe that the moniker refers to a real person, however, and that "Lao Ai," whoever he was, played a role in the ultimate downfall of Lü Buwei.

According to the *Records of the Historian*, Lü Buwei recruited Lao Ai as a retainer for his one outstanding asset: an extraordinarily large penis. After Lao Ai joined Lü's household, the prime minister began throwing frequent gatherings marked by wine and music, at each of which Lao Ai was called upon to perform a "party trick." He would strip naked, hang a wooden chariot wheel from his erect penis through the hole in the hub, and walk about displaying the strength of his virility to the hilarious appreciation of his patron's guests.

Lü hoped that when news of this feat reached the Queen Dowager she would be tempted, and he was not disappointed. The Queen Dowager asked Lü Buwei to transfer Lao Ai to her household. Lü thus accused Lao Ai of a crime, so that he would be sentenced to castration. On his instruction the

Queen Dowager bribed the officers charged with executing orders of castration, so that Lao Ai would be released, his facial hair removed but otherwise unmutilated. In this way Lao Ai was legally presumed to be a eunuch and could serve the Queen Dowager in the privacy of her bedchambers.[35]

The above story, though titillating, is probably not true. It is clear from other sources that Lao Ai eventually became very powerful in his own right through his association with the Queen Dowager, being awarded titles and estates as "Marquis Changxin" and gathering a household of 1,000 retainers.[36] Those facts do not square with accounts of Lao's public debasement and faux-castration. If the Queen Dowager had gone to such trouble to keep her relationship with Lao Ai discrete, why would she have called attention to him by making him a Lord? The scenario becomes even less plausible when one contemplates the scandal that would have erupted by raising a condemned and castrated criminal to the rank of marquis.

Thus, the very lurid stories about Lao Ai preserved in the *Records of the Historian* were most likely concocted to defame the Qin court. But the evidence does suggest that the queen did take a lover, with whom she had two illegitimate sons. Like Mi Bazi before her, the Queen Dowager would have had the means to conceal her issue. When she was pregnant she reportedly would have an "unfavorable" divination cast that required her to leave the baleful influences in Xianyang and remove to her alternative residence in the old Qin capital of Yong, returning to Xianyang only when she had given birth. The Queen Dowager's building of a new family and her maneuvering to see her lover given title and wealth are again signs that her motives in her relationships with "Lao Ai" were simultaneously personal and political. She desired a lover but also, understandably, given the egregiously patriarchal nature of Warring States society, felt she needed a male ally of real power in the political realm. When Lü Buwei became unwilling to fill at least one of these roles for her (making his commitment to the second role suspect), she took steps to see that Lao Ai could fill both of them.

For the Queen Dowager, the children she had with Lao Ai were most likely cherished as a concrete embodiment of their personal and political bond. The chronicles report that Lao Ai harbored ambitions of making his eldest son by the Queen Dowager King of Qin, but that could only have been true if Lao Ai was himself rather daft. The Mi-clan clique, which had put much of the power and wealth of Qin into the hands of non-Qin natives, had required the participation of a full-blood member of the Qin royal line, and even it had unraveled when King Zhao finally tired of his kin's selfishness. It would have been rash folly to try and place a scion of some random bloodline on the Qin throne over the objections of the whole royal clan (who most likely would have found many sympathetic collaborators in the civil bureaucracy and military). If he attempted such a feat, Lao Ai would have been assuming that he could compress into a matter of days or weeks the kind of political transition that it had taken the Tian clan of Qi and the ruling clans of Wei, Han, and Zhao generations to achieve. The only way such a plot on Lao Ai's part would have been feasible is if, in reality, Lao was himself a member of the Qin royal clan (perhaps one of the king's uncles or cousins). Though that is possible (given the fact that the chronicles do not give us his real name), there is no way we could ever corroborate (or definitively disprove) such a hypothesis from the existing evidence.

Whatever the case may have been, the revelation of the existence of the king's secret half-brothers was political dynamite, especially in the immediate wake of the defection of the Lord of Changan to Zhao. Lao Ai was exposed to immediate danger. Whether he had ever intended to usurp the throne, he was now exposed as having profaned the Queen Dowager, and the king would be honor-bound to make him pay. In an attempt to save himself and his sons, Lao Ai fabricated orders under the royal seal and that of the Queen Dowager, to mobilize the soldiers and militia in and around the royal palace along with cavalry under the command of both regular officers of the Qin military and lords of the Rong and Di tribes.

A sign of how much disaffection there was with the position of Lü Buwei at the Qin court can be seen in the fact that Lao Ai was not alone in this rebellion. The Commander of the Palace guard and 19 other high officers of the Qin court joined in the uprising. They may not all have been Lao Ai's co-conspirators from the outset—they may have been drawn in to the action by the forged orders that Lao Ai had drawn up under official seal. But their willingness to follow orders from the Queen Dowager that were a betrayal of the king shows that they must have had longstanding grievances with the conditions of the court.

Lao Ai led an attack with the object of seizing the king. It is not clear what "end game" he envisioned. Any genuine escape from his predicament would have required that Lü Buwei be killed, or at least deposed, and Lao Ai made prime minister. Above and beyond that, Lao's security would almost certainly have required that the king (the son of Lao Ai's lover, the Queen Dowager) be killed and replaced by another scion of the royal clan.

The king was prepared, however, and mobilized forces under Lü Buwei and two loyal courtiers to counter Lao Ai's assault. Lao's forces were defeated and he fled, but he and his confederates were captured. Lao Ai himself was torn to pieces by horses, the court officers who had aided him were decapitated and their heads displayed on poles. All of Lao's household retainers were punished. The less guilty were demoted in rank and set to work as woodcutters in the royal funerary park. More serious offenders were transported to hard labor in Sichuan, which served as a penal colony for the Qin state. The Queen Dowager was sent out of the capital in Xianyang and kept under house arrest in her residence at the old capital of Yong. Her sons by Lao Ai were killed.[37]

Though Lü Buwei had rallied to the defense of the king, the Lao Ai affair proved his undoing. A royal investigation after the rebellion had been put down revealed Lü's role in having brokered the affair between Lao Ai and the Queen Dowager. The king wanted to execute Lü Buwei according to the law, but so many of Lü's retainers came forward to plead their lord's merit and virtue that the king settled for Lü's dismissal from office. Lü left Xianyang and took up residence in his fief along with his retinue of knights.

It was the repetition of a pattern seen in the careers of Tian Wen, Zhao Sheng, Wei Wuji, and Huang Xie. Like all the other Warring States, power in the kingdom of Qin was shared between a strictly regulated civil-military bureaucracy and an aristocratic order rooted in tradition, kinship, and ritual. Though mechanisms like written law codes and the use of seals and tallies helped enforce compliance with established routines and rules, the charismatic influence that an individual like the Queen Dowager, Lao Ai, or Lü Buwei wielded could frequently circumvent the regular operation of the system (as when the Queen Dowager gave her seal to her lover, or perhaps had it stolen) and create unpredictable disruptions. Someone like Lü Buwei, who successfully harnessed both matrices of power (that of the bureaucracy as prime minister, that of the aristocracy as Marquis Wenxin and great patron) invariably proved capable of great achievements, but just as certainly fell victim to the instability that his contradictory roles engendered.

The cracks that had opened up beneath Lü Buwei widened as his position became more untenable. Like the retinues of the other great patrons, that of Lü Buwei proved portable. His retainers followed him to his fief, where he set up court and (most likely) continued the literary activities that he had overseen successfully while he and his knights resided in Xianyang. Lü's household was a constant buzz of activity, wandering scholars and emissaries from all over the world continued to come in and out, seeking Lü's advice and sounding him out on his future plans.[38]

The hostility to Lü Buwei continued to mount in Xianyang. In 237 BCE, the year after Lü Buwei had been dismissed from office, a proposal was memorialized to the throne by members of the Qin royal clan and debated in court, calling for expulsion of all foreign-born people from the state of Qin. The proposal warned of the danger of espionage and cited the example of a case that had transpired early in Lü Buwei's tenure as prime minister. A knight from Han had been hired by the Qin court as a hydraulic engineer, for the purpose of building a system of canals and irrigation ditches.[39] In 246 BCE, while work was already underway, it was discovered that the knight was a paid spy working for the Han court, and that one of his missions was to exhaust the resources and people of Qin with his project. The king had desired to execute the knight, but he pleaded that his work was of real benefit to Qin, and so it was allowed to continue.[40]

The point of raising the "Canal Affair" in 237 BCE was by way of insinuating that Lü had proven in that instance that he could not be trusted: he had sheltered a foreign spy then just as later he would keep the secret of the Queen Dowager and her illicit affair. Lü had been at the helm for a decade, in which time he had attracted many knights to Qin to serve in his retinue and at the Qin court. All of them were now suspect. If all foreigners were not expelled (which would of course entail the expulsion of Lü and his retinue), Qin would be in constant peril.[41]

In the course of this debate a knight distinguished himself as a forceful persuader. His name was Li Si (d. 208 BCE), and he was one of those who would have been expelled if the proposal had been mandated as law, since he was a native of Chu. Li Si had begun his public career as a petty officer in the local government of Chu. In his work at that post he is supposed to have observed that the rats who lived in the privy ate filth and were terrified by human beings and dogs, while the rats who lived in the tax granary lofts ate sweet grain and had no fear of people or dogs. This taught him that no one is born superior or inferior to others: we derive our character from the circumstances in which we live.

Li Si had departed Chu in search of better circumstances. His travels took him first to the gate of Xun Kuang, whom he studied with and served as a disciple. After completing his studies, he traveled to Qin, where he first joined the household of Lü Buwei. Lü was impressed with Li's talent and appointed him as a "Court Gentleman," a low-ranking attendant official at court. In this capacity he was able to advise the throne, and he sent up periodic memorials to the young king.

The king was impressed with Li Si, and made him Chief of Scribes. He was in that position when the proposal was put forward to expel all foreigners from Qin. Li Si himself would have been a victim of this plan, and wrote a long and expertly crafted memorial in response. He reviewed the long history of Qin rulers and their use of foreign talent: Duke Mu's employment of Baili Xi, Duke Xiao's employment of Shang Yang, King Huiwen's employment of Zhang Yi, King Zhao's employment of Fan Sui. He asked the king how many useful objects and fine luxuries his court would lack if he used only products native to Qin. Finally, he inquired what would happen if all the foreign personnel currently at the Qin court gave their talents to other lords and the knights outside of Qin now who yearned to be subjects of Qin were told to give up hope.

Li Si was a fine writer, but he obviously had the better part of this argument. His last point was his most cogent. The Warring States had become a very cosmopolitan society, and the Qin court of 237 BCE was no exception in that regard. The Qin princes may have resented the power of foreign interlopers like Li Si and Lü Buwei, but the entire bureaucratic structure that had helped make Qin so predominantly powerful could not run in their absence. The proposal was struck down, and Li Si himself was promoted to Commandant of Justice.[42]

Though the members of the royal clan and the titled aristocracy of Qin had overreached in their efforts to exert power over the civil bureaucracy and meritocracy with a ban on foreign personnel, their setback did not save Lü Buwei from the forces that were gathering to pull him down. The constant flow of fawning visitors in and out of Lü's court finally broke the king's patience. He sent a letter asking Lü Buwei: By what merit he had really earned his titles and estates? On the basis of what kinship was he called "Second Father"? At the end of the brief letter he declared that Lü and his household would be relocated to Sichuan. Lü, seeing the writing on the wall, took poison rather than waiting for a summons to the executioner.[43]

With Lü Buwei's dismissal from office, the young King Ying Zheng stepped out from under his prime minister's shadow and began to truly rule in his own right. Ying Zheng arguably belongs on any list of the 10 most important figures in world history, having been the first to establish and hold a position (the Dragon Throne of the unified Empire) which would persist in various forms for more than 2,100 years,[44] and which, for much of recorded history, would hold one-quarter of humanity under its sway. Like many figures who played such a pivotal role, the written record about him is complex.

Fig. 23. The famous terra cotta army buried to guard the approaches of the First Emperor's tomb give us a clear sense of what the massed infantry armies of the Warring States period would have looked like on campaign. (Source: Wikimedia Commons.)

It can be difficult, sometimes impossible, to separate fact from fiction and history from mythology where stories of the First Emperor are concerned. Accounts of the fabulous splendor of his tomb, for example, were long dismissed by many scholars as obvious hyperbole. According to the *Records of the Historian*, Ying Zheng was sealed in a tumulus the size of a large hill, the hollow center of which was shaped as a model of the cosmos in miniature. On the floor of the tomb, all of the mountains, valleys, rivers, and seas of the known world were sculpted in exacting detail, with the bodies of the water being represented by an enormous quantity of mercury. On the ceiling the stars of the night sky were arrayed in precise patterns of rare gemstones. The body of Ying Zheng himself is said to be kept in a sarcophagus that floats on a sea of mercury in the very center of the tomb.[45] All of these descriptions understandably aroused skepticism on the part of scholars.

In 1974 a group of farmers digging a well in Shaanxi province discovered the first of a group of man-made pits in which hundreds of life-size terra cotta figures were buried (see Fig. 23). Most of the figures are soldiers, sculpted to accurately depict the uniforms and gear of the Qin army, each of them originally painted in lifelike colors and provided with working armaments and equipment. This buried army was one of the most labor- and resource-intensive public works projects of antiquity, rivaling the Great Pyramids of Egypt in sheer effort and expense.

No word about the terra cotta soldiers had been preserved in the ancient chronicles, but this enormous army (which has been only partially excavated even now) was found to be guarding the eastern approaches to Ying Zheng's tomb. Given that this latter, enormous feature of the tomb complex escaped inclusion in the written record, scholars are no longer confident that early descriptions of the tomb mound itself are exaggerated. It has not been excavated yet, but ground samples in the area show a high degree of mercury contamination.[46]

The archaeological record corroborates the impression left by the written record, that Ying Zheng was a forceful and distinctive character who left a powerful and lasting personal imprint on the work of his court and, more broadly, on the world in which he reigned, first as king, then as emperor. The chronicles describe him as a dynamic but sometimes volatile or even capricious figure, capable of penetrating insight and strong leadership but prone to occasional bouts of paranoia or rage. Given the experience of his formative years, this can hardly be surprising. He was born and spent the first years of his life in captivity, having been left by his father in a city where he and his mothers were objects of hatred. When he was finally freed and brought to live in luxury and splendor, he had less than four years to adjust to his change of fortunes before the weight of history was laid upon him at the age of 12. The mere fact that he did not collapse under such strains shows him to have been a truly exceptional individual.

The distinct personal orientation of Ying Zheng to political affairs is perhaps best exemplified by his affinity for the counsel of Li Si. When Li Si joined the Qin court he offered advice to Ying Zheng that departed radically from the world view and governing ethos expressed in Lü Buwei's *Lüshi chunqiu*. Where Lü Buwei had advocated a conciliatory approach to the elites and rulers of the Warring States, Li Si, by contrast, argued that now was not the time to appease or reconcile. The widening power differential between Qin and its rival kingdoms presented a historic opportunity. Qin could, if it went aggressively on the offensive in this moment, subdue the other Warring States and unite the world. If Qin hesitated or shrank from the harsh methods necessary, the moment would pass and the chance to unify the world be lost.

Li Si's preference for confrontation over reconciliation was not confined to the macropolitical realm. Unlike Lü Buwei, who sought to woo knights with promises of respectful treatment, patronage, and employment, Li Si favored the use of intimidation and manipulation. He advised Ying Zheng to send out clever agents, well provided with funds, who would be directed to bribe those knights serving in other courts that proved willing to be corrupted, and arrange the assassination of anyone who could not be so co-opted.[47] Whether because he was persuaded by Li Si's arguments or because Li's perspective spontaneously accorded more closely with Ying Zheng's than that of the former prime minister, as Ying Zheng took a more independent hand in affairs, Qin policy came to embody the principles outlined in Li Si's advice to the throne much more than anything expressed in the *Lüshi chunqiu*.

In 238 BCE, the same year as the Lao Ai affair, military aggression paid enormous dividends for Qin. Qin's armies marched south and east from their bases in the newly formed Eastern Commandery that had been established in territory conquered from Qin's old nemesis of Wei. The campaign of 238 BCE brought more than six new districts under Qin's control. By the time these campaigns halted, Qin's domain had been extended so far that it shared a boundary with Yan in the north and Qi in the east.[48] Qin was thus closing in on the vision outlined in Huang Xie's memorial presented to King Zhao of Qin 25 years before, in which he described a future in which Qin's frontiers would reach the Pacific Ocean and cut the Zhou realm in two.

In the same year as these conquests in Wei, the King of Zhao came to pay court to Ying Zheng, seeking a peace compact. Ying Zheng entered into an agreement with Zhao, affirming publicly that the King of Yan was "without the Way" and that Zhao would be correct to exterminate the kingdom of Yan altogether. When in 237 BCE the armies of Zhao invaded Yan, the Yan court sent an emissary to Qin pleading for rescue.[49] Ying Zheng seized the opportunity. He sent his most trusted commanders, Wang Jian and Huan Bo, to invade Zhao. While the armies of Zhao advanced across Yan, scoring successive victories, the armies of Qin did the same within the territory of Zhao. By the time Zhao's armies could be recalled from Yan, six of Zhao's districts had been lost and Zhao's king had died in bitterness and frustration.[50]

Despite the ever-mounting threat of Qin's power, the eastern courts continued to pursue conflicts with one another. In 235 BCE the Wei court pleaded with Qin for assistance in a campaign against Chu, aiming to conquer some of the territory that Chu had acquired from the partition of the domain of Song. A joint Qin-Wei expeditionary force marched into Chu. The campaign did not achieve its objective, but the fighting took a much greater toll on both Wei and Chu than it did on Qin, if only in relative terms.[51]

Having abandoned the campaign in Chu, Ying Zheng turned his focus back on Zhao. In 234 BCE he raised a major levee of new soldiers and ordered an assault that carved two new commanderies out of conquered Zhao terrain.[52] The following year General Huan Qi set out from Upper Commandery and took his soldiers across the Taihang Mountains, striking toward the region north of Handan to cut off communication between the Zhao court and its territories on the Inner Asian steppe. The new Zhao king gave command of the counter-attack to Li Mu (d. 229 BCE), a general who had proven himself in campaigns against the Xiongnu, a steppe confederation of growing power that had been threatening Zhao along its northern frontier.[53] Li Mu destroyed Huan Qi's invasion force. Huan Qi himself, cut off from the return route to Qin and fearing reprisals if he returned home, fled to the court of Yan in search of refuge.[54]

Despite this setback Qin remained on the offensive. In 233 BCE Ying Zheng mobilized to invade Han. Fearful and desperate, the King of Han turned to diplomacy. Ying Zheng had read and admired some of the writings of Master Han Fei, the brilliant prince of the Han royal house who had been a disciple of Xun Kuang. Li Si, having been Han Fei's co-disciple, informed Ying Zheng about the Master whose writings he had appreciated. When word reached Han of Ying Zheng's respect for Han Fei, the King of Han sent him as an envoy to plead for peace.[55]

In audience with Ying Zheng, Han Fei did not disappoint the young king. Ying Zheng was impressed with Han Fei, leaving the literatus hopeful that he could persuade the king with logic and eloquence. He wrote a long and impassioned memorial pleading with Ying Zheng to see the folly of destroying Han, which is preserved in the eponymous text attributed to Han Fei and is entitled "Preserving Han" (*Cun Han*). The memorial argues, in effect, that the existence of Han meant only benefit to Qin, while its destruction could only bring woe. Han already paid tribute to Qin and followed its directives as if it were one of Qin's own commanderies, thus the expense of destroying Han was doubly wasteful. Moreover, the long-term impact of destroying Han would be even more harmful. The other eastern states would realize that the same fate awaited them unless they resisted, and rather than emulate Han in being more submissive to Qin, they would unite in hostility and destructive wrath.[56]

Han Fei was effectively trying to replicate the feat accomplished by Huang Xie in 273 BCE, and in the terms by which the larger literati community understood the world, it should have been possible. Huang Xie had been a gifted writer, but Han Fei was a genius whose mastery of all dimensions of the literatus's craft was unmatched. If "worth" as the Masters and their disciples understood it had as much influence as they thought it should, Han Fei should have prevailed.

Unfortunately, there were more things in Heaven and Earth than were dreamed of in the Masters' teachings. If Lü Buwei had still been in charge of the Qin court, Han Fei's arguments might have carried the day, as they comported well with the conciliatory ideas expressed in the *Lüshi chunqiu*. But Ying Zheng was inclined to the more cynical and hard-bitten strategic outlook articulated by Li Si.

Li Si, for his part, lobbied aggressively against the efforts of his former co-disciple. His written response to Han Fei's memorial is also preserved in the *Han Feizi*. At the heart of Li Si's thesis was a classic ad hominem argument. Li Si declared that as a prince of the Han royal house, Han Fei's interests would always be aligned with the interests of Han, he could never be trusted to give any advice that would genuinely be of advantage to Qin.

Ying Zheng was persuaded by Li Si to reject Han Fei's advice, but he remained so personally impressed with Han Fei that Li Si grew alarmed. One of Li Si's retainers observed that the rapport between the king and Han Fei had grown so warm that the latter man might ultimately persuade the king to offer him a post at the Qin court. If that happened, he would almost surely rise quickly to outrank Li Si, perhaps even becoming prime minister.

Li Si took his retainer's warnings to heart. He approached Ying Zheng with advice, cautioning the king that a man as brilliant as Han Fei was a keen observer whose gaze missed nothing of significance. If he was allowed to return to Han after having been at the Qin court for so long, Han would have vital intelligence that would undermine all of Qin's plans. Li Si urged the king to have Han Fei killed on some pretext.

Li Si's urgings convinced Ying Zheng, who issued an order for Han Fei to be detained. Li Si sent poison to Han Fei in his cell, offering him the chance to commit suicide. Han pleaded for an opportunity to make his case for clemency to the king, but he was denied an audience. Eventually Ying Zheng regretted his decision and ordered that Han Fei be released, but by that time Han had despaired of his chances and taken Li Si's poison.[57] The annals of the Warring States present us with many ironies, but perhaps none is greater than the fact of Han Fei falling victim to the destructive forces of court politics that he himself had analyzed so brilliantly.

In the end the fate of Han bore out Li Si's arguments better than those of Han Fei. On the word that Han Fei's embassy had failed, the King of Han pleaded with Qin to become a vassal, despite the humiliation of doing so after his own envoy and kinsman had been killed on thin justification.[58] Demoralization and defeatism gripped Han. In 231 BCE a knight surnamed Teng, who was the Acting Prefect of Han's Nanyang Commandery, surrendered his territory to Qin. For this act of betrayal he was promoted to the rank of Palace Scribe of the Qin court. The following year he led his regional forces in a march on the Han capital, taking the King of Han (his former monarch) prisoner.[59] This brought a final end to the sovereign state of Han, 223 years after it had first been created from the partition of the state of Jin.

The destruction of Han was a major turning point. It demonstrated that Li Si's recommended tactics of intimidation and subversion could work just as well as (or better than) the conciliatory policies advocated by Lü Buwei. The augmentation of Qin's power that it effected is difficult to overstate. The territory of Han was centrally situated and strategically critical, affording Qin's armies freedom to strike virtually any of its rival states without having to worry that its supply lines would become overextended or impeded.

The manner of Han's fall was as devastating as its material strategic impact. The fact that the ancient state had imploded, with one of its own officials serving as the agent of the downfall of its king, shook the foundations of the political world. In 262 BCE Zhao's attempt to accept the defection of one of Han's Prefects had brought cataclysmic consequences down on the Zhao court. If no similar consequences were suffered by Qin now, the resulting precedent would be corrosive of the coherence of all the eastern states. The King of Qin would be shown as the only sovereign whose writ was truly effective, the loyalty of all of the other regional officials of the world then became negotiable. Acid had been thrown on the ties holding each of the respective eastern states intact, and they proved lacking in the political will to mount an effective response.

Having destroyed Han, Ying Zheng once again focused on Zhao. Zhao had begun experiencing draught and famine, and Qin took advantage of its weakened state to attack. In 229 BCE General Wang Jian once again led armies out of Upper Commandery across the Taihang Mountains, seeking to cut off the Zhao capital from the steppe lands that were the source of Zhao's elite cavalry. Li Mu was sent to meet the invading force, but spies at the Zhao court who had been bribed by Qin, among whom was the Queen Dowager of Zhao, reported that Li Mu was planning to rebel. The Zhao king ordered Li Mu killed and replaced him as commander with a member of the Zhao royal clan.[60]

In 228 BCE, after a hard-fought campaign, Wang Jian destroyed the Zhao army that had been commanded by Li Mu (killing the Zhao prince who had assumed command) and marched south on Handan. In a panic, the Zhao king sent an emissary to inquire whether Lian Po, the famed Zhao commander who had served so ably against both Qi and Qin, was still healthy enough to lead. Lian Po had fled to Wei after a feud with a rival commander in Zhao. One of the same Qin spies who had undermined Li Mu bribed the Zhao king's emissary to give a bad report of Lian Po. Though Lian Po had eaten a full meal, donned full armor and leaped onto his horse to show his fitness, the emissary told the Zhao king only that Lian Po had gotten up to relieve himself three times while they ate together. The Zhao king believed Lian Po had grown too old and did not summon him.[61]

Wang Jian's forces overran the Zhao capital and captured the Zhao king. Ying Zheng personally went to Handan and oversaw a manhunt for all those who had mistreated him and his mother when they lived in Zhao as hostages. These unfortunates were rounded up and executed.

One of the Zhao king's brothers fled the capital accompanied by several hundred members of the royal clan and court officials, and established himself in the Dai Commandery. Dai was the territory that Zhao Wuxu had first conquered by murdering the King of Dai in 476 BCE, and which had served traditionally as a fief of the current Zhao Heir Apparent. The fugitive Zhao prince had himself coronated as the new King of Dai. The territory that had once been the Zhao heartland became Qin's new Handan Commandery.[62]

The desperation and chaos that reigned among the eastern states was expressed in an affair that transpired in 227 BCE. In that year Ying Zheng sent two commanders leading separate armies in a "pincer move" to assault both Yan and the rump kingdom of Dai. The campaign advanced rapidly, driving a combined Yan-Dai army to the banks of the Yi River, where it was defeated.[63]

Alarm seized the elites of Yan, but the only leader among its ruling class who formulated a robust response was its Heir Apparent, the Crown Prince Dan. Crown Prince Dan of Yan had arrived as a hostage in Qin in 244 BCE, thanks to negotiations initiated by Lü Buwei. The Crown Prince had previously been a hostage in Zhao, where he and Ying Zheng had played together as boys. On coming to Qin the Crown Prince felt snubbed by Ying Zheng, who refused to treat him with any of their former intimacy. He escaped from Qin in 232 BCE and returned to Yan, where he harbored his grudge against Ying Zheng. As Qin grew more powerful and encroached ever more inexorably on the eastern states, the Crown Prince became convinced that his vendetta was not merely personal, but a matter of ultimate urgency to the world.[64]

He sought counsel from some of the officials of Yan that he most revered and trusted. The first advice they offered him was to abandon his dream of revenge. When pressed further, they allowed that there was a slim chance an alliance could be formed between the rulers of the remaining eastern states. When the Crown Prince rejected that idea as too slow to satisfy his impatience for revenge, he was finally advised that an assassin might be procured for the mission. The Crown Prince was thus recommended to seek the service of Jing Ke.

Jing Ke was a romantic and quixotic figure, virtually the apotheosis of his era. A knight born in Wey, he had wandered through the former Zhou realm, acquiring all the skills that were most celebrated among knights and developing a reputation for passion and eccentricity. He was both a literatus and a swordman, a student of statecraft and a dreamer. He had made friends among the wealthy and powerful in many states, but he had settled in the marketplace of Yan, where he spent his time drinking and singing songs in the company of a dog butcher and a musician. His name was given to the Crown Prince as the knight whose spirit was up to the task of assassinating the King of Qin.

Crown Prince Dan sought out Jing Ke and wooed him in all the ways that had become the hallmark of great patrons like Wei Wuji and Zhao Sheng, showering him with riches and honors and treating him with exaggerated courtesy. When Jing Ke finally agreed that the time was right for him to undertake his mission, he asked that he be given some "tokens of trust" that could win him entry into the presence of the King of Qin. He was furnished with two objects to aid in the prosecution of his mission. The first was a detailed map of one of the most strategic regions of Yan.

The second object was the head of Huan Qi, the Qin general who had fled to Yan after being defeated by Li Mu in Zhao. Ying Zheng had executed Huan's family and confiscated his estates. Huan had been offered refuge in Yan and become the personal friend of the Crown Prince, but when Huan heard of Jing Ke's objective, he readily cut his own throat so that his head could be used to take revenge on the King of Qin.

Jing Ke was given one of the bravest warriors in Yan to serve as his assistant. When he set off for Xianyang in 227 BCE, as the armies of Qin descended on the Yi River, the high nobles of Yan saw him off wearing robes of mourning white. His friend the marketplace musician played a sorrowful song about heroes who set off, never to return.

When he arrived in Qin the objects that he had brought won Jing Ke an audience at the royal court. Coming into Ying Zheng's throne room, the brave warrior assisting Jing Ke began to tremble, but Jing Ke remained calm and explained that his servant was merely awed to be in the presence of the "Son of Heaven." Ying Zheng asked to see the map that the trembling servant carried.

Jing Ke removed the map from its casings and handed it to Ying Zheng, who began to unroll it and peer at its depictions. When the king reached the point in the scroll that concealed a dagger, Jing Ke, who had been standing before the throne while the king perused the map, grabbed Ying Zheng's sleeve with his left hand and snatched the dagger with his right. Jing Ke aimed a thrust at the King of Qin's heart, but Ying Zheng's reflexes were quick. He sprang from his throne and twisted clear of the knife, leaving his ripped sleeve in Jing Ke's left fist.

Chaos erupted in the court as Jing Ke pursued Ying Zheng around the pillars of the upper hall. None of the courtiers in the upper hall were allowed to bear arms, so they pummeled at Jing Ke with their fists in confusion. The royal physician threw his satchel of medicines at the assassin. There were armed guards in the lower hall of the throne room, but they were not allowed to ascend without a royal command, and in the adrenaline rush of the moment Ying Zheng did not pause to issue an order.

Ying Zheng had a sword on his belt, but it was long and fitted tightly into his ornamental scabbard. He tried several times to draw it, but could not get enough leverage while the sword was on his hip. Finally one of the courtiers shouted at Ying Zheng to shift the sword to his back. The king adjusted his belt so that the sword could be drawn over his shoulder, and when he did so it came free of his scabbard. He slashed at Jing Ke and opened a gash in his left thigh. Jing Ke threw his dagger at the king and missed, hitting one of the pillars in the upper hall.

Ying Zheng stabbed Jing Ke repeatedly until the knight collapsed against a pillar, his legs splayed. Laughing, Jing Ke mocked the king. He claimed that the only reason Ying Zheng had survived was that Jing Ke was trying to force him into a peace pact at knife-point that he could have taken back to offer the Crown Prince of Yan.[65]

If the assassination attempt on Ying Zheng had worked, it might have bought the eastern states some time to regroup, depending on how much disorder attended the King of Qin's death. But the failed assassination attempt only managed to throw fuel on the bonfire of Qin's aggression. By resorting to the same coercive tactics Qin had been employing, moreover, Crown Prince Dan had helped foster cynicism and malaise among the knights of the east.

Qin's armies crossed the Yi River and overran the Yan capital of Ji. The King of Yan moved his capital to Liaodong, in present-day Manchuria. He executed his son the Crown Prince Dan and offered his head to the armies of Qin in exchange for an armistice.[66]

While Qin's armies advanced in the northeast, their recently conquered subjects in the former state of Han rebelled. The city of Xinzheng, the former Han capital, expelled its Qin garrison and declared a revived Han throne. Qin's armies put down the rebellion quickly, killing the dethroned King of Han in the process.[67]

While all of these operations were transpiring in the north, a third Qin expeditionary force went on the offensive in the southern kingdom of Chu.[68] An inflection point had been reached. The productivity of Qin's former conquests (especially its colonial possessions in Sichuan) had given Qin a replenishable surfeit of men and materials. At the same time, the territorial expansion of Qin along its active battle fronts had made its supply lines easier to maintain, bringing the costs of aggression down even as its revenues rose. A cycle that was virtuous from the perspective of Qin, vicious from that of its opponents had been activated. The more Qin conquered, the easier conquest became.

In 225 BCE the armies of Qin attacked Wei. For all of the mistakes of its leaders, Wei had remained a vital state with a robust mystique well into the last half of the third century BCE. But with the fall of both its neighboring brother states, Han and Zhao, Wei's strategic position was hopeless. The armies of Qin were able to quickly surround Greatbridge, secure in the knowledge that no state would come to Wei's rescue.

The one power that might have rallied to Wei's defense was Qi, but that state was under the rule of the particularly weak-minded King Jian. King Jian's mother (the daughter of the Grand Astrologer of Ju) had tried to warn him of ministers in his court that could not be trusted as she was on her deathbed (as discussed in Chapter 11), but had given up on seeing that he did not have the capacity to understand. He had given leadership of his court to a prime minister, Hou Sheng, who most likely would have headed his mother's list of suspect characters. Hou Sheng, like his counterparts in Han and Zhao, had accepted bribes from Qin for many years. He not only refused to mobilize Qi's armies to the defense of any of the other eastern states, he deliberately neglected the necessary preparations for the defense of Qi itself.[69]

The Qin commander assaulting the Wei capital breached the dikes on the Yellow River and the ingenious system of canals that served as the city's transport network. The city flooded, undermining the foundations of the city walls, which collapsed. The last king of Wei surrendered, and the dynasty founded by Marquis Wen of Wei ended. All of the princes of the Wei house were hunted down by Qin soldiers and killed. The last surviving prince was spirited out of the palace by his wet nurse, but she was spotted on the road by a former minister of the Wei court, who turned her in to the Qin army for a reward. The wet nurse fled deeply into a marsh pursued by Qin soldiers, and vainly attempted to shield the prince with her own body, but both she and the infant were pierced by dozens of arrows.[70]

With the fall of Wei, and with Qi safely neutralized, Qin was able to direct all of its resources to the margins of the former Zhou realm. Armies simultaneously assaulted Yan and Dai in the North and Chu in the south. The campaign in Chu initially met with more difficulty. The first commander entrusted with the operation did not request enough men and supplies, and was defeated by the treacherous terrain and tenacious armies of the South. Wang Jian was called out of retirement and, after demanding a larger force and promises of ample reward for success, he pressed forward. In 223 BCE, two years after the fall of Wei, Wang Jian entered the Chu capital and took the last King of Chu prisoner, ending the long history of that southern imperium.[71]

The campaign in the north took longer but met with fewer setbacks. In 222 BCE, one year after Wang Jian entered the Chu capital, Liadong fell. The Yan king was captured and the kingdom of Yan extinguished. After conquering Yan, Qin's armies doubled back and overran Dai. The same year that Yan was conquered, the "first and last" Zhao clan King of Dai was taken prisoner, bringing the Zhao royal line to a final end.[72]

With the destruction of Yan and Dai, Qi stood alone. From their positions in Yan, Qin troops poured across the northern frontier of Qi in 221 BCE and advanced on Linzi, the Qi capital. Thanks to the deliberate malfeasance of prime minister (and Qin double-agent) Hou Sheng, the Qin invaders met only token resistance.

King Jian, on inquiring of his prime minister, was told that resistance was futile. Mounting a chariot to go meet the Qin armies and surrender, he purportedly met a knight who asked him how he could be so shameless as to give up his birthright so compliantly. The impressionable king turned his chariot around and returned to court, where he sought out one of his more honest courtiers and asked what could be done other than surrender. The courtier explained that Qi still had thousands of men in arms, and if the king rallied them they might be joined by thousands of others from Han, Wei, Zhao, and Chu who desired to resist. He urged the king to take up the fight.

The king contemplated this, but was soon approached by a Qin agent who promised that the king would be granted a fief of 500 square *li* if only he would head west toward Qin. The king decided that this would secure him a good future for much less trouble, so he did as the Qin agent proposed. When he had traveled some distance and was at a point between two Qin military checkpoints, Qin soldiers surrounded him and would not allow him to continue. They held him in place until he starved to death.[73]

The story of King Jian's demise is most likely apocryphal, but it expresses an impression that must have haunted many of the literati who observed the decade between 231 and 221 BCE. If eastern leaders had rallied their elites and peoples to effectively resist, the juggernaut advance of Qin power might have been interrupted. But the divisiveness, greed, arrogance, callousness, and venality displayed by eastern leaders hollowed out the legitimacy of their regimes just as their material resources were likewise ebbing away. Leaders in the east were not only losing land, people, and resources, they were losing the ability to conjure in people's imaginations a future in which states such as Wei, Qi, or Chu were still meaningful.

With the final destruction of Qi, the last independent kingdom apart from Qin was eliminated, and the Warring States came to an end.[74] Ying Zheng had conquered "all under Heaven," and was the uncontestable founder of a new dynasty.

Epilogue and Conclusions

> The vapors of Heaven and Earth mingle, and the myriad things are distilled.
>
> *The Classic of Change*

As the dust settled from the last of Ying Zheng's wars of conquest, the shock and awe that pervaded what had once been the Zhou realm were profound. From the fall of neighboring Han in 229 BCE, Qin's destruction of the Warring States had taken just under eight years. Successive generations had been born, fashioned lives and careers around, and been buried in the hallowed ground of the kingdoms of Wei, Zhao, Han, Chu, Yan, and Qi. The urban centers and monumental architecture of those states surpassed anything hinted at in ancient texts. Their respective armies were many times more powerful than those of the "world-conquering" sage rulers of antiquity. Who would have guessed that in less than eight years such political behemoths could be swallowed whole? Believing would have waited upon seeing.

The sense of disorientation ranged up to the conqueror Ying Zheng himself and his court. Language did not exist with which to describe the Qin ruler's new position in the political order. Continuing to refer to him as "king" rang hollow. In the more than 120 years following the summit between Wei Ying and Tian Yinqi at Xuzhou in 334 BCE, the concept of "kingship" had been redefined. A king was now a sovereign who moved and operated among peers in a multipolar world. The position of Ying Zheng, emerging as it had from that multi-regnal system, was unique and unprecedented.

Deliberations were held on Ying Zheng's orders. Tradition held that five sage rulers of the distant past had taken the title "Thearch" (*di*) or "High Lord." This was the same title ascribed to the ruler of the gods, and that Wei Ran had proposed the rulers of Qin and Qi should grant to one another in 288 BCE. On reflection, Ying Zheng's courtiers determined that none of the Thearchs of high antiquity had exercised power equivalent to that of the current Qin ruler. They thus proposed that Ying Zheng should assume the title of a group of demigods who had ruled the human realm in the hazy mists of time before the era of the Five Thearchs: "Supreme August One" (*taihuang*).

Ying Zheng provisionally accepted the findings of his officials. He ordered that the qualifier "supreme" (*tai*) should be dropped and the designation "thearch" (*di*) added, creating a new compound title, "August Thearch" (*huangdi*). It is this title that would be held by every ruler claiming to possess ultimate sovereignty within the Chinese-speaking world for slightly more than two millennia, and which, following an apt analogy to the history of the Roman world, has generally been translated in English as "emperor."

Ying Zheng further declared that since his dynasty would effectively be unique and eternal, there would be no need to distinguish between different rulers as the old system of posthumous titles had done. That could be dispensed with in favor of a simple numbering protocol. He would be referred to henceforth as the "First Emperor," to be followed in succession by the "Second Emperor," "Third Emperor,"..."Ten Thousandth Emperor," and so on. Thus was born the designation by which Ying Zheng has been known to history ever since: the First Emperor of Qin (Qin Shihuangdi) (see Fig. 24).[1]

Ying Zheng and his ministers present a picture of mixed confidence and insecurity that might be invoked by the familiar symbol of the *yin-yang*. On the side of confidence, they boldly remade the political world in defiance of tradition and precedent. The creation of new titles and nomenclature was only the beginning.[2]

In the immediate aftermath of the conquest Chancellor Wang Wan and other courtiers proposed that new kings should be established as hereditary regional lords over the former territories of Yan, Qi, and Chu, since they were so distant from the Qin capital and would be difficult to pacify and administer from afar. These new kings would presumably have been chosen from among the emperor's sons or brothers. Ying Zheng placed the proposal before the whole court to be debated. Li Si, still serving as Commandant of Justice, wrote a memorial arguing against the proposal, noting that though most of the regional lords established at the beginning of the Zhou dynasty had been close kin, within a few generations their descendants had taken to warring with one another as bitter enemies, and the Zhou rulers had been powerless to keep the peace. Ying Zheng sided with Li Si. The system of regional lords was abolished, and the entire territory of what had at one time been the seven Warring States

Fig. 24. The First Emperor Ying Zheng (r. 221–210 BCE), as depicted in an imperial-era collection of royal portraits. (Source: Smith Archive/Alamy Stock Photo.)

was divided between 38 commanderies (*jun*), each under a team of centrally appointed officials headed by a prefect, (*shou*).³

It is difficult to overstate how ambitious and audacious this territorial reorganization of the realm was. This degree of regularization and centralization had not been attempted even on the scale of a single Warring State: in each of the competing kingdoms centrally administered local government had existed alongside fiefs held in the hereditary trust of titled families. Such a mixture of governing systems had been considered a function of administrative necessity. Monitoring the activities of multiple regional magistrates was a strain on the bureaucratic faculties of any pre-industrial government. It was assumed that such duties would have to be divided between the central court and satellite courts operating under the hegemony of the throne, in order to keep corruption and abuse within manageable limits. The division of the entirety of "All Under Heaven" into routine, centrally appointed and controlled regional governments was so unprecedented as to be almost inconceivable.

That aggressive confidence marked the administrative policies of Ying Zheng's entire tenure as emperor. He mandated a complete overhaul of the standards of the empire. Embracing the correlative cosmological systems that had inspired King Hui of Liang, the court declared that in the cyclical evolution of the "five phases of *qi*" the establishment of Qin corresponded to the ascending predominance of water, having overcome the "fire *qi*" which had predominated during the Zhou era. On that basis, black (the color produced by and correlated to "water *qi*") was adopted for the insignia, wardrobe, and official equipment of the court, and the number six was made the basis of the dimensions of official gear and the derivation of standard measurements.[4] Units of volume, weight, and length were made uniform throughout the empire.[5]

Standardization extended beyond equipment and material. The writing system of the Zhou realm had been versatile but fragmented, with many variant forms of individual logographs in use and conventions varying from region to region. The Qin court mandated a general unification of the writing system, fixing the standard form of all individual graphs and establishing uniform scribal conventions throughout the empire.[6] The forms of the Chinese logographs in use today are largely a product of this comprehensive reform.

Other ambitious centralizing projects marked Ying Zheng's reign. Weapons were collected from all corners of the empire and melted down to make statues that adorned the capital in commemoration of the emperor's establishment of interregional peace. The system of roads connecting all parts of the empire was extended and coordinated, forming a transit web that radiated from the capital at Xianyang, with special corridors reserved exclusively for imperial use.[7] The length of cart axles was made uniform, to facilitate even wear of road surfaces and ease of travel. A universal system of corvée labor was instituted throughout the realm. All adult men owed a yearly fixed term of service to the state, in which they were employed in the construction and maintenance of public works.[8]

Aside from the expansive road network, this pool of labor was applied to the fortification of the northern frontier. Yan, Zhao, and Qin had all constructed systems of long walls to impede the mobility and combat power of northern steppe cavalry. Under unified Qin rule these systems of fortification were strengthened and extended, linking them together to fashion the original Great Wall.[9]

Fiscal consolidation was accompanied by legal and judicial coordination. The Qin Code first promulgated by Shang Yang and elaborated upon by his successors became binding for the entire empire. The enforcement of law and the administration of justice was made uniform throughout the empire, overseen by a disciplined and orderly cadre of officials and scribes.[10]

This intensive program of centralization and integration yielded dramatic gains in military power. The Qin armed forces, already formidable before the conquest, made the Qin empire a potentate like nothing ever seen before in greater East Asia. The empire remained on an expansionary war footing for all of Ying Zheng's reign. Qin forces pushed the frontiers of the dynasty's control as far north and east as what is now Korea, as far south as the coast of the South China Sea, and as far out into the Inner Asian steppe as what are now the autonomous region of Inner Mongolia and the western precincts of Gansu Province, establishing an enduring and expanding imperial presence along the eastern stretches of what would, over time, develop into the Silk Road.[11] This imperial system founded by Qin would become a shaping influence on all of East and most of Southeast Asia, driving a dynamic network along which goods, people, and ideas have been exchanged down to the present day.

The political, religious, linguistic, economic, social, and artistic life of Asia and the world were forever altered by the legacy of the Warring States and the Qin unification. We take it for granted, for example, that we now live in a world in which Chinese script appears on every page of every newspaper in both Korea and Japan, in which a temple dedicated to Confucius is pictured on the back of the ₫100,000 note in Vietnam,[12] or in which one in every five people on earth lives within the borders of the People's Republic of China. But those realities are contingent products of a long historical process that began with the Warring States and the rise of the Qin dynasty.

Ying Zheng died in the summer of 210 BCE. Just over a year later, the first of the rebellions against Qin rule broke out. A commoner named Chen She (d. 208), the leader of a group of convict laborers who had been delayed in reporting for duty by heavy rains and thus faced punishment, declared himself a general (later "king") fighting for the revived state of Chu. What had probably begun as an act of desperation soon turned into a tidal wave of revolt. Local groups across the periphery of the empire rose up to challenge the Qin court. Soon the Second Emperor of Qin was facing a rapidly swelling coalition of rebel forces. Within three years the Qin army, which had conquered the largest empire East Asia had yet known, had been defeated, and Xianyang overrun.

The Qin dynasty thus presents us with a paradox. It was undeniably one of the most transformative regimes in the long history of the Chinese-speaking world. Yet in a society where such profound historical legacies generally mature over the course of centuries (as would later be the case of great dynasties such as the Han and Tang), Qin rule lasted for only 15 short years. As recounted in the Introduction, the dynasty Ying Zheng founded would only outlive him by four years, and indeed began to disintegrate as soon as he expired.

Why did Qin fall so quickly? The mystery has preoccupied historians virtually since the event itself transpired. During the Han dynasty that quickly succeeded to the mantle of Ying Zheng's court, a scholar-official named Jia Yi (d. 169 BCE) composed a famous prose essay outlining "The Faults of Qin." Many of the answers that Jia Yi proposed to the conundrum of Qin's fall have been echoed by historians in Asia and abroad ever since.

Qin, by Jia Yi's account, had relied too much on military power and economic wealth, and neglected the moral mission that must animate any truly legitimate government. If only Qin had tried to do right with its might, its throne might have endured, but its rule proved too draconian to be borne by the "black-headed people."

Though Jia Yi's explanations have been influential over the centuries, they work better as ideological rhetoric than as historical empirical analysis. A comparison of the legal codes and administrative practices of the Qin dynasty and the succeeding Han dynasty, for example, does not show a stark difference in political cultures. If the harshness of Qin rule caused the dynasty to collapse, the Han should not have endured for more than 400 years.

In similar fashion, any explanation of the Qin fall that heavily emphasizes the personal character of Ying Zheng is dubious. There is much evidence that he was a volatile character, but if he were totally unsuited to rule as some have suggested, it is difficult to explain the scope of his achievements. If Qin was able to recover from the chaotic rule of Ying Zheng's great-great-uncle King Wu and the nepotistic policies of Ying Zheng's great-aunt and great-uncles of the Mi-clan clique to go on and conquer the other Warring States, the Qin empire should have been able to survive the personal foibles of Ying Zheng himself.

Perhaps the greatest evidence that the dynasty was brought down by forces beyond its control are the signs of real insecurity that marked the entire span of Ying Zheng's reign. A court that felt truly confident in the sustainability of its imperial enterprise would not have been so strident in asserting its supremacy. For example, Ying Zheng had replicas of the palaces of his defeated enemies built on the slopes of the hills overlooking the capital.[13] Construction of his mausoleum began shortly after the final conquest, and apart from the enormous scale on which the tomb was built, its design incorporated elements from the mortuary traditions of all six of the conquered Warring States.[14] It was as if the First Emperor felt the need to convince not only his subjects, but even himself, that unification had really happened.

The most telling sign of insecurity on the part of the Qin throne were the persistent and frenetic imperial tours of inspection undertaken by Ying Zheng over the course of his reign. There is no record that Ying Zheng felt compelled to tour the Qin realm frequently when he was a regional lord. During his 11 years as universal sovereign, however, he made tours of the eastern commanderies of the empire at least four times (in 219 BCE, 218 BCE, 215 BCE, and 210 BCE).[15]

Such excursions were costly affairs. The emperor had to be accompanied by a huge retinue of civil and military officials, armed guards, and servants. The shortest of the tours had the enormous imperial cortege travel more than 1,000 kilometers from the Qin capital. It was on the last of these tours that Ying Zheng died in 210 BCE, creating the conditions that gave Li Si, by then serving as Chancellor, and his co-conspirator Zhao Gao, the Prefect of Palace Vehicles, the opportunity to stage a coup giving them effective control of the court (as described in the Introduction).

To call these tours signs of anxiety or insecurity is not to suggest that they had no basic strategic logic. Such displays of "soft power" naturally aided in the consolidation of Qin authority. By transiting peacefully through the length and breadth of his newly united realm, Ying Zheng demonstrated to his subjects that the era of conflict was well and truly over. Anyone harboring dreams of reviving the regional "kingdoms" would be discouraged to see that the new emperor felt secure enough to leisurely travel through lands where it would have been death (or worse) for him to trespass before.

But the ritual dimensions of these tours undermine the sense that their impetus flowed solely or even chiefly from a place of confidence. Each tour took Ying Zheng to various sacred mountains of his eastern territories, where he ascended and made sacrificial offerings to the gods and spirits. This program was modeled on ancient legends of the sage kings of high antiquity, who had demarcated the sacred geography of "All Under Heaven" and who had undertaken similar tours to commune with the spirit realm.

Though legends provided precedent for Ying Zheng's tours, they do not explain the high priority placed on them and the extraordinary expense of their execution. If the goal had simply been to fulfill a traditional obligation bequeathed by the ancient sages, one tour would presumably have sufficed. Ying Zheng was as much inventing tradition as he was following it. He was leveraging the ancient legends in an attempt to serve the urgent needs of the present.[16]

What was at stake? The problems being engaged by the inspection tours were numerous and complex. At the most basic level, the sheer speed and suddenness of the Qin conquest had created a kind of "strategic deficit." The overwhelming success of Qin's military had robbed the Qin court of the opportunity to achieve political "closure" of the kind that Wei Ying had been seeking through interstate summits like the one he held at Welcome Pond in 344 BCE (as described in Chapter 9). There had been no formal abdication of the Zhou throne, no austere surrender or submission offered by the gathered sovereigns of the Warring States. No human agents were left who could effectively solemnify the transition from one era to another, thus Ying Zheng had to go directly to the gods and spirits to authenticate an inaugural rite of passage.

Such formalities were important in setting a climate of expectations. Absent ceremonies that persuaded a critical mass of people and elites that the world had "turned the page," Qin hegemony would have to be maintained through constant, costly application of coercive force. The apprehensions of Qin rulers in this regard proved prescient. The rebellions that broke out in 206 BCE and that would ultimately bring the dynasty down were exactly the kind of contingency that the inspection tours (vainly, as it turned out) had sought to dissuade.

More was at stake, however, than political closure. The Qin conquest had created a religious crisis as well. By destroying the cult complex of seven royal houses, Qin rulers had deprived material support to the spirits of dozens of dead kings. Making so many powerful enemies in the spirit world in so short a period of time was dangerous work, and would necessarily have created the perception that the Qin court and its sovereign were in dire jeopardy. Ying Zheng and his officials, moreover, would not necessarily have had to believe that they were threatened by spirits for them to have understood that the religious crisis they had initiated was a problem. Allowing the general perception to persist that Qin was spiritually "doomed" would have been political folly of the highest order.[17]

Many of the policies of the Qin court manifest the seriousness of the problem. We can see the mark of the crisis in the fabulous terra cotta army that guards Ying Zheng's tomb. The tomb itself is protected by mountains, forests, and water on three sides. The principles of *fengshui* require that one side be left open, leaving Ying Zheng vulnerable to attack by his spiritual enemies. The terra cotta army solved the problem, albeit at great expense.[18]

Even Ying Zheng's purported search for immortality was tied to the religious implications of his conquest. Shortly after his first tour of inspection, he adopted the plan proposed by Xu Fu, a native of Qi, to fund an expedition to search for the three islands of "immortals" (*xian*) off the eastern coast of the empire. Thousands of children were recruited and loaded on ships that set out to find the fabled isles.[19]

Traditions concerning the immortals varied, but they were commonly conceived of as beings who did not require ordinary nourishment to survive (hence *xian* is sometimes translated into English as "transcendent"). This made the immortals, in some sense, more powerful than the ancestral spirits or even the gods, who depended upon the food offered up in sacrifice by human beings.[20]

Somone who had offended as many powerful ancestral spirits as Ying Zheng could potentially find useful allies among the immortals. Thus, his repeated attempts to find the immortals (or become one himself), though they may appear to us as mere superstition or egotism, had a clear political logic from the perspective of the third century BCE. However much the notion of immortality may have appealed to Ying Zheng personally, in the eyes of his subjects someone in his position and with his resources would have looked foolish if he had not sought the aid of the immortals, and the First Emperor could not afford to look foolish.

Like the terra cotta army and search for the immortals, the tours of inspection were aimed at redressing the perceived vulnerabilities of Ying Zheng's throne. This can be seen most clearly in the poetic inscriptions that Ying Zheng erected at each of the sacred mountains where he stopped and performed austere rites on his imperial tours.[21] The first inscriptions were erected on Mount Yi, which overlooks the birthplace of Confucius, the first Master, and on nearby Mount Tai, the most sacred mountain in the spiritual geography of All Under Heaven. While sojourning in Confucius's former home state, Ying Zheng convened a summit of the Master's latter-day disciples and sought their advice concerning the text of the first stelae inscriptions.[22] The inscriptions thus were aimed at effecting a "grand reconciliation." They present a comprehensive justification for the imperial enterprise that Ying Zheng had accomplished, laid out so that all beings in both the human and spirit realms could see the incontestable arguments in favor of Ying Zheng's new order.

The inscriptions are not iconoclastic, draconian, or dogmatically "Legalist" in tone. They faithfully continue the venerable traditions of the ancestral religion inherited from the Zhou dynasty and embrace the moral concepts (humaneness, rightness, filial piety) that animated the teachings of Confucius and other Masters. They extol the virtues of peace and prosperity, and express an obligation to vouchsafe the welfare and harmony of all people. Great care and effort were expended in the composition of these inscriptions. Despite the later tarnished reputation of Ying Zheng and his court, for many centuries the stelae inscriptions themselves were admired by literati for their beauty and elegance of composition. The text of the first inscription, erected on Mount Tai, gives a sense of these writings' tone, a haunting mixture of bombast and gentle pleading:

> His precepts and principles reach all around,
> The distant and near are completely well ordered
> And all receive his sage will.
> The noble and the mean are distinguished and made clear,
> Men and women embody compliance,
> Distinctly demarcated are the inner and outer spheres,
> Nothing that is not clear and pure
> Extending down to later descendants.
> His transforming influence reaches without limit:
> May [later ages] respect and follow the decrees He bequeaths
> And forever accept His solemn writings.[23]

Why, then, did these artful communications not work? We should be open to the possibility that the inscriptions did not achieve their object because such success was not possible. The problems that made the erection of the stelae necessary ultimately proved too intractable to be redressed even by such thoughtful and eloquent means.

As discussed earlier, there were many challenges confronting Ying Zheng and his court, and thus the fall of Qin cannot ultimately be put down to any one factor exclusively. But the stelae inscriptions give us a clue as to the issue that most vexed Qin leaders. As exemplified in the text quoted above, in presenting the justifications for Qin rule, the inscriptions repeatedly assert that the new dynasty had "clarified the division between the noble and the base."[24] The persistent foregrounding of this assertion marks it as a problem. It is as if Ying Zheng and his officials hoped that insisting emphatically enough that all questions of social status had been settled by their regime would make it so. If that in fact was their thinking, they were wrong.

In effect, the Qin court continued to be plagued by the same social contradictions that had destabilized the politics of the Zhou world for more than two centuries. The Qin government was organized as a regularized bureaucracy in which authority was dispensed to individuals on the basis of talent, skill, and learning. Qin elites, however, still believed in a social hierarchy that placed power naturally into the hands of people of ancient lineage and elevated birth. With its system of "merit ranks" the kingdom (and succeeding empire) of Qin had taken more aggressive steps to unify each person's "official status" with his or her general "social status" than had been attempted by any other regime in the Sinitic world, but there were still families who enjoyed traditional prestige that operated independently of the power of the state. In the first year of his reign Ying Zheng reportedly moved "120,000 great and wealthy households" from across the former Zhou domain to the imperial capital at Xianyang.[25] These aristocrats now lived on state stipends rather than on the income from their own estates, but their very existence created a kind of Socratic dilemma about the nature of personal status: were these families great because the state supported them, or did the state support them because they were great? Above and beyond these émigré eastern nobles, who served as a form of "human regalia" for the Qin throne, there was the very large and very wealthy family of the emperor himself.

The sensitivity of the issue ultimately served as the tripwire for policies that would do the greatest damage to Qin's legacy. In 213 BCE Ying Zheng hosted the imperial Erudites to a banquet at the palace. The Erudites were a group of 70 Masters, similar to the denizens of Jixia in the former state of Qi, who were housed at the imperial court on public expense, and whose only official duties were to study and teach "the Way." The Erudites were dedicated to an eclectic array of teachings, including sources that would form the basis of many of the "Confucian classics," and their existence further undermines conventional notions of the Qin as a dogmatically "Legalist" regime.[26]

On this occasion late in Ying Zheng's reign, however, the relationship between the throne and the Erudites took a bad turn. During the festivities the leader of the Erudites stepped forward to offer a homily in praise of the First Emperor's achievements, in which he especially congratulated the ruler for having done away with feudal domains in favor of regular "commanderies and districts," predicting that this would bring the blessings of peace for myriads of generations. When this flattery was done, another erudite named Chunyu Yue (perhaps a descendant of the famed gadfly, Chunyu Kun) stepped forward to contradict his colleague. The current situation, in which the emperor's sons and brothers were all "ordinary men," posed a great danger to the throne. If a traitor like Tian Chang were to appear, who would come to the emperor's rescue? The emperor would be well advised, according to Chunyu Yue, to revive the ways of antiquity and reinstitute feudal ranks and domains.

It is remarkable that Tian Chang, the traitor of 481 BCE, still cast a shadow more than 260 years later. The same tensions between hereditary status and earned merit that had driven the conflict between Tian Chang and Zai Wo were at the crux of the argument between the Erudites at Ying Zheng's banquet. Certainly, times had changed. All of the Erudites at the banquet had much more in common with Zai Wo than they did with Tian Chang. None of them were the sons of marquises or could boast huge estates, yet their learning had lifted them to the privilege of dining with the most powerful man in the world.

Yet though the world of 213 BCE was very different than that of 481 BCE, it was still one in which hereditary status retained great mystique. The host of the banquet was the living embodiment of that mystique: Ying Zheng could count kings and marquises among his direct forbears going back dozens of generations. He had tried to denude his own status of personal implications by abolishing posthumous titles in favor of simple numbering. By calling himself the "First Emperor" he had tried to insist that his authority derived solely from his relationship to the state, rather than from his origins in an ancient family. But that idea was too novel to achieve much traction.

The force of hereditary prestige that had empowered great patrons like Zhao Sheng and Wei Wuji in the decades after the lifting of the siege of Handan in 257 BCE was still a living memory in 213 BCE. Indeed, in their youth many of the Erudites present at the banquet with the First Emperor that night may have enjoyed the hospitality of one or more of the great patrons. Though the elimination of feudal domains had radically diminished the power of the ancient families, there was always a chance that things might go back to the way they had been before, especially in the case of the emperor's close kin.

This was one reason that someone like Chunyu Yue would argue in favor of the return of feudal domains. He (like everyone else in Qin society) was caught in a paradox. Collectively knights like the Erudites had little to gain (and much to lose) from a restoration of the power of the highborn aristocracy. But if and when the old system was reinstated, those individuals who had served the interests of the titled aristocracy stood to benefit enormously, and as long as the Ying clan was on the throne (and the imperial court was filled with well-connected Ying clan scions), there was a chance that the old status norms would be revived. Even Li Si was vulnerable to such concerns. Despite his early epiphany that status distinctions were the product of arbitrary chance, he made sure to hedge his bets by marrying all of his children to princes and princesses of the imperial clan.[27] Thus, try as they might, Ying Zheng and his officials could never truly and finally clarify "the division between the noble and the base."

The question was so sensitive that this (seemingly) casual contretemps at a festive occasion set off a formal debate. The emperor placed the arguments of the two Erudites before the court for deliberation. Once again it was Li Si, now serving as Chancellor, who formulated the winning argument. He condemned the basic logic of Chunyu Yue's thinking. Each generation of past leaders had adopted new policies suited to the conditions of the age: to condemn present policies on the basis of ancient precedent was fraud.

But Li Si went beyond indicting Chunyu Yue's assertions. He proposed that all such arguments should be proscribed by law. To support such a ban, Li Si advised that all records produced by scribes not in the employ of the Qin court be burned. Furthermore, all of the writings of the ancient sages and Masters other than those in the personal use of the court Erudites should be confiscated and destroyed. Discussion or invocation of ancient writings such as the *Classic of Songs* or the *Classic of Documents* outside of the imperial court should be punishable by death.[28]

Ying Zheng accepted and instituted Li Si's proposals, earning the Qin regime eternal ignominy for the subsequent "burning of the books." Censorship led to harsher measures. In 212 BCE two of the occult specialists employed by Ying Zheng in the search for the immortals became disenchanted with the emperor and fled the court. Furious at having been humiliated this way, Ying Zheng ordered a general investigation of the literati community. Under interrogation, Masters began to turn on one another, "naming names" of those who had retained or discussed banned writings in defiance of imperial prohibitions. More than 460 Masters were arrested and brought to the capital, where they were all publicly executed.[29]

This event, two years before Ying Zheng's final demise in 210 BCE, did much to destroy the trust cultivated between the throne and the literati community by the first imperial tour into the homeland of Confucius. The danger of this error was perceived by the Heir Apparent, who remonstrated with his father, criticizing the disrespect he had shown to the learned by such harsh treatment. This angered Ying Zheng, who sent the heir out to the frontier to join General Meng Tian in his campaigns against the people of the steppe.[30] This alienation of father and son helped set the stage for Li Si's and Zhao Gao's coup upon the death of the First Emperor.

When Ying Zheng died during his final inspection tour, Li Si's choice to seize power was driven by the same tensions that had troubled the court since the final conquests of the Warring States. Li knew that he was returning to a capital city filled with imperial kinsmen whose wealth and power had been curtailed by policies Li Si had championed. He was thus compelled to consolidate power in his own hands and use it to preemptively destroy those members of the imperial family who threatened him, further destabilizing a dynasty that had already been weakened by internal conflict.

In the final analysis, the paradox of Qin may not be a paradox at all. The 15 years of Qin rule were an extension and culmination of the revolution of the Warring States. Like Robespierre in eighteenth-century France, Ying Zheng was both a key leader and a victim of the larger historical movement of which he was a part. He consolidated and institutionalized many of the key changes of the Warring States revolution, but ultimately could not change the structural factors that put him and his family on the wrong side of history.

What had the revolution of the Warring States produced? The changes that the era effected in the economy, culture, political life, and even the physical geography of the former Zhou world are virtually too numerous to list. In very general terms, however, the struggles of the Warring States culminated in four key developments that would have an enduring influence on the region and the world. The best way to understand the impact of the Warring States is by reference to questions that animated the controversies of the time, and the answers at which the society of the former Zhou realm ultimately arrived.

The first great question that engendered much conflict during the Warring States was over the choice between two models of the state: one of which envisioned the government as an impersonal bureaucracy organized to achieve material goals, the other of which viewed the state as the patrimony of its ruling clan and an instrument of the honor of its lord and ancestral spirits. The revolution of the Warring States largely settled the question of legitimate government in favor of routine bureaucracy. Predictability and regularity were not always and invariably achieved in governance, but they were basic ideals pursued by successive regimes in imperial times and beyond. In the grand sweep of imperial history most leaders of broad and enduring impact would have more in common with technocrats like Li Kui or Fan Sui than with warrior-aristocrats such as Zhi Yao or courtly patrons such as Tian Wen.

Another great question of the Warring States involved regional sovereignty. Is society best served by centralized unity or multipolar regional autonomy? Here again, the question was never fully settled over the long span of imperial history. But the Warring States, during which fully sovereign regional governments temporarily developed elaborate systems of "international relations," established centralized unity as the ideal and the norm. Debates would persist over time (and continue today) over how much autonomy should rest in the hands of regions and localities, but a general consensus has prevailed that a reversion to the balkanized conditions of the "Warring States" should be avoided (though that has not always proved possible).

A third great question of the Warring States involved the relationship between education and government. Were literati the treasure of the state or its bane? Were they indispensable to the maintenance of good order, or an extraneous drain on resources? Tensions between the state and literati persisted over successive generations throughout time and down to the present day. But the Warring States settled for good and all that government could not be functional or legitimate without the participation of the educated. The strategy pioneered by Marquis Wen of Wei and elaborated upon by other Warring States leaders remained crucial to government success from that era onward, and was a defining factor of the various forms of political system that evolved within the Chinese-speaking world and greater East Asia. Nothing like the civil service exam instituted during the Song dynasty, for example, existed in any of the Warring States. But the "deep historical" processes that would lead to the development of the civil service exam system over time were rooted in the struggles of the Masters and their disciples to enter and shape the political realm during the Warring States.

Finally, the era of the Warring States and Qin dynasty saw one of the most intensely transformative social revolutions in world history. With the collapse of the Qin regime (and upon the conclusion of the civil wars that transpired in its immediate aftermath), the former Zhou realm was transformed from a society dominated by an ancient hereditary aristocracy to one in which hereditary aristocracy no longer existed in meaningful terms, and in which such social groups would effectively never exist again.[31] It is difficult to overestimate the importance of this development for the history of Chinese-speaking society, the broader East Asian region, and the world. It created possibilities and unleashed energies within a large and expanding social sphere that persisted in reshaping the cultural, political, and economic life of the global human community for more than two millennia in ways that continue to this day.

It is important to reiterate that none of these transformations were "complete and final" at any point during or in the immediate aftermath of the Warring States. The Warring States revolution did not, for example, completely replace traditional patrimonial government with bureaucratic political structures, but created such enduring social traction for bureaucratic governance that it would persist through many struggles over and reworkings of the social contract of successive imperial regimes. The Han dynasty that emerged from the civil wars following the collapse of the Qin regime initially elected to repudiate Qin's complete division of the realm into "commanderies and districts." The eastern half of the Han empire was divided between feudal domains apportioned to regional "kings," drawn from among the kin and allies of the founding emperor, Liu Bang (r. 203 BCE–195 BCE). The western half of the empire was divided into regular commanderies and districts overseen by centrally appointed magistrates.[32]

Though this was heralded as a revival of the ancient Way of the Zhou sages, the more traditional dimensions of the Han political system were vexed from the outset and steadily deteriorated as time passed. By the end of Liu Bang's short reign all of the regional kings who were not members of the imperial clan had been eliminated. Over the first decades of Han rule, through a succession of rebellions and civil conflicts, the fiefs of the regional kings were steadily weakened and reduced, so that the Han government progressively grew closer in form to that of its Qin predecessor and drifted ever further from the ancient model of Zhou rule. Though occasional revivals of and debates over the value of such regional "kingdoms" would persist for all of imperial history, the normative organization of imperial government had largely been anticipated by the Qin restructuring and the novel Warring States models on which it was based.

In similar fashion, the social revolution of the Warring States, though profoundly significant, was provisional and subject to variation over time. The idea of hereditary status did not perish altogether with the fall of Qin. But the Chinese-speaking world would never again see the emergence of a group whose hereditary privileges were as dominant as those of the Zhou-era aristocracy.

The government of the Han dynasty, for example, bestowed inheritable titles upon officials and subjects who rendered extraordinary service to the throne, and the imperial clan itself was composed of the progeny of emperors and kings. But this new imperial aristocracy did not possess anything like the venerable pedigree of the Zhou nobility. The Han founder Liu Bang had effectively been a common farmer, thus those at the very apex of the Han social order could never, even in the last decades of Han rule, count highborn figures among their ancestors for more than 15 or 20 generations.[33]

In that climate, the earned status that flowed from education and personal merit could compete on a par with, even surpass in importance, that of birth and lineage. From the Han dynasty on, the effective ruling class of the empire was composed primarily of *shi*. *Shi* never had to worry that their dignity was so far beneath that of a "marquis" that they could not meet (and be commonly expected to treat one another) as peers in the context of state service. Moreover, *shi* identity itself was explicitly understood and celebrated as an *earned* status. Birth played little or no part (in an ideal sense, at least) in determining one's place as a *shi*; one became a *shi* through effort and education. It is from this point on that it no longer makes sense to translate *shi* as "knight." From the Han dynasty on, translations of *shi* such as "scholar-official" or "scholar-gentry" more accurately convey the cultural significance of the label and the social position of those to whom it was applied.

Was the revolution of the Warring States a heroic epic or an epic tragedy? I am inclined to invoke Zhuangzi (Master Zhuang), who would insist that any answer to such a question is entirely a matter of perspective. The long-term impacts of the Warring States revolution on hundreds of millions throughout East Asia were intensely diverse. The new social, cultural, and political forms that emerged from the Warring States produced harmony and prosperity for some, strife and deprivation for others, some combination of all of these for different regions and peoples at different times.

Whatever one's normative judgment, there can be no doubt that an understanding of the Warring States is critical not only to an understanding of the history of China or East Asia, but to that of humanity writ large. One cannot possibly develop a comprehensive understanding of the kinds of change that can transpire in human societies unless and until one examines the evidence of the Warring States.

For many centuries historians in Europe and America wrote off China as a place "beyond history," where people were so hidebound by tradition and subservient to authority that genuine political and cultural change never transpired. Any brief look at the conditions of the Warring States shows that this conventional view was profoundly false. It was not the case, moreover, that Chinese society was vibrant and dynamic during the Warring States but stagnated afterwards. As can be seen in the lives and works of figures such as Confucius, Marquis Wen of Wei, and Lü Buwei, one of the key achievements of the Warring States revolution was the development of versatile and sophisticated cultural tools to link past, present, and future. Using the techniques, textual legacy, and conceptual models developed by Warring States cultural and political leaders, successive generation of literati were able to imagine and construct the novel and creative projects in which they were engaged as an extension of "the Way of high antiquity."[34]

The continuities that these generations of literati created cannot be dismissed as illusory. Continuity, after all, is a foundational building block of state power and stability, and if there is any one agenda most broadly served by the revolutionaries of the Warring States, from Confucius to the First Emperor, it was the nurturing and preservation of state power and stability, albeit for different reasons and to different ends. But the record of the Warring States shows us a society engaged in constant self-reinvention and reconstruction. It was in this capacity to respond to, direct, and harness change that the Warring States revolution found its most consummate expression, and that dynamism has animated the legacy of the Warring States in China, East Asia, and the larger world down to the present day.

Appendix A
Historical Timeline

ca. 1045 BCE	Founding of the Zhou dynasty (1045–256 BCE) after the defeat of the last Shang king (ca. 1570–1045 BCE).
771 BCE	The western Zhou capital overrun by a non-Sinitic people known as the Xianyun, forcing the Zhou kings to move into their eastern capital of Luoyi.
771–481 BCE	The Spring and Autumn period.
667 BCE	Duke Huan of Qi (r. 685–643 BCE) becomes the first Lord Protector of the Zhou realm.
632 BCE	Duke Wen of Jin (r. 636–628 BCE) becomes the second Lord Protector of the Zhou realm.
584 BCE	Military advisors from the northern state of Jin travel to the Lower Yangzi region of Wu, to teach the leaders and warriors of Wu the battle tactics of the Zhou realm and enlist the forces of Wu as allies against the southern state of Chu.
527 BCE	Wu Zixu's father, tutor to the Heir Apparent of Chu, is slandered by his deputy and killed by the King of Chu. Zixu flees.
522 BCE	Zixu arrives in Wu.
514 BCE	King Helü (r. 514–496 BCE) ascends the throne of Wu after assassinating his own brother, with the help of Zixu. Zixu is appointed Minister of Foreign Affairs.
513 BCE	A group of Jin nobles forges the Penal Cauldron, inscribing a set of laws aimed at regularizing power and authority among leaders of the state of Jin.
506 BCE	King Helü of Wu invades Chu, cripples the army of Chu at the battle of Cypress Rise, and overruns the Chu capital of Ying. Zixu digs up the grave of the Chu king who had murdered Zixu's father and brother. The reigning King of Chu flees, and his throne is only saved when Helü's own brother rebels back home in Wu.
496 BCE	King Helü of Wu dies from wounds sustained while campaigning to put down a rebellion in Yue, and is succeeded by his son, Fuchai.
494 BCE	King Fuchai of Wu invades Yue to avenge his father's death. He defeats but spares King Goujian of Yue, who is forced to serve a term as a slave in Fuchai's court.
485 BCE	Duke Dao of Qi is murdered by one of his own courtiers, and he is succeeded by his son Lü Ren. Lü Ren appoints Tian Chang and Zai Wo as co-prime ministers.
484 BCE	King Fuchai of Wu launches an expedition to save Lu from aggression by Qi. Zixu warns that Wu should not strike northward but south, at Yue. The campaign against Qi is a great success, culminating in victory over Qi at the battle of Mugwort Hill. Zixu so offends his king that he is forced to commit suicide.

482 BCE	A covenant ceremony held at Yellow Pond (*Huangchi*) attended by many of the regional lords of the Zhou domain elevates King Fuchai of Wu to the title of Lord Protector (*ba*). While the covenant ceremony is being held, King Goujian of Yue attacks Wu. Fuchai rushes home to defend his state, but is only able to secure Goujian's withdrawal with the payment of a large ransom.
481 BCE	Tian Chang murders Lü Ren, the Duke of Qi, and his co-prime minister, Zai Wo. This coup gives the Tian clan effective control of the state of Qi, an event that is often taken as the beginning of the Warring States period (481–221 BCE).
475 BCE	Yue invades Wu and surrounds its capital. A two-year siege ensues. Zhao Wuxu, newly elevated head of the Zhao clan in Jin, tricks and kills his brother-in-law, the King of Dai, and annexes the land of the non-Sinitic Dai people.
473 BCE	The state of Wu is destroyed by the invading armies of Yue. King Fuchai of Wu commits suicide. In a covenant ceremony attended by the regional lords at Xuzhou, King Goujian of Yue is named Lord Protector of the Zhou realm.
458 BCE	The united warriors of the Zhi, Han, Zhao, and Wei clans, under the overall leadership of Zhi Yao, assault the Fan and Zhonghang clans in the state of Jin. The Fan and Zhonghang clans are destroyed and their territory divided among the four victors.
455 BCE	Zhi Yao demands that the leaders of the Han, Wei, and Zhao clans surrender territory to him. Zhao refuses. Zhi Yan leads a coalition of warriors from the Zhi, Han, and Wei clans against Zhao. Zhao Wuxu is besieged in the city of Jinyang.
453 BCE	The Wei and Han clans break with Zhi Yao and join with Zhao Wuxu. Zhi Yao is killed and the Zhi clan wiped out. The Zhao, Han, and Wei clans divide the territory of the Zhi clan.
441 BCE	"Year of Four Kings." Two successors to the Zhou throne are killed by their younger brothers within a few months of being crowned. One prince is finally established as "Duke of Zhou" and head of a newly sovereign cadet branch of the royal clan in part of the royal domain, which thenceforward is divided into "West Zhou" and "East Zhou."
439 BCE	Mo Di uses the threat of his counter-siege technology to halt the invasion of Song by the state of Chu.
409–408 BCE	Wu Qi is given command of Wei's forces along its western frontier and conquers the territory on "West of the Yellow River" (*Hexi*) for Wei.
408 BCE	A Wei army under the command of Yue Yang invades Zhongshan.
406 BCE	After a two-year siege of the Zhongshan capital, Yue Yang destroys the state. It is annexed by Wei.
405 BCE	Tian He (r. 404–384 BCE) becomes clan leader through a coup in Qi. A Tian clan kinsmen defects to Zhao. Qi attacks Zhao, activating the trilateral defensive pact between Wei, Han, and Zhao forged by Wei Si.
404 BCE	The coalition forces of Wei, Han, and Zhao break through Qi's defensive walls at Pingyin and threaten the siege capital. Qi sues for peace.

HISTORICAL TIMELINE

403 BCE	The Duke of Qi petitions the Zhou king to elevate the leaders of the Wei, Han, and Zhao clans to the rank of "marquis." The petition is granted, and three new Warring States are officially born.
397 BCE	To avenge his friend Yan Sui, Nie Zheng assassinates Han Gui, the Prime Minister of Han.
389 BCE	Wu Qi joins the Chu court, rising rapidly to the post of prime minister.
386 BCE	Marquis Wu of Wei, under pressure from Qi, petitions the Zhou king to transfer to Tian He the title of "Duke of Qi." The king accedes, and the Tian clan is finally able to rule Qi in their own name.
384 BCE	Ying Lian, having returned home from exile, is crowned Duke of Qin. He is known posthumously as Duke Xian (r. 384 BCE–362 BCE).
383 BCE	Zhao invades Wey. Wey pleads for assistance from Wei. Marquis Wu of Wei breaks the decades-long peace and assaults Zhao in defense of Wey. A protracted conflict ensues.
381 BCE	At the request of Zhao, Chu sends forces to attack Wei under the command of Wu Qi. Wu Qi is victorious and deeply penetrates the territory of Wei. The King of Chu dies. When Wu Qi returns to the Chu court to pay his respects to the deceased Chu king, he is murdered by rebellious nobles.
375 BCE	In Qi, Tian Wu kills his brother and ruler Tian Yan. Tian Yan's infant heir is also killed in the coup. Tian Wu (r. 374–357 BCE) is crowned Duke of Qi.
370–369 BCE	Marquis Wu of Wei dies, setting off a succession struggle among his sons. Han and Zhao intervene in favor of Wei Huan, the younger claimant to the Wei throne, but the older son Wei Ying becomes ruler.
361 BCE	Tian Wu holds sacrifices to his birth mother in the state ancestral temples.
	Wei Ying moves the capital of Wei from Anyi (Peace) in Wei's Hedong region to Greatbridge (Daliang, modern-day Kaifeng) in Wei's Henei region.
359 BCE	Shang Yang memorializes the Duke of Qin proposing reforms and is promoted to the post of "Left Chief of Staff."
356 BCE	Wei Ying hosts the rulers of Lu, Wey, Song, and Han at a summit held in the Wei capital of Greatbridge (Daliang), where they honor Wei Ying as their "Lord." The Zhou king punishes the ruler of Wey by demoting him from the formal rank of "duke" to that of "marquis."
354 BCE	Zhao assaults Wey. Wei sends an army to rescue Wey and besieges the Zhao capital of Handan.
353 BCE	In response to request for aid from Zhao, Qi attacks Wei and defeats a Wei army at Cassia Hill.
350 BCE	Shang Yang moves the capital of Qin from Yueyang to Xianyang.
344 BCE	In Wei, Wei Ying hosts a meeting of the rulers of 12 states at Welcome Pond, a park outside of Greatbridge. The assembled lords pay homage to Wei Ying as the "King of Xia."
342 BCE	Wei sends an army to attack Han, which had refused to attend the conclave at Welcome Pond.
341 BCE	Qi attacks Wei, defeating its armies soundly at Horse Hill (Maling).

338 BCE	Shang Yang defeats Wei and is enfeoffed as "Lord of Shang." Shortly after that, Duke Xiao dies. His son and heir, Ying Si (r. 337–311 BCE), accuses Shang Yang of rebellion, leading to Shang's death.
336 BCE	Hui Shi becomes Prime Minister of Wei. On Hui Shi's advice, Wei Ying dons commoner's garb and pleads to become the vassal of the ruler of Qi, to secure peace.
334 BCE	Wei Ying and Tian Yinqi meet in a summit at Xuzhou in which they honor one another as "kings," setting off a "royal revolution."
333 BCE	Gongsun Yan is appointed "Great Excellent Charioteer" in Qin. He attacks his home state of Wei and forces it to cede territory to Qin.
328 BCE	Zhang Yi becomes Prime Minister of Qin. Gongsun Yan returns to Wei, where he is employed as a military official.
327 BCE	The kingdom of Yiqu submits to Qin as a vassal state.
325 BCE	The rulers of Wei, Han, and Qin meet to acknowledge one another as "kings."
323 BCE	The five rulers of Wei, Han, Zhongshan, Zhao, and Yan meet to acknowledge one another as "kings."
322 BCE	After debates, Wei joins a "Horizontal Alliance" with Qin. Zhang Yi is made Prime Minister of Wei. He exiles Hui Shi.
321 BCE	Zhang Yi becomes simultaneously Prime Minister of Qin and Wei.
320 BCE	A Qin army crosses Han and Wei to attack Qi. The Qin invasion force is defeated. Zhang Yi resigns as Prime Minister of Wei and returns to Qin.
319 BCE	Under pressure from multiple foreign courts, the King of Wei makes Gongsun Yan Prime Minister of Wei. He invites Hui Shi to return to Wei.
318 BCE	The ruler of Song declares himself "king."
	A Vertical Alliance of Wei, Han, Zhao, Yan, and Chu attacks Qin. It is defeated and repulsed at the Hangu Pass.
	King Kuai of Yan abdicates his throne to his prime minister, Zizhi.
316 BCE	The Marquis of Zu flees from Shu (in the Sichuan basin) to Qin and pleads for aid. Qin dispatches an army and conquers the entire Sichuan basin by 314 BCE.
315 BCE	Qin invades Han and wins a decisive victory at Muddy Marsh (*Zhuoze*). The King of Han sends a peace emissary to Qin, but is persuaded not to make peace by false offers of aid from the King of Chu.
	The former Crown Prince of Yan rebels against "King" Zizhi. His forces storm the royal palace but are repulsed.
314 BCE	Qin goes on the offensive and again defeats the Vertical Alliance army at Rivergate; the Vertical Alliance collapses.
	The Crown Prince of Yan is killed. An army from Qi invades Yan, conquering it in 50 days. King Xuan of Qi decides to annex Yan.
313 BCE	A prince of the royal clan raises a rebellion that drives Qi's armies out of Yan. The prince becomes King Zhao of Yan.
307 BCE	King Wu of Qin (r. 310–307 BCE) hemorrhages and dies while trying to lift one of the Nine Tripods of Zhou. A succession struggle ensues at the Qin court.

HISTORICAL TIMELINE

	King Wuling of Zhao holds deliberations at the Zhao court over the policy of adopting "barbarian dress" (*hu fu*).
306 BCE	The state of Yue is destroyed by the armies of Chu.
301 BCE	Tian Wen, Prime Minister of Qi, mobilizes a coalition of the armies of Qi, Han, and Wei to assault Chu. Chu is defeated at Hanging Sands and cedes significant territory, which is all given to Han and Wei.
300 BCE	Huang Qiao rebels in Chu. Qin assaults Chu.
299 BCE	King Huai of Chu (r. 328–299 BCE) accepts the invitation of the Qin court to travel to Qin for peace negotiations. He is held hostage in Qin and never returns home to Chu.
	King Wuling of Zhao (r. 325–299 BCE) abdicates in favor of his young son, retaining the title of "Ruling Father" (*zhufu*).
	Tian Wen travels to Qin, where he is appointed prime minister.
298 BCE	Despite the fact that King Huai of Chu is still alive and hostage in Qin, his son is crowned and reigns as King Qingxiang of Chu.
	Tian Wen returns to Qi. He mobilizes an alliance of Han, Wei, and Qi to assault Qin. The allied armies blockade the Hangu Pass, allowing no commerce between Qin and the states to the east.
296 BCE	Tian Wen's allied army marches through the Hangu Pass and threatens the Qin capital. Qin sues for peace and agrees to the return of conquered territory.
	War breaks out between Yan and Qi. Qi is victorious, killing 10,000 Yan soldiers and capturing two of its top commanders.
	Zhao conquers and annexes Zhongshan.
295 BCE	A failed coup at the Zhao court ends with the former King Wuling of Zhao starved to death in one of his own palaces.
294 BCE	King Min of Qi is briefly kidnapped by a member of the royal clan. He suspects his prime minister, Tian Wen, who flees Qi and takes up the post of prime minister in Wei.
288 BCE	Prime Minister Wei Ran of Qin proposes to King Min of Qi that Qin and Qi recognize one another as "Thearchs" (*di*) of the West and East, respectively. King Min initially agrees, but on the advice of Su Qin, he unilaterally renounces the new title and begins organizing a Vertical Alliance of eastern states to punish Qin.
287 BCE	Su Qin leads a five-state coalition against Qin. The assault army becomes bogged down on the route to the Hangu Pass. Qi attacks Song while its allies are distracted by the campaign against Qin. The anti-Qin coalition dissolves.
286 BCE	As Qin goes back on the offensive against Qi's former allies, Qi launches another invasion of Song. Song is destroyed; King Yan dies in Wei.
285 BCE	Angered by King Min's greedy pursuit of profit in Song, Qi's former allies join Qin in a coalition to attack Qi. A five-state coalition (Wei, Zhao, Qin, Yan, and Han) invades Qi.
284 BCE	Qi is overrun, its capital of Linzi sacked. King Min takes refuge in Ju, one of two Qi cities to hold out against the invaders, but he is killed brutally by a rebel commander.

279 BCE	Tian Dan, a former market clerk, breaks the siege of Jimo in Qi. Within a year he drives all foreign forces from Qi and restores King Xiang of Qi to his throne in Linzi. He is enfeoffed as Lord Anping.
	Qin armies under Bai Qi capture the Chu capital of Ying, forcing the Chu court to move further east.
272 BCE	The King of Yiqu is ambushed and killed in Xianyang on his way to an assignation with Mi Bazi (the Qin Queen Dowager). A yearlong war follows.
269 BCE	Qin invades Zhao in an attempt to capture the district of Eyu, but is defeated by forces commanded by Zhao She.
266 BCE	Fan Sui is made Prime Minister of Qin and raised to the rank of marquis. Wei Ran and the other male members of the Mi-clan clique are sent through the Hangu Pass to reside in their own fiefs.
262 BCE	Han cedes its Upper Commandery to Qin. The Prefect of the Upper Commandery convinces the elders and elites of the region to join him in offering their allegiance to the King of Zhao. The Zhao court accepts.
	Huang Xie risks his life to help the Chu Heir Apparent return home from Qin. The prince is crowned and rules as King Kaolie of Chu, making Huang Xie his prime minister.
260 BCE	A Qin army invades Upper Commandery. Zhao forces deploy to resist the invasion. The two armies face off along fortified lines at Changping. After a long period of attrition, the Zhao army is trapped and destroyed, suffering massive casualties.
258 BCE	Qin besieges the Zhao capital of Handan.
257 BCE	The siege of Handan is lifted with the help of forces sent by Wei and Chu. The great patrons play a key role.
256 BCE	Qin annexes the small state of "West Zhou." King Nan of Zhou (314–256 BCE) dies. No heir is crowned king.
250 BCE	After less than a year on the throne, King Xiaowen of Qin dies, and is succeeded by Ying Yiren, the adopted son of the Lady of Huayang. Lü Buwei becomes prime minister.
249 BCE	Qin annexes "East Zhou," ending the last remnants of the Zhou dynasty.
247 BCE	Wei Wuji becomes Prime Minister of Wei. He assembles a coalition of five states and marches on Qin, forcing the Qin army to shelter behind the Hangu Pass.
	King Zhuangxiang of Qin (Ying Yiren) dies and is succeeded by his 11-year-old son, Ying Zheng. Lü Buwei remains prime minister, and is given the title of "Second Father" (*zhongfu*).
246 BCE	A slander campaign by Qin agents convinces the King of Wei to dismiss Wei Wuji. In his absence, the anti-Qin coalition falls apart.
241 BCE	Huang Xie helps organize another five-state coalition to attack Qin, but it is repulsed.
	Lü Buwei unveils the *Lüshi chunqiu*.
239 BCE	Lord Changan, a Qin prince, defects to the state of Zhao.
238 BCE	King Kaolie of Chu dies. Huang Xie is murdered by one of his former clients.

	An informant reveals to the Qin court that the Queen Dowager has secretly had two sons with Lao Ai. Lao Ai attempts a palace coup and is killed. A subsequent investigation reveals that Lü Buwei had introduced the Queen Dowager to Lao Ai. He is dismissed from office.
237 BCE	A proposal is made to ban all foreign residents from Qin. Li Si argues successfully against the proposal and is promoted to Commandant of Justice.
235 BCE	Lü Buwei is sentenced to exile in Sichuan and commits suicide.
234 BCE	Qin invades Zhao. Its armies are repulsed by forces commanded by Li Mu.
233 BCE	Qin mobilizes for war with Han. Han Fei is sent as an envoy to Xianyang to plea for peace. Li Si convinces King Zheng to sentence Han Fei to death.
231 BCE	The Prefect of Han's Nanyang Commandery defects to Qin.
230 BCE	The former Prefect of Nanyang turns his armies on the Han capital and captures the Han court, effectively destroying the state of Han.
229 BCE	Qin invades Zhao. Qin agents convince the Zhao king to execute Li Mu.
228 BCE	Qin forces overrun the Zhao capital and capture the Zhao king. A brother of the king flees and establishes himself as the King of Dai.
227 BCE	Crown Prince Dan of Yan dispatches Jing Ke upon an unsuccessful mission to assassinate King Zheng of Qin.
226 BCE	Qin forces take the Yan capital of Ji. The Yan court moves east to Liaodong. The Yan king offers Qin the head of Crown Prince Dan, pleading for peace.
225 BCE	Qin forces take Greatbridge and destroy the kingdom of Wei.
223 BCE	Qin forces conquer Chu.
222 BCE	Qin forces destroy the remnants of both Yan and Dai.
221 BCE	Qin forces conquer Qi, bringing the Warring States period to an end.
219 BCE	Ying Zheng undertakes the first of four tours of the eastern prefectures of the Qin empire, in which he erects inscribed stelae describing the merits of his rule for both his people and the gods.
213 BCE	At a banquet with the court Erudites, Chenyu Yue pleads that aristocratic fiefs should be revived. A controversy erupts that leads ultimately to the burning of proscribed books and the execution of scholars who violate the ban.
210 BCE	Death of the First Emperor (Ying Zheng).
206 BCE	Fall of the Qin empire.
203 BCE	Founding of the Han dynasty (203 BCE–220 CE) under its first ruler, Liu Bang (Han Gaodi, r. 203–195 BCE).

Appendix B
Glossary of Historical Figures

Bai Qi 白起 (d. 257 BCE). A military commander of Qin, responsible for some of its greatest victories, including the battle of Changping.

Bo Pi 伯嚭 (d. 473 BCE). A native of Chu, he became Grand Steward of the state of Wu under King Fuchai. He accepted bribes from King Goujian of Yue and plotted the demises of Wu Zixu.

Chen She 陳涉 (d. 208). A commoner who as head of a gang of conscript laborers first raised the flag of rebellion against the Qin empire in 209 BCE.

Chen Zhong 陳仲 (ca. 350–ca. 260 BCE). A knight of Qi famous for withdrawing from state and society to live as a hermit. He was honored by many as "Master Chen Zhong" (Chen Zhongzi), roundly critiqued by others, including Mencius and Xun Kuang.

Chunyu Kun 淳于髡 (ca. 385–ca. 305 BCE). A Master of Qi, famous for using satire and riddles. He was one of the most famous denizens of the Jixia patronage community.

Chunyu Yue 淳于越 (fl. ca. 215 BCE). A court Erudite during the Qin dynasty. He urged the First Emperor to restore feudal domains.

Concubine Ru 如姬 (fl. ca. 258 BCE). Consort of King Anxi of Wei. She aided Wei Wuji in lifting the siege of Handan.

Confucius 孔夫子 (Kong Qiu 孔丘, Zhongni 仲尼) (551–479 BCE). A teacher in the state of Lu, the first in history to don the mantle of a "Master 夫子."

Duke Dao of Qi 齊悼公 (r. 488–485 BCE). Father of Lü Ren. He lived much of his life in exile and reigned briefly before being assassinated by one of his own courtiers.

Duke Huan of Qi 齊桓公 (r. 685–643 BCE). (For the second Duke Huan of Qi, see Tian Wu). The most celebrated and powerful of the Lü dukes of Qi. With the help of his minister, Guan Zhong he became the first Lord Protector (*ba* 霸) of the Zhou realm.

Duke Jian of Qi (see Lü Ren).

Duke Mu of Qin 秦穆公 (r. 659–621 BCE). The most powerful Qin ruler of the Spring and Autumn era. He conquered the territory on the west bank of the Yellow River from the state of Jin.

Duke of Shao 召公 (fl. ca. 1050 BCE). A son of King Wen of Zhou. Founding ancestor of the clan and state of Yan 燕.

Duke of Zhou 周公 (fl. ca. 1050 BCE). A son of King Wen of Zhou. One of the main architects of the concept of the "Mandate of Heaven," and founding ancestor of the clan and state of Lu.

Duke Ping of Qi (r. 480–456 BCE). The scion of the Lü clan who was made duke after Tian Chang killed Lü Ren.

Duke Wen of Jin (r. 636–628 BCE). The most celebrated ruler of the state of Jin, the second ruler to hold the title of Lord Protector.

Duke Xian of Qin 秦獻公 (Ying Lian 嬴, r. 384–362 BCE). The first reformist ruler of Qin. He returned from exile in 384 BCE and instituted a number of changes to Qin state and society after observing reforms in neighboring Wei.

Duke You of Jin (r. 433–416 BCE). One of the last of the ducal line of Jin. He was waylaid on the road to an assignation, and his death was avenged by Wei Si.

Fan 范 clan. A powerful grandee clan of the state of Jin, finally wiped out by a coalition led by Zhi Yao in 458 BCE.

Fan Sui 范雎 (d. 255 BCE). A knight of Wei who, disgraced in his home state, rose under the pseudonym Zhang Lu to become a dynamic reforming Prime Minister of Qin.

First Emperor of Qin (see Ying Zheng).

Fuchai, King of Wu 吳王夫差 (r. 495–473 BCE). Ruler of the southern state of Wu. He rose to become Lord Protector of the Zhou realm before being conquered by his former vassal Goujian.

Gongshu Ban 公輸盤 (fl. ca. 440 BCE). A famous military engineer, designer of a "cloud ladder" for assaulting walled cities. He lost a famous debate against Mo Di in 439 BCE.

Gongsun Long 公孫龍 (ca. 320–ca. 250 BCE). A Master famous for his abstruse propositions concerning language and logic, such as "a white horse is not a horse."

Gongsun Yan 公孫衍 (ca. 360–ca. 300 BCE). A minister and military commander, often known by his sobriquet of "Xishou" (Rhinoceros-Head General 犀首). He became Zhang Yi's great rival and chief advocate of the Vertical Alliance in opposition to Qin.

Gongsun Yang (see Shang Yang).

Gongzhong Huan (see Wei Huan).

Grand Steward Bo Pi (see Bo Pi).

Guan Zhong 管仲 (d. 645 BCE). Prime Minister of Qi under Duke Huan. During his life he conceived the title of Lord Protector and won it for his ruler. During the fourth century BCE he was reimagined as a "Master" whose teachings projected the world view and ruling ideology of the Tian clan rulers of Qi. He became the eponym of a Masters text, the *Guanzi* 管子.

Han Fei 韓非 (Han Feizi, 韓非子) (ca. 280–233 BCE). A scion of the royal family of Han. He became famous as a Master whose innovative writings were much admired by the First Emperor of Qin. He fell victim to court intrigue on an embassy to Qin.

Han Gui 韓傀 (d. 397 BCE). Prime Minister of Han who feuded with Yan Sui and was assassinated by Nie Zheng.

Helü, King of Wu 吳王闔閭 (r. 514–496 BCE). Ruler of the southern state of Wu. He vastly expanded the power of Wu, so that he was able to invade neighboring Chu and occupy its capital of Ying. He died of wounds incurred during a rebellion by Goujian, ruler of Yue.

Hou Sheng 后勝 (fl. ca. 230 BCE). The last Prime Minister of Qi. He was a paid agent of Qin, and purposefully neglected the defenses of his home state.

Hou Ying 侯嬴 (d. 258 BCE). A poor knight and gate warden of Wei who became the valued client and advisor of Wei Wuji.

Huan Qi 桓齮 (d. 227 BCE). A general of Qi, sentenced and forced to flee because he was defeated in Zhao. He gave his head to help the assassin Jing Ke get close to Ying Zheng.

Huang Xie 黃歇 (Lord of Chunshen 春申君) (d. 238 BCE). A knight of Chu who, because of his extraordinary service to King Kaolie of Chu, became Prime Minister of Chu and one of the greatest patrons of the Warring States.

Huhai 胡亥 (Second Emperor 二世皇帝) (r. 209–207 BCE). A younger son of Ying Zheng, placed upon the throne by Li Si and Zhao Gao after Ying Zheng's death in 210 BCE.

Hui Shi 惠施 (ca. 380–310 BCE). A native of Song and a Master famous for posing logical paradoxes. He was the intellectual sparring partner of Zhuangzi. As Prime Minister of Wei he initiated the royal revolution in 334 BCE.

Jing Ke 荊軻 (d. 227 BCE). A knight and swordsman of Wei, enlisted by Crown Prince Dan of Yan in an unsuccessful attempt to assassinate Ying Zheng.

King Anxi of Wei 魏安釐王 (Wei Yu 魏圉) (r. 276–243 BCE). The brother of Wei Wuji, ruler of Wei during the lifting of the siege of Handan and the Vertical Alliance of 247 BCE.

King Cuo of Zhongshan 中山譻王 (d. ca. 308 BCE). Ruler of Zhongshan during the abdication affair in Yan. Bronze inscriptions describe his reluctant execution of Prime Minister Sima Zhou.

King Fuchai of Wu (see Fuchai, King of Wu).

King Helü of Wu (see Helü, King of Wu).

King Huai of Chu (Xiong Huai 熊槐) (r. 328–299 BCE). Ruler of Chu who was tricked into attending a diplomatic summit in Qin at which he was taken prisoner and effectively held hostage. He never returned home, dying in 297 BCE.

King Hui of Liang (or Wei, see Wei Ying).

King Huiwen of Zhao 趙惠文王 (Zhao He 趙何) (r. 298–266 BCE). Successor of King Wuling. He came to the throne as a minor, but oversaw a period of burgeoning power for his state, appointing talented ministers such as Lian Po, Lin Xiangru, and Zhao She.

King Jian of Qi 齊王建 (r. 264–221 BCE). The last King of Qi. The sources portray him as so naïve and foolish that even his mother the Queen Dowager despaired of advising him.

King Kaolie of Chu 楚考烈王 (Xiong Wang 熊完) (r. 262–238 BCE). Ruler who as Crown Prince escaped being hostage in Qin thanks to the bravery of Huang Xie, who served as prime minister during all of King Kaolie's reign.

King Kuai of Yan 燕王噲 (r. 320–318 BCE, d. 314 BCE). Ruler whose abdication to Prime Minister Zizhi plunged Yan into civil war.

King Min of Qi 齊湣王 (Tian Di 田地) (r. 300–284 BCE). Ruler of Qi whose venal policies led to Qi's disastrous defeat of 284 BCE.

King Qingxiang of Chu 楚頃襄王 (Xiong Heng 熊橫) (r. 298–263 BCE). Ruler of Chu who first employed Huang Xie as a state envoy and later as chief of staff to the Crown Prince.

King Wei of Qi (see Tian Yinqi).

King Wen of Zhou 周文王 (d. 1050 BCE). "The Civil King." The first leader of the Zhou to rebel against the King of Shang 商. Posthumously declared king and honored as founder of the Zhou dynasty.

King Wu of Zhou 周武王 (r. ca. 1045–1043 BCE). "The Martial King." Son of King Wen of Zhou. He defeated the last King of Shang and was the first to rule as King of the Zhou dynasty.

King Wuling of Zhao 趙武靈王 (Zhao Yong 趙雍) (r. 325–299 BCE). Ruler of Zhao who initiated the adoption of "barbarian dress" (*hufu* 胡服) and who radically increased the power of Zhao through the development of cavalry forces.

King Xiang of Qi 齊襄王 (Tian Fazhang 田法章) (r. 283–265 BCE). Successor of King Min. He is distinguished by his brilliant wife, Queen Jun, who sheltered him when he was a refugee, advised him as king, and remained actual ruler after his death.

King Xiaocheng of Zhao 趙孝成王 (Zhao Dan 趙丹) (r. 265–245 BCE). The ruler of Zhao whose dream vision led him to accept the cession of Han's Upper Commandery, precipitating the battle of Changping.

King Xiaowen of Qin (see Lord of Anguo).

King Xuan of Qi 齊宣王 (Tian Pijiang 田辟彊) (r. 319–301 BCE). Successor of Tian Yingqi as King of Qi. He successfully invaded and occupied neighboring Yan after the abdication of King Kuai, but failed in his attempt to annex Yan.

King Yan of Song 宋王偃 (r. 328–286 BCE). Sometimes known as King Kang 康. The last independent ruler of Song, famous for his erratic and obscene behavior.

King of Yiqu 義渠王 (d. 272 BCE). Ruler of a non-Sinitic kingdom to the northwest of the heartland of Qin in the Wei River valley. His personal name is unknown. By his rule Yiqu had submitted to Qin as a vassal. He had an affair with Queen Dowager Mi Bazi of Qin and was the father of two of her sons. His murder in 272 BCE set off a war between Yiqu and Qin.

King You of Chu 楚幽王 (Xiong Han 熊悍) (r. 237–228 BCE). Successor of King Kaolie, King You was purportedly the natural son of Huang Xie. He was the last ruler of Chu to receive a posthumous title.

King Zhao of Qin 秦昭王 (Ying Ji 嬴稷) (r. 306–251 BCE). Also known as King Zhaoxiang 昭襄. He came to the throne as a youth through the machinations of his mother, Mi Bazi, and her brothers, who controlled the court for the first decades of his reign. He ultimately exerted his independence and reigned successfully with the aid of his Prime Minister Fan Sui.

King Zhao of Yan 燕昭王 (Yan Zhi 燕職) (r. 312–279 BCE). Prince of Yan who successfully restored the Yan throne after the abdication of his father, King Kuai, to Prime Minister Zizhi. He employed Su Qin as a double-agent in a successful campaign to undermine the state of Qi.

King Zhuangxiang of Qin (see Ying Yiren).

Kong Qiu (see Confucius).

Lady of Huayang 華陽夫人 (d. 230 BCE). Wife of the Lord of Anguo, she adopted Ying Yiren as her son on the advice of Lü Buwei. When she became Queen of Qin, Ying Yiren became Heir Apparent.

Lao Ai 嫪毐 (d. 238 BCE). The secret lover of the Queen Dowager of Qin, with whom he fathered two sons. The discovery of his sons set off a rebellion in 238 BCE and ultimately led to the downfall of Lü Buwei.

Lao Dan 老聃 (fl. ca. 500 BCE). The legendary archivist of the Zhou royal court, said to have been the teacher of Confucius. Some literati in the early third century BCE appropriated him as the putative author of the teachings contained in the *Daodejing* 道德經.

Li Kui 李悝 (fl. ca. 410 BCE). Influential Prime Minister of Wei whose *Classic of Laws* served as the basis of many subsequent legal codes, well into imperial times.

Li Mu 李牧 (d. 229 BCE). General of Zhao who successfully resisted the encroachment of Qin until he was brought down by the slander of Qin agents at the Zhao court.

Li Si 李斯 (ca. 280–208 BCE). Influential minister of Qin who made a profound mark on Qin policy during the reign of Ying Zheng.

Li Yuan 李園 (fl. ca. 240 BCE). A wily client of Huang Xie, who curried favor with his patron and later murdered him.

Lian Po 廉頗 (fl. ca. 275 BCE). A talented military commander of Zhao who first feuded with and then became the sworn comrade of Lin Xiangru.

Lin Xiangru 藺相如 (d. ca. 260 BCE). A talented minister of Zhao, famed for his bravery on sensitive diplomatic missions to Qin.

Liu Bang 劉邦 (Han Gaozu 漢高祖) (r. 203–195 BCE). First Emperor of the Han dynasty.

Lord Changan 長安君 (Ying Chengjiao 嬴成蹻) (fl. ca. 240 BCE). A Qin prince and Ying Zheng's younger brother whose defection to Zhao shocked the Qin court in 239 BCE.

Lord Jingguo (see Tian Ying).

Lord Mengchang (see Tian Wen).

Lord of Anguo 安國君 (King Xiaowen of Qin 秦孝文王 Ying Zhu 嬴柱) (d. 250 BCE). Prince of Qin who reigned as king for less than one year. His queen's adoption of Ying Yiren as her son led eventually to the accession of Ying Zheng as First Emperor of Qin.

Lord of Chunshen (see Huang Xie).

Lord of Xinling (see Wei Wuji).

Lord of Yangcheng 陽成君 (fl. ca. 385 BCE). A grandee of Chu. When he was implicated in the coup that killed Wu Qi, he fled and his fief was defended by Mohists under the command of Grand Master Meng Sheng.

Lord Pingyuan (see Zhao Sheng).

Lü Buwei 呂不韋 (d. 235 BCE). A merchant who became a powerful Prime Minister of Qin during the minority of Ying Zheng. He was a great patron whose literati clients produced a compendium known as the *Lüshi chunqiu*.

Lü Dai 呂貸 (Duke Kang of Qi 齊康公) (d. 379 BCE). The last duke of Qi from the ancient Lü clan. In 392 BCE he was exiled to the Qi coast by Tian He, where he died without an heir.

Lü Ren (Duke Jian of Qi 齊簡公) (r. 484–481 BCE). The ruler of Qi whose ouster by Tian Chang is often taken as the beginning of the Warring States era.

Luzhong Lian 魯仲連 (ca. 305–ca. 245 BCE). A famed Master of the late Warring States period. His teachings were preserved in an eponymous text, fragments of which survive.

Mao Sui (fl. ca. 260 BCE). A talented client of Zhao Sheng. He persuaded the King of Chu to assist in relieving the siege of Handan.

Marquis Cheng of Zhao 趙成侯 (趙種) (r. 374–350 BCE). Ruler of Zhao. He unsuccessfully intervened, along with Marquis Yi of Han, to try and prevent Wei Ying from succeeding to the throne of Wei.

Marquis Lie of Han 韓烈侯 (Han Qu 韓取) (r. 399–387 BCE). The ruler of Han who was an early patron of Yan Sui. He was wounded when Nie Zheng assassinated his uncle and prime minister, Han Gui.

Marquis Sunnyside 山陽侯. The god of the Huotai Mountains, whose emissaries sent Zhao Wuxu a prophecy about the demise of Zhi Yao.

Marquis Wen of Wei (see Wei Si).

Marquis Wu of Wei 魏武侯 (Wei Lu 魏陸) (r. 395–370 BCE). Son of Wei Si and father of Wei Ying. His reign is distinguished by his war against Zhao in 383 BCE and the succession struggle that broke out among his sons on his death.

Marquis Yi of Han 韓懿侯 (Han Ruoshan 韓若山) (r. 373–363 BCE). The ruler of Han who, in conjunction with Marquis Cheng of Zhao, attempted to prevent Wei Ying from succeeding to the throne of Wei.

Mencius (Meng Ke 孟軻 or Mengzi, "Master Meng" 孟子) (ca. 390–ca. 305 BCE). The first of Confucius's great latter-day disciples. His eponymous text became part of the standard exam curriculum during imperial times.

Meng Sheng 孟勝 (d. 381 BCE). Grand Master of the Mohist order. He died defending the fief of his friend and patron, the Lord of Yangsheng, in Chu.

Meng Tian 蒙恬 (d. 210 BCE). A highly successful commander of Qin, spanning the late kingdom and empire. He fell victim to the machinations of Li Si and Zhao Gao. He has his own biography at *Shi ji* 88.

Mi Bazi 羋八子 (Queen Dowager Xuan 宣太后) (d. 265 BCE). A lower-ranking wife of King Hui of Qin. When King Wu of Qin died without leaving an heir, Mi Bazi maneuvered successfully, with the aid of her brothers Wei Ran and Mi Rong, to place her son on the throne as King Zhao of Qin.

Mi Rong 羋戎 (d. 262 BCE). Younger brother of Mi Bazi. As a military commander in the capital garrisons of Qin, he helped his sister take control of the court after the death of King Wu. Afterwards he was enfeoffed as Lord of Huayang and was part of the ruling clique centered on his sister, the Queen Dowager.

Mo Di 墨翟 (Mozi or "Master Mo" 墨子) (ca. 480–ca. 390 BCE). Most likely a native of Lu. In the mid-fifth century BCE Mo Di claimed the title of Master, gathered disciples, and began promulgating a doctrine based on the concepts of "profit" and "Heaven's will." His fellowship grew and offered robust opposition to the followers of Confucius (among others) for the whole Warring States period.

GLOSSARY OF HISTORICAL FIGURES

Nao Chi 淖齒 (d. 283 BCE). A Chu general sent to "rescue" King Min of Qi during the invasion of Qi by the coalition of Qin, Wei, Zhao, Han, and Yan. Nao Chi briefly served as prime minister of King Min's court in exile at Ju, but later killed King Min in grisly fashion. Nao Chi himself was killed when the people of Ju rebelled.

Nie Zheng 聶政 (d. 397 BCE). A knight of Han forced by an unavenged insult to live as a common butcher in Qi. He killed Prime Minister Han Gui to avenge the insult done to his friend Yan Sui.

Prince Guang (see Helü, King of Wu).

Queen Dowager Xuan (see Mi Bazi).

Queen Jun 君王后 (fl. ca. 280 BCE). Wife of King Xiang of Qi. Daughter of the Chief Astrologer of Ju, she sheltered King Xiang when he was a fugitive prince in 284 BCE. She advised her husband during his life and was in effective control of the Qi court after he died.

Shang Yang 商鞅 (aka Gongsun Yang 公孫鞅, Wey Yang 衛鞅) (ca. 390–338 BCE). A knight of Wey who, passed over for promotion in Wei, answered the recruitment call put out by Duke Xiao of Qin. He rose to become effective Prime Minister of Qin, one of the most powerful and influential ministers in that state's history. He led a set of administrative and legal reforms that vastly increased Qin's power, extending over several generations.

Shen Dao 慎到 (ca. 350–274 BCE). A native of Zhao and a renowned Master, whose teachings centered on statecraft theory. He is most famous for articulating the concept of "political force (shi 勢)." He was a resident at Jixia. A text in his name survives in fragments.

Shen Nong 神農 (ca. third millennium BCE). The "Divine Farmer." A mythical sage of high antiquity, credited with inventing farming. A movement of literati during the Warring States invoked his name in urging that all people must return to the land and engage in farming, even kings and aristocrats.

Shen Buhai 申不害 (d. 337 BCE). Prime Minister of Han. He oversaw an effective reform of Han's governing institutions, and as "Master Shen" promulgated teachings on statecraft theory. He is famous for articulating the doctrine of "forms and names," which enjoins rulers to empirically test the performance of their ministers against the formal powers and duties of each minister's office. A text in his name survives in fragments.

Shun 舜 (ca. third millennium BCE). A mythical sage king of high antiquity. His predecessor Yao was said to have sought the wisest man in the realm, found Shun living as a common farmer, and abdicated the throne to him.

Sima Cuo (fl. ca. 315 BCE). An official and military commander of Qin. He advocated for Qin's intervention in the affairs of the kingdom of Shu, and co-commanded the forces that conquered the Sichuan basin on Qin's behalf.

Sima Guang 司馬光 (1019–86 CE). A famous Song literatus and historian. His *Comprehensive Mirror for the Aid of Government* (*Zizhi tongjian* 資治通鑑) is a masterpiece of historiography, and takes as its starting point the elevation of Wei, Han, and Zhao to the rank of marquis in 403 BCE.

Sima Qian 司馬遷 (b. 145 BCE). Grand Historian of the Han dynasty and putative author of the *Records of the Historian* 史記, a vital source for the history of the Warring States.

Sima Zhou 司馬賙 (d. 314 BCE). Prime Minister of Zhongshan. Bronze inscriptions discovered in the tomb of King Cuo revealed that Sima Zhou was executed for lèse majesté because of his actions during the abdication affair in neighboring Yan.

Su Qin 蘇秦 (d. 284 BCE). A native of East Zhou, the most famous of the "wandering persuaders" of the Warring States. He succeeded in forming a Vertical Alliance against Qin and held the prime ministerial seal of at least three states at once, but he was ultimately revealed to be acting as a double-agent in the service of King Zhao of Yan. He was executed in Qi.

Sun Wu (fl. ca. 520 BCE). A successful military commander in the armies of King Helü of Wu. His reputation for brilliance inspired some later literati to appropriate him as "Master Sun," the putative proponent of the teachings collected in the *Art of War of Master Sun* (*Sunzi bingfa* 孫子兵法).

Supreme Duke of Qi (See Tian He).

Tian Chang 田常 (Viscount Cheng of Tian 田成子) (fl. ca. 485 BCE). Grandee of Qi and leader of the Tian clan. In 481 BCE he led a coup that gave his clan effective control of the state of Qi.

Tian Dan 田單 (fl. ca. 285 BCE). A low-ranking government clerk who demonstrated a genius for military command when Qi was overrun by invaders in 284 BCE. He rallied forces that drove out the invading armies and restored Qi to independence.

Tian Fazhang (see King Xiang of Qi).

Tian He 田和 (Supreme Duke of Qi 齊太公) (r. 404–384 BCE). After taking over the Tian clan by murdering his own brother, Tian He proved an effective leader. He maneuvered to have the Tian clan appointed formal rulers of Qi by the Zhou Son of Heaven, and thus was posthumously honored as the "Supreme" founder of a new ducal line.

Tian Pian 田駢 (ca. 350–ca. 275 BCE). One of Jixia's resident Masters, an advocate of the macrobiotic inner cultivation practices (such as sitting meditation) associated with early sources such as the *Laozi* and the *Zhuangzi*.

Tian Pijiang (see King Xuan of Qi).

Tian Wen 田文 (Lord Mengchang 孟嘗君) (fl. ca. 300 BCE). Prime Minister of Qi, briefly of Qin, and ultimately of Wei. He pioneered a new political and military strategy, and as the first of the "great patrons" of the Warring States he was widely emulated.

Tian Wu 田午 (Duke Huan of Qi 齊桓公) (r. 374–357 BCE). After coming to the throne through the murder of his half-brother and nephew, and killing his stepmother to defend his position, he oversaw the development of a new ruling ideology, promulgated through the state ancestral cult and in the teachings of figures such as "Master Guan" and "Master Yan."

Tian Xiang 田襄 (fl. ca. 380 BCE). A Master in the Mohist order, he became Grand Master upon the death of Meng Sheng in Chu.

Tian Xu 田需 (fl. ca. 320 BCE). Chosen as Prime Minister of Wei after the failure of the first Horizontal Alliance, his position was undermined by the machinations of Gongsun Yan.

Tian Yan 田剡 (r. 384–375 BCE). The ruler of Qi after the death of his father, Tian He, the "Supreme Duke." He led Qi in several unsuccessful wars before being murdered by his half-brother Tian Wu, who had him expunged from the historical record.

Tian Ying 田嬰 (Lord Jingguo 靖郭君) (fl. ca. 340 BCE). Prime Minister of Qi, father of Tian Wen.

Tian Yinqi 田因齊 (King Wei of Qi 齊威王) (r. 356–320 BCE). After succeeding his father, Tian Wu (Duke Wu), Tian Yinqi led Qi for 36 years. By the end of that time he had increased Qi's power and reputation sufficiently to succeed in claiming the title of "king" at a summit with the ruler of Wei in 334 BCE.

Viscount Huan of Wei 魏桓子 (Wei Ju 魏駒) (d. 446 BCE). Head of the Wei clan during the turbulent years of Zhi Yao's leadership of the Jin court, father of Wei Si. He colluded with the leaders of Zhao and Han to destroy Zhi Yao.

Viscount Jian of Zhao 趙簡子 (Zhao Yang 趙鞅) (d. 475 BCE). Charismatic leader of the Zhao clan who led the Jin aristocracy in the forging of the Penal Cauldron. Father of Zhao Wuxu.

Wang He 王齕 (fl. ca. 265 BCE). A Qin general, original commander of the forces at the battle of Changping.

GLOSSARY OF HISTORICAL FIGURES

Wang Jian 王翦 (fl. ca. 225 BCE). A Qin general, the victorious commander in the conquests of both Zhao and Chu.

Wei Huan 魏緩 (aka Gongzhong Huan 公仲緩) (d. 369 BCE). Younger brother of Wei Ying. On their father's (Marquis Wu of Wei's) death, Wei Huan fought, with the help of the armies of Zhao and Han, to claim the throne, but was killed in battle.

Wei Ji (see Marquis Wu of Wei).

Wei Ran 魏冉 (Marquis of Rang 穰侯) (fl. ca. 290 BCE). The younger half-brother of Mi Bazi. He helped his half-sister take control of the Qin court and served as his nephew's prime minister for many years. His self-serving policies led King Zhao to banish Wei Ran and the other members of the Mi-clan clique from the home territories of Qin, to take up residence in the lucrative fiefs they had carved for themselves from the conquered territory of the eastern kingdoms.

Wei Si 魏斯 (Marquis Wen of Wei 魏文侯) (r. 445–396 BCE). The most celebrated ruler in the history of Wei, and perhaps the whole of the Warring States. He engineered the accession of the Wei, Han, and Zhao clans to independent sovereignty, and oversaw a dynamic program of reforms that made Wei a leading power of and model for the rest of the Zhou realm for several generations.

Wei Wuji 魏無忌 (Lord Xinling 信陵君) (d. 243 BCE). A prince of Wei and one of the great patrons of the Warring States. He helped lift the siege of Handan and forged a Vertical Alliance that managed to temporarily check the rising power of Qin.

Wei Ying 魏罃 (King Hui of Wei [or Liang] 魏[梁]惠王) (r. 369–319 BCE). A ruler who exerted broad influence on the history of his time. He failed in his hopes of becoming Son of Heaven, but initiated the royal revolution under the guidance of Hui Shi in 334 BCE.

Wey Yang (see Shang Yang).

Wu Qi 吳起 (d. 381 BCE). A native of Wey who served with distinction in both Wei and Chu. In Wei he pioneered new methods of military command. As Prime Minister of Chu he oversaw reforms that vastly increased the kingdom's power. He was killed by conservative nobles in Chu on the death of the king by whom he had been recruited.

Wu Zixu 伍子胥 (d. 484 BCE). A refugee noble of Chu who became a powerful courtier in the state of Wu. The hero of many stories, novels, and plays, he helped develop the power of Wu in a quest to revenge the murder of his family. He died warning his ruler of the danger of Yue, but his words were unheeded.

Xi Shi 西施 (fl. ca. 490 BCE). A famed beauty of Yue. She and another beauty, Zheng Dan, were given as gifts by King Goujian of Yue to King Fuchai of Wu, to seduce the latter king into neglecting affairs of state.

Ximen Bao 西門豹 (fl. ca. 410 BCE). A famed official of Wei. As Magistrate of Ye, Ximen Bao was scrupulously honest, working diligently to increase the prosperity of the people under his administration and to suppress evil customs that were plaguing his district.

Xu Fu 徐市 (fl. ca. 218 BCE). A native of Qi who convinced the First Emperor to fund an expedition that he led in search of the island of the immortals. He departed, never to return.

Xu Jia 須賈 (fl. ca. 275 BCE). A grandee of Wei and an early patron of Fan Sui.

Xu You 許由 (fl. ca. third millennium BCE). A famed hermit, known for having refused to accept the abdication of the royal throne from the sage Yao.

Xun Kuang 荀況 (Xunzi or Master Xun 荀子) (ca. 340–ca. 245 BCE). The second great latter-day disciple of Confucius, sometimes called the "Aristotle of China."

Yan Sui 嚴遂 (fl. ca. 399 BCE). A knight of Han who enjoyed the favor of its ruler before the ruler's uncle and prime minister publicly insulted him, forcing him into exile and withdrawal from public life. He enlisted Nie Zheng to revenge his honor.

Yan Ying 晏嬰 (d. 500 BCE). A famed courtier of Qi, known for his rectitude and integrity. He served three of the Lü dukes in turn. In the fourth century he was appropriated as the mouthpiece of new doctrines by literati serving the Tian rulers of Qi, who formulated and circulated teachings in the name of "Master Yan 晏子." A text that purports to record these teachings, the *Yanshi chunqiu*, is still extant.

Yang Zhu 楊朱 (ca. 395–ca. 335 BCE). Little is known about the biography of this Master, but he is frequently cited as the leader of a fellowship of literati who promulgated a doctrine rooted in the principle of "valuing life." There is evidence that he and/or his latter-day disciples were active at the court of Wei Ying, and again later in the retinue of Lü Buwei.

Yao 堯 (fl. circa third millennium BCE). A legendary sage king, famed for passing over his own son in favor of abdicating to Shun, the wisest among his subjects.

Yellow Thearch (fl. ca. fourth millennium BCE). The legendary first ruler in human history.

Ying Chengjiao (see Lord Changan).

Ying Lian (see Duke Xian of Qin).

Ying Si 嬴駟 (King Huiwen of Qin 秦惠文王) (r. 337–311 BCE).

Ying Yiren 嬴異人 (King Zhuangxiang of Qin 秦莊襄王, d. 247 BCE). The successor of King Xiaowen (the Lord of Anguo) and the father of Ying Zheng (the First Emperor). He came to the throne thanks to his partnership with Lü Buwei.

Ying Zheng 嬴政 (First Emperor of Qin 秦始皇帝) (259–210 BCE). The ruler of Qin who ultimately conquered all of the other Warring States and founded the Qin dynasty.

Yu Qing 虞卿 (ca. 305–ca. 235 BCE). A literatus who served as a minister in Zhao and who is reported to have written a lengthy treatise entitled the *Yushi chunqiu*. The text was lost after the Han dynasty,

Yue Yang 樂羊 (fl. ca. 410 BCE). A military commander of Wei. Under Marquis Wen he led Wei's conquest of Zhongshan and was rewarded with a fief in the defeated state.

Yue Yi 樂毅 (fl. ca. 290 BCE). A native of Zhongshan and a descendant of Yue Yang. He served simultaneously as Prime Minister of Zhao and Wei, and commanded the allied armies that invaded Qi in 284 BCE.

Yurang 豫讓 (fl. ca. 455 BCE). A knight of Jin who went to extraordinary lengths to avenge the death of his ruler, Zhi Yao.

Zai Wo 宰我 (aka Zai Yu 宰予) (d. 481 BCE). A disciple of Confucius who was appointed co-Prime Minister of Qi, along with Tian Chang, by Lü Ren. Zai Wo and Lü Ren both died in the coup that gave Tian Chang control of Qi.

Zeng Shen 曾參 (aka Zengzi or Master Zeng 曾子) (b. 505 BCE). A disciple of Confucius famed for his filial piety. The Master of Wu Qi.

Zhang Deng 張登 (fl. ca. 320 BCE). A knight of Zhongshan who successfully used diplomacy to avoid a conflict with Qi and secure recognition of Zhongshan's ruler as "king."

Zhang Yi 張儀 (d. 310 BCE). A knight of Wei who rose to become Prime Minister of Qin and the first champion of the Horizontal Alliance.

Zhao Gao 趙高 (d. 207 BCE). A eunuch who served as the Prefect of Palace Vehicles under the First Emperor. On the First Emperor's death, he helped Li Si engineer a coup that gave the two men effective control of the Qin court.

Zhao He (see King Huiwen of Zhao).

Zhao Kuo 趙括 (d. 260 BCE). A military commander of Zhao, son of Zhao She. After replacing Lian Po as commander at the battle of Changping, he led the Zhao army into a disastrous defeat.

Zhao She 趙舍 (fl. ca. 270 BCE). A knight who rose from being a tax collector to being one of the most celebrated military commanders in Zhao. He led Zhao's armies to victory over Qin in the campaign to defend Eyu.

Zhao Sheng (Lord Pingyuan 平原君) (d. 252 BCE). A prince of Zhao and one of the great patrons of the Warring States. He was instrumental in lifting the siege of Handan in 258 BCE.

Zhao Wuxu 趙无恤 (Viscount Xiang of Zhao 趙襄子) (r. 475–425 BCE). Heir of Viscount Jian of Zhao. His resistance to the coercion of Zhi Yao ultimately led to the latter's downfall and to the partition of Jin by the three clans of Zhao, Han, and Wei.

Zhao Yang (see Viscount Jian of Zhao).

Zhao Yong (see King Wuling of Zhao).

Zheng Dan (see Xi Shi).

Zhi Yao 知瑤 (d. 453 BCE). Leader of the Zhi clan in the state of Jin. He briefly consolidated paramount power his own hands before being brought down by avarice and overreach.

Zhonghang clan 中行氏. A grandee clan of Jin, allied with the Fan clan. The Fan and Zhonghang clans were destroyed by a coalition of the four clans of Zhi, Han, Wei, and Zhao in 458 BCE.

Zhu Hai 朱亥 (fl. ca. 260 BCE). A butcher in the marketplace of Greatbridge and a friend of the knight Hou Ying. He assisted Wei Wuji in the latter's mission to relieve the siege of Handan.

Zhuang Qiao 莊蹻 (fl. ca. 300 BCE). A Chu noble who rose up in rebellion and threatened the Chu capital in 301 BCE. Later he was re-enlisted as a general of Chu and in 279 BCE was sent west to try and dislodge the forces of Qin from the Sichuan basin. His mission was impeded, but he used his army to conquer the region of Dianchi 滇池 (in present-day Kunming Province), establishing himself as the independent King of Dian.

Zhu Ying (fl. ca. 240 BCE). A client of Huang Xie. He tried to warn his lord about the threat posed by Li Yuan, to no avail.

Zilu 子路 (ca. 540–480 BCE). A disciple of Confucius known for his courage and martial zeal. He briefly held high office in Wey, but was killed amid palace intrigue.

Zixia 子夏 (510–ca. 420 BCE). A disciple of Confucius. In later life he was invited to the Wei capital of Anyi, to serve as the teacher of Wei Si (Marquis Wen of Wei).

Zixu (see Wu Zixu).

Zou Ji 鄒忌 (fl. ca. 350 BCE). Prime Minister of Qi under Tian Yinqi (King Wei of Qi).

Zou Yan 鄒衍 (ca. 305–ca. 240 BCE). A prolific Master whose works are now largely lost, but who was celebrated for having systematized the teachings concerning *yin*, *yang*, and the five phases of *qi*.

Notes

INTRODUCTION

The following abbreviations are used for commonly cited sources:

SJ	Sima Qian 司馬遷. *Shi ji* 史記. Beijing: Zhonghua shuju, 1959.
HS	Ban Gu 班固. *Han shu* 漢書. Beijing: Zhonghua shuju, 1962.
HHS	Fan Ye 范曄 (398–446 CE), *Hou Han shu* 後漢書 Beijing: Zhonghua shuju, 1965
ZGS	Yang Kuan 楊寬. *Zhangguo shi* 戰國史. Shanghai: Shanghai Renmin chubanshe, 2019.
ZZ	*Zuo zhuan* 左傳 (various editions and translations, cited below)
ZZTJ	Sima Guang 司馬光 (1019–86 CE). *Zizhi tongjian* 資治通鑑. Beijing: Zhonghua shuju, 1956.

All other citations of Chinese-language primary sources, unless otherwise noted, are to the ICS Ancient Chinese Text Concordance Series editions edited by D. C. Lau and Chen Fangzheng (see the Bibliography), with citations in the form of chapter/page/line.

1. "Knights" is a translation of the Chinese word *shi* 士. *Shi* were the lowest-level aristocrats of early China.
2. The *Analects*, the text which reports this incident, does not specify that Confucius and his followers were traveling when it transpired. The context may be inferred, however. Lau 1979, 170–77; Chin 2007, 85–118.
3. Lau and Chen, eds., 2006, 9.12/21/5–7. All subsequent references to Chinese texts other than official histories will be to ICS Ancient Chinese Text Concordance Series editions, and will be in the form of chapter/page/line. The publication date will be given for the first citation of a text. When chapters are notated as *juan* rather than *pian*, the number of the *pian* will be provided in parentheses. For example *Mozi* 2.1(8)/9/7–9.
4. The following account is drawn from SJ 6:260–69, 87:2547–54. This and all subsequent citations of the *Shi ji* are in the form of chapter:page. For an English translation of this source, see Cheng, Liu, Nienhauser, and Reynolds, trs., 1994 (subsequently Nienhauser 1994a), 151–58; Cheng et al., trs.; Nienhauser, ed., 1994 (subsequently Nienhauser 1994b), 341–47.
5. As in many ancient societies, eunuchs were employed in early China to guard the personal quarters of the ruler. This particular official, the Prefect of Palace Vehicles, served in this capacity because some of the emperor's wives would accompany him on tour.
6. Counting from the first year of his ascendancy as King of Qin in 247 BCE.
7. See Kern 2000, 1–49.
8. Later tradition granted Confucius thousands of disciples, but that was a reverent exaggeration.
9. Aisin-Gioro Puyi, the last emperor of the Qing dynasty (est. 1644 CE), abdicated in 1911 CE.

CHAPTER 1

1. Since earliest imperial times it has been conventional to divide the history of the Zhou into the earlier Western Zhou (ca. 1045–771 BCE), a period in which the Zhou kings themselves were relatively powerful, and the Eastern Zhou (770–221 BCE), a period after the Zhou were forced to abandon their western capital, in which the power of the Zhou kings steadily declined. This latter era is then further broken down into two "sub-periods." The earliest record of the periodization of the Eastern Zhou dynasty into "Spring and Autumn 春秋" and "Warring States 戰國" eras is found in the "Bibliographical Notice" of Liu Xiang 劉向 (77–6 BCE) to his redaction of the *Zhangguo ce* 戰國策. See Fan 2006, 1–3. See also the discussion of "periodization" in Wilkinson 2022, 1287–88.
2. These events are recorded in several different sources. See SJ 32:1508–12 (Knickerbocker, tr., Nienhauser 2006, 114–19), 46:1883–4. These accounts share much material with that of ZZ Ai 14: Lau and Chen, eds., 1995, B12.14.3/456/28–457/19 (hereafter cited as ZZ), Durrant et al., trs., 2016, 1923–27. The account in SJ 46:1883–84 differs slightly from that of SJ 32 and the ZZ, but the latter are more reliable and will be cited below.
3. For a sense of the material conditions of life, see Mu-chou Poo 2018. See also Li Xueqin 1985, 295–446.
4. Fu Xinian 2017, 1–30; Wu Hung 1999, 651–744.
5. Excellent surveys of the historical background of the Warring States may be found in Li Feng 2013, 1–182; Major and Cook 2016, 1–145.
6. Anderson 1988, 9–22; Lander 2021, 32–73; ZGS, 61–95.
7. For the Shang bronze industry that was the antecedent of the Zhou, see Bagley 1999, 136–57.
8. Lam 2020, 595–614; Shelach-Lavi 2015, 291–93.
9. Yuan Jing 2008, 1–7.
10. Peng Hao 2012, 65–114.
11. Mithen 2012, 150–75.
12. For a general review of the history and historiography of the Shang, see Keightley 1999, 232–91.
13. Dickens 1859.
14. For the early institutions of the Zhou, see Creel 1970. See also Li Feng 2008.
15. For a discussion of the fall of the Western Zhou, see Li Feng 2006.
16. The idea of the Mandate of Heaven was articulated by the Zhou founders and their descendants in various writings, some of which are preserved in the *Class of Odes* 詩經 (sometimes translated as the *Book of Songs*) and the *Classic of Documents* 書經 (sometimes translated as the *Book of Documents*). See Legge 1960a, 427–64, 1960b, 281–508. For a discussion of the early Zhou concept of the Mandate of Heaven in modern scholarship, see Schwartz 1985, 40–55; Shaughnessy 1999, 313–17; Matsui 2002; Puett 2002, 31–79.
17. Cho-yun Hsu 1965, 2–5.
18. SJ 32:1508, Knickerbocker, 114–15; SJ 46:1883; ZZ Ai 8 (B12.8.6/446/17–19); Ai 10 (B12.10.3/448/29), Durrant et al., trs., 2016, 1884–85, 1892–93.
19. The brother is known in chronicles as "Yan Ruzi 宴孺子" ("Child of Yan," after his mother's clan name, r. 486 BCE): ZZ Ai 6 (12.6.3/441/16–24, B12.6.6/442/15–31), Durrant et al., trs., 2016, 1864–65, 1868–71; SJ 32:1506–7; Knickerbocker, 112–14; SJ 46:1881–82. The *Zuo zhuan* and *Shi ji* accounts diverge in some details, but agree on the general facts about Duke Dao's accession.
20. As, for example, the feud of 532 BCE: *Zuo zhuan* Zhao 10 (B10.10.2/345/31–346/19), Durrant et al., trs., 2016, 1452–59.
21. Duke Dao's father was Duke Jing 景 (r. 547–490 BCE). He came to the throne upon the murder of his brother Duke Zhuang 莊 (r. 553–548 BCE) *Zuo zhuan* Xiang 25

(B9.25.2/282/24–284/3), Durrant et al., trs., 2016, 1137–41. *Shi ji* 32:1500–2; Nienhauser 2006, 98–102.

22. The Qing scholar Gu Donggao 顧棟高 (1679–1759 CE), in his massive study of the *Chunqiu*, compiled a "Chart of Rebels and Bandits in the *Chunqiu* 春秋亂賊表." He records 32 separate instances of rulers being murdered and 35 instances of rulers being usurped (Gu Donggao 1995, 2500–2521). A partial survey of such instances can be found in Cho-yun Hsu 1965, 26–31. See also Watson, tr., 1989.
23. Judge Dee is based on a historical figure, Di Renjie 狄仁傑 (630–704 CE), who was memorialized in a Chinese novel of the eighteenth century. He was introduced to readers of modern English language fiction in a series of novels beginning with van Gulik 1956. "Dr. Fu-Manchu" is a fictional character first introduced to English-language readers in Rohmer 1913. Fu-Manchu subsequently appeared in myriad movies and radio programs.
24. See Li Feng 2011, 271–301.
25. See Lewis 1990, 15–52. Many sources dating to the Western Zhou express the warrior traditions of the Bronze Age aristocracy. For example, the *Duoyou ding* 多友鼎 *Yin Zhou jinwen jicheng* 殷周金文集成, no. 2835. For an annotated transcription, see Ma Chengyuan 1988, 112–13 (#172). It is translated in Shaughnessy 2000, 4–5.
26. Lewis 1990, 17–46. For an example of an encounter between aristocrats marked as "without incident," see the "Square Beaker of Mai" (*Mai fangzun* 麥方尊) inscription, translated in Li Feng 2008, 261–62.
27. von Falkenhausen 2006, 71. See also Zhu Fenghan 1990, 361–80; Matsui 2002, 208–42.
28. See Chang 1983, 9–15.
29. For a discussion of the development of the ideas and practices behind these traditions, see Puett 2002, 31–79.
30. Zhu Fenghan 1990, 361–80. Also Matsui 2002, 208–42.
31. A classic example of can again be seen in Li Feng 2008, 261–62.
32. ZZ Cheng 13 (B13.2/209/24), Durrant et al., trs., 2016, 802–3.
33. See McNeal 2012, 13–39.
34. von Falkenhausen 2006, 244–54, 87–88. Also Rawson 2023, 119–230.
35. Rawson 1999, 352–449.
36. Li Feng 2008, 235–70.
37. Blakeley 1977, 307–43, 1979, 81–118.
38. For the mirroring of component structures in the fiefs (*fengjian* 封建) of the regional rulers and the estates (*caiyi* 采邑) of their grandees, see Zhao Guangxian 1980, 110–20.
39. Cho-yun Hsu 1965, 53–62.
40. See for example ZZ Yin 1 (B1.1.4/2/3–30), Durrant et al., trs., 2016, 8–13.
41. Chen Shen 2003, 290–310.
42. SJ 45:1879–80; ZZ Zhuang 22 (B3.22.1/56/3–7), Durrant et al., trs., 2016, 192–97.
43. SJ 36.1575; Knickerbocker 2006, 221.
44. SJ 46:1880–81. The *Shi ji* first begins recording Tian clan heads with both a posthumous temple name and a rank of "viscount" with the fourth patriarch, Tian Xuwu 田須無, Viscount Wen 文.
45. ZZ Zhao 3 (B10.3.3/323/23–29), Durrant et al., trs., 2016, 1348–49; *Yanzi chunqiu* (1994) 4.17/35/20–36/1, 7.10/64/1–11. The *Shi ji* only mentions the institution of separate grain measures during the headship of Tian Chang's father, Tian Qi 田乞 (SJ 46:1881), but the these earlier texts places a report of these policies in 539 BCE, during the headship of Tian Wuyu 田無宇 (see ZGS, 142; Wang and Tang 1992, 623).
46. Evidence for this trend is documented in Cho-yun Hsu 1965, 31–37.

47. *Guo yu* 4.120/95/3–9.
48. *SJ* 46:1885.
49. The *Shi ji suo yin* 索引 records the medieval scholar Qiao Yunnan 譙允南 (201–70 CE) as opining that even a figure as reprehensible as Tian Chang would not act like a beast (*Shi ji* 46:1885n).
50. For an account of the Tian rise to supremacy in Qi, see Wang and Tang, 360–63. For the larger trend of which the Tian usurpation was a part, see ZGS, 139–51.
51. The *Shi ji*, following the *Zuo zhuan*, frequently gives Zai Wo's name as Kan Zhi, but Qian Mu persuasively demonstrated, this confusion is only a product of the politics among Confucius's latter-day disciples (Qian 1935, 54–58). Many pre-Qin and Han texts place Zai Wo in Qi in 481 BCE (e.g. *Han Feizi* 韓非子 3/5/28; *Lüshi chunqiu* 17.6/106/19–23; *Huainanzi* 18/195/14–16). SJ 67:2195 (Nienhauser, ed., 1994b, 70) notes that Zai Wo's family had been wiped out because of the rebellion in Qi. There can be little doubt that Zai Wo was indeed Tian Chang's counterpart as joint leader of the Qi court.
52. SJ 32:1508 (Knickenbocker 115–16), 46:1883; *Zuo zhuan* Ai 14 (12.14.3/456/28–29), Durrant et al., trs., 2016, 1922–23.
53. See Jensen 1997, 31–134.
54. The sources for the ancestry, birth, and early life of Confucius are scattered and fragmentary. See Lau, tr., 1979, 161–65; Chin 2007, 1–21; Nylan and Wilson 2010, 1–11.
55. The evidence for early forms of elite education is reviewed in Chan 2004, 103–13.
56. For this discussion of the teachings of Confucius I will be relying on the *Lunyu* 論語 or *Analects*, the best witness we have of what Confucius taught during his lifetime. For the date and authorship of the *Analects*, see Anne Cheng 1993, 313–23. A different view is presented in Brooks and Brooks 1998. An even more skeptical view can be found in Hunter 2017. I am more inclined to agree with Goldin 2018, 92–115.
57. *Lun yu* 16.2/45/25–46/1; Lau, tr., 139. There is much English-language scholarship on the thought of Confucius. Interested readers may consult Fingarette 1972, 56–134; Graham 1989, 9–32; Sterckx 2019, 221–66; Goldin 2020, 31–53. See also the essays collected in Van Norden, ed., 2002.
58. *Lun yu* 7.1/14/22.
59. *Lun yu* 3.14/5/29, Lau, tr., 69.
60. *Lun yu* 4.8/7/23.
61. *Lun yu* 1.12/2/6–7, Lau, tr., 61; 3.3/4/29, Lau, tr., 67; 9.5/20/15–16, Lau, tr., 96.
62. *Lun yu* 12.1/30/17–18, Lau, tr., 112.
63. This dimension of Confucius's thought has been most insightfully outlined in Fingarette 1972, 1–17.
64. This insight is articulate at several points in the *Analects*, for example *Lun yu* 4.5/7/12–14, Lau, tr., 72.
65. *Lunyu* 1.1/1/3, Lau, tr., 59; 5.28/11/24, Lau, tr., 80; 8.17/19/18, Lau, tr., 94; 14.24/39/17, Lau, tr., 128; 16.13/47/3–9, Lau, tr., 141–42.
66. *Lunyu* 16.1/45/7–15; Lau, tr., 138.
67. A good example of this type of critique can be seen in Lu Xun 2009, 21–36.
68. *Lun yu* 12.11/32/3–4.
69. See Li Chenyang 2000.
70. See Csikszentmihayli 2001, 267–72.
71. ZZ Ai 8, B12.8.3–7/446/6–21, Durrant et al., trs., 2016, 1882–83.
72. *Lun yu* 11.3/26/16; Lau, tr., 106.

73. SJ 32:1508 (Knickerbocker 2006, 116); 46:1888; ZZ Ai 14 (B12.14.3/456/28-29), Durrant et al., trs., 2016, 1922-23.
74. This man was Tian Ni 田逆, who also appears in bronze inscriptions dating to the early fifth century BCE: Yang Bojun 1993, 1683.
75. SJ 32:1508 (Knickenbocker 2006, 116); ZZ Ai 14 (B12.14.3/456/31-457/1), Durrant et al., trs., 2016, 1922-23.
76. This was Chen Bao 陳豹, a first cousin once removed of Tien Chang (Yang Bojun 1993, 1683).
77. SJ 32:1508 (Knickerbocker 2006, 116); ZZ Ai 14 (B12.14.3/457/3-7), Durrant et al., trs., 2016, 1924-25.
78. SJ 32:1510 (Knickerbocker 2006, 117).
79. SJ 32:1510-12 (Knickerbocker 2006, 117-18); ZZ Ai 14 (B12.14.3/457/14-19, B12.14.5/458/9), Durrant et al., trs., 2016, 1926-27, 1930-31. For questions on the location of the Duke's death, see Knickerbocker 2006, 118n641.
80. SJ 32:1512 (Knickerbocker 2006, 118).
81. SJ 46:1884.
82. ZZ Ai 14 (B12.14.5/458/9-12), Durrant et al., trs., 2016, 1930-31; *Lun yu* 14.21/39/5-9, Lao, tr., 127-28.
83. *Yi Zhou shu* 54/278/2.
84. *Lun yu* 17.21/50/1-9.
85. *Lun yu* 5.10/10/1-3, Lau, tr., 77.
86. Goldin 2000, 77-81, notes the penchant for chroniclers to use this type of "appellation that could not be [a] birth name."
87. See for example *Han Feizi* 44/133/1, 49/148/15; *Zhuangzi* 29/89/10; *Lüshi chunqiu* 25.1/160/13; *Huainanzi* 13/123/8, to name only a few.
88. Zilu was cut down for his defiance of rebels in the state of Wey, where he was employed: ZZ Ai 15 (B12.15.5/459-460/14), Durrant et al., trs., 2016, 1938-41; *Shi ji* 67:2193-4 (Nienhauser, ed., 1994b, 68-69).
89. *Lun yu* 9.9/20/29.
90. Achebe 1959.

CHAPTER 2

1. An exhaustive list of the different products of popular culture spun from the saga of Wu and Yue would require a monograph-length catalogue on its own. Some sense of the sheer volume of these works can be garnered from: Johnson 1980, 93-156, 465-505; Cohen 2009; Milburn 2013b, 23-53.
2. The phrase "Above there is Heaven, below there is Su[zhou] and Hang[zhou] 上有天堂，下有蘇杭" has been a common adage since the Yuan 元 dynasty (1271-1368 CE). See Luo Zhufeng 羅竹風 et al. 1990, 1-271B. The Qing emperor Qianlong 乾隆 (r. 1735-96 CE) was so enamored of Suzhou that he built a replica "Suzhou Street 蘇州街" in the Summer Palace at Beijing, a rebuilt version of which can still be visited today.
3. See Milburn 2013b.
4. "Non-Han" distinguishes those citizens of the People's Republic of China (hereafter PRC) who do not speak some form of one of the major language families referred to as "dialects" of Chinese (for example, Mandarin, Cantonese, Shanghainese, etc.). See Ramsey 1987, 157-59. "Non-Han" citizens of the PRC include Uighurs, Mongols, Tibetans, and other linguistic minorities.

5. See Brindley 2015, 45–61. The PRC citizens whose current languages are most likely descendant from that spoken in Wu and Yue include members of the Miao, Yao, and Zhuang minorities (Ramsey, 234–43, 278–85).
6. The penchant of the Wu-Yue people for wearing their hair short and body tattooing is well attested in the sources, being recorded at ZZ Ai 7 (B12.7.3/443/28); *Shi ji* 31:1445 (Nienhauser, ed., 2006, 2) and 41:1739; *Zhanguo ce* 222/117/14–15 (Crump 1996, 290 [note that Crump follows a different numbering of the component anecdotes of the *Zhanguo ce* than do Lau and Chen]); and in numerous other texts. Their preference for clothes made of plant fibers is noted at *Shi ji* 41:1739. See also Falkenhausen 2006, 271–84, 1999, 525–38.
7. This explanation is recorded in the "Monograph on Geography" of Ban Gu 班固 (32–92 CE), HS, 28B:1669.
8. See Taylor 1983, 43. My thanks to Eric Henry for his insights on ancient Yue language and ethnicity.
9. For the identity of the people of Yue, see Brindley 2015, 21–44.
10. On distinctions like "barbaric" and "civilized," see Brindley 2015, 115–40. See also Meacham 1983, 147–75.
11. ZZ Cheng 7, A8.7.2/198/16, Durrant et al., trs., 2016, 762–63. The *Zuo zhuan* commentary has an earlier mention of Wu and Yue, in an entry for 602 BCE (ZZ Xuan 8, B7.8.3/165/17, Durrant et al., trs., 2016, 622–23). The *Spring and Autumn Annals* does not mention Yue until an entry for 537 BCE: ZZ Zhao 5, A10.5.8/330/31, Durrant et al., trs., 2016, 1384–85.
12. Overview and analysis of the rise of (and clash between) Wu and Yue may be found in Brindley 2015, 85–92; Milburn 2013a, 19–115. See also Millburn 2010, 1–36.
13. For the history of the *ba* 霸 ("Lord Protector," sometimes translated as "hegemon") system, see Rosen 1978, 99–114.
14. Veeck et al. 2011, 116–19.
15. The earliest preserved census by the Han (202 BCE–220 CE) imperial government, taken in 2 CE, showed 44 million people living in northern China and 13.7 million people living in southern China. See Bielenstein 1947, 125–63, 1986, 241–42.
16. Lattimore 1988; Di Cosmo 2002.
17. Schafer 1967, 11–16.
18. 南船北馬. See Xie Xiuzong 謝秀宗, ed., 1990, 165–66. See also Major et al. 2010, 420.
19. For a survey of the unique geography and ecology of the South, see Marks 2012, 24–28.
20. von Falkenhausen 2006, 271–84.
21. The legendary origins and early history of the ruling Xiong 熊 clan of Chu are recorded in SJ 40:1689–92 (Cao 2006, 381–84).
22. von Falkenhausen 2006, 262–71; Flad and Chen 2013, 108–39.
23. Falkenhausen 2006, 264–65. Also Blakeley 1999, 9–10.
24. SJ 30:1691–92 (Cao 2006, 384).
25. SJ 4:134; Nienhauser, ed., 1994a, 66. *Zhushu jinian* (1998), 1.57.5/26/15–16. Shaughnessy 1991, 205–8, 245.
26. SJ 40:1695 (Cao 2006, 388).
27. SJ 40:1695–1703 (Cao 2006, 388–400; Blakeley 1999, 12–14). Sources on the expansion of Chu by conquest are collected in Ma Su 馬驌 2002, Vol. 3, 980–91.
28. von Falkenhausen 2005, 79–123. The trade tallies analyzed in this study were of late date (323 BCE), but their design indicates that they were bronze-cast models of similar safe-transit pass tallies that had earlier been issued on bamboo.
29. Peng 2000, 208–12.
30. See *Wu Yue chunqiu* 10/47/26–28.

31. For the origins and history of this rivalry see Hsu 1999, 558–62.
32. Peters 1999, 99–117.
33. ZZ Cheng 7 (B8.7.5/199/27–30; Durrant et al., trs., 2016, 766–67).
34. See Milburn 2013a, 20–4. The earliest source that specifically reports Taipo fleeing to the South to live among "barbarians" is the Han-era SJ 31:1445 (Chen and Nienhauser, 2006, 1–2).
35. The wide distribution of weapons and ceramics manufactured in Wu and Yue testifies to these states' intense commercial activity. See Falkenhausen 2006, 271, 282.
36. For the cult of Zixu as a god, see Johnson 1980 (Part II), 465–505. The Wugong Temple 伍公廟, where Zixu is enshrined as the principal deity, is still active in the city of Hangzhou: https://www.trip.com/travel-guide/attraction/hangzhou/wugongmiao-13684627/.
37. In Chu the official titled the *shi* 師 held the same office that in other states was called the *fu* 傅. See Gu Dongguo 1995, Vol. 2, 1059–60.
38. ZZ Zhao 19 B10/19.2/370/14–16, Durrant et al., trs., 2016, 1560–61; SJ 40:1712; Cao 2006, 410; SJ 66:2171, Nienhauser, ed., 1994b, 49.
39. ZZ B10.20.2/372/15–28 (Durrant et. al., trs., 2019, 1568–70); SJ 66:2172–73 (Nienhauser, ed., 1994b, 49–50); SJ 40:1712–14 (Cao 2006, 410–11).
40. Accounts of the fate of the Chu Heir and the point at which his son became Zixu's ward are inconsistent across the early sources. See SJ 66:2173 (Nienhauser, ed., 1994b, 50–1, 51n10); *Wu Yue chun qiu* 3/5/8–6/1; SJ 31:1461 (Chen and Nienhauser, trs., 2006, 14–15; SJ 42:1774). The Heir of Chu's son Sheng 勝 (d. 479 BCE) was enfeoffed as the Duke of Bo. He is notorious for having led a very destructive rebellion against the Chu court in 479 BCE (ZZ Ai 16, B12.16.5/461/16–462/23, Durrant et al., trs., 2016, 1946–53).The Duke of Bo's biography is joined to that of Wu Zixu in SJ 66:2181–83, Nienhauser, ed., 1994b, 59–60.
41. The story of the fisherman does not appear in all versions of Zixu's tale, and it is not the same in all accounts. See SJ 66:2173 (Cao 2006b, 51); *Wu Yue chunqiu* 3/5/19–6/1; *Lüshi chunqiu* 10.4./51/1–9 (Knoblock and Riegel, trs., 2000, 235). See also Milburn 2010, 85–6. For a parallel story, see ZZ Zhao 20 B10.20.2/372/17–21, Durrant et al., trs., 2016, 1570–71.
42. See Milburn 2013a, 259–60.
43. The material and economic sophistication of Wu and Yue are well attested in the archaeological record, which also bears witness to the historicity of the major figures in the saga of the South. Mirrors, bells, and weapons bearing the names of Helü and Fuchai have been discovered. See Dong Chuping 1992, 45–53, 71–75, 117–21, 133–34. One of the most spectacular ancient artifacts ever discovered in China is an extraordinarily well-preserved sword bearing an inscription identifying it as having been manufactured at the orders of King Goujian for his own use (Dong Chuping, 1992, 202–5).
44. Wallace-Hadrill 1998, 79–91.
45. The succession of kings from King Shoumeng to his grandson King Liao 僚 (526–515 BCE) is outlined in SJ 31:1447–64 (Chen and Nienhauser 2006, 4–16). See also Milburn 2004, 195–214. For the lore surrounding Shoumeng's youngest son, the Prince Jizha 季札, see Milburn 2013a, 30–49.
46. SJ 31:1461 (Chen and Nienhauser 2006, 14); ZZ Zhao 17 B10.17.6/367/18–24 (Durrant et al., trs., 2016, 1548–49).
47. SJ 31:1461 (Chen and Nienhauser 2006, 15).
48. SJ 31:1462 (Chen and Nienhauser 2006, 15), Zhao 20 (B10.20.2/372/30–31; Durrant et al., trs., 2016, 1572–73). The knight recommended by Zixu was Zhuan Zhu 專諸, a warrior of famous strength and courage whose biography is included among those of the "Assassin Retainers" (SJ 66:2516–18; Nienhauser, ed., 1994b, 320–21).

49. *Wu Yue chunqiu* 3/7/14–15.
50. ZZ Zhao 27 (B10.27.2/394/27–395/12; Durrant et al., trs., 2016, 1672–75); SJ 31:1463–65 (Chen and Nienhauser 2006, 16); SJ 66:2174 (Nienhauser 1994b, 52).
51. Accounts in the ZZ and SJ differ. SJ 66:2175 reports that the Wu princes surrendered on the news of their brother's assassination. ZZ Zhao 30 (B10.30.3/401/37–B10.30.4/402/11; Durrant et al., trs., 2016, 1708–9) reports that the Wu princes rebelled only after King Helü ordered them seized by two of Wu's vassals.
52. SJ 66:2174–75 (Nienhauser 1994b, 52–53).
53. ZZ Zhao 30, 31, Ding 11 (B10.30.5/402/13–16, B10.31.4/403/22–4B11.2.2/408/20–21; Durrant et al., trs., 2016, 1708–11, 1714–15, 1738–93).
54. ZZ Ding 4 (B11.4.3/412/3–413/21; Durrant et al., trs., 2016, 1752–57); *Shi ji* 31:1466 (Chen and Nienhauser, trs., 2006, 17–18), 66:2175–76 (Nienhauser, ed., 1994b, 53).
55. SJ 31:1466 (Chen and Nienhauser, trs., 2006, 18); SJ 66:2176 (Nienhauser, ed., 1994b, 54).
56. See Cook 2006.
57. Accounts of the rape of the women of Ying occur in *Yuejue shu* 4/14/10, 19/54/11–12 (Milburn 2010, 131, 384) and in *Wu Yue chunqiu* 4/14/24–25. Confucius's commentary appears at *Yuejue shu* 19/54/22–23 (Milburn 2010, 385). These accounts are corroborated in the *Chunqiu Guliang zhuan* 11.4.13/138/10–12. The *Lienü zhuan* contains an alternative version of events in which the Queen Dowager resisted being violated by threatening to commit suicide when accosted by King Helü: *Gu Lienü zhuan* 4.9/36/23–37/12 (Kinney, tr., 2014, 76–78). See Milburn 2023, 277–91. My thanks to Paul Goldin for alerting me to the interpretive issues elucidated by Milburn.
58. This of course does not absolve ancient literati and modern scholars of responsibility. See Milburn 2023, 288.
59. ZZ Ding 4 (B11.4.2/413/1–13, Durrant et al., trs., 2016, 1756–59).
60. ZZ Ding 4 (B11.4.2/413/15–21, Durrant et al., trs., 2016, 1760–61); SJ 66: 2176–77 (Nienhauser, ed., 1994b, 54).
61. SJ 31:1467 (Chen and Nienhauser, trs., 2006, 18).
62. ZZ Zhao 5 (A10.5.8/330/31, B10.5.8/333/18–334/2, Durrant et al., trs., 2016, 1384–85, 1398–1401).
63. ZZ Zhao 32 (B10.32.2/404/28–9, Durrant et al., trs., 2016, 1718–19).
64. SJ 31:1467 (Chen and Nienhauser, trs., 2006, 18); SJ 66:2177 (Nienhauser, ed., 1994b, 55).
65. SJ 66:2177 (Nienhauser, ed., 1994b, 55).
66. *Wu Yue chunqiu* 4/16/15–17/2.
67. ZZ Ding 14 (B11.14.5/430/12–18, Durrant et al., trs., 2016, 1816–19); SJ 41:1739–40.
68. SJ 31:1465, 1469 (Chen and Nienhauser, trs., 2006, 17, 19); SJ 66:2174, 2178 (Nienhauser, ed., 1994b, 52, 55).
69. ZZ Ai 1 (B12.1.2/433/14–24, Durrant et al., trs., 2016, 1832–5); *Guo yu* 7.1/111/20–7.2/112/25; SJ 31:1469–70 (Chen and Nienhauser, trs., 19–21), 41:1740–1, 66:2178 (Nienhauser, ed., 1994b, 55–56).
70. ZZ Ai 2 (B12.2.4/436/16–17, Durrant et al., trs., 2016, 1848–49), Ai 6 (A12.6.3.440/24; Durrant et al., trs., 1862–63), Ai 7 (B12.7.3/443/19–29, Durrant et al., trs., 2016, 1872–77), Ai 8 (A12.8.2/444/30, B12.8.2/445/16–446/4, Durrant et al., trs., 2016, 1878–83). For the canal linking the Yangzi and Huai, see Ai 9 (B12.9.5/447/16); Durrant et al., trs., 2016, 1886–87 and 1886n186).
71. *Wu Yue chunqiu* 9/40/20–41/20; *Yuejue shu* 6/20/1–23/16 (Milburn 2010, 161–78).
72. SJ 41:1742. The *Shi ji*'s account of Goujian "tasting gall" was augmented later by the image of him "sleeping on sticks." The expression "sleeping on sticks and tasting gall" is a common

idiomatic expression today for working strenuously toward some goal, and alludes to Goujian's tribulations.
73. *Wu Yue chunqiu* 9/40/7–18. See also *Zhuangzi* 2/4/26 (Watson, tr., 1968, 161–62); *Mozi* 1.1[1]/1/22 (Johnston, tr., 2010, 7).
74. A review of the lore surrounding Xi Shi may be found in Milburn 2013a, 93–96.
75. See for example *Guanzi* 管子 (2001) 16.3(51)/118/22 (Rickett, tr., 1998, 187); *Xunzi* 荀子 9/37/7 (Hutton, tr., 2014, 72).
76. Duke Dao had asked for an alliance with Wu against Confucius's home state of Lu, then withdrew his offer of alliance. King Fuchai had then entered into a covenant with Lu and joined the hostilities between Lu and Qi on the side of Lu. See ZZ Ai 8, 9 (B12.8.5/446/11, B12.9.1/447/8–10, Durrant et. al., trs., 2016, 1884–87).
77. ZZ Ai 10 (B12.10.2/448/27, B12.10.3/448/29–30, Durrant et al., trs., 2016, 1890–93).
78. ZZ Ai 11 (B12.11.3/450/21–451/2, Durrant et al., trs., 2016, 1898–1901). The date of the battle of Mugwort Hill (Ailing 艾陵) is variously reported in different sources. See Nienhauser, ed., 1994, 56n59.
79. ZZ Ai 11 (B12.11.4/451/4–12, Durrant et al., trs., 2016, 1900–1903); *Guo yu* 7.5/113/25–114/10; SJ 66:2178–80 (Nienhauser, ed., 1994, 55–58). I have conflated the details in these accounts, especially the chronology.
80. SJ 5:198 (Nienhauser, ed., 1994a, 105), 39:1685, 43:1792–93, 66:2181 (Nienhauser, ed., 1994b, 58); ZZ Ai 13 (B12.13.2/454/16, Durrant et al., trs., 2016, 1915–17). *Guo yu* 7.7/115/5–116/14 reports that Jin only acceded to Fuchai being recognized as Lord Protector after a military standoff at Huangchi.
81. ZZ Ai 13 (B12.13.3/18–24, Durrant et al., trs., 2016, 1914–15); SJ 31:1474 (Chen and Nienhauser, trs., 2006, 23).
82. SJ 31:1474 (Chen and Nienhauser, trs., 2006, 23), 41:1744.
83. ZZ Ai 17 (B12.17.2/463/7–9, Durrant et al., trs., 2016, 1954–55).
84. ZZ Ai 20 (B12.20.3/465/21–31, Durrant et al., trs., 2016, 1966–69); *Guo yu* 7.9/117/3–8.1/18, 8.8/124/18–125/10; SJ 31:1475 (Chen and Nienhauser, trs., 2006, 24), 41:1745–46.
85. SJ 41:1746.
86. SJ 41:1746–51. For the determination of the date of Yue's destruction in 306 BCE, see Yang Kuan 2002, 630–34. cf. Henry 2007, 1–36.

CHAPTER 3

1. ZGS, 310–11.
2. For a discussion of the social composition of Jin elites, see Blakeley 1979, 81–118. Gu Donggao 1995, Vol. 2, 1245–83 gives a list of 15 clans of Jin, along with chronological lists of their recorded members. Blakeley 1979, 83n8, lists 30 independent clans of Jin.
3. The Lords of the Land (*zhuhou* 諸侯) is a collective term for the set of aristocrats that exercised effective sovereignty over the territory on which they resided.
4. SJ 39:1635 (Zhao Hua and William H. Nienhauser Jr., trs., "Chin, Hereditary House 9." In Nienhauser, ed., 2006, 297–98).
5. ZZ Xiang 29 (B9.29.11/302/19–24, Durrant et al., trs., 2016, 1240–41); Hsu 1999, 567–58.
6. For the territorial scope of Jin, see Tan Qixiang, ed., 1982, 22–23.
7. SJ 39:1638–40 (Zhao Hua and William H. Nienhauser Jr., trs., 2006, 301–4).
8. SJ 39:1666–67 (Zhao Hua and William H. Nienhauser Jr., trs., 2006, 340–42). Translations of the most important sources for the career of Duke Wen of Jin (r. 636–628 BCE) are collected in Watson 1989, 40–72.
9. Rosen 1978, 107–11.

10. Barry Blakeley notes that Jin was exceptional among the Zhou states for having very few collateral clans that were offshoots of the ruling clan (Blakeley 1979, 82–83). He counts only the Han clan among this group, but other evidence suggests that the Luan 欒 and Xi 郤 clans were also offshoots of the ruling clan (Ma Su 2002, Vol. 5, 2181).
11. See SJ 43:1780; SJ 44:1835; Ma Su 2002, Vol. 5, 2181. For more information about the origins of Jin grandee clans, see Blakeley 1979 and Gu Donggao 1995.
12. See Hsu 1965, 80–92. For conflict specific to the state of Jin, see Ma Su 2002, Vol. 5, 2104–38.
13. "Counselor" (*qing* 卿) was a rank that marked the courtiers closest to the ruler of one of the Zhou states in both status and personal intimacy, in theory a step above ordinary "grandees" (*dafu* 大夫). See Hsu 1965, 5–9.
14. Yang Bojun 1993, Vol. 1, 474–75.
15. In 588 BCE a "new army" was added to each of the existing "three armies" (for a total of six), but the "privy council" of ruling clans seems to have been generally fixed at "Six Counselors." See ZZ Cheng 3 (B8.3.8/193/3–4, Durrant et al., trs., 2016, 742–43).
16. ZZ Zhao 29 (B10.29.5/400/26–401/5, Durrant et al., trs., 2016, 1702–3). The text of the Penal Cauldron was not preserved. A similar penal code was cast onto a bronze cauldron earlier by the Prime Minister of Zheng 鄭, Zichan 子產, in 536 BCE. See Hsu 1999, 584–85; ZZ Zhao 6 (B10.6.3/334/32–335/18, Durrant et al., trs., 2016, 1402–5).
17. For the nature and use of covenant texts, see Weld 1997, 125–60. For the date of the Houma texts, see Weld 1997, 137–39; Williams 2012–13, 247–75.
18. This is a pledge text recording an oath in the name of a knight named An Zhang 盦章, who is otherwise unknown from the historical records. See Weld 1997, 146–48.
19. SJ 41:1746.
20. For the genealogy and rank of the Zhi clan, see Gu Donggao 1995, Vol. 2, 1264–67.
21. See Ames 1993, 174–76.
22. *Guo yu* 4.125/96/1–7.
23. Yang Bojun, Vol. 2, 1721; *Mozi* 5.2(18)/32/23 (Johnston 2010, 179).
24. Takigawa 1999, Vol. 6, 2652–53.
25. ZZ Ai 23 (B12.13.2/466/26–467/1, Durrant et al., trs., 2016, 1972–73). Zhi Yao is identified here alternatively as Xun 荀 Yao and Zhi Bo 伯 ("Earl Zhi"). The Zhi clan was an offshoot of the Xun clan following the *zongfa* 宗法 traditions of the Zhou aristocracy (Blakeley 1979, 82–3). More will be said about the frequently used title of "Earl Zhi" below.
26. ZZ Ai 27 (B12.27.3/470/6–13, Durrant et al., trs., 2016, 1988–91).
27. *Shuo yuan* 說苑 (1992) 15.9/119/11–13.
28. ZZ Ai 27 (B12.27.5/470/25–27, Durant et al., trs., 2016, 1992–93).
29. SJ 43:1789.
30. SJ 43:1789.
31. ZZ Ai 27 (B12.27.5/470/27–29, Durant et al., trs., 2016, 1992–93). An alternate version of this story is found at SJ 43:1793.
32. SJ 42:1775.
33. The independent state of Wey 微 is spelled differently to distinguish it from the Jin grandee clan domain of Wei 魏.
34. *Zhanguo ce* 448A,B/220/12–19 (Crump 1996, 518–19).
35. *Han Feizi* 韓非子 (2000) 23/54/12–14; *Lüshi chunqiu* 呂氏春秋 (1992) 15.2/82/8–14 (Knoblock and Riegel, trs., 2000, 345–46).
36. *Zhushu jinian* 竹書紀年 (1998) 2.5.20.7/73/15. For the textual evidence to place this event in 462 BCE, see Yang Kuan 2002, 110.

37. ZZ Ai 5 (B12.5.1/439/31–440/4, Durrant et al., trs., 2016, 1858–61). The *Zuo zhuan* records that the heads of the Fan and Zhonghang clans fled Jin in 490 BCE after a rebellion, but their clans seem to have continued to operate within the Jin territory under new leadership.
38. SJ 39:1686–87 (Zhao and Nienhauser, trs., 2006, 366), 43:1794. See also *Han Feizi* 10/15/20–17/1, 21/42/12–13, 38/134/9–16; *Zhanguo ce* 83B/38/30–39/5, 89/43/8,142/72/27–73/1, 203/103/22–105/14, 204B/106/5–29; *Lüshi chunqiu* 12.5/61/5–17, 12.6/62/14–18.
39. Yang Kuan argues that Duke Chu of Jin did not die in 458 BCE, but must have lived for another six years and fled Jin for refuge in Chu in 452 BCE (Yang Kuan 2002, 139–40). Even if that was the case, it would have meant that Zhi Yao took effective control of the Jin court in 458 BCE after leading the other clans in defiance of the ducal house.
40. For the etymology of *bo*, see Goldin 2021, 478.
41. Cf. Pines 2020, 714–20. While the title may have been in use internally to the Zhi clan (meaning, effectively "elder") before Zhi Yao's time, it became associated with Zhi Yao persistently in the wake of his tenure as Zhi clan head.
42. Zhi Yao's campaign of 455 BCE to seize back land from the Wei, Han, and Zhao clans is recounted in many sources. See *Zhanguo ce* 203/103/23–104/2, 264A/140/4–12 (Crump 1996, 273, 351); *Han Feizi* 22/47/1–7. For a collection and critical textual evaluation of these and other sources, see Yang Kuan 2002, 119–26.
43. *Han Feizi* 10/15/20–16/11; *Zhanguo ce* 203/104/4–12 (Crump 1996, 273–74).
44. *Han Feizi* 10/16/11–13; *Zhanguo ce* 203/104/14–15 (Crump 1996, 274); *Guo yu* 4.127/96/15–23. See also Yang Kuan 2002, 123–24.
45. *Han Feizi* 10/16/13–17/2; *Zhanguo ce* 203/104/15–105/14 (Crump 1996, 274–76).
46. *Zhanguo ce* 204B/106/7–8 (Crump 1996, 279), 38/124/22–23; *Lüshi chunqiu* 14.4/74/9–13 (Knoblock and Riegel 2000, 318); SJ 86:2519 (Nienhauser, ed., 1994a, 321).
47. SJ 39:1686 (Zhao and Nienhauser, trs., 2006, 366).
48. *Zhanguo ce* 204B/106/5–29 (Crump 1996, 279–81); SJ 86:2519–21 (Nienhauser, ed., 1994a, 321–23); *Lüshi chunqiu* 8.2/39/9–10, 12.5/61/4, 12–17, 12.6/62/14–18, 20.1/129/11–16 (Knoblock and Riegel 2000, 195, 268, 269, 271, 513). The correct romanization of Yurang's 豫讓 name is open to interpretation. I have followed Crump in Romanizing his name as Yurang (rather than Yu Rang, as Knoblock and Riegel do), on the assumption that this was his personal name, his surname being uncertain.
49. Qian Mu 1935, 89–90, 616. For figures among the Masters for whose birth and death dates we have no firm evidence, I have generally followed Qian Mu's determinations unless I have found evidence to contradict his assessments.

CHAPTER 4

1. For the "Mandate of Heaven" (*tian ming* 天命), see Jiang 2011.
2. See also Luo and Pines 2023, 1–47.
3. See for example Cook 2012, 521–64.
4. Though the promotion of these ideas by an ostensible vassal of the Zhou king, who claimed to rule on the basis of the mandate of Heaven, they reflected very old popular expectations about the nature of the gods and ancestors, dating back to before the Zhou conquest. See Keightley 2000.
5. For the early history of the Mohist movement, see Graham 1978, 1–24; Knoblock and Riegel 2013, 1–15.
6. SJ 4:158 (Nienhauser, ed., 1994a, 78).
7. SJ 43:1793–94; *Lüshi chunqiu* 14.5/75/14–22 (Knoblock and Riegel 2000, 322–23). The two accounts vary slightly in details.

8. SJ 34:1569 (Nienhauser, tr., 2006, 205), 36:1584 (Wang, tr., 2006, 234), 40:1719 (Cao, tr., 2006b, 418). I have Latinized the state of Qii 杞 with two i's to distinguish it from the much larger state of Qi 齊.
9. ZGS, 311–13.
10. This was the state of Song, the ruling house of which were the ancestors of Confucius. See SJ 38:1607–20 (Zhang, tr., 2006, 267–76).
11. SJ 43:1786–89. The prophecies offered to Viscount Jian by the "stranger" in the *Shi ji* include predictions of the conquests undertaken by King Wuling of Zhao 趙武靈王 (r. 325–299 BCE), about whom we will read in Chapter 12. My account infers that the *Shi ji* preserves a later iteration of a tradition that had begun during Zhao Wuxu's tenure (see also below).
12. SJ 43:1794–96. Here again the prophecies offered by the spirit emissaries contain predictions that apply to the later King Wuling. Nakai Sekitoku (1732–1817 CE) argues that this proves the anecdote to be of late provenance (Takigawa 1999, Vol. 6, 2656). But for the prophecy to be plausible its association with institutions like the cult of Mount Huotai would have to be believable, thus a late origin is unlikely.
13. *Lun yu* 7.14/15/25 (Lau, tr., 1979, 87); *Mozi* 8.4 (32)/55/17–57/25 (Johnston, tr., 306–17).
14. See for example *Lun yu* 17.19/49/25–6 (Lau, tr., 1979, 146). On the cultivation of Potency, see *Lun yu* 2.3/2/29–30 (Lau, tr., 1979, 63). For the continued currency of such ideas in the fifth century, see Cook, tr., 2012, Vol. 1, 429–64. See also Meyer 2012, 53–72, 269–82.
15. For Mo Di's origins and life, see SJ 74:2350 (Nienhauser, ed., 1994b, 185). See also Sun Yirang 1987, 629–30; Qin Yanshi 2002, 1–18. See also Hsiao 1979, 214–24. For evidence that Mo Di was a knight, see *Mozi* 2.1[8]/9/5–2.3[10]/16/3 (Johnston, tr., 2010, 54–89). These chapters repeatedly declaim that the "worthy" can be found among the world's knights.
16. On the thought of Mo Di, see Schwartz 1985, 135–72; Graham 1989, 33–52; Ren Jiyu 2011; Fraser 2016.
17. *Mozi* 7.1(26)/42/6–7.3(28)/50/8 (Johnston, tr., 2010, 232–77).
18. *Mozi* 2.1(8)/9/5–2.3(10)/16/3 (Johnston, tr., 2010, 54–89).
19. *Mozi* 6.6(25)/38/16–40/26 (Johnston, tr., 2010, 211–23). The *Mozi* only specifies that mourning should be of "short duration." Other texts report that the Mohists prescribed three months of morning as a general rule. For example *Han Feizi* 50/150/26 (Watson, tr., 1963, 119).
20. *Mozi* 4.1(14)/23/27–4.3(16)/30/10 (Johnston, tr., 2010, 130–65).
21. *Mozi* 8.4 (32)/55/17–57/25 (Johnston, tr., 2010, 306–17).
22. *Mozi* 9.3(35)/58/11–9.4(36)/61/25 (Johnston, tr., 2010, 318–37).
23. *Mozi* 8.3(31)/50/20–55/15 (Johnston, tr., 2010, 278–305).
24. Meyer 2015, 271–97.
25. *Mozi* 5.1(17)/30/14–5.3(19)/35/28 (Johnston, tr., 2010, 166–97).
26. *Mozi* 15.3(70)/139/15–24 (Johnston, tr., 2010, 888–89). My thanks to Robin Yates for alerting me to this passage.
27. *Mozi* 14.1(52)/123/17–24, 14.6(62)/127/25–128/9 (Johnston, tr., 2010, 772–5, 800–803). For more discussion of counter-siege technology in the *Mozi*, see Yates 1982, 409–52; Qi Yanshi 2002, 60–75.
28. *Mozi* 13.2(50)/115/29–116/20 (Johnston, tr., 2010, 724–29); *Lüshi chunqiu* 21.5/142/11–17 (Knoblock and Riegel 2000, 560–61). For the evidence to site the event in 439 BCE, see Yang Kuan 2002, 152–54.

CHAPTER 5

1. Yang Kuan 2002, 142–44, demonstrates that the notices of Wei Si's accession in SJ 15:703, 39:1687, and 44:1838 all preserve scribal errors.
2. See ZGS, 205–8, 313–17.
3. von Falkenhausen 1996, 1–22.
4. It put Wei Si on a par with the second Lord Protector, posthumously known as Duke Wen of Jin (r. 636–628 BCE).
5. SJ 44:1835.
6. The first clan head was known as Bi Wan 畢萬. In subsequent generations the clan used the name of its fief, Wei 魏, as its surname. See Gu Donggao 1995, Vol. 2, 1255.
7. *Shuo yuan* 8.34/66/20–23; *Huainanzi* 12/119/8–12 (Major et al., 479–80).
8. SJ 3:709, 44:1839; *Lüshi chunqiu* 21.2/139/24–25 (Knoblock and Riegel 2000, 552). For the chronology of Zixia's tenure in Wei, see Yang Kuan 2002, 146–49; Qian Mu 1935, 124–25.
9. HS 30:1724.
10. The Qing 清 dynasty (1644–1911 CE) scholar Ma Guohan 馬國翰 (1794–1857 CE) produced a "reconstruction" of a partial *Wen Wenhou* 魏文侯, but we cannot know whether it accurately reflects the content of the original text. See Ma Guohan, *Yuhan shanfang jiyishu* 玉函山房輯佚書. 8 vols. Yangzhou: Jiangsu guangling guji keyingshe, 1990, Vol. 6, 176–82.
11. For evidence of Zixia's reputation, see for example *Li ji* 禮記 (1992)3.36/14/18–22; Qian Mu 1935, 125–29.
12. These were Wu Qi 吳起, Li Ke 李克, and Tian Zifang 田子方. See Qian Mu 1935, 129–37.
13. SJ 44:1837; *Lüshi chunqiu* 21.3/140/17–141/2 (Knoblock and Riegel 2000, 555–56).
14. See Schaberg 2001; Wai-yee Li 2007; Leung 2019.
15. SJ 44:1840; *Hanshi waizhuan* 韓詩外傳 (1992) 3.6/16/29–17/14.
16. For Li Kui's origins and identity, see ZGS, 204n1.
17. *Han Feizi* 30/67/7–9; 32/89/13–18.
18. See HS 24:1124–26; Swann 1950, 136–44; SJ 30:1442, 129:3258–9 (in both SJ passages Li Kui is mistakenly referred to as "Li Ke"). See also von Glahn 2016, 55.
19. ZGS, 205–6.
20. For the *Classic of Laws*, see *Jin shu* 30:922; Zhangsun Wuji et al. 1983, 2 (Johnson 1979, 52–53). For debates over the historicity of the *Classic of Laws*, see Barbieri and Yates 2015, 53–54, 72. See also Ikeda 2008, 76–146; Yang Kuang 2002, 210–16.
21. Johnson 1979, 9.
22. For the origin and structures of commanderies and districts, see ZGS, 245–49; Creel 1970, 121–59.
23. *Han Feizi* 94/18/23.
24. SJ 126:3211–12. The version of the story preserved in the *Shi ji* is a Han-era redaction, I have transposed anachronistic titles to fit the conditions of the fifth century BCE.
25. SJ 29:1408, 126:3213–14. Other sources divide the credit between Ximen Bao 西門豹 and a later Wei magistrate named Shi Qi 史起. See *Lüshi chunqiu* 16.5/95/7–20 (Knoblock and Riegel 2000, 391–93); Yang Kuan 2002, 202.
26. ZGS, 327–41; Lewis 1999a, 620–32; Graff 2002, 17–34; Lorge 2012, 13–52; Galvany 2020, 637–56.
27. SJ 5:200, 44:1838.
28. SJ 44:1838, 65:2166 (Nienhauser, ed., 1994b, 42). See also ZGS, 313–14; Yang Kuan 2002, 193–94. For the participation of Han and Zhao, see Yang Kuan 2002, 216–17; Zhang Yachu 張亞初, ed., 2001, 7:1.157–61.

29. SJ 39:1687 (Zhao and Nienhauser, trs., 2006, 366–67).
30. *Han Feizi* 23/54/26–28; *Zhanguo ce* 264B/140/14–18 (Crump, tr. 1996 352); *Zizhi tongnian* 1:18. The *Zizhi tongjian* testimony suggests that the tripartite covenant must have preceded 408 BCE.
31. SJ 15:1709, 43:1797, 44:1838.
32. Wu 2017, 1–133.
33. The *Shi ji* records the heir as commander at several points, but this is not likely to have been the case. See Yang Kuan 2002, 195.
34. *Han Feizi* 22/49/7–9; *Zhanguo ce* 265/140/20–24, 460/225/22–25 (Crump, tr. 1996, 352, 523).
35. SJ 80:2427; *Lüshi chunqiu* 19.5/124/16–20 (Knoblock and Riegel 2000, 494). For a full discussion, see Yang Kuan 2002, 199–200.
36. *Zhushu jinian* 1.82.12/43/26–8; SJ 15:709, 32:1512, 46:1886; *Lüshi chunqiu* 15.6/87/1–7 (Knoblock and Riegel 2000, 361–62).
37. *Zhushu jinian* 1.82.13/44/1. The *Zhushu jinian* reports that the "Three Jin" coalition invaded Qi on the orders of the Zhou king, presumably to punish the behavior Qi's Tian leaders.
38. *Lüshi chunqiu* 15.3/83/26–7; *Huainanzi* 18/190/22–191/4 (Major et al., trs., 730).
39. *Zhushu jinian* 1.82.14/44/3; SJ 43:1797, 44:1839, 45:1867.
40. SJ 4:158 (Nienhauser, ed., 1994a, 79), 15:709.
41. ZZTJ 1:2.

CHAPTER 6

1. *Zhanguo ce* 385/186/8. Han Gui 韓傀 is known by several different names across various sources, but they all refer to the same figure. See Yang Kuan 2002, 234–39.
2. See *Lüshi chunqiu* 16.8/98/11–13 (Knoblock and Riegel 2000, 401–2); Lewis 2021, 27–28.
3. See *Zhuangzi* 1/2/11 (Watson 1968, 33).
4. SJ 86:2519 (Nienhauser 1994b, 321); *Zhanguo ce* 204B/106/8 (Crump 1996, 279); *Shuo yuan* 6.17/44/5 (Henry 2021 314–15).
5. The story of Nie Zheng appears in several sources. The fullest accounts are found in *Zhanguo ce* 385/185/16–186/25 (Crump 1996, 423–26) and SJ 86:2522–26 (Nienhauser 1994b, 323–25). *Han Feizi* 31/77/6–7 gives a brief account, but puts the event in the reign of the wrong ruler of Han. See Chen Qiyou 2000, 646n1. The date of Nie Zheng's assassination attempt on Han Gui in 397 BCE is given at SJ 15:711, 45:1867.
6. The following account of Wu Qi's life is drawn from SJ 65:2165–69 (Nienhauser 1994b, 41–45), unless otherwise noted.
7. *Lüshi chunqiu* 2.4/10/14 (Knoblock and Riegel 2000, 90). Cf. Qian Mu 1935, 156–57.
8. A war between Qi and Lu is recorded in 412 BCE (SJ 15:707), See Qian Mu 1935, 161–62.
9. Cf. Goodrich 1981–83, 197–233. All evidence shows that Wu Qi made enough of an impact on the Zhou world to become a figure of enormous controversy.
10. An example of the typical aristocratic mode of command can be seen in *Mao Shi* 178/81/9–25 (Legge 1960b, 284–87).
11. SJ 65:2166 (Nienhauser 1994b, 65). A parallel account is found in *Shuo yuan* 6.26/46/17–19 (Henry 2021, 332–35).
12. On the authenticity of the *Wuzi*, see Yang Jialuo 1973, 943–44; Sawyer 1993, 191–224, 453–55n4).
13. SJ 40:1716–20 (Cao, tr., 2006, 415–19).
14. Henry 2007, 1–36.
15. SJ 42:1776–77, 45:1868.

16. *Shuo yuan* 15.4/117/23–118/6 (Henry 2021, 866–69); *Huainanzi* 12/112/1–11 (Major et al. 2010, 459); Yang Kuan 2002, 250–53.
17. For Wu Qi's reforms in Chu, see ZGS, 209–12.
18. These new forms of status ranking were tied to the development of what scholars call the "*fengjun* 封君 system" of the Warring States. See ZGS, 280–90.
19. For archaeological evidence of the continued segmentation of Chu society, see Weld 1999, 77–98; von Falkenhausen 2006, 395–96; Habberstad 2014, 181–219; He and Liu 1991, 569–79.
20. *Lüshi chunqiu* 21.6/143/7–8 (Knoblock and Riegel 2000, 563).
21. *Han Feizi* 13/23/19–21.
22. *Lüshi chunqiu* 14.4/73/22–23 (Knoblock and Riegel 2000, 315–16).
23. SJ 65:2168 (Nienhauser 1994b, 44–45); HHS, 86:2831; Yang Kuan 2002, 267.
24. SJ 43:1798.
25. SJ 43:1798; *Zhanguo ce* 142/71/8–15 (Crump 1996, 201); Yang Kuan 2002, 266–67.
26. SJ 65:2168 (Nienhauser, ed., 1994b, 45); *Lüshi chunqiu* 21.6/143/7–11 (Knoblock and Riegel 2000, 563). The *Shiji*'s version of the story is slightly different than that of the *Lüshi chunqiu*. For the fate of Wu Qi's body, see *Han Feizi* 3/5/26, 13/23/21, 14/26/7; *Zhanguo ce* 81/37/3 (Crump 1996, 141); *Huainanzi* 10/91/19 (Major et al. 2010, 384).
27. *Lüshi chunqiu* 19.3/122/12–23 (Knoblock and Riegel 2000, 487–88).
28. See Weld 1999, 77–97.

CHAPTER 7

1. Tian Wu 田午 and Tian Yinqi 因齊 are rarely referred to by their personal names in the sources, but by the posthumous titles Duke Huan 桓公 and King Wei 威王, respectively. I will refer to all Tian clan leaders by their personal names by way of avoiding chronological confusion.
2. SJ 32:1510 (Knickerbocker 2006, 117).
3. SJ 46:1885.
4. Wu Hung 2001, 248–49.
5. *Xunzi* 7/25/8–9 (Hutton 2014, 47) reports that Duke Huan of Qi alone subjugated 35 states. For Qi's "Marquises within the Passes 關內之侯," see *Guanzi* 7.1(18)/55/1, 8.2(20)/64/25–26 (Rickett 1985, 297n89, 342).
6. *Zhushu jinian* 2.2.23.6/27–28.
7. SJ 46:1886n1.
8. SJ 46:1886.
9. SJ 15:713, 44:1841.
10. SJ 46:1886; ZZTJ 1:27.
11. SJ 15:713–14, 46:1886.
12. SJ 15:714, 46:1887. The chronological gaps here reflect the doctoring of the record by the Qi court itself.
13. See SJ 46:1887n2, quoting the *Zhuzi jinian* (*Bamboo Annals*).
14. *Zhushu jinian* 2.6.1.6/77/3.
15. For the campaign of 384 BCE, see SJ 43:1798. Tian Yan similarly met with defeat in campaigns in 380 and 378 BCE. See SJ 15:715.
16. SJ 32:1512 (Cao 2006, 119).
17. *Zhushu jinian* 2.6.1.11/77/14. For questions of chronology, see Yang Kuan 2002, 278.
18. SJ 15:717, 46:1888. For a discussion of the chronology, see Yang Kuan 2002, 282–85. See also Wang and Tang 1992, 367.
19. *Zhushu jinian* 2.6.2.7/78/19–20.

20. The information we have about these ceremonies comes from a series of bronze inscriptions. See Zhang Yachu, ed., 2001, 99:9.4646–48.
21. For bronze vessels and their role in the sacrificial rites of the Zhou period, see Rawson 2023. See also Cook 2020, 436–70.
22. *Guanzi* 2.1(6)/14/32–15/3, 6.1(16)/47/18, 6.1/49/13 (Rickett 1985, 131, 260, 261, 266).
23. See Meyer 2010–11, 37–99.
24. See *Lun yu* 6.24/14/3 (Lau, tr., 1979, 84); *Mencius* 3.1/14/6–29 (Lau, tr., 1970, 74).
25. See Csikszentmihalyi 2001, 267–68.
26. *Mozi* 4.1 (14)/23/27–4.3(16)/30/10 (Johnston, tr., 2010, 131–65).
27. For a detailed analysis of the construction of "Master Guan" see Meyer 2010–11, 42–59. See also Guo Moruo 1996, 156–59; Lin Li'e 1992, 252–56.
28. For the historical figure of Guan Zhong 管仲, see Rosen 1976, 431–40. Guan Zhong's "official" biography is found in SJ 62:2131–34 (Nienhauser, ed., 1994b, 9–14).
29. For the origins and textual history of the transmitted *Guanzi*, see Rickett, tr., 1985, 3–43; Rickett 1993, 244–51.
30. For the origins of "Shepherding the People" (*Mu min* 牧民), see Rickett, tr., 1985, 51–52.
31. *Guanzi* 1.1 (1)/1/7–9 (Rickett, tr., 1985, 52).
32. *Guanzi* 1.1 (1)/1/7 (Rickett, tr., 1985, 52). The virtues themselves are outlined in *Guanzi* 1.1 (1)/1/16–19 (Rickett, tr., 1985, 53–54).
33. *Guanzi*, 7.1(18)/51/16–52/27 (Rickett, tr., 1985, 284–90).
34. *Guanzi* 8.2(20)/59/5–17 (Rickett, tr., 1985, 319–20).
35. For the historical Yan Ying 晏嬰, see Milburn, tr., 2016, 68–114. Yan Ying's "official" biography is found at SJ 62:2134–37 (Nienhauser, ed., 1994b, 14–17).
36. See Meyer 2010–11, 59–66. See also Wu Zeyu 1962, 23–30; Pian Yuqian 2000, 9–15, 229–41, 257–68; Lin Li'e 1992, 248–52.
37. *Yanzi chunqiu* 5.21/46/21–27, accepting the proposed emendation at note 4 (Milburn, tr., 2016, 328–29).
38. For the true length of Tian Wu's reign, see Qian Mu 1935, 198–200.
39. For the correct orthography of Tian Yinqi's name, see Yang Kuan 2002, 322.
40. For the bronze inscription expressing Tian Wu's new formulations, see Zhang Yachu 2001, 99:9.4649. See also Doty 1982, 616–37; Puett 1998, 450n64.
41. For a general survey of the reforms helmed by Zou Ji in Qi, see ZGS, 215–17.
42. *Xin shu* 新序 (1992) 2.7/8/1–2. The *Xin xu* incorrectly gives the ruler served by Zou Ji as King Xuan 宣 (r. 319–301 BCE), Tian Yinqi's son and heir. A more complex variant of this story is found at SJ 46:1889.
43. SJ 46:1888–89.
44. See Creel 1974.
45. These are found at SJ 74:2347 (Nienhauser, ed., 1994b, 182–83) and 126:3197–200 (Baccini and Barenghi, trs., 2019, 150–55).
46. SJ 126:3197 (Baccini and Barenghi, trs., 2019, 150). The text notes that Chunyu Kun 淳于髡 was less than seven *chi* 尺 tall, which would have made him less than 1 meter, 60 centimeters in stature.
47. SJ 74:2347 (Nienhauser, ed., 1994b, 182–83).
48. For Jixia, see Qian Mu 1935, 227–35; Lin Li'e 1992, 140; Wang and Tang 1992, 509–12; Sato 2003, 72–84.
49. *Shi ji*, 46.1895n6; Lin Li'e 1992, 232–39; Zhang Bingnan 1991.
50. *Sima Wengong wenji* 司馬文公文集, "Juan shisi 卷十四." The text is transcribed in Lin Li'e 1992, 148.

51. *Xin xu* 2.7/8/2–11. See also Weingarten 2015, 283–307.
52. See for example *Zhanguo ce* 125/61/5–15 (Crump, tr., 1996, 191).
53. SJ 65:2160 (Nienhauser, ed., 1994b, 35).
54. SJ 65:2157–58 (Nienhauser, ed., 1994b, 32–34).
55. These debates stimulated the developed of a large volume of writings on military affairs. See Yates 1988, 211–48.
56. See the discussion in Gawlikowski and Loewe 1993, 446–55. See also Sawyer 1993, 149–57; Goldin 2020, 153–65.
57. Zhang Zhenze 1984; Ames and Lau 1996.
58. The following analysis is outlined in more detail in Meyer and Wilson 2003, 95–113; Meyer and Wilson 2008, 151–68; Meyer 2017, 1–24.
59. *Sunzi* A11/12/4–6 (Sawyer 1993, 180).
60. *Sunzi* A2/1/25–29, A5/4/18–19 (Sawyer 1993, 159, 165).
61. *Sunzi* A12/13/20–23 (Sawyer 1993, 184).
62. *Sunzi* A3/2/22–25 (Sawyer 1993, 161).
63. *Sunzi* A12/13/11–20 (Sawyer 1993, 183–84).
64. *Sunzi* A11/13/5–7, A13/14/1–27 (Sawyer 1993, 183, 184–86).
65. *Sunzi* A11/13/5–7 (translation my own).
66. *Zhanguo ce* 102/50/19–26 (Crump, tr., 1996, 161–62).
67. SJ 65:2162–63 (Nienhauser, ed., 1994b, 39–40).
68. Zhang Zhenze 1984, 1–2; Sawyer 1995, 81–82.
69. SJ 44:1845; *Zhushu jinian* 2.6.2.17/79/20–2.6.2.18/79/25.

CHAPTER 8

1. Lieu 2024, 12–68.
2. Pines et al. 2014, 4–5.
3. *Zuo zhuan* B6.6.3/131/19 (Durrant et al., trs., 2016, 492–93). For discussion of this prediction, see Yang Bojun 1993, 38 (前言); Pines 2002, 224.
4. For a survey of the scholarly debates surrounding the origins and early evolution of the Qin state, see Pines et al. 2014, 1–34, 37–51, 141–54; Lander 2021, 14–31, 114–53.
5. The geographic advantages enjoyed by the early Qin state have been remarked upon since ancient times. See for example Yan Zhenyi and Zhong 2000,1–13. For a recent survey of the geographic foundations of Qin power, see Lander 2021, 126–33.
6. Li Feng 2006, 27–232.
7. SJ 5:173–79 (Nienhauser, ed., 1994b, 87–91).
8. Pines et al. 2014, 11.
9. An example of an argument for the "eastern origins" theory of Qin's founding elite can be seen in Lin Jianming 1981, 14–34. For a survey of the difficulties deciding between "eastern origin" and "western origin" theories of the founding Qin elite on the basis of archaeological evidence, see von Falkenhausen 2006, 233–43.
10. See Zhao 2014, 53–70. Also Lander 2021, 124.
11. *Zuo zhuan* B.6.6.3/131/11–19 (Durrant et al., trs., 2016, 490–93).
12. Lin Jianming 1981, 35–54; ZGS, 322; Di Cosmo 2002, 132–33, 139, 142, 150–51; Lander 2021, 126–29.
13. See for example the analysis in Wu Xialong 2017, 22–23; Sian Jones 1997.
14. See Zhang Yachu 2001, 12–13 (1.262–1.270), 87 (8.4315). For a translation and discussion of the inscriptions, see Kern 2016, 243–48.
15. SJ 5:200 (Nienhauser, ed., 1994a, 106), 15:705, 44:1838.

16. SJ 15:708, 44:1838, 65:2166 (Nienhauser, ed., 1994b, 42–43).
17. SJ 5:199–200 (Nienhauser, ed., 1994a, 106–7), 15:706.
18. SJ 5:200 (Nienhauser, ed., 1994a, 107).
19. *Lüshi chunqiu* 24.4/157/21–29 (Knoblock and Riegel 2000, 615–16); SJ 5:200 (Nienhauser, ed., 1994a, 107), 15:714.
20. The entries at SJ 5:201 (Nienhauser 1994a, 107); SJ 5:201n2. See also Wang Guowei 1984, 19:627; Li Fang 1994, 155:9 (Vol. 2, 531); Lin Jianming 1981, 173–74; Yang Kuan 2002, 263–64.
21. Lander 2021, 142.
22. SJ 5:201 (Nienhauser, ed., 1994a, 107).
23. SJ 6:289 (Nienhauser, ed., 1994a, 173. The translation gives the wrong date for this event).
24. SJ 15:715.
25. SJ 6:289 (Nienhauser, ed., 1994a, 173. The translation gives the wrong date for this event).
26. For evidence of the uniquely diverse structure of Qin elite society, see Teng 2014, 71–112.
27. SJ 15:719, 44:1844.
28. SJ 5:201 (Nienhauser, ed., 1994a, 108), 15:719, 43:1799; ZZTJ 2:42. These accounts vary in small details, but a coherent picture can be extrapolated. See Yang Kuan 2002, 299.
29. SJ 43:1799.
30. SJ 5:201 (Nienhauser, ed., 1994a, 108), 15:720, 43:1799. For discrepancies in these accounts, see Yang Kuan 2002, 301–2.
31. SJ 5:201–2 (Nienhauser, ed., 1994a, 108–9).
32. The following account the life of Shang Yang 商鞅 (a.k.a. Wei 衛 Yang, Gongsun 公孫 Yang), unless otherwise noted, is drawn from his biography in the *Shi ji*: SJ 68:2227–36 (Nienhauser, ed., 1994b, 87–95).
33. This story may of course be fabricated.
34. SJ 5:203 (Nienhauser, ed., 1994a, 109).
35. For Qin legal code, see Lin Jianming 1981, 224–33; Hulsewé 1985; Yates 1985–87, 243–75; Yates 2018, 403–45.
36. A discussion of the Qin merit-rank system can be found in ZGS, 273–79. See also *Shangjun shu* (1992) 19/25/1–26/8 (Pines, tr., 2017, 221–26). Evidence of the operation of the merit-rank system can be seen in Hulsewé 1985, 82–83, 118, 191–93 (A 90, A 91, C 24, E 13, E14). See also Yates 1987, 211–48. For the evolution of the merit-rank system into imperial times, see Barbieri-Low and Yates 2015, Vol. 2, 873–81.
37. Loewe 1960, 97–174.
38. SJ 5:203 (Nienhauser, ed., 1994a, 109), 15:722.
39. Yang Kuan 2002, 360.
40. SJ 15:723.
41. For Shang Yang's new land and taxation policy, see ZGS, 221–22; Lander 2021 170–73.
42. SJ 15:723.
43. See Hsing 2014, 155–65.
44. SJ 68:2232 (Nienhauser, ed., 1994b, 91).
45. Zhang Yachu 2001, 160/16.10372. A picture of the measure and its inscription can be seen at ZGS, 224–25.
46. Lewis 1999a, 589. See also his discussion of "Writing the State" in Lewis 199b, 13–52.
47. SJ 4:160, 5:203 (Nienhauser, ed., 1994a, 79, 110).
48. SJ 5:203 (Nienhauser, ed., 1994a, 110), 15:725; HHS 87:2876.
49. SJ 68:2232–33 (Nienhauser, ed., 1994b, 91–92), *Lüshi chunqiu* 22.2/145/8–16 (Knoblock and Riegel 2000, 570–71).
50. SJ 5:204 (Nienhauser, ed., 1994a, 110).

51. Shang Yang's biography in the *Records of the Historian* exaggerates his achievement, claiming that in 338 BCE Wei ceded back all of the conquered Hexi territory to Qin. Though that was not so, Wei did make some territorial concessions to Qin in seeking an armistice. See Wang Shumin 1982, 68:2178.
52. SJ 68:2236–37 (Nienhauser, ed., 1994b, 95).
53. For the composition and history of this text, see Levi 1993, 368–75; Pines 2017, 25–58.
54. For a discussion of this phenomenon, see Lewis 1999, 29.
55. SJ 68:2228 (Nienhauser, ed., 1994b, 88).
56. SJ 2233–35 (Nienhauser, ed., 1994b, 92–95).

CHAPTER 9

1. SJ 44:1842–43; ZZTJ 1:38. See discussion in Yang Kuan 2002, 285.
2. *Zhushu jinian* 2.6.1.1/76/22 reports that in his first year on the throne, Marquis Wu invested Wei Huan with his own fief. This may be an indication of an unstable family dynamic that undermined the peaceful succession, but we do not know the details of the situation.
3. SJ 15:718, 43:1799, 44:1843–44; ZZTJ 1:39–40; *Zhushu jinian* 2.6.2.1/78/5.
4. SJ 44:1843; *Zhushu jinian* 2.6.2.1/78/6. See discussion in Yang Kuan 2002, 287–88.
5. SJ 44:1843; *Zhushujinian* 2.6.2.1/78/6; ZZTJ 1:40.
6. The longest reigning monarch was King Nan of Zhou 周赧王 (r. 314–256 BCE), followed by King Zhao of Qin 秦昭王 (306–251 BCE).
7. A review of early reform programs in Zhao and Han, respectively, may be found at ZGS, 208–9, 212–15.
8. For example *Mencius* 1.3/1/23 (Lau, tr., 1970, 51); SJ 44:1847.
9. The frequency of conflict during Wei Ying's tenure can be seen most easily in the chronological tables found at ZGS, 772–74.
10. *Xunzi* 15/70/1–9 (Hutton 2014, 149).
11. SJ 15:719, 44:1844, 45:1868.
12. SJ 15:719, 44:1844.
13. SJ 15:720, 43:1799; *Zhanguo ce* 270/142/3–10 (Crump 1996, 355–56); *Zhushu jinian* 2.6.2.8/78/22.
14. *Zhushu jinian* 2.6.2.9/78/25.
15. Wang Guowei, *Shuijing zhujiao* 1984, 5:177, 22:722; Yang Kuan 2002, 310–11.
16. *Zhushu jinian* 2.6.2.11/79/1–2. The three cities extended in a line south from the White Horse Ford 白馬之口 on the Yellow River in present-day Henan Province. For the critical strategic value of the White Horse Ford, see *Zhanguo ce* 42/16/20, 220/115/23, 422/204/5 (Crump 1996, 144, 286, 493). For discussion of the chronology, see Fan Xiangyong 1956, 59; Yang Kuan 2002, 318–19.
17. SJ 44:1847n2. For discussion of the chronology, see Yang Kuan 2002, 308–10.
18. *Zhushu jinian* 2.6.2.10/78/27–8; Yang Kuan 2002, 312.
19. *Zhushu jinian* 2.6.2.12/79/4–5; Zhang Shuangdi 1997, 1768, 1771n11 (Major et al. 2010, 683); Yang Kuan 2002, 317–18. For a general discussion of wall building as a strategy during the Warring States period, see Di Cosmo 2002, 138–58.
20. *Zhushu jinian* 2.6.2.14/79/10; SJ 15:721, 44:1844.
21. Drawing his figures from reports in the *Zhanguo ce*, Yang Kuan puts the strength of Wei's military at 700,000 infantry, 600 chariots, and 5,000 cavalry. At the time the combined strength of Han ("no more than 300,000 infantry"), Zhao ("several hundred thousand infantry, 1,000 chariots, 10,000 cavalry"), and Qi ("several hundred thousand infantry") would have been about the same. Given the efforts Wei Ying had exerted to produce elite

forces, his armies had a tactical edge (ZGS, 333–35). See also Lewis 1999a, 626–27; Sawyer 1995, 29.
22. SJ 80:2427 (Nienhauser, ed., 1994b, 255).
23. Poundstone 1993.
24. SJ 37:1604 (Cook 2006, 260). For the siting of this event in 356 BCE, see Yang Kuan 2002, 323.
25. SJ 15:721, 43:1801.
26. *Zhushu jinian* 2.6.2.16/79/17; SJ 15:722, 43:1801, 44: 1845.
27. *Zhushu jinian* 2.6.2.18/79/24–25; SJ 15:722–23, 43:1801, 44:1845.
28. SJ 44:1847.
29. For the name and possible location of the "Fan Pavilion 范臺," see Dong Shuo 1987, 371.
30. *Zhanguo ce* 307/155/25–156/6 (Crump 1996, 358–59).
31. For Yang Zhu, see for example Fung 1952, 133–43; Graham 1989, 53–64; Defoort and Lee, eds., 2022. My own understanding of the sources is distinctive. See Meyer, forthcoming.
32. *Lüshi chunqiu*, 1.3/3/27–4/1 (Knoblock and Riegel 2000, 69–70).
33. As the Latinized name by which he is known in English attests, Mencius eventually became highly revered, second only to Confucius in the esteem of Confucian scholars of the imperial era. The *Mencius*, the text which bears his name and records his teachings, was one of the "Four Books" that all literati were ultimately required to commit to memory in preparation for the imperial examinations. This is why the European Jesuits who first resided at the court of the Ming empire (1368–1644 CE) gave Master Meng the sobriquet "Mencius," so that they could inform the pope in Rome about his doctrines. See Fontana 2011, 104–6.
34. A key source for the life of Mencius is SJ 74:2343 (Nienhauser, ed., 1994b, 179). See also Lau 1970, 205–13.
35. There is an extensive and growing scholarly literature on the teachings of the *Mencius*. See for example Fung 1952, 106–31; Lau 1970, 7–48, 223–64; Schwartz 1985, 255–90; Graham 1989, 111–31; Denecke 2010, 153–79; Goldin 2020, 79–105. See also the essays collected in Chan, ed., 2002.
36. *Mencius* 6.9 (III B.9)/34/30–35/10 (Lau 1970, 114–15).
37. *Mencius* 3.6 (II A.6)/18/4–12 (Lau 1970, 82–83).
38. *Mencius* 1.5 (I A.5)/2/28–30 (Lau 1970, 53).
39. *Mencius* 1.1 (I A.1)/1/3–9 (Lau 1970, 49).
40. *Mencius* 1.5 (I A.5)/3/5 (Lau 1970, 53).
41. *Mencius* 14.1 (VII B.1)/73/6–12 (Lau 1970, 194).
42. *Zhuangzi* 2/7/21–3 (Watson 1968, 49).
43. *Zhuangzi* 17/47/11–14 (Watson 1968, 188).
44. See for example Ma Guohan 1990, Vol. 7, 135–36. See also Ruan Tingzhuo 1980, 141–56.
45. For the development of correlative cosmological thought in the Warring States, see Henderson 1983; Schwartz 1985, 350–82; Graham 1989, 315–69; Aihe Wang 2000.
46. For a more detailed discussion of qi, see Goldin 2020, 229–44.
47. Wang Meng'ou 1991, 329–53.
48. Our most substantive early source for Zou Yan is SJ 74:2344–46 (Nienhauser, ed., 1994b, 180–82).
49. SJ 74:2345 (Nienhauser, ed., 1994b, 181).
50. For the approximate chronology of Zou Yan's life, see Qian Mu 1935, 438–41. Unless he lived much earlier than Qian Mu inferred, the meeting between Wei Ying and Zou Yan could not have happened.
51. We do not have a complete list of attendees. The number 12 is reported at *Zhanguo ce* 142/73/27 (Crump 1996, 206). Song, Wey, Zou, Lu, Chen, Cai, and Qin are all variously mentioned as having attended. The other attendees are unrecorded.

52. SJ 5:204 (Nienhauser, ed., 1994a, 110) and 15:725 both put the meeting at Welcome Pond in 342 BCE and give the credit for gathering the "Lords of the Land" together to Duke Xiao of Qin. But this is a distortion introduced into the record by Qin scribes in their efforts to exalt the achievements of Qin and efface those of Wei. Entries at SJ 4:160 (Nienhauser, ed., 1994a, 79) and 15:724 give the correct date for the meeting as 344 BCE, though the former still erroneously credits Qin for calling the meeting. See Yang Kuan 2002, 384–85.
53. *Zhanguo ce* 142/73/22–74/7 (Crump 1996, 206–7).
54. *Zhanghuo ce* 88/42/20–21, 142/74/2–3 (Crump 1996, 156–57, 207).
55. See K. C. Chang 1999, 71–73.
56. This assumes a consistency of cosmological thought over time. Since Wei Ying was using forms of cosmological lore that antedated Zou Yan, it is possible that the "cosmic cycle" theory informing Wei Ying's iconography did not adhere to the "five-phase" model ultimately articulated by Zou Yan.
57. SJ 5:203 (Nienhauser, ed., 1994a, 110).
58. *Han Feizi* 22/46/21–22.
59. SJ 5:203 (Nienhauser, ed., 1994a, 110).
60. *Zhushu jinian* 2.6.2.27/80/19–20. The ICS editors have reversed the order of the battles of Horse Hill and Southbridge. See Yang Kuan 2002, 391.
61. *Zhanguo ce* 103/50/18–7 (Crump 1996, 165–66); SJ 49:1893–94. Some of the chronological details in the *Shi ji* account are distorted. See Yang Kuan 2002, 392–93.
62. SJ 65:2164–65 (Nienhauser, ed., 1994b, 40–41).
63. SJ 5:204 (Nienhauser, ed., 1994a, 110),15:725, 45:1845–46, 68:2232 (Nienhauser, ed., 1994b, 91), 75:2351 (Nienhauser, ed., 1994b, 190); Zhang Zhenze, *Sun Bin bingfa jiaoli*, 42 (Sawyer 1995, 95).
64. *Zhushu jinian* 2.6.2.28/80/22–23.
65. SJ 68:2236–37 (Nienhauser, ed., 1994b, 95).
66. *Zhanguo ce* 104/51/10–106/52/3 (Crump 1996, 163–64, 166–67).
67. Qian Mu 2011, 12, estimates that Hui Shi died in 309 BCE at the age of 60. I would argue that this puts the birth of Hui Shi too late, but all such determinations are somewhat speculative.
68. Unlike Chunyu Kun or Mencius, Hui Shi did not receive his own biographical notice in the *Records of the Historian*. The evidence concerning his life is collected in Qian Mu 2011, 1–38.
69. These two descriptions of Hui Shi give us some of the most detailed reports of his teachings. One is found at *Xunzi* 6/22/3–6 (Hutton 2014, 41). The other is found at *Zhuangzi* 33/100/14–101/2 (Watson 1968, 374–77). Another informative critique of Hui Shi's teachings is found at *Xunzi* 3/9/1–3 (Hutton 2014, 16).
70. *Zhuangzi* 33/100/17 (Watson 1968, 374). The same paradox is adopted as an example of faulty reasoning at *Zhuangzi* 2/4/10 (Watson 1968, 39), perhaps affirming that the historical Zhuang Zhou and Hui Shi were, in fact, affectionate rivals.
71. Gödel 1986, 346–71.
72. *Zhuangzi* 33/100/18–19 (Watson 1968, 375).
73. *Han Feizi* 30/63/9.
74. For scholarly discussion of Hui Shi's teachings, see Fung 1952, 192–203; Graham 1989, 75–82; Hansen 1992, 261–63.
75. Gao You's commentary to the *Lüshi chunqiu* identifies Hui Shi as Wei Ying's prime minister. See Wang Liqi 2002, 2616. See also *Zhuangzi* 17/47/6 (Watson 1968, 188).
76. *Zhanguo ce* 103/51/6–7, 142/74/3–4, 301/153/1–16 (Crump 1996, 166, 207, 360–61).
77. *Lüshi chunqiu* 18.5/114/21–24 (Knoblock and Riegel 2000, 459–60).
78. SJ 5:205 (Nienhauser, ed., 1994a, 110). 15: 727, 44:1848, 46:1894. Several reports mistakenly identify the respective rulers of Qi and Wei who met at Xuzhou. See Yang Kuan 2002, 421–24.

79. For the change of "origin year" see Kong Yingda 2000, Vol. 19, 1983. See also Fan Xiangyong 1956, 65; Yang Kuan 2002, 424–28.

CHAPTER 10

1. *Lüshi chunqiu* 21.5/142/23–28 (Knoblock and Riegel 2000, 561–62).
2. See Macdonald 1982, 267–75.
3. Hassan 2013, 75–89.
4. SJ 4:160n3, 5:206 (Nienhauser 1994a, III), 15:730. See also Yang Kuan 2002, 455–56.
5. *Zhanguo ce* 454/222/13–223/2 (Crump 1996, 523–25), SJ 15:730, 33:1546 (Cao, tr., 160), 40:1722 (Cao, tr., 2006, 422). Crump emends "five states" to "three states," following Yokota Ikō 1911, *ken* 10, 10. But Yang Kuan 2002, 462–65 demonstrates that there were five: Wei, Han, Zhao, Zhongshan, and Yan.
6. SJ 38:1632 (Zhang, tr., 2006, 290).
7. This can be seen in the sources regarding the institution of "enfeoffed lords" (*fengjun* 封君) that developed over the Warring States period. See ZGS, 738–49; more detailed collection of source materials pertaining to the individual lords of whom we have records for can be found in Yang Kuan and Wu, eds., 2005, 566–617. For a knight who became a marquis, see SJ 79:2401–18 (Nienhauser, ed., 1994b, 233–46).
8. See for example Wai-yee Li 2014, 241–61.
9. For the use of seals and tallies, see ZGS, 233–35. See also the sources collected in Yang and Wu 2005, 300–308.
10. A good example of the use of tallies in diplomatic negotiations can be seen in *Zhanguo ce* 431/209/25–29 (Crump 1996, 497–98).
11. A good example of the use of a hostage to secure an agreement in rapid diplomacy can be seen at *Zhanguo ce* 63/25/26–29 (Crump 1996, 111–13).
12. These conditions are well-evinced by *Han Feizi* 49/149/4–19 (Watson, tr., 1963, 113), where such "wandering persuaders 游說之士" are listed among "five vermin" who plague the state.
13. A good example of a wandering persuader effecting policy on his own initiative can be seen at *Zhanguo ce* 51/21/21–22/3 (Crump 1996, 95).
14. The recognition of diplomacy as a fundamental constituent of power is best exemplified by *Sunzi bingfa* 3/2/22 (Sawyer 177): "The superior soldier attacks plans, the next best attacks alliances…"
15. *Zhanguo ce* 455/223/4–29 (Crump 1996, 525–26).
16. Many scholars have noted the inconsistencies and anachronisms in the *Shi ji*'s account of Su Qin's life. See for example Maspero 1925, Vol. 2, 127–41; Qian Mu 1935, 285–94; Crump 1964, 29–39; Tang Lan 1976, 123–53; Durrant 1995, 103–4; Lewis 1999a, 633; Yang Kuan 2002, 447–48, 505. Cf. Fan Xiangyong 1985, Vol. 5, 1–25.
17. Zhang Yi's biography is found at SJ 70:2279–99 (Nienhauser, ed., 1994b, 123–38). Gongsun Yan is given a brief biography at SJ 2302–4 (Nienhauser, ed., 1994b, 141–42).
18. For the title of "Xishou 犀首", see Dong Shuo 1987, 144; Yang and Wu 2005, 543.
19. SJ 69:2241 (Nienhauser, ed., 1994b, 97) and SJ 70:2279 (Nienhauser, ed., 1994b, 123).
20. SJ 5:205 (Nienhauser, ed., 1994a, III); 15:728.
21. SJ 15:728.
22. SJ 5:205, 15:728.
23. SJ 5:205–6 (Nienhauser, ed., 1994a, III). For the Qin prince, "Master Shuli," see SJ 71:2307–10 (Nienhauser, ed., 1994b, 145–47). These events are also recorded at SJ 15:729, 44:1848.
24. SJ 5:206 (Nienhauser, ed., 1994a, III), 15:729, 44:1848.

25. *Lüshi chunqiu* 15.4/84/20 (Knoblock and Riegel 2000, 354) refers to Zhang Yi as a "spare son" of the Wei clan. The *Suoyin* commentary of the *Shi ji* infers that he was the scion of a cadet branch of the royal clan given the surname "Zhang," for whom we have the names of two other grandees that served the Wei court. See SJ 70:2279n1.
26. SJ 70:2279 (Nienhauser, ed., 1994b, 123).
27. SJ 40: 1721 (Cao, tr., 2006, 421).
28. *Zhanguo ce* 47/18/28–19/2 (Crump 1996, 87), 367/180/26–181/9 (Crump 1996, 449–50).
29. SJ 5:206 (Nienhauser, ed., 1994b, 111), SJ 40:1721 (Cao, tr., 2006, 421). See also Zhang Yachu 2001, 171:17.11394.
30. *Zhanguo ce* 291/149/7–15 (Crump 1996, 374); ZGS, 378.
31. SJ 5:206 (Nienhauser, ed., 1994a, 111), 15:729, 70:2284 (Nienhauser 1994b, 126).
32. SJ 15:729, 44:1848.
33. SJ 5:206 (Nienhauser, ed., 1994a, 111), 15:729–30.
34. SJ 5:206–7 (Nienhauser, ed., 1994a, 111), 15:30.
35. SJ 5:206 (Nienhauser, ed., 1994a, 111), 15:730, 70:2284 (Nienhauser, ed., 1994b, 126).
36. *Zhanguo ce* 454/222/13–223/2 (Crump 1996, 523–25).
37. For "the Vertical and the Horizontal," see Yang and Wu 2005, 1205–25; Ma Su 2002, 2934–46, 3002–17, 3047–78. See also Lewis 1999a, 632–34.
38. *Lüshi chunqiu* 18.4/113/11–13 (Knoblock and Riegel 2000, 455–56).
39. See for example *Han Feizi* 51/154/23–25; Wang Chong 1990, 33:526.
40. For the basic parity between Lu and Zhongshan, see Yan Shoucheng 1997, 23.
41. *Zhanguo ce* 302/153/18 (Crump 1996, 362); *Zhuzi jinian* 2.6.2.38/81/19, 2.6.2.40/81/23.
42. SJ 5:207 (Nienhauser, ed., 1994a, 111), 15:730, 40:1722 (Cao, tr., 2006, 422), 44:1849, 46:1896, 70:2284 (Nienhauser, ed., 1994b, 126–27).
43. SJ 15:730, 40:1721 (Cao, tr., 2006, 421).
44. *Zhanguo ce* 116/57/1–7 (Crump 1996, 186).
45. *Zhanguo ce* 282/147/4–8 (Crump 1996, 316); *Han Feizi* 30/63/9–15. By contrast, Zhang Yi's explicit plan was to join Qin, Wei, and Han together for the purpose of assaulting Qi and Chu.
46. *Zhanguo ce* 273/143/20–144/21 (Crump 1996, 376–78).
47. SJ 5:207 (Nienhauser, ed., 1994a, 111), 15:730–31, 44:1849; *Zhanguo ce* 184/95/6–15 (Crump 1996, 247).
48. *Zhanguo ce* 281/146/24–147/2 (Crump 1996, 370).
49. *Zhanguo ce* 33/11/10–14, 368/181/11–16 (Crump 1996, 60–61, 442–43).
50. *Zhanguo ce* 116/57/1–7 (Crump 1996, 186).
51. SJ 70:2284–85 (Nienhauser, ed., 1994b, 126–27).
52. See Yang Kuan 2002, 479–80. *Zhanguo ce* 282/147/4–9 (Crump 1996, 366) makes clear that though Zhang Yi may have wanted to serve simultaneously as Prime Minister in both Wei and Qin, this was not initially the case.
53. *Zhanguo ce* 109/53/4–15 (Crump 1996, 162). For the dating of this anecdote in 320 BCE, see Yang Kuan 2002, 486–87.
54. *Zhanguo ce* 276/145/9–24 (Crump 1996, 371–72); SJ 70:2300–2301 (Nienhauser 1994b, 139–40).
55. For the teachings of Shen Dao 慎到, see Thompson 1979; Harris, tr., 2016. Modern translators will often render the concept of *shi* 勢 as it is used in Shen Dao's teachings as "political advantage" or "political purchase."
56. *Zhushu jinian* 2.6.2.43/82/1.

57. *Lüshi chunqiu* 21.1/138/20–139/2 (Knoblock and Riegel 2000, 549–50); *Zhanguo ce* 296/150/17–151/3 (Crump 1996, 362–63).
58. SJ 5:208 (Nienhauser, ed., 1994a, 112), 15:731, 34:1555 (Hongyu Huang, tr., "The Duke of Shao, Hereditary House 4," in Niehauser, ed., 2006, 177), 40:1722–23 (Cao, tr., 2006, 422–3), 44:1850, 70:2304n7; *Zhanguo ce* 352/175/1–10 (Crump 1996, 453–54).
59. SJ 5:208 (Nienhauser, ed., 1994a, 112), 15:732, 43:1804, 45:1870.
60. *Zhanguo ce* 185/95/19–28 (Crump 1996, 238–39).
61. SJ 70:2303 (Nienhauser, ed., 1994b, 139).
62. SJ 15:732, 44:1850, 46:1896.
63. *Zhanguo ce* 292/149/17–23 (Crump 1996, 374–75).
64. *Zhanguo ce* 298/152/12–16 (Crump 1996, 379). The beginning of the text has been corrupted here. Either the three graphs "魏文子" (In Wei, Wenzi...) have been added erroneously or, as Fan Xiangyong proposes, the opening of the passage originally read "魏犀首文子相善" (In Wei the *xishou* and Wenzi had good relations...). See Fan Xiangyong 2006, 1334n1.
65. Mawangdu Hanmu boshu zhengli xiaozu 馬王堆漢墓帛書整理小組, ed., *Mawangdui Hanmu boshu Zhanguo zonghengjia shu* 馬王堆漢墓帛書戰果從橫家書. Beijing: Wenwu chubanshe, 1976, 106–7; *Zhanguo ce* 357/176/13–177/7 (Crump 1996, 430–31); SJ 45:1870–71.
66. *Han Feizi* 31/75/3–4. Accounts of Gongsun Yan's later life vary. Other sources have him surviving Tian Xu. Common to all accounts is the fact that Gongsun Yan never rose to the heights of power he had reached before the defeat at Rivergate.
67. SJ 5:208 (Nienhauser, ed., 1994a, 112).
68. SJ 45:1871.
69. SJ 15:733, 44:1851. The prince, Gongzi Zheng 公子政, did not ultimately succeed to the Wei throne.
70. Two detailed accounts of this affair are preserved in the sources. My narrative follows the more spare record found in *Zhanguo ce* (Crump 1996, 93–95). A more elaborate story is found in SJ 40:1723–25 (Cao, tr., 2006, 423–26).
71. For the office of *zongzhu* 宗祝, see Dong Zhuo 1987, 25.
72. For the text of the *Zu Chu wen* 詛楚文 (*Imprecations Against Chu*), see Chavannes 1893, 475–82; Guo Moruo 1947, 606–25.
73. See for example *Zhanguo ce* 422/204/9–10, 433/211/21–22 (Crump 1996, 494, 482).
74. SJ 70:2281 (Nienhauser, ed., 1994b, 124).
75. Morrish 1997, pp. 3–4; Flad and Chen, 2013, 22–27.
76. Sage 1992, 14–28; Flad and Chen 2013, 71–107.
77. Chen De'an 1994; Bagley 2001.
78. Sage 1992, 53–60; Rowan and Chen 2013, 140–42.
79. Sage 1992, 60–66.
80. Sage 1992, 31–34; Rowan and Chen 2013, 72.
81. SJ 5:205 (Nienhauser, ed., 1994b, 110).
82. Sage 1992, 109–10, 252–53n68.
83. Chang Qu 1987, 123.
84. Chang 1987, 126; SJ 70:2281 (Nienhauser, ed., 1994b, 124).
85. *Zhanguo ce* 44/17/19–18/9 (Crump 1996, 91–92); SJ 70:2281–83 (Nienhauser, ed., 1994b, 124–26).
86. *Zhanguo ce* 44/18/9–12 (Crump 1996, 92); SJ 70:2283 (Nienhauser, ed., 1994b, 126).
87. Chang 1987, 126.

88. SJ 70:2283 (Nienhauser, ed., 1994b, 126); Chang 1987, 126.
89. Sage 1992, 120–56.
90. Anderson 1988, 204–5.
91. Sage 1992, 4–5.
92. SJ 34:1549–50 (Huang, tr., 2006, 169–71). For the geographic parameters of the state of Yan, see ZGS, 302.
93. See for example SJ 34:1555 (Huang, tr., 2006, 177).
94. SJ 15:732 puts the abdication to Zizhi 子之 in 316 BCE, but Yang Kuan (2002, 510) extrapolates from the totality of the evidence that it transpired in 318 BCE.
95. For an extended exploration of this phenomenon, see Allan 1981.
96. For a discussion of the origins of Potency (*de* 德) as a concept within the ancestral traditions of the Zhou elite, see Cook 2017, 52–90.
97. For example *Han Feizi* 7/10/11–16 (Watson 1963, 33–34).
98. An exemplary account of this legend can be found at *Zhuangzi* 1/2/5–11 (Watson 1968, 32–33).
99. *Zhanguo ce* 416A/199/1–29 (Crump 1996, 475–77); SJ 34:1555–56 (Huang, tr., 2006, 176–78).
100. For example *Han Feizi* 35/110/9–13.
101. For Chen Zhongzi, see *Xunzi* 6/21/17–18 (Hutton 2014, 40); *Zhanguo ce* 138/69/21–22 (Crump 1996, 220); *Mencius* 6/35/12–25 (Lau 1970, 115–16). For the hermit ideal during the Warring States period, see Vervoorn 1990; Berkowitz 2000, 1–63.
102. The one concrete example of such a literatus who appears in the sources is Xu Xing 許行 (ca. 390–ca. 315 BCE), whose teachings are used to challenge Mencius at *Mencius* 5.4/27/11–30/5 (Lau 1970, 100–101). See also Graham 1979, 66–100.
103. *Zhanguo ce* 416A/199/20–29 (Crump 1996, 478–77); SJ 1556–57 (Huang, tr., 2006, 178–79).
104. Zhongshan's participation is not recorded in any transmitted sources; we know about it exclusively from the archaeological record. See Wu 2017, 134–48.
105. *Zhanguo ce* 114/56/7–8 (Crump 1996, 183) gives the time as 30 days. *Mencius* 2.18/11/24 (Lau 1970, 69) reports 50 days.
106. *Zhushu jinian* 2.6.3.3/82/10.
107. *Mencius* 2.10/11/23–2.11/12/8 (Lau 1970, 68–70) makes clear that King Xuan of Qi moved to annex Yan in the wake of his conquest.
108. SJ 43:1804; *Zhushu jinian* 2.6.3.3/82/10–11.
109. *Mencius* 4.9/22/21 (Lau 1970, 91).
110. SJ 34:1558 (Huang, tr., 2006, 179).
111. *Mencius* 4.8/22/6–19 (Lau 1970, 90–91).
112. For example, *Lüshi chunqiu* 18.7/116/19–22 (Knoblock and Riegel 2000, 466). He is known as Sima Xi 司馬喜 in the *Lüshi chunqiu*, but scholars generally agree that he is the same figure mentioned on the bronzes discovered in the tomb of King Cuo. See Yang Kuan 2002, 530–31.
113. The inscriptions can be found in Zhang Yachu 2001, 5–56:5.2840, 146:15.9734–147:15.9735. They are translated in Wu 2017, 183–97. One inscription is translated at Cook 2016, 289–95.
114. *Sunzi* 8/7/29 (Sawyer 1994, 203).
115. SJ 70:2998–99 (Nienhauser, ed., 1994b, 137–38).
116. SJ 15:734.
117. For example *Laozi* 41 (Lau 1963, 122); *Mencius* 1.6/3/4–18 (Lau 1970, 8–9).
118. This is evinced, for example, by *Han Feizi* 51/154/23–26; *Zhanguo ce*, 86/40/18, 167/85/26–27 (Crump 1996, 156, 232).

CHAPTER 11

1. SJ 46:1893, 69:2257n1; *Zhushu jinian* 2.6.2.42/81/27–28. SJ 46 gives records Tian Yinqi dying in 321 BCE, but that can be corrected on the basis of testimony preserved in the *Zhushu jinian*. See Yang Kuan 2002, 487–88.
2. Lewis 1999a, 595; Yan 1997, 21–23.
3. Harrington and Frolich 2018 used data collected by the Yale School of Forestry to determine that Linzi was the ninth-largest city of the pre-industrial period.
4. Wu Hung 1999, 655–57, 662–64.
5. *Zhanguo ce* 112/54/25–29 (Crump 1996, 169). For the game of "kickball" 蹴鞠 (踏毬), see Mu-chou Poo 2018, 182.
6. Dong Shuo 1987, 337–39.
7. *Mencius* 2.5/9/22–24 (Lau 1970, 65).
8. *Mencius* 2.11/11/30 (Lau 1970, 69).
9. Lewis 1999a, 594–95; ZGS, 302.
10. *Mencius* 2.11/12/1–9 (Lau 1970, 69–70).
11. This social reality is evinced by Mencius reported urging of King Yan to "plan with the masses of Yan, establish a ruler and withdraw [your army] 謀於燕眾, 置君而去之" (*Mencius* 2.11/12/7).
12. SJ 34:1558 (Huang, tr., 2006, 179), 43:1804; *Zhushu jinian* 2.6.3.3/82/10–11.
13. *Mencius* 4.9/22/21 (Lau 1970, 91).
14. *Mencius* 4.10/23/15–24/5 (Lau 1970, 92–93).
15. SJ 75:2351 (Nienhauser, ed., 1994b, 190). The royal chronology of Qi is confused in the *Shi ji*. We can know from the sources in aggregate that Tian Ying 田嬰 served as prime minister under King Wei. See Yang Kuan 2002, 421–24.
16. SJ 46:1896, 75:2351 (Nienhauser, ed., 1994b, 191). The *Shi ji* account of the Qi court has the reign year wrong, but we can again reconstruct the chronology from other evidence. For the sources pertaining to the history of Xue, see Qian Mu 2001, 445–46.
17. SJ 75:2352 (Nienhauser, ed., 1994b, 191).
18. *Han Feizi* 25/55/4–9; *Huainanzi* 18/190/13–19 (Major et al. 2010, 729–30).
19. SJ 75:2353–54 (Nienhauser, ed., 1994b, 191–92).
20. Zhang and Wang 1993, 264n3.
21. Extrapolating from what became common practice among great patrons. See *Zhanguo ce* 198/101/4 (Crump 1996, 268).
22. SJ 75:2354 (Nienhauser, ed., 1994b, 192).
23. In this I am following the interpretive logic of Yang Kuan (ZGS, 394–95).
24. SJ 40:1725–26; ZGS, 395–96.
25. SJ 71:2318 (Nienhauser, ed., 1994b, 153); *Zhanguo ce* 166/85/1–11 (Crump 1996, 252–53; Yang Kuan 2002, 630–34).
26. SJ 5:209 (Nienhauser, ed., 1994a, 113). The two royal uncles appointed as co-Chancellors were Master Shuli (discussed in the previous chapter) and Gan Mao 甘茂, whose biography accompanies that of Master Shuli at SJ 71:2310–18 (Nienhauser, ed., 1994b, 147–53).
27. SJ 5:209 (Nienhauser, ed., 1994a, 114).
28. SJ 5:209 (Nienhauser, ed., 1994a, 114), 43:1805. Fragments of a text known as the *Diwang shiji* 帝王世紀 (*Genealogy of Thearchs and Kings*) preserve the details of the king's eyes bleeding. See Yang Kuan 2002, 610–11.
29. Dong Shuo 1987, 45.
30. SJ 72:2323 (Nienhauser, ed., 1994b, 156).

31. SJ 5:210 (Nienhauser, ed., 1994a, 116), 15:735, SJ 72:2323 (Nienhauser, ed., 1994b, 156); *Zhuzi jinian* 2.6.3.11/83/5.
32. SJ 5:209 (Nienhauser, ed., 1994a, 114).
33. SJ 40:1727 (Cao, tr., 2006, 429). The alliance was secured by a royal marriage, though the details of this event are muddled in the sources. Yang Kuan and other commentators argue that Chu sent a princess who became King Zhao of Qin's queen (Yang Kuan 2002, 645; Cao, tr., 2006, 429n474; SJ 15:735).
34. SJ 40:1727 (Cao, tr., 2006, 429), 75:2356 (Nienhauser, ed., 1994b, 194); Mawangdui boshu zhengli xiaozu 1976, 27; *Zhanguo ce* 22/8/3 (Crump 1996, 59).
35. SJ 40:1727 (Cao, tr., 2006, 429).
36. *Lüshi chunqiu* 12.5/61/19–62/2 (Knoblock and Riegel 2000, 269–71); *Zhanguo ce* 134/66/1–17 (Crump 1996, 216–17).
37. SJ 5:210 (Nienhauser, ed., 1994a, 115), 15:736, 40:1727 (Cao, tr., 2006, 429), 45:1872; Shuihudi Qinmu zhujian zhengli xiao zu 睡虎地竹簡整理小組. *Shuihudi Qinmu zhujian* 睡虎地竹簡. Beijing: Wenwu chubanshe, 1990, 4.
38. SJ 5:210 (Nienhauser, ed., 1994a, 115), 15:736, 40:1727 (Cao, tr., 2006, 429); 44:1852, 45:1872; *Lüshi chunqiu* 25.5/164/23–28 (Knoblock and Riegel 2000, 638–39); *Shangjun shu* 20/27/20; *Xunzi* 15/72/14–15 (Hutton 2014, 157); *Zhanguo ce* 179/93/20–21 (Crump 1996, 236); Yang Kuan 2002, 666. The Chu commander Tang Mei is listed at SJ 27:1343 among outstanding "transmitters of the astronomical arts 傳天數者."
39. SJ 40:1727 (Cao, tr., 2006, 430).
40. SJ 5:210 (Nienhauser, ed., 1994a, 115).
41. *Shangjun shu* 20/27/20; *Xunzi* 15/72/15 (Hutton 2014, 157); SJ 23:1164.
42. SJ 5:210 (Nienhauser, ed., 1994a, 115), 15:739, 40:1727 (Cao, tr., 2006, 429–30).
43. SJ 5:210 (Nienhauser, ed., 1994a, 115), 15:737, 40:1727–28 (Cao, tr., 2006, 430–31).
44. SJ 40:1728 (Cao, tr., 2006, 431); *Zhanguo ce* 176/91/25–177/93/6, 195/99/7–12 (Crump 1996, 255–57, 258).
45. SJ 43:1812.
46. SJ 75:2354 (Nienhauser, ed., 1994b, 192).
47. *Zhanguo ce* 124/60/21–61/2 (Crump 1996, 190–91); *Shuoyuan* 9.5/68/21–69/2 (Henry 2021, 504–505); SJ 75:2354 (Nienhauser, ed., 1994b, 193).
48. SJ 5:210 (Nienhauser, ed., 1994a, 116), 15:737, 46:1898; 75:2354 (Nienhauser, ed., 1994b, 193). SJ 46 reports that in the same year Tian Wen traveled to Qin, Qi returned the Qin prince who had been sent as hostage to the Qi court. This may have provided the pretext for Tian Wen's commission: he was sent to escort the prince home.
49. *Zhanguo ce* 260/138/14–17 (Crump 1996, 298); SJ 5:210 (Nienhauser, ed., 1994a, 116), 75:2354 (Nienhauser, ed., 1994b, 193).
50. SJ 75:2354–55 (Nienhauser, ed., 1994b, 193–94).
51. SJ 15:737, 44:1852, 45:1876, 46:1898, 75:2355–56 (Nienhauser, ed., 1994b, 194); *Zhanguo ce* 18/7/4–8 (Crump 1996, 74–75).
52. *Zhanguo ce* 22/8/1–11 (Crump 1996, 59–60).
53. SJ 5:211 (Nienhauser, ed., 1994a, 116), 15:737–38, 44:1852, 45:1876, 46:1898; *Zhanguo ce* 83A/38/11–21 (Crump 1996, 107–8); *Han Feizi* 2/4/16–17, 30/68/15–20.
54. *Zhanguo ce* 119/57/27–58/4, 142/71/21, 72/12–13; *Xunzi* 11/50/12–15 (Hutton 2014, 101).
55. For a translation of "On the White Horse 白馬論" and other putative writings of Gongsun Long 公孫龍, see Wing-tsit Chan 1963, 235–43. On the thought of Gongsun Long and its influence upon the discourse of the Warring States, see Fung 1952, 203–22; Graham 1990, 125–215; Indraccolo 2016, 67–88; She 2024, 273–308.

56. *Han Feizi* 32/82/6–7.
57. For a study and complete translation of the "logic" chapters of the *Mozi*, see Graham 1978.
58. An early biography of Xun Kuang 荀況 is found in SJ 74:2348 (Nienhauser, ed., 1994b, 184). For a detailed modern critical study of the sources for his life, see Knoblock 1988, 3–35. Also Knoblock 1982–83, 28–52.
59. For modern critical study of Xunzi's thought, see Fung 1952, 279–311; Guo Moruo 1982, 218–59; Schwartz 1985, 290–320; Graham 1989, 235–67; Goldin 1999. See also the collected essays in Hutton, ed., 2016.
60. *Xunzi* 9/36/10–37/17 (Hutton 2014, 70–73).
61. It of course must be noted that "the teachings of Xun Kuang" can only ever be an approximation from the vantage of the twenty-first century. Our best evidence of Xun Kuang's teachings is the transmitted text of the *Xunzi*, which like all other transmitted Masters texts is an imperial-era compilation.
62. An extended argument to this effect is presented in *Xunzi* 23/113/1–118/1 (Hutton 2014, 248–57).
63. See for example *Xunzi* 1/1/3–8, 19/92/13–19, 95/1–4, 23/113/3–7 (Hutton 2014, 1, 205–6, 210–11, 48).
64. *Xunzi* 1/3/7–15 (Hutton 2014, 5).
65. We have very little information about the facts of Zhuang Zhou's life. See SJ 63:2143–45 (Nienhauser, ed., 1994b, 23–24).
66. An excellent study of the cross-currents that can be perceived between the *Xunzi* and sources such as the *Zhuangzi* can be found in Stalnaker 2003, 87–129.
67. For an alternative view, see Klein 2010, 299–369. I perceive more consistency in the material collected in the "Inner Chapters," though it is undeniable that we cannot know what form that material might have circulated in during the Warring States period.
68. For modern critical study of the teachings of Zhuang Zhou, see Fung 1952, 221–45; Graham, tr., 1981; Schwartz 1985, 215–37; Liu Xiaogan 1994; Cook, ed., 2003.
69. *Zhuangzi* 1/1/1–12, 2/6/14 (Watson 1968, 29–30, 46).
70. *Zhuangzi* 2/4/16–20 (Watson 1968, 39–40).
71. *Zhuangzi* 6/19/17–22 (Watson 1968, 90–91).
72. For extensive critical discussion of the evidence for the practice of meditation and macrobiotic yoga among early advocates of teachings like those found in the *Zhuangzi*, see Roth 1991, 599–650. Also Roth 2021.
73. This is especially evident in, for example, *Zhuangzi* 4/8/26–10/9 (Watson 1968, 54–61), but is also expressed in anecdotes like the one found at *Zhuangzi* 1/2/5–11 (Watson 1968, 32–33).
74. Examples of this can be seen in the story of the "Spirit-like Person 神人 of Gushe Mountain 姑射山" (*Zhuangzi* 1/2/13–21, Watson 1968, 33–34), or that of Cook Ding 庖丁 (*Zhuangzi* 3/7/30–4/11, Watson 1968, 50–51).
75. A biography of Lao Dan is included at SJ 63:2139–43 (Nienhauser, ed., 1994b, 21–23). The lore about Lao Dan had already grown complicated and internally contradictory by the time that the *Shiji* was composed, thus the text admits at several points that the truth of certain claims about Lao Dan could not be verified.
76. For a critical study of the lore surrounding Lao Dan, see Graham 1990, 111–24.
77. Good examples of the *Daode jing*'s intense engagement with the politics of the Warring States can be found at *Daode jing* 61, 75, and 80 (Lau 1963, 68, 82, 87), to name only a few. For modern explorations of the thought of the *Daode jing*, see for example Fung 1952, 170–91; Hsiao 1979, 273–318; LaFargue 1992; Goldin 2020, 109–28. See also the essays

collected in Csikszentmihalyi and Ivanhoe, eds., 1999. The *Daode jing* is among the most translated texts on earth. For a sense of the scope of global "Laozegetics," see Tadd 2022.
78. *Daode jing* 20 (Lau 1963, 24).
79. *Xunzi* 17/79/14–83/7 (Hutton 2014, 175–82).
80. The first instance of the use of a label that might be translated as "Daoist" (*Daojia* 道家) to refer to a collective movement is in SJ 130:3292, ca. 100 BCE. The label eventually was appropriated as a bibliographical category with which texts like the *Daode jing* and *Zhuangzi* were classified. See HS 30:1729–32.
81. Seidel 1969.
82. For a critical discussion of these issues, see Hoffert 2015, 165–78.
83. For a critical discussion of and review of the historiography surrounding these questions, see Raz 2012.
84. Tian Pian 田駢's interest in the "arts of the Way" (*Daoshu* 道術) is recorded at *Lüshi chunqiu* 17.8/107/23-6 (Knoblock and Riegel 2000, 435–36). For more sources concerning Tian Pian and the practice of meditative and macrobiotic arts at Jixia, see Zhang Bingnan 1991, 100–104, 176–77, 197–211; Roth 1995.

CHAPTER 12

1. SJ 15:738, 75:2357 (Nienhauser 1994b, 195). The *Shiji* gives the name of the kidnapper as Tian Jia 田甲, but nothing is known of him. As Nienhauser, ed., 1994b, 195n38 observes, "Jia" is often used as a placeholder for an unknown name (akin to "Mr. X"), thus "Tian Jia" may mean "one of the Tians."
2. *Han Feizi* 34/100/23–30; *Zhanguo ce* 14A/5/26–6/2; SJ 75:2358 (Nienhauser, ed., 1994b, 196); Yang Kuan 2002, 730.
3. SJ 5:210 (Nienhauser, ed., 1994a, 116), 15:738, 72:2324 (Nienhauser 1994b, 158).
4. SJ 5:212 (Nienhauser, ed., 1994a, 116), 15:738–9, 40:1729 (Cao, tr., 2006, 432), 44:1853, 45:1876, 72:2325, 73:2331 (Niennauser, ed., 1994b, 159, 167).
5. SJ 5:212 (Nienhauser, ed., 1994a, 116–17), 72:2325, 73:2331 (Niennauser, ed., 1994b, 159, 167).
6. The status of Su Qin as a double-agent for Yan is made very explicit in "Account Four" discovered among the "Zhanguo zonghengjia shu" found at Mawangdui (Mawangdui Hanmu boshu zhengli xiaozu 1976, 9–11). For a translation, see Blanford 1994, 77–82.
7. SJ 69:2265 (Nienhauser, ed., 1994b, 111). As noted above, the chronology of the *Shiji* biography of Su Qin does not tally even with its own account of events.
8. *Zhanghuo ce* 168/87/17–19 (Crump 1996, 244).
9. *Zhanguo ce* 420/202/12–203/14 (Crump 1996, 484–86); Mawangdui Hanmu boshu zhengli xiaozu 1976, 16–17. The text in the *Zhanguo ce* makes Su Dai 蘇代 (Su Qin's brother) the King of Yan's interlocutor. But in the silk manuscripts it is Su Qin who addresses the king.
10. Mawangdui Hanmu boshu zhengli xiaozu 1976, 9–11 (Blanford 1994, 77–79).
11. SJ 69:2241 (Nienhauser 1994b, 97).
12. *Zhanguo ce* 204B/106/8 (Crump 1996, 279); SJ 86:2519 (Nienhauser, ed., 1994b, 321).
13. SJ 129:3257 (Durrant, tr., 2019, 270).
14. For the issues surrounding the name and title of Song's king, see Wang Jing, tr., 2006, 290n214.
15. SJ 38:1632 (Wang Jing, tr., 2006, 290).
16. *Zhanguo ce* 248/132/3–5 (Crump 1996, 307).
17. *Zhanguo ce* 422/204/9–10, 433/211/21–22 (Crump 1996, 494, 482); *Lüshi chunqiu* 23.4/152/27–29 (Knoblock and Riegel 2000, 597–98).

18. ZGS, 411. See also *Zhanguo ce* 210/109/5–8, 247/131/18–248/132/28 (Crump 1996, 305–8).
19. Sage rulers of high antiquity such as Yao and Shun were occasionally referred to as *di* 帝, but even the founding rulers of the Zhou dynasty were virtually never given a title higher than "*wang* 王" (king).
20. SJ 5:212 (Nienhauser, ed., 1994a, 117), 15:739, 40:1729 (Cao, tr., 2006, 432), 44:1853, 46:1898, 72:2325, 79:2428 (Nienhauser, ed., 1994b, 159, 256); *Han Feizi* 31/76/16.
21. *Zhanguo ce* 141A/70/8–141B/70/25 (Crump 1996, 199–200).
22. In the subsequent account of events I have generally followed the reconstructed timeline proposed by Yang Kuan in ZGS, 417–19. See also the sources collected and analyzed in Yang Kuan 2002, 779–208.
23. *Mawangdui Hanmu boshu zhengli xiaoxu* 1976, 9.
24. *Mawangdui Hanmu boshu zhengli xiaoxu* 1976, 35–36.
25. *Mawangdui Hanmu boshu zhengli xiaoxu* 1976, 38–40, 46–48.
26. *Zhanguo ce* 209/108/8–109/3 (Crump 1996, 311–13); *Mawangdui Hanmu boshu zhengli xiaoxu* 1976, 91–93.
27. SJ 5:212 (Nienhauser, ed., 1994a, 117), 15:740.
28. *Zhanguo ce* 41B/15/1–5, 297/151/8–11 (Crump 1996, 109, 391).
29. SJ 15:740, 38:1632 (Wang, tr., 2006, 290), 46:1900.
30. SJ 5:212 (Nienhauser, ed., 1994a, 117), 15:740, 40:1729–30 (Wang, tr., 2006, 432–33).
31. SJ 75:2358 (Nienhauser, ed., 1994b, 196).
32. SJ 43:1816, 79:2428 (Nienauser, ed., 1994b, 256).
33. The specific fate of Su Qin is recorded at *Zhanguo ce* 168/87/18, 220/116/1 (Crump 1996, 244, 286), as well as in later sources. It is possible that Su Qin did play a significant role in the diplomacy that led to the events of 284 BCE, and that he was acting as a double-agent the whole while. Whatever the case may be, we can be certain, given the contradictions and inconsistencies of the record, that the legend that grew around the historical "core" of Su Qin's story is vast in scope, though we may never know its exact dimensions without finding new evidence.
34. SJ 5:212 (Nienhauser, ed., 1994a, 117), 15:740, 46:1900.
35. SJ 79:2428 (Nienhauser, ed., 1994b, 256), 43:1816; *Lüshi chunqiu* 15.2/82/17–19 (Knoblock and Riegel 2000, 146).
36. *Lüshi chunqiu* 15.2/82/19–21 (Knoblock and Riegel 2000, 146–47); *Zhanguo ce* 143/74/13–14 (Crump 1996, 207).
37. SJ 15:740–41, 43:1816, 44:1853; 45:1876, 46:1900, 79:2428–29 (Nienhauser, ed., 1994b, 256); *Zhanguo ce* 418/201/8–10 (Crump 1996, 481).
38. SJ 46:1900.
39. *Zhanguo ce* 73B/34/5, 143/74/16–24 (Crump 1996, 126, 207–8), SJ 46:1900, *Xin xu* 5.21/29/9–25.
40. *Zhanguo ce* 144/74/26–75/2 (Crump 1996, 208–9); SJ 46:1901. The *Zhanguo ce* reports that the uprising in Ju killed Nao Chi. The *Shiji* reports that he left the city.
41. SJ 82:2453–55 (Nienhauser, ed., 1994b, 275–76); *Zhanguo ce* 143/74/23–24 (Crump 1996, 208).
42. SJ 75:2358 (Nienhauser, ed., 1994b, 197).
43. *Zhanguo ce* 149B/78/26–79/15 (Crump 1996, 221–22), SJ 46:1901.

CHAPTER 13

1. The phrase *qi xiong* 七雄 was first used to designate the seven most powerful of the Warring States in Ban Gu's account of his own biography at HS 100:4227.

2. SJ 43:1779.
3. ZGS, 322; SJ 5:206 (Nienhauser, ed., 1994a, 111), 15:729–30.
4. SJ 5:206 (Nienhauser 1994a, 111).
5. SJ 15:434–35, 43:1806–11, 110:2885; *Zhanguo ce* 221/116/13–224/120/19 (Crump 1996, 288–98). See also ZGS, 400–401; Yang Kuan 2002, 622–30; Di Cosmo 2002 134–38.
6. The evidence of this sensitivity on the part of Warring States authors is too abundant to catalogue. See for example *Lun yu* 4.9/7/25, 5.26/11/18–19, 6.4/12/13, 8.21/19/29, 9.27/22/11; *Mencius* 2.16/13/26, 3.9/18/25, 5.4/27/16, 10.1/50/23–24, 14.6/73/27–28; *Mozi* 1.6(6)/6/23, 1.6(6)/7/1–15, 4.2(15)/26/1–3, 8.4/(32)/56/26–29, 12.1(47)/105/25–29, 12.2(48)/107/11–18, 13.1(49)/114/13; *Zhuangzi* 28/82/14–17, 28/83/25–27, 28/85/7–8, 32/97/1–2; *Xunzi* 10/48/10–11, 27/136/1–2, 29/142/28–143/6, 31/144/27–145/5; *Lüshi chunqiu* 15.3/82/25–83/4, 15.5/86/1–8, 19.8/128/10–17, 20.2/130/18–23, 20.5/134/6–11.
7. Wu 2017, 26–133.
8. SJ 43:1806.
9. *Zhanguo ce* 221/116/29 (Crump 1996, 289).
10. *Huainanzi* 9/77/25 (Major et al. 2010, 327) describes these "barbarian" elements of the court dress adopted by King Wuling of Zhao. Such adornments became customary in later imperial cavalry uniforms. See Yang Kuan 2002, 622. On the spread of cowrie shells to Inner Asia, see Bin Yang 2018.
11. *Zhanguo ce* 222/119/1–22 (Crump 1996, 296–97).
12. SJ 43:1811–13; *Han Feizi* 32/86/22–28.
13. SJ 43:1815–16. The text claims that King Wuling planned to establish Zhao Zhang as King of Dai, though how a record of that would have been preserved is dubious.
14. SJ 43:1815.
15. *Zhanguo ce* 366/180/7–24 (Crump 1996, 448–49).
16. SJ 72:2323–29 (Nienhauser, ed., 1994b, 157–63).
17. SJ 5:213 (Nienhauser, ed., 1994a, 118), 15:742, 73:2331 (Nienhauser, ed., 1994b, 168).
18. SJ 79:2401–3 (Nienhauser, ed., 1994b, 233–34).
19. SJ 110:2885.
20. SJ 110:2885.
21. HHS 87:2874; Yang Kuan 2002, 922.
22. SJ 79:2406 (Nienhauser, ed., 1994b, 236); *Zhanguo ce* 73A/29/19–20 (Crump 1996, 122).
23. On this phenomenon, see Crump 1964, 88–106.
24. SJ 79:2404–10 (Nienhauser, ed., 1994b, 234–40); *Zhanguo ce* 72/28/26–73A31/22 (Crump 1996, 120–25).
25. SJ 72:2329, 79:2411–12 (Nienhauser 1994b, 163, 240–41); *Zhanguo ce* 73B/31/25–74/33/2 (Crump 1996, 125–28).
26. SJ 72:2329 (Nienhauser, ed., 1994b, 164).
27. *Zhanguo ce* 73B/32/10 (Crump 1996, 126) records that she was "repudiated" (*fei* 廢, i.e. stripped of her official title of Queen Dowager), but most historians agree that was unlikely, given that the *Shiji* reports her being buried with state honors (see Fan Xiangyong 2006, 331n125).
28. SJ 5:213 (Nienhauser, ed., 1994a, 119), 15:745.
29. *Zhanguo ce* 64/26/17–22 (Crump 1996, 129).
30. This is corroborated by the chronicle discovered among bamboo texts interred in the tomb at Shuihudi. See Shuihudi Qinmu zhujian zhengli xiaozu 1990, 5.
31. SJ 79:2413–16 (Nienhauser, ed., 1994b, 241–45).
32. For further discussion of this phenomenon, see Lewis 2021.

33. SJ 43:1816, 80:2427–28 (Nienhauser, ed., 1994b, 255–56).
34. SJ 43:1820–21; 81:2439 (Nienhauser, ed., 1994b, 263).
35. The legend of the origins of the Circular Jade of the He Clan 和氏璧 is recounted in *Han Feizi* 13/23/4–17 (Watson 1963, 80–81).
36. See for example *Zhanguo ce* 127/61/26 (Crump 1996, 192); *Lüshi chunqiu* 12.5/61/27–28 (Knoblock and Riegel 2000, 271).
37. SJ 81:2439–43 (Nienhauser, ed., 1994b, 263–67).
38. SJ 5:213 (Nienhauser, ed., 1994a, 119), 15:744. The *Shiji* gives the wrong date for the campaign and erroneously sites Eyu in Han. See Yang Kuan 2002, 936.
39. *Zhanguo ce* 228/121/24–122/5 (Crump 1996, 313–14).
40. SJ 2445–56 (Nienhauser, ed., 1994b, 267–68).
41. *Zhanguo ce* 228/122/5 (Crump 1996, 314).
42. SJ 79:2412 (Nienhauser, ed., 1994b, 241) gives 266 BCE as the year that Fan Sui became Marquis of Ying 應侯. which indicates that he became prime minister in that year.
43. SJ 5:213–14 (Nienhauser, ed., 1994a, 119–20); 15:745–46.
44. SJ 43:1822.
45. SJ 43:1824–25; 73:2332–33 (Nienhauser, ed., 1994b, 169).
46. *Zhanguo ce* 211/109/28 (Crump 1996, 321).
47. *Zhanguo ce* 211/109/11–110/17 (Crump 1996, 320–22); SJ 43:1824–25.
48. SJ 43:1826, 73:2333 (Nienhauser, ed., 1994b, 169).
49. SJ 43:1826, 73:2333 (Nienhauser, ed., 1994b, 170).
50. *Sunzi* A13/14/9–12, 21–24 (Sawyer 1994, 231).
51. SJ 73:2333–34, 81:2446 (Nienhauser, ed., 1994b, 170, 269).
52. SJ 81:2447 (Nienhauser, ed., 1994b, 269); *Lienü zhuan* 3.15/31/16–32/2 (Kinney 2014, 64–65).
53. See Meyer and Wilson 2003, 112–13; Meyer 2017, 4–5.
54. *Sunzi* A11/13/7 (Sawyer 1994, 224).
55. Several passages in the *Zhanguo ce* give evidence of these types of calculations being made in the capitals of the various Warring States. See for example *Zhanguo ce* 120/58/6–15, 327/166/7–13 (Crump 1996, 218, 411).
56. SJ 73:2334–5, 81:2447 (Nienhauser, ed., 1994b, 170–71, 269–70).
57. *Wenwu* 1996.6, 33–40.

CHAPTER 14

1. Sage 1992, 119–56; ZGS, 433.
2. von Glahn 2016, 44–83.
3. Picketty 2020.
4. As an example that demonstrates the general phenomenon, see SJ 2506–7 (Nienhauser, ed., 1994b, 312).
5. SJ 76:2365–66 (Nienhauser, ed., 1994b, 203–4).
6. The most extreme example of this is the libel against Tian Chang (discussed in Chapter 1), which held that he gave his clients "free use" of his wives and concubines by way of remunerating their loyalty (SJ 46:1885).
7. Milburn 2007, 1–22. See also the essays collected in Rom, ed., 2025.
8. SJ 75:2351–78:2399 (Nienhauser, ed., 1994b, 189–231).
9. SJ 2335–36 (Nienhauser, ed., 1994b, 171–72).
10. SJ 2336–37 (Nienhauser, ed., 1994b, 172–73).
11. SJ 77:2379 (Nienhauser, ed., 1994b, 216–17).
12. SJ 77:2378–81 (Nienhauser, ed., 1994b, 215–18).

13. SJ 76:2366–69 (Nienhauser, ed., 1994b, 204–6). The outcome of the siege of Handan is corroborated at SJ 5:214 (Nienhauser, ed., 1994a, 121), 15:747, 43:1827, 44:1862, 78:2395 (Nienhauser, ed., 1994b, 228); *Zhanguo ce* 236/126/11–128/8, 339/169/11–18 (Crump 1996, 327–31, 416).
14. The biography of Yu Qing 虞卿 (or "Counselor Yu") is found at SJ 76:2371–76, that of Lu Zhonglien 魯仲連 at (Nienhauser, ed., 1994b, 207–13, 281–86). The *Yushi chunqiu* and the *Lu Zhonglianzi* are both recorded at HS 30:1736, listed among the "Confucian 儒" Masters writings 子書. Scholars have made efforts to reconstruct these writings from surviving fragments. See Ruan 1980, 65–92; Ma 1990, Vol. 6, 204–16.
15. SJ 5:212 (Nienhauser, ed., 1994a, 119), 15:743–44, 73:2331 (Nienhauser, ed., 1994b, 168).
16. SJ 15:746–50, 40:1735 (Cao, tr., 2006, 438–39), 78:2387–94 (Nienhauser, ed., 1994b, 223–28).
17. SJ 78:2395 (Nienhauser, ed., 1994b, 228).
18. SJ 15:748, 33:1547 (Cao, tr., 2006, 160), 78:2395 (Nienhauser, ed., 1994b, 228).
19. SJ 74:2348 (Nienhauser, ed., 1994b, 184).
20. *Xunzi* 13/63/28–64/9, 13/66/1–6 (Hutton 2014, 135, 139). Zhao Sheng is mentioned in the former passage as an exemplar of virtuous leadership.
21. SJ 63:2146–56 (Nienhauser, ed., 1994b, 25–29).
22. For a good critical discussion of the vexations of the label "Legalism," see Goldin 2011, 88–104.
23. For modern critical study of Han Feizi's thought, see Fung 1952, 312–36; Hsiao 1979, 368–424; Wang and Chang 1986; Du Heng 2017, 193–228. See also the essays collected in Goldin, ed., 2013.
24. *Han Feizi* 8/12/7–11 (Watson 1963, 41–42).
25. *Han Feizi* 7/9/13–10/16 (Watson 1963, 30–34).
26. The one possible exception is Huang Xie. A character named "Lord of Chunshen" appears at *Han Feizi* 14/25/30, but that figure is identified as the younger brother of King Zhuang of Chu (r. 613–591 BCE), and none of the details of his story match exactly with other accounts of Huang Xie's life.
27. *Hanshi waizhuan* 4.25/31/24–32/12.
28. *Xunzi* 26/126/1–3 (Hutton 2014, 286–87).
29. Qu Yuan 屈原 is commemorated with his own biography at SJ 84:2481–91 (Nienhauser, ed., 1994b, 295–302). See also Schneider 1980.
30. See the essays collected in Kern and Owen, eds., 2023.
31. *Chu ci* 1/1/3–4/13 (Hawkes, tr., 1985, 67–95).
32. Shuihudi Qinmu zhujian zhengli xiaozu, 6, records the death of Fan Sui in 255 BCE, though he is referred to as Zhang Lu.
33. SJ 77:2382–83 (Nienhauser, ed., 1994b, 218–20).
34. SJ 43:1827.
35. SJ 5:218–19 (Nienhauser, ed., 1994a, 121–22).
36. SJ 4:169 (Nienhauser, ed., 1994a, 83).
37. SJ 15:749–50.
38. SJ 5:219 (Nienhauser, ed., 1994a, 122), 15:750, 44:1863, 77:2283–84 (Nienhauser, ed., 1994b, 220).
39. 77:2284 (Nienhauser, ed., 1994b, 220–21).
40. SJ 6:224 (Nienhauser, ed., 1994a, 128), 15:752, 40:1736 (Cao, tr., 2006, 439).
41. SJ 78:2395 (Nienhauser, ed., 1994b, 228–29).
42. SJ 78:2395–99 (Nienhauser, ed., 1994b, 229–31). A parallel account of Huang Xie's demise is found at *Lienü zhuan* 7.14/72/21–73/13 (Kinney, tr., 2014, 154–55). A different version of the story appears at *Yuejue shu* 17/50/24–51/22 (Milburn 2010, 356–57), but the chronology of that narrative is garbled.

CHAPTER 15

1. SJ 4:169 (Nienhauser, ed., 1994a, 83).
2. A stylized biography of Cai Ze is recorded at SJ 79:2418–25 (Nienhauser 1994b, 246–53).
3. Ying Dao 嬴悼, King Zhao's heir, died in the state of Wei in 267 BCE. See SJ 5:213 (Nienhauser, ed., 1994a, 119).
4. Zhuanguo ce 93/18–20 (Crump 1996, 151).
5. SJ 85:2505–8 (Nienhauser, ed., 1994b, 311–13).
6. Of course, the story could have been a fabrication in the case of both Huang Xie and Lü Buwei. The chance that the story has some historical basis is higher in the case of Huang Xie, however, because Huang Xie himself was a participant, and might have confided in some trusted retainer, who let the secret out after Huang Xie was murdered.
7. SJ 6:223 (Nienhauser, ed., 1994a, 127), 15:749–50, 85:2509 (Nienhauser, ed., 1994b, 313).
8. SJ 5:219 (Nienhauser, ed., 1994a, 122).
9. SJ 5:219 (Nienhauser, ed., 1994a, 122), 15:750.
10. SJ 85:2509 (Nienhauser, ed., 1994b, 314).
11. SJ 6:224 (Nienhauser, ed., 1994a, 128), 15:751, 43:1829.
12. SJ 34:1559–62 (Huang, tr., 2006, 181–83), 43:1827–31.
13. SJ 79:2425 (Nienhauser, ed., 1994b, 252).
14. SJ 6:224 (Nienhauser, ed., 1994a, 128), 15:751, 44:1863, 45:1877, 88:2565 (Nienhauser, ed., 1994b, 361).
15. SJ 6:224 (Nienhauser, ed., 1994a, 128), 15:752, 40:1736 (Cao, tr., 2006, 439).
16. SJ 85:2510 (Nienhauser, ed., 1994b, 314).
17. For the mechanics of bamboo manuscripts, see Tsien 2004, 96–125.
18. For modern critical studies of the *Lüshi chunqiu*, see Kalinowski 1980, 155–208; Tian Fengtai 1986; Lewis 1999b, 302–8; Sellman 2002; Cook 2002, 307–45; Jacoby 2022, 5–26; Jacoby and Sellman, forthcoming.
19. *Lüshi chunqiu* 12.6/6–12 (Knoblock and Riegel 2000, 272–73).
20. The "Twelve Records" correspond to the 12 months of the year, the "Eight Expositions" correspond to the eight cardinal directions, the "Six Discourses" correspond to the "six coordinates" (*liu he*: up, down, left, right, front, back). In this way each section of the work presents itself as being "modeled" upon and textually embodying a foundational cosmic structure: the "Twelve Records" embody Heaven, the "Eight Expositions" embody Earth, and the "Six Discourses" embody human beings.
21. For a detailed discussion of "cosmic resonance" (*ganying* 感應), see Leblanc 1985, 191–206.
22. *Lüshi chunqiu* 9.5/46/19–27 (Knoblock and Riegel 2000, 218–19) describes the basic operation of cosmic resonance.
23. *Lüshi chunqiu* 4.1/17/9–10 (Knoblock and Riegel 2000, 115).
24. This structure can be seen in any Table of Contents of an edition of the text, i.e. Knoblock and Riegel 2000, xiii–xv.
25. See for example *Lüshi chunqiu* 2.4/10/11–16, 26.1/166/3–167/3 (Knoblock and Riegel 2000, 90, 644–47).
26. *Lüshi chunqiu* 7.2/34/7–14 (Knoblock and Riegel 2000, 175–76).
27. *Lüshi chunqiu* 7.5/36/25–37/16 (Knoblock and Riegel 2000, 184–87).
28. For a detailed study of the persistent influence of the *Lüshi chunqiu* during the Han dynasty, see Xu Fuguan 1979, 1–84.
29. cf. Sivin 1995, 4:1–33.
30. *Zhouyi* 周易 55/85/6; Lynn, tr., 1994, 488.
31. SJ 6:226 (Nienhauser, ed., 1994a, 129), 44:1863.

32. SJ 6:226 (Nienhauser, ed., 1994a, 129), 43:1831. The original text of SJ 6 is corrupted and mistakenly reads that "[Ying] Chengjiao 成蟜, Lord Changan 長安君 died." SJ 43:1831, which records the enfeoffment of Lord Changan, shows the character "died" in SJ is a scribal error. See Yang Kuan 2002, 1104–5.
33. SJ 85:2512 (Nienhauser, ed., 1994b, 315).
34. For "Lao Ai," see Goldin 2002, 84–85.
35. SJ 85:2511 (Nienhauser, ed., 1994b, 314–15).
36. SJ 6:227 (Nienhauser, ed., 1994a, 129), 15:752. *Zhanguo ce* 342/170/26–171/9 (Crump 1996, 420) suggests that Lao Ai had factional support within the Qin government to rival that of Lü Buwei, which would not have been possible if Lao Ai had accepted the sentence of a convicted criminal and eunuch, even in pretense.
37. SJ 6:227 (Nienhauser, ed., 1994a, 130), 15:752, 85:2512 (Nienhauser, ed., 1994b, 315).
38. SJ 6:227 (Nienhauser, ed., 1994a, 130), 15:753, 85:2512 (Nienhauser, ed., 1994a, 315).
39. SJ 15:751.
40. SJ 29:1408.
41. SJ 6:230 (Nienhauser, ed., 1994a, 131), 87:2541 (Nienhauser, ed., 1994b, 336).
42. SJ 87:2539–46 (Nienhauser, ed., 1994b, 335–40).
43. SJ 6:231 (Nienhauser, ed., 1994a, 131), 15:753, 85:2513–14 (Nienhauser, ed., 1994b, 315–16).
44. The last ruler to hold the title of emperor, Aisin-Giorio Puyi 愛新覺羅浦儀 (r. 1908–11 CE), was the final monarch of the Qing dynasty 清 (1644–1911 CE).
45. SJ 6:265 (Nienhauser, ed., 1994a, 155).
46. There is an extensive literature on the tomb of the First Emperor, which continues to be investigated. See for example Wang Xueli 1994; Ciarla, ed., 2005; Portal, ed., 2007; Wu Hung 2010, 109–18; Burman 2018.
47. SJ 87:2540–41 (Nienhauser, ed., 1994b, 335–36). For modern critical studies of Li Si 李斯, see Bodde 1967; Goldin 2005, 66–75.
48. 15:752, 44:1863.
49. *Zhanguo ce* 439/214/3–14 (Crump 1996, 502–3); ZGS, 462.
50. SJ 43:1831; *Han Feizi* 19/31/31–32/3.
51. SJ 15:753, 40:1736 (Cao, tr., 2006, 440); *Zhanguo ce* 88/42/25–27 (Crump 1996, 157).
52. SJ 6:232 (Nienhauser, ed., 1994a, 132), 15:753. 43:1831.
53. SJ 81:2449–50 (Nienhauser, ed., 1994b, 271–72). For the history of the Xiongnu 匈奴, see Miller 2024.
54. SJ 43:1832, 81:2450 (Nienhauser, ed., 1994b, 272). The testimony here differs from what is recorded in SJ 6 and 15, but Yang Kuan makes the case that the testimony of SJ 43 and 81 is more reliable. He also argues persuasively that the general identified here as Huan Qi 桓齮 is the general identified as Fan Wuqi 樊於期 in SJ 86. See Yang Kuan 2002, 1132–34.
55. SJ 6:232 (Nienhauser, ed., 1994a, 132), 15:754, 45:1876, 63:2155 (Nienhauser, ed., 1994b, 29).
56. *Han Feizi* 2/3/3–5/4.
57. SJ 6:232 (Nienhauser, ed., 1994a, 132), 63:2155–56 (Nienhauser, ed., 1994b, 29).
58. SJ 15:754.
59. SJ 6:232 (Nienhauser, ed., 1994a, 132), 45:1878.
60. SJ 6:233 (Nienhauser, ed., 1994a, 132–33), 43:1832, 81:2451–52 (Nienhauser, ed., 1994b, 272); *Zhanguo ce* 263/139/25–140/2, 95/46/13–47/17 (Crump 1996, 346–49); *Lienüzhuan* 7.15/73/15–29 (Kinney 2014, 155–56).
61. SJ 81:2448–49 (Nienhauser, ed., 1994b, 270–71).
62. SJ 6:233 (Nienhauser, ed., 1994a, 133), 15:755, 43:1832–33, 73:2338 (Nienhauser, ed., 1994b, 173).
63. SJ 6:233 (Nienhauser, ed., 1994a, 133), 15:755.

64. SJ 34:1560–61 (Huang, tr., 2006, 183), 86:2528 (Nienhauser, ed., 1994b, 326).
65. SJ 34:1561 (Huang, tr., 2006, 184), 86:3526–38 (Nienhauser, ed., 1994b, 325–33), *Zhanguo ce* 440/214/16–217/28 (Crump 1996, 503–11).
66. SJ 6:233 (Nienhauser, ed., 1994a, 133), 34:1561–62 (Huang, tr., 2006, 184).
67. SJ 6:233 (Nienhauser, ed., 1994a, 133), Shuihudi Qinmu zhujian zhengli xiaozu 1990, 7.
68. SJ 6:233 (Nienhauser, ed., 1994a, 133), 40:1736 (Cao, tr., 2006, 440).
69. SJ 46:1902–3; *Zhanguo ce* 149A/79/14–15 (Crump 1996, 221–22).
70. SJ 6:234 (Nienhauser, ed., 1994a, 134), 15:756, 44:1864; *Lienüzhuan* 5.11/48/4–20 (Kinney 2014, 102–3).
71. SJ 6:234 (Nienhauser, ed., 194a, 134), 15:756, 40:1736–37 (Cao, tr., 2006, 440–41), 73:2339–41 (Nienhauser, ed., 1994b, 174–75).
72. SJ 6:234 (Nienhauser, ed., 1994a, 134), 15:757, 34:1561–62 (Huang, tr., 2006, 184–85).
73. *Zhanguo ce* 150/79/17–29 (Crump 1996, 22–23).
74. 6:235 (Nienhauser, ed., 1994a, 134), 15:757, 44:1902–3.

EPILOGUE

1. SJ 6:235–36 (Nienhauser 1994a, 134–36).
2. For a more detailed review of the policies of the Qin dynasty, see Bodde 1986, 21–102. See also Lewis 2007.
3. SJ 6:238–39 (Nienhauser 1994a, 137).
4. SJ 6:238 (Nienhauser 1994a, 136).
5. SJ 6:239 (Nienhauser 1994a, 137).
6. SJ 6:239 (Nienhauser 1994a, 137); Xu Shen 許慎 (ca. 55–ca. 149 CE), *Shuowen jiezi zhu* 說文解字注. Shanghai: Shanghai guji chubanshe, 1981, 758.
7. SJ 6:241 (Nienhauser 1994a, 138); Lewis 2007, 55–57 (see esp. the map of the Qin road system on p. 56).
8. For sources on the corvee administration of Qin, see Hsing I-t'ien 2014, 155–86. For a systemic discussion of the recruitment of labor for public works under Qin, see Shelach 2014, 113–38.
9. SJ 88:255–56 (Nienhauser 1994b, 361–62).
10. For this dimension of Qin governance, see Yates 2014, 141–54.
11. SJ 6:239–40, 252–53 (Nienhauser 1994a, 137–38, 145–46).
12. The note pictures the gate of the "Temple of Literature" (*Văn Miếu* 文廟) built by the rulers of the Lý dynasty in Hanoi in 1070 CE.
13. SJ 6:240 (Nienhauser 1994a, 138).
14. Jie Shi 2014, 359–91.
15. SJ 6:242–64 (Nienhauser 1994a, 138–54). For a map of the routes of these tours, see Lewis 2007, 58. The map includes a fifth route of a tour taken in 220 CE that was confined to the territory of the former kingdom of Qin.
16. Kern 2000, 106–18.
17. For a more detailed discussion of the political and cultural dimensions of the imperial tours, see Sanft 2014, 77–100.
18. Ciarla 2005, 133.
19. SJ 6:247 (Nienhauser 1994a, 142).
20. For the history of immortals and their lore, see Pirazzoli-t'Serstevens 2009, 988–94. See also Campany 2009.

21. My discussion of the Qin stelae inscriptions owes much to the scholarship of Martin Kern. See his translation and historical analysis of the inscriptions: Kern 2000, 10–49, 154–96. My thanks for his comments on this chapter.
22. SJ 6:242–43 (Nienhauser 1994a, 138–39).
23. Translated in Kern 2000, 22–23.
24. Kern 2000, 166. Specific reference to the distinction between "the noble and the base 貴賤" occurs three times in the seven inscriptions (Kern 2000, 22, 30, 47).
25. SJ 6:239 (Nienhauser 1994a, 138).
26. For the Erudites (*bo shi* 博士), see Ma 1982, 893–901.
27. SJ 87:2547 (Nienhauser 1994b, 341).
28. The banquet at which Chunyu Yue delivered his critique and its aftermath is reported at SJ 6:254–55 (Nienhauser 1994a, 146–8). An alternate account appears at SJ 87:2546 (Nienhauser 1994b, 340–41).
29. SJ 6:258 (Nienhauser 1994a, 149–50).
30. SJ 6:258 (Nienhauser 1994a, 150).
31. Forms of aristocracy did emerge during imperial times, but such groups never exercised the sheer degree of social dominance enjoyed by the aristocracy of the pre-imperial world.
32. Loewe 1986, 123–27. See esp. the map on p. 125.
33. T'ung-tsu Ch'u 1972, 63–159.
34. For a detailed analysis of this phenomenon, see Puett 2001.

Bibliography

Achebe, Chinua. *Things Fall Apart*. New York: Astor-Honor, 1959.
Allan, Sarah. *The Heir and the Sage: Dynastic Legends in Early China*. San Francisco: Chinese Materials Center, 1981.
Ames, Roger. *Sun-tzu: The Art of Warfare: The First English Translation Incorporating the Recently Discovered Yin-ch'üeh-shan Texts*. New York: Ballantine Books, 1993.
Ames, Roger, and D. C. Lau, trs. *Sun Pin: The Art of Warfare*. New York: Ballantine, 1996.
Ahern, Emily M. "The Power and Pollution of Chinese Women." In Margery Wolf and Roxane Witke, eds., *Women in Chinese Society*. Stanford: Stanford University Press, 1975, 193–214.
Anderson, E. N. *The Food of China*. New Haven: Yale University Press, 1988.
Baccini, Giulia, and Maddalena Barenghi. "The Witty Courtiers, Memoir 66." In Nienhauser, ed., 2019, 149–96.
Bagley, Robert. "Shang Archaeology." In Loewe and Shaughnessy, eds., 136–57.
Bagley, Robert. *Ancient Sichuan: Treasures From a Lost Civilization*. Seattle: Seattle Art Museum, 2001.
Ban Gu 班固 (32–92 CE), *Han shu* 漢書. Beijing: Zhonghua shuju, 1962.
Barbieri, Anthony J. and Robin D. S. Yates. *Law, State, and Society in Early Imperial China: A Study with Critical Edition and Translation of the Legal Texts from Zhangjiashan Tomb No. 247*. 2 vols. Leiden: Brill, 2015.
Berkowitz, Alan J. *Patterns of Disengagement: The Practice and Portrayal of Reclusion in Early Medieval China*. Stanford: Stanford University Press, 2000.
Bielenstein, Hans. "The Census of China during the Period 2–742 A.D." *Bulletin of the Museum of Far Eastern Antiquities* 19 (1947): 125–63.
Bielenstein, Hans. "Wang Mang, the Restoration of the Han Dynasty, and Later Han." In Twitchett and Loewe, eds., 1986, 223–90.
Blakeley, Barry B. "Functional Disparities in the Socio-Political Traditions of Spring and Autumn China." *Journal of the Economic and Social History of the Orient* 20.2 (1977): 208–43; 20.3 (1977): 307–43; 22.1 (1979): 81–118.
Blakeley, Barry B. "The Geography of Chu." In Constance A. Cook and John Major, eds., *Defining Chu: Image and Reality in Ancient China*. Honolulu: University of Hawaii Press, 1999, 9–20.
Blanford, Yumiko F. "Discovery of Lost Eloquence: New Insight from the Mawangdui 'Zhanguo zonghengjia shu.'" *Journal of the American Oriental Society* 114.1 (1994): 77–82.
Bodde, Derk. "Feudalism in China." *Essays on Chinese Civilization*. Princeton: Princeton University Press, 1956.
Bodde, Derk. *China's First Unifier: Li Ssu*. Hong Kong: Hong Kong University Press, 1967.
Bodde, Derk. "The State and Empire of Ch'in." In Twitchett and Loewe, eds., 1986, 21–102.
Brindley, Erica Fox. *Ancient China and the Yue: Perceptions and Identities on the Southern Frontier, c. 400 BCE–50 CE*. Cambridge: Cambridge University Press, 2015.
Brooks, E. Bruce, and A. Taeko Brooks. *The Original Analects: Sayings of Confucius and His Successors*. New York: Columbia University Press, 1998.
Burman, Edward. *The Terracotta Warriors: Exploring the Most Intriguing Puzzle in Chinese History*. New York: Pegasus, 2018.

Campany, Robert Ford. *Making Transcendents: Ascetics and Social Memory in Early Medieval China*. Honolulu: University of Hawaii Press, 2009.

Cao Weiguo, "The Duke of Chou and of Lu: Hereditary House 3" and "Ch'u: Hereditary House 10." In Nienhauser, ed., 2006, 1–29, 131–61, 381–447.

Chan, Alan K. L., ed. *Mencius: Contexts and Interpretations*. Honolulu: University of Hawaii Press, 2002.

Chan, Shirley. *The Confucian Shi: Official Service and the Confucian Analects*. Lampeter: The Edwin Mellen Press, 2004.

Chan, Wing-tsit 陳榮捷 (1901–94 CE). *A Sourcebook in Chinese Philosophy*. Princeton: Princeton University Press, 1963.

Chang, K. C. 張光直. *Art, Myth and Ritual: The Path to Political Authority in Ancient China*. Cambridge, MA: Harvard University Press, 1983.

Chang, K. C. 張光直. "China on the Eve of the Historical Period." In Loewe and Shaughnessey, eds., 1999, 37–73.

Chang Qu 常璩 (291–361 CE). *Huayang guozhi jiaobu tuzhu* 華陽國志校補圖注. Ren Naiqiang (1894–1989 CE), ed. Shanghai: Shanghai guji chubanshe, 1987.

Chavannes, Édouard. "Les Inscriptions des Ts'in." *Journal Asiatique* 1 (1893): 473–521.

Chen De'an 陳德安. *Shang dai Shu ren mibao: Sichuan Guanghan Sanxingdui yiji* 商代蜀人秘寶：四川廣漢三星堆遺蹟. Beijing: Wenwu, 1994.

Chen Qiyou 陳奇猷. *Lüshi chunqiu jiaoshi* 呂氏春秋校釋. Shanghai: Xuelin chubanshe, 1995.

Chen Qiyou. *Han Feizi xinjiaozhu* 韓非子新校注. 2 vols. Shanghai: Shanghai guji chubanshe, 2000.

Chen Shen. "Compromises and Conflicts: Production and Commerce in the Royal Cities of Eastern Zhou, China." In Monica L. Smith, ed., *The Social Construction of Ancient Cities*. Washington, D.C.: Smithsonian, 2003, 290–310.

Chen Zhi and William H. Nienhauser, trs. "Wu T'ai-po, Hereditary House 1." In Nienhauser, ed., 2006, 1–30.

Cheng, Anne. "Lun yu." In Michael Loewe, ed., *Early Chinese Texts: A Bibliographical Guide*. Berkeley: The Society for the Study of Early China, 1993, 313–23.

Childs-Johnson, Elizabeth, ed. *The Oxford Handbook of Early China*. Oxford: Oxford University Press, 2020.

Chin, Annping. *The Authentic Confucius: A Life of Thought and Politics*. New York: Scribner, 2007.

Ciarla, Roberto, ed. *The Eternal Army: The Terracotta Soldiers of the First Emperor*. Vercelli, Italy: White Star, 2005.

Cohen, Paul. *Speaking to History: The Story of King Goujian in Twentieth Century China*. Berkeley: University of California Press, 2009.

Cook, Constance A. "Moonshine and Millet: Feasting and Purification Rituals in Ancient China." In Roel Sterckx, ed., *Of Tripod and Palate: Food Politics, and Religion in Traditional China*. New York: Palgrave MacMillan, 2005, 9–33.

Cook, Constance A. *Death in Ancient China: The Tale of One Man's Journey*. China Studies 8. Leiden: Brill, 2006.

Cook, Constance A. "Zhongshan Wang Cuo Ding." In Cook and Goldin, eds., 2016, 289–95.

Cook, Constance A. *Ancestors, Kings, and the Dao*. Cambridge, MA: Harvard University Press, 2017.

Cook, Constance A. "Western Zhou Rites and Mortuary Practice (Inscriptions and Texts)." In Childs-Johnson, ed., 2020, 436–50.
Cook, Constance A., and John Major, eds. *Defining Chu: Image and Reality in Ancient China*. Honolulu: University of Hawaii Press, 1999.
Cook, Constance, and Paul R. Goldin, eds. *A Source Book of Ancient Chinese Bronze Inscriptions*. Berkeley: Society for the Study of Early China, 2016.
Cook, Scott. "The *Lüshi chunqiu* and the Resolution of Philosophical Dissonance." *Harvard Journal of Asian Studies* 62.2 (2002): 307–45.
Cook, Scott, ed. *Hiding the World in the World: Uneven Discourses on the Zhuangzi*. Albany: SUNY Press, 2003.
Cook, Scott. "K'ang Shu of Wey, Hereditary House 7." In Nienhauser, ed., 2006, 241–64.
Cook, Scott. *The Bamboo Texts at Guodian: A Study and Complete Translation*. 2 vols. Ithaca: Cornell East Asia Series, 2012.
Creel, Herrlee Glessner. "The Beginnings of Bureaucracy in China: The Origin of the *Hsien*." In *What Is Taoism? and Other Studies in Chinese Cultural History*. Midway Reprint. Chicago and London: University of Chicago Press, 1970, 121–59.
Creel, Herrlee Glessner. *The Origins of Statecraft in China*. Chicago: University of Chicago Press, 1970.
Creel, Herrlee Glessner. *Shen Pu-hai: A Chinese Political Philosopher of the Fourth Century B.C.* Chicago and London: University of Chicago Press, 1974.
Crump, J. I. *Intrigues: Studies of the Chan-kuo Ts'e*. Ann Arbor: University of Michigan Press, 1964.
Crump, J. I., tr. *Chan-kuo Ts'e*. Revised edition. Michigan Monographs in Chinese Studies 77. Ann Arbor: University of Michigan Press, 1996.
Csikszentmihalyi, Mark. "Confucius." In David Noel Freedman and Michael J. McClymond, eds., *The Rivers of Paradise: Moses, Buddha, Confucius, Jesus, and Muhammad as Religious Founders*. Grand Rapids and Cambridge: William B. Eerdmans, 2001, 233–308.
Csikszentmihalyi, Mark, and Philip J. Ivanhoe, eds. *Religious and Philosophical Aspects of the Laozi*. Albany: SUNY Press, 1999.
Defoort, Carine. "Ruling the World with Words: The Idea of *Zhengming* in the *Shizi*." *The Bulletin of the Museum of Far Eastern Antiquities* 73 (2001): 217–42.
Defoort, Carine, and Nicolas Standaert, eds. *The Mozi as an Evolving Text: Different Voices in Early Chinese Thought*. Leiden: Brill, 2013.
Defoort, Carine, and Ting-mien Lee, eds. *The Many Lives of Yang Zhu: A Historical Overview*. Albany: SUNY Press, 2022.
Denecke, Wiebke. *The Dynamics of Masters Literature: Early Chinese Thought from Confucius to Han Feizi*. Cambridge, MA: Harvard University Press, 2010.
Di Cosmo, Nicola. *Ancient China and Its Enemies: The Rise of Nomadic Power in East Asian History*. Cambridge: Cambridge University Press, 2002.
Dickens, Charles. *A Tale of Two Cities*. London: Chapman and Hall, 1859.
Dong Chuping 董楚平. *Wu Yue Xu Shu jinwen jishi* 吳越徐舒金文集釋. Hangzhou: Zhejiang guji chubanshe, 1992.
Dong Shuoyuan 董說 (1620–86 CE). *Qiguo kao ding bu* 七國考訂補. 2 vols. Miao Wenyuan 繆文遠, ed. Shanghai: Shanghai guji chubanshe, 1987.
Doty, Paul Darrel. "The Bronze Inscriptions of Ch'i: An Interpretation." Ph.D. Dissertation, University of Washington, 1982, 616–17.

Du Heng. "From Villains Outwitted to Pedants Out-Wrangled: The Function of Anecdotes in the Shifting Rhetoric of the *Han Feizi*." In van Els and Queen, eds., 2017, 193–228.

Durrant, Stephen W. *The Cloudy Mirror: Tension and Conflict in the Writings of Sima Qian*. Albany: SUNY Press, 1995.

Durrant, Stephen W., tr. "Those Whose Goods Increase, Memoir 69." In Nienhauser, ed., 2019, 263–310.

Durrant, Stephen, Wai-yi Lee, and David Schaberg, trs. *Zuo Tradition/Zuozhuan* 左傳: *Commentary on the "Spring and Autumn Annals."* 3 vols. Classics of Chinese Thought. Seattle: University of Washington Press, 2016.

Fan Xiangyong 范祥雍. *Guben zhushu jinian jijiao dingbu* 古本竹書紀年輯校訂補. Shanghai: Xinzhishi chubanshe, 1956.

Fan Xiangyong. "Su Qin hezong Liuguo niandai kaoxin 蘇秦合縱六國年代考信." *Zhonghua wenshi luncong* 中華文史論叢 1985.5: 1–25.

Fan Xiangyong. *Zhanguo ce jian zheng* 戰國策箋證. 2 vols. Shanghai: Shanghai guji chubanshe, 2006.

Fan Ye 范曄 (398–446 CE). *Hou Han shu* 後漢書 (HHS). Beijing: Zhonghua shuju, 1965.

Fang Shouchu 方授楚. *Moxue yuanliu* 墨學源流. Shanghai: Zhonghua shuju, 1937.

Fingarette, Herbert. *Confucius: The Secular as Sacred*. New York: Harper and Row, 1972; rpt, Schwartz, 1985.

Flad, Rowan, and Chen Pochan. *Ancient Central China: Centers and Peripheries along the Yangzi River*. Cambridge: Cambridge University Press, 2013.

Fontana, Michela. *Matteo Ricci: A Jesuit in the Ming*. Lanham: Rowan and Littlefield, 2011.

Fraser, Chris. *The Philosophy of the Mòzǐ: The First Consequentialists*. New York: Columbia University, 2016.

Fu Xinian 傅熹年. *Traditional Chinese Architecture: Twelve Essays*. Nancy S. Steinhardt, tr. Princeton: Princeton University Press, 2017.

Fung Yu-lan 馮友蘭. *A History of Chinese Philosophy*, Vol. I. Derk Bodde, tr. Princeton: Princeton University Press, 1952.

Galvany, Albert. "The Army, War, and Military Arts during the Warring States Period." In Childs-Johnson, ed., 2020, 637–56.

Gawlikowski, Krzysztof, and Michael Loewe. "*Sun tzu ping fa* 孫子兵法." In Loewe, ed., 1993, 446–55.

Gödel, Kurt. "On Undecidable Proposition of Formal Mathematical Systems." In Feferman, Solomon, et al., eds. *Collected Works*, Vol. I: *Publications 1929–1936*. New York: Oxford University Press, 1986, 346–71.

Goldin, Paul R. *Rituals of the Way: The Philosophy of Xunzi*. Chicago and La Salle: Open Court, 1999.

Goldin, Paul R. "Personal Names in Early China: A Research Note." *Journal of the American Oriental Society* 120.1 (2000): 77–81.

Goldin, Paul R. *The Culture of Sex in Ancient China*. Honolulu: University of Hawaii Press, 2002.

Goldin, Paul R. "Li Si: Chancellor of the Universe." In *After Confucius: Studies in Early Chinese Philosophy*. Honolulu: University of Hawaii Press, 2005, 66–75.

Goldin, Paul R. "Persistent Misconceptions about Chinese 'Legalism.'" *Journal of Chinese Philosophy* 38.1 (2011): 88–104.

Goldin, Paul R., ed. *Dao Companion to the Philosophy of Han Fei*. Dao Companions to Chinese Philosophy 2. Dordrecht: Springer, 2013.

Goldin, Paul R. "Confucius and His Disciples in the *Lunyu*: The Basis for the Traditional View." In Michael Hunter and Martin Kern, eds., *Confucius and the* Analects *Revisited: New Perspectives on Composition, Dating, and Authorship*. Studies in the History of Chinese Texts 11. Leiden and Boston: Brill, 2018, 92–115.

Goldin, Paul R. *The Art of Chinese Philosophy: Eight Classical Texts and How to Read Them*. Princeton: Princeton University Press, 2020.

Goldin, Paul R. "Etymological Notes on Early Chinese Aristocratic Titles." *T'oung Pao* 107.3–4 (2021): 475–80.

Goodrich, Chauncey S. "Ssu-ma Ch'ien's Biography of Wu Ch'i." *Monumenta Serica* 35 (1981–83): 197–233.

Graff, David. *Medieval Chinese Warfare 300-900*. London: Routledge, 2002.

Graham, Angus. *Later Mohist Logic, Ethics and Science*. Hong Kong: Chinese University Press, 1978.

Graham, Angus. "The 'Nung-chia' 農家 'School of the Tillers' and the Origins of Peasant Utopianism in China." *Bulletin of the School of Oriental and African Studies* 42.1 (1979): 66–100.

Graham, Angus, tr. *Chuang-tzǔ: The Inner Chapters*. London and Boston: George Allen & Unwin, 1981.

Graham, Angus. *Disputers of the Dao*. La Salle: Open Court, 1989.

Graham, Angus. *Studies in Chinese Philosophy and Philosophical Literature*. Albany: SUNY Press, 1990.

Gu Donggao 顧棟高 (1679–1759 CE). *Chunqiu dashibiao* 春秋大事表. 3 vols. Wu Shuping 吳樹平 and Li Jiemin 李解民, eds. Beijing: Zhonghua shuju, 1995.

Guo Moruo *Tiandi xuanhuang* 天地玄黃. Shanghai: Dafu chubanshe, 1947.

Guo Moruo 郭沫若 (1892–1978 CE). " *Shi pipan shu* 十批判書. Beijing: Dongfang chubanshe, 1996.

Guo Qingfan 郭慶藩. *Zhuangzi jishi* 莊子集釋. Beijing: Zhonghua shuju, 1985.

Habberstad, Luke. "Texts, Performance, and Spectacle: The Funeral Procession of Marquis Yi of Zeng, 433 BCE." *Early China* 37 (2014): 181–219.

Hansen, Chad. *A Daoist Theory of Chinese Thought*. New York: Oxford University Press, 1992.

Harrington, John, and Thomas C. Frolich, "Forty-Two Mega Cities of the Ancient World." *24/7 Wall Street*. August 6, 2018, https://247wallst.com/special-report/2018/08/06/42-mega-cities-of-the-ancient-world/.

Harris, Eirik Lang, tr. *The* Shenzi Fragments*: A Philosophical Analysis and Translation*. New York: Columbia University Press, 2016.

Hassan, Zheger. "Kurdish Nationalism: What Are Its Origins?" *International Journal of Contemporary Iraqi Studies* 7.2 (2013): 75–89.

Hawkes, David, tr. *The Songs of the South: An Anthology of Ancient Chinese Poems by Qu Yuan and Other Poets*. Harmondsworth: Penguin, 1985.

He Hao 何浩 and Liu Binhui 劉彬徽, "Baoshan Chujian fengjun shidi 包山楚簡封君釋地." Hubeisheng Jingsha tielu kaogudui, 1991, 569–79.

Henderson, John B. *The Development and Decline of Chinese Cosmology*, New York: Columbia University Press, 1983.

Henry, Eric. "The Submerged History of Yuè." *Sino-Platonic Papers* 176 (2007): 1–36.

Henry, Eric. *Garden of Eloquence (Shuoyuan* 說苑*)*. Seattle: University of Washington Press, 2021.

Hoffert, Brian. "Beyond Life and Death: Zhuangzi's Great Awakening." *Journal of Daoist Studies* 8 (2015): 165–78.

Hsiao, Kung-chuan. 蕭公權, *A History of Chinese Political Thought*, Vol. I: *From the Beginning to the Sixth Century A.D.* F. W. Mote, tr. Princeton: Princeton University Press, 1979.

Hsing I-t'ien 邢義田, "Qin-Han Census and Tax and Corvée Administration." In Pines et al., eds., 2014, 155–86.

Hsu Cho-yun 許倬雲. *Ancient China in Transition*. Stanford: Stanford University Press, 1965.

Hsu Cho-yun. "The Spring and Autumn Period." In Loewe and Shaughnessy, eds., 1999, 545–86.

Huang, Honyu, tr. "The Duke of Shao, Hereditary House 4." In Niehauser, ed., 2006, 169–90.

Hulsewé, A. F. P. *Remnants of Ch'in Law: An Annotated Translation of the Ch'in Legal and Administrative Rules of the 3rd century B.C. Discovered in Yün-meng Prefecture, Hu-pei Province, in 1975*. Sinica Leidensia 17. Leiden: Brill, 1985.

Hunter, Michael. *Confucius beyond the* Analects. Studies in the History of Chinese Texts. Leiden and Boston: Brill, 2017.

Hunter, Michael, and Martin Kern, eds. *Confucius and the* Analects *Revisited: New Perspectives on Composition, Dating, and Authorship*. Studies in the History of Chinese Texts 11. Leiden and Boston: Brill, 2018.

Hutton, Eric L. *Xunzi: The Complete Text*. Princeton: Princeton University Press, 2014.

Hutton, Eric L., ed. *Dao Companion to the Philosophy of Xunzi*. Dordrecht: Springer, 2016.

Ikeda Yuichi 池田雄一. *Chūgoku kodai no ritsuryō to shakai* 中國古代の律令と社會. Tokyo: Kyūko shoin, 2008.

Indraccolo, Lisa. "The 'White Horse,' the 'Three-Legged Chicken' and Other Paradoxes in Classical Chinese Literature." *Antiquorum Philosophia* 10 (2016): 67–88.

Jacoby, Marcin. "*Lüshi chunqiu* and the Value-Based Leadership Model in Ancient China." *Roczniki humanistyczne* 70.9 (2022): 5–26.

Jacoby, Marcin, and James Sellman, eds. *Dao Companion to the Philosophy of the* Lüshi Chunqiu 呂氏春秋: *Political Thought, Metaphysics, and the Ethics of Leadership in Ancient China*. Dordrecht: Springer, forthcoming.

Jensen, Lionel. *Manufacturing Confucianism: Chinese Traditions and Universal Civilization*. Durham: Duke University Press, 1997.

Jia Yi 賈誼 (d. 169 BCE.). *Xin shu jiaozhu* 新書校注. Beijing: Zhonghua shuju, 2000.

Jiang Yonglin. *The Mandate of Heaven and the Great Ming Code*. Seattle: University of Washington Press, 2011.

Johnson, Wallace. *The T'ang Code*, Vol. I: *General Principles*. Princeton: Princeton University Press, 1979.

Johnson, David. "The Wu Tzu-hsü *pien-wen* and Its Sources." *HJAS* 40.1 (1980): 93–156; 40.2 (1980): 465–505.

Johnston, Ian, tr. *Mozi: A Complete Translation*. Hong Kong: Chinese University Press, 2010.

Jones, Sian. *The Archaeology of Ethnicity*. New York: Routledge, 1997.

Kalinowski, Marc. "Les justifications historiques du gouvernement ideal dans le *Lüshi chunqiu*." *Bulletin de l'Ecole Française d'Extrême-Orient* 68 (1980): 155–208.

Keightley, David N. "The Shang: China's First Historical Dynasty." In Loewe and Shaughnessy, eds., 232–91.

Keightley, David N. *The Ancestral Landscape: Time, Space, and Community in Late Shang China (ca. 1200–1045 B.C.)*. China Research Monograph 53. Berkeley: Institute of East Asian Studies, 2000.

Kern, Martin. *The Stele Inscriptions of Ch'in Shih-Huang: Text and Ritual in Early Imperial Representation*. New Haven: American Oriental Society, 2000.

Kern, Martin, ed. *Text and Ritual Context in Early China*. Seattle: University of Washington Press, 2005.

Kern, Martin. "Qin Gong *Bo*, Qin Gong *Gui*, and Qing Gong *Yongzheng*." In Cook and Goldin, eds., 2016, 243–48.
Kern, Martin, and Stephen Owen, eds. *Qu Yuan and the* Chuci*: New Approaches*. Leiden: Brill, 2023.
Kinney, Anne Behnke, tr. *Exemplary Women of Early China*. New York: Columbia University Press, 2014.
Klein, Esther. "Were There 'Inner Chapters' in the Warring States? A New Examination of Evidence about the *Zhuangzi*." *T'oung Pao* 96.4–5 (2010): 299–369.
Knickerbocker, Bruce, tr. "T'ai-kung of Ch'i, Hereditary House 2." In William Nienhauser Jr., ed., *The Grand Scribe's Records*, Vol. V.1: *The Hereditary Houses of Pre-Han China*, Part 1. Bloomington: Indiana University Press, 2006.
Knoblock, John. "The Chronology of Xunzi's Works." *Early China* 8 (1982–83), 28–52.
Knoblock, John. *Xunzi: A Translation and Study of the Complete Works*, Vol. I. Stanford: Stanford University Press, 1988.
Knoblock, John, and Jeffrey Riegel, trs. *The Annals of Lü Buwei*. Stanford: Stanford University Press, 2000.
Knoblock, John, and Jeffrey Riegel. *Mozi: A Study and Translation of the Ethical and Political Writings*. China Research Monograph 68. Berkeley: Institute of East Asian Studies, 2013.
Kong Yingda 孔穎達. *Chunqiu Zuozhuan zhengyi* 春秋左傳正義, in Ma Xinming 馬辛民, ed., *Shisanjing zhushu* 十三經注疏. 26 vols. Beijing: Beijing daxue chubanshe, 2000, vols. 16–19.
LaFargue, Michael, tr. *The Tao of the Tao Te Ching: A Translation and Commentary*. Albany: SUNY Press, 1992.
Lagerway, John, and Marc Kalinoski, eds. *Early Chinese Religions: Shang through Han (1250 BC–220 AD)*. Leiden: Brill, 2009.
Lam, Wengcheong. "Iron Technology and Its Regional Development during the Eastern Zhou Period." In Childs-Johnson, ed., *The Oxford Handbook of Early China*, 2020, 595–614.
Lander, Brian. *The Kings Harvest: A Political Ecology of China from the First Farmers to the First Empire*. Yale: Yale University Press, 2021.
Lattimore, Owen. *Inner Asian Frontiers of China*. New York: American Geographical Society, 1940; rpt, Oxford: Oxford University Press, 1988.
Lau, D.C., tr. *Lao Tzu: Tao Te Ching*. Harmondsworth: Penguin, 1963.
Lau, D. C., tr. *Mencius*. Harmondsworth: Penguin, 1970.
Lau, D. C., tr. *The Analects*. Harmondsworth: Penguin, 1979.
Lau, D. C. 劉殿爵, and Chen Fangzheng 陳方正, eds. *Bing shu si zhong zhuzi suoyin* 兵書四種逐字索引 (The ICS Ancient Chinese Text Concordance Series). Hong Kong: Commercial Press, 1992.
Lau, D. C., and Chen Fangzheng, eds. *Chu ci zhuzi suoyin* 楚辭逐字索引 (The ICS Ancient Chinese Text Concordance Series). Hong Kong: Commercial Press, 2000.
Lau, D. C., and Chen Fangzheng, eds. *Chunqiu Zuozhuan zhuzi suoyin* 春秋左傳逐字索引 (The ICS Ancient Chinese Text Concordance Series). Hong Kong: Commercial Press, 1995.
Lau, D. C., and Chen Fangzheng, eds. *Gongyang zhuan zhuzi suoyin* 公羊逐字索引 (The ICS Ancient Chinese Text Concordance Series). Hong Kong: Commercial Press, 1995.
Lau, D. C., and Chen Fangzheng, eds. *Guanzi zhuzi suoyin* 管子逐字索引 (The ICS Ancient Chinese Text Concordance Series). Hong Kong: Commercial Press, 2001.
Lau, D. C., and Chen Fangzheng, eds. *Guliang zhuan zhuzi suoyin* 穀梁傳逐字索引 (The ICS Ancient Chinese Text Concordance Series). Hong Kong: Commercial Press, 1995.

Lau, D. C., and Chen Fangzheng, eds. *Gulienüzhuan suoyin* 古列女傳逐字索引 (The ICS Ancient Chinese Text Concordance Series). Hong Kong: Commercial Press, 1993.

Lau, D. C., and Chen Fangzheng, eds. *Guo yu zhuzi suoyin* 國語逐字索引 (The ICS Ancient Chinese Text Concordance Series). Hong Kong: Commercial Press, 1999.

Lau, D. C., and Chen Fangzheng, eds. *Han Feizi zhuzi suoyin* 韓非子逐字索引 (The ICS Ancient Chinese Text Concordance Series). Hong Kong: Commercial Press, 2000.

Lau, D. C., and Chen Fangzheng, eds. *Hanshi waizhuan zhuzi suoyin* 韓詩外傳逐字索引 (The ICS Ancient Chinese Text Concordance Series). Hong Kong: Commercial Press, 1992.

Lau, D. C., and Chen Fangzheng, eds. *Huainanzi zhuzi suoyin* 淮南子逐字索引 (The ICS Ancient Chinese Text Concordance Series). Hong Kong: Commercial Press, 1992.

Lau, D. C., and Chen Fangzheng, eds. *Li ji zhuzi suoyin* 禮記逐字索引 (The ICS Ancient Chinese Text Concordance Series). Hong Kong: Commercial Press, 1992.

Lau, D. C., and Chen Fangzheng, eds. *Lunyu zhuzi suoyin* 論語逐字索引 (The ICS Ancient Chinese Text Concordance Series). Hong Kong: Commercial Press, 2006.

Lau, D.C., and Chen Fangzheng, eds. *Lüshi chunqiu zhuzi suoyin* 呂氏春秋逐字索引 (The ICS Ancient Chinese Text Concordance Series). Hong Kong: Commercial Press, 2004.

Lau, D.C., and Chen Fangzheng, eds. *Maoshi zhuzi suoyin* 毛詩逐字索引 (The ICS Ancient Chinese Text Concordance Series). Hong Kong: Commercial Press, 1995.

Lau, D.C., and Chen Fangzheng, eds. *Mengzi zhuzi suoyin* 孟子逐字索引 (The ICS Ancient Chinese Text Concordance Series). Hong Kong: Commercial Press, 1995.

Lau, D.C., and Chen Fangzheng, eds. *Mozi zhuzi suoyin* 墨子逐字索引 (The ICS Ancient Chinese Text Concordance Series). Hong Kong: Commercial Press, 2001.

Lau, D.C., and Chen Fangzheng, eds. *Shangjun shu zhuzi suoyin* 商君書逐字索引 (The ICS Ancient Chinese Text Concordance Series). Hong Kong: Commercial Press, 1992.

Lau, D.C., and Chen Fangzheng, eds. *Shenzi, Shizi, Shenzi zhuzi suoyin* 申子, 尸子, 慎子逐字索引 (The ICS Ancient Chinese Text Concordance Series). Hong Kong: Commercial Press, 2000.

Lau, D.C., and Chen Fangzheng, eds. *Shuo yuan zhuzi suoyin* 說苑逐字索引 (The ICS Ancient Chinese Text Concordance Series). Hong Kong: Commercial Press, 1992.

Lau, D.C., and Chen Fangzheng, eds. *Wu Yue chunqiu zhuzi suoyin* 吳越春秋逐字索引 (The ICS Ancient Chinese Text Concordance Series). Hong Kong: Commercial Press, 1993.

Lau, D.C., and Chen Fangzheng, eds. *Xin xu zhuzi suoyin* 新序逐字索引 (The ICS Ancient Chinese Text Concordance Series). Hong Kong: Commercial Press, 1992.

Lau, D.C., and Chen Fangzheng, eds. Yanzi chunqiu zhuzi suoyin 晏子春秋逐字索引 (The ICS Ancient Chinese Text Concordance Series). Hong Kong: Commercial Press, 1994.

Lau, D.C., and Chen Fangzheng, eds. *Yi Zhou shu zhuzi suoyin* 逸周書逐字索引 (The ICS Ancient Chinese Text Concordance Series). Hong Kong: Commercial Press, 1992.

Lau, D.C., and Chen Fangzheng, eds. *Zhanguo ce zhuzi suoyin* 戰國策逐字索引 (The ICS Ancient Chinese Text Concordance Series). Hong Kong: Commercial Press, 1992.

Lau, D.C., and Chen Fangzheng, eds. *Zhouyi zhuzi suoyin*. 周易逐字索引 (The ICS Ancient Chinese Text Concordance Series). Hong Kong: Commercial Press, 1995.

Lau, D.C., and Chen Fangzheng, eds. *Zhuangzi zhuzi suoyin* 莊子逐字索引 (The ICS Ancient Chinese Text Concordance Series). Hong Kong: Commercial Press, 2000.

Lau, D.C., and Chen Fangzheng, eds. *Zhushu jinian zhuzi suoyin* 竹書紀年逐字索引 (The ICS Ancient Chinese Text Concordance Series). Hong Kong: Commercial Press, 1998.

Leblanc, Charles. *Huai Nan Tzu: Philosophical Synthesis in Early Han Thought*. Hong Kong: Hong Kong University Press, 1985.

Legge, James. *The Chinese Classics*, Vol. 3: *The Shoo King, or Book of Historical Documents*. Hong Kong: Hong Kong University Press, 1960a.
Legge, James. *The Chinese Classics*, Vol. 4: *The She King*. Hong Kong: Hong Kong University Press, 1960b.
Leung, Victor S. *The Politics of the Past in Early China*. Cambridge: Cambridge University Press, 2019.
Levi, Jean. "*Shang chün shu*." In Loewe, ed., 1993, 368–75.
Lewis, Mark Edward. *Sanctioned Violence in Early China*. Albany: State University of New York Press, 1990.
Lewis, Mark Edward. "Warring States Political History." In Loewe and Shaughnessy, eds., 587–650.
Lewis, Mark Edward. *Writing and Authority in Early China*. Albany: State University of New York Press, 1999b.
Lewis, Mark Edward. *The Early Chinese Empires: Qin and Han*. Cambridge, MA: Harvard University Press, 2007.
Lewis, Mark Edward. *Honor and Shame in Early China*. Cambridge: Cambridge University Press, 2021.
Li Chenyang 李晨陽, ed. *The Sage and the Second Sex: Confucianism, Ethics, and Gender*. Chicago and La Salle: Open Court, 2000.
Li Fang 李昉 (925–996 CE), et al. *Taiping yulan* 太平御覽. 9 vols. Shanghai: Shanghai guji chubanshe, 1994.
Li Feng 李峰. *Landscape and Power in Early China: The Crisis and Fall of the Western Zhou*. Cambridge: Cambridge University Press, 2006.
Li Feng 李峰. *Bureaucracy and the State in Early China: Governing the Western Zhou*. Cambridge: Cambridge University Press, 2008.
Li Feng 李峰. "Literacy and the Social Contexts of Writing in the Western Zhou." In Li Feng and David Prager Branner, eds. *Writing and Literacy in Early China: Studies from the Columbia Early China Seminar*. Seattle: University of Washington Press, 2011, 271–301.
Li Feng 李峰. *Early China: A Social and Cultural History*. New Approaches to Asian History 12. Cambridge: Cambridge University Press, 2013.
Li Xueqin. *Eastern Zhou and Qin Civilizations*. K. C. Chang, tr. New Haven: Yale University Press, 1985.
Li, Wai-yee. *The Readability of the Past in Early Chinese Historiography*. Harvard East Asian Monographs 253. Cambridge, MA: Harvard University Press, 2007.
Li, Wai-yee. "Poetry and Diplomacy in the *Zuozhuan*." *Journal of Chinese Literature and Culture* 1 (2014): 241–61.
Liang Yusheng 梁玉繩 (1744 CE–1792 CE). *Shiji zhiyi* 史記志疑. 3 vols. Beijing: Zhonghua shuju, 1981.
Lieu, S. N. C. "From Qin (Ch'in) to Cathay: Names for China and the Chinese on the Silk Road." *Medieval History Journal* 27.1 (2024): 12–68.
Lin Jianming 林劍鳴. *Qinshi gao* 秦史稿. Shanghai: Shanghai renmin chubanshe, 1981.
Lin Li'e 林麗娥. *Xian Qin Qixue kao* 先秦齊學考. Taibei: Commercial Press, 1992.
Liu, James J. Y. 劉若愚. *The Chinese Knight-Errant*. Chicago: University of Chicago Press, 1967.
Liu Xiaogan 劉笑敢. *Classifying the Zhuangzi Chapters*. William E. Savage, tr. Ann Arbor: Michigan University Press, 1994.
Liu Yang, ed. *China's Terracotta Warriors: The First Emperor's Legacy*. Minneapolis: Minneapolis Institute of Arts, 2012.

Liu Zehua 劉則華. *Xian Qin shi ren yu shehui* 先秦士人與社會 (revised). Tianjin: Tianjin renmin chubanshe, 2004.
Loewe, Michael. "The Orders of Aristocratic Rank of Han China." *T'oung Pao* 48.1–3 (1960): 97–174.
Loewe, Michael. "The Former Han Dynasty." In Twitchett and Loewe, eds., 1986, 103–222.
Loewe, Michael, ed. *Early Chinese Texts: A Bibliographical Guide*. Berkeley: The Society for the Study of Early China, 1993.
Loewe, Michael and Edward L. Shaughnessy, eds. *The Cambridge History of Ancient China: From the Origins of Civilization to 221 B.C.* Cambridge: Cambridge University Press, 1999.
Lorge, Peter A. *Chinese Martial Arts: From Antiquity to the Twenty-First Century*. Cambridge: Cambridge University Press, 2012.
Lu Xun 魯迅. *The Real Story of Ah Q and Other Tales of China: The Complete Fiction of Lu Xun*. Julia Lovell, tr. London: Penguin, 2009.
Luo, Xinhui 羅新慧 and Yuri Pines 尤銳. "The Elusive Mandate of Heaven: Changing Views of Tianming 天命 in the Eastern Zhou Period." *T'oung Pao* 109.1–2 (2023): 1–47.
Luo Zhufeng 羅竹風 et al., eds. *Hanyu dacidian* 漢語大辭典. 12 vols. Shanghai: Hanyudacidian chubanshe, 1990.
Lynn, Richard John, tr. *The Classic of Changes*. New York: Columbia University Press, 1994.
Ma Chengyuan 馬承源, ed. *Shang Zhou qingtong mingwen xuan* 商周青銅器銘文選. Beijing: Wenwu chubanshe, 1988.
Ma Febai 馬非百. *Qin jishi* 秦集史. Beijing: Zhonghua shuju, 1982.
Ma Guohan 馬國翰 (1794–1857 CE). *Yuhan shanfang jiyishu* 玉函山房輯佚書. 8 vols. Yangzhou: Jiangsu guangling guji keyingshe, 1990.
Ma Su 馬驌 (1621–73 CE), *Yi shi* 繹史. 10 vols. Beijing: Zhonghua shuju, 2002.
Macdonald, Barry. *Cinderellas of Empire: Towards a History of Kiribati and Tuvalu*. Canberra: Australian National University Press, 1982.
Mair, Victor H., ed. *The Shorter Columbia Anthology of Traditional Chinese Literature*. New York: Columbia University Press, 2000.
Mair, Victor H., tr. *The Art of War: Sun Zi's Military Methods*. New York: Columbia University Press, 2007.
Major, John S., Sarah A. Queen, Andrew Seth Meyer, and Harold D. Roth, trs. *The Huainanzi: A Guide to the Theory and Practice of Government in Early Han China*. Translations from the Asian Classics. New York: Columbia University Press, 2010.
Major, John S., and Constance A. Cook. *Ancient China: A History*. London and New York: Routledge, 2016.
Mann, Michael. *The Sources of Social Power*, Vol. 1: *A History of Power from the Beginning to A.D. 1760*. Cambridge: Cambridge University Press, 1986.
Marks, Robert. *China: Its Environment and History*. Lanham: Rowman and Littlefield, 2012.
Maspero, Henri. "Le Roman de Sou Ts'in." *Études Asiatiques Publieé à l'occasion vingt-cinquieme anniversaire de l'École Français d'Extrême Orient*, Vol. 2. Paris: G. Van Oest, 1925, 127–41.
Matsui Yoshinori 松井嘉德. *Shū dai kokusei no kenyū* 周代國制の研究. Kyūko sōsho, Vol. 34. Tokyo: Kyūko Shoin, 2002.
Mawangdu Hanmu boshu zhengli xiaozu 馬王堆漢墓帛書整理小組, ed. *Mawangdui Hanmu boshu Zhanguo zonghengjia shu* 馬王堆漢墓帛書戰果從橫家書. Beijing: Wenwu chubanshe, 1976.
McNeal, Robin. *Conquer and Govern: Early Chinese Military Texts from the* Yi Zhou shu. Honolulu: University of Hawaii Press, 2012.

Meacham, William. "Origins and Development of the Yüeh Coastal Neolithic: A Microcosm of Culture Change on the Mainland of East Asia." In David N. Keightley, ed., *The Origins of Chinese Civilization*. Berkeley: University of California Press, 1983, 147–75.

Meyer, Andrew. "'The Altars of the Soil and Grain are Closer Than Kin' 社稷戚於親: The Qi 齊 Model of Intellectual Participation and the Jixia 稷下 Patronage Community." *Early China* 33–34 (2010–11): 37–99.

Meyer, Andrew. "What Made Mo Di A Master? Exploring the Construction of a Category in Warring States Sources." *T'oung Pao* 101.4–5 (2015): 271–97.

Meyer, Andrew. "Reading 'Sunzi' as a Master." *Asia Major* (third series) 30.1 (2017): 1–24.

Meyer, Andrew. "Yangism, 'Valuing Life,' and the *Lüshi chunqiu*." In Jacoby and Sellman, eds., forthcoming.

Meyer, Andrew, and Andrew Wilson. "*Sunzi bingfa* as History and Theory." In Bradford A. Lee and Karl F. Walling, eds., *Strategic Logic and Political Rationality: Essays in Honor of Michael I. Handel*. London: Frank Cass, 2003, 95–113.

Meyer, Andrew, and Andrew Wilson. "Inventing the General: A Reappraisal of the *Sunzi bingfa*." In Mark L. Perry, ed., *War, Virtual War and Societies: The Challenge to Communities*. Leiden: Brill, 2008, 151–68.

Meyer, Dirk. *Philosophy on Bamboo: Text and the Production of Meaning in Early China*. Studies in the History of Chinese Texts 2. Leiden: Brill, 2012.

Milburn, Olivia. "Kingship and Inheritance in the State of Wu: Fraternal Succession in Spring and Autumn Period China (770–475 BC)." *T'oung Pao* (2nd series) 90.4/5 (2004): 195–214.

Milburn, Olivia. "Marked for Greatness? Perceptions of Deformity and Physical Impairment in Ancient China." *Monumenta Serica* 55 (2007): 1–22.

Milburn, Olivia. *The Glory of Yue: An Annotated Translation of the* Yuejue shu. Leiden: Brill, 2010.

Milburn, Olivia. *Cherishing Antiquity: The Cultural Construction of an Ancient Chinese Kingdom*. Cambridge: Harvard University Press, 2013a.

Milburn, Olivia. "The Silent Beauty: Changing Portrayals of Xi Shi, from *zhiguai* and Poetry to Ming Fiction and Drama." *Asia Major* (third series) 26.1 (2013b): 23–53.

Milburn, Olivia. *The Spring and Autumn Annals of Master Yan*. Sinica Leidensia 128. Leiden and Boston: Brill, 2016.

Milburn, Olivia. "Rape in Early China: Two Case Studies." *Bulletin of the School of Oriental and African Studies* 86.2 (2023): 277–91.

Miller, Brian K. *Xiongnu: The World's First Nomadic Empire*. Oxford: Oxford University Press, 2024.

Mithen, Steven. *Thirst: Water and Power in the Ancient World*. Cambridge, MA: Harvard University Press, 2012.

Morrish, Mike. "The Living Geography of China." *Geography* 82.1 (1997): 3–16.

Mu-chou Poo. *Daily Life in Ancient China*. Cambridge: Cambridge University Press, 2018.

Nienhauser, William H. Jr., ed. *The Grand Scribe's Records*, Vol. I: *The Basic Annals of Pre-Han China*. Bloomington: Indiana University Press, 1994a.

Nienhauser, William H. Jr., *The Grand Scribe's Records*, Vol. VII: *The Memoirs of Pre-Han China*. Bloomington: Indiana University Press, 1994b.

Nienhauser, William H. Jr., *The Grand Scribe's Records*, Vol. V.1: *The Hereditary Houses of Pre-Han China*, Part 1. Bloomington: Indiana University Press, 2006.

Nienhauser, William H. Jr., *The Grand Scribe's Records*, Vol. XI: *The Memoirs of Han China*, Part IV. Bloomington: Indiana University Press, 2019.

Nylan, Michael, and Thomas Wilson. *Lives of Confucius: Civilization's Greatest Sage through the Ages*. New York: Doubleday Religion, 2010.

Peng Ke. "Coinage and Commercial Development in Eastern Zhou China." Ph.D. dissertation, University of Chicago, 2000, 208–12.

Peng Hao 彭浩. "Sericulture and Silk Weaving from Antiquity to the Zhou Dynasty." In Dieter Kuhn, ed., *Chinese Silks*. New Haven: Yale University Press, 2012, 65–114.

Peters, Heather A. "Towns and Trade: Cultural Diversity and Chu Daily Life." In Cook and Major, eds., 1999, 99–117.

Pian Yuqian 骿宇騫. *Yinque shan zhujian "Yanzi chunqiu" jiaoshi* 銀雀山竹簡 "晏子春秋" 校釋. Taibei: Wanjuan lou, 2000.

Picketty, Thomas. *Capital and Ideology*. Arthur Goldhammer, tr. Cambridge, MA: Harvard University Press, 2020.

Pines, Yuri. *Foundations of Confucian Thought: Intellectual Life in the Chunqiu Period, 722–453 BCE*. Honolulu: University of Hawaii Press, 2002.

Pines, Yuri. *Envisioning Eternal Empire: Chinese Political Thought of the Warring States*. Honolulu: University of Hawaii Press, 2009.

Pines, Yuri, tr. *The Book of Lord Shang: Apologetics of State Power in Early China*. Translations from the Asian Classics. New York: Columbia University Press, 2017.

Pines, Yuri. "Names and Titles in Eastern Zhou Texts." *T'oung Pao* 106.5–6 (2020): 714–20.

Pines, Yuri, Lothar von Falkenhausen, Gideon Shelach, and Robin D. S. Yates, eds. *Birth of an Empire: The State of Qin Revisited*. Berkeley: University of California Press, 2014.

Pirazzoli-t'Serstevens, Michèle. "Death and the Dead: Practices and Images in the Qin and Han." Tr. Margaret McIntosh. in Lagerway and Kalinowski, eds. 2009, 988–94.

Portal, Jane, ed., *The First Emperor: China's Terracotta Army*. Cambridge, MA: Harvard University Press, 2007.

Poundstone, William. *Prisoner's Dilemma*. New York: Anchor Books, 1993.

Puett, Michael. "Sages, Ministers and Rebels: Narratives from Early China Concerning the Initial Creation of the State." *Harvard Journal of Asiatic Studies* 58.2 (1998): 425–79.

Puett, Michael. *The Ambivalence of Creation: Debates Concerning Innovation and Artifice in Early China*. Stanford: Stanford University Press, 2001.

Puett, Michael. *To Become a God: Cosmology, Sacrifice and Self-Divinization in Early China*. Harvard-Yenching Institute Monograph Series 57. Cambridge, MA, and London: Harvard University Press, 2002.

Puett, Michael. "The Offering of Food and the Creation of Order: The Practice of Sacrifice in Early China." In Roel Sterckx, ed., *Of Tripod and Palate: Food Politics, and Religion in Traditional China*. New York: Palgrave MacMillan, 2005, 75–95.

Qian Mu 錢穆. *Xian Qin zhuzi xinian* 先秦諸子繫年. Shanghai: Shangwu, 1935.

Qian Mu. *Shi ji diming kao* 史記地名考. 2 vols. Beijing: Shangwu yingshu guan, 2001.

Qian Mu. *Mozi, Hui Shi, Gongsun Long* 墨子惠施公孫龍. Beijing: Jiuzhou chubanshe, 2011.

Qin Yanshi 秦彥士. *Mozi kaolun* 墨子考論. Chengdu: Bashu shuju, 2002.

Ramsey, S. Robert. *The Languages of China*. Princeton: Princeton University Press, 1987.

Rawson, Jessica. "Ancient Chinese Ritual as Seen in the Material Record." In Joseph P. McDermott, ed., *State and Court Ritual in China*. Cambridge: Cambridge University Press, 1999, 20–49.

Rawson, Jessica. *Life and Afterlife in Ancient China*. Seattle: University of Washington Press, 2023.

Raz, Gil. *The Emergence of Daoism: Creation of Tradition*. London and New York: Routledge, 2012.

Ren Jiyu 任繼愈. *Mozi yu Mojia* 墨子與墨家. Beijing: Beijing chubanshe, 2011.

Rickett, W. Allyn. *Guanzi: Political, Economic, and Philosophical Essays from Early China*, Vol. 1. Princeton: Princeton University Press, 1985.

Rickett, W. Allyn. "Kuan tzu." In Loewe, ed., 1993, 244–51.
Rickett, W. Allyn. *Guanzi: Political, Economic, and Philosophical Essays from Early China*, Vol. 2. Princeton: Princeton University Press, 1998.
Rohmer, Sax. *The Mystery of Doctor Fu-Manchu*. London: Methuen, 1913.
Rom, Avital H., ed. *Disability and Impairment in Early China: Other Bodies*. London: Routledge, 2025.
Rosen, Sydney. "In Search of the Historical Kuan Chung." *Journal of Asian Studies* 35.3 (1976): 431–40.
Rosen, Sydney. "Changing Conceptions of the Hegemon in Pre-Ch'in China." In David T. Roy and Tsuen-hsuin Tsien, eds., *Ancient China: Studies in Early Civilization*. Hong Kong: Chinese University Press, 1978, 99–114.
Roth, Harold D. "Psychology and Self-Cultivation in Early Daoistic Thought." *Harvard Journal of Asiatic Studies* 51.2 (1991): 599–650.
Roth, Harold D. *Original Dao: Inward Training and the Foundations of Daoist Mysticism*. New York: Columbia University Press, 1995.
Roth, Harold D. *Contemplative Foundations of Classical Daoism*. Albany: SUNY Press, 2021.
Rouzer, Paul. *Articulated Ladies: Gender and the Male Community in Early Chinese Texts*. Cambridge, MA: Harvard University Asia Center, 2001.
Ruan Tingzhuo 阮廷焯 (1936–93 CE). *Xian Qin zhuzi kaoyi* 先秦諸子考佚. Taibei: Dingwen shuju, 1980.
Sage, Steven F. *Ancient Sichuan and the Unifications of China*. Albany: SUNY Press, 1992.
Sanft, Charles. *Communication and Cooperation in Early Imperial China: Publicizing the Qin Dynasty*. Albany: SUNY Press, 2014.
Sato, Masayuki. *The Confucian Quest for Order: The Origin and Formation of the Political Thought of Xunzi*. Leiden: Brill, 2003.
Sawyer, Ralph. *The Seven Military Classics of Ancient China*. Boulder: Westview Press, 1993.
Sawyer, Ralph D., tr., with the collaboration of Mei-chün Lee Sawyer. *Sun Tzu: The Art of War*. Boulder: Westview, 1994.
Sawyer, Ralph. *Sun Pin: Military Methods*. Boulder: Westview Press, 1995.
Schaberg, David. *A Patterned Past: Form and Thought in Early Chinese Historiography*. Cambridge, MA: Harvard University Arts Center, 2001.
Schafer, Edward H. *The Vermillion Bird: T'ang Images of the South*. Berkeley: University of California Press, 1967.
Schneider, Laurence. *A Madman of Ch'u: The Chinese Myth of Loyalty and Dissent*. Berkeley: University of California Press, 1980.
Schwartz, Benjamin. *World of Thought in Ancient China*. Cambridge, MA: Harvard University Press, 1985.
Shaughnessy, Edward L. *Sources of Western Zhou History: Inscribed Bronze Vessels*. Berkeley: University of California Press, 1991.
Shaughnessy, Edward L., ed. *New Sources of Early Chinese History*. Early China Special Monograph Series 3. Berkeley: University of California Press, 1997.
Shaughnessy, Edward L. "Western Zhou History." In Michael Loewe and Edward L. Shaughnessy, eds. *The Cambridge History of Ancient China: From the Origins of Civilization to 221 B.C.* Cambridge: Cambridge University Press, 1999, 292–351.
Shaughnessy, Edward L. "A Bronze Inscription of the Western Chou." In Victor Mair, ed. *The Shorter Columbia Anthology of Traditional Chinese Literature*. New York: Columbia University Press, 2000, 4–5.
Seidel, Anna K. *La divinization de Lao Tseu dans le Taoisme des Han*. Paris: École Française d'Extrême-Orient, 1969.

Sellman, James. *Timing and Rulership in Master Lü's Spring and Autumn Annals (Lüshi chunqiu)*. Albany: SUNY Press, 2002.

She Sheqin. "Why Is 'A White Horse Not a Horse'? A New Perspective on Gongsun Long's 'A Discussion on the White Horse.'" *Asian Studies* 24.2 (2024): 273–308.

Shelach, Gideon. "Collapse or Transformation? Anthropological and Archaeological Perspectives on the Fall of Qin." In Pines et al., eds., 2014, 113–38.

Shelach-Lavi, Gideon. *The Archaeology of Early China: From Prehistory to the Han Dynasty*. Cambridge: Cambridge University Press, 2015.

Shi, Jie 施傑. "Incorporating All for One: The First Emperor's Tomb Mound." *Early China* 37 (2014): 359–91.

Shuihudi Qinmu zhujian zhengli xiao zu 睡虎地竹簡整理小組. *Shuihudi Qinmu zhujian* 睡虎地竹簡. Beijing: Wenwu chubanshe, 1990.

Sima Guang 司馬光 (1019–86 CE). *Zizhi tongjian* 資治通鑑. Beijing: Zhonghua shuju, 1956.

Sima Qian 司馬遷. *Shi ji* 史記. Beijing: Zhonghua shuju, 1962.

Sivin, Nathan. "The Myth of the Naturalists." In *Medicine, Philosophy and Religion in Ancient China*. Aldershot: Variorum, 1995, 4:1–33.

Smail, Daniel Lord. "Common Violence: Vengeance and Inquisition in Fourteenth Century Marseilles." *Past and Present* 151 (1996): 28–59.

Stalnaker, Aaron. "Aspects of Xunzi's Engagement with Early Daoism." *Philosophy East and West* 53.1 (2003): 87–129.

Sterckx, Roel. *Chinese Thought: From Confucius to Cook Ding*. London: Pelican, 2019.

Sun Yirang 孫詒讓 (1848–1908 CE). *Mozi jiangu* 墨子閒詁. Taibei: Huazheng shuju, 1987.

Swann, Nancy Lee. *Food and Money in Ancient China: The Earliest Economic History of China to A.D. 25*. Princeton: Princeton University Press, 1950.

Tadd, Misha. *The Complete Bibliography of Laozi Translations*. Tianjin: Nankai University Press, 2022.

Takigawa Sukenobu 瀧川資言 (1865–1946 CE), ed. 史記會注考證. 10 vols. Taiyuan: Beiyue wenyi chubanshe, 1999.

Tan Qixiang 譚其驤, ed. *Zhongguo lishi dituji* 中國歷史地圖集, Vol. 1. Shanghai: Ditu chubanshe, 1982.

Tang Lan 唐蘭 (1901–79 CE). "Sima Qian suo meiyou Jianguo de zhengui shiliao 司馬遷所沒有見過的珍貴史料." In Mawangdu Hanmu boshu zhengli xiaozu 馬王堆漢墓帛書整理小組, ed., *Mawangdui Hanmu boshu Zhanguo zonghengjia shu* 馬王堆漢墓帛書戰果從橫家書. Beijing: Wenwu chubanshe, 1976, 123–53.

Tao Xisheng 陶希聖. *Bianshi yu youxia* 辨士與遊俠. Shanghai: Commercial Press, 1933.

Taylor, Keith Weller. *The Birth of Vietnam*. Berkeley: University of California Press, 1983.

Teng Mingyu 滕銘予. "From Vassal State to Empire: An Archaeological Examination of Qin Culture." Susanna Lam, tr. In Pines et al., eds., 2014, 71–112.

Thompson, Paul M. *The Shen Tzu Fragments*. Oxford: Oxford University Press, 1979.

Tian Fengtai 田鳳台. *Lüshi chunqiu tanwei* 呂氏春秋探微. Taibei: Taiwan Xuesheng shuju, 1986.

Tsien, Tsuen-hsuin. *Written on Bamboo and Silk: The Beginnings of Chinese Books and Inscriptions*. Chicago: University of Chicago Press, 2004.

T'ung-tsu Ch'u 瞿同祖. *Han Social Structure*. Seattle: University of Washington Press, 1972.

Twitchett, Dennis, and Michael Loewe, eds. *The Cambridge History of Ancient China*, Vol. I: *The Ch'in and Han Empires 221 B.C.–A.D. 220*. Cambridge: Cambridge University Press, 1986.

van Els, Paul, and Sarah A. Queen, eds. *Between History and Philosophy: Anecdotes in Early China*. Albany: SUNY Press, 2017.

van Gulik, Robert H. *The Chinese Maze Murders*. The Hague: W. Van Hoeve Ltd., 1956.

Van Norden, Brian W., ed. *Confucius and the Analects: New Essays*. New York: Oxford University Press, 2002.

Veeck, Gregory, Clifton W. Pannell, Christopher J. Smith, and Huang Youqin. *China's Geography: Globalization and the Dynamics of Political, Economic, and Social Change*. 2nd ed. London: Rowman and Littlefield, 2011.

Vervoorn, Aat. *Men of the Cliffs and Caves: The Development of the Chinese Eremitic Tradition to the End of the Hand Dynasty*. Hong Kong: Chinese University Press, 1990.

von Glahn, Richard. *The Economic History of China: From Antiquity to the Nineteenth Century*. Cambridge: Cambridge University Press, 2016.

von Falkenhausen, Lothar. "The Concept of Wen in the Ancient Chinese Ancestral Cult." *Chinese Literature: Essays, Articles, Reviews (CLEAR)* 18 (1996): 1–22.

von Falkenhausen, Lothar. "The E Jun Metal Tallies: Inscribed Texts and Ritual Contexts." In Kern, ed., 2005, 79–123.

von Falkenhausen, Lothar. *Chinese Society in the Age of Confucius (1000–250 BC): The Archaeological Evidence*. Los Angeles: Cotsen University of Archaeology, 2006.

Wallace-Hadrill, A. "To Be Roman, Go Greek: Thoughts on Hellenization at Rome." *Bulletin of the Institute of Classical Studies. Supplement* 71 (1998): 79–91.

Wang, Aihe. *Cosmology and Political Culture in Early China*. Cambridge: Cambridge University Press, 2000.

Wang Chong 王充 (27–97 CE). *Lunheng jiaoshi* 論衡校釋. Huang Hui 黃暉, ed. Beijing: Zhonghua shuju, 1990.

Wang Gesen 王閣森 and Tang Zhiqing 唐致卿. *Qi guo shi* 齊國史. Jinan: Shandong renmin chubanshe, 1992.

Wang Guowei 王國維 (1877–1927 CE). *Shuijing zhujiao* 水經注校. Shanghai: Shanghai renmin chubanshe, 1984.

Wang Hsiao-po 王曉波 (1943–2020 CE) and Leo S. Chang (1935–2022). *The Philosophical Foundations of Han Fei's Political Theory*. Honolulu: University of Hawaii Press, 1986.

Wang Jing 王靜, tr. "Sung Wei-tzu, Hereditary House 8." In Nienhauser, ed., 2006, 267–95.

Wang Liqi 王利器 (1912–98 CE). *Lüshi chunqiu zhu shu* 呂氏春秋注疏. 4 vols. Chengdu: Ba Shu chubanshe, 2002.

Wang Meng'ou 王夢鷗 (1907–2002 CE). "Zou Yan wude zhongshi lun de gouzao 鄒衍五德終始論的構造." Xiang Weixin 項維新 and Liu Fuzeng 劉福增, eds., *Zhongguo zhexue sixiang lunji* 中國哲學思想論集, Vol. 2. Taibei: Shuiniu chubanshe, 1991, 329–53.

Wang Shumin 王叔岷 (1914 C.E.–2008 C.E.), *Shiji jiaozheng* 史記斠證 (10 vols.). Taibei: Zhongyang yanjiuyuan, 1982.

Wang Xueli 王學理. *Qin Shihuang ling yanjiu* 秦始皇陵研究. Shanghai: Renmin chubanshe, 1994.

Wang Zhaoyuan 王照圓. *Lienü zhuan buzhu* 列女傳補注. Shanghai: Huadong shifan daxue chubanshe, 2012.

Watson, Burton. *Han Fei Tzu: Basic Writings*. New York: Columbia University Press, 1963.

Watson, Burton, tr. *The Complete Works of Chuang Tzu*. New York: Columbia University Press, 1968.

Watson, Burton. *The Tso chuan: Selections from China's Oldest Narrative History*. Translations from the Oriental Classics. New York: Columbia University Press, 1989.

Weingarten, Oliver. "Debates around Jixia: Argument and Intertextuality in Warring States Writings Associated with Qi." *Journal of the American Oriental Society* 135.2 (2015): 283–307.

Weld, Susan R. "The Covenant Texts from Houma and Wenxian." In Edward L. Shaughnessy, ed., *New Sources of Early Chinese History*. Early China Special Monograph Series 3. Berkeley: University of California Press, 1997, 125–60.

Weld, Susan R. "Chu Law in Action: Legal Documents From Tomb 2 at Baoshan." In Major and Cook, eds., 1999, 77–97.

Williams, Crispin. "Dating the Houma Covenant Texts: The Significance of Recent Findings from the Wenxian Covenant Texts." *Early China* 35–36 (2012–13): 247–75.

Wilkinson, Endymion. *Chinese History: A New Manual*. 6th ed. 2 vols. Harvard-Yenching Institute Monograph Series 127. Cambridge, MA, and London: Harvard University Press, 2022.

Wu Hung. "From Temple to Tomb: Ancient Chinese Art and Religion in Transition." *Early China* 13 (1988): 78–115.

Wu Hung 巫鴻. "The Art and Architecture of the Warring States Period." In Loewe and Shaughnessy, eds., 1999, 651–744.

Wu Hung. "Rethinking Warring States Cities: An Historical and Methodological Proposal." *Journal of East Asian Archaelogy* 3.1–2 (2001): 237–57.

Wu Hung. *The Art of the Yellow Springs: Understanding Chinese Tombs*. Honolulu: University of Hawaii Press, 2010.

Wu, Xialong. *Material Culture, Power, and Identity in Ancient China*. Cambridge: Cambridge University Press, 2017.

Wu Zeyu 吳則虞. *Yanzi chunqiu jishi* 晏子春秋集釋. Beijing: Zhonghua shuju, 1962.

Xie Xiuzong 謝秀宗, ed. *Shiyong chengyu cidian* 實用成語辭典. Taibei: Leigu chubanshe, 1990.

Xu Fuguan 徐復觀 (1904–82 CE). *Liang Han sixiang shi* 兩漢思想史, Vol. 2. Taibei: Taiwan xuesheng shuju, 1979.

Xu Shen 許慎 (ca. 55–ca. 149 CE). *Shuowen jiezi zhu* 說文解字注. Shanghai: Shanghai guji, 1981.

Yan Buke 閻步克. *Shi dafu zhengzhi yansheng shigao* 士大夫政治演生史稿. Beijing: Beijing Daxue chubanshe, 1996.

Yan Shoucheng 閻守誠. *Zhongguo renkou shi* 中國人口史. Taibei: Wenjin chubanshe, 1997.

Yan Sun. "Bronze Vessels: Style, Assemblages, and Innovations of the Western Zhou Period." In Childs-Johnson, ed., 2020, 451–70.

Yan Zhenyi 閻振益 and Zhong Xia 鍾夏. *Xin shu jiaozhu* 新書校注. Beijing: Zhonghua shuju, 2000.

Yang Bin 楊斌. *Cowrie Shells and Cowrie Money: A Global History*. Milton Park: Routledge, 2018.

Yang Bojun 楊伯峻. *Chunqiu Zuozhuan zhu* 春秋左傳注. 2 vols. Beijing: Zhonhua shuju, 1993.

Yang Jialuo 楊家駱 (1912–91 CE). *Weishu tongkao* 偽書通考. 2 vols. Taibei: Dingwen shuju, 1973.

Yang Kuan. *Zhanguo shiliao biannian jizheng* 戰國史料編年輯證. Taibei: Commercial Press, 2002.

Yang Kuan 楊寬. *Zhangguo shi* 戰國史. Shanghai: Shanghai Renmin chubanshe, 2019.

Yang Kuan 楊寬 and Wu Haokun 吳浩坤, eds. *Zhanguo huiyao* 戰國會要. 2 vols. Shanghai: Shanghai guji chubanshe, 2005.

Yates, Robin D. S. "Siege Engines and Late Zhou Military Technology." In Li Guohao, Zhang Mengweng, and Cao Tianqin, eds., *Explorations in the History of Science and Technology in China: A Festschrift in Honour of Dr. Joseph Needham*. Shanghai: Shanghai Guji, 1982, 409–52.

Yates, Robin D. S. Some Notes on Ch'in Law." *Early China* 11–12 (1985–87): 243–75.

Yates, Robin D. S. "Social Status in the Ch'in: Evidence from the Yün-meng Legal Documents. Part One: Commoners." *Harvard Journal of Asiatic Studies* 47.1 (1987): 211–48.

Yates, Robin D. S. "New Light on Ancient Chinese Military Texts: Notes on Their Nature and Evolution, and the Development of Military Specialization in Warring States China." *T'oung Pao* 74.4–5 (1988): 211–48.

Yates, Robin D. S. "Introduction: The Empire of the Scribes." In Pines et al., eds., 2014, 141–54.
Yates, Robin D. S. "Evidence for Qin Law in the Qianling County Archive: A Preliminary Survey." *Bamboo and Silk* 1.2 (2018): 403–45.
Yinque shan Bamboo Slip Collation Group. *Yinqueshan Han mu zhu jian zhengli xiaozu* 銀雀山漢墓竹簡整理小組. *Sun Bin bingfa* 孫臏兵法. Beijing: Wenwu chubanshe, 1975.
Yokota Ikō 橫田惟孝 (1774–1829 CE). *Senkokusaku Seikai* 戰國策正解. Tokyo: Seizando, 1911.
Yu Yingshi 余英時. *Shi yu Zhonguo wenhua* 士與中國文化. Shanghai: Shanghai renmin chubanshe, 2000.
Yuan Jing, "The Origins and Development of Animal Domestication in China." Rowan Flad, tr. *Chinese Archaeology* 8 (2008): 1–7.
Zhang Bingnan 張秉楠. *Jixia gouchen* 稷下鉤沉. Shanghai: Shanghai guji, 1991.
Zhang Shuangdi 張雙棣. *Huainanzi jiaoshi* 淮南子校釋. 2 vols. Beijing: Beijing University Press, 1997.
Zhang Yachu 張亞初, ed. *Yin Zhou jinwen jicheng yinde* 殷周金文集成引得. Beijing: Zhonghua shuju, 2001.
Zhang, Zhenjun. "Sung Wei-tzu, Hereditary House 8." In Nienhauser, ed., 2006, 267–92.
Zhang Zhenze 張震澤. *Sun Bin bingfa jiaoli* 孫臏兵法校理. Beijing: Zhonghua shuju, 1984.
Zhangsun Wuji 長孫無忌 (d. 659 CE) et al. *Tang lü shuyi* 唐律疏議. Beijing: Zhonghua shuju, 1983.
Zhao Guangxian 赵光贤. *Zhoudai shehui bianxi* 周代社会辨析. Beijing: Remin chubanshe, 1980.
Zhao Hua and William H. Nienhauser Jr., trs. "Chin, Hereditary House 9." In William H. Nienhauser Jr., ed., *The Grand Scribe's Records*, Vol. V.1: *The Hereditary Houses of Pre-Han China*, Part 1. Bloomington: Indiana University Press, 2006, 297–380.
Zhao Huacheng 趙化成. "New Explorations of Early Qin Culture." Andrew H. Miller, tr. In Pines et al., eds., 2014, 53–70.
Zhang Qingchang 張清常 and Wang Yandong 王延棟. *Zhanguo ce jianzhu* 戰國策箋注. Tianjin: Nankai daxue chubanshe, 1993.
Zhong Wenzhong 種文烝. *Chunqiu Guliang jingzhuan buzhu* 春秋穀梁經傳補注. Beijing: Zhonghua shuju, 1996.
Zhu Fenghan 朱鳳瀚. *Shang Zhou jiazu xingtai yanjiu* 商周家族形態研究. Tianjin: Tianjin Guji chubanshe, 1990.

Index

For the benefit of digital users, indexed terms that span two pages (e.g., 52–53) may, on occasion, appear on only one of those pages.

abdication 244–5, 264, 280, 285, 306, 340–1, 440–1
  abdication "myths" 280, 282–3. *See also*: King Kuai of Yan, Shun, Xu You, abdication affair of 318 BCE; Yao, Zizhi
abdication affair of 318 BCE
  as challenge to the world view of literati 285–7
  as history 280–1, 283–6, 288, 292, 335. *See also*: King Kuai of Yan, SIma Zhou, Yan (state), Zizhi
adoption 403–4, 416
agricultrual revolution 8–9
agriculture 8–9, 19–20, 116–17
  distinct by region 45
  reform under Li Kui 116–18
Ailing. *See* Mugwort Hill
Alcibiades 303
alcohol, *See*: wine
Alexander the Great 3–4
All Under Heaven (tian xia 天下) 433, 436, 440, 442
Altars of the Soil and Grain are closer than kin 社稷戚於親, the 160, 163, 167. *See also*: Guanzi, Master Guan
Altars of the Soil and Grain 社稷 160, 286
  Altar of the Grain 176
American Revolution 7, 207
Analects 論語 13, 27–32, 39, 113–14, 409
ancestor worship 33, 83, 157–60, 441
ancestors, ancestral spirits 13–14, 21, 26–7, 55, 58, 98, 118, 154–5, 159–60, 188, 274, 324, 330, 441–2
ancestral temple, *See*: temple
Anhui Province 45–6
Anyi 安邑 (Peace, early capital of Wei) xviii, xxi–xxii, 112–15, 144–5, 197–8, 205, 223–4, 329
archers 122–3, 145–6
architecture 193, 219, 225–6, 434

aristocracy 47–8
  as warrior-priests 13–18, 118, 122, 356
  courage as a value of 13–14, 81, 83, 91, 135–7, 139, 354–5, 358, 364–5, 381–2
  culture of honor among 13, 15, 59–60, 75, 80–1, 83, 89–91, 118, 131–2, 147, 172–3, 182–3, 265, 273, 352, 381–2
  descended from the gods 14, 98–100, 188, 371, 393–4
  emergence of great patrons among 296–7, 309–10
  evolution of 17–18, 20–1, 50, 87–8, 90, 107, 126–8, 142, 152
  feuds among 13, 15, 18, 20–2, 75, 77–9, 98–100, 126–7, 201–2, 297, 357
  grandee families among 16–18, 77–9, 142–3, 195–6
  lifestyle of 8–9, 51, 80, 91, 158–9, 166, 337–8, 350–1
  physical beauty as characteristic of 83, 91
  position of the knights (shi) within 23, 25, 31, 88–91, 136–7, 158, 383, 445
  power of 1, 41, 75, 195, 445
  social hierarchy of 24–5, 30, 99–100, 114–15, 126–7, 173, 179, 337–8, 445
  social role and hereditary privileges of 12–16, 28–9, 51–2, 83, 99–100, 160, 179–80, 195, 394, 398–9, 419, 443–4
  traditional education of 26, 51–2, 389
Aristotle 313
  Xun Kuang as the "Aristotle of China" 313
Art of War by Master Sun, *See*: Sunzi bingfa
artisans 8–9, 51–2, 88, 95–6, 225
assassination 54–5, 88–90, 95–6, 104–5, 135, 379, 391, 429–31
assassins 54–5, 88, 111, 135–6, 380, 429. *See also*: Jing Ke, Nie Zheng, Yurang
astronomy 231
Athens 25

INDEX

Ba 巴 (state) xviii, xxii–xxiii, 274–8
Bai Qi 白起 (Qin general)
   campaigns against Chu 324, 344
   campaigns against Han and Wei 323–4, 383, 387–8
   paragon of the new model military commander 364–5, 369
   refusal to serve in siege of Handan and execution 375–6, 381
   service in Changping campaign 364–7, 369, 375, 387–8
Baiyi 百邑 (town) xxi, 98–9, 101
barbarians. *See* non-Sinitic peoples
barley 45
beggars 89
Beijing 北京 xxiv, 279
bells 83. *See also*: bronze, bronze ritual vessels
benefit (利 *li*) 102–3, 163, 228–30
Bi River 沘水 xxiii, 302
Bo Pi, *See*: Grand Steward Bo Pi
boats, ships 45, 53, 68, 121, 442
Boju, *See*: Cypress Rise, battle of
Book of Lord Shang 商君書 208
bronze
   as material resource 158–9
   as technology 8–9, 249, 274
Bronze Age 118, 371
bronze ritual vessels 15, 158–9
   inscriptions on 15, 159, 191
broomcorn 116
Buddha 25
bureaucracy 128, 169–72, 195, 220, 267–8, 349, 352, 357, 361–2, 367–8, 386–7, 398–9, 401, 414, 419, 421, 447
   importance of orderly transfer of power to 204–5, 212–13, 283, 401
butchers 132–3, 377

Caesar's crossing of the Rubicon 7–8
Cai Ze (prime Minister of Qin) 401, 407
Cai 蔡 (state) 96
calendrics 231–2. *See also*: state (*guo*), calendrical system of
canals 65–6, 122, 194, 219–20, 370, 432
   "Canal Affair" of 246 BCE 420–1
Cantonese 42
carriage
   as a marker of aristocratic status and rank 2, 114–15, 139, 351, 356, 377

   as a mode of transport 1, 4–5, 66, 89, 98, 299
   as a symbol of state 234
Cassia Hill (Guiling 桂陵, battle site) xxi, 185–6, 223–4, 291
cavalry 338–40, 358–9, 365, 427. *See also*: horses, King Wuling of Zhao
ceramics 8
Ceramictown. *See* Tao
Changping (Longpeace 長平, battle site) xxi
   campaign of 260 BCE 363–7, 369, 374–5, 403, 414–15
charioteering, chariots 80–1, 96, 122
Chen She 陳涉 (rebel against Qin empire) 438
Chen 陳 (state) 19, 159
Chengdu 成都 (capital of Shu) xiv, xviii, xxii, 274, 278–9
Chinese cuisine 279, 438
Chinese origins, questions of 110, 187, 190–1, 335–6
Chinese script 51–2, 437
Chinua Achebe 39–40
Chu 楚 (state) xviii–xxi, xxiii–xxiv, 45–6, 51–4, 63–4, 185–6, 238–9, 263–4
   alliances 61, 262, 267, 270, 272, 298, 300–1, 379–81, 383–4
   as multi-ethnic empire 46–8, 59
   conflict with northern states 46–9, 75, 106–7, 141, 223–4, 240, 272–4, 301–4, 307, 344, 387, 424
   conflict with Wu 51, 53–4, 56–62, 66, 71
   court intrigue within 50–1, 145–6
   destruction of 432
   employment of Wu Qi 141–6
   expansion of 46–7, 96, 141, 143, 275, 386–8
   importance of commerce to 47, 49
   kidnapping of King Huai 304–7, 353–4
   kings of 106–7, 145–6, 300, 380–2
   loss of territory to Qin 324, 335
   origins of 46–7
   perceived as alien or "barbarian" by northerners 47–8, 75, 233, 243–4, 387–8
   persistence of titled aristocratic oligarchy in 142–3, 145
   rebellion of Zhuang Qiao (301 BCE) and aftermath 303–4, 335, 386–7
   reforms in 142–4, 147, 215–16, 386–7
   relations with vassal states 46–9, 57, 59–60, 66

ruling clan 46, 59–60, 300, 393–4
social evolution of 50
use of title "king" 47–8, 233, 246
Chuci 楚辭 (Verses of Chu) 392–4
"Encountering Sorrow 離騷" 392–4
Chuci 楚辭 (Verses of Chu). *See also*: Huang Xie, Qu Yuan
Chunyu Kun 淳于髡 173
 as a "model Master" 174–7, 224
 as a denizen of Jixia 176–7
 as emissary of the Qi court 177–8
 as teacher in riddles 173, 176–7, 260–1, 444
Chunyu Yue 淳于越 (imperial Erudite) 444–6
cinnabar 48
Circular Jade of the He Clan, *See*: jade
civil tradition (wen 文) 15–18. *See also*: wen and wu (the civil and the martial)
Classic of Change (Yi jing 易經) 231–2, 410, 414, 434
Classic of Documents 書經 446
Classic of Laws (Fa jing 法經) 117–18
Classic of Songs 詩經 446
classics 經 112–13, 444, 446
clothing
 as a basic need 102–3, 116–17, 163, 298
 as a key marker of status 139, 337–40, 351, 377, 386, 394, 404
 as military gear 338
 cultural differences in 42, 337, 340–1
 of commoners 240, 350–1, 354–5, 385
 of the aristocracy 139, 308, 351
cock-crow knight 308–9, 382
commanderies (*jun* 郡) and districts (*xian* 縣) 118–19, 123, 161–2, 194–6, 298, 304, 340, 349–50, 386–7, 407, 424–8, 435–6
 facilitation of diplomacy 248
commerce (trade)
 growth of 18, 49, 130, 275, 325
 in the South 47–9, 59–60, 71, 275–6
 rising political and social importance of 19–20, 41–2, 48, 56–7, 67, 71, 194, 218, 277–8, 311, 402. *See also*: Linzi (capital of Qi), merchants, Tao (city)
commoners 14, 18, 20, 36–7, 99–100, 134, 196, 302
 as defining assets of the titled aristocracy 19–20, 152

as exemplary figures in literature 51, 109
as paid laborers 31, 91, 132–4, 377–8, 429
as targets of exploitation by elites 121
courted by grandee clans 19–20, 36–7, 151
courted by the state 122, 160, 194–5, 203, 219, 232–3
growing role in military affairs 122–3, 139, 174, 178, 180, 182–3
lacking education or literacy 101
perceived as prone to pollution 133
produced by physical disability 184, 374
produced by the downward social mobility of aristocrats 70–1, 89–90, 110, 130, 132–4, 143, 203, 350–1
targets of aristocratic condescension or contempt 131, 240, 256
ugliness as characteristic of 83
upward mobility among, from slaves to independent farmers 130
valorized in the teachings of the Masters 282–3. *See also*: clothing, artisans, labor, merchants, Nie Zheng, Zhu Hai
Comprehensive Mirror for the Aid of Government 資治通鑑 127
Concubine Ru 如姬 378
Confucian fellowship 5, 91–2, 101–2, 104, 113, 131, 167–8, 170, 388, 414
 partnership with Wei court 113–15, 127. *See also*: Lu (state), Mencius, Xun Kuang
Confucius 孔子 33, 45–7, 68, 72, 104, 106, 162
 as "Master Kong" 1, 5–6, 24–5, 93–4, 100–1, 168–9, 208, 411, 442
 compared to Jesus, Buddha, and Socrates 25
 critiqued by other Masters 102–3, 165, 167–8, 226, 317–18
 death of 6, 39, 102, 113
 disciples of 1–3, 5, 25–31, 68, 91, 101–2, 112, 114, 168–9
 in historical memory 24–5, 28, 113, 438
 latter-day disciples of 113–15, 138, 167–8, 280, 388, 412, 442
 on Penal Cauldron 77–8
 on Wu Zixu 59
 origins and early life 25–6
 resistance to transactional models of state service 162–3, 175

Confucius 孔子 (*Continued*)
  response to coup in Qi 37–8, 127
  teachings of 26–32, 91, 101–2, 127–8, 162–3, 390, 442–3
  travels of 1–3. *See also*: Confucian fellowship, learning, Lu (state), Mencius, music, ritual, Way (Dao), the, Xun Kuang
conscription 117, 123, 195, 425
correlative cosmology 231–5, 410–11, 436–7. *See also*: cosmic resonance, dynastic cycle, five phases of qi, qi, Wei Ying, Zou Yan
corruption, bribery 71, 87, 95, 118, 120–1, 171, 331–2, 364, 396, 405, 416–17, 423–4, 427–8, 431, 436
corvée labor 195, 204, 437
cosmic resonance (*ganying*) 410–11
Counselor 卿 (rank) 77–9, 81–2, 98, 110, 324. *See also*: Six Counselors
courage, *See*: aristocracy (courage as a value of)
covenant ceremony 33, 69, 78–9, 103–4, 124–5, 155, 185–6, 207, 380–1
covenant texts 78–9
Crooked Ditch (Quwo 曲沃, alternative capital of Jin State) xxi, 75, 87
Crooked Ditch (Quwo 曲沃, town in Wei) xxi, 272
Crown Prince Dan of Yan 燕太子丹
  as hostage in Qin 407, 428–9
  early life and personal animosity toward Ying Zheng 428–9
  plan to assassinate Ying Zheng 429–31
Crown Prince of Qin 4–5
Cypress Rise (Boju 柏舉), battle of xxiii, 57, 61

Daba 大巴 Mountains xviii, xxii, 275–6
dafu, *See*: grandees
Dai 代 (state, non-Sinitic people) xx, 82, 233
  as a feudatory within the Zhao state 96, 336, 428
  conquest by Zhao 95–9, 125, 428
  final destruction of, by Qin 432
  reestablished as sovereign kingdom under Zhao clan scion 428
Daliang 大梁 (Greatbridge, capital of Wei) xviii, xxi, xxiv, 185, 198, 218–19, 223, 225, 227, 234, 236–8, 269, 377–8
  as a commercial hub 218–19
  See also: Kaifeng

dancing 97
Danyang 丹陽 (town) 46
Dao, the. *See* Way, the
Daodejing 道德經 (text), or Laozi 老子
  lore surrounding 319–20
  poetic qualities and broad influence of 320–1. *See also*: Daoist Church, Master Lao, personal cultivation
Daoist movement 230–1, 321
  Daoist Church 105, 321
de, *See*: Potency
defensive walls 65, 126, 216, 218–19, 270, 296, 301–3. *See also*: Great Wall, Qi Great Wall, Square Great Wall
demographics 44–6, 116
Di 狄 (non-Sinitic people) 82, 110, 206–7, 259. *See also*: Dragon Gate, Winter Feast; Turks
diplomacy 84–5, 301, 337, 353, 355, 383–4, 425
  "vertical-horizontal (zongheng 縱橫)" as an early signifier for 260–1
  during Spring and Autumn period 247–8
  evolution over fourth century BCE 248
  increasing strategic power of 250–2, 254, 257–8, 327
  revolutionized after summit of 334 BCE 247, 249–50
  used by Fuchai of Wu 66, 68
  used by Tian Chang of Qi 37, 70. *See also*: Horizontal Alliance, hostages, Gongsun Yan, Su Qin, Vertical Alliance, Zhang Yi
disease 45
District Magistrate 令 (office) 119, 123, 128, 161–2, 248
  seal of office 120–1
  yearly review 120–1, 171
divination 81, 237–8, 361
  omens 39, 77–8, 299, 363, 414–15
Divine Hill (Lingqiu 靈丘, battle site) xx, 330
dog thief 308–9, 382
dragon 42, 249, 361, 393–4
Dragon Boat festival 392
Dragon Gate (Longmen 龍門, city) xxi
  Winter Feast held for Rong and Di chieftains at 259, 336
duels 13, 20, 137–8, 141, 301, 356
Duke (*gong* 公, rank) 222–3
Duke (*gong* 公, title) 8, 29, 101
  as primes inter pares among grandee clans 16

INDEX

Duke Dao of Qi 齊悼公 12, 67–8
Duke Huan of Qi (Tian clan), See: Tian Wu (Duke Huan of Qi)
Duke Huan of Qi 齊桓公 (Lü clan)
  as Lord Protector 43, 111–12, 169, 210
  as protégé of Master Guan 164, 198
  first patron of Tian clan 19
  in the Guanzi 166–8
Duke Jian of Qi 齊簡公. See Lü Ren
Duke Jing 景 of Qi 179
Duke Mu 穆 of Qin 190, 198–9
Duke of Zhou 周公 (ruler of West Zhou) 94–5
Duke of Zhou 周公 (son of King Wen of Zhou) 137
Duke Ping 平 of Qi 37
Duke Wen of Jin 晉文公 47–8, 75
Duke Xian of Qin 秦獻公 (Ying Lian)
  abolition of "following in death" 193–4
  administrative reforms of 192, 194–5, 197, 205
  at war with Wei 197–8, 216
  death and legacy of 198–9
  early life and exile 192–7, 200
  move of capital 193–4, 197
Duke Xiao of Qin 秦孝公 (Ying Quliang)
  continuation of his father's policies 198, 214, 225
  death of 207–8, 237
  employment of Shang Yang 199–200, 204–5, 209–10
  inaugural edict of 198–200, 207
  made "Lord Protector" 206–7, 235.
    See also: Shang Yang (Lord Shang)
Duke You 幽 of Jin 124
dynastic cycle 232, 234–5. See also: five phases of qi, qi

Earl (*bo* 伯, rank) 85, 142
Earth 地 78, 410, 434
East Asia 5–6, 71, 175, 229–32, 274, 438, 450
  impact of the Warring States upon 73, 115–16, 155–6, 178
East Bank Commandery 河東郡 xxi, 257, 259
East Zhou 東周 (domain) xxii, 253, 395, 400
economy, economics
  accelerating economic competition among Zhou elites 18, 28, 311
  economic distinctness of the South 45
  steady economic growth of Zhou society 18, 117, 119, 142, 154–5, 205, 219, 292, 370. See also: agriculture, artisans, commerce, farmers, merchants, Qin (economic advantages from the conquest of Shu)
Emperor (huangdi 皇帝, title) 3–6, 435
Encountering Sorrow, See: Chuci
Erudites 444–5
espionage (spies) 57, 64, 69, 87, 105, 183, 331–2, 364, 396, 407, 423–4, 426–8. See also: Master Sun, Su Qin
eunuchs
  role in Zhou elite society 4–5, 8, 17–18, 34, 192–3, 209, 353
  Zhao Gao as 3–4
Europe 243–4
Eyu 閼與 xx
  campaign of 269 BCE 358–60, 363, 396

Fan Pavilion 范臺, drinking party at 225–7
Fan Sui 范睢 (prime minister of Qin, aka Zhang Lu)
  as champion of meritocracy and routinization 348, 357, 362, 368–9, 447
  as prime minister of Qin 349–50, 352, 384–6, 401–2, 407
  death of 394
  early career and humiliation 344–6, 350
  leadership during Changping campaing 364, 366, 375
  made marquis 349–50, 352, 406
  migration to Qin 345–6
  policy of "befriending the far and attacking the near" 349–50, 360, 362
  use of assumed identity of "Zhang Lu" 345, 350–1
Fan 范 clan (of Jin) 84–5, 88–91, 98–9, 195
farmers 8–9, 19–20, 54, 76, 116–17, 123, 130, 139, 194–5, 201–2, 219, 282–3
Fen 汾水 River xxi, 86–7
fengshui 風水 (geomancy) 231, 441
fief (feng 封) 161–2. See also: Warring States, establishment of fiefs and "feudal lords" in
Filial King of Zhou (Zhou Xiaowang 周孝王) 188–9
filial piety 孝 26–7, 50–1, 111–12, 325, 442–3
first audience stories, genre of 170, 174–5, 209–10

First Emperor of Qin. *See* Ying Zheng
fiscal-military state 195, 277–8, 357, 367, 370, 398–9
fish, fishing 4–5, 20, 51, 55, 219
five phases of qi 五行 231–2, 234–5, 410, 436–7
food
    as a basic need 102–4, 123, 163, 298
    as a component of health 225–6
    as a marker of status 139, 226, 297–8
    in religious observance 121, 159, 442
food aid 65
Forest Hu 林胡 people 98–9, 340
forms and names, *See*: Shen Buhai
French Revolution 7, 9–10
fu, *See*: rhyme-prose
Fu Manchu 12–13
Fuchai 夫差 (King of Wu) 42–3, 62, 69, 71
    as Lord Protector 43, 69, 71, 79, 88
    death of 42–3, 70–1, 73, 383–4
    northern strategy 65–9, 88
    rivalry with Goujian 63–4, 67
funerals 135, 145, 269
Fuzhou 43–4

Gao Yang (god) 393–4
Gaoliang. *See* Highbridge
gentleman (*junzi* 君子) 1, 31, 229, 283
geography 7, 45–6, 447
    impact on strategy and diplomacy 261–2, 274, 277, 427, 431
    sacred geography 440
George Washington 109
ghosts
    in the teachings of Mo Di 103–4
gods 31, 55, 58, 98–100, 118, 155, 160, 269, 393–4, 440–2
    as bestowers of Mandate of Heaven 11, 291–2
    River God cult (in Wei) 121–2, 127–8, 194. *See also*: spirits, spirit world
gold 47–8, 134–6, 174–5, 404
Gongsun Long 311–12
Gongsun Yan 公孫衍
    as chief advocate of the "Vertical Alliance" 260–1, 266–7, 269–72, 295–6, 337
    as head of the Qin court 255–7
    as prime minister of Han 271, 295–6, 311
    as prime minister of Wei 267–8
    as protégé of Hui Shi 260, 268
    brokerage of "meeting of five kings" in 323 BCE 259–62
    failure and demise 271–2
    origins and early career 253–4
    return to Wei, use of diplomacy to frustrate Zhang Yi's strategy 258–62, 264–5
    rivalry with Tian Xu 266–7, 270–2
    use of "political force" 264–8. *See also*: diplomacy, Master Shen Dao, Verticle Alliance, Zhang Yi
Gonshu Ban 公輸盤 106–7
Goujian 勾踐 (King of Yue) 62–3
    as Lord Protector 71, 79
    destruction of Wu 70–1, 73
    determination to seek revenge 65–6, 69–71
    submission to Wu 63–4, 67
    use of honey traps 64–6
    use of spies 64, 69, 87
government
    reform of 112, 115–18
grain 19–20, 45, 116, 201–2
    government price-stabilization of 116–17, 194
grain wine, *See*: wine
Granary Hill (Linqiu 廩丘, town) xx, 126
Grand Master, Grand Master, *See*: Mohist order
Grand Steward Bo Pi 太宰伯嚭
    chief minister of Wu 63, 65
    paid agent of Yue 64–5, 69–71, 87
grandees (*dafu* 大夫)
    as patrons of knights from outside the clan 12, 21, 23–7, 29–31, 39, 79, 152
    competition between grandee clans 20–2, 76–9, 87–8
    in the state of Jin 76, 110, 196
    in the state of Qi 16–17, 19, 196
    rising power of 18, 29. *See also*: Individual clans (Fan, Han, Tian, Wei, Zhao, Zhi, etc...)
Great Excellent Charioteer 大良造 (office)
    Shang Yang as 205–6, 208
Great Exellent Charioteer
    Gongsun Yan as 255
great patrons
    ca. 260-240 BCE as the "age of the great patrons" 371–2, 374–5, 381–2, 386–8, 391, 394, 398, 445

competitive displays of humility and concern for the dignity of knights 373–4, 380–2, 395
competitive displays of wealth and conspicuous consumption 373, 377, 386, 392–3
coordinated effort of Zhao Sheng, Wei Wuji, and Huang Xie to lift siege of Handan 375–6, 379–81, 387–9
cultural impact of 388, 391, 394
deliberate formulation and broadcasting of a self-justifying world view 381–3
endorsement of vigilantism 378, 383
rejection of transactional, bureaucratic norms of service in favor of personal reciprocity 379, 381–2
sociopolitical origins of 310, 369, 382–3, 398–9. See also: Huang Xie, patron-client retinues, Tian Wen, Wei Wuji, Zhao Sheng
Great Wall, the 44, 219, 437
Greatbridge. See Daliang
Greece, Hellenistic world 75, 303, 313
relations with ancient Rome 51–2
Gu 顧 (capital of Zhongshan) xix, xxi, 125
Guan Zhong 管仲 111–12, 301
as historical inspiration for "Master Guan" 164–5, 198, 210, 406
divergence of historical figure from constructed "Master Guan" 164–5, 167. See also: Master Guan
Guangzhou 43–4
Guanzhong 關中 (region, "Land with the Passes") 187–8
Guanzi 管子 (Master Guan), transmitted text 164, 314, 321–2
"Sheperding the People" (Guanzi Chapter 1) 165–6
narratives within 166–8

Hairpin Mountain 96, 101
Han clan 韓氏 84–7, 98, 109, 111, 151, 154, 389
Han Fei 韓非 (Master Han, Han Feizi)
as a disciple of Xun Kuang 389, 425
as a scion of the Han royal clan 389, 425
as envoy for the Han court 425–7
relationship to great patrons 391
teachings of 389–91, 425
Han Feizi 韓非子 (text) 390–1, 425–6
Han Gui 韓傀 (Prime Minister of Han) 131–2, 135, 147

Han 漢 dynasty 93, 97, 122, 168, 204, 211, 253–4, 392, 409, 439, 448–9
archaeology of 325, 329–30
imperial library of 112–13, 163, 381
Han 漢 River xxii, 45–7, 57, 275
Han 韓 (state) xviii–xxi, xxiv, 124, 131, 134, 213–14
assumption of title of "king" 246
at war with Qin 270–2, 407
deterioration and ultimate destruction of 335, 426–7, 434
internal conflict within 131–2
origins in partition of Jin 87–8, 151
political reform in 131, 171–2, 215–16
relations with Qin 263, 266, 271–2, 343–4, 383–4
relations with Wei 124, 126–8, 131, 185, 197, 219, 225, 233, 235, 263–4, 267
Handan 邯鄲 (capital of Zhao) xviii–xxi, 183–5, 223–4, 338, 358–9, 372, 403–4, 427–8
siege of 258 BCE 375–7, 379–82, 405
Hanging Sands (Chuisha 垂沙, battle site) xxiii, 302–5
Hangu 函谷 Pass xviii, xxi–xxiii, 208, 270, 308, 310–11, 328, 349–50, 396–7, 406–7
Hanzhong 漢中 Commandery 273, 298, 301–2. See also: Square Great Wall
He River 菏水 xx, xxiii, 325
Heaven 天 3–5, 33, 78, 94–5, 97, 102, 296, 326
in general folk belief and cosmology 295, 404, 410, 434
in the aristocratic theology of the fifth century BCE 94
in the teachings of Confucius and Mencius 101–2, 293
in the teachings of Mo Di 102–4, See also: Mandate of Heaven, Son of Heaven, Heaven's Will
Heaven's Will 天志, Mo Di's teaching of 94, 102–4
Hebei Province xxiv, 4, 279–80
Hedong, Hedong territory, See: Wei (state)
Helü 闔閭 (King of Wu)
death of 63
early rise as "Prince Guang" 53–5, 83
founder of Wu's "Golden Age" 62–3
struggles with Yue 61–3
wars against Chu 56–62, 66, 68–9, 141
hemp 116

Henan Province 45–6
Henei, *See*: Wei (state) Henei territory
hermits 281, 283
High God Di 帝 14, 97–8, 100–1, 188, 326–7
Highbridge (Gaoliang 高陵, town in Han, once capital of Zhi Yao) xxi, 84
Highmount (Xiangling 襄陵, city in Wei) 155, 223
Himalayas 6
historical chronicles 51–2, 96, 176, 238–9, 309, 347, 350, 381, 385–6
  falsification of 154, 156, 215, 234, 416–17. *See also*: literati (role in historiography of), *Records of the Historian*, wandering persuaders (distortions in the historiography of), *Zhanguoce*.
historical geography 43–6
historiography of the Warring States Period, *See*: literati, role in historiography
Hong Kong 香港 43–4
honor, *See*: aristocracy (culture of honor among)
Horizontal Alliance 從 260–1
  conception and significance 260
  first Horizontal Alliance of 322–320 BCE 263–6, 272, 274, 310
  five-state coalition of 285 BCE 329–30
  persistence as strategic model in Late Warring States period 288
  second Horizontal Alliance of 313 BCE 272–4, 298
  strategic dynamics of 261. *See also*: Zhang Yi
Horse Hill (Maling 馬陵, battle of) xx–xxi, 237–40, 244–5, 291
horses 45, 95, 188, 311–12, 338–40, 428
hostages 249, 262, 303, 305–7, 384–5, 407
Hou Sheng 后生 (prime minister of Qi) 431–2
Hou Ying 侯嬴 (gate warden of Daliang) 376–9, 412
Hu Hai 胡亥 (Second Emperor) 4–5, 438
Huai 淮 River xiii, xx, xxix, 44–6, 385–6
Huan Qi 桓齮 (Qin general and defector) 425, 429
Huang Xie 黃歇 (Lord Chunshen)
  as a distinguished literatus and patron of belles lettres 383–4, 391–4
  as a great patron 372, 381, 385–8, 402
  as a humble envoy of Chu and chief retainer of the Heir Apparent 383–5, 405, 425–6
  as prime minister of Chu 381, 385–7, 396–7, 405–6
  death 398. *See also*: Chu (state), Chuci, King Kaolie of Chu, Li Yuan, Xun Kuang, Zhu Ying
Huangchi 黃池 (town), 3 43. *See also*: Yellow Pond
huangdi, *See*: Emperor, title
Hubei Province 45–6
Hui Shi 惠施 (Master Hui), Prime Minister of Wei
  as a Master, teachings of 238–41, 244, 269, 311–12, 371–2, 386
  brokerage of Xuzhou summit of 334 BCE 241, 243–6
  exile from Wei 263, 265, 270–1
  proponent of a defensive "Vertical" alliance with Qi to "rest Wei's military" 260–3
  relationship with Zhuang Zhou 238–9, 316
  rescue of Wei from the aftermath of Horse Hill 240–1, 265
  resistance to Horizontal Alliance with Qin 260, 262–3
  return to Wei from exile 268–9. *See also*: Gongsun Yan, logic (in the teachings of the Masters), Wei Ying
humaneness (仁 ren) 26–8, 127–8, 165, 228–9, 442–3
Hundred Yue 百越 (Viet) 143
hunting 13, 15, 97, 174–5, 219
Huotai 霍太 Mountains xxi, 98–9, 101

immortals (仙 xian) 441–2
India 243–4
Inner Asian steppe 1–2, 6, 44, 97, 110, 336–40, 427, 438
  as alien frontier, 64 44–5, 74, 164
interstate relations 29, 41, 43
iron
  as technology 8–9, 290–1
irrigation works 8–9, 117, 122, 219–20, 420

jade 48, 174–5, 353, 386
  Circular Jade of the He Clan 353–5. *See also*: regalia
Japan 118, 438

INDEX 535

Jean-Paul Sartre 239–40
Jesuits 24–5
Jesus 25
Ji (capital of Yan) xix–xx, 279, 431
Ji clan, *See*: Zhou royal clan
Jia Yi 賈誼 (Han dynasty literatus) 439
Jiangsu Province 45
Jimo 即墨 (city) xx
   resistance to occupation of Qi 331–2
Jin successor states (Wei, Han and Zhao, aka "Three Jin") 107–8, 114, 124, 126–8, 141, 147, 213–14, 270, 334
   as "brother states" 124, 126–9, 149–50, 154, 191, 213, 221, 236, 244–5, 335–6, 362, 431
   social leveling in 142–3. *See also*: Marquis Wu, breach of the defensive pact with Zhao and Han
Jin 晉 (state) 52, 88, 98, 107–8, 111, 117, 128, 151, 190, 254–5
   "three armies" of 77
   conflict with Chu 47–9, 144–5
   dukes of 73–6, 79, 84–5, 87, 110, 124, 126–7, 197
   internal conflict within 76–8, 84, 195
   origins and early expansion of 74–5
   particpation in covenant of Yellow Pond 69, 79
   partition of 73–4, 87–8, 92–5, 109, 151, 154–5, 417–18
   relations among the aristocratic clans of 72, 74–5, 83–4
   social evolution of 74, 79, 87–91
   structure of aristocratic society within 76–7
   wars with neighboring states 76, 80–3
Jing Ke 荊軻 (assassin) 429–30
Jing 涇 River 205–6
Jinyang 晉陽 (city) xx, 86, 98
Jisun 季孫 clan 25, 28, 30–3, 37–8
Jixia 稷下 patronage community, the
   as an intellectual center of the Warring States 175–7, 311–12, 322, 330
   as an organ of Qi state policy 177–9, 199, 413–14
   currency of teachings of Zhuang Zhou and Master Lao at 316, 321–2
   setting and organization of 175–6, 294
   tensions between Jixia Masters and Qi officials 176–7. *See also*: logic, Master-disciple fellowships, Mencius, Xun Kuang

Ju 莒 (city) xx
   site of Qi "court in exile" 331–2
Judge Dee 12–13
junzi. *See* "gentleman"
Jurchens 44

Kaifeng 開封 xxiv, 218
Khitans 44
King Anxi of Wei 魏安釐王
   inertia during siege of Handan 376
   relationship with Wei Wuji 372, 395–6
King Cuo of Zhongshan 中山王
   early tutelage under Sima Zhou 286
   execution of Sima Zhou 286–7
   tomb of 286
King David 10
King Goujian of Yue, *See*: Goujian (King of Yue)
King Helü of Wu, *See*: Helü of (King of Wu)
King Huai of Chu 楚懷王
   kidnapping of 304–5, 307, 343–4, 355
   succession crisis 304–6
King Huiwen of Qin 秦惠文王 (Ying Si)
   assumption of title of "king" 246, 259
   death 288, 298–9
   employment and promotion of Zhang Yi 257–8, 265, 343
   employment of Gongsun Yan 255–7
   husband of Mi Bazi 299–300
   participation in summit of Welcome Pond, as Heir Apparent 235
   rancor with Shang Yang 204–5, 207–8
   relations with Shu 274–8
   succession to Duke Xiao 207–8, 275–6
King Huiwen of Zhao 趙惠文王 (Zhao He)
   death of 361
   leadership of the Zhao court 342, 352, 358–9
   succession to the throne as a child 340–2
King Jian of Qi 齊王建 333–4, 431–3
King Kaolie of Chu 楚考烈王
   as hostage in Qin 384–5
   relationship to Huang Xie 385, 397, 405
King Kuai of Yan 燕王噲
   in historiography 280–1
   practical impact of abdication 283–4
   rationale for abdication 281–3. *See also*: abdication affair
King Min of Qi 齊湣王 (Tian Di)
   accession to the throne and employment of Tian Wen 305–7

King Min of Qi 齊湣王 (Tian Di)
  (*Continued*)
  ambition to conquer Song 324–5
  assaults on and eventual destruction of
    Song 325–6, 328–9
  assent to and unilateral withdrawal from
    the partition plan of Wei Ran 327–8
  break with Tian Wen 307, 323–4
  defense of Qi against coaltion of
    285 BCE 330
  flight and death 331
  oversaw golden age of Jixia 311–12, 320–2
  relationship with Su Qin 324–5, 327–8
  reputation for venality and greed 333–4, 344
King Nan of Zhou 周赧王 395, 400
King of Yiqu 義渠王 346–7
King Qingxiang of Chu 楚頃襄王
  as hostage in Qi 305–6
  employment of Huang Xie 383
King Wen of Zhou 周文王 46, 110, 137, 269
King Wu of Qin 秦武王
  death under extraordinary circum-
    stances 299
  eccentricity of 298–9, 304, 309, 439
  hostility to foreign-born officials
    288, 298–9
King Wu of Zhou 周武王 110, 212, 328
King Wuling of Zhao 趙武靈王
  (Zhao Yong)
  abdication and assumption of title "Father
    of the Ruler (zhufu)" 306, 340–1, 352
  adoption of "barbarian dress" 337–41
  campaign to conquer
    Zhongshan 338, 340–1
  engagement with steppe peoples and
    culture 336–7, 340–1, 362
  family relations of 341–2
  ouster and death 341–2, 352. *See also*:
    Zhao (state), relations with non-Sinitic
    steppe people
King Xiang of Qi 齊襄王 (Tian Fazhang)
  as refugee in Ju 331
  marriage to Queen Jun 332
King Xiang of Wei 魏襄王 269–71
King Xiaocheng of Zhao 趙孝成王
  accession to the throne 361, 371–2
  annexation of the Uppery Commandery
    of Han 362–3, 427
  dream of 262 BCE 361, 363
  leadership during the Changping
    campaign 364, 366

King Xiaowen of Qin 秦孝文王
  (Lord of Anguo)
  as Heir Apparent 403–4
  coronation and death 405–6
King Xuan of Qi 齊宣王 (Tian Pijiang)
  annexation of Yan 285, 292–4
  coronation and early reign 290
  death of 305–6
  expulsion from Yan 285
  invasion of Yan in 314 BCE 272–3,
    292–3, 310
  relations with military commanders 302
  relationship with Mencius 291–4
King Yan of Song 宋王偃
  exile and death 329
  sacrilege and profanity of 326
  tyrranical behavior and belligerence of 326
King Yi of Yan 燕易王 280
King You of Chu 楚幽王 398
King Yu 禹王 225
King Zhao of Qin 秦昭王
  annihilation of the Zhou dynasty 395, 400
  death of 395, 401, 405
  hostage in Yan and succession to King
    Wu 299–300, 343
  leadership during the Changping
    campaign 366, 375
  leadership in foreign affairs diplo-
    macy 383–5
  relations with Chu 304
  relations with Fan Sui 347–9, 351–2, 401
  relations with mother, Mi Bazi, and
    uncles 300, 343–4, 346–7, 352, 401
  relations with Tian Wen 301, 303, 306
King Zhao of Yan 燕昭王 (Yan Zhi)
  expulsion of Qi occupiers from
    Yan 285, 294
  formally crown king of Yan
    in 311 BCE 294
  recuriked and supported by Zhao
    court 285, 294
  use of Su Qin as a double agent 324–5
King Zhuangxiang of Qin 秦莊襄王,
  (Ying Yiren)
  as Heir Apparent and King 405–6
  as hostage in Zhao 403–5, 407–8
  death of 406, 415–16
King 王 (title, rank) 10, 47–9, 233–4, 236,
  241, 243, 245–7, 262, 434
  enhanced diplomatic powers of a
    king 247–9

enhanced power of a king through control over status hierarchy 246–7
kinship 77–8, 128, 137, 160, 398–9
  changing attitudes towards 21, 35–6, 49, 77, 152
  forging of kinship bonds through ritual 14–15, 159–60
  resilience of kinship networks in the face of routinizing reform 293–4, 419
Kiribati 245–6
Kissinger, Henry 263
knights (士 *shi*) 23–5, 31, 78–9, 122, 142
  among the Masters and disciples 1, 23, 94, 101–2, 114–15, 131
  as clients of great patrons 296–8, 301, 308, 373, 377–82, 391, 394–8, 407–8, 412–14
  as retainers of grandee clans 20–2, 31, 79, 88–90, 98
  as state servitors 100–1, 104–5, 131–2, 142, 179, 195, 338–40, 353, 357, 427
  courted by rulers of the Warring States 114–15, 119, 121, 130–1, 282, 287, 342, 412–14
  declining social position of 31, 74, 88, 91, 101, 107, 172, 195, 254, 268
  held in contempt by titled nobility 132–4, 136–7
  honor bound to reciprocate recognition from social superiors 90, 133–5, 325, 379
  literati among 100–1, 115, 163, 167–8, 172–5, 254–5, 285–6, 340
  resistance to highborn aristocratic domination 90–1, 94, 101, 136–7, 162–3, 173, 282–3, 395
  vulnerability to status assault 131–4, 172–3, 256, 268, 273, 337–8, 373–4, 394.
  See also: aristocracy, social mobility, status
knights of feudal Europe 13
Kong clan 孔氏 (family of Confucius) 25
Korea 118, 279–80, 438
Kuaiji 會稽 (early capital of Yue) xix, xxiii, 63–4
Kurdistan 245–6
Kurt Gödel 239

labor
  as the hallmark of common status 91, 133–4, 350–1
lacquer 8, 48, 89

Lady of Huayang 華陽夫人 403–5, 407–8, 416
Lake Tai 太湖 xxiii, 45
land
  as foundation of aristocratic power 20, 76–7, 195
  revenue from 14, 79, 119, 142, 154–5, 342, 363
Langya 郎雅 (city) xx, 330–1
Lanling Commandery 蘭陵 387–8, 392. *See also*: commanderies and districts, Huang Xie, Lu (state), Xun Kuang
Lao Ai 嫪毐 (Marquis Changxin)
  power and political ambitions of 417–19
  rebellion against Ying Zheng 418–19, 424
  salacious lore and open questions surrounding 416–18. *See also*: Lü Buwei, Queen Dowager (mother of Ying Zheng)
Lao Dan, *See*: Master Lao
Laozi, *See*: Master Lao
Laozi (text), *See*: *Daodejing*
law codes 77–8, 80, 145–6, 439
  collective responsibility within 132, 135–6, 195, 364
  developed by Shang Yang 118
  development by Li Kui 117–19, 128
learning 114–15, 383, 394
  in the teachings of Confucius, Mencius and Xun Kuang 27–8, 101–2, 228–9, 292, 294, 313–16, 321–2, 394, 411
  opposed in the teachings of Zhuang Zhou and "Lao Dan" 316, 318–22
Legalist, Legalism 389, 442–4. *See also*: Master Han
Lesserbridge. *See* Shaoliang
Li Kui 李悝 (Prime Minister of Wei) 115–16, 127, 147, 169, 371–2, 447
  administrative reforms of 119, 149–50, 194, 221–2
  agricultural policies of 116–17, 122–3, 142–3
  legal reforms of 117–19, 123, 128, 201
  rise from local administrator 116
Li Mu 李牧 (Zhao commander) 425, 427
Li Si 李斯
  as Chancellor of the Qin Empire 4–5, 440, 446–7
  as Commandant of Justice in Qin court 421, 423–4, 426, 435–6

Li Si 李斯 (*Continued*)
  attitudes toward social status 420, 445
  disciple of Xun Kuang 420, 425
  early life and education 420
  role in Qin court debates 421, 423–4, 426–7, 435–6, 446
Li Yuan 李園
  as a client of Huang Xie 397
  plot to seize control of Chu court 397–8
  sister of 397–8
Liadong 遼東 (region) xx, 431
Lian Po 廉頗 (general of Zhao)
  enmity and reconciliation with Lin Xiangru 356–7
  in the Changping campaign 363–4
  military leadership of 358–9, 428
  recruitment and early career 353
Lin Xiangru 藺相如 (Zhao official)
  as a pargon of courage 354–7
  background and early career 353
  enmity and reconciliation with Lian Po 356–7
  service as diplomat for Zhao 353–6
Lingqiu. *See* Divine Hill
Linqiu. *See* Granary Hill
Linzi 臨淄 (capital of Qi) xix–xx, 11, 37, 126, 150, 154–6, 164, 171–2, 178, 290–1, 322, 329–30
  archaeology of 152–3, 290–1
  sacked in 284 BCE 330, 353
Liqiu, *See*: Plough Hill (Liqiu), battle of
literacy 12–13
literati
  as members of Master-disciple fellowships 113–14, 167–9, 199, 239, 389
  as servitors of the state 100–1, 109, 112–13, 119, 160, 163–4, 167–9, 233, 244–5, 448
  in the service of great patrons 296, 374, 388, 407–8
  role in historiography 7, 51, 59–60, 109, 115, 189–90, 206, 209–11, 221, 225, 229–30, 273, 347–8, 367–9, 375, 381
  urgently recruited by governments of the Warring States 162, 172–3, 175, 177–8, 199, 282, 287, 314–15, 342. *See also*: historical chronicles, Master-disciple fellowships, Masters writings, Records of the Historian, scribes
Liu Bang 劉邦 (founder of Han dynasty) 448–9
local elites 16, 112, 118–22, 128, 142, 195, 293–4, 361–2

local government, restructuring of 119–20, 122–3, 194–5, 361–2. *See also*: commanderies and districts, District Magistrates, Prefects
logic (in the teaching of the Masters) 239
  "a white horse is not a horse" 311–12
  dialectical chapters of the Mozi 312. *See also*: Chunyu Kun, Gongsun Long, Hui Shi, Jixia patronage community, Xun Kuang
Longmen. *See* Dragon Gate
Longpeace. *See* Changping
Lord Changan 長安君 (Ying Chengjiao) 414–15
Lord of Anguo, *See*: King Xiaowen of Qin
Lord of Yangcheng 陽成君 146–7
Lord Protector (*ba* 霸, title) 43, 47–8, 66–8, 75, 77, 85, 111–12, 151, 206–7, 210, 235, 349
  in the teachings of Master Guan 164, 169–70
  in the teachings of Xun Kuang 313–14, *See also*: Fuchai, Goujian, Guan Zhong, Duke Huan of Qi, Duke Wen of Jin
Lower Yangzi region 45, 48–9, 52
Lower Yangzi River 45
loyalty 20, 26–7, 89, 111–12, 135
Lü Buwei 呂不韋 (prime minister of Qin)
  as "Second Father" and regent to Ying Zheng 406–8, 421
  as a great patron 402, 407–8, 414, 419
  as a merchant 402–4, 406
  as eponymous sponsor of the Lüshi chunqiu 408, 410–12
  as Marquis of Wenxin 405–6, 419
  as pioneer of a new hybrid form of communal political organization 413–14
  as prime minister of Qin 405–7, 414, 419
  background and historical role 401–2
  dismissal, exile, and demise 419–21
  early signs of political trouble 414–15
  parallels to and emulation of Huang Xie 405, 408, 413–14
  relationship with Prince Yiren (King Zhuangxiang of Qin) 403–5
  relationship with the Queen Dowager 404, 415–17. *See also*: Lao Ai, Li Si, Lüshi chunqiu, Queen Dowager (mother of Ying Zheng)

INDEX

Lü clan 呂氏 10, 35, 109, 151, 153–4, 156–7, 165, 197. *See also*: Qi (state), Lü dukes of
Lü Dai 呂貸 (last Lü duke of Qi)
  death 155–6
  exile 154–6
Lü Ren (Duke Jian of Qi 齊簡公)
  death of 37, 39–40
  exile in Lu 22–3, 31–2
  in historical memory 38
  relationship with Zai Wo 23–4, 31–3
  role in coup of 481 BCE 8, 10, 34–7
Lü Ren 呂壬 (Duke Jian of Qi 齊簡公)
  as ruler of Qi 9–10, 12, 16, 22, 34, 43, 68
Lu Zhonglian 魯仲連 381
Lu 魯 (state) xix–xx, xxiii–xxiv, 22–3, 36–7, 47, 68, 84–5
  as home of Confucius and descendants 1–2, 25, 102, 162, 168–9, 387–8
  as native state of Mo Di 92, 102
  as unofficial "headquarters" of the Confucian fellowship 227, 387
  destruction of 387–8
  dukes of 1, 27, 37–8, 138, 168–9, 262, 387
  employment of Wu Qi 137–8
  participation in the summit at Welcome Pond 233, 235
  participation in Wei summit of 356 BCE 219, 225–6, 233
  rivalry with Qi 22–3, 68, 138, 162, 262, 331
  structure of aristocratic society within 76, 246–7
Luoyi 洛邑 (Zhou royal capital) xxii, 10, 299, 406
Lüshi chunqiu 呂氏春秋 (*The Annals of the House of Lü*)
  claims and rhetorical organization 410
  geopolitical agenda 412–13, 423–7
  in the political strategy of Lü Buwei 413–14
  production, display and structure of 408–9
  reception and impact 413–14
  use of correlative cosmology 410–12. *See also*: correlative cosmology, Lü Buwei
Lyndon Johnson 239–40

malaria 45
Maling. *See* Horse Hill
Manchus 44
Mandarin (language) 42
Mandate of Heaven 天命 47–8
  as justification for Zhou rule 11, 14, 93, 96, 215, 233, 291–2, 400
  declining faith in 93–5, 99
  in the discourse of the imperial era 93
  in the teachings of Confucius and Mencius 72, 93–4, 101–2, 227, 229, 291–2
  Wei Ying's attempted transfer of 215, 233, 237, 240. *See also*: dynastic cycle, Heaven, gods, sage, Son of Heaven
Mao Sui 毛遂 (client of Zhao Sheng) 380–1
Marco Polo 24–5
Marquis (*hou* 侯, rank) 10, 101, 109, 126–8, 143, 153–6, 159, 222–3, 241, 246–7, 351
Marquis Cheng of Zhao 趙成侯 213–14
Marquis Lie of Han 韓烈侯 131–2, 135
Marquis Sunnyside 陽侯 (god of the Huotai Mountains) 98–9, 101
Marquis Wen of Wei, *See*: Wei Si
Marquis Wu of Wei 魏武侯 129, 140–1, 145, 155
  breach of the defensive pact with Zhao and Han 144–5, 213, 221–2
  death and ensuing succession crisis 212–13
Marquis Yi of Han 韓懿侯 213–14
Marshal of Horse 司馬 16, 179
Marshal Rangju 司馬穰苴 (Tian Rangju)
  paragon of military reform 179–81
Martial Fortress (Wucheng 武城) xxiii, 216
Master Chen Zhong (陳仲子 Chen Zhongzi) 282–3
Master Gongsun Long 公孫龍子 311–12. *See also*: Jixia patronage community, logic (in the teaching of the Masters)
Master Guan 管子
  as a product of the Tian Qi court 163–5, 167, 177–9
  as a prototypical "Master" 165, 174, 208
  as a symbol and embodiment of the Qi state 164–5, 167, 169, 179, 413–14
  contra Confucius and Mo Di 165–8, 170, 172
  putative teachings of 165–7, 169, 314–15
Master Kong, *See*: Confucius
Master Lao (Laozi 老子, Lao Dan)
  political agenda of 319–21
  putatively teacher of Confucius and author of *Daodejing* 319–21
Master of Punishments 司寇 16–17
Master Shen Dao 267–8, 270–1

Master Sun 孫子 (Sunzi, aka Sun Tzu)
  advocate for rethinking the forms, nature and uses of military power 182–5, 360, 411
  as a construction of the Warring States 181–2, 315
  as critic of the aristocratic ethos 182–3, 364–5
Master Xun, *See*: Xun Kuang
Master Yan 晏子 174
  as a critic of Confucius and the Confucian fellowship 168–9, 172, 314
  as a product of the Tian Qi court 168–9, 177–9, 414
Master Zhuang, *See*: Zhuang Zhou
Master 夫子 (title)
  as teacher of "the Way" 1, 30, 102, 163, 165, 173, 313, 390, 413–14
  diverse conceptions of 164, 230, 239
  novelty in fifth century BCE 30, 39.
  See also: Master-disciple fellowships
Master-disciple fellowships 91–2, 113, 131, 172
  as a form of collective resistance to aristocratic condescension 173–5, 210, 374–5, 413–14
  increasing doctrinal diversity among, over time 91–2, 94, 227–30, 313–15, 322. *See also*: Confucian fellowship, Jixia patronage community, Mohist order
Masters writings 112–13, 239, 381, 388, 408–9
Mawangdui 馬王堆 silk manuscripts 325, 329–30
media manipulation (ancient) 114, 164–5
meeting of "five kings" of 323 BCE 246, 250–2, 259–62, 280, 291
Mencius 孟子 (Master Meng) 24–5
  at the court of King Xuan of Qi 213, 291–4, 312–13
  at the court of Wei Ying 227, 229–31
  criticism of Mo Di and Yang Zhu 227–9, 314–15
  doctrine of the goodness of human nature 228, 315
  grand ambition 227, 229
  ideal of a True King 229, 291–2, 294
  origins in Zou and Lu 227
Mencius 孟子, the (text) 227, 229–30, 291–2, 294
Meng Sheng 孟勝, Mohist Grand Master 146–7

Meng Tian 蒙恬 4–5
merchants 18, 47, 49, 201–2, 402, 406.
  See also: Lü Buwei
merit, meritocracy 31, 88, 90, 102–4, 107, 112, 114, 119, 131, 137, 161, 169–72, 198–200, 280, 287, 294, 342, 345–6, 353, 367–8, 389, 394, 398–9, 443–4
Mi Bazi 芈八子 (Queen Dowager Xuan)
  affair with the King of Yiqu and aftermath 346–7, 350, 360
  conduct of foreign affairs and institution of "pay to play" rules 300, 343–4
  control of Qin court 299–300, 343, 345–6
  death 350
  relationships with sons and brothers 300, 303–4, 323, 347, 350
Mi Rong 芈戎 (Qin official) 343
Mi-clan clique
  challenge to and fall of 344, 349–50
  control of Qin court and nepotism of 343–7, 439
  early inexperience of 304, 309
  engrossment of fiefs 324, 343, 348–50, 358, 362
Middle East, the 243–4
military culture
  in Zhou tradition 13–16, 43, 51, 54, 139
  reform of 28–30, 55–6, 139–40, 178–80, 182–3, 239, 286, 302, 337, 364–5, 379
Military Methods of Marshal Rangju 179
military power 3, 10–11, 20, 47–9, 116, 386–7
  enhanced by administrative reform 123, 194–5, 198, 292, 342
  enhanced by new technology 8–9, 48–9, 105, 181–2
  growing importance of infantry 122–3, 139, 182–3
  limits of 47, 266, 292–4, 374–5
millet 45, 116
Ming 明 dynasty 12–13, 24–5
ministers 109, 111–12
Mo Di 墨翟
  as Master Mo (Mozi) 92, 94, 102, 113, 165, 315
  ban on music 100–1, 103
  critic of Confucius 94, 102–3, 113–14, 120
  critiqued by other Masters 166–8, 226–9, 317–18
  defense of Song 106–7
  disciples of 94, 104–5, 107
  origins and early life 92, 94, 102

INDEX 541

teachings of 94, 102–5, 163, 390, 411
use of "benefit" as cardinal value 102, 163, 228–30. *See also*: Heaven's Will, Mo Di's teaching of, Mohist order
Mohist order 92, 94, 102, 131, 146, 167–8, 280, 412, 414
  and defensive warfare 105, 146–7
  Grand Master 105, 146–7, 163
  unique organization of 104–5, 146–7, 163
Mon-Khmer language family 42
Mongols 44
Mount Chang 長山 iii, 82
Mount Hua 華山 xxii, 219
Mount Kuaiji 會稽山, 5 63
  as destination of Qin imperial tour 3–4
Mount Tai 泰山 xx, 291–2, 442–3
mourning 38–9, 55, 102–3
  duty of a new ruler 54, 62–3, 67–8, 95, 257, 269
Mozi 墨子 (text) 312, 409
Muddy Marsh, *See*: Zhuoze
Mugwort Hill (Ailing 艾陵), battle of xx, 68–9
music 樂 1, 12–13, 26, 170, 174–5, 240–1, 416
  as an adjunct to health, in the teachings of Yang Zhu 226
  banned by Mo Di 100–1, 103, 170, 226
  in the conduct of affairs of state 355–6, 429
  in the teachings of Confucius 26–7, 100–1, 226, 228
  in the teachings of Mencius 228
  in the teachings of Xun Kuang 315
  of the gods 97, 100–1
mutual responsibility groups 195, 202

Nanjing 43–4
Nanyang Commandery 南陽郡 (Han) xxi, 426–7
Nao Chi 淖齒 (Chu general) 331
New York 132
Nie Zheng 聶政 132–7, 147, 172–3, 256, 325
  sister of 135–7
Nine Tripods 九鼎 127, 264, 277, 299
non-Sinitic people
  absorption into the Zhou realm 15–16, 51–2, 74–5, 189
  as "barbarians" 1–2, 14, 42–5, 59, 68–9, 71, 79, 83, 110, 164, 188, 233, 276
  culturally distinct from the Zhou 13, 41, 44, 82, 125, 196, 425

  integration into the political matrices of the Warring States 336, 367
  of the South 41–3, 52, 67, 143, 274. *See also*: Dai (state), Hundred Yue, King Wuling of Zhao, Rong, Shu (state), Turks, Xianyun, Yiqu (state), Zhongshan (state)
North (region) 42, 46
  as Zhou heartland 44, 73
  population of 44
  relations with South 48, 66–7, 69–70
North China plain 8–9, 18, 44, 75, 117, 126, 243

oriental despotism
  as a myth 361–2

Pacific Ocean 6, 43–5
Pang Juan 龐涓 (Wei general)
  leadership in campaign of 354-351 BCE 185
  leadership in campign of 341 BCE 236–7
  rivalry with Sun Bin 184, 237, 254. *See also*: Cassia Hill, Horse Hill (battles of)
pastoralism 44
patronage retinues 372
patron-client retinues
  as autonomous centers of power 374–5, 382–3, 386–7, 419
  employment of literati for public relations 309, 372, 374
  organization of 297, 309–10, 372, 374–5
  proliferation and growing social importance of over time 371–2, 404, 407–8
patrons, *See*: grandees (as patrons...), great patrons
Peace (city). *See* Anyi
pearls 48, 386, 393–4
Penal Cauldron 77–8, 80, 82, 84, 117–18
People's Republic of China 43–4
personal cultivation 228, 394
  "the arts" of the mind and meditation 318–19, 321–2, 411
Phillip of Macedon 62
phoenix 39
physical disability
  as a forfeiture of status 89, 184, 372–4
physicians 97
Pingyang 平陽 (battle site) xxii, 214
Pingyuan Ford 平原津 xx, xxii, 4
Plough Hill (Liqiu 梨丘), battle of 81

poetry 12–13, 26–7, 166, 228, 320, 391–4, 442–3, 446
pollution 91, 133–4, 139, 350, 406
Pope, the 24–5
population, *See*: North (region), South (region), individual states
population growth 18, 117, 143, 205
posthumous titles 3–4, 38, 110, 154–6, 169, 212, 245, 280, 290, 405, 435, 445
Potency (*de* 德)
  as a necessary quality of rulers and leaders 280, 286, 314, 353, 363
  in the teachings of Confucius 101–2
  in the teachings of Master Lao 320
  in the teachings of Xun Kuang 313–14, 322
power sharing as a feature of Warring States politics 107, 268, 361–2
Prefects (*Shou* 守, administrators of commanderies) 119, 123, 138, 142, 193, 278, 361–3, 388, 426–7
Prince Guang, *See*: King Helü of Wu
profit, *See*: benefit (*li*)
prophecy texts 97–102
public works 116–17, 194–5, 216, 437
punishments 16–17, 166, 172, 201–2, 204–5, 207–8, 228
Puyang 浦陽 (capital of Wey) xix–xxi

Qi Great Wall xx, 126, 330–1
qi 氣 231–2, 234–5, 410. *See also*: five phases of *qi*
Qi 齊 (state) xix–xx, xxiii–xxiv, 39–40, 47, 55–6, 84–5, 113, 132–3, 147, 151, 173, 223, 263
  "second revolution" of 374 BCE 150, 160–2, 169
  administrative reforms in 147–8, 161–2, 169–72, 215–16, 292
  agricultural economy 19–20, 37, 290, 293
  allied with Chu 272, 298, 319–20
  allied with Han and Wei 298, 301–3, 310, 328
  allied with Yan 325, 328
  as Lord Protector of Zhou realm 151
  as the key state in any Vertical Alliance 261, 272
  at war with Chu 240, 300, 344, 424
  at war with Jin 80–2
  at war with Lu 22–3, 38, 68, 138, 157, 162, 262
  at war with Qin 266, 300, 310–11, 328, 330, 432
  at war with Wei 126, 154–7, 184–6, 223–4, 236–7, 270, 291
  at war with Wu 67–9
  at war with Yan 157, 284–5, 292, 302, 310–11, 323
  at war with Zhao 144, 154, 156–7
  calendrical system of 155
  commercial economy of 290–1, 293
  coup of 481 BCE 8, 11–12, 22, 28, 33–7, 41, 43, 49, 80, 94–5, 150, 152–3, 267–8, 329
  destruction of 432–3
  establishment of "Capital Grandees" 152, 203
  geographic vulnerability of 261–2
  instability within 12, 17, 20, 22, 126, 151–2, 154–7
  Lü dukes of 8, 10, 16–17, 37, 126, 151, 153–4, 179
  near-extinction, restoration, and irreversible decline 330–5, 353, 387–8
  occupation of Yan 292–4
  population of 290–1
  religious reforms within 157–60
  rising power of 289, 291–2, 311, 322
  social evolution of 11–12, 19, 31–2, 39–41, 72–3, 152
  structure of aristocratic society within 16–17, 76, 79, 158–9, 163
  succession crisis of 405 BCE 126, 154
  transfer of state title from Lü clan to Tian clan 155, 159. *See also*: Jixia patronage community, Linzi (capital of Qi), Lü clan, Mencius, Tian clan, individual rulers
Qii 杞 (state) 96
Qin 秦 (state) xviii, xxi–xxiv, 54, 58, 60–1, 147, 254–5
  "cold war" with Zhao 342, 353–6, 358, 361
  allied with Chu 300–1
  allied with Wei 257, 260, 263–4, 424
  allied with Zhao 308–10, 323, 329, 335, 424
  annihilation of Zhou dynasty 395, 400, 406
  aristocracy of 196–7
  assumption of the title of "king" 246, 259
  at war with Chu 303–4, 307, 424, 431–2
  at war with Han 270–2, 406–7

INDEX

at war with Qi 291, 310–13
conquest of Sichuan (Shu and Ba) 276–9, 292–3, 298
dukes of 97, 189–90, 192, 198
early capitals 188, 193
economic advantages from conquest of Shu 277, 279, 370
endemic hostility of titled aristocracy for foreign-born literati bureaucrats 207–8, 298–9, 345–6, 418, 420–1
expansion of 191, 326, 329, 344–6, 349, 360, 406–7, 414, 424, 431
geography of 187–208, 261
implementation of mutual responsibility groups 195, 202
instability at court 192–3, 196–7, 212–13, 299–300, 401
merit rank system 203–4, 443–4
origins in the collapse of the Western Zhou 188
origins of English word "Chinese" 187
perceived as a "semi-barbarian" backwater 187, 198–9, 211, 362
question of "Chinese ethicity" 187, 189–91
rebellion of Lao Ai 418–19
reforms in 147–8, 186, 192, 215–16
relations with non-Sinitic steppe people 190, 193, 259, 336, 418
reorganization into commanderies and districts 194–6, 205, 347, 349–50
rising power of 197–8, 206–7, 258, 266, 289, 334, 367, 398, 407
ruling clan 144, 197, 203
socially and culturally distinct 187, 190–1, 193–7, 201
strategic rivalry with Wei 124–5, 186, 193, 197–8, 205–6, 216, 219, 223–4, 237, 255–6, 258, 265, 395, 407, 431
strategic rivalry with Zhao 334, 367, 395, 424–5
strategic use of diplomacy 257–9, 262–3
throne of 3–4
use of scribes and cultivation of official bureaucracy 205, 349, 401. *See also*: Mi-clan clique, Yiqu, names of individual leaders
Qin 秦 dynasty
centralization and standardization under 435–7
collapse of 438–9
military expansion of 438
new nomenclature of 435
paradox of 438, 447
signs of insecurity during 439–40, 442–3
Qin-Chu curse texts 273–4
Qinling 秦岭 Mountains xviii, xxii–xxiii, 187–8, 275–6
Qinzhou 秦周 (city) xx, 330
Qiuyou 仇由 (state) xx, 83
Qu Yuan 屈原 392. *See also*: Chuci
Queen Dowager (mother of Ying Zheng)
affair with Lao Ai and birth of two sons out of wedlock 415–19
formal authority as Regent 415–16, 418–19
Queen Dowager Xuan, *See*: Mi Bazi
Queen Jun of Qi 君王后
as mother of King Jian 333–4, 431
early life and birth family 332–3
leadership of Qi court 332–4
marriage to King Xiang of Qi 332–4
Qufu 曲阜 (capital of Lu) xix, 388
Quwo. *See* Crooked Ditch

rape 58–61
Records of the Historian 史記 97, 173, 179, 188–9, 194, 198, 209, 211, 224–5, 253–4, 325, 335–6, 375, 404–5, 408, 416–17
regalia 158–9, 299, 353, 400, 443–4. *See also*: Circular Jade of the He Clan, Nine Tripods
regional lords (aka zhuhou 諸侯, "Lords of the Land") 10, 126, 232–3, 449
debate over retention in Qin empire 435–6, 444–5
power of 11–12, 16. *See also*: Marquis (*hou*), rank; Duke (*gong*), title
revenge 50–1, 53–4, 58–9, 63, 65, 88, 90–1, 132–5, 351–2, 357, 378
rewards and punishments
in the teachings of the Masters 228, 391
rhyme-prose (*fu* 賦) 391–2
rice 45
riddles 82
rightness (*yi* 義) 106, 163, 228–9, 442–3
ritual 禮 1, 26, 51–2, 66, 77–8, 233–4, 241, 244–5, 273, 340
as a mechanism of social cohesion 14–15, 79
employed by the great patrons, as a display of humility and/or wealth 373, 377–8

ritual 禮 (*Continued*)
  in the ancestral cult 14–15, 83, 157–60
  in the operation of the state 114–15, 341, 354–5, 398–9, 419
  in the teachings of Confucius 26–7, 33, 128, 228–9
  in the teachings of Master Guan 165
  in warfare 81, 182–3, 197–8. *See also*: covenant ceremony, funerals, mortuary customs, mourning, music
River Gate (Anmen), battle of 271–2
River God, *See*: gods
roads 194, 219–20, 370, 437
Rome 24–5, 46–7
  relations with ancient Greece 51–2
Rong 戎 (non-Sinitic people) 189–90, 206–7, 259, 270, 335–6. *See also*: Dragon Gate, Winter Feast
routinization, routine authority 4–5, 120–1, 128, 132, 147, 152, 161–2, 171–2, 179–80, 194–5, 203, 205–6, 248–9, 267–8, 357, 361–2, 378–9, 387, 398–9, 435–7, 449
royal revolution 241, 243–4, 246, 258, 281, 285, 288, 296, 326
rulers 109

sacred mountains 28, 440, 442
sacrifice 13–18, 27–8, 33, 69, 78–9, 98–9, 103–4, 133, 154–5, 157–60, 163, 165, 169, 176, 273–4, 291–2, 312–13, 331, 387, 413, 442
  human sacrifice 121–2, 127–8, 190, 193–4, 350, 373
saga of the South
  as history 41–2, 49, 72, 94–5
  in literature 41
sages 聖, sage kings 96, 100–1, 188, 212, 225, 227–9, 240–1, 246–7, 269, 279–80, 282–3, 315–16, 320–1, 328, 362–3, 388, 392, 411, 434, 440, 449
  sagehood as a goal of personal cultivation 316
samurai 13
Sandalwood Terrace 檀臺 (Linzi) 8, 11–13, 16–19, 34
scholar-official or scholar-gentry (as translation of shi 士, "knights") 13, 439, 449–50
scholar-officials, scholar gentry (imperial era) 12–13

scribes 51–2, 115, 189–90. *See also*: Qin (state), use of scribes
seals 璽
  authority of office invested in 3–5, 120–1, 266, 281, 361–2, 418–19
  use in diplomacy 248–9, 361–2
self-mutilation 89, 91, 133–5
Seven Titans (*qi xiong* 七雄) 335
Shang Yang 商鞅 (Lord Shang)
  death and dismemberment 208, 211, 237, 284
  drawn to Qin 199–200, 255
  encouragement of farming and military service 201–4, 257
  enfeoffed at Shang 207–8
  in historical memory 208–11, 234, 301, 389–90
  legal code of 118, 201–2, 204, 208
  merit rank system of 203–4
  military campaigns against Wei 205, 207, 223–4
  move of capital to Xianyang 205–6
  origins in Wey and early career in Wei 199–201, 224–5
  reform proposals and administrative reforms 200–1, 205–6, 208, 334, 349
  relations with Ying Si (Qin Heir Apparent and future King Huiwen) 204–5, 207–8
  use of rewards and punishments 201–5. *See also*: Book of Lord Shang
Shang 商 (town in Qin) xxi–xxii, 207, 264, 272
Shang 商 dynasty 9, 209, 212, 232
  Shang kings 10, 14, 96, 106, 110, 188, 328
Shanghai 43–4
Shaoliang 少梁 (Lesserbridge, city) xxii, 124, 219
Shaqiu 沙丘 (city) xx, 4
Shen Buhai 申不害 389–90
  concept of "forms and names" 171–2. *See also*: bureaucracy, Han (state), routinization
Shen Dao 慎到 389–90
  concept of political "force (勢 *shi*)" 267–71. *See also*: force (shi), Gongsun Yan
Shen Nong 神農 282–3
shi. *See* knights
Shimen. *See* Stone Gate
shrines 76, 101. *See also*: temple

Shu 蜀 (state) xviii, xxii
    as a strategic frontier between Qin and Chu 277, 304
    crisis of 316–314 BCE 276–8
    descended from Sanxingdui culture 274
    divisions and instability 275
    early relations with Qin 274–6
    King of 276–8
    under Qin rule 278–9, 370
    unique geography and climate 274, 277.
        See also: Ba, Daba Mountains, Qin (state), Qinling Mountains, Stone Cattle Road, Zu
Shun 舜 (sage king) 19, 280–3
Sichuan basin (Sichuan Province),
    See: Shu (state)
Sichuanese cuisine 279
siege warfare 86, 106–7, 125, 432
    Mohist strategies for 105. See also: Gongshu Ban, Handan (siege of 258 BCE), Mo Di, Mohist order
silk 8, 42, 116, 121, 174–5, 234, 290–1, 350–1, 438
Silk Road 438
Sima Cuo 司馬錯 (Qin minister)
    argument in favor of Shu campaign 277, 279
    as military commander in Sichuan campaign 278
Sima Guang 司馬光 127, 176
Sima Qian 司馬遷 211
Sima Zhou 司馬𩰚, prime minister of Zhongshan
    death my execution 286–7
    inititiave to punish Zizhi of Yan 284, 286
    model servant of the throne 286–7
    source concerning 286
Simon Bolivar 109
Sinitic (Sino-Tibetan) languages 42, 46
Six Counselors 六卿 77, 84–5
slaves, bondservants 83, 88, 117, 201–2
social mobility 30–2, 76, 119, 121, 130, 136–7, 253, 280–1, 338–40, 349–50, 352–3, 360, 382, 405–6
    forces limiting social mobility 382
Socrates 25
soldiers 76, 81, 87, 139, 178, 201–2, 220–1, 273, 302, 342
Son of Heaven 天子
    as leader of the Zhou realm 52, 66–7, 69, 71–3, 75, 79, 81, 126, 154–5, 206–7, 221, 243, 246, 248–9, 264, 299

title of 10, 19, 47–8, 109, 188, 233–5, 243, 265, 277, 289, 301, 328, 400, 430.
    See also: Zhou kings
Song dynasty 127, 176, 273
    civil service exam 448
Song 宋 (state) xix–xxi, xxiii, 146–7, 185, 216–17, 221–5
    assumption of title of king 246
    destroyed by Qi 329, 387
    home of Confucius's ancestors, native home of Hui Shi and Zhuang Zhou 25, 106, 238–9
    participation in summit at Welcome Pond 233, 235
    relations with Qin 308, 310–11
    threatened by Chu 106–7. See also: King Min of Qi, King Yan of Song, Tao (Ceramictown, city)
sorghum 45
South (region) 41–2, 49, 52, 60, 62, 71, 143
    as alien frontier 44–5, 68–9, 73, 233
    ecology of 45, 142–3
    population of 44–7, 142–3
    relations with North 48, 79, 147
    zones of 45–6
South China Sea 43–5, 438
Southeast Asia 42, 438
sovereignty 128, 245–6, 248–9, 447–8
soybeans 116
spirits, spirit world 78, 81, 97–100, 103–4, 331. See also: gods, temple, ritual, mourning
Spring and Autumn 春秋 Period 7, 73–4, 151, 190, 296
    escalating political violence of 12, 18, 153–4
Square Great Wall (defensive wall of Chu) xxiii, 301–4, 307
state (guo 國)
    as a public trust, an abstract focus of loyalty 160–3, 165–7, 348–9, 357, 447
    as the patrimony of its ruling clan 160, 344, 347, 360, 447
    calendrical system of 155–6, 241, 405–6
    dedicated to "sacrifice and warfare" 15, 118, 447
    in the political economy of the Zhou dynasty 11
    in the teachings of Master Guan 166–7
    internal structure of 17, 51

state (*guo* 國) (*Continued*)
  progressively conceived in more economic and strategic terms 83–4, 88, 95, 107, 182–3
  sovereignty of 58
  state titles of 155. *See also*: aristocracy, knights, literati, temple
statecraft theory 172
  "forms and names" doctrine of Shen Buhai 171–2
status
  by birth 91, 137, 172–3, 280, 287, 367–8, 381–2, 394, 443–5
  contradiction between hereditary and earned forms of status 90–1, 131–2, 296–7, 367–9, 398–9, 443–5, 449–50
  earned 91, 137, 280, 379–82, 394, 443–4
  extreme consciousness of in Zhou society 114–15, 131–3, 137, 246, 282, 337–8, 356
  growing role of the state in determining 142, 203, 246–7, 281, 285, 445
  steepening bifurcation of the status hierarchy 296–7, 371–2, 445.
    See also: aristocracy, commoners, clothing, great patrons, physical disability, Qin (state) merit rank system, King (title, rank), temple, Warring States (establishment of fiefs and feudal lords)
stelae inscriptions, *See*: Ying Zheng (stelae inscriptions)
Stone Cattle Road 石牛道 xxii, 276–7
Stone Gate (Shimen 石門, battle site) xxi–xxii, 197–8, 216–17, 219
Stone of Scone 158–9
Su Qin 蘇秦
  advice to Tian Wen 307–8
  as a double agent for Yan 324–5, 329–30
  exposure and dimemberment 329–30
  mythologization of 253–5, 324
  negotiation of the vertical alliance of 287 BCE 328–9
suicide
  compulsory, as punishment 4–5, 69, 351–2, 376, 385
  for duty or honor 41, 43–4, 50–1, 73, 90, 96, 135–6, 146, 297–8, 379
Suiyang 睢陽 (capital of Song) xx–xxi, xxiii, xxix, 106–7
Sun Bin bingfa 孫臏兵法 182

Sun Bin 孫臏, Commandant (shuai) of Qi
  origins and early education 182, 184, 254
  strategic leadership of campaign of 341 BCE 236–8
  strategic leadership of campaign of 354-351 BCE 184–5, 223–4. *See also*: Cassia Hill, Horse Hill (battles of); Pang Juan
Sun Tzu, *See*: Sunzi bingfa
Sun Wu 孫武 (Master Sun, Sunzi)
  in history 55–7, 59, 65
  See also: Sunzi bingfa
Sunzi bingfa 孫子兵法 (*The Art of War by Master Sun*, the *Sun Tzu*) 55–6, 59, 140, 303, 314, 364–5
  provenance 181–2
Supreme August One (taihuang 泰皇) 434–5
Suzhou xxiv, 42–4, 386
swords
  as family heirlooms 51, 386
  as weapons 430

Tai-Kadai language family 42
Taihang Mountains 太行山 xx, xxix, 425, 427
Taiwan Strait 43–4
tallies 符 4, 146, 378–9, 389
  use in diplomacy 248–50
Tang Code 118
Tang 唐 (sage king, aka Yao) 328
Tao 陶 (Ceramictown, city) xx–xxi
  as commercial center 325, 348
  as fief of Wei Ran 348–50, 360, 362
tattoos 42
taxation 79, 206, 216, 363. *See also*: land (revenue from)
temple
  as a marker of social status 17, 20, 26, 28–9, 76, 84, 87–8, 99, 101, 119, 137, 142, 172–3, 195–6
  as a site of religious practice 58, 78–9, 98–9, 101, 103–4, 291–2, 388
  in the ancestral cult of the state 14–15, 46, 51–2, 58, 76–7, 157–8, 160, 169
  site of military planning 183. *See also*: gods, ritual, sacrifice, shrines, spirits
terra cotta army 422–3, 441–2
territorial consolidation 46
textiles 201–2

Thearch (*di* 帝, rank)
    plan for Qi and Qin to bestow upon one-another 326–8, 434–5
    rulers of high antiquity 209, 434–5
Things Fall Apart 39–40
Three Jin, *See*: Jin successor states
Tian Chang 田常 48
    as clan leader 8, 21, 32–6
    as co-priminister with Zai Wo 32–3
    as de facto ruler of Qi 37–8, 72, 81–2
    in historical memory 39, 110, 444–5
    role in coup of 481 BCE 8, 18–19, 33–7, 41–3, 70, 80, 93
Tian Dan 田單 (Qi commander)
    organization of the defense of Jimo 331–2
    revival of Qi kingdom and title of Lord Anping 332
    social background and flight from Linzi 331, 357
Tian Daozi 田悼子 (The Mournful Viscount) 154
Tian He 田和 ("Supreme Duke" of Qi)
    death of 155–6
    leadership of Qi as Prime Minister 154–5
    transfer of Qi title to the Tian clan 151–5
Tian Ji 田忌 (General of Qi) 184–5, 236–8, 240
Tian Pian 田駢 (Master) 321–2
Tian Pijiang, *See*: King Xuan of Qi
Tian Rangju, *See*: Marshal Rangju
Tian Wen 田文 (Lord Mengchang)
    "kidnapping" of King Min, the, and exile from Qi 323–4, 414
    as a great patron 297–8, 301–3, 307, 309–10, 371–2, 447
    as Marquis of Xue 297, 301, 332
    as prime minister of Qi 298, 300–2, 305–7, 310–11, 323
    as prime minister of Qin 307–9
    as prime minister of Wei 271, 295–7, 323–4, 326, 329
    character and mindset 295–8, 306–7
    departure from Qin 308, 310, 323, 343–4
    early life and education 295–6
    journey to and sojourn in Qin 306–9
    policy of strategic magnanimity 302–3, 305, 326
    public image 303–4, 309–10. *See also*: great patrons, patronage retinues King Min of Qi, King Xuan of Qi, King Zhao of Qin, Qi (state), Vertical Alliance

Tian Wu 田午 (Duke Huan of Qi)
    coup of 374 BCE 154, 156, 193
    in the ancestral cult of Qi 169
    inclusion of mother in ancestral cult of Qi 157–60, 163, 165, 169
    promotion of new doctrine for recruitment of literati 162–4, 167–9, 172, 177–8, 294, 312–13
    reinvention of Qi state under 150, 157–62, 165–6, 169, 178, 198
    relations with Tian Yan and family 156–9
Tian Xiang 田襄 (Mohist Grand Master) 146–7
Tian Xu 田需 266, 270–1
Tian Yan 田剡 (unrecorded ruler of Qi) 156
Tian Ying 田嬰 (Lord Jingguo)
    conservative outlook 295–6
    cultivation of Tian Wen 271, 297
    service as prime minister of Qi 295–7
Tian Yinqi 田因齊 (King Wei of Qi) 150, 162
    adminstrative reforms 169–72, 178
    as a patron of literati 170, 173, 178, 294
    continuation of his father's policies 169–70, 172, 177–8, 198, 214
    continued advocacy of new Qi doctrines of state 169–70, 312–13
    death of 267, 290, 295–6
    employment of literati for public relations 170, 175
    encouraged growth of Qi military power 178, 186
    military campaigns of 183–6, 236–7
    millitary reform under 178–9
    opposition to "kingship" of Zhongshan 250–3, 261–2, 291
    participation in Xuzhou summit of 334 BCE 241, 243, 295, 434
    resistance to strategic alignment with other states 262–3, 291
Tian 田 clan 8, 33–4
    as ruling oligarchy of Qi 126, 151–4, 156, 158, 161, 163, 168, 203, 308, 417–18
    evolution of 19, 36
    internal divisions within 126, 151–4, 156–7, 212–13
    origins in state of Qi 19, 196
    recruitment of clients from outside the clan 20–1, 151
    rising power of 22, 31, 37

Tian 田 clan (*Continued*)
  use of markets to cultivate power 19–20, 36–7, 41–2, 118–19, 151, 162–3. *See also*: Qi (state), individual Tian clan leaders
tigers 28, 249, 356–7
Timothy Leary 239–40
tombs (graves) 47, 58, 188, 190, 196, 286, 439
  mortuary customs 190–1, 196, 439
trade. *See* commerce
True King, *See*: Mencius, Xun Kuang
Turks, Turkic peoples 44, 97, 125, 338. *See also*: Dai, Di

United Nations 43
United States of America, the 16, 51, 60, 73–4, 79, 207, 239–40
universal love (jian ai) 103, 163
Upper Commandery (of Han)
  as staging area for the Qin invasion of Zhao 425, 427
  final conquest by Qin 407, 414–15
  secession from Han and submission to Zhao 361–3
  site of Changping campaign 363–5
Upper Commandery (Zhao) 414–15
Upper Commandery 上黨郡 (Wei) xxi, 259
Upper Yangzi region 45–7, 49, 60, 63
  as "alien" region 46
urbanization 62, 219, 290–1, 325, 434

Venerable of Ghost Gorge (Guigu 鬼谷) 184, 254
Vertical Alliance 橫 260–1, of 318 BCE 269–70
  "three kingdom" alliance of 298 BCE 310–11, 323–4
  coalition of 287 BCE 328–9, 344
  conception and significance 260
  of 241 BCE 396–7, 400, 407, 414
  of 247 BCE 396, 399–400, 406
  persistence as model in Late Warring Stes period 288
  strategic dynamics of 261–2. *See also*: Gongsun Yan, Hui Shi, Tian Wen
Vietnam 42, 118, 438
  Vietnam War 239–40, 263
Viscount (*zi* 子, rank) 19, 85, 101, 110, 142
Viscount Huan of Wei 魏桓子 109
Viscount Jian 趙簡子 of Zhao 77–8, 80, 82, 84
  in the prophecy texts of Zhao 97–8, 100–1, 326–7

wandering persuaders
  distortions in the historiography of 253–4
  prestige among literati 252–5, 384
  role in diplomacy 249–52, 324–5
  Su Qin as the epitome of 253, 324
Wang He 王齕 (Qin general) 363–5
Wang Jian (Qin commander) 424, 427–8
war
  as a stimulus to insitutional innovation 119, 128, 221–2
  opposition to, in the teachings of the Masters 28–9, 105–7
  progressively intensifying nature of 17–18, 20, 59–60, 101. *See also*: military culture, military power.
Warring States Period 5–6, 8, 11, 41, 44, 90, 106–7, 118–19, 137, 164, 176, 179, 190, 274, 392, 399
  archaeology of 152–3, 182, 189–90, 196, 273–4, 286, 367, 423
  changing attitudes toward the Mandate of Heaven during 93–4
  crisis of, political versus military solutions to 277–9, 288–9, 401
  periodization of 7–8
  persistence of aristocratic ethos during 352, 357, 398–9
  revolution of 5–7, 11–13, 18–19, 28, 59–60, 178, 182, 215, 241, 243, 367–9, 447–51
  shifting values during 67, 71–2, 88, 91–2, 109, 136–7, 285–6, 313, 352. *See also*: historical chronicles
Warring States 戰國
  as form of polity 11–12, 73, 77–8, 109, 116–19, 241–2, 248–9, 263, 267–8, 283–4, 335, 398–9
  changing political economy and social dynamics of 107, 119–21, 268, 309–10, 313–15, 336, 342, 352, 357, 361–2, 367, 398–9, 401, 419, 427, 448
  establishment of fiefs (feng) and "feudal lords (feng jun)" in 203, 207, 246–7, 295, 297, 301, 324, 332, 341, 343, 348–50, 358, 363–4, 385–6, 394–5, 405–6
  exchange of ideas, people, and influences between 129–31, 145, 199, 253, 322, 421
  geography of 6, 130, 261, 277, 336–8, 427. *See also*: bureaucracy, commanderies and districts, fiscal-military state, meritocracy, state (guo)

INDEX

Way (Dao 道), the
  as an alternate to aristocratic standards of value 173, 388, 390
  as the reunified "Way of high antiquity" of the Lüshi chunqiu 411–12
  in teachings of Confucius 1, 26–8, 31–3, 39, 93–4, 101–2, 114–15, 127, 162–3, 228, 230, 313
  in the discourse of the Qin and Han empires 444, 449
  in the parlance of interstate diplomacy 424
  in the teachings of Master Guan and Master Yan 163, 166, 170
  in the teachings of Mencius 227–9, 292, 294
  in the teachings of Mo Di 102, 147, 163
  in the teachings of Xun Kuang 313–15
  in the teachings of Zhuang Zhou and Master Lao 316–21
wealth inequality 268, 371–2
wealth inequality, growth of 88, 101
Wei Huan 魏緩 (Gongzhong Huan) 212–14, 216–17
Wei Ran 魏冉 (Marquis Rang)
  as prime minister of Qin 323–4, 344, 348
  dismissal, exile and death 349–50
  expansionist aggression of 329, 344–6
  hostility to foreign-born officials 345–6
  partition proposal to Qi 326–8, 344
  role in the rise of the "Mi-clan clique" 300, 344–6
  self-dealing and self-enrichment of 348–50, 358, 360, 362. See also: Eyu (campaign of 269 BCE), Tao (Ceramictown, city)
Wei Si 魏斯 (Marquis Wen of Wei) 108, 149–50, 163
  acquisition of title of "Marquis" 109, 126–7, 149–50, 154–5
  capture of Qin "West Bank" territory 124, 138, 147, 149–50, 311
  conquest of Zhongshan 125, 221
  death 127, 129, 138
  disciple of Zixia and partner of Confucian fellowship 112–15, 127–8, 162, 229–30, 312–13, 448
  early reign 111–15, 131
  expansion of Wei military power 116, 124, 191
  in historical memory 109–10, 114–15, 211, 224–5
  legacy and broad influence of 129–31, 145, 154, 162, 169–70, 192, 197, 201, 213–15, 219–21, 229–30
  promotion of "worthies" (i.e. commitment to meritocracy) 112, 114–16, 119, 121, 124, 138, 171
  relations with Zhao and Han 124–8, 143–5, 213
  self-promotion of 112–14, 128. See also: Jin successor states, Li Kui, Wei (state), Wei Ying Wu Qi, Ximen Bao
Wei Wenhou 魏文侯 (text) 112–13
Wei Wuji 魏無忌 (Lord Xinling)
  as a great patron 372, 376–9, 381, 386, 412, 429
  as Prime Minister of Wei 396, 399, 406
  dismissal, reclusion and death 396–7, 414
  exile in Zhao 394–6
Wei Ying 魏罃 (King Hui of Liang/Wei)
  ambition to become Son of Heaven 212, 214–15, 222, 224, 229, 233, 235–7, 240, 243, 265, 291, 400, 440–1
  as a patron of literati 174–5, 200, 224–5, 227, 229–31, 238
  assent to alliance with Qin and employment of Zhang Yi 263, 269
  at war with Qi 184–6, 223–4, 236–7
  building of defensive walls 216, 218–20
  campaigns against Han 216–17, 236–7
  campaigns against Qin 197, 259
  campaigns against Zhao 183, 216–17, 223–4
  death of 268–9
  disputed succession to the throne of Wei 212–14, 283
  economic policies of 216, 222
  in historical memory 216, 224–5, 229–30, 238–40
  legacy of 211, 241–2, 335, 434
  military strengthening policies of 216, 218–20
  move of capital 198
  participation in Xuzhou summit of 334 BCE 241, 243
  relationship with Hui Shi 238–42, 265
  relationship with Mencius 227–31
  summit of 356 BCE 219–20, 223, 225, 233
  use of ceremonial summits 219–20, 222
  use of ruler-to-ruler diplomacy to negotiate territorial exchanges 216–18, 248. See also: Welcome Pond (Fengze)

Wei 渭 River xviii, xxii, 188–9, 205–6, 219
  original homeland of the Zhou kings 188
  Wei River Valley 10, 188–9, 261
Wei 魏 (clan) 84–7, 98, 109–11, 140–2, 151, 154, 195–6, 256
Wei 魏 (state) xviii–xxiv, 108, 138–41, 205–6, 234, 254–5, 383–4
  administrative reform in 119–22, 149–50, 199–200
  agricultural productivity 116, 124, 220
  agricultural reforms in 116–17, 122
  allied with Qi 258–9
  allied with Qin 257, 260, 263–6
  as a model for reform in other states 129–31, 169, 192, 199–201, 215–16, 221–2, 253, 344
  as an intellectual center 114–15, 174–5, 225–32, 256
  as the key player in any interstate alliance 261
  at war with Qi 126, 154–6, 207, 223–4, 236–7, 270
  at war with Qin 197–8, 205, 207, 216, 219, 223–4, 237, 255–6, 258–9, 265, 329, 407
  at war with Zhao 144–5, 183, 185, 258–9
  alternative name of "Liang (Bridge)" 218
  changing relationship between state and aristocracy in 142–3, 203
  conquest of territory from Qin 124, 192, 197, 207, 237–8
  decline of 211, 215–16, 258, 261, 289, 335
  destruction of 432
  geographical boundaries of 217–18
  Hedong territory of 217–18
  Henei territory of 217–18, 270
  invaded by Chu 144–5, 147, 262
  legal reforms in 117–18
  origins in partition of Jin 87–8, 109–10, 142, 151, 217–18
  population 116, 220. See also: Wei Si, Wei Ying
weights and measures 206
Welcome Pond (Fengze 逢澤) 219
  as a "public" park 219, 232–3
  summit of 344 BCE 232–6, 241, 244–5, 440–1
wen and wu 文武 (the civil and the martial) 15–16
Wen 文 ("Civil," posthumous title) 110
West Bank Commandery 河西郡 xxii, 257
West Zhou 西周 xxii, 395
Western Zhou 西周 period 16, 188, 296
wet-rice agriculture 45
Wey 衛 (state) xx–xxi, xxix, 83, 113, 135, 137, 219, 225, 331
  conflict with Zhao 144, 183
  demotion of ruling clan from "duke" to "marquis" 222–3, 246–7
  participation in summit at Welcome Pond 233, 235
  war with Wei 185, 223–4
wheat 45, 116
White Deer Mountain 白鹿山 xxiii, 278
White Turks, See: Turks
wine 8, 32, 55, 61, 95–6, 111–12, 134, 225–6, 404, 416
women
  as "daughters-in-law" 416
  as concubines 8–9, 18, 21, 82, 225, 295, 299–300, 308, 354, 372, 374, 404, 415
  as daughters 32, 60–1, 121, 332–3
  as figures venerated in the ancestral cult 157–60
  as grandmothers 169, 414
  as initiators of a romantic liaison 332, 346–7, 350, 415–16
  as mothers 58, 133–5, 157–60, 192–3, 295, 299–300, 303, 333–4, 341, 343, 346–7, 364, 403–4, 415, 431
  as participants in court politics 157, 299–300, 308, 427
  as political leaders 192–3, 300, 332–4, 343–4, 346–7, 350, 415–16, 431
  as sisters 95, 135–7, 300, 323, 343, 397–8, 404
  as spies and double agents 65–6, 427
  as stepmothers 157–9
  as unmarried girls 183
  as wet-nurses 432
  as wives 8–10, 13, 17–18, 21, 35, 50, 58–9, 95, 138, 140, 157, 332–3, 341, 354, 403–4, 415
  female shamans 121
  subject to patriarchal gender norms 29, 59, 121, 332, 343–4, 373. See also: Lady of Huayang, Mi Bazi, Queen Jun of Qi, Xi Shi
World War II 207
Wu (town in Qin) xxi, 272
Wu Pass 武關 xii–xiii, xviii, 304, 307
Wu Qi 吳起

as a military reformer 139–40, 143–4, 178, 182–3
as a prototypical "wanderer" 157, 162, 172–3
commander, warden, and minister in Wei 124, 137–8, 140–2, 192
death of 145–7, 207–8
early life in Wey 137–8, 199–200
invasion of Wei 144–5, 149–50, 217–18
prime minister of Chu 142–7
social and administrative reforms of 142–3, 215–16
tenure in Lu 138, 141. *See also*: Chu (state), reforms in; Wei Si, capture of Qin's "West Bank" territory
Wu Zixu 伍子胥
as a god 69
as Minister of Foreign Affairs in Wu 55–6, 68
brother of 50–1
disgrace and death in Wu 69, 71
early life and exile 49–51, 142–3
early years in Wu 51–4, 83
father of 49–51, 63
in historiography 49, 51
leader of Wu campaigns against Chu 56–61, 145
opposition to peace with Yue 64–5, 67–8, 70–1
rape of Queen Dowager of Chu 58–61
Wu 吳 (city, site of Wu state capital) xiii–xiv, xix, 62, 386. *See also*: Suzhou
Wu 吳 (state) 41, 45, 69, 71
as alien culture to Zhou realm 41, 43, 59, 79, 189–90, 233
assimilation to Zhou political culture 49, 51–2
at war with Qi 67–9
capital of 45, 51, 53, 69–70
conflict with Chu 48–9, 53–4, 56–62, 65
conflict with Yue 41–2, 61–5, 69–71
customs of 42, 52
destruction of 41–4, 70–3, 93, 141, 330
origins of 42–3, 49, 73
relations within the royal clan 52–7, 61
rise of 42–4, 48–9, 51, 56–7, 62–3, 76–7
royal succession within 52–3, 63
social and political evolution of 51–2, 55–6
use of Chu and northern émigrés 51–6, 63
Wucheng. *See* Martial Fortress
Wuzi (Master Wu) 140

Xi Shi 西施 65–6
Xia 夏 dynasty
as eponym of "Xia" people 191
in the political rhetoric of Wei Ying's court 234–5, 244–5
in traditional historiography of the Zhou 234
Xianyang 咸陽 (capital of Qin) xviii, xxii–xxiii, 3, 205–6, 304–5, 311, 404, 408–9, 419–20, 429, 438
Xianyun 獫狁 (Inner Asian people) 15–16
destruction of the Western Zhou 10, 189–90
Ximen Bao 西門豹
as "model Magistrate" 119–22, 128, 171, 194–5
as Magistrate of Ye 120–2, 127–8, 194, 213
Xinzheng 新鄭 (capital of Han) xviii, xxi, 236, 361–2
move of Han court to 141
rebellion of, after Qin conquest 431. *See also*: Zheng (state), capital of
Xiong clan, *See*: Chu (state), ruling clan
Xu Jia 須賈 (official of Wei)
early patron of Fan Sui 345, 350
embassy to Qin during Fan Sui's premiership 350–1
Xu You 許由 281–3
Xue (fief), *See*: Xuzhou
Xun Kuang 荀況 (Master Xun, Xunzi)
as a poet 391–2, 394
as latter-day disciple of Confucius 312–13, 322
as leader of the Confucian fellowship 312, 413–14
as Prefect of Lanling 388, 392
as resident of Jixia 312–13, 315, 388
ideal of a True King 313–14
origins in Zhao and early education 312
relationship with Huang Xie and other great patrons 388–9
syncretisic dimensions of the teachings of 313–16, 320–1
teaching that "human nature is evil" 315–16, 321–2. *See also*: Han Fei, Li Si
Xunzi, *See*: Xun Kuang
Xunzi 荀子, the (text) 313–14, 316, 389, 394

Xuzhou 徐州 (town), also known as Xue 薛 (fief seat) xx, xxiii
　as seat of the fief of Tian Ying and Tian Wen 295, 332
　site of Xuzhou summit of 334 BCE 241, 243–8, 253–5, 260–1, 288, 291, 326, 434

Yan Sui 嚴遂
　as minister in Han 131–2, 147
　disgrace and exile 132–3, 172–3, 256
　friendship with Nie Zheng 132–5
Yan 燕 (state) xix–xxi, xxiv
　assumption of title of "king" 246, 250–2
　at war with Qi 157, 284–5, 292, 302, 310, 324
　at war with Qin 270, 428–9, 431–2
　at war with Zhao 407
　destruction of 432
　geography of 279–80, 293, 336
　occupied by Qi 285, 292–3, 324, 335
　participation in "Vertical Alliance" against Qin 267
　relations with non-Sinitic people 279–80
　relative power of 279–80. See also: abdication affair of 318 BCE, King Kuai, Sima Zhou, Zizhi
Yang Zhu 楊朱 (Master Yang)
　critic of Confucius and Mo Di 226
　evidence of teachings at Wei Ying's court 225–7
　opposed by Mencius 227–9
　teachings on "valuing life" 225–6, 228, 411
Yangzi River delta. See Lower Yangzi River
Yangzi River 揚子江 xviii–xix, xxii–xxiv, 7, 42–7, 49, 51, 62, 275, 298
Yanzi chunqiu 晏子春秋 (Annals of Master Yan) 168, 314
Yao 堯 (sage king) 280–3
Ye 鄴 (District of Wei) xxi, 120–2, 213
year of four kings (441 BCE), the 94–5, 400
Yellow Pond 黃池 43, 69–70
　covenant meeting of 482 BCE at 69. See also: Huangchi (town)
Yellow River 黃河 xviii–xxiv, 7–9, 42–4, 197–8, 218, 279–80, 330
　dikes and irrigation works 8–9
　West Bank (Hexi) territory of 192, 197–9, 207, 237

Yellow River plain 10, 44–8, 75, 143–4, 147, 233, 248. See also: gods, River God cult (in Wei)
Yellow Sea 44
Yellow Thearch 黃帝 410
Yi jing, See: Classic of Change
yin-yang 陰陽 symbol 435
Ying Lian, See: Duke Xian of Qin
Ying Si, See: King Huiwen of Qin (Ying Si)
Ying Yiren, See: King Zhuangxiang of Qin
Ying Zheng 嬴政 (First Emperor of Qin, Qin Shihuangdi)
　accession to the throne of Qin 399, 404–6, 415–16
　as First Emperor 3–6, 188, 399, 404–5, 435–7, 440–1
　conquests of 3–4, 407, 424–8, 432–4
　death of 10, 438
　early upbringing and character 404–5, 423, 439
　family of 4–5
　grand tours 3–4
　historical image and legacy 401, 421–2
　imperial tours of 3, 439–43
　relationship to Han Fei 425–6
　relationship with imperial literati 442, 444–6
　relationship with Li Si 131, 421, 423–4, 446
　relationship with Lü Buwei 406, 415–16, 418–19, 421, 423–4
　search for immortals of 441–2, 446
　stelae inscriptions of 442–3
　tomb of 188, 422–3, 439, 441
Ying 嬴 clan
　ancestors of Zhao clan 144, 335–6
　origins of 188–9, 335–6
　ruling clan of Qin 188–90, 196–7, 212–13, 335–6, 445
Ying 郢 (capital of Chu) xviii, xxiii, 46–7, 56–8, 62, 106, 141, 143, 145–6, 303–4
　fall to Qin in 279 BCE 344
　sack of 473 BCE 58–61, 68–9
Yingcheng plates 47
Yinjin 陰晉 254
Yinqueshan 銀雀山 (tomb excavation) 182
Yiqu Affair 346–7
Yiqu 義渠 (non-Sinitic state) xxii
　submission to Qin as vassal 259, 270, 336, 346
　war with Qin 270, 336, 346–7, 360

INDEX

Yong 雍 (city) xxii, 193
Yu Qing 虞卿 381
Yue Yang 樂羊 125, 142, 203
Yue Yi 樂毅
    field commander in coalition invasion of Qi 329-32
    joint prime minister of Zhao and Yan 352-3
Yue 越 (state) xiv, xix-xx, xxiii, 45, 51, 69, 71, 76-7, 239
    alliance with Chu 61
    as alien culture to Zhou realm 41-2, 189-90, 233
    as vassal of Fuchai 64-8
    customs of 42
    destruction by Chu 71, 298
    early defiance of Wu hegemony 61-2
    invasion of Wu 41-2, 69-71, 141
    origins 61
    rival of Chu 141
    use of émigrés 63, 71
Yueyang 櫟陽 (city) 193
Yurang 豫讓 88-91, 101, 104, 111-12, 133-4, 325

Zai Wo 宰我 (disciple of Confucius) 23-4, 26, 31, 444-5
    as co-priminister of Qi 32-7, 68, 113, 142
    as disciple of Confucius 23, 32-3, 294
    death of 36-7, 39-40
    in historical memory 38-9
Zeng Shen 曾參 138
Zhang Deng 張登 251-3, 262
Zhang Lu, See: Fan Sui
Zhang Yi 張儀
    as chief advocate of a "Horinzontal Alliance" 260-5, 269, 272, 327, 337, 344
    as prime minister of Qin 258-9, 266, 272-3, 303, 311
    as prime minister of Wei 263-5, 270-1
    demotion, expulsion and death 254, 288, 298-9
    employment in Qin and advocacy of a Wei-Qin alliance 257-8, 260
    humiliation in Chu and subsequent revenge 256, 272-4, 301-2
    origins and early education 253, 256
    role in conquest of Shu 277-8
    tactics to pressure Wei into alliance with Qin 259, 262-3. See also: diplomacy, Gongsun Yan, Horizontal Alliance

Zhanguoce 戰國策 (text) 325
Zhao Gao 趙高 4-5, 440
Zhao Kuo 趙括 (Zhao general)
    background and training 364
    his own mother's opposition to 342, 364
    in the Changping campaign 364-6
Zhao She 趙奢 (Zhao official and commander)
    as a paragon of the new military doctrines 358-60, 396
    champion of meritocracy and routinization 357-8, 368-9
    enfeoffed as Lord of Mafu 360, 364
    humble origins and early career 357-8. *See also*: Eyu (campaign of 269 BCE)
Zhao Sheng 趙勝 (Lord Pingyuan)
    as a great patron 372-4, 379-81, 386, 395, 429
    birth and high rank 351-2, 357-8
    recognition of merit 358, 380-1
Zhao Wuxu 趙无恤
    as first de facto rule of Zhao 91, 95-6, 104, 107, 125, 428
    as head of Zhao clan 82-4
    in the prophecy texts of Zhao 98-9
    parentage of 82-3, 336
    rivalry with Zhi Yao 82-3, 85-8, 95, 213
    role in the development of Zhao state doctrine 96-7, 99, 103
    target of Yurang 88-90
Zhao Zhang 趙章 (prince of Zhao) 341-2
Zhao 趙 (state) xviii-xxi, 108, 124, 213-14
    "cold war" with Qin 342, 353-6, 358, 361
    assumption of title of "king" 246, 250-2
    at war with Qi 126, 154, 156, 329-31, 342
    at war with Qin 270, 328, 358-60, 363-7, 424-5
    at war with Wei 183-5, 223-4, 337
    at war with Yan 407
    conflict with Wey 144, 223, 337
    destruction of 428
    geography of 336-8
    origins in the partition of Jin 87-8, 151
    reform in 215-16
    relations with non-Sinitic steppe people 98-9, 336-7, 339-40, 425, 427
    relations with Qin 304-5, 308-11, 327, 335-6, 340-2

Zhao 趙 (state) (*Continued*)
  relations with Wei 124–8, 144–5, 197–208, 223, 264, 267
  resistance to Qi occupation or exploitation of Yan 285, 293, 311
  rising military power of 336–8, 341
  strategic rivalry with Qin and castrophic defeat 334, 367, 370
Zhao 趙 clan 77–8, 83–7, 98–101, 109, 111, 144, 151, 154, 428
Zheng Dan 65–6
Zheng 鄭 (state)
  at war with Jin 81, 83
  capital of xix, xxi, 81–2 (marked on map as "Xinzheng")
  destruction by Han 141, 221–2. *See also*: Xinzheng (capital of Han)
Zhi Yao 知瑤
  ambition to unite Jin under his rule 81–3, 85–6, 88, 124
  as "Earl Zhi" 85–6
  as a warrior and military leader 80–2, 86–7, 447–8
  as head of Zhi clan 79–80, 85, 87–8, 90
  death of 87–8, 95, 98–9, 109, 133, 151
  early life 80
  in historical memory 93, 383–4
  legacy of, in the Jin successor states 111–12, 114, 127–8, 213–14, 221–2
Zhi 知 clan 79, 84–7, 98–9, 151
Zhonghang clan 中行氏 (of Jin) 84–5, 88–91, 98–9, 195
Zhongshan 中山 (state) xix, xxi
  assumption of title of "king" 246, 250–2, 291
  destruction by Wei 125, 221
  destruction by Zhao 341, 387
  geography of 338
  kings of 286–7, 341
  non-Sinitic origins of 125, 338
  relations with Zhao 338, 340
  revival 221. *See also*: Gu (capital of Zhongshan), King Cuo, King Wuling of Zhao, Sima Zhou
Zhou kings 1–4, 7, 9, 16, 41, 43, 45, 66, 155, 164, 188, 197–8, 277
  descent from the High God Di 14
  disorder surrounding 94–5
  exertion of control over status hierarchy 222–3, 235
  expelled from their original capital 10, 16, 46–7, 188–9, 191
  power of 10–11, 16, 29, 37, 47–8, 222–3, 264. *See also*: Son of Heaven, Year of Four Kings, the
Zhou royal clan (Ji clan) 14, 74–5, 94–5, 126, 144, 400
Zhou royal domain xviii–xxi, xxiv, 94–5, 253, 264, 299
Zhou traditional culture 46–7, 51–2, 67, 91–2, 147, 196–8, 381–2, 398–9
  declining influence of 95, 149
Zhou world 7–10, 12, 17, 19, 22, 26, 39–43, 45, 49, 51–2, 59–60, 62, 67–71, 74, 76, 91, 93, 101–2, 137, 147, 149, 162, 248, 335
Zhou 周 dynasty
  anticipated end 149–51, 215, 233
  division into periods 7
  end of 395
  expansion 15–16
  founding 11–12, 16, 66, 91, 95, 126–7, 188, 209, 212, 232, 328
  revered by Confucius 26–7
  territorial realm 3–4, 10–11, 13, 16, 48, 71, 73, 75, 88, 117–18, 136–7, 164
  traditional hierarchy 17–18, 23–4, 29, 32, 76, 154. *See also*: Mandate of Heaven, Son of Heaven, year of four kings
Zhu Hai 朱亥 (butcher of Wei) 377–9
Zhu Ying 397–8
Zhuang Qiao 莊蹻 303–4
Zhuang Zhou 莊周 (Master Zhuang, Zhuangzi)
  influence on/critiqued by Xun Kuang 316–17
  origin, travels, and association with Hui Shi 230–1, 239, 316
  teachings 317–19, 450
  teachings, counter-political nature of 316–17, 319. *See also*: Daoist movement, personal cultivation, Way (Dao), the
Zhuangzi, the 莊子 (text) 316–17, 319
Zhuoze 濁澤 (Muddy Marsh) xxii, 213, 271–2
Zilu 子路 (disciple of Confucius) 2–3, 113
Zixia 子夏 (disciple of Confucius) 112–14, 125, 162
Zixu. *See* Wu Zixu

Zizhi 子之, prime minister of Yan
  defeat and execution 284
  role in the abdication affair of 318
    BCE 280–1, 292
Zou Ji 鄒忌
  champion of meritocracy and bureaucracy
    169–70, 176–7
  Prime Minister of Qi 169–70, 184, 209

Zou Yan 鄒衍 (Master Zou)
  association with Wei Ying's court 231–2
  origins, work, and travels 231–2
  teachings on correlative cosmology
    231–2
Zou 鄒 (state) 227
Zu 苴 (city in Shu) xxii, 276, 278
  Marquis of Zu 276–8